Crime, Criminal Justice and Masculinities

International Library of Criminology, Criminal Justice and Penology - Second Series
Series Editors: Gerald Mars and David Nelken

Titles in the Series:

Gender and Prisons
Dana M. Britton

Quantitative Methods in Criminology
Shawn Bushway and David Weisburd

Insurgent Terrorism
Gerald Cromer

Criminal Courts
Jo Dixon, Aaron Kupchik and Joachim J. Savelsberg

Crime and Immigration
Joshua Freilich and Graeme Newman

Crime and Security
Benjamin Goold and Lucia Zedner

Crime and Regulation
Fiona Haines

Recent Developments in Criminological Theory
Stuart Henry

Gun Crime
Robert Hornsby and Richard Hobbs

The Criminology of War
Ruth Jamieson

The Impact of HIV/AIDS on Criminology and Criminal Justice
Mark M. Lanier

Burglary
Robert Mawby

Domestic Violence
Mangai Natarajan

Women Police
Mangai Natarajan

Crime and Globalization
David Nelken and Suzanne Karstedt

Crime and Immigration
Graeme Newman and Joshua Freilich

Surveillance, Crime and Social Control
Clive Norris and Dean Wilson

Crime and Social Institutions
Richard Rosenfeld

The Death Penalty, Volumes I and II
Austin Sarat

Gangs
Jacqueline Schneider and Nick Tilley

Corporate Crime
Sally Simpson and Carole Gibbs

Green Criminology
Nigel South and Piers Beirne

Crime, Criminal Justice and Masculinities
Stephen Tomsen

Crime and Deviance in Cyberspace
David Wall

Crime, Criminal Justice and Masculinities

Edited by

Stephen Tomsen

University of Western Sydney, Australia

ASHGATE

Published by
Ashgate Publishing Limited
Gower House
Croft Road
Aldershot
Hampshire GU11 3HR
England

Ashgate Publishing Company
Suite 420
101 Cherry Street
Burlington, VT 05401-4405
USA

Ashgate website: http://www.ashgate.com

British Library Cataloguing in Publication Data
Crime, criminal justice and masculinities. – (International
library of criminology, criminal justice and penology.
Second series)
1. Crime – Sociological aspects 2. Criminal justice,
Administration of 3. Masculinity
I. Tomsen, Stephen
364'.081

Library of Congress Cataloging-in-Publication Data
Crime, criminal justice and masculinities / edited by Stephen Tomsen.
p. cm. – (International library of criminology, criminal justice and penology. Second Series)
Includes index.
ISBN 978–0–7546–2740–1 (alk. paper)
1. Crime–Sex differences. 2. Masculinity. 3. Criminal behavior. 4. Criminology.
I. Tomsen, Stephen

HV6158.C75 2008
364.2'4–dc22

2007009771

ISBN: 978–0–7546–2740–1

Printed in Great Britain by TJ International Ltd, Padstow, Cornwall

Contents

Acknowledgements vii
Series Preface ix
Introduction xi

PART I THEORETICAL PERSPECTIVES

1 Steve Hall (2002), 'Daubing the Drudges of Fury: Men, Violence and the Piety of the "Hegemonic Masculinity" Thesis', *Theoretical Criminology*, **6**, pp. 35–61. 3
2 Tony Jefferson (2002), 'Subordinating Hegemonic Masculinity', *Theoretical Criminology*, **6**, pp. 63–88. 31
3 R.W. Connell (2002), 'On Hegemonic Masculinity and Violence: Response to Jefferson and Hall', *Theoretical Criminology*, **6**, pp. 89–99. 57
4 James W. Messerschmidt (1999), 'Making Bodies Matter: Adolescent Masculinities, the Body, and Varieties of Violence', *Theoretical Criminology*, **3**, pp. 197–220. 69
5 Richard Collier (1997), 'After Dunblane: Crime, Corporeality, and the (Hetero-) Sexing of the Bodies of Men', *Journal of Law and Society*, **24**, pp. 177–98. 93

PART II THE SPECTRUM OF MASCULINE CRIME

6 Joachim Kersten (1996), 'Culture, Masculinities and Violence against Women', *British Journal of Criminology*, **36**, pp. 381–95. 117
7 Elizabeth A. Stanko and Kathy Hobdell (1993), 'Assault on Men: Masculinity and Male Victimization', *British Journal of Criminology*, **33**, pp. 400–15. 133
8 Karen Franklin (2004), 'Enacting Masculinity: Antigay Violence and Group Rape as Participatory Theater', *Sexuality Research and Social Policy*, **1**, pp. 25–40. 149
9 Heith Copes and Andy Hochstetler (2003), 'Situational Construction of Masculinity among Male Street Thieves', *Journal of Contemporary Ethnography*, **32**, pp. 279–304. 165
10 James W. Messerschmidt (1995), 'Managing to Kill: Masculinities and the Space Shuttle Challenger Explosion', *Masculinities*, **3**, pp. 1–22. 191
11 David Gadd and Stephen Farrall (2004), 'Criminal Careers, Desistance and Subjectivity: Interpreting Men's Narratives of Change', *Theoretical Criminology*, **8**, pp. 123–56. 213

PART III CULTURAL AND ETHNOGRAPHIC ANALYSES

12 Richard Sparks (1996), 'Masculinity and Heroism in the Hollywood "Blockbuster": The Culture Industry and Contemporary Images of Crime and Law Enforcement', *British Journal of Criminology*, **36**, pp. 348–60. 249

13 Mike Collison (1996), 'In Search of the High Life: Drugs, Crime, Masculinities and Consumption', *British Journal of Criminology*, **36**, pp. 428–44. 263

14 Philippe Bourgois (1996), 'In Search of Masculinity: Violence, Respect and Sexuality among Puerto Rican Crack Dealers in East Harlem', *British Journal of Criminology*, **36**, pp. 412–27. 281

15 Stephen Tomsen (2005), '"Boozers and Bouncers": Masculine Conflict, Disengagement and the Contemporary Governance of Drinking-Related Violence and Disorder', *Australian and New Zealand Journal of Criminology*, **38**, pp. 283–97. 297

16 Lee F. Monaghan (2002), 'Hard Men, Shop Boys and Others: Embodying Competence in a Masculinist Occupation', *Sociological Review*, **50**, pp. 334–55. 313

17 Katie Mooney (1998), '"Ducktails, Flick-knives and Pugnacity': Subcultural and Hegemonic Masculinities in South Africa, 1948–1960', *Journal of Southern African Studies*, **24**, pp. 753–74. 335

PART IV CRIMINAL JUSTICE SETTINGS

18 Anastasia Prokos and Irene Padavic (2002), '"There Oughtta Be a Law Against Bitches": Masculinity Lessons in Police Academy Training', *Gender, Work and Organization*, **9**, pp. 439–59. 359

19 Yvonne Jewkes (2005), 'Men Behind Bars: "Doing" Masculinity as an Adaptation to Imprisonment', *Men and Masculinities*, **8**, pp. 44–63. 381

20 Sara Willott, Christine Griffin and Mark Torrance (2001), 'Snakes and Ladders: Upper-Middle Class Male Offenders Talk About Economic Crime', *Criminology*, **39**, pp. 441–66. 401

21 Sally Holland and Jonathan B. Scourfield (2000), 'Managing Marginalised Masculinities: Men and Probation', *Journal of Gender Studies*, **9**, pp. 199–211. 427

22 Laureen Snider (1998), 'Towards Safer Societies: Punishment, Masculinities and Violence Against Women', *British Journal of Criminology*, **38**, pp. 1–39. 441

Name Index 481

Acknowledgements

The editor and publishers wish to thank the following for permission to use copyright material.

Australian Academic Press for the essay: Stephen Tomsen (2005), '"Boozers and Bouncers": Masculine Conflict, Disengagement and the Contemporary Governance of Drinking-Related Violence and Disorder', *Australian and New Zealand Journal of Criminology*, **38**, pp. 283–97.

Blackwell Publishing for the essays: Richard Collier (1997), 'After Dunblane: Crime, Corporeality, and the (Hetero-)Sexing of the Bodies of Men', *Journal of Law and Society*, **24**, pp. 177–98. Copyright © 1997 Blackwell Publishing; Lee F. Monaghan (2002), 'Hard Men, Shop Boys and Others: Embodying Competence in a Masculinist Occupation', *Sociological Review*, **50**, pp. 334–55. Copyright © 2002 Editorial Board of the Sociological Review; Anastasia Prokos and Irene Padavic (2002), '"There Oughtta Be a Law Against Bitches": Masculinity Lessons in Police Academy Training', *Gender, Work and Organization*, **9**, pp. 439–59. Copyright © 2002 Blackwell Publishing.

Copyright Clearance Center for the essays: Karen Franklin (2004), 'Enacting Masculinity: Antigay Violence and Group Rape as Participatory Theater', *Sexuality Research and Social Policy*, **1**, pp. 25–40. Copyright © 2004 National Sexuality Resource Center, San Francisco State University; Sara Willott, Christine Griffin and Mark Torrance (2001), 'Snakes and Ladders: Upper-Middle Class Male Offenders Talk About Economic Crime', *Criminology*, **39**, pp. 441–66.

Oxford University Press for the essays: Joachim Kersten (1996), 'Culture, Masculinities and Violence against Women', *British Journal of Criminology*, **36**, pp. 381–95; Elizabeth A. Stanko and Kathy Hobdell (1993), 'Assault on Men: Masculinity and Male Victimization', *British Journal of Criminology*, **33**, pp. 400–15; Richard Sparks (1996), 'Masculinity and Heroism in the Hollywood "Blockbuster": The Culture Industry and Contemporary Images of Crime and Law Enforcement', *British Journal of Criminology*, **36**, pp. 348–60; Mike Collison (1996), 'In Search of the High Life: Drugs, Crime, Masculinities and Consumption', *British Journal of Criminology*, **36**, pp. 428–44; Philippe Bourgois (1996), 'In Search of Masculinity: Violence, Respect and Sexuality among Puerto Rican Crack Dealers in East Harlem', *British Journal of Criminology*, **36**, pp. 412–27; Laureen Snider (1998), 'Towards Safer Societies: Punishment, Masculinities and Violence Against Women', *British Journal of Criminology*, **38**, pp. 1–39.

Sage Publications, Inc for the essays: Heith Copes and Andy Hochstetler (2003), 'Situational Construction of Masculinity among Male Street Thieves', *Journal of Contemporary Ethnography*, **32**, pp. 279–304. Copyright © 2003 Sage Publications; James W. Messerschmidt

(1995), 'Managing to Kill: Masculinities and the Space Shuttle Challenger Explosion', *Masculinities*, **3**, pp. 1–22. Copyright © 1995 Sage Publications; Yvonne Jewkes (2005), 'Men Behind Bars: "Doing" Masculinity as an Adaptation to Imprisonment', *Men and Masculinities*, **8**, pp. 44–63. Copyright © 2005 Sage Publications.

Sage Publications Ltd for the essays: Steve Hall (2002), 'Daubing the Drudges of Fury: Men, Violence and the Piety of the "Hegemonic Masculinity" Thesis', *Theoretical Criminology*, **6**, pp. 35–61. Copyright © 2002 Sage Publications; Tony Jefferson (2002), 'Subordinating Hegemonic Masculinity', *Theoretical Criminology*, **6**, pp. 63–88. Copyright © 2002 Sage Publications; R.W. Connell (2002), 'On Hegemonic Masculinity and Violence: Response to Jefferson and Hall', *Theoretical Criminology*, **6**, pp. 89–99. Copyright © 2002 Sage Publications; James W. Messerschmidt (1999), 'Making Bodies Matter: Adolescent Masculinities, the Body, and Varieties of Violence', *Theoretical Criminology*, **3**, pp. 197–220. Copyright © 2002 Sage Publications; David Gadd and Stephen Farrall (2004), 'Criminal Careers, Desistance and Subjectivity: Interpreting Men's Narratives of Change', *Theoretical Criminology*, **8**, pp. 123–56. Copyright © 2004 Sage Publications.

Every effort has been made to trace all the copyright holders, but if any have been inadvertently overlooked the publishers will be pleased to make the necessary arrangement at the first opportunity.

Preface to the Second Series

The first series of the International Library of Criminology, Criminal Justice and Penology has established itself as a major research resource by bringing together the most significant journal essays in contemporary criminology, criminal justice and penology. The series made available to researchers, teachers and students an extensive range of essays which are indispensable for obtaining an overview of the latest theories and findings in this fast-changing subject. Indeed the rapid growth of interesting scholarly work in the field has created a demand for a second series which, like the first, consists of volumes dealing with criminological schools and theories as well as with approaches to particular areas of crime criminal justice and penology. Each volume is edited by a recognized authority who has selected twenty or so of the best journal essays in the field of their special competence and provided an informative introduction giving a summary of the field and the relevance of the essays chosen. The original pagination is retained for ease of reference.

The difficulties of keeping on top of the steadily growing literature in criminology are complicated by the many disciplines from which its theories and findings are drawn (sociology, law, sociology of law, psychology, psychiatry, philosophy and economics are the most obvious). The development of new specialisms with their own journals (policing, victimology, mediation) as well as the debates between rival schools of thought (feminist criminology, left realism, critical criminology, abolitionism etc.) make it necessary to provide overviews that offer syntheses of the state of the art.

GERALD MARS
Honorary Professor of Anthropology, University College, London, UK

DAVID NELKEN
Distinguished Professor of Sociology, University of Macerata, Italy
Distinguished Research Professor of Law, University of Cardiff, Wales
Honorary Visiting Professor of Law, LSE, London, UK

Introduction

Male offenders carry out the great majority of crimes. Although criminal justice agencies focus heavily on detecting, prosecuting and punishing the offending of working-class, poor and minority males, it is apparent that high levels of recorded and reported offending reflect a real and pervasive social phenomenon of disproportionate male criminality. The reasons for this have been a puzzle for researchers, officials and commentators. Since its origins at the end of the 1800s, criminology has had ongoing difficulty explaining the link between masculinity and crime. Much traditional criminological discourse had a close concern with the study and control of 'dangerous' forms of masculinity, particularly working-class male delinquency, but did not tackle the relation between criminality and the socially varied attainment of male status and power. It studied crime by a male norm and never developed a sufficiently critical view of the link to gender, especially to non-pathological and widespread forms of masculine identity that are tied to offending. The result of this has been a tendency to naturalize male offending, and accounts often revert to gender essentialism by explaining male wrongdoing as an inherent and pre-social phenomenon that men are drawn to.

The positivist stress on individual biology and psychological and sociological accounts which disregard the link between crime and masculinity have been challenged by contemporary research on the social construction of masculinities and the 'everyday' qualities of its aggressive and destructive forms. This shift since the 1980s has been a response to the wider reflection on gender and identity from global social movements that include feminism, gay and lesbian activism and elements of 'the men's movement'. In the academy, there has been a growth of feminist research on violence against women and an expansion of research on masculinity or 'men's studies' (see Kimmel 1987; Connell, Kimmel and Hearn, 2005). In the 'new masculinities' approach there is an emphasis on the relations between different masculinities, the causes and patterns of most criminal offending and victimization, and the broader workings of the wider criminal justice system of public and private policing, criminal courts, corrections and prisons (Newburn and Stanko, 1994).

Most influentially for this new approach, 'hegemonic masculinity' has been defined not as a particular character type but a whole complex of historically evolving and varied social practice in societies which either legitimate, or attempt to guarantee, the shoring up of patriarchy and male domination of women (Connell, 1995). Any attainment or approximation of this empowered hegemonic form by individual men is highly contingent on the uneven levels of real social power in different men's lives. Dynamic relationships and tensions exist between the hegemonic and other subordinated or marginalized forms of masculinity with different masculinities and a gender politics within masculinity. A key marginalized form is 'protest masculinity'. This is a term that has been used before by criminologists and it appropriates the psychoanalytic description of 'masculine protest'. It describes a gender identity that is characteristic of men in a marginal social location with the masculine claim on power contradicted by economic and social weakness. Protest masculinity may be reflected in hypermasculine aggressive display, anti-social, violent and criminal behaviour. Frequently, it exhibits a juxtaposition of overt misogyny, compulsory heterosexuality and homophobia.

For some, this model could seem too closely tied to Marxist ideas about an overarching dominant ideology as a ruling set of oppressive masculine beliefs. Or it can appear to result in a narrow view of true masculinity as a negative set of personal attributes, or the tautological and imprecise notion that masculinity comprises whatever men do (Jefferson, 1997; Collier 1998).[1] Moreover, any simple understanding of this approach may disregard the ways in which criminalized masculinities are produced in tension with the official forms of masculinity inscribed in policing and criminal justice systems (Tomsen, 1996).

Nevertheless, this model of hegemonic and marginalized masculinities has been deployed in a range of criminological studies. Critical work has emphasized that masculinity is linked to more than just violent crime by less powerful men and relates widely to such matters as motor vehicle offences, theft, drug use and dealing, white collar offending or official corruption. As there are different forms of masculinity that are differently linked to the attainment of social power, crime itself is a means or social resource to achieve masculinity, and analyses must balance consideration of structural forces and human agency (Messerschmidt, 1993, 1997).

This volume features the leading contemporary essays that are either part of or related to the 'new masculinities' approach in this sphere. They comprise an impressive range of theoretical and empirical work including important cultural and ethnographic analyses. All of this material is taken from flagship international journals, and was produced by a global mix of researchers with diverse disciplinary backgrounds. These scholars now share the view that masculinities are plural, socially constructed, reproduced in the collective social practices of different men and embedded in institutional and occupational settings. Furthermore, masculinities are intricately linked with struggles for social power that occur between men and women and among different men. Crime, criminal justice and their cultural representation are the key terrain for these masculine contests.

The material is organized in four parts. 'Theoretical Perspectives' illustrates the important influence of 1970s/1980s feminist views about male crime as well as the notion of 'hegemonic masculinity' and the debate this set off in criminology during and since the 1990s. Research in this field has had to balance stress on the structural effects of gender hierarchies and ongoing forms of social division such as those arising from social class, race/ethnicity, age, and sexualities. The central importance of social class is the kernel of Hall's view (Chapter 1). He argues that class divisions have remained fundamental in contemporary industrialized societies. And this is especially so in post-Fordist conditions with a decline of manual labour, a shift to finance capital, and a cultural emphasis on consumption above production. These social changes make the tough traditional masculinities cultivated by early capitalism appear increasingly redundant. In addition, these changes have occurred alongside the rise of a radical/cultural variant of feminism that depicts men as destructive and violent. Feminists are divided about such generalized and essentialist accounts of male power that conflate violence and masculinity (Segal, 1990). For Hall, the model of 'hegemonic masculinity' is substantially the same as this form of radical feminism. It also echoes views from media and middle-class

---

[1] For a comprehensive overview of a very wide related literature and a reply to key criticisms, see Connell and Messerschmidt (2005).

commentators that offer a distorted and degrading view of all working-class and marginal men as the actual or likely perpetrators of crime and violence.

This piece does draw attention to the interrelation of different masculinities and how problematic conceiving the differences between hegemonic and potentially criminal protest masculinities has become for criminologists with an elastic use of these terms in some discussions of male criminality. Furthermore, the commentator hypocrisy that he refers to suggests that there is still an insufficient understanding of the condoning and cultivation of violent forms of manhood by capitalist, imperial and contemporary post-colonial states. Male violence is deployed internally and externally in a range of state forms, and is both legitimated and denounced in different historical and social circumstances. Ultimately though, it is Hall's approach that may be too limited by its central focus on social class as this leaves him without a notion of the gendered power that men from a range of different social classes and groupings may collectively benefit from. Hall may also leave his readers wanting a more sufficient social explanation of the origins of male violence and destructiveness, including the widespread violence directed at men as victims that he regards as overlooked by researchers. Connell (Chapter 3) argues in reply, that Hall's attack is a rhetorical one and only pillories a narrow version of the masculinities model that is a reductionist sketch of male oppression drained of subtlety and nuance.

From a different angle, Jefferson (Chapter 2) suggests Connell's model is too focused on negative individual attributes and hard to reconcile with evidence of an apparent contemporary 'crisis' of male identity. Moreover, any overall concern with understanding male violence and criminality requires a more complex model of human motivation and (unconscious) subjectivity that is not deterministic and can balance structure and agency to explain both offending and non-offending by men. Obviously, he has in mind the complexity of his own life history account of Mike Tyson that has traced the evolution of a vulnerable boy into a champion athlete and convicted rapist, a hypermasculine though racially marginal male. In reply to this, Connell insists on having produced a model of masculinities that are dynamic and relational, global and local, and melding social and psychological elements.

A more sympathetic response and expanded use of this model is evident in Messerschmidt's own influential account (Chapter 4) of crime as 'doing masculinity' within a structured action framework incorporating differences of class, race/ethnicity, age, sexuality and the shared concern with attaining power. Here, a dynamic interplay of hegemonic and other masculinities is demonstrated by discussion of the lives of two juvenile offenders from a working-class American neighbourhood. This interplay occurs against the backdrop of different relations to the body and achievable masculinities, as social understandings of the body shape offending in two different criminal pathways.

Collier's account (Chapter 5) of official and media discourses surrounding a massacre by a lone gunmen that took place in a Scottish town in 1996 suggests another approach to the relation between criminal acts and the male body. It provocatively suggests a parallel between the perpetrator's murderous violence and a broad range of other forms of violence in male-dominated societies. The evidence gathered is secondary and no unconscious motives are suggested. Collier is critical of the 'masculinities/gender' approach and this notorious crime is instead framed within the 'sexed bodies/corporeal feminist' approach that has intellectual roots in Continental philosophy. Nevertheless, for some readers, this detailed analysis would not dissolve doubts about whether this latter theory can itself avoid overstating and reifying gender differences or sufficiently explain the diversity, contradictions and subtleties of social forms of masculinity.

'The Spectrum of Masculine Crime' introduces the breadth of analyses that cover both violent and non-violent male offending and victimization. As feminist researchers have so often observed, sexual violence has a collective effect in reinforcing the subordinated group position of women. Among cultural feminists this has been taken to suggest a uniform and absolute pattern of patriarchal control, though this is not confirmed by detailed analyses from research on male violence. Kersten (Chapter 6) maps out cross-cultural evidence to illustrate an underlying link between male domination and a wide range of reported and unreported rapes, forms of sexual harassment and coercion from both male strangers and acquaintances. Additionally, he stresses the national differences in gender relations in order to argue that, although these assaults are related to a range of social and historical factors, they are higher in nations (for example Australia, rather than Germany or Japan) with an overtly aggressive public masculine culture. Such violence is viewed as a means of asserting or seeking a male identity that is increasingly under threat of change from new social forces.

Analyses of the effects of violence on women have lit the pathway for research on the results of victimization and an associated regulation of gender/sexual identities among men. Stanko and Hobdell (Chapter 7) note that the very wide level of male violence against other men has not been well researched or examined as a form of gendered violence. There are major gaps regarding the criminological study of male victims, with a reliance on models that attribute equal blame to all men involved in violence. Similarly, there has been little analysis of masculine attitudes towards subjection to violence beyond the general finding that men as a group tend to be less fearful in relation to crime. This study of the experience of violence traces the role of victimization in establishing power relations between men, and the mixed effects on victims that both undermine and reinforce conventional ideas of manhood.

The control of both women and certain men by violence suggests a strong parallel. Franklin (Chapter 8) argues that assaults on women and anti-gay violence enforce sex/gender conformity on victims and a wider social audience. And both forms of crime clearly concern the establishment of masculine identity and status among groups of perpetrators. This parallel is most obvious in the cases of anti-gay gang attacks and group rape of female victims where a collective production of masculinity among perpetrators prevails.This similarity of particular forms of anti-female and anti-gay male violence is convincing and illuminating, though the importance of masculine sexual desire in ostensibly non-sexual anti-gay attacks may be downplayed here. Her account of an overlap of a masculinity built around misogyny and homophobia brings to mind the recent contribution of queer theorists concerned with the generation of modern Western notions of manhood around the homosexual/heterosexual binary (Sedgwick, 1994). It may also conflate aspects of sexism and homophobia in a way that has been a source of contention and debate in gay and lesbian analyses. The eventual focus is on the treatment of actual and potential individual offenders. This is a different concern from some of the most interesting observations in this piece. The latter are made in regard to the overlap between the masculinities of various marginal and more socially empowered male groups (that include many police and soldiers) as perpetrators of sexual abuse and anti-gay attacks.

Accounts of the gendered patterns of economic and corporate offending serve to correct the narrow view of masculine crime as just comprising acts of physical violence. The insights drawn from an interview study of street thieves conducted by Copes and Hochstetler (Chapter 9) give further understanding of the motivations and processes involved in the male attraction to a range of non-violent offending. A strong stress on the situational construction of masculinity is linked to those branches of contemporary criminology that emphasize the spontaneity of offending and its quasi-rational and voluntary nature. This explores group interactions and exchanges that precede collective offending, including robbery, burglary and vehicle theft by groups of young risk-taking males. Ad hoc decisions to engage in crime often result from challenges to the masculinity of recruits. Even more broadly, a reader could conclude that much collective male offending of this sort arises from masculine 'honour' contests occurring among offenders and prior to a criminal act akin to those that other crime researchers find so frequently in occasions of male on male violence.

What about the masculine attractions of criminal risk at higher levels of social class and privilege? Clues about this are offered in Messerschmidt's classic account (Chapter 10) of an instance of serious corporate crime. The Challenger disaster of 1985 killed seven people and seriously undermined public and political confidence in the United States Space Shuttle programme. Institutional crime by collective decision-making or oversight does not fit the classic liberal notion of a single reasoning (presumptive male) criminal actor. This study clearly demonstrates how the fatal decision to launch against strong evidence of equipment failure reflected the dominance of a particular managerial masculinity that valued risk and decisiveness and discounted human consequences. Messerschmidt's insights into the masculinity of corporate crime might well inform the recent criminological interest in state crime. There is a range of major public institutional offending, including internal and external official violence, paramilitary activity and warfare, that is also deeply masculine and it remains a fertile field for researchers with this approach.

If crime is a ready resource for attaining masculinity and this is particularly the case among socially marginal or highly competitive groups of men, we could wonder what this means for the masculinity of non-offenders. Gadd and Farrall (Chapter 11) explore the subjective significance of 'desistance' for two male working-class offenders. Ending criminal offending and criminal careers is a puzzle for conventional criminology that the masculinities approach could help to unravel. Following the signposts in Jefferson's analysis of violence and the masculine unconscious, and research on desistance balancing individual agency with structural determination of the sort stressed in research on social risk factors or life course stages, they conclude that desistance is a complex gendered process. A detailed discussion of life circumstances draws out the contradictory nature of this desistance. An apparent ending of criminality is shaped around heroic male discourses of redemption and protectiveness and the uncertain possibilities of male renunciation of actual or phantasized violence, with the latter being more widespread and commonly shared by offenders and other males alike.

The significance of a general vicarious masculine interest in violence, crime and wrongdoing is evident from the contributions of researchers exploring the status of cultural messages and meanings in a range of societies. 'Cultural and Ethnographic Analyses' reflect how a particular highlight of the new crime and masculinities research has been the discursive analysis of masculine cultural representations and a variety of ethnographic studies that seek out the viewpoints that inform masculine social action in relation to crime and criminal justice.

Sparks (Chapter 12) explains how popular film depictions of male heroism as a critical aspect of policing and law enforcement shape and skew public understanding of crime and the law. Additionally, the strident assertion of masculinity in recent Hollywood movies about crime reflects the instability of current gender identities. In these, the suffering and striving crime-fighter heroes have an exaggerated muscularity and physical toughness. Some of their audience and international success resides in the populist appeal of vigilantism by anti-establishment individuals who nevertheless resolve and punish wrong and protect the weak and innocent.

Sparks does not elaborate on the point, but this could mean that some core tensions and attractions of both hegemonic masculinity that is official, pro-state and respecting authority and the protest masculinity that more usually animates the identity of criminal offenders are inscribed within these heroic characters and triumphant narratives. Even more broadly, we could ask what is the cultural significance of these and similar pro-law and criminalized representations of aggressive masculinity in the cultural sphere? Do they reflect or shape public consciousness about men, violence and crime? Sparks takes care to avoid any simple reading of these as mere ideology. He acknowledges that audience identifications and reactions are always uncertain. In fact, this is so much the case that in the end it may be too simple to talk of these as just 'dodgy blokes' films' that only truly attract the interest of particular male viewers.

This cultural studies emphasis on the establishment of social identities in patterns of leisure and consumption rather than by the traditional means of the workplace and occupation, informs Collison's account (Chapter 13) of a group of young British males. Social disadvantage persists and shapes offending in new forms. Establishing a respected masculine street identity through a range of public criminal activities and poly-drug use occurs against a social backdrop that strictly limits the possible mechanisms for establishing male status. The same tension between individual agency and objective factors in masculine criminal activity and the value of an insider understanding of this are very evident in the fully ethnographic picture drawn by Bourgois's study (Chapter 14) of New York crack dealers from a deprived Puerto Rican neighbourhood.

These are men who also struggle for respect in their wrongdoing. Drug-dealing, violence and sexual assaults provide a distorted mirror of the limited empowerment that was won by male forebears in a traditional rural patriarchy where protection and provision for women and families were vital aspects of gender dominance. The structures of immigration to a colonial centre undergoing rapid de-industrialization drastically altered the possibilities for attainment of male respect. The insider accounts and graphic snapshots of brutality, gang rapes and other crimes are convincing and disturbing. At the same time, the author is well aware of the pitfalls of ethnographic voyeurism. Cultural detail gathered by painstaking and dangerous fieldwork fleshes out the racialized, criminal masculinities assumed by these young gang members. Bourgois insists that they must be balanced by the acknowledgement of the structural disadvantage behind them. Furthermore, he notes that there are dire human consequences in the mass criminalization and incarceration of large numbers of Latino and other racial/ethnic minority males in the contemporary United States (see also Miller, 1996).

The further value of insider understanding in accounts of masculine offending and non-offending is signalled by Tomsen's study (Chapter 15) of young Australian men and security officers involved in regular episodes of drinking violence and disorder. This study points out that, although the link between masculinity and criminality has been newly emphasized, researchers have little understanding of the means by which a withdrawal from violence can sit with a socially respected masculine identity. 'Disengagement' is understood here as a process of situational decision-making and withdrawal from conflicts and offending that may characterize a broad population of 'non-criminal' men rather than as any full desistance from a set criminal pathway and identity. Involvements in drinking-related public violence are tied to matters of male group status, the protection of honour in episodes involving insults and slights that must be responded to, and the collective pleasure of carnival-like rule-breaking in public disorder. Yet an awareness of danger and a disengagement from occasions of conflict can sit with rational and restrained models of a masculine self. This may even be cultivated by public safety campaigns that give an exaggerated belief that individual agency always prevails in avoiding violence.

So what is the broader potential of research that explores the masculine, rather than emasculating, possibilities of not offending? There is some overlap here with Gadd and Farrall's detailed account of men who have begun to offend less frequently. They have only a mixed optimism about criminological understanding of this process. Furthermore, the social structures behind these gendered patterns of drinking-related offending are not only the 'de-industrial' threat to the traditional male worker's identity. Tomsen's findings refer to masculinities that have a long trajectory through historical time and attach to an ongoing dichotomy of established 'respectable' and more marginal 'disrespectable' sectors of the working class.

The theme of masculinity and de-industrialization has been pursued by British researchers studying night-time leisure and related offending and its policing (Winlow, 2001; Hobbs *et al.* 2003). There are sensual attractions in the liminal 'night-time' economy for its many young participants, and an allied official ambivalence towards the male aggression and disorder that characterize it. This is drawn out by Monaghan's insider account (Chapter 16) of 'bouncing' in a study of private security officers working in nightclubs and pubs in city centres in South-West Britain. In this workplace, physicality and violent potential are transformed into a workplace skill built on the importance of forceful bodies. The mixed official response to the economic benefits and social costs of the expanding night economy that fosters drunkenness, male conflicts and disorder problems is also evident in the discomfort with, and reliance on, the aggressive masculinity of security officers instructed to maintain a semblance of public order.

Monaghan demonstrates that there are occupational norms of controlled violence that might exclude 'nutters' and 'psychos'. The danger of this work generates hierarchies of male physical ability within private policing, particularly the contrasts between 'hard men', 'shop boys' coming from security work in retail stores and 'glass collector types' that are less physically imposing and are unable to deal with the risks of violent encounters. The same masculine hierarchy inflects the positioning of the minority of women working in this occupation; these are either denigrated as unmasculine and physically incapable or in fewer cases given a marginal position in a masculine hierarchy.[2]

---

[2] There is growing research evidence and debate about masculine performance and appropriation of fluid elements of masculinity by women in criminal justice occupations or criminal activities (see Miller's (2002) critique of 'gender dualism' in this field and her discussion of female street crime and girls 'doing masculinity'). For most researchers, masculinity still refers to social identities and practices that are substantially monopolized by men and they are given their fullest social meaning in these contexts.

This is a specific form of masculinity that has global manifestations and corresponds with images from a general culture. It also seems to involve a form of private policing that is laxly regulated and reproduces forms of masculine identity that are close to the original aggressive physicality of traditional unreformed public policing. With the fine line between legitimate force and actual assault, bouncing itself encapsulates a gendered identity at the edge of the protest and official masculinities that criminal justice systems so often express the tensions and convergence between.

The importance of cultural history and oral evidence for the analysis of crime and masculinities is attested to by Mooney's study (Chapter 17) of the 'Ducktails', a white and mostly young male delinquent subculture that appeared in South African urban centres in the 1940s and 1950s. This retrospective account consciously exceeds the class-oriented concerns of early British research on youth subcultures to explore the dimensions of class and race such as 'whiteness' and racial superiority, and gender and sexuality including male aggression, hedonism and crime, sexist exploitation, promiscuity and violent homophobia. It demonstrates how a particular white masculine identity is consolidated around distinct attire and speech and characteristic episodes of petty offending and resistance to authority.

Violent and anti-social behaviour by the Ducktails took place against the backdrop of important local and global changes. White privilege for Afrikaans speakers was affirmed in this era, alongside international cultural influences such as a youth culture of distinct leisure and rebellion. Most interestingly, the contradictions of hegemonic and protest masculinity emerge here as mixed rebelliousness and conformity. The continuities between these rival forms of masculinity are tellingly revealed in an occasionally expressed view from white police and authorities; such aggressive and racist youth were likely recruits for state service if military discipline could mould a more useful pattern of controlled violence and official masculinity.

'Criminal Justice Settings' concerns the wider context of the generation of different masculinities in criminal justice systems and related dilemmas for programmes of punishment, correction and crime prevention. The paradox of regulating criminalized masculinities with the formally law-abiding, though sexist and aggressive, official masculinities of criminal justice systems is reflected in research on policing. Prokos and Padavic (Chapter 18) draw attention to the heightened male domination and masculinity of this occupation. This is confirmed by an observational study of police academy training in the rural South-East of the United States where a 'hidden curriculum' of sexist professional socialization remains a powerful force against ostensibly gender-neutral classes. An aggressive masculinity is already constructed at the recruit level in the various interactions of students and instructors, and the harassment and exclusion of women. Hard masculinity is equated with policing and its presumed characteristics including state-licensed aggression and violence, guns and crime fighting, and a denial or disdain for the social service forms of police work. There is a typical view of women as hapless crime victims. The depiction that is drawn here has little room for contradiction and nuance, yet the central point that this socialization serves to accentuate entrenched and rigid forms of official masculinity is convincing.

Responses to criminal justice intervention that foster and reproduce masculinities with a direct or indirect relation to criminality are uncovered in contemporary studies. The general failure of prisons to deter crime or to rehabilitate inmates with any certainty is now informed by accounts of masculinity in these. Jewkes (Chapter 19) illustrates the sharp struggles over male power and status and the masculine hierarchies that characterize prison subcultures and the lives of incarcerated men. From an interview study with British prisoners, she argues that a specific form of 'manliness' that is hard, aggressive, bullying and conformist is a usual adaptation to prison. There is a dehumanizing impact of prisons as total institutions that threaten personal identity with a climate of 'mortification and brutality'. This engenders a hard public masculine social performance among inmates.

The hard and performed prison masculinity may contrast with individual understandings of a more private inner self and some alternative forms of male identity, such as the prison tradesman, scholar or activist. But a tough exterior is the more common means of retaining personal dignity. Even the frequent muscularity that is attained by vigorous exercise and valued by inmates for signalling a powerful masculine physique preserves some sense of self as a significant individual in the face of institutionally imposed surveillance, discipline and regulation. This analysis and related work on prison masculinities cogently suggest that it is aspects of the intervention process itself that affirm destructive forms of male identity to which criminal justice systems are ostensibly opposed (Sabo, Kupers and London, 2001).

The failure of prisons to reform and their apparent reinforcement of masculine identities that excuse offending are evident from a small study of middle-class inmates. Willott, Griffin and Torrance (Chapter 20) unveil the masculine qualities of an expanded 'breadwinner' discourse in the rationalizations for offending voiced by male professionals incarcerated for fraud matters. This stresses notions of responsibility and paternal caring towards a broad range of family members, employees and colleagues to excuse illegal behaviour. This response is a form of male resistance to the penal process that is distinct from the reactions to the brutalization of poor and marginal males studied by Jewkes. Here, there is a denial of actual belonging in prison and an insistence on social and moral difference from the prisoner mainstream of 'foul-mouthed sadistic riff-raff'. The recidivism rates for imprisoned white-collar offenders may be modest, but there is very little evidence of remorse in this configuration of maleness.

The important matter of the contradictions of intervention directed at male offenders is explored by Holland and Scourfield (Chapter 21) in relation to justice professionals' responses to the violence of impoverished men and the ruinous effects of their offending on partners, families and communities. This draws out some of the dilemmas in the state and political response to destructive masculinities. Their study of male and female probation officers working with offenders in South Wales found opposed professional discourses about masculinity and its relation to offending and rehabilitation. These oppositions echoed the professional quandary about the contemporary swing to greater punitiveness and away from an emphasis on offender welfare and non-intervention with clients.

The violence of these men living in council estates located in regions of industrial decline occurs in communities that are more heavily policed and stigmatized by officials. Regardless of this, the violence remains deeply problematic with gender identity central to matters of offending. Probation officers react to this with three distinct discourses. A traditional probation discourse accepts aggressive masculinity and gender identity in a commonsense way that denies agency. It seeks mitigation for offending with an anti-carceral viewpoint that eschews intervention. By contrast, an explicit discursive challenge to violent masculinity fully stresses offender agency and focuses on the needs of victims. Between these responses, an implicit challenge to masculinity can arise from a discourse aimed at achieving cooperative involvement in offender therapy and programmes that reflect on matters of male identity and behaviour. Holland and Scourfield seem to imply that this may be the best professional option. The traditional discourse is sympathetic to the disadvantage of offenders, but essentialist in its view of gender and it does nothing practical to deal with violence. The explicit challenge approach ironically overlaps with the macho punitiveness of contemporary law and order politics.

Finally, Snider (Chapter 22) affirms the overall value of the acknowledgement of the link between crime and masculinities for criminological understanding by feminist and male researchers. From a perspective with apparent ties to restorative justice, she also discusses the many contradictions inherent in exclusively punitive responses to male crime that disregard racial and social class contexts. She further explains the political and professional dilemmas of potentially counterproductive anti-violence agitation by a narrow fostering of criminal justice intervention. For her, there is a need to move beyond criminalization with its reliance on legal sanctions and criminal justice system solutions to social problems as the key response to male violence and criminal offending.

This criminalization is a common strategy in a contemporary era of post-left new social movement activism around crime that may dovetail with punitive law-and-order politics. Globally, this has encouraged an American-style penality in expanding and now often privatized police and prisons, and the imposition of longer and often mandatory sentences with an erosion of commitment to alternative punishments. This has the pernicious effects of net-widening, mass incarceration and punishment for 'vengeance' rather than reform or rehabilitation. It particularly targets and brutalizes poor, African-American/black and Hispanic men with further divisive and negative impacts on their own fragile communities. With these outcomes, it is mistaken for feminists and 'progressives' to disregard wider measures of control and crime prevention, and the potential value of social amelioration to enhance public safety. At worst, the criminalization strategy may reflect white middle-class concerns and an individualistic focus that is unlikely to change the bulk of offenders, especially by further brutalizing men with incarceration. Additionally, this has not empowered women or improved their feelings of safety.

These claims may seem to be generalized, yet the global trend to mass incarceration and criminalization has gone further since this was penned. Snider's writing returns readers to the core issues that run through other pieces in this collection. These include the plurality of masculinities, the significance of social class, race/ethnicity and other axes of power and inequality in considerations of masculinity and crime, the degree of causality from social structures in offending, and the real and wider effects of criminal justice intervention. Most importantly, she directly addresses the matter of the actual likelihood of ever reconstructing problematic masculine identities. Snider advocates the importance of measures directed against the inequalities of capitalism and patriarchy such as provision of basic social security in disadvantaged communities and collective efforts to educate and promote diverse and non-violent masculinities among marginalized boys and men.

Such an approach may appear optimistic in light of the potency of the law-and-order trend she describes and the global shift to neo-liberalism. Furthermore, there is a widespread public belief in a commonsense view about masculinity as a force inevitably leading millions of men to involvement in crime and violence. But, as most of these contributors insist, to acknowledge the uneven influences of culture, social history and structures of inequality in producing masculine criminality can sit alongside a recognition of agency and social change. This offers to readers a measure of optimism that some instances of human choice and certain forms of collective action can and do weaken and transform the masculinity and crime nexus.

References

Collier, R. (1998), *Masculinities, Crime and Criminology: Men, Heterosexuality and the Criminal(ised) Other*, London: Sage.

Connell, R.W. (1995), *Masculinities,* St. Leonards: Allen and Unwin.

Connell, R.W., Kimmel, M. and Hearn, J. (2005) (eds), *Handbook of Studies on Men and Masculinities,* Sage.

Connell, R.W. and Messerschmidt, J. (2005), 'Hegemonic Masculinity – Rethinking the Concept', *Gender and Society*, **19**, 6, pp. 829–59.

Hobbs, D., Hadfield, P., Lister, S. and Winlow, S. (2003), *Bouncers: Violence and Governance in the Night-time Economy*, Oxford: Oxford University Press.

Jefferson, T. (1997), 'Masculinities and Crime', in M. Maguire, R. Morgan and R. Reiner (eds), *The Oxford Handbook of Criminology*, Oxford: Clarendon Press.

Kimmel, M.S. (1987) (ed.), *Changing Men: New Directions in Research on Men and Masculinity*, Newbury Park, CA: Sage.

Messerschmidt, J. (1993), *Masculinities and Crime: Critique and Reconceptualization of Theory,* Lanham, MD: Rowman and Littlefield.

Messerschmidt, J. (1997), *Crime as Structured Action: Gender, Race, Class, and Crime in the Making*, Thousand Oaks, CA: Sage.

Miller, J. (1996), *Search and Destroy: African-American Males in the Criminal Justice System,* Cambridge, UK/ New York: Cambridge University Press.

Miller, J. (2002), 'The Strengths and Limits of "Doing Gender" for Understanding Street Crime', *Theoretical Criminology*, **6**, 4, pp. 433–60.

Newburn, T. and Stanko, E. (1994) (eds), *Just Boys Doing Business? Men, Masculinities and Crime,* London: Routledge.

Sabo, D., Kupers, T. and London, W. (2001) (eds), *Prison Masculinities*, Philadelphia: Temple University Press.

Sedgwick, E.K. (1994), *Epistemology of the Closet*, London: Penguin.

Segal, L. (1990), Slow M*otion: Changing Masculinities, Changing Men,* London: Virago.

Tomsen, S. (1996), 'Ruling Men', *The Australian and New Zealand Journal of Criminology*, **29**, 2, pp. 191–4.

Winlow, S. (2001), *Badfellas: Crime, Tradition and New Masculinities*, Oxford: Berg.

Part I
Theoretical Perspectives

[1]

Daubing the drudges of fury:

Men, violence and the piety of the 'hegemonic masculinity' thesis

STEVE HALL

University of Northumbria at Newcastle, UK

Abstract

A substantial body of empirical work suggests that young, economically marginalized males are the most likely perpetrators and victims of serious physical violence. Interpreting these findings in a historicized way that has been neglected by the criminological discourses of the moment suggests that physical violence has become an increasingly unsuccessful strategy in the quest for social power in liberal-capitalist societies. Although it has been displaced by symbolic violence as the principal domineering force in capitalism's historical project, physical violence has not been genuinely discouraged but harnessed as a specialist practice in a pseudo-pacification process. From this perspective, violence has a complex relationship with liberal-capitalism. Can the concept of 'hegemonic masculinity' help criminology to deal with this complexity and inform violence reduction strategies? This article argues that, in the context of pseudo-pacification, the notion that violent males 'rework the themes' of an institutionally powerful 'hegemonic masculinity' inverts and distorts the concept of hegemony, which for Gramsci was the self-affirming cultural production of the dominant political-economic class. Thus the concept of 'hegemonic masculinity' tends to downplay political economy and class power, which suggests that it is too far removed from historical processes and material contexts to either justify the use of the term hegemony itself or explain the striking social patterns of male violence. This intellectual retreat is representative of a general political evacuation of capitalism's global socio-economic processes, a move that is allowing sparsely regulated market forces to continue the economic insecurity, specialist roles and corresponding cultural forms that reproduce the traditional male propensity to physical violence.

Key Words

dimorphic violence • hegemony • masculinity • neocapitalism • pseudo-pacification

Introduction: scrutinizing the terms of the 'hegemonic masculinity' discourse

The claim that men commit most acts of physical violence is possibly the nearest that criminology has come to producing an indisputable fact. There is now a measure of consensus in the discipline that men's violence has undergone a real increase in the past three decades (James, 1995; Levi, 1997), or alternatively that more penetrative analyses are revealing a traditionally high level (Newburn and Stanko, 1994). Working from this platform, criminology has made a major contribution to the placement of masculinity under the scrutiny of a number of critical standpoints, many of which have been influenced by varieties of feminism and profeminism. The intellectual tribunal emerging from this 'gender turn' has coincided with the gradual but seemingly irreversible erosion of the traditional male's predominance in politics, culture and the labour market. For many commentators violence is a traditional masculine method of maintaining dominance and responding to challenges, and thus it follows that an upward trend in male violence is one of the clearest indicators that the masculine gender order is under threat and showing a 'tendency to crisis' (Ingham, 1984; Connell, 1987,1995; Kimmel, 1987, 1996; Brittan, 1989).

In this climate of transition and crisis, the sociologist Bob Connell's (1987, 1995) notion of 'hegemonic masculinity' has become highly influential in the study of the relationship between men, masculinity and violence. Connell, aided by a number of collaborators in the general profeminist project (see Kimmel, 1987, 1996; Morgan, 1992; Messerschmidt, 1993), has tried to support yet problematize the pivotal feminist claim that violence is an instrument of transhistorical male or 'heteropatriarchal' dominance and oppression in the gender order. His claim that '[a] structure of inequality on this scale . . . is hard to imagine without violence . . . [perpetrated by] . . . the dominant gender who hold and use the means of violence' (1995: 83) is balanced by an awareness that, on the one hand, many acts of violence could be expressions of the continuity of that oppressive power or, on the other, reactions to its perceived discontinuity.

Connell's introduction of the 'threatened male' into the discourse allows the totalizing image of the transhistorically oppressive male to be juxtaposed against its vulnerable *alter ego*. He builds on this tension by claiming that a diversity of 'subordinated' masculinities shadows the traditional oppressive norm, offering men alternative gendered identities that can contest this norm in progressive ways. Following Gramsci (1971), he names the traditional, oppressive gender form 'hegemonic' because it utilizes cultural production to reproduce ideologically its institutionalized dominance over 'subordinated' men as well as women (1995: 78–9). This reinforces his earlier claim that both the gender *and* internal masculine orders are structured by '. . . a historically constructed pattern of power relations between men and women and definitions of femininity and masculinity' (1987: 184).

Summarizing this complex position would risk oversimplification, but it does rest on the pivotal concept of 'hegemony'. The Italian neo-Marxist Antonio Gramsci reformulated this old term to mean the use of popular cultural production—texts, images and ideas—to engineer among the subordinate proletarian mass a fragile consensus that the bourgeoisie's power, wealth and privilege was the product of 'natural' values, forces and circumstances. Thus hegemony helped to reproduce the class order by incorporating the bulk of the working class *mentally and emotionally* into the dominant belief-system, preventing a conscious appraisal of their material exploitation and politico-cultural subjugation that might have led to the politics of social transformation. Gramsci furnished the intellectual world with a vital insight; how class and corporate power is no longer reproduced principally by crude, coercive means, but by the naturalizing, legitimizing and mystifying ideological production of institutions such as the state, the family, religion, art and mass media. The influence of this ideology on everyday life can be seen in practices such as politics, wage negotiations, social policies, family relationships, schooling and child-rearing.

According to Connell (1995), traditional males mobilize similar ideological techniques to reproduce their real dominance over women in the gender order and, more notably, over 'subordinated masculinities' in the masculine order. 'Legal violence' and 'street violence' combine with 'economic discrimination' to constitute a set of '. . . quite material practices' (1995: 78) by means of which structures of dominance and subordination are enacted in real social and economic relations. Male-dominated cultural production 'exalts' these practices, giving men the impression that they have a legitimate right to call upon violence when it is deemed essential to the maintenance of the traditional order. In reality this often means in a brutal and arbitrary manner. This right has been distributed across the class order as one of a cluster of 'patriarchal privileges'. Hegemonic cultural production, in conjunction with the recurring enacted practices that it encourages (Butler, 1993), reproduces the belief that it is legitimate and natural for men to use violence as a means of oppressing women and less belligerent males. Thus male violence is the brutal core of a politico-cultural strategy that is deployed to sustain an illegitimate position of dominance. Men who intimidate or physically attack women, gay men or less assertive heterosexual men '. . . usually feel they are entirely justified, that they are exercising a right. . . authorised by an ideology of supremacy' (Connell, 1995: 83). Whether or not they are involved directly as '. . . the frontline troops of patriarchy' (1995: 79), 'complicit' males in all class positions benefit from it because it distributes a 'patriarchal dividend' of privileged and legitimated entitlements throughout the traditional masculine order, one of which is the right to use violence. Thus what Messerschmidt (1993) labels 'destructive masculinity' can take its place as one of the hegemonic forms that dominate both the gender order and the social order.

Connell (1995) goes on to draw what could have been useful distinctions in the masculine order. He divides it roughly into three main groups, which bear some resemblance to those that make up the class structure. First, the specialist producers and circulators of culture; second, the complicit, aggressive (but not necessarily violent) mainstream redeemers of the 'patriarchal dividend'; and third, the frequently violent 'protest masculinities' that inhabit the socio-economic margins. The members of this third group are the most likely to mobilize their entitlements to violence as a crude reaction to economic redundancy and the perceived threat of supersession by what they believe should be 'subordinate' gender forms.

However, although these formal distinctions give the impression that class divisions are not being entirely overlooked, they simply describe the differing ways in which class-based groups of men tend to 'rework' the same universal privileges and strategies of domination. The basic totalizing premise is retained: real male powers and privileges are hegemonically reproduced and distributed in the form of a universal 'patriarchal dividend' that *permeates the class divisions of the masculine order*. The central claim seems to be that traditional masculine culture has some sort of unifying, distributive property that overrides class divisions in order to maintain its dominant social position for the benefit of all traditional males.

However, Connell does not delve too deeply into the question of the *real value* that the privileged right to use intimidation and violence might carry, and whether it is enough to warrant such prodigious cultural production and a cherished place in the traditional male's inventory of power strategies. The debate on whether or not social power is based on abstract rights and beliefs is too expansive to discuss here, but suffice it to say that Pierre Bourdieu's (1984, 1990) economic metaphor is possibly more convincing. For him, the main purpose of displaying, enacting and reproducing the customary beliefs, rights, practices and expressive capacities that make up symbolic and cultural capital is that not only can they aid the maintenance of a perceived dominant social position, but also that they can be transferred eventually into *economic* capital. Although this might elicit a cry of 'economic reductionism' from some temporarily in-vogue theorists of the 'cultural turn', this protest often throws a smokescreen over their own tendency to reduce analyses of social power to the much less convincing premise of domination for its own sake. At least Bourdieu's perspective furnishes us with an objective material purpose for the struggle over cultural privileges. If this is the case, does the specific privilege of using intimidation and violence allow men to redeem this 'patriarchal dividend' politically and economically, or does it limit them to the fleeting liminal satisfaction of wielding pointless, destructive force over others? If indeed a unified 'patriarchy' does exist as a real social power, then its 'dividends' must be in some real sense exchangeable across class divisions. Put simply, it must be possible for lower-class men to *cash them in* for some of the real privileges and benefits enjoyed by those men who—alongside many women and 'subordinated masculinities'—inhabit the higher class or occupational echelons. If profitable exchange is infrequent rather than routine, then, in the case of violence, the personal is quite possibly *not* very political.

Connell (1995) glosses over this question of material reward in two main ways. First, he expresses the disparity of wealth between men and women in terms of a crude mean average income. This move ignores class divisions, not only allowing him to place a £3.60 per hour security guard or a £50 per night doorman in the same politico-economic category as a male billionaire, but also in a position of 'structural' dominance over a £300,000 per year female Q.C. or 'subordinated masculine' media executive. It also carries the tacit suggestion that, in the project of liberating homosexuality, a gay security guard might share mutual *political* interests with a gay media executive, an intellectual position in which the cultural politics of sex and gender override rather than 'intersect with' the economic politics of class, making his claim to give '. . . full weight to their class as well as their gender politics' (1995: 75) sound rather hollow. If this statistical average were to be broken down, it would become quite obvious that it is heavily skewed by the vast fortunes owned by a very small number of men.

It is also difficult to see how the 'patriarchal privileges' enjoyed by the lower classes can be expressed even in purely *cultural* terms. How, for instance, could the notion that '. . . [m]en gain a dividend from patriarchy in terms of honour, prestige and the right to command' (Connell, 1995: 82) be applied to the security guard, apart from the honour and prestige of wearing a peaked cap adorned with the firm's logo and the right to command his Alsatian dog? Connell, in an attempt to retain some notion of class, claims that the class and gender orders 'intersect' (1995: 75). However, he seems reluctant to explain exactly how, or provide any thick description of everyday life in the nodes of intersection, preferring instead to illustrate his argument with rather rare examples of working-class masculinities that might be experiencing some form of 'gender vertigo' (1995: 142). The inconspicuous majority—the comfortably heterosexual, quietly traditional and far less exotic young males who populate the streets, pubs and clubs of every western town and city—are conveniently ignored.

Second, he fails to apply even this crude economic analysis to the *internal masculine order* itself, the very focus of his study. This exercise would furnish us with a rough sketch of the general economic class positions occupied by those masculinities that he posits as 'culturally subordinated' in the masculine order. However, as far as I know, no such research exists. Until it does we have very little idea of the offices of social power that these 'subordinated' forms might have held across the history of liberal-capitalism.

Although Connell's notion of 'protest' highlights the overall frustration in lower-class locations, it does not explain why these men would protest so forcefully over the loss of specific 'privileges' that, in what will be argued is a normative climate of pacification, have never been really valuable and are now virtually worthless. This problem is an indicator of fundamental contradictions in the concept of 'hegemonic masculinity', especially its connection to violence. In Gramsci's formulation of hegemony, cultural production was designed to engineer an *inclusive consensus*, and one important aspect of this was the creation of a secularized faith that would encourage the lower orders to emulate and aspire to the values and practices of their 'natural leaders'. If we remember that the bourgeoisie itself rose from the lower ranks of feudalism, then practising the entrepreneurial faith that grew around the developing economic logic of the market, as so many peasants and workers did (Hobbs, 1995), could always enhance prospects of status and wealth. Embracing bourgeois hegemony could produce *real results* for the active believer, and *real subordination* for the working-class passive believer or dissenter.

Does the *active believer*—and violent males are nothing if not active—in traditional masculine hegemony benefit in a similar way? Something approaching the *inverse* of this might be the case. Although the bourgeoisie aspired to create an inclusive yet hierarchal society in its own image, it seems to have made a significant exception in the case of those lower-class men who were required to construct and defend the physical infrastructure on which its power and prosperity ultimately depended. Crude, aggressive masculinity was constituted primarily by enforced and brutalizing practical experience (Horne and Hall, 1995) and culturally reproduced by *exclusive* subaltern anti-norms, which are difficult to label 'hegemonic' in a capitalist project where socially and politically powerful men increasingly abandoned physical violence for a form of sublimated, codified aggression. If this *pseudo-pacified* elite controlled the means of cultural production, it is difficult to depict the crude caricature of 'destructive masculinity' as part of the elite's attempt to engineer a legitimizing consensus by affirming itself as the pinnacle of a 'natural order'. Rather—and this is in keeping with the historical and anthropological tradition of many cultures (see Gilmore, 1990)—the purpose might have been to constitute and reproduce at a safe distance an archaic hyper-masculine 'other', whose insecure and peripheral social inclusion actually depended on his serviceability.

These problems need to be examined in more detail, because they suggest that Connell's overall theory suffers from some elementary misconceptions. First, the claim that '. . . members of the privileged group use violence to sustain their dominance' (1995: 83) is excessively simplistic in its direct association of violence and social domination, and it neglects the complex dimorphic nature of violence as both a symbolic and a material practice (see Hall, 2000). Second, his one-dimensional conceptions of cultural hegemony, violence, state formation and the logic of capital accumulation do not bear the mark of deep exploration. The correspondences that he draws between them, summed up in the quotation below, seem to be informed by a notion of consumer-driven neocapitalism as the old Wright–Millsian *military–industrial complex* that characterized the productivist–imperialist form of classical capitalism. As such, they are quite stunningly simplistic and dated:

> Nevertheless, hegemony is likely to be established only if there is some correspondence between cultural ideal and institutional power, collective if not individual. So the top levels of business, the military and government provide a fairly convincing *corporate* display of masculinity, still very little shaken by feminist women or dissenting men. It is the successful claim to authority, more than direct violence, that is the mark of hegemony (though violence often underpins or supports authority).
>
> (Connell, 1995: 87, emphasis in original)

This rather vague statement tells us little about precisely how, when, by whom and for what purposes 'direct violence' is exercised, or exactly who is really benefiting from it. Complex and divergent institutionalized authorities, cultural ideals and class practices, between which he posits nothing more detailed than 'some correspondence', are being conflated in the questionable notion of a unified masculine authority. Perhaps this ambiguity can be addressed by emphasizing that capitalism has from its beginnings deemed the *physical pacification* of the internal territory to be essential to its economic expansion and social reproduction (a position reflected clearly and consistently in bourgeois high culture and law). Viewed from this perspective, the claim that enacted violence was ever a valuable 'power' and 'privilege' reflecting the sort of multi-dimensional and paradoxical authorities that capitalism required seriously neglects its complex institutional, moral and functional contexts.

To support a connection between violence as a valuable 'privilege' and a patriarchal order that is sufficiently unified and organized to be able to distribute this privilege as part of a general 'dividend', Connell's three patriarchal groups must be shown to have common interests. Then, to avoid reducing the issue entirely to culture and gender, the patriarchy's ability to distribute real social, political and economic benefits among its members without too much class and racial discrimination must be clearly demonstrated. Also, the real value of physical violence across capitalism's history, over and above its obvious ability to establish temporary interpersonal dominance over other individuals, must be appraised. Finally, if violence is to be connected firmly to institutional power, the claim that the 'hegemonic' cultural encouragement to practise it does actually represent the distribution of a dividend that has real value in the *current* socio-economic context must be rigorously examined. If there are reasonable doubts about any of this then quite clearly criminology should defer the use of 'hegemonic masculinity' as an explanatory tool in its research into violence and masculinity.

Patterns of violence

Can we find empirical support for the claim that men who indulge in acts of crude aggression or violence really benefit from patriarchal power and privilege? Analyses that are based on the intersection of class and race teem with evidence to the contrary. Even if feminist criminology's important disclosure of hidden domestic violence in all class echelons is taken into account, a broad sweep of research findings suggests that the more serious forms of interpersonal violence—especially murder—are more conspicuous among the marginalized fragments of the (former) working class. Even if all the usual phenomenological and political problems of data construction and interpretation are acknowledged (see Maguire, 1997), we will see shortly that both statistical and ethnographic studies of serious and fatal violence show an undeniable concentration in specific social and geographical locations.

There are four main sources of contemporary positivist data: police records of arrests and convictions, government victimization surveys, self-report surveys and health service statistics.

Basing his conclusions on official statistics, while taking some account of their unreliability, the psychologist Oliver James (1995) claims that there was an 'unprecedented rise' in interpersonal violence among 14–16-year-olds between 1987 and 1993 in England and Wales. He focuses predominantly on the legal category 'violence against the person', which constitutes 75 per cent of all violent crimes that appear in the annual Home Office publication, *Criminal Statistics*. Although this category covers recorded incidents from homicide to domestic assaults, he notes that the bulk of the cases concern '. . . young men from poor backgrounds punching, kicking and stabbing each other' (1995: 1). The idea that similar levels and forms of violence occur in comfortable middle-class suburbs is a myth (Wilson, 1987; Lea, 1992; Currie, 1993). James' work indicates that some cohorts of working-class males from economically abandoned areas have become up to 30 times more violent in the period 1955 to 1995.

Attempts to deny or explain away working-class violence have been less than successful. The general feeling expressed by most non-idealist criminologists is that the incidence of serious violence is likely to be far higher than the average in specific economically impoverished areas (Wilson, 1987; Currie, 1993). Although it must be made quite clear that this is by no means a general practice permeating either *all* or *whole* poor areas (Horne and Hall, 1995), these findings cannot simply be dismissed. The likelihood is that the under-reporting of violence might well understate the reality of the situation *in specific areas*, perhaps even more than unjustified police or media attention might exaggerate the general picture (Currie, 1993; Hall, 1995, 1997). This makes political sense if we remember that *understatement*, with its emotional effect *complacency*, is just as effective as *exaggeration*, with its emotional effect *anxiety*, as a metonymic device in the construction of establishment rhetoric. As usual, the reality seems to be more complex and spatially specific. Recent work on the 'fear of crime' indicates that a decrease in the fear of being on the street after dark in more salubrious locales contrasts with an increase in fear—and in the actual risk of victimization—in economically abandoned locales (see Lea and Young, 1993: 45–9). The 'average risk' calculation, which claims that in Britain a 'statistically average' person can expect to be the victim of violence once every 100 years, ignores the extreme variation of victimhood across social and geographical space and the reality of '. . . the daily spontaneous outbursts of violence in the margins . . .' (Lea and Young, 1993: 39).

A recent medical study conducted in the Accident and Emergency departments of large urban hospitals in England (Hutchinson et al., 1998) offers striking support for this sort of interpretation. According to this work, some of the larger hospitals are treating up to 1000 serious facial injuries per year, usually inflicted during 'drink-related' fighting between young, working-class males. In 1998, the 16–25-year-old cohort constituted the bulk of admissions. A national total of something like 18,000 per year are suffering lifetime scarring of the face. What used to be a bit of stitching up after a fist-fight is now more serious because of the increased use of weapons such as reinforced boots, knuckle dusters, baseball bats, scaffold poles, knives and the occasional firearm.

The relatively comprehensive statistical overview of North American crime compiled by Dobrin et al. (1996) indicates that the USA suffers from the highest murder rate in the industrialized West; 37 per 100,000 for young men between the ages of 15 and 24 compared to less than 2 per 100,000 for the same group in England and Wales. This is five times the average of the other industrialized nations and twice that of Northern Ireland during the 'troubles'. Given that men do most of the killing, it is quite telling that 17,949 males were also the *victims* of homicide, compared to 5278 women. This male number constitutes 77 percent of the total, and the vast majority of incidents occur outside the domestic sphere among the most impoverished male members of the lower classes and ethnic groups. It is, in other words, being practised predominantly among the most powerless and socio-economically devalued male groups in American society, very often catalysed by alcohol or drugs and occurring among young men who know each other (Gibbs and Merighi, 1994). There is no need to downplay the gravity of domestic and sexual violence, homophobic bullying or workplace intimidation to appreciate that the redemption of this 'patriarchal privilege' (or the supposed protest lodged against its unavailability) is more often than not manifested in *materially and politically pointless* inter-male violence. The only discernible reward that the audience of fellow marginals can bestow is *applause*, a brief moment of approval that, because it delivers only a fleeting shadow of the glory it promises, becomes a highly addictive but ultimately futile pursuit. Some 'privilege'.

A helpful cross-cultural comparison emerges from Zimring and Hawkins' (1997) statistical analysis of assault and death. Compared to other industrialized western nations, the North American rate of assault is not unusual, but the death rate is. It seems that young American males are no more prone to petty altercations than their counterparts in other parts of the world, but because of the prolific use of firearms and other weapons they are certainly more likely to carry an argument to its most lethal conclusion. Therefore a lower murder rate in Western Europe does not indicate a lower violence rate. Although cultural and legal factors such as gun ownership can cause variations in the rate of death and serious injury, the general rise in *assault rates* among young men of the former working class across the industrialized West confirms the probability that they might be in the grip of similar socio-historical forces (Wilson, 1987; Hall, 1995, 1997; Currie, 1997; Taylor, 1999).

A brief look at the circumstances in which murders are committed also casts an empirical shadow of doubt over the direct linking of violence to institutional power, the 'patriarchal dividend' or 'reworked cultural privileges'. Alongside murders in 'unknown circumstances' (5059 men and 1352 women), the highest victim categories for both sexes were 'escalation of trivial arguments' (4698 and 1590), 'non-specified violence' (2071 and 989), 'robbery' (1950 and 351), and 'drug-related violence' (1180 and 105). Taken together, these categories towered above the others, totalling 19,388, which constituted 83 percent of the total of 23,271 in 1993 (Dobrin et al., 1996). Regionally, the highest murder rates—calculated as homicides per 100,000 of the population—were to be found in the economically troubled 'downtown' areas of Washington (80+), New Orleans (80+) and Detroit (60+). Black males are by far the most likely victims of murder, over 100 per 100,000 in the early 1990s compared to 20 for black females, nine for white males and two for white females. Newburn and Stanko's (1994) reminder of the high incidence of sexual and physical assaults against young males supports the claim that they tend to be the main victims as well as the perpetrators of physical violence. Adler (1992) and King (1992) suggest that male victimization tends to be under-reported mainly because of the taboo against 'informing' in lower-class male cultures, while Lister et al. (2000) attribute under-reporting to the rational avoidance, by both victims and perpetrators, of unpredictable police actions and legal outcomes. This, in combination with the silencing effect of intimidation, suggests that the actual number of assaults and injuries might be considerably higher. However, the vast majority of murders *do* enter the statistical record, and the victimization figures for black males have spiked upwards since the early 1980s, while those for white males have declined. This rise coincides with a number of major changes in the socio-economic fabric, such as high post-industrial unemployment, the intensified socio-economic exclusion and ghettoization of working-class racial minorities, and increased activity in the drug, nocturnal leisure and general criminal markets. Although intimidation and less physically injurious forms of violence are more evenly distributed across the social structure, most serious or lethal violence occurs in demographic clusters of poor, young, urban, minority males (Zimring and Hawkins, 1997).

Many ethnographic studies also tend to support the link between serious physical violence and socio-economic subordination. Gibbs and Merighi (1994) point to the multiple marginalization—in terms of race, age and class—of young lower-class blacks in American urban areas that have been deserted by the forces of capital. Some time ago Hannerz (1969) noted the drift into a 'compulsory masculinity' in impoverished and 'hypersegregated' neighbourhoods; a form characterized by sexual aggression, ostentation, high-risk behaviour and confrontational violence. In conditions of pragmatic social and economic stress, it displayed a tendency to become almost self-parodying, and many of the more committed individuals followed the stereotypical progression into gangs, crime, drugs and violence. Winlow (2001) notes that in some equivalent British locales the drug and theft industries are now providing more occupational positions for this 'pseudo-masculinity' than the mainstream economy. The probability that so many young, lower-class males continue to scratch a living in such impoverished conditions yet carry in their hearts and minds this parody of patriarchal authority suggests that violent hyper-masculinity is both an ideologically induced delusion (MacInnes, 1998) and a liminal fixation (Hall, 1995, 1997; Winlow, 2001) that emerged—or were cultivated—as complementary, sub-rational reproductive agents of an enforced practical relationship with specific material conditions (Hall, 1995, 1997; Horne and Hall, 1995). Or, to apply Bourdieu's (1990) more succinct formulation, rather than the product of cultural narratives or synchronic psychodynamic relations, it is a set of beliefs and dispositions carried in the body, a *habitus* that is the product of generations of recurring practical experiences in unforgiving material conditions, a brutal art of living supported by internalized but *externally constructed* cultural narratives (see also Hall, 1997; Winlow, 2001). The more committed subjects of this deeply entrenched form now seem to be falling deeper into a social cul-de-sac where these delusions and fixations are best able to sustain themselves (Hall, 1995, 1997; Horne and Hall, 1995).

Earlier ethnographic studies from the USA and Britain in the 1970s and 1980s (Chambliss, 1973; Willis, 1977; Schwendinger and Schwendinger, 1985) also support the idea that violence is associated with cultural vilification and a lowly social position. One of the most valuable insights to emerge is Paul Willis' notion that persistent displays of aggression attracted condemnation from authority figures and pacified yet more successful peers. This tended to shunt the perpetrators towards 'dead-end jobs', the most unrewarding positions in the occupational hierarchy. It raises the point that 'symbolic violence' (expressions of derogation that are part of the cultural suffocation and subsequent reconstitution of provincial working-class cultures—see Bourdieu, 1984, 1990, 1991) emanating from the pacified mainstream order is a powerful force in the sociogenesis, reproduction and socio-economic structuring of 'visceral cultures' (Hall, 1997, 2000).

Another common ethnographic finding on the theme of cultural derogation is that violence often flares up among men when sleights are made concerning the *performance* of traditional roles (Katz, 1988; Ptacek, 1988; Frieze and Browne, 1989). Polk (1994) confirms Wolfgang's (1958) finding that insults thrown at the traditional objects of male protection and provision—wives, girlfriends, family, close friends—are more likely to trigger violence than those directed at the person. Many cultural theorists have tended to underplay the importance of the way in which micro-interactions in the gender order—energized by powerful emotional dynamics such as expectation, judgement, honour and humiliation—are grounded and referenced in the logic of socio-economic performance (Gilmore, 1990). They operate with an impenetrable, preoccupying intensity in the worst material circumstances—where honour is constantly offended and humiliation is a structural condition of existence—which tends to restrict the practising or even imagining of alternatives (Horne and Hall, 1995).

Physical violence is also more likely to occur in front of a male audience. This indicates that many lower-class males are anxious to secure admiration in sub-cultures that are characterized by mimetic rivalry, where young men judge each other quite ruthlessly on their performances of normative sub-cultural expectations (Gilmore, 1990; Polk, 1994; Winlow, 2001). But if the perpetrators somehow feel or believe that violence is a privilege that can be contextually reworked for their own benefit, why are they predominantly *attacking each other*, and why are their everyday relationships characterized by so much anxiety, irritability and interpersonal hostility? Does membership of the supreme patriarchy—which supposedly authorizes access to the cultural resources and privileges that ensure continuing domination of the social world—engender feelings of triumph, solidarity and security, or express itself in the smug, elegant posture and celestial sneer of a timeless ruling elite? Miraculously, it appears not.

If this desolate mess is the only real result of the 'reworking of privileges', there might be a need for the patriarchy to introduce some sort of quality control on both its craftsmanship and its material. What is at its worst a forlorn cycle of socio-economic exclusion, foolish bickering, emotional combustion, violence, death and imprisonment does not seem to indicate the successful application of an institutionalized dominance strategy, the redemption of a 'patriarchal dividend', or the lodging of an effective 'protest'. Alternatively, it could be seen as the spontaneous fury that tends to follow a sense of betrayal as young men realize that, in this current socio-economic shift, most of their 'privileges' are—and in crucial ways always have been—bogus, obsolete and unredeemable for anything really valuable. Reactions such as this are quite common when the subject first catches a glimpse of itself as the victim of a deception that it barely understands; a deception that for some reason continues to be culturally promoted even though its material and political purposes have evaporated. There is an increasing tendency for young working-class men to do very badly in the acquisition of qualifications, rewarding occupations and wealth when compared to other social groups, including young working-class women (Amin, 1994; Taylor, 1999). If the powerful producers of patriarchal culture have at heart common interests that transcend class, why, rather than reaching down and pulling their lower-class brothers out of trouble, do they persistently sell them a hollow, useless fake? Why do they ply a trade in parodies of an obsolete power that cannot furnish these supposed beneficiaries with any tangible rewards unless they have access to traditional class privileges or neocapitalism's new offices? And, more disturbingly, why do those who are sold short continue to buy?

The evidence itself, with or without these alternative interpretations, casts some doubt on the idea that men with a propensity for crude aggression or physical violence are in receipt of cultural privileges that carry any material or structural exchange value in western societies. Some recent ethnographic studies conducted by Hobbs (1994, 1995), Horne and Hall (1995) and Winlow (2001) have begun to address this problem by contextualizing masculine practice in the nascent post-industrial, neocapitalist economy. In this rather novel context, physically violent men confront a '... post-traditional order that is by definition hostile to modes of authority based upon the eternal recurrence of male hegemony' (Hobbs, 1994: 120), an order that places high value on '.... *precisely the opposite sorts of dispositions*' (Hall, 1997: 468, emphasis in original). This insight demands some consideration of exactly what this mutating order actually *is* and, if it has an element of continuity, how it has been implicated in capitalism's historical process.

Classical capitalism, neocapitalism and the pseudo-pacification process

A telling problem with the hegemonic masculinity discourse is that earlier radical liberal and feminist arguments, which staged a one-dimensional critique of both capitalism and patriarchy as unremittingly oppressive tyrannies driven by the 'masculine traits' of aggression, intimidation and physical violence (see Messerschmidt, 1993), have not really been shaken off. Connell (1987, 1995) does hint that these traits cannot be posited as the cause or reproductive agent of modern violence, because social institutions both encourage and discourage them in complex and ambivalent ways (see also MacInnes, 1998), but again he fails to tell us precisely how. Theorists as disparate as Gramsci (1971) and Elias (1994) have acknowledged that capitalism and some of its patriarchal agents retained the right to use intimidation or violence in the international disputes that inevitably accompanied the pursuit of national power and wealth, and as a last resort in techniques of internal regulation such as policing and corporal punishment. However, they also recognized that the most strenuous politico-cultural effort was applied to the *elimination* of these practices in the internal state territory. The establishment of a more stable rule by enrolment into the social order—backed up by the rule of law—was both inferred by capitalism's market logic and preferred by its more committed and institutionally powerful agents. In short, a sort of expedient, selective *pacification process* in the internal territory vitally enhanced the market-capitalist project's capacity to maintain order and create wealth.

There is a good deal of empirical and historiographical evidence to support the claim that, compared to what preceded it, this pacification process was notably successful in reducing serious violence in the internal state territory. Historian Ted Gurr's (1981) classic empirical study of murder in England found that the overall rate decreased significantly from just under 20 per 100,000 at the beginning of the 13th century to less than 2 per 100,000 in 1950. Hanawalt (1976) demonstrates that the London rate was higher than average during the economic and political upheavals of the late 14th century, somewhere between 36 and 52. Although the point was made earlier in this article that the link between the murder rate and a general climate of violence is tenuous when cross-cultural comparisons are being made, these two phenomena correspond more precisely in the same cultural and geographical space. Gurr comments:

> . . . [T]hese early estimates of homicide rates sketch a portrait of a society in which men were easily provoked to violent anger, and were unrestrained in the brutality with which they attacked their opponents. Interpersonal violence was a recurring fact of rural and urban life.
>
> (1981: 307)

A number of historical studies show that most incidents of serious assault and murder followed arguments and flare-ups—especially between neighbouring families—in a general social climate where '. . . [h]atred, fear and violence were endemic in rural England before the Industrial Revolution' (MacDonald, 1981: 109). Girard's (1977) anthropological and literary studies support the salutary observation that much of the history of the pre-capitalist agricultural settlement was made against a permanent backdrop of petty hostility and mistrust. Bouts of violence erupted regularly, often ensnaring the protagonists in interminable cycles of revenge (Trompf, 1994; Hall, 2000). In contrast, the capitalist project has been characterized by a sustained downward trend in murder and serious interpersonal violence in the internal state territories of Europe from the mid-14th century to the mid-20th century. Remarkably, this occurred in spite of the intensification of conditions that, initial logic suggests, should have sent it spiralling upwards: increased socio-economic competition and class division; political, religious and economic upheaval; increased warfare; the structural consolidation of patriarchy, nationalism and racism; brutal state-administered class repression; and the creation of large numbers of landless labourers, some of whom in the midst of recession expanded the ranks of violent criminal bands (Beier, 1983; Briggs et al., 1996; Hill, 1996).

Despite these apparently countervailing conditions, early and high capitalism's hegemonic cultural power seems to have achieved some success in establishing a 600-year internal pacification process in emergent European states. However, it is wholly inaccurate to claim that this was the product of the reformist lobbying of pacifists, liberal humanists, philanthropists, religious groups or feminists. These movements played a role in arranging and monitoring pacifying codes, or introducing piecemeal reforms, but the claim that they were prime movers is quite simply erroneous. Behind the pacification process was capitalism's central purpose: the expansion of the commercial market economy. This simply could not proceed under the rigid patriarchal tyrannies administered by partially Christianized warlords in the seigniorial-feudal eras. In Early Modern Europe these elite groups, whose family-centred political power was maintained by the deployment of privatized intimidation and physical violence, began a steep political descent. In fact, capital's logic demanded a wholesale revaluation and modification of both physical and symbolic violence. This signalled the demise of the independent or ordained warrior as an arbitrarily violent territorial tyrant (Bolton, 1980; Maddern, 1992; Elias, 1994). It also ended the monopoly that the religious and royal *ministeria* traditionally held on the deployment of symbolic violence. In an interesting historical reversal, the physical violence that had permeated civil society was monopolized by the emerging state, while the symbolic violence that had been monopolized by the elite was quasi-democratized in civil society in the sense that it was placed by the ascending bourgeoisie under the authority of market logic (Hall, 2000). Although external warfare in some respects proliferated, this emergent elite was determined to cultivate internal peace alongside an aggressive but sublimated socio-economic dynamic.

Classical historians from Herodotus to Gibbon (1972 [1788]) knew that it is impossible to expand trade and increase prosperity under conditions of general disorder, hostility and violence, and that the attempt to restore order by means of centralized tyrannies creates only the most fragile, ephemeral peace. Throughout its reign the original bourgeoisie's interest in establishing the crucial *internal* pacification process markedly outweighed its interest in maintaining the right to exercise arbitrary physical violence, and the corporate management class that succeeded it has, for precisely the same reasons, retained this preference. Violent masculine customs that had established themselves in the seigniorial hierarchies, but which were deemed to be dysfunctional in the nascent capitalist economy, were either repressed by altered cultural coding, commercialized and heavily regulated or outlawed (Holt, 1989). There is no space here for a detailed exposition of the pacification process, and at this juncture the reader could be pointed towards Norbert Elias' work *The Civilizing Process* (1994 [1939]) and its burgeoning secondary literature (see Mennell, 1992; Fletcher, 1997). Very briefly—and with apologies for the crudity of this synopsis—of interest to this thesis is the way in which bourgeois society, establishing itself between the 16th and 19th centuries, based behavioural codes on the strict control of the visceral emotions. This process was supported by the state's monopolization of violence, the cultural prompting of individuals to psychosomatically internalize 'refined' behavioural codes as 'sensibilities', and the proliferation of 'figurations', long chains of social interdependencies in the expanding market and industrial economies in which individuals learnt to value each other. These expanding chains enabled and encouraged the traditionally despised lower orders to achieve more rewarding and valued social positions by displaying 'polite' postures and adopting non-violent forms of social and economic interaction.

However, in early capitalism's socio-economic environment, the process of distributing these behavioural codes was competitive, selective and uneven. A new class hierarchy grew around pacification because a convincing outward display of refined sensibilities became a vital requirement for entry to the expanding bourgeois social networks, which in turn lubricated personal access to the higher echelons of politics, trade and industry. The display of civility, manners, cultural knowledge and, most importantly, a reputation for being able to *sublimate aggressive liminal urges* became the main cultural criteria for social ascent (Bourdieu, 1984; Elias, 1994; Fletcher, 1997; Mellor and Shilling, 1997; Hall, 2000).

However, the capitalist socio-economic dynamic could not be fuelled by gentle sensibilities alone; if they had permeated every dimension of human interaction the dynamic might well have stalled. The velvet glove needed its iron fist, but the old, brittle fist of physical violence was to be replaced by a stronger and more flexible alloy. This was fashioned from what was known and available; in this case 'symbolic violence'. As explained earlier, this traditional form of symbolic derogation and cultural suffocation of the lower-class 'other' had for centuries been the exclusive privilege of religious, monarchical and aristocratic elites as a social ordering and control technique. Quasi-democratizing symbolic violence was a reasonably effective method of retaining aggressive interpersonal, familial and social competition in a modified form while simultaneously reducing trade-inhibiting forms of physical intimidation and violence. Thus the stimulation of those aggressive or fearful liminal urges and desires that could be translated into commodities and acceptable social ambitions, together with their diversion from physical expression by constant sublimation, gradually established itself as a core dynamic process (Hall, 2000). The personal adoption and expression of these elaborately coded sensibilities and practices signified the most valued mode of being in the classical capitalist project: 'Social advancement became less dependent upon one's ability to wield arms and more dependent upon one's ability to compete with words and planned strategies with which to win the favour of social superiors' (Fletcher, 1997: 35).

As a dynamic social and economic drive, symbolic violence proved itself to be infinitely more effective than the abandonment of the body in the ecstatic religious fervour and physical violence that had characterized so much of the past. Any requirements or opportunities for naked intimidation and physical violence were palmed off onto a residue of dislocated males, and discarded ex-warriors found themselves competing with dispossessed peasants in a new, 'democratized' set of specialist violent careers in war, adventuring, internal regulation and banditry (Beier, 1983).

This realignment and revaluation of the physical and the symbolic can be seen as a reworking of the essential *dimorphic* nature of violence (Hall, 2000), in other words the capacity of violence to operate as both a physical and a symbolic form of social power. Despite the utilization of ancient religious sublimating and ordering techniques (see Girard, 1977; Mellor and Shilling, 1997) in capitalist cultural production, the underlying utilitarian logic of the market's requirements meant that maximum effort was applied not to the exciting transformation of some Hegelian 'spirit of the age', but to the practical reduction of physical violence in the mundane public places and activities that were vital to commodity exchange: streets, marketplaces, fairs, taverns, highways, sea-lanes, etc. It would have been simultaneously over-ambitious *and* counter-productive to be totally democratic by applying strenuous efforts to the 'liberation' of all displaced men from the grip of the traditional masculine norms and habits that could provide specialist services to the capitalist project. Although a vestige of the old warrior culture was retained and rebriefed to perform supervisory roles in military expansion, a proportion of the hegemonic output from the increasingly domesticated elite was focused on modifying *already existing* serviceable masculine and feminine forms among the lower classes; what Connell names 'hegemonic masculinity' might make more sense if it is seen as a dimension of this output. However, because the limited social mobility in the quasi-democratized order did offer some escape routes, the gendered cultural reproduction of the 'visceral habitus' (see Hall, 1997) could only be even reasonably effective and reliable among those who were already consigned to a brutalizing existence in impoverished locations and physically demanding occupations by means of political repression, economic dispossession and the vagaries of the labour market. This paradox between the simultaneous needs for pacification and the retention of serviceable practices of physical violence is at the heart of bourgeois cultural deception and class structuring. What does not seem to be emerging from this perspective is a picture of capitalism as yet another epochal manifestation of the ancient civic entitlement to exercise physical violence to further personal, familial or 'gender' interests, or indeed the endurance of privatized violence as an effective strategy in the reproduction of real social power in the internal territory. What we might be looking at here, rather than Elias' general civilizing process *or* Connell's oppressive tyranny, is an extremely complex market-driven *pseudo-pacification process* that has been supported by paradoxical, inconsistent and duplicitous cultural activity.

Neocapitalism is the recent outcome of profound shifts in the basal productive mode and motive forces of its predecessor, classical capitalism. In the industrialized West, the acquisition and extraction of raw materials, their manufacture into commodities and the militarized defence and internal regulation of the political group's territory are now performed by sophisticated machines and robots rather than onerous muscular labour and physical violence. Information processing, commodity circulation and consumption and the attachment of artificial symbolic and aesthetic value to otherwise mundane commodity objects, have replaced productive, domestic and militaristic work as primary economic activities. A cursory glance at the post-industrial wage structure confirms the fact that even very basic technological, informatic, aesthetic and consumptive skills are much more valuable than traditional physical and practical skills (Amin, 1994; Horne and Hall, 1995; Rifkin, 1995; Taylor, 1999). This shift has set in motion *automatically* a systematic revaluation of the marketable dispositions, desires, beliefs, skills, qualities and appearances that constitute the *habitus* of diverse groups and individuals. In this culturally driven economy of symbols and aesthetic surfaces, the symbolic violence that the more powerful classes have honed to a fine edge can now dominate over all other forms of aggression as an instrument of social power and the focus of lower-class emulation. However, it would be grossly naïve to portray specialist cultural producers as permanent 'family members' of a specific ruling class or gender alongside which they rise and fall. Over the preceding 20 years the rather slippery behaviour of the press, broadcasting and general cultural industries suggests quite strongly that, within the parameters of market logic, they are adaptable, durable and independent power brokers with a keen eye for changes in the *zeitgeist*. Their allegiances to incumbent powers—ethico-religious, monarchical, patriarchal, governmental, corporate or otherwise—tend to slip and slide in a rather expedient manner (Hall, 2000). Symbol specialists operating in and around the commodity market now have the opportunity to reign over discredited, semi-redundant soldier-producers, domestic workers, politicians and old high-cultural *connoisseurs* (Gorz, 1989; Lasch, 1996; Hall, 2000); rather than continuing to serve ruling elites, they are rapidly *becoming* the ruling elite.

Some readers might suspect that the extent of symbolism's current dominance over material forces is being exaggerated. If so, perhaps the following quotation from Jeremy Rifkin's assiduously researched study on employment and social restructuring—which shows the rapid and permanent elimination of manual workers from the production process and the circulatory economy in the 'third industrial revolution'—might help to dispel some of the doubts:

> The information and communications technologies and global market forces are fast polarising the world's population into two irreconcilable and potentially warring forces—a new cosmopolitan elite of 'symbolic analysts' who control the technologies and forces of production, and the growing number of permanently displaced workers who have little hope and even fewer prospects for meaningful employment in the new high-tech global economy. (1995: xviii)

Connell (1995) recognizes that familiar models of working-class masculinity that were cultivated around the stable forms of practical-manual employment are now being discarded in this socio-economic transition. However, he fails to update his conception of the dominant elite, ignoring prosperous new groups and therefore also failing to locate marginality in the *full context* of neocapitalism's radically altered social relations. The intermittent employment, unemployment and severe deprivation experienced by traditional males must be seen *in relation* to the accelerating accumulation of wealth, security and status enjoyed by the physically pacified symbol specialists and their attendant service class (Amin, 1994; Lasch, 1996; Taylor, 1999; Hall, 2000). In this context, what are 'protest masculinities' actually protesting about? His claim that '[p]rotest masculinity is a marginal masculinity, which picks up themes of hegemonic masculinity in society at large but reworks them in a context of poverty' (Connell, 1995: 114) ignores the probability that the specific 'themes' of violence and crude aggression enacted among lower-class masculinities have never reflected any of the *sublimated* strategies required to achieve real political and economic success in capital's social hierarchy (Horne and Hall, 1995; Hall, 1997, 2000), and now they are becoming obsolete even as menial auxiliary tasks. Rather than playing a variation on their self-composed 'hegemonic' theme, redundant masculinities are being erased from the score by the newly appointed composer.

Underneath the crassly metonymic accounts of 'living fast and dying young' presented by Connell (1995) and others, there is little evidence of a cultural or psychodynamic logic of protest in the violence practised by young working-class men. There is even less evidence that this violence is 'underpinning or supporting' an institutionalized authority, to which strategic pseudo-pacification is far more important than persistent violence. Rather, there is some ethnographic evidence (James, 1995; Hobbs et al., 2000)—supported strongly by police and health service statistics—which shows that the politically pointless detonations of violence that occur among the young men who wander the streets, pubs and clubs of the deindustrialized zones are often triggered by the frustrations experienced in struggles over inadequate material resources. The majority of serious violence occurs in crowds and queues around night club doors, bars, taxi ranks, fast-food outlets and sporting events, or in the acquisition or distribution of drugs and other illegal commodities. These incidents are often catalysed by excessive intakes of intoxicants (James, 1995; Hobbs et al., 2000), and in some instances can be racially or ethnically motivated (Webster, 1996). Young men of more entrepreneurial leanings have become extremely adept in the pragmatic use of traditional forms of intimidation and violence to establish operations and generate cash in criminal or quasi-legal enterprise (Winlow, 2001). As the robust *habitus* enacts its limited dispositions and strategies in pressing socio-economic circumstances, psycho-cultural gender discourses do not provide the principal generative or reproductive forces, only vindicating narratives.

Conclusions

One constant requirement for the stability and prosperity of any past society based on trade and exchange was a complex structure of practical norms that could maintain interpersonal pacification in tension with aggressive social competition, while also being able to call on physical force and violence when required. From this perspective, 'destructive masculinity' is simply an archaic form that was modified to service capitalism's political economy. Higher-class groups seem to have invested in pacification because they eventually recognized that, in the longer term, this was a much more durable source of real political power because it was more effective in creating wealth, expanding markets, accruing legitimate political capital and maintaining stability. This group dominated cultural production to manufacture the archaic image of 'destructive masculinity' specifically for serviceable lower-class males, along with any others who were sufficiently gullible actively to adopt it as a narrative that justified the practices of their allocated roles, and, eventually, when culture was fully mediated and commercialized, spend their money buying it.

If genuine bourgeois hegemony was an affirming cultural image of its own existing social order (even though Gramsci agreed with Marx—who might not have been wrong about everything—that this social order itself was an inversion of real productive values and relations), the image of the violent macho male in eternal sovereignty over the pacified was certainly not. Rather, 'hegemonic masculinity' was an important element of the original ideological mystification of *real* productive relations, a ruse that helped to legitimize and reproduce *existing* inverted social relations. If lower-class males were to be simultaneously motivated and exploited, the machismo-myth had to be extravagantly inflated in the gender and cultural orders both to disguise and compensate for the fact that the ascending pseudo-pacified elite, and the economic logic they served, were in reality exploiting physically aggressive males as part of the class of materially productive males and females. This was a risky cultural ruse constructed simultaneously to mollify and motivate working-class males who had little alternative but to *do* the violent and dirty work allocated to them; to inspire them as active participants in their own subordinated functions and eventually to neutralize the dangerous political opposition that emerged in later stages of the project in the form of labour movements. Modernist 'femininity' was, of course, a complementary ruse encouraging working-class women to perform very different but equally onerous and unrewarding functions. The mass cultural output that attempts to reproduce the classic models of aggressive masculinity or passive femininity is a deception initially contrived by a genuine hegemonic elite to harness the violence and hard labour of the politically and culturally powerless. Because its function is not to distribute the dominant class' own beneficial, pseudo-pacified way of life across the social landscape, but rather to engineer through a one-way mirror an alternative consensus among a subordinate class 'other' about its own much less rewarding way of life, this cultural output cannot be described as 'hegemonic'.

In this light it becomes clear that there is no overall 'crisis of masculinity' across neocapitalism's reconfiguring class order. In the reality of the pseudo-pacification project, the class factions of the masculine order have never been united under a patriarchal flag in the first place. What Connell claims to be a gender relation in which an institutional 'hegemonic' masculinity uses violence to oppress reconstructing 'subordinate' masculinities is, in terms of real politico-economic power and success, *the inverse of the real class relation* that continues to structure the masculine order. Now, in the neocapitalist order, the economic function in which traditional masculinities were grounded has largely evaporated, which means that these so-called 'subordinate' masculinities are not 'reconstructing' but rather recognizing that the time has come to reveal and fully assert themselves. His fundamental mistakes are first to ignore that the pacified have learnt how to exert a fragile rule over the violent, and second to posit physically pacified, non-macho masculinities as new, alternative or revolutionary: at the beginning of the bourgeois revolutions 600 years ago he would have been correct.

Thus there is no real 'crisis' among the mainstream cohort of pseudo-pacified, commodity-circulating and symbol-processing males, only a bit of pique, nervous apprehension and inconvenience as female and educated working-class incomers flood in to their privileged spaces in a period of rapid expansion and disruption. They will get over it. The *real social and economic crisis* is being experienced by traditional working-class men and women who inhabit the former heavy industrial heartlands that once relied on sex-specific variations of physical labour in the productivist, domestic and military spheres. These locations, cut off both geographically and culturally from the centres and arteries of mainstream commodity circulation and symbol processing, are now the heart of nowhere.

Connell acknowledges that the 'destructive' masculine form is a caricature that can be embraced quite gullibly by working-class men (see Taylor, 1999). However, he ignores the contextualizing fact that the pseudo-pacified mainstream has for 600 years exploited the brutalizing practices of hard labour, violence and the stultifying practices of domestic drudgery that working-class men and women performed in the name of their respective caricatures. From this perspective, the notion that the right to exercise violence was at any time in this historical epoch a 'privilege' that promoted the interests of anyone but these pseudo-pacified rulers has to be suspect. Absent from Connell's account is the most obvious and extensively evidenced source of violence: that it was a brutal skill and a common livelihood practised by expendable lower-class males across the millennia of our hostile and physically demanding agricultural-industrial history; a form of enforced service to incumbent elites who manipulated the symbolic to reproduce their real wealth and political dominance (Hall, 2000). Connell's claim that the '. . . members of the privileged group use violence to sustain their dominance' (1995: 83) is correct as far as it goes, but it omits the crucial qualification that the dominant classes *avoid actually doing violence themselves*. Put simply, until very recently the lower classes have been ruled not only with the surplus products of their own labour but also with their own violence.

The altered, disorganized neocapitalist commodity market still has a use for intimidation, 'hardness' and physical violence, although the corresponding occupational fields, like others based on physical labour, have been severely 'downsized'. The remaining fields are in the general areas of criminality and the increasingly privatized methods of regulating it. Here the cultural ideal of hyper-masculinity continues to be generated and reproduced in economic reality, more intensely than ever because, compared to their predecessors, these new fields offer limited opportunities. The localized need to display 'hardness' as a marketable skill would at least partly explain the predominance of male-on-male violence and the preference for an audience through which the reputation of the 'hardest' can be transmitted. There are large numbers of former working-class individuals who, as Crowther (2000) suggests very persuasively, are very unlikely to find a place in the radically altered neocapitalist mode of production. Some have sunk into a general apathy that is punctuated by detonations of politically pointless interpersonal hostility (Horne and Hall, 1995), while others seek economic opportunities in those sectors of the economy where the boundary between criminal and legal commodity circulation is blurred (Hobbs, 1995; Ruggerio, 1996). Large numbers of young men are engaging with criminal and quasi-legal occupations such as property theft, selling stolen goods, drug distribution, protection racketeering, private security and varieties of temporary, unofficial physical labour. In some areas these fields of activity are providing more 'job' opportunities than the mainstream economy (Hudson, 1986; Winlow, 2001), and here hyper-masculinities number among the gendered forms that are deeply embedded in new capital–labour relations (Taylor and Tyler, 2000) and market imperatives (Hall, 1997; Winlow, 2001).

Once again, much of this is the dirty, violent, unrewarding work that members of the pseudo-pacified elite would rather not do, and which has traditionally been serviced by their very own subaltern social construction, *the drudges of fury*. To expect pious proposals of reconstructed masculine positions or progressive parenting to be taken seriously enough to have a transforming effect in these brutal spaces would be to push the boundaries of credibility, while in the socio-economic mainstream they amount to little more than pointless sermonizing to those who are already being slowly but inexorably converted by historical forces. However, these reformist cultural schemes—touted by self-appointed priests of pacifism who bask in the security of the symbol-processing mainstream—transcend mere piety. They are also *active* in the process of socio-economic exclusion because the very act of identifying an inadequate 'other' in need of reform reverberates around the 'symbolically violent' and socially competitive value system at the heart of neocapitalism. No matter how sympathetically and delicately this is done, it translates itself *automatically* into a process of deselection in the new occupational and social networks. Thus too many traditional males are debarred from the real processes that are gradually promoting 'change', and the overall culturalist project colludes in the intensified reproduction of that which it wishes to reform.

In this bleak climate western governments are left with only two choices. The first, and possibly still preferable among the Left's less fashionable and vocal majority, would be more serious political intervention in the forces of the market and capitalism's culture machine. The return of full employment in the form of 'decent' tenured jobs and the retraction of consumer pressure —at an opportune time when brutalizing occupations are no longer required functions—could afford working-class men the time, security, practical incentives and cultural refuge needed to reflexively change their ways of being. It might be preferable, but under the present political regime it is also highly unlikely (Habermas, 1989; Hall, 1997; Taylor, 1997, 1999). This leaves us with only the restoration of the state's capacity to prevent and reduce male violence in the spaces where it occurs, which tend to be against other males in public and against women in private. This means simply more accountable and effective policing.

Left-liberal criminology, with its voyages into the oxymoronic world of 'cultural politics', is suffering the same fate as the general progressivist-reformist movement to which it belongs: paralysed in the negative double-bind that it brought upon itself when its initial rejection of old interventionist socio-economic strategies was followed by its subsequent distaste for the fragmented authoritarian measures that are being applied to clear up the social mess that appeared after political economy was meekly handed over to neoliberalism and market forces. In this hiatus it is forced to save face, so it feigns a preference for the only position that its political capitulation allows; one of repose to chatter about whether or not the intellectual flotsam and jetsam washed up by obsolete radical liberal currents can sustain its utopian yearnings. Quite simply, it no longer fulfils its function as a credible opposition. In a market-driven neocapitalist order that can transpose all sweet dreams into lifestyle commodities and competitive social hierarchies Connell's '. . . politics of pure possibility' (1995: 243) are a part of this clutching at straws. Meanwhile, pointless hostility flourishes in the social margins that neocapitalism has left gasping for breath, and at its reconstructed economic heart privatized violence inexorably revises its tactics, alters its forms and expands its endeavours.

Acknowledgements

Thanks to Tony Jefferson and Simon Winlow for valuable comments on earlier drafts, without whose help and patience these ideas could not have been presented in a comprehensible form. Nevertheless, despite what Jacques Derrida said, only the author is to blame for it.

References

Adler, Z. (1992) 'Male Victims of Sexual Assaults— Legal Issues', in G.C. Mezey and M.B. King (eds) *Male Victims of Sexual Assaults*. Oxford: Oxford University Press.

Amin, A. (ed.) (1994) *Post-Fordism: A Reader*. Oxford: Blackwell.

Beier, A.L. (1983) *Masterless Men*. London: Methuen.

Bolton, J.L. (1980) *The Medieval English Economy 1150–1500*. London: J.M. Dent.

Bourdieu, P. (1984) *Distinction*. London: Routledge.

Bourdieu, P. (1990) *The Logic of Practice*. Cambridge: Polity.

Bourdieu, P. (1991) *Language and Symbolic Power*. Edited by J.B. Thompson and translated by G. Raymond and M. Adamson. Cambridge: Polity.

Briggs, J., C. Harrison and A. McInnes (1996) *Crime and Punishment in England*. London: UCL Press.

Brittan, A. (1989) *Masculinity and Power*. Oxford: Basil Blackwell.

Butler, J. (1993) *Bodies That Matter*. London: Routledge.

Chambliss, W.J. (1973) 'The Saints and the Roughnecks', *Society* 11(1): 24–31.

Connell, R.W. (1987) *Gender and Power: Society, the Person and Sexual Politics*. Cambridge: Polity Press.

Connell, R.W. (1995) *Masculinities*. Oxford: Blackwell.

Crowther, C. (2000) 'Thinking about the Underclass: Towards a Political Economy of Policing', *Theoretical Criminology* 4(2): 149–67.

Currie, E. (1993) *Reckoning: Drugs, the Cities and the American Future*. New York: Pantheon.

Currie, E. (1997) 'Market, Crime and Community: Toward a Mid-Range Theory of Post-Industrial Violence', *Theoretical Criminology* 1(2): 147–72.

Dobrin, A., B. Wiersema, C. Loftin and D. McDowall (1996) *Statistical Handbook on Violence in America*. Phoenix, AZ: Oryx Press.

Elias, N. (1994 [1939]) *The Civilizing Process*. Oxford: Basil Blackwell.

Fletcher, J. (1997) *Violence and Civilization*. Cambridge: Polity.

Frieze, I.H. and A. Browne (1989) 'Violence in Marriage', in L. Ohlin and M. Tonry (eds) *Family Violence*. Chicago, IL: University of Chicago Press.

Gibbon, E. (1972 [1788]) *The Decline and Fall of the Roman Empire*. New York: Dell.

Gibbs, J.T. and J.R. Merighi (1994) 'Young Black Males: Marginality, Masculinity and Criminality', in T. Newburn and E.A. Stanko (eds) *Just Boys Doing Business*. London: Routledge.

Gilmore, D.D. (1990) *Manhood in the Making: Cultural Concepts of Masculinity*. London: Yale University Press.

Girard, R. (1977) *Violence and the Sacred*. Baltimore, MD: John Hopkins University Press.

Gorz, A. (1989) *Critique of Economic Reason*. London: Verso.

Gramsci, A. (1971) *Selections from Prison Notebooks*. London: New Left Books.

Gurr, T.R. (1981) 'Historical Trends in Violent Crime: A Critical Review of the Evidence', *Crime and Justice: An Annual Review of Research* iii: 295–353.

Habermas, J. (1989) 'The New Obscurity: The Crisis of the Welfare State and the Exhaustion of Utopian Energies', in J. Habermas (ed.) *The New Conservatism*, edited and translated by Shierry Weber Nicholsen. Cambridge: Polity Press.

Hall, Steve (1995) 'Grasping at Straws: The Idealisation of the Material in Liberal Conceptions of Youth Crime', *Youth and Policy* 48: 49–63.

Hall, Steve (1997) 'Visceral Cultures and Criminal Practices', *Theoretical Criminology* 1(4): 453–78.

Hall, Steve (2000) 'Paths to Anelpis, 1: Dimorphic Violence and the Pseudo-Pacification Process', *Parallax: A Journal of Metadiscursive Theory and Cultural Practices* 6(2): 36–53.

Hanawalt, B.A. (1976) 'Violent Death in Fourteenth and Early Fifteenth Century England', *Comparative Studies in Society and History* xviii.

Hannerz, U. (1969) *Soulside: Inquiries into Ghetto Culture and Community*. New York: Columbia University Press.

Hill, C. (1996) *Liberty aganist the Law*. London: Allen Lane.

Hobbs, D. (1994) 'Mannish Boys: Danny, Chris, Crime, Masculinity and Business', in T. Newburn and E.A. Stanko (eds) *Just Boys Doing Business? Men, Masculinities and Crime*. London: Routledge.

Hobbs, D. (1995) *Bad Business: Contemporary Professional Crime, Culture and Change*. Oxford: Oxford University Press.

Hobbs, D., P. Hadfield, S. Winlow, S. Lister and S. Hall (2000) 'Receiving Shadows: Governance and Liminality in the Night-Time Economy', *British Journal of Sociology* 51(4): 701–17.

Holt, R. (1989) *Sport and the British: A Modern History*. Oxford: Clarendon.

Horne, R. and S. Hall (1995) 'Anelpis: A Preliminary Expedition into a World without Hope or Potential', *Parallax: A Journal of Metadiscursive Theory and Cultural Practices* 1(1): 81–92.

Hudson, R. (1986) 'Producing an Industrial Wasteland: Capital, Labour and the State in the North East of England', in R. Martin and B. Rowthorn (eds) *The Geography of De-Industrialisation*. London: Macmillan.

Hutchinson, I.L., P. Magennis, J.P. Shepherd and A.E. Brown (1998) B.A.O.M.S. United Kingdom Survey of Facial Injuries, Pt. 1: Aetiology and the Association with Alcohol Consumption. *British Journal of Oral and Maxillofacial Surgery* 36: 3–13.
Ingham, M. (1984) *Men: The Male Myth Exposed.* London: Century.
James, O. (1995) *Juvenile Violence in a Winner–Loser Culture.* London: Free Association.
Katz, J. (1988) *Seductions of Crime.* New York: Basic Books.
Kimmel, M.S. (ed.) (1987) *Changing Men.* London: Sage.
Kimmel, M.S. (1996) *Manhood in America.* New York: Free Press.
King, M.B. (1992) 'Male Sexual Assault in the Community', in G.C. Mezey and M.B. King (eds) *Male Victims of Sexual Assaults.* Oxford: Oxford University Press.
Lasch, C. (1996) *The Revolt of the Elites and the Betrayal of Democracy.* New York: Norton.
Lea, J. (1992) 'The Analysis of Crime', in J. Young and R. Matthews (eds) *Rethinking Criminology: The Realist Debate.* London: Sage.
Lea, J. and J. Young (1993) *What Is to Be Done about Law and Order?* London: Pluto.
Levi, M. (1997) 'The Risk of Violence', in M. Maguire, R. Morgan and R. Reiner (eds) *The Oxford Handbook of Criminology.* Oxford: Clarendon.
Lister, S., D. Hobbs, S. Hall and S. Winlow (2000) 'Violence in the Night-Time Economy: Bouncers: The Reporting, Recording and Prosecution of Assaults', *Policing and Society* 10: 383–402.
MacDonald, M. (1981) *Mystical Bedlam.* Cambridge: Cambridge University Press.
MacInnes, J. (1998) *The End of Masculinity.* Buckingham: Open University Press.
Maddern, P. (1992) *Violence and Social Order: East Anglia 1422–1442.* Oxford: Oxford University Press.
Maguire, M. (1997) 'Crime Statistics, Patterns and Trends', in M. Maguire, R. Morgan and R. Reiner (eds) *The Oxford Handbook of Criminology.* Oxford: Clarendon.
Mellor, P.A. and C. Shilling (1997) *Re-forming the Body.* London: Sage.
Mennell, S. (1992) *Norbert Elias: An introduction.* Oxford: Basil Blackwell.
Messerschmidt, J.W. (1993) *Masculinities and Crime.* Lanham, MD: Rowman & Littlefield.
Morgan, D. (1992) *Discovering Men.* London: Routledge.
Newburn, T. and E.A. Stanko (1994) 'When Men Are Victims: The Failure of Victimology', in T. Newburn and E.A. Stanko (eds) *Just Boys Doing Business.* London: Routledge.
Polk, K. (1994) 'Masculinity, Honour and Confrontational Homicide', in T. Newburn and E.A. Stanko (eds) *Just Boys Doing Business.* London: Routledge.
Ptacek, J. (1988) 'Why Do Men Batter Their Wives?', in K. Yllo and M. Bograd (eds) *Feminist Perspectives in Wife Abuse.* Newbury Park, CA: Sage.

Rifkin, J. (1995) *The End of Work: The Decline of the Global Labour Force and the Dawn of the Post-Market Era.* New York: Tarcher/Putnam.

Ruggerio, V. (1996) *Organised and Corporate Crime in Europe.* Aldershot: Dartmouth.

Schwendinger, H. and J. Schwendinger (1985) *Adolescent Sub-Cultures and Delinquency.* New York: Praeger.

Taylor, I. (1997) 'Crime, Anxiety and Locality: Responding to the "Condition of England" at the End of the Century', *Theoretical Criminology* 1(1): 53–75.

Taylor, I. (1999) *Crime in Context.* London: Sage.

Taylor, S. and M. Tyler (2000) 'Emotional Labour and Sexual Difference in the Airline Industry', *Work, Employment and Society* 14(1): 77–95.

Trompf, G.W. (1994) *Payback: The Logic of Retribution in Melanesian Religions.* Cambridge: Cambridge University Press.

Webster, C. (1996) 'Local Heroes: Violent Racism, Localism and Spacism among Asian and White Young People', *Youth and Policy* 53: 15–27.

Willis, P. (1977) *Learning to Labour.* Farnborough: Saxon House.

Wilson, W.J. (1987) *The Truly Disadvantaged.* Chicago, IL: Chicago University Press.

Winlow, S. (2001) *Badfellas: Crime, Violence and New Masculinities.* Oxford: Berg.

Wolfgang, M.E. (1958) *Patterns in Criminal Homicide.* New York: Wiley.

Zimring, F.E. and G. Hawkins (1997) *Crime Is Not the Problem: Lethal Violence in America.* Oxford: Oxford University Press.

STEVE HALL is a Senior Lecturer in Sociology and Criminology at the University of Northumbria at Newcastle. He recently co-directed a research project called 'The Art and Economics of Intimidation', part of the ESRC Violence Research Programme.

[2]

Subordinating hegemonic masculinity

TONY JEFFERSON
Keele University, UK

Abstract

This article starts with a paradox, namely, the widespread talk of a 'crisis of masculinity' alongside the strong endorsement of Bob Connell's concept of 'hegemonic masculinity', a term which implies (following Gramsci's use of hegemony) the opposite of crisis. This produces the article's first objective, namely, a critical look at the origins of the term hegemonic masculinity and its subsequent usage. This finds it problematic on several grounds: its tendency to be used attributionally (despite Connell's insistence on the relational nature of masculinity) and, within criminology, focused specifically on negative attributes; its use in the singular, implying it is not a contingent, context-specific notion; and its oversociological view of masculinity. This last problem produces the article's second objective, namely, to begin to develop a more adequate, psychosocial view of masculinity. It does this in several stages. It starts with two attempts to produce more psychologically complex accounts of masculinity: one by Wetherell and Edley, which argues for the (Lacanian-inspired) idea of a psycho-discursive subject, but fails to produce an authentic inner world; another by MacInnes which distinguishes between sexual *genesis* (being born *of* a woman *and* a man) and sexual *difference* (being born *as* a woman *or* a man). This recognizes an inner world 'beyond social construction' (sexual *genesis*), but fails to address how this is related to particular investments in positions within gender relations (the social ideology of biological sexual *difference*). The final section attempts to put together the rudiments of a more adequate psychosocial understanding of masculinity, starting with the importance of sexual genesis and the early vulnerabilities and anxieties to which this gives rise, and the unconscious defences necessarily precipitated. Contrasting accounts of the unconscious follow: Freud's Oedipal, repression-based account in which gender is inherently implicated versus Klein's pre-Oedipal splitting/ projection-based account in which gender is not implicated. The problems with Freud's gendered account provide the basis for taking the Kleinian route. Thereafter, how to conceptualize the link between (psychic) anxiety and (social) gender is explored through the writings of Chodorow, Layton and (especially) Benjamin. It is on this terrain, I contend, where both fantasy and the social are co-present but irreducible, that a more adequate, psychosocial understanding of masculinity needs to be produced.

Key Words

anxiety • crisis of masculinity • hegemonic masculinity • identification • psychosocial • sexual difference • sexual genesis

The title of Susan Faludi's book, *Stiffed: The Betrayal of the Modern Man* (1999), aptly summarizes its core thesis. Based on six years of research and countless interviews with US men from all walks of life, *Stiffed* is a feminist-inspired investigation into the widely shared notion of a contemporary 'crisis of masculinity'. In essence, she conceptualizes the crisis as a 'betrayal' characterized by the replacement of a culture of useful production with an 'ornamental culture. . . [C]onstructed around celebrity and image, glamour and entertainment, marketing and consumerism', a culture in which there are 'almost no functional public roles' and hence no 'model of masculinity' showing 'men how to be part of a larger social system'. In such a culture, men are effectively rudderless: 'In an age of celebrity, the father has no body of knowledge or authority to transmit to the son. Each son must father his own image, create his own Adam' (1999: 35). Skilfully interweaving her interview materials with historical and socio-cultural data, the result is a compelling contemporary exploration of the 'American male dilemma' (1999: 594), one worthy of a writer who has won both a Pulitzer Prize for journalism and the National Book Critics Circle Award for non-fiction for *Backlash* (1992), her previous book on women.

Though it operates on a larger canvas, Faludi's *Stiffed* brings to mind the examination of the 'crisis of masculinity' affecting young men on a poor, declining estate in the north-east of England by the British award-winning journalist Bea Campbell. Young men's various anti-social responses to a world which no longer appeared to have much use for them, provides the core of the book *Goliath* (Campbell, 1993), an influential intervention in the British debate on men and masculinity, especially in criminological circles. *Stiffed* also reminds me of Mairtin Mac an Ghaill's excellent ethnographic study investigating 'the social construction and regulation of masculinities in a state secondary school' (1994: 3) in the West Midlands. In this he talks of different class- and race-based crises of masculinity. For Mac an Ghaill's 'white macho lads', a working-class group who rejected the 'three Rs' and embraced the 'three Fs—fighting, fucking and football' (1994: 58), the source of the crisis was the same economic restructuring affecting Faludi's American males and Campbell's north-eastern young men: 'the disruption and accompanying restructuring of the students' transitions from school to waged work, with the collapse of the local economy's manufacturing base, appeared to be creating a crisis in traditional white working-class forms of masculinity' (1994: 71).

Three important and influential texts from both sides of the Atlantic, all based on detailed empirical material, variously talking about contemporary crises of masculinity.[1] Though none define their use of the term 'crisis', all imply that the traditional masculine order—in terms of models, roles, practices, transitions, opportunities and institutions—has become thoroughly destabilized with the result that what it means to 'be a man' has become both a real personal problem for large numbers of men, and a pressing social problem for the societies in question, not least (for criminologists) because males for whom societies have no use will usually find anti-social 'uses' to plug the gap, like 'joy-riding', drug-taking or fighting (in the cases of Campbell's and Mac an Ghaill's young men). Though one might argue the detail or question the conceptual framing, it seems difficult to deny that something unsettling is happening to many men and their milieux in the present period.

On the other hand, Bob Connell, the most cited social scientist currently researching masculinity to whom we owe the enormously influential term 'hegemonic masculinity' (1987, 1995) would seem to be downplaying the significance of these seismic shifts in gender relations. Writing the lead article in the launch issue of the new journal *Men and Masculinities*, he has recently argued the need for students of masculinity to move beyond the 'ethnographic moment' (1998: 4) and begin to think in global terms. To assist this transition, he sketches a framework for this new agenda and proposes:

> that the hegemonic form of masculinity in the current world gender order is the masculinity associated with those who control its dominant institutions: the business executives who operate in global markets, and the political executives who interact (and in many contexts, merge) with them.
>
> (1998: 16)

This he wants to call 'transnational business masculinity', and tentatively suggests it is 'marked by increasing egocentrism, very conditional loyalties . . . a declining sense of responsibility to others. . . a limited technical rationality (management theory) [and]. . . increasingly libertarian sexuality' (1998: 16). He goes on to argue that although the 'gradual creation of a world gender order has meant many local instabilities of gender' (1998: 16) (a reference which might encompass the investigations of Faludi, Campbell and Mac an Ghaill), the Right-wing, neo-liberal agenda, which is restructuring economies everywhere, will not fund the kind of measures needed to sustain the reform of gender relations since they are too costly. The result is that 'the patriarchal dividend to men is defended or restored' (1998: 17). In other words, despite 'local instabilities', the world gender order remains substantially crisis-free, and a new hegemonic masculinity is emerging. Now while it would be foolish to deny the continuance of male domination across the globe, what is more contestable is whether such dominance is also hegemonic, a perhaps unintended elision that is fairly common in writings on the subject.[2] Dominance is a necessary but by no means a sufficient condition of hegemony, since, as I spell out below, a notion of consent is crucial to the latter. Thus, while the new 'transnational business masculinity' may be dominant in the world gender order (though I, personally, am not persuaded since I have difficulty conceptualizing a single 'world gender order' and *one* dominant masculinity), it is certainly not, in my understanding of the term, hegemonic.

What we appear to have here then is a paradox: one influential group of writers on men and masculinity talking in terms of a contemporary crisis (or crises) of masculinity (or masculinities) brought about fundamentally by the enormous changes precipitated by the advent of a truly global capitalism; and the influential Bob Connell (and his many followers) talking in terms of hegemonic masculinity; in Connell's case of one which is successfully riding the waves (and the 'many local instabilities of gender' these create) of the new global disorder, even benefiting from it (Connell's 'patriarchal dividend'). Can masculinity be 'in crisis' and 'hegemonic' (as opposed to merely dominant) at the same time? Doesn't the use of the term 'crisis', with its connotations of change, of breakdown, of instability, preclude the use of the term 'hegemonic' with its opposite connotations of successful (i.e. relatively stable, consensually achieved, crisis-free) domination? Certainly we thought so when, in *Policing the Crisis* (Hall et al., 1978), we discussed changing class relations in post-war Britain and contrasted the hegemonic 1950s with the crisis-laden 1970s when hegemony had broken down. Given this, and given the widespread use (and abuse) of the term hegemonic masculinity across the social sciences, including criminology, the time appears to be ripe for a bit of conceptual stock-taking, a view which seems to be shared by others, given the emergent dissatisfaction being registered with the term (see Donaldson, 1993; Collier, 1998; Wetherell and Edley, 1999; Whitehead, 1999, Hearn, 2000). To look critically at the concept 'hegemonic masculinity' is thus the first objective of this article.

The second objective, which grows out of the first, is to argue for an understanding of masculinity which takes seriously the psychic as well as the social dimension of masculinity, which sees the psychic and the social as irrevocably intertwined: both necessary to an adequate understanding, neither reducible to the other. Anthony Elliott, in proposing 'that without a psychoanalytical concept of fantasy—of the representational expression of desires and passions—we are unable to grasp the inseparability of society and subjectivity in the late modern age' (1996a: 2), boldly makes the psychic realm of fantasy foundational to an understanding of the contemporary world. In doing so he acknowledges the influence of Castoriadis (1987) and his 'concept of the *radical imaginary*, by which he means a purely originary architecture of representations, drives, and passions through which self and society are constituted and reproduced' (Elliott, 1996b: 191, emphasis in original). In a certain sense, this suggestion of the need to take fantasy seriously might be seen as an implicit challenge to Connell's suggested move in the other direction, namely, from ethnography to the global. More directly germane to the study of masculinity is the work of Pattman et al. (1998) into boys' gendered identities. They highlight the importance of having something to look down upon in consolidating such identities, which is what they mean by the phrase 'producing and traducing the Other' (1998: 127). They conceptualize the 'Other' in psychoanalytic terms 'as a fantasy structure into which difference is projected' (1998: 127). In so doing, they make the case for psychic investments to be an object of study alongside boys' 'everyday practices. . . agency and the meanings boys attach to their actions [and]. . . the discursive positions available to them' (1998: 127). My purpose will be to show that attention to the importance of this psychic dimension is still only fitfully (and mostly inadequately) recognized, yet desperately important if we do want to unravel the complex links between men and their masculinities in the present period. For criminologists, the posited links between masculinity and crime make this a particularly pertinent task. Consequently, my argument can be seen as a direct challenge to Connell's suggestion that we need:

> a reconsideration of research methods, since the life-history and ethnographic methods that have been central to recent work on masculinities give limited grasp on the very large scale institutions, markets and mass communications that are in play on the world scale.
>
> (1998: 19)

Since life-history and ethnographic methods have been all but universally conducted within a variant of social constructionism, to my mind there is much still to be learned about masculinity by such methods, not least about the difficulties of living with 'large scale institutions, markets and mass communications' (1998: 19).

Looked at from the underside, the ending of the Cold War, the collapse of communism and the triumph of global capitalism (which is what underpins Connell's 'transnational business masculinity' as the new, current hegemonic masculinity) has been accompanied by a new world disorder characterized by nationalism, fundamentalism, xenophobia, war and genocide. Without attempting to connect all these developments, nor to link them to ideas about the fragmentation of the social and the growing importance of identity and difference, what this vantage point suggests is the proliferation of difference rather than the consolidation of a hegemonic project. To understand how these differences variously implicate gender will require more attention, not less, to the local, the particular, the everyday, the mundane (as well as to the larger developments that Connell points towards). In short, we must attend to the psychosocial dynamics of gender if we are serious about contemporary masculinities. 'Scale and complexity' (1998: 19) are not simply a function of size, as Connell, in this context, might be accused of suggesting.

What is hegemonic masculinity?

Hegemonic masculinity brings together two terms, neither of which is easily defined, given the chequered and contested intellectual history of each. No doubt some of the current problems of 'hegemonic masculinity' can be traced to these.

The notion of hegemony was originally deployed by Gramsci (1971) to try to make sense of class relations in democratic societies; in particular, to understand how a dominant class manages to legitimate its rule in societies characterized by class inequality.[3] When the ruling class (or alliance of classes) managed to sustain its ascendancy predominantly through the production of consent to its moral and intellectual leadership, rather than through the use of coercion or force, Gramsci used the term hegemonic. However, given the underlying class inequality, periods of hegemony were never fixed but were always contingent (upon prevailing historical conditions, some being more favourable than others) and contested, given the presence of subordinated classes. From this starting point, Connell (1987, 1995) set himself the task of understanding how an unequal gender order manages to reproduce itself: how hierarchies of dominance and subordination among men and between men and women come to be commonly accepted at any particular historical moment.

The idea of gender relations was also central to Connell's understanding of masculinities. Rejecting traditional ideas of masculinity as the differential psychological attributes that purportedly distinguish males from females, or as the sex-appropriate norms that males learn in a host of socializing institutions, Connell's brief definition emphasized gender relations, practices and the importance of the cultural (as well as the individual) level: '"Masculinity" is simultaneously a place in gender relations, the practices through which men and women engage that place in gender, and the effects of these practices in bodily experience, personality and culture' (1995: 71). Putting the two notions together, Connell went on to define hegemonic masculinity as 'the configuration of gender practice which embodies the currently accepted answer to the problem of legitimacy of patriarchy, which guarantees (or is taken to guarantee) the dominant position of men and the subordination of women' (1995: 77). If hegemonic masculinity is the 'currently accepted' legitimization of male domination, it is always historically contingent and contested; by women, and by men whose gender practices are at odds with the hegemonic configuration. The masculinities of such men Connell calls 'subordinate' (1995: 78–9). Given the widespread cultural ascendancy of heterosexuality, the idea of homosexual masculinities as subordinate, Connell's key example (1995: 78–9), is unsurprising. Additionally, and relatedly, the long-standing, well-nigh general subordination of women makes those masculinities that can be represented as effeminate easy to expel 'from the circle of legitimacy' (1995: 79).

In his later volume, Connell also introduced two new terms, 'complicit' and 'marginalized' masculinities (1995: 79–81). The former refer to those large numbers of men who neither practice nor challenge the hegemonic version of masculinity but are its 'complicit' beneficiaries (1995: 79). Marginalized masculinities result from '[T]he interplay of gender with other structures such as class and race' (1995: 80). Given the relations of domination/subordination between ethnic groups, for example, the masculinities of such subordinate groups will always be subject to the authority of the hegemonic masculinity of the dominant group, which has the power to marginalize or to authorize admission to the hegemonic project. Certain black US athletes, for example, may be 'authorized' exemplars of hegemonic masculinity, though this has no effect on the social authority of black men more generally (1995: 80–1).

Evaluating hegemonic masculinity

Connell's introduction of the term hegemonic masculinity has been widely taken up. It has inspired and influenced much contemporary writing on men and masculinity, including that conducted by criminologists. Its appeal is manifold because it manages to acknowledge something of the diversity of men's lives (which early feminist writings on male violence, like Brownmiller's 1976 classic, *Against Our Will*, signally failed to do), while hanging on to the feminist stress on the importance of power. Within criminology, the importance of power structuring relations among men enabled Messerschmidt (1993, 1997) to explore not only how, for some men, 'doing crime' is a form of 'doing masculinity', but also why men occupying different positions in the hierarchies of power constituted by gender, race and class commit different crimes. The importance attached to the cultural level permitted interesting new analyses of criminal justice organizations and cultures, in terms of their gendered practices (Newburn and Stanko, 1994; Walklate, 1995). The emphasis on competing masculinities, the resistance that power always engenders, provides a new vantage point from which to think about police/youth relations, or the meaning of departmental hierarchies within the police (why the CID enjoys higher status than Community Relations, for example).

Despite these, and other, positive outcomes of Connell's subtle theorizing, hegemonic masculinity is a problematic concept. Not all of the problems can be laid directly at Connell's door, since some stem from its subsequent usage rather than Connell's careful definitions. However, since a concept carefully fashioned to be of use for social scientific purposes only remains so to the extent that it is used with care, the fate of such concepts, how they are commonly used, is an important and relevant object of critique. In this instance, for all Connell's emphasis on the relational nature of 'masculinity' ('No masculinity arises except in a system of gender relations' (1995: 71)), it is still common to see masculinity used attributionally, as if it referred simply to a list of 'manly' attributes—competitive, aggressive, risk-taker, strong, independent, unemotional, and so on, perhaps even more so once the term 'hegemonic' is added, given the usual considerable overlap between this list and some cultural norm, ideal or stereotype of masculinity.

Specifically within criminology, the search for connections between masculinity and crime (and criminal justice) has highlighted some of the more negative attributes at the expense of the more positive, caring ones underpinning, for example, the father who protects and provides (Gilmore, 1993). Richard Collier, in suggesting how intractable is the idea of a normative gender order, puts his finger on the problem nicely: 'Hegemonic masculinity appears to open up an analysis of the diversity of masculinities (subordinate, effeminate, non-capitalist?) whilst simultaneously holding in place a normative masculine "gender" to which is then assigned the range of (usually undesirable/negative) characteristics' (1998: 21). The reductive consequence of this Collier also notes: '[T]he argument that "real men" (that which is ascribed the status of "hegemonic" masculinity) are inherently oppressive continues to override any investigation of the complexity of behaviour of men in their everyday relations with women and other men' (1998: 22).

Messerschmidt's (1993, 1997) catalogue of criminals might fit this criticism. They may all be doing masculinity differently, depending on their location in gender, race and class relations, but they are all indubitably doing bad not good. A more specific example can be found in the work of Jeff Hearn, one of Britain's leading writers on men and masculinities. After a lengthy and comprehensive overview of approaches to defining and explaining men's violence, he concludes with a list of five characteristics which he argues are specific to 'men's violence to known women' (1998: 37). The first of these certainly seems to demonstrate Collier's concern: 'First, it is an inherently *gendered* way of men referring to themselves and to violence. Men's doing of violence to women simultaneously involves "being a man" and symbolically showing "being a man"' (1998: 37, emphasis in original). Without wishing to downplay the horror of male violence against women, nor to gainsay Hearn's prolific contribution (using his preferred term) to 'Critical Studies on Men' (Hearn, 2000), this particular formulation seems to me to be reductive because (ironically, in the light of his earlier comprehensive overview) it ignores the complexity of the relations under study. In particular, it overlooks at least three pieces of relevant evidence that undermine it. First, the remorse and shame that some research (e.g. Gadd, 2000) has shown abusers attest to, not the pride that should be associated with 'being a man'. Second, and following on from that, batterers rarely boast of their exploits but rather keep them a (guilty) 'secret'; again, the opposite of what would be predicted if such violence connoted 'being a man'.[4] Third, and linked to both previous points, wife/partner batterers are not cultural heroes. While they may get away with such violence more than they should, this is not because such men are looked up to as exemplars of hegemonic masculinity. Far from 'being a man', the resort to violence against women is commonly regarded as a failure of manhood (certainly in my experience of growing up male) since it displays both a (feminine) inability to control emotions and cowardice in attacking someone (usually) weaker than oneself: a *gentle*man, I learned, never hits a woman (even if, as we now know, this was often observed only in the breach).[5] This reductiveness occurs, I contend, through not giving sufficient weight to what O'Sullivan (1998: 105) calls the 'emotional component'. This, for me, effectively equates with the absent psychic dimension that I deal with below.

One consequence of reducing hegemonic masculinity to a set of traits or characteristics is to render the notion static, not something which is incessantly struggled over as Connell's theoretical usage insists. However, and notwithstanding such insistence, the problem may have its roots in the original notion because, although Connell talks of a range of subordinate masculinities, hegemonic masculinity is always used in the singular.[6] Does this mean that there is only ever one hegemonic strategy at any given historical moment, or is hegemonic masculinity a much more contingent, context-specific notion, as Wetherell and Edley ask as part of their critical interrogation of the term?[7]

> It is. . . unclear whether there is only one hegemonic strategy at any point in time or whether hegemonic strategies can vary across different parts of a social formation, creating conflicts or tensions for individual men between different hegemonic forms as they move across social practices.
>
> (1999: 337)

This goes to the heart of the relational versus attributional understanding of the term. The thoroughgoing relational approach implied by the theory does suggest multiple, context-specific strategies. This contradicts the consistent use of the term in the singular. It also accords with empirical commonsense. Take Bill Gates, for example. Is he someone who embodies/personifies/practises Connell's 'transnational business masculinity', i.e. someone 'marked by increasing egocentrism, very conditional loyalties . . . a declining sense of responsibility to others . . . a limited technical rationality . . . [and] . . . increasingly libertarian sexuality' (Connell, 1998: 16)? Perhaps, though I am not sure who would be in a position to judge.

However, there are several things that are known publicly about Bill Gates—his philanthropic concerns, his very public opposition to Bush's huge tax cuts favouring the rich, and his background in computers with all its connotations of 'nerdish' enthusiasm and daunting expertise—which at least complicate the picture of his 'masculinity'. Perhaps the idea of context-specific hegemonic strategies can help reconcile these difficulties, if we envisage him 'performing' 'transnational business masculinity' to business audiences, a version of Gilmore's 'selfless' masculinity (1993: 229) in philanthropic contexts, and a specific, knowledge-based, 'whizz-kid' masculinity when confronted with a gathering of fellow experts.

The point can be made more dramatically if we attempt to think about the relationship between hegemonic and subordinate, complicit or marginalized masculinities in particular contexts. In school playgrounds up and down the country, the masculinity that is hegemonic is more likely to be the physical, anti-intellectual (but subordinate, in Connell's terms) masculinity of Paul Willis's (1977) 'lads' (or Mac an Ghaill's 'white macho lads') than that of the computer 'nerd' or 'boffin' (Willis's ' 'ear-oles'). Or, imagine Bill Gates parachuted (alone) into Manhattan's Bronx district or Chicago's southside. Would being an ordinary-looking, bespectacled, white, middle-class, male 'carrier' of global, hegemonic masculinity count for much in black-dominated public scenarios where a certain ostentatious stylishness and physical presence constitute one visible, strong (but marginalized, in Connell's terminology) masculine standard? Might not being rich, white, middle-class and male in a poor, black neighbourhood create 'conflicts or tensions', not to say fear (justified or not)? Tom Wolfe's (1988) novel *Bonfire of the Vanities* starts with just such a tension. Sherman McCoy, the super-rich white stockbroker (one of Wolfe's 'Masters of the Universe'), takes the wrong exit off the expressway only to discover that he, his mistress and his expensive Porsche are suddenly in alien territory, namely, in the Bronx. Uncertain what to do, and increasingly fearful of the black faces all around, they eventually race off in panic when two young black men appear, offering to help McCoy remove a tyre from the road which was blocking the car's progress. This hasty retreat caused a serious injury to one of the young men, which they subsequently failed to report. What help was hegemonic masculinity in that situation? As it happens, the complex race and judicial politics of New York City in the 1980s ensured, at least in Wolfe's novel, the humbling of this 'Master of the Universe' with a prison sentence for his fearful failure to report. So, even outside the ghetto, hegemonic masculinity carried no guarantees, and, on this (fictional) occasion was successfully contested. If, then, hegemonic masculinity is a contingent notion, dependent on context, this poses a far more complex series of questions in understanding how masculinities and crimes are related than has been attempted hitherto.

A further problem is the oversocialized view of the male subject that users of the concept have generally taken. It is as if, having outlined what constitutes hegemonic masculinity within a particular culture, there is no need to attend to how actual men relate to this notion. Yet, the idea of a range of masculinities—subordinate, marginalized and complicit—constantly competing with hegemonic masculinity would seem to make unavoidable the question of how actual men, with their unique biographies and particular psychic formations, relate to these various masculinities. Connell (1995) certainly recognized this issue when he insisted that the depth and complexity of Freud's study of the Wolf Man constituted a challenge to all subsequent researchers interested in masculinity, a sentiment which now reads somewhat ironically, given his current shift to the global level. Several other writers have also noted the importance of not ignoring the psychic or subjective dimension of masculinity (Jefferson, 1994; Collier, 1998; MacInnes, 1998; Pattman et al., 1998; Wetherell and Edley, 1999), though mostly from different theoretical traditions. In the section that follows, then, I take up my second objective by looking at two contrasting attempts to rectify the omission of this psychic dimension before laying out the contours of a more adequate 'psychosocial' understanding of masculinity.

Conceptualizing an inner world

In stressing the importance of psychic investments, Pattman et al. (1998) show they are mindful of the need to address the psychological complexity of the male subject, though they do not offer a detailed elaboration of the theoretical resources needed to do so. Likewise Collier, who sets himself the more 'modest' (though still important) task of exploring 'subjectivity as embodiment, subjectivity as the lived experience of a (specifically masculine) body as it is socially and culturally inscribed' (1998: 32). By contrast, Wetherell and Edley (1999) and MacInnes (1998) do engage the psychological dimension of masculinity in some detail. Hence it is to their work I turn first. Wetherell and Edley criticize Connell for 'a lack of specification on how hegemonic masculinity might become effective in men's psyches' (1999: 337). However, their own solution to the problem falls somewhere short of what is required. In my view, their Lacanian-inspired 'psycho-discursive' solution, though interesting and imaginative, fails to produce an authentic inner world.

Basing themselves on their tape-recorded interviews with 61 men, conducted by Nigel Edley and volunteers in the early 1990s, they described the patterns of identification they detected in some parts of their interviews as examples of 'imaginary positioning' (1999: 342). By that they mean, following Lacan and Barthes, that '[A]n external voice from without is. . . mispresented [hence "imaginary"] as a voice from within' (1999: 343), though they do go on to differentiate themselves from Lacan and Barthes by reserving this idea 'for a specific set of appearances of the "I" in talk rather than all instances of self-description' (1999: 343). Given the diverse and sometimes mixed positions their interviewees variously took up, their attempt to understand 'the nitty gritty of negotiating masculine identities and men's identity strategies' (1999: 336) led them to propose that Connell's hegemonic 'norms are in fact discursive practices' (1999: 353) and that:

> identification is a matter of the procedures in action through which men live/talk/do masculinity. . . these procedures are intensely local (situationally realized) and global (dependent on broader conditions of intelligibility). They represent the social within the psychological. . . What we mean by character or identity is partly the differential, persistent and idiosyncratic inflection of these procedures over time in the course of a life. . . These procedures are a particular class of discursive practice which we call psycho-discursive.
>
> (1999: 353)

In short, their attempt to understand '[w]hat happens psychologically' (1999: 337) in the interaction between actual men and hegemonic masculinity, to combine 'insights from the ethnomethodological/conversation tradition. . . with those stemming from poststructuralist and Foucauldian notions of discourse' (1999: 338), remains resolutely social ('the social within the psychological'). Their male interviewees might negotiate and wriggle, but there is no escaping the iron hand of discourse in this account. Men's masculinities are the (discursive) accounts through which they communicate them. Effectively, we are the sum of our talk. Since there is a resolute refusal to 'get behind' discourse, to talk of a pre-discursive or non-discursive realm, all psychological processes, including the motives, emotions and desires that may underpin the crucial question of identification (the take-up of one discursive position rather than another) are reduced to forms of 'discursive accomplishment' (1999: 335). For all its sophistication, this is a social psychology without an authentic (and irreducible) inner world.

Which brings me to MacInnes (1998), whose efforts are directed towards answering 'three interrelated questions', namely,

> Why is. . . masculinity. . . an obvious concept. . . yet is incapable of any precise empirical definition. . . [capable of describing] empirically existing men?. . . What is male about masculinity?. . . How is it that a system that does not depend on biological differences nevertheless leads to the oppression of one biological sex by the other?
>
> (1998: 15–16)

His answer to the first of these (a question which, incidentally, echoes one of the concerns of both Collier and Wetherell and Edley with the term hegemonic masculinity) is, in essence, that masculinity does not exist, except as an ideology to explain the continuing subordination of women in the era of modernity, the 'core principle' of which is 'that all human beings are essentially equal (regardless of their sex)' (1998: 11). This novel solution to the problematic idea of masculinity rests, in turn, upon

MacInnes's crucial distinction between 'sexual difference' and 'sexual genesis' (1998: 17). It is this distinction, which is premised on the recognition of an inner world 'beyond social construction' (1998: 22), that is of particular interest to us.

The ideological solutions which 'explain' masculinity, its continuing monopolization by men, and patriarchal oppression in an era of formal equality, all

> depended upon a systematic confusion of sexual *difference* with sexual *genesis*, such that what are in reality issues of the natural generation of individuals (about the relationship between parents and infants) have been displaced onto issues of social differences between sexes (about the production of 'masculine' and 'feminine' from male and female). We have come to systematically confuse what results from us all being born *of* a man *and* a woman with what results from us all being born *as* a man *or* a woman, so that the natural limits to our social identities come to appear to be the fact that we are all born of one sex or another, rather than being set by the inexorable fact that we are the products of biological sexual reproduction.
> (1998: 17, emphases in original)

MacInnes then elaborates on the idea of sexual genesis:

> The sexual genesis of individuals is the process whereby helpless, dependent infants arrive originally as products of nature, sexually produced by a father and a mother and fused with them, but come to develop into relatively autonomous selves with a distinct identity, capable of forming social relations with others and constructing societies. This process of 'generation' addresses the problem of the natural limits to social construction by analysing how the production of independent selves. . . is possible in the first place. . . The identity of any self that emerges from this process can only ever be understood as a combination of contradictory potential capacities (such as love and hate, empathy and independence), whose expression and management comprise the stuff of life, the inevitably anxious biography of a self conscious of its vulnerability and mortality.
> (1998: 18)

In this account, the tasks of individuation, of separating self from other, of coping with the vulnerability and anxiety this produces, are universal, human tasks of generation, the product of sexual genesis, not sexual difference.[8] His subsequent account of (sexual) genesis,[9] since broadly persuasive, is less an issue for me than the question of the relationship between (sexual) genesis and sexual difference (conceived as either discourse or, for MacInnes, ideology). Put another way: what have particular individual (or biographical) experiences of (sexual) genesis to do with the identifications men and women make with particular discursive positions (which in a world still constituted by oppressive gender relations will be encoded masculine or feminine, albeit that such encodings will differ somewhat by situation)? In short, who is likely to identify with the hegemonically masculine position in a given discourse, on particular occasions, and why? Unfortunately, MacInnes cannot help us here since he is more interested in the social construction of the ideology of sexual difference. It is probably also true that he cannot help us with this question since he wishes to make a clear distinction between a private, non-social world of 'persons'—the proper province of psychology—and a public, social world of 'societies'—the proper province of sociology (1998: 148). In other words, my question is improperly posed since it risks mixing up 'two distinct kinds of subject matter: societies and persons'. I must disagree, for without mixing them up, we shall never properly understand how persons beget, challenge, reproduce or change societies. So, here I part company with MacInnes, but without rancour since he has provided an essential element missing from Wetherell and Edley's oversocialized conversational/discursive account—an inner world that is genuinely psychological. The question of how to understand that inner world as psychological but not 'beyond social construction' (1998: 22), as simultaneously a product of psychology and sociology, or psychosocial, remains. That is our next and final task.

For a psychosocial understanding of masculinity

I am now in a position to piece together the rudiments of a psychosocial understanding of masculinity. Following MacInnes, I start with the importance of (sexual) genesis and 'the inevitably anxious biography of a self' (1998: 18), the product of early attachments, to which this gives rise. This is what makes each of us unique, each 'fucked up' in our own particular way, as the poet, Philip Larkin, once tellingly put it.[10] It is that unique, 'inevitably anxious biography' that we can never escape; whether we like it or not, whether we will it or not, we take it with us through life. We can start a new job, a new relationship or a new 'way of life', but we never do so tabula rasa because we cannot change our unique (sexual) genesis. Consequently, the vulnerabilities, dependencies and anxieties resulting from this early process of becoming human continue to haunt our entry into new social situations, part-shaping our responses. It is this co-presence of the-past-in-the-present, what Pontalis (1993: 30) aptly expressed in the idea that 'one never gives up anything', which makes psychological change so difficult to effect, despite our best, conscious intentions.[11]

MacInnes argues that 'as products of sexual genesis, we must by definition possess an unconscious' (1998: 22), which is a reminder of his debt to psychoanalytic theory, all of which 'takes for granted the existence of an unconscious which is seen as what is repressed, split off or dissociated' (Minsky, 1998: 15). Pontalis's notion of never forgetting anything obviously depends on an unconscious, since we clearly cannot recall everything to consciousness, and the idea that our conscious intentions are often undermined by our particular biographical legacies seems inexplicable without one. However, my task here is not to argue the case for the importance of the unconscious but, rather, to show how a particular understanding of the unconscious can contribute to an understanding of hegemonic masculinity. This requires that we distinguish between different psychoanalytical accounts of the phenomenon.

For Freud, the unconscious 'is created as a result of repression [which]. . . is a blocking mechanism through which consciouness shuts off potentially painful aspects of our early experience and produces an entirely separate place in our psyche' (Minsky, 1998: 21). Though inaccessible to language, 'sudden eruptions of unconscious loss and desire. . . often emerge as physical or psychological "symptoms". . . in the symbolic language of dreams. . . jokes and bungled speech and action' (1998: 21). The therapeutic task of psychoanalysis, in a nutshell, is to find means to render the unconscious conscious and amenable to language, and hence rob it of its potential to disrupt who we think we are. Freud links the moment of the formation of the unconscious with the acquisition of an autonomous and gendered identity via the idea of the Oedipal conflict, the moment, somewhere between the ages of 3 and 5, when we are forced 'from our merged, narcissistic identity with the mother' (1998: 27) into selfhood proper. What precipitates the crisis in boy children is a combination of the fantasy of becoming the mother's lover in preference to the father and other rivals, and the simultaneous discovery of sexual difference, through noticing which bodies do or do not possess a penis. These discoveries produce both guilt, in relation to the father-rival, and fear that this rivalry will end with the loss of his penis, as he thinks has already happened to girls, at the hands of his father. This castration anxiety is both physical and symbolic (or 'psychical annihilation'); in the latter case the fear is of the 'extinction of his fragile and emergent sense of identity which at that time centres around the pleasure derived from his penis' (1998: 27). In order to avoid this terrifying, imagined fate, the boy gives up both his identifications with and desire for the mother, deferring the latter until adulthood and the finding of a mother-substitute of his own, and begins to identify with the father, and the culturally masculine that he represents, which then becomes psychically internalized through the formation of the superego.

In this version, the repression which forms the unconscious is inherently gendered. It is the pain of having to give up love for the mother, for fear of the castrating father, that requires both that the memory be repressed and an alternative, 'masculine' source of identification be found. Two problems immediately present themselves. The first has to do with the centrality accorded the penis and sexual difference—and the (too easy) elision of the two. Herein lies one source of Freud's oft-imputed biologism. The second has to do with the fact that the pattern of identifications of actually existing boys (and girls) is less straightforward than one reading of this account would allow, the case of the homosexual male being but one obvious example that has given psychoanalysis problems over the years (Lewes, 1988). Freud did not entirely dissent from this understanding since he recognized the necessarily ambivalent feelings caused for boys by having to identify with someone who inspires love, guilt and fear simultaneously. He also had a notion that this crisis could be resolved more or less successfully, positively or negatively, meaning that some boys would fail to identify sufficiently with the father to enable successful separation from the mother, and hence could store up problems for subsequent relationships. Given these problems, it is hard not to agree with Hood-Williams that they 'immediately. . . undermine the complex as an account of sexual difference' (2001: 53).

Consequently, and particularly with the advent of post-structuralist and feminist thinking, there has been a move away from the equation 'penis = sexual difference = gender' and a refocusing on the pre-Oedipal period and the role of the mother, especially the moment of an infant's beginning to distinguish its own boundaries from those of its mother's. Here, the work of Melanie Klein (1988a, 1988b) has been central, especially her attention to how infants defend against anxiety.[12] Where Freud made sexuality, desire and the father central to his account of Oedipal conflict, the child's acquisition of identity and its entry into culture, 'Klein argues that it is the baby's anxiety arising out of its instinctive emotional ambivalence towards the mother. . . that is the major problem with which the small baby, and later the adult, have to contend' (Minsky, 1998: 33). Coping with this anxiety arising from the struggle in relation to the mother (and later, others), leads to the construction of fantasies of love and hate, driven by the primitive defence mechanisms of splitting and projection, which provide the basis of an early fragile identity. The breast rather than the penis is central to this process:

> Loving and hating phantasies of the breast are the baby's first experience of relating to the mother and (since the baby's identity is fused with the breast because it does not have an identity of its own) of filling itself up with a good or bad phantasy of the breast thus creating a primitive sense of having a self.
>
> (Minsky, 1998: 35)

Thus, feelings which become too distressing may be split off as 'bad', separated from both the internal and external 'good' fantasy objects, and projected onto the mother's breast, which then becomes 'bad'. Such defences, stemming from persecutory anxiety, are characteristic of a baby's early months and what Klein called the paranoid-schizoid position (though anyone can operate from such a position). As the baby learns to take in whole objects, to perceive the mother as the source of both love and hate and to live with the resulting ambivalence, Klein talks of the baby entering the depressive position. Such an achievement is never absolute; we never entirely relinquish paranoid-schizoid defences, although our particular experience of early nurturing will affect both our level of general anxiety and our characteristic ways of defending against it.

One important difference between the Freudian and Kleinian analyses of the psyche is that Freud's Oedipal moment implicates gender, albeit unsatisfactorily, whereas Klein's anxiety, splitting and ambivalence are all gender-neutral terms (Hood-Williams, 2001): in MacInnes's terms they concern (sexual) genesis but not, following Freud, sexual difference. The question then remains, how to understand the relation between anxiety and gender, or, as I suggested earlier in the discussion of MacInnes, that between (sexual) genesis and sexual difference.

Before addressing this, it is worth reiterating that taking this particular route to an understanding of masculinity involves breaking definitively with any hint that masculinity is something essentially, biologically or psychically, to do with actual men. This also puts paid to the idea that masculinity is a set of attributes possessed by men. A further advantage is that it forces us into the realm of the social to explain sexual difference,[13] but without denying the (irreducible) significance of the psyche (or (sexual) genesis). In short, this particular route requires an explanation that is neither psychic nor social, but psychosocial.

If the Oedipal complex is not an adequate account of sexual difference, it is nonetheless significant as the moment when the exclusivity (from the child's point of view) of the dyadic mother–child relationship is broken, once he or she becomes aware of the presence of someone, usually the father, who also has a relationship with the mother. From that point on, the child must begin to accommodate to the complexity of triangular relationships, and the loss of the feelings of omnipotence which are characteristic of the mother–child relation, a trauma comparable to the earlier discovery of one's separateness from the mother. To the extent that boy children, at this point, identify with the masculine, it is not the penis but its cultural power with which they identify. This cultural power, symbolized in language by the phallus, Lacan's master signifier, is inherently social, external to the psyche.

But this still leaves unanswered the question of how to think the connection between psychic processes and the performance of social gender. One of the most influential attempts to do so has been made, unsurprisingly perhaps given her dual interests, by the sociologist and now practising analyst, Nancy Chodorow (1978). This centred on the differential timing of the separation (from the mother) of boy and girl children. As Craib (1987: 729) somewhat brusquely put it (thereby echoing the nature of the process), 'the core of Chodorow's argument is that the little boy is pushed into an early psychic separation from the mother', the effect of which (put baldly since I have no space for the fuller argument) is the development of strong ego boundaries[14] and an unwillingness to 'risk themselves in relationship' (Craib, 1987: 730). More colloquially, we might call this the 'flight from the feminine'. Though criticized (by herself among others) as overgeneralized, her later work (Chodorow, 1994) wrestles only inconclusively with the problems of a more multiple, less generalized understanding.

Lynne Layton's recent defence of this 'object relational' (as opposed to postmodern) way of theorizing gender redefines the trauma of the boy child's separation from (rejection by?) the mother as 'narcissistic injury', but the importance of the turning away from the feminine remains crucial: '[B]oys are narcissistically injured by the cultural demand, mediated by subtle and not-so-subtle parent–child relational patterns, to abjure dependency, emotionality, nurturance, and the primary affectional ties with their mothers' (Layton, 1998: 41).

This approach is genuinely psychosocial: it offers some account of the specifically psychic processes underpinning what Layton still wants to call, contra postmodern theory, 'core gender identity' (1998: 56) in combination with the idea of the social pre-existence of gender difference. As Chodorow puts it, 'most men and women must come to psychological terms with male dominance. . . Somewhere along the line. . . part of learning the meanings of masculinity and femininity includes learning not just difference but differential value and asymmetrical power and hierarchy' (1994: 79). In other words, an internal process, early psychic separation, provides the (psychic) preconditions for entry into the (social) world of male domination. But, unless we accept the reductive, generalizing version of this, there is more to be unravelled about the nature of the connection between the psychic and the social, between (sexual) genesis and sexual difference.

The writer who has most consistently addressed this connection in a resolutely non-reductive fashion is Jessica Benjamin (1995, 1998). It is, thus, to her work we need now to turn. Benjamin (1998) recognizes the psychic constellation underpinning Chodorow's account of the boy's early separation from the mother, which she characterizes as 'the boy's oedipal posture in which the identification with the mother is repudiated, and the elements associated with his own babyhood are projected onto the girl, the daughter' (1998: xvii). However, crucially for her it is only one possible constellation. For Benjamin, Chodorow's 'mistake' (and that of the 'maternal relational thesis' (1998: 51) generally) was not her reversal of Freud's phallic logic by the focus on pre-Oedipal maternal identifications but the failure to transcend its binary splitting of identificatory love (the desire to be like) from object love (the desire for). To transcend this exclusionary logic requires that the account of the mother–child relation be supplemented by an account of the pre-Oedipal father and of the child's identifications with him.[15] This redefines the pre-Oedipal position as one characterized by multiple identifications with both mother and father (or substitutes) and what they symbolize culturally. These multiple, bisexual identifications Benjamin (1998: 60), following Fast (1984, 1990), calls 'overinclusive'. From this perspective, what determines Oedipal outcomes is the extent to which this overinclusive bisexuality is given up. When it is given up decisively in favour of the mutual exclusivity of gender difference, with its overvaluation of the masculine and denigration of the feminine, it is not hard to follow Benjamin's reasoning that this Oedipal posture is built psychically on a foundation of defensive repudiation: 'without access to the overinclusive identifications, the oedipal renunciation [of the possibility of being both sexes] inevitably elides into repudiation, splitting the difference, rather than truly recognizing it' (1998: 64).

But, less defensively exclusive outcomes are possible. In such cases, psychic oscillations between pre-Oedipal overinclusiveness and Oedipal gender complementarity loosen 'the oedipal opposition between object love and identification' (Benjamin, 1998: 67) and, hence, the polarization of heterosexuality and homosexuality. Where pre-Oedipal identificatory tendencies are sustained alongside object love, this 'creates a different kind of complementarity, and a different stance towards oppositional differences', not 'a simple opposition, constituted by splitting, projecting the unwanted elements into the other', but one based on reintegrating 'elements of identification, so that they become less threatening, less diametrically opposite, no longer cancelling out one's identity' (Benjamin, 1998: 69–70). This ability to tolerate gender ambiguity and uncertainty 'relies on the psychic capacity to symbolically bridge split oppositions as well as on preoedipal overinclusiveness. It allows for transgression that recognizes rather than manically denies the necessity of separation and difference' (Benjamin, 1998: 73). But, since, for Benjamin, identification and a tendency towards splitting are unavoidable, being part of our psychic make-up, we cannot simply abolish gender categories. The question then becomes, how to prevent the polarizations of gender from becoming 'reified, congealed in massive cultural formations, perceived as the Law' (Benjamin, 1998: 75).

The question of how (sexual) genesis and sexual difference are related can now be answered in a non-reductive, psychosocial fashion, in a way which encompasses both the messy reality of actually existing gender relations, the diversity of actual men and women's relationships to discourses of masculinity and femininity and the underlying psychological processes. For Benjamin, (sexual) genesis might be summarized as the universal task of separating from a particular mother, or substitute (and her particular relationship to gender) and learning to share her with a particular father, or substitute (and his particular relationship to gender) against a backdrop of managing the inevitable excitement and anxiety generated by loving attachments, both the desire for (object love) and the desire to be like (identificatory love). The timing and management of these universal (and irreducibly psychic) tasks will determine how any particular individual relates to questions of (socially produced) sexual difference.

In conclusion

This, of course, is not the end of our psychosocial story; merely a (hopefully persuasive) beginning. Inevitably, loose threads remain. On the psychic side, we may have the contours of an explanation, but we still have much to learn about who is likely to take up the Oedipal posture and who might transcend it. And, even within the Oedipal posture, there are clearly more or less benign versions to be understood. On the social side, I believe Benjamin leaves us with a paradox. On the one hand she convincingly demonstrates the essential 'ambiguity of gender', how 'masculinity and femininity can each be construed as the negation of the other—its opposite, its complementary other', a 'view. . . that gender as we now know it works through a mutual and symmetrical determination of opposing terms, [masculinity/femininity; mother/father; active/passive, etc.] which can shift in tandem, rather than through essential, fixed qualities' (Benjamin, 1998: xvi). In short, she shows that gender has no content as such. On the other hand, as she correctly recognizes, 'patriarchal culture has historically given certain contents to these gender categories' (1998: xvi). It is of course her tracing of the psychic constellation underpinning patriarchal culture that enables her to conclude that 'the [present] cultural form of femininity [as passive object]. . . may be seen, broadly speaking, as the effect of a male construction of culture in accord with the oedipal boy's anxieties' (1998: 57). The question that this paradox poses for me is how to comprehend gender as both shifting and fixed at the same time. Her answer, following Mitchell (1991), centres on the idea that there may be

> two different epistemological positions here, one aiming for a centered ontology of the psychic origins of sexual difference, in which subjectivity is constituted through a single major division; the other aiming for a decentered phenomenology of the psychic, in which subjectivity emerges through shifting, multiple identifications that refer to an inconsistent though pervasive binary.
>
> (Benjamin, 1998: 47)

But this epistemological answer misses something. If we recall her earlier formulation about the passive femininity characteristic of patriarchal culture being in accord with the Oedipal boy's anxieties, what also needs an answer is with what it is within contemporary social reality that the less defensive psychic constellation that she spends so much space outlining is 'in accord'.[16]

This, finally, returns us to our starting point and the question of whether or not masculinity is 'in crisis' and how this concept relates to hegemonic masculinity in the present period. The affirmative answer offered by Faludi, Campbell and Mac an Ghaill with which I started this article rested upon the idea of a contemporary crisis of capitalism—the massive global restructuring of the economy and its consequent general impact on the social and sexual division of labour. To my mind we should add to that the whole range of social and cultural changes collectively captured by the term 'postmodern', which we might conceptualize as a crisis of modernity.[17] These dual crises (whether or not underpinned by a single 'logic' as Jameson (1991) would have it), or what I called earlier 'a new world disorder characterized by nationalism, fundamentalism, xenophobia, war and genocide', would seem to point towards (again, to repeat my earlier words) 'the proliferation of difference rather than the consolidation of a hegemonic project'. If this is right, it is with this contemporary social reality that Benjamin's less defensive psychic constellation is 'in accord'.

But, to end here would be to end only on an optimistic reading of the present, a reading of its psychic potential under optimal conditions. In doing so, it risks ignoring with what it is in contemporary social reality that the masculinities in crisis with which I started this article—Faludi's American males, Campbell's joy-riders and Mac an Ghaill's 'white macho lads'—are also 'in accord'. Here it is necessary to remind readers, qua Bauman, that postmodernity does not signal the end of modernity. As Elliott puts it:

> Rather than attempting a historical periodization of the modern and post-modern eras, Bauman argues that contemporary culture, not without certain tensions and contradictions, deploys both orders simultaneously. Contemporary society revolves around a modernist impulse for creating order, boundaries and classifications as well as a postmodern tolerance for plurality, difference and uncertainty. Contemporary society, it might be said, embraces and avoids ambivalence in equal measure.
>
> (1996a: 21)

Faced with such a world, buffeted between order and plurality, boundaries and difference, classifications and uncertainty, it should not be hard to see how the potential for a new openness to 'gender ambiguity and uncertainty' (Benjamin, 1998: 72–3) is the same potential under the worst psychic and social conditions for a defensive hardening of differences and the restaking of firm boundaries. In these terms, the various crises of masculinity referred to earlier might be better seen as so many 'crisis masculinities', grim permutations of Benjamin's 'Oedipal boy', the downside of the postmodern symbolic with its 'openness as regards contemporary social processes' (Elliott, 1996a: 36).

Either way, then, whether read through its upside, through Benjamin's 'postoedipal boy' able to live with 'gender ambiguity and uncertainty' (Benjamin, 1998: 72–3), or through its downside, through the inability to live with Bauman's 'modernity without illusions', the concept of hegemonic masculinity (and its moment of hegemony within the social sciences) would seem to be, terminally, 'in crisis'.

Notes

1. I could of course have cited a whole range of other texts, as well as countless journalistic pieces, which either presuppose or refer to this 'crisis'.
2. Harry Brod complained as long ago as 1994 that hegemonic masculinity, 'as it became popularized . . . seemed to lose [even] the dimension of power and simply signify plurality and diversity' (1994: 86). For one example of equating hegemonic masculinity simply with dominance or power, see

Kimmel: 'The hegemonic definition of manhood is a man *in* power, a man *with* power, and a man *of* power' (1994: 125, italics in original).

3. Gramsci was not the originator of the term. He took up and expanded Lenin's narrow usage of the term in the phrase 'hegemony of the proletariat', where it referred to political leadership within a class alliance, to think about class-based political leadership across the social formation as a whole.
4. After an eight-year study of campus gang rape and extensive work on wife battering, O'Sullivan concluded thus: 'Battering, while in some cases a show put on for other men to demonstrate dominance in the family, is more often *a private exercise of power* with an emotional component' (1998: 105, emphasis added).
5. Again, O'Sullivan would appear to concur: 'Battering [in comparison to gang rape] more often operates from a deficit position when men feel a loss of control in the family, *a failure to share in male dominance in society*, or both' (1998: 106, emphasis added).
6. Perhaps in the light of the recent publication of Messerschmidt's (2000) book, *Nine Lives*, 'always' should now read 'usually', since he has begun to speak as if there is more than one hegemonic masculinity. However, he does this in a way which fails to acknowledge that this is breaking with Connell's original usage, and without exploring the implications (for the concept) in so doing. Consequently, it is more confusing than clarifying.
7. Their first criticism of Connell is that '[T]he exact content of the prescriptive social norms which make up hegemonic masculinity is left unclear' (1999: 336), which only goes to show how difficult it is to think concretely about the idea in purely relational terms.
8. In an earlier version of this article delivered to staff and students at Lancaster University in May 2000, I was asked why MacInnes used the term sexual genesis if it had nothing to do with being a man or a woman. I did not know the answer then and still do not. It would seem that 'human genesis' might be a more accurate term. However, it might constitute an implicit (albeit unconscious) recognition by MacInnes of just how early matters of sexual difference/gender impact on the infant. In other words, genesis in a gender-differentiated world will always take place in the shadow of sexual difference, even if, for heuristic purposes, it is necessary to separate them out, as MacInnes does. To signify this difficulty, all subsequent references to MacInnes's term will read thus: (sexual) genesis (except when I am quoting him directly).
9. See endnote 8.
10. The wonderful line, 'They fuck you up, your mum and dad' comes from the poem 'This be the verse' (Larkin, 1974: 30).
11. This is also what gives the lie to the idea of the fragmented subject of postmodernism. Without wishing to deny that we can, and do, produce different social identities for different social occasions, our responses are often more (drearily) predictable and fixed (not to say stuck) than we care to admit.

12. This does not mean that I am compelled to follow Klein's belief in the role of 'early biological instincts. . . reflected in her assumption that "masculinity" and "femininity" are. . . biologically determined but reinforced during early childhood' (Minsky, 1998: 34). This 'all or nothing' approach to theorists serves only to stifle theoretical innovations which, it seems to me, must inevitably be somewhat eclectic (witness the theoretical fruitfulness of Klein's own revisionism). See Jefferson (1994) for my own attempt to appropriate Klein eclectically in a social fashion, following the lead of the authors of the classic *Changing the Subject* (Henriques et al., 1998 [1984]).
13. At this point, it is important to note, Collier's stress on the social and cultural inscriptions that produce 'the lived experience of a (specifically masculine) body' (1998: 32), or Wetherell and Edley's 'psycho-discursive practices' (1999: 353), or the idea of masculinity as 'accomplishment' (Messerschmidt, 1993) or as 'performative' (Butler, 1990), can all be usefully revisited as ways of grasping the social dimension of sexual difference.
14. Craib (1987: 730) thinks she means not strong but 'well-defined and rigid'.
15. In Chodorow's (1978) account it is the common absence of the father from the caretaking role which accounts for the tendency of boys to identify with cultural stereotypes of masculinity during the Oedipal stage.
16. See also the earlier work of Craib (1987) who, in pondering the relationship between what he called 'gender personality and the wider social division of labour' (1987: 735), talked of an 'elective affinity' (1987: 737) between the two.
17. Or, as Bauman more eloquently put it, '[p]ostmodernity is modernity coming to terms with its own impossibility' (quoted in Elliott, 1996a: 5).

References

Benjamin, J. (1995) *Like Subjects, Love Objects: Essays on Recognition and Sexual Difference*. New Haven, CT: Yale University Press.

Benjamin, J. (1998) *Shadow of the Other: Intersubjectivity and Gender in Psychoanalysis*. New York: Routledge.

Brod, H. (1994) 'Some Thoughts on Some Histories of Some Masculinities', in H. Brod and M. Kaufman (eds) *Theorizing Masculinities*, pp. 82–96. London: Sage.

Brownmiller, S. (1976) *Against Our Will: Men, Women and Rape*. Harmondsworth: Penguin.

Butler, J. (1990) *Gender Trouble: Feminism and the Subversion of Identity*. London: Routledge.

Campbell, B. (1993) *Goliath: Britain's Dangerous Places*. London: Virago.

Castoriadis, C. (1987) *The Imaginary Institution of Society*. Cambridge: Polity.
Chodorow, N.J. (1978) *The Reproduction of Mothering: Psychoanalysis and the Sociology of Gender*. Berkeley, CA: University of California Press.
Chodorow, N.J. (1994) *Femininities, Masculinities, Sexualities: Freud and Beyond*. Lexington, KY: The University Press of Kentucky.
Collier, R. (1998) *Masculinities, Crime and Criminology*. London: Sage.
Connell, R.W. (1987) *Gender and Power*. Cambridge: Polity.
Connell, R.W. (1995) *Masculinities*. Cambridge: Polity.
Connell, R.W. (1998) 'Masculinities and Globalization', *Men and Masculinities* 1(1): 3–23.
Craib, I. (1987) 'Masculinity and Male Dominance', *Sociological Review* 34(4): 721–43.
Donaldson, M. (1993) 'What is Hegemonic Masculinity?', *Theory and Society* 22: 643–57.
Elliott, A. (1996a) *Subject to Ourselves: Social Theory, Psychoanalysis and Postmodernity*. Cambridge: Polity.
Elliott, A. (1996b) 'Psychoanalysis and Social Theory', in B.S. Turner (ed.) *A Blackwell Companion to Social Theory*, pp. 171–93. Oxford: Blackwell.
Faludi, S. (1992) *Backlash: The Undeclared War against Women*. London: Chatto & Windus.
Faludi, S. (1999) *Stiffed: The Betrayal of the Modern Man*. London: Chatto & Windus.
Fast, I. (1984) *Gender Identity*. Hillsdale, NJ: The Analytic Press.
Fast, I. (1990) 'Aspects of Early Gender Development: Toward a Reformulation', *Psychoanalytic Psychology* 7(supplement): 105–18.
Gadd, D. (2000) 'Deconstructing Male Violence: A Qualitative Study of Male Workers and Clients on an Anti-Violence Programme', unpublished Ph.D. dissertation, Keele University, Staffs.
Gilmore, D. (1993) *Manhood in the Making: Cultural Concepts of Masculinity*. New Haven, CT: Yale University Press.
Gramsci, A. (1971) *Selections from the Prison Notebooks*. London: Lawrence & Wishart.
Hall, S., C. Critcher, T. Jefferson, J. Clarke and B. Roberts (1978) *Policing the Crisis*. London: Macmillan.
Hearn, J. (1998) *The Violences of Men*. London: Sage.
Hearn, J. (2000) 'The Hegemony of Men: On the Construction of Counter-Hegemony in Critical Studies on Men', in P. Folkersson, M. Nordberg and G. Smirthwaite (eds) *Hegemoni och Mansforskning: Rapport från Nordiska Workshopen i Karlstad, 19–21 mars 1999*, pp. 17–35. Karlstad: Universitetstryckeriet.
Henriques, J., W. Hollway, C. Urwin, C. Venn and V. Walkerdine (1998 [1984]) *Changing the Subject: Psychology, Social Regulation and Subjectivity*. London: Routledge.

Hood-Williams, J. (2001) 'Gender, Masculinities and Crime: From Structures to Psyches', *Theoretical Criminology* 5(1): 37–60.

Jameson, F. (1991) *Postmodernism, or the Logic of Late Capitalism.* Durham, NC: Duke University Press.

Jefferson, T. (1994) 'Theorising Masculine Subjectivity', in T. Newburn and E.A. Stanko (eds) *Just Boys Doing Business?: Men, Masculinities and Crime*, pp. 10–31. London: Routledge.

Kimmel, M. (1994) 'Masculinity and Homophobia', in H. Brod and M. Kaufman (eds) *Theorizing Masculinities*, pp. 119–41. London: Sage.

Klein, M. (1988a) *Love, Guilt and Reparation and Other Works, 1921–1945.* London: Virago.

Klein, M. (1988b) *Envy and Gratitude and Other Works, 1946–1963.* London: Virago.

Larkin, P. (1974) *High Windows.* London: Faber & Faber.

Layton, L. (1998) *Who's That Girl? Who's That Boy?: Clinical Practice Meets Postmodern Gender Theory.* Northvale, NJ: Jason Aronson.

Lewes, K. (1988) *Psychoanalysis and Male Homosexuality.* Northvale, NJ: Jason Aronson.

Mac an Ghaill, M. (1994) *The Making of Men: Masculinities, Sexualities and Schooling.* Buckingham: Open University Press.

MacInnes, J. (1998) *The End of Masculinity: The Confusion of Sexual Genesis and Sexual Difference in Modern Society.* Buckingham: Open University Press.

Messerschmidt, J.W. (1993) *Masculinities and Crime.* Lanham, MD: Rowman & Littlefield.

Messerschmidt, J.W. (1997) *Crime as Structured Action: Gender, Race, Class and Crime in the Making.* Thousand Oaks, CA: Sage.

Messerschmidt, J.W. (2000) *Nine Lives: Adolescent Masculinities, the Body and Violence.* Boulder, CO: Westview.

Minsky, R. (1998) *Psychoanalysis and Culture: Contemporary States of Mind.* Cambridge: Polity.

Mitchell, J. (1991) 'Commentary on "Deconstructing Difference": Gender, Splitting and Transitional Space', *Psychoanalytic Dialogues* 1: 353–9.

Newburn, T. and E.A. Stanko (eds) (1994) *Just Boys Doing Business?: Men, Masculinities and Crime.* London: Routledge.

O'Sullivan, C. (1998) 'Ladykillers: Similarities and Divergences of Masculinities in Gang Rape and Wife Battery', in L.H. Bowker (ed.) *Masculinities and Violence*, pp. 82–110. Thousand Oaks, CA: Sage.

Pattman, R., S. Frosh and A. Phoenix (1998) 'Lads, Machos and Others: Developing "Boy-Centred" Research', *Journal of Youth Studies* 1(2): 125–42.

Pontalis, J.-B. (1993) *Love of Beginnings.* London: Free Association Books.

Walklate, S. (1995) *Gender and Crime.* London: Prentice Hall/Harvester Wheatsheaf.

Wetherell, M. and N. Edley (1999) 'Negotiating Hegemonic Masculinity: Imaginary Positions and Psycho-Discursive Practices', *Feminism and Psychology* 9(3): 335–56.

Whitehead, S. (1999) 'Review Article: Hegemonic Masculinity Revisited', *Gender, Work and Organization* 6(1): 58–62.

Willis, P. (1977) *Learning to Labour.* Aldershot: Gower.

Wolfe, T. (1988) *Bonfire of the Vanities.* London: Jonathan Cape.

TONY JEFFERSON is a Professor of Criminology in the Department of Criminology, University of Keele. He has researched and published widely on questions to do with youth subcultures, the media, policing, race and crime, masculinity and fear of crime. His most recent book is *Doing Qualitative Research Differently: Free Association, Narrative and the Interview Method* (2000, with Wendy Hollway).

[3]

On hegemonic masculinity and violence:

Response to Jefferson and Hall

R.W. CONNELL
University of Sydney, Australia

The articles in this issue by Tony Jefferson and Steve Hall raise important issues about men and violence. Since a number of these issues centre on the idea of 'hegemonic masculinity' I should start with some notes on this concept and how it operates in the analysis of gender relations.

The question of how an unequal and oppressive system of social relations stabilizes itself arises in many cases: class relations, gender relations, race relations, imperialism and neocolonialism among them. Gramsci was not the first European radical to address this question—Bakunin had dealt with it repeatedly—but Gramsci provided brilliant examples of how to think the problem through in historically concrete terms, so his discussions of hegemony have been paradigmatic. I would stress 'historically concrete'. Hegemony has many different configurations, and may be local as distinct from general (there are certainly examples in masculinity research of distinctive local constructions). Like class relations, gender relations change historically, and the pattern and depth of hegemony changes also.

This is partly a matter of social struggle. Hegemony in gender relations can be contested and may break down—as it has, at least partially, in various communities impacted by late 20th-century feminism. This is not just among those meek and dreamy intellectuals whom Hall traduces at the end of his article. Gender struggles occur in many social contexts and around issues ranging from violence to pollution, education and housing (Naples, 1998). Jefferson is right to call attention to discussions of 'crisis' among men, and to suggest that this has important implications for the concept of hegemony (though his reading of those discussions, as I will suggest, is debatable).

The concept of 'hegemonic masculinity' appeared in the 1980s as a convergence of ideas from three main sources: women's political experience and research on gender hierarchy; gay men's political experience and theorizing of oppression; and empirical research with boys and men in locales such as schools and workplaces (Carrigan et al., 1985.) It was part of a critique of 'sex role' notions about gender, and particularly the concept of an undifferentiated 'male sex role' which at that time prevailed in discussions of men and gender (Kimmel, 1987). The concept recognized the political importance of differences among men *in gender terms* as well as in terms of class and race. It recognized a connection between two important social patterns, hierarchy between men and women and hierarchy among men. And it recognized the historically mutable character of these relationships, the possibility of struggle for the hegemonic position and contestation of hegemony overall.

The problem of the stabilization of the gender order had already been extensively discussed in feminist research, but overwhelmingly in relation to the construction of femininity and women's assent to patriarchal gender relations (e.g. Ferguson, 1983). The distinction between 'hegemonic' and various marginalized, subordinated or complicit masculinities (hegemony is always a relational concept) expresses the idea that the cultural dynamic of gender among men is also important in the overall politics of the gender order.

The most visible form of this dynamic is the circulation of models of admired masculine conduct, which may be exalted by churches, narrated by mass media, celebrated by the state or embedded informally in local cultures. It is familiar from analyses of ideology that such cultural formations refer to, but also in various ways distort, the everyday realities of social practice. Thus exemplary masculinities may be constructed (e.g. in commercial sport) which do not correspond closely to the lives of the majority of men, or even correspond closely to the actual lives of the richest and most powerful men (Donaldson, 1998), but which in various ways express ideals, fantasies and desires, provide models of relations with women and solutions to gender problems and above all 'naturalize' gender difference and gender hierarchy.

However, the distinctions between masculinities do not only occur in the dimension of generalized imagery. It is very important that they also operate in the context of institutions. For instance, dominant patterns of masculinity become embedded in the organizational culture of corporations and bureaucracies, where they are important in the life and work of managers (Roper, 1994). Socially legitimated models of masculinity are in play in families, where men's gender strategies shape negotiations around housework and the 'second shift' (Hochschild, 1989). Dominant patterns of masculinity are both engaged with, and contested, in child and adolescent development, where the construction of masculinity is played out in peer group structure, control of school space, dating patterns, homophobic speech, harassment (Thorne, 1993; Mac an Ghaill, 1994). Such processes can be found in other sites as well.

As Jefferson notes, the concept of 'hegemonic masculinity' has been widely used in recent years. It has found application in fields ranging from social psychology, education and media studies to research on sport, the military and crime, and it has found application in quite a number of countries. Not all of its uses have been consistent. This discussion, like others in the gender field, faces problems of reification, shifting definitions, and uneven empirical support. Nevertheless, the fact that the concept has been widely used suggests that it meets a need. From my reading of the literature, the key issues for which this concept has been providing a useful tool are the pervasiveness of relatively narrow cultural constructions of masculinity, the diversity of men's real experiences and trajectories, the significance of power relations among men and between men and women, and above all the varying *combination* of these factors in real-life situations.

Jefferson's article begins with an empirical question: the depth of contemporary crisis in masculinity. He cites three books which provide descriptions of crises in groups of men in the UK and the USA, and contrasts this with my downplaying of these 'seismic shifts in gender relations', and my tentative account of a new hegemonic project emerging in global arenas.

We have a straightforward difference of opinion about the significance of this evidence. I think Faludi's story of 'the betrayal of the modern man' is exaggerated, and I think Mac an Ghaill's excellent ethnography provides evidence of the continuity of constructions of masculinity (as do other school ethnographies, discussed in Connell, 2000) as much as evidence of crisis. An important control over exaggerating the significance of local studies is national-level survey data. In fields such as sexual practice and gender attitudes, the evidence supports the notion of historical change, but not the notion of a sudden crisis (e.g. Laumann et al., 1994—USA; Zulehner and Volz, 1998—Germany). Another important control is institutional data. Here the evidence is unequivocal. Contrary to what Hall seems to think, men as a group maintain their control over the dominant institutions of capitalism, the corporations and the state—as seen in the 1995 US 'Glass Ceiling Report', the 2001 ILO report, the Inter-Parliamentary Union's annual surveys, business magazines' 'Rich Lists' and indeed any other data source one cares to examine.

I have learnt to be sceptical of claims about 'men in crisis' or a 'crisis of masculinity', which have been the stock in trade of the 'mythopoetic' men's movement since the early 1980s, and various 'men's rights' groups in the 1990s. As an example, in 1995 there was a media outcry over a supposed men's health crisis in Australia, which led to agitation for men's health services, men's health policy, etc.—at a time when the statistical indicators showed unequivocally that men's health, on a society-wide scale, was improving, not getting worse. There has been an even bigger outcry over a supposed boys' educational crisis—with headlines and television specials on the theme that 'the girls are beating the boys!'—when the evidence shows that the great majority of boys are doing about as well as they usually have done, and gender differences in educational outcomes are fairly small. Therefore I am not inclined to accept the idea of a 'seismic shift in gender relations' (assuming that 'seismic' implies society-wide) which has rendered the concept of hegemonic masculinity empirically irrelevant.

It is undoubtedly true that hegemony in gender relations has been contested in the last generation, above all by the world-wide presence of women's movements (Bulbeck, 1998). Men in rich western societies, and beyond, are widely aware of this challenge: I agree with Jefferson that 'something unsettling' is happening to many men. We have passed what I (rather pompously) called in *Masculinities* (1995) a horizon of historicity in relation to masculinity. I would also argue that over the last 20 years the challenge from feminism in the metropolitan countries has in some measure been absorbed or rolled back (partly by a transformation of institutions in which the processes of globalization have been crucial). Yet local upheavals, even crises, in gender relations continue to occur, which may give rise to renewed general challenges in the future.

That, I would suggest, is the broad context in which we must attempt to understand contemporary masculinities. Jefferson sees the world disorder and 'proliferation of difference' in contemporary society, but does not see (at least in relation to gender) the transnational power structures, the interlinked market dynamics, and systems of cultural domination which operate in the same space. I think one must see both, and for that reason argue for an increased attention to global arenas in analyses of gender. Jefferson has difficulty conceptualizing a single world gender order, and he is not alone—this is a difficult shift of analytic focus to make, and of course the world gender order is not 'single' in the sense of obliterating local patterns. Rather, global arenas and institutions develop in complex interaction with local cultures and institutions, in gender relations as in sexuality (Marchand and Runyan, 2000; Altman, 2001; Connell, 2002).

Hall cannot see the historical argument at all. He claims that the work of masculinity researchers (Connell, Morgan, Messerschmidt and Kimmel are cited) rests on a model of transhistorical male oppression—a theme Hall repeats with variations through his article. If true, this would be a damaging criticism, but in fact it is quite false. *All* the authors named are clear about the historically constructed character of masculinities and gendered power. (Curiously it is Gilmore, an ethnographer Hall cites with approval, who proposes a transhistorical model of masculinity.) Indeed the profound historicity of gender relations is a *major* theme of the account of gender in *Gender and Power* and *Masculinities*, the two works of mine that Hall cites. The 'transhistorical patriarchy', 'archaic lust for power', and 'timeless ruling elite' that he ridicules are Hall's own inventions. This is, I regret to say, only one of Hall's misrepresentations of other people's views, and I hope that readers coming new to these questions will read the original contributions rather than relying on his account of them.

Gender processes, and the groupings of men that arise in them, have multiple and sometimes divergent connections with violence. There is no such thing as '*the* hegemonic masculinity thesis', outside of Hall's text. 'Hegemonic masculinity' is a concept which may function in a number of ways in analyses of violence. Used with awareness of historical context—and not as a catch-all formula—it may help explain the cultural embedding and specific shape of violence in communities where physical aggression is expected or admired among men. It may help explain broad differences in rates of violence between men and women. It may help understand motive and emotion in domestic violence and homophobic violence, and in certain patterns of confrontation among men. It may be useful in understanding the dynamics of violent organizations, for instance the ways armies function and produce violence. It may help in understanding the difficulties of peacemaking and conflict resolution.

Hall sets up his own straw-man model of patriarchal violence, which he proceeds with some relish to refute (and rightly so, as it is a fairly bad model). His presentation misses much of the complexity just noted because he drastically narrows what is taken into account as men's violence. He focuses on the case of face-to-face fighting between individual men. Hall practically ignores domestic violence against women (unbelievably, when he mentions 'wives, girlfriends' it is to claim that they are 'objects of male protection', p. 46). He totally ignores rape and child sexual abuse. He never discusses homophobic murders or assaults (and in a long article manages one dismissive allusion to 'homophobic bullying'). He practically ignores military violence (and the significance of the fact that in the current time of 'peace' there are about 20 million soldiers in the world). Hall practically ignores police violence, and totally ignores incarceration. He does not seem to regard industrial injury as violence against workers, nor does he detect physical violence in any other kind of white-collar crime. Most strikingly, given his invocation of changing capitalism, he totally ignores the violence of imperialism, the prevalence of post-colonial war, the international arms trade, the 'defence' industry, the gun lobby and the corporate 'security' industry. In short, Hall's conception of 'violence' substantially excludes violence against women, organizational violence and international violence. It is not surprising that he has difficulty understanding the relationships of violence to hegemonic masculinity.

Jefferson recognizes the issue of violence against women but, in a discussion of Hearn's work, finds it difficult to see this as an enactment of (in Hearn's terminology) 'being a man'. I agree that in the public realm men who batter wives/partners are not cultural heroes. However, Jefferson misses the extent to which (in Anglophone communities at least, and probably others) in the informal culture of neighbourhoods, workplaces and pubs, husbands have been expected to keep wives in their place, and a man who cannot do this has been regarded by other men with a degree of contempt ('henpecked', 'she wears the pants', etc.). A controlled use of force, or the threat of force, has been widely accepted as part of men's repertoire in dealing with women and children ('a woman is like a rug . . .'; 'wait until your father gets home . . .'), as well as with other men ('the test of manhood . . .'). It is precisely this assumption that campaigns against domestic violence are *still*, in 2001, trying to contest. Research with batterers and rapists indeed detects remorse and shame, as Jefferson says, but *also* detects feelings of entitlement, justifications and the intention to establish control (e.g. Ptacek, 1988; Lea and Auburn, 2001). It does not seem difficult to understand at least part of the violence Hearn documents in terms of men's relationship with hegemonic masculinity, provided we see masculinities (as I have consistently argued) as projects, not fixed patterns. The relationship of men to hegemonic masculinity is often fraught, the enactment partial, contested and capable of shifting into violence.

Jefferson raises the possibility, which has been increasingly discussed in the recent literature, that we might understand masculinities and femininities as discursive strategies or performances. This would allow easy acknowledgement of the different strategies taken by an individual subject (Jefferson's example of Bill Gates) in different situations addressed to different audiences. I think this a useful idea, which has already led to some fascinating educational, cultural and psychological research (e.g. Davies, 1993; Buchbinder, 1998; Wetherell and Edley, 1999).

But I have problems with those poststructuralist formulations which see discursive strategies or performances as the *only* reality of gender. Questions of material inequality are important in understanding what is at stake in these strategies. Questions of embodiment are essential to understanding their consequences—violence is, after all, a relation between bodies. The gendered character of institutions is essential to understanding how gender operates on the scale of contemporary societies, including understanding collective violence. I would argue, also, that understanding institutions is essential to understanding the limits of discursive diversity. Even Mr Gates is not free to take up any discursive position he likes, because some of them, given the way capitalist businesses operate, would lose him his organizational power.

Hall's view of social relations and history places much more emphasis on materiality, but sees it only in one dimension. To Hall, capitalism is the central reality, and class is the fundamental social division; everything else is epiphenomenal. It is difficult to engage with Hall on the subject of masculinities because he cannot really 'see' gender as a structure of social relations, a system of material practices resulting in material inequalities. (For a useful recent survey of gender relations and inequalities in the UK see Walby, 1997.) Hall is evidently not familiar with the data about gender inequalities. If he were, he would hardly make the suggestion that income disparities between women and men can be disregarded because the statistics are 'heavily skewed by the vast fortunes owned by a very small number of men'. In fact, gender income differentials, and the differences in occupational pay rates, chances of promotion, rates of part-time and casual employment and workforce participation rates that produce them, are very widespread and are found in the working class of metropolitan countries as well as the ruling class.

This point is important because one of Hall's key moves is to deny that working-class men get any benefit from current gender arrangements, so in his view their violence can have nothing to do with patriarchy. I do not think much is to be gained by discussing such rhetorical comparisons as the £50 per night male doorman versus the £300,000 per year female QC. The important issue is how gender relations operate in practice. There seems a good deal of evidence, from many sources, of working-class men being involved in issues where the concept of hegemonic masculinity is relevant: concern with men's status and authority, affirmations of toughness and power, assertions of men's freedom, anxieties about men's position as breadwinner and head of household, assertions of men's rights to sexual gratification and to domestic service, contempt and fear of effeminate and homosexual men, insistence on the masculinity of industrial jobs and the masculinity of many leisure activities. (As examples from a large literature: Donaldson, 1991; Hearn, 1998; Tomsen, 1998.) There is also evidence that such patterns play out in domestic violence, industrial injury, public confrontations among men, rape and homophobic violence and violent sports. Hall himself cites some of this evidence, when describing the prevalence of what he can only understand as 'pointless' violence among marginalized working-class men. It is *also* true, as I have pointed out in case-study material (Connell, 1995), that we can find egalitarianism, innovation and tolerance in working-class communities, sometimes in the same families and households. 'Hegemony' does not mean totalitarian dominance.

Hall has difficulty with 'the hegemonic masculinity thesis' partly because he has constructed an unbelievable version of the argument about masculinity and violence, a thesis that violence is always and only a direct expression of power. In another odd expression he represents masculinity researchers as arguing that violence is a 'privilege'. Hall seems to have missed the point, though it is carefully formulated by Messerschmidt (1993) in a text Hall cites, that violence often arises in the *construction* of masculinities, as part of the practice by which particular men or groups of men claim respect, intimidate rivals, or try to gain material advantages. Violence is not a 'privilege', but it is very often a means of claiming or defending privilege, asserting superiority or taking an advantage. (By ignoring organizational violence, and most violence against women and gay men, Hall makes this more difficult to see.)

Hall's discussion of the 'pacification' of social relations in the development of capitalism is interesting and suggestive. Shorn of Bourdieu's deeply misleading concepts of 'symbolic violence' and 'habitus', this discussion traces the development of techniques of social organization and control that certainly reduce violence in one direction, but augment it in another.

For the very societies that were being 'pacified' internally (and we should not exaggerate the smoothness or success of this project) were simultaneously launching projects of global conquest and, from time to time, increasingly destructive wars against each other.

Imperialism and war are, of course, gendered projects which depend on large-scale organization. They have been important in the shaping of modern western masculinities while, conversely, the institutionalization of particular masculinities has been important in sustaining the organization and legitimacy of collective violence. There is a close interplay between military heroism and hegemonic masculinity both in the metropole and the colonial world. Hall's claim that the pacified class elite has avoided the direct use of physical violence must be heavily qualified in the light of the history of imperialism. Doubtless J. Pierpont Morgan did not tote a gun, but quite a lot of generals, admirals, police chiefs, colonial governors and plantation owners did. The militarization of world capitalism is not exactly a thing of the remote past. In the week I have been writing this article, President Bush has responded to the mass murder at the World Trade Center by declaring 'We are at war', and doing his best to mobilize support across the capitalist world for a violent US response to the problems of the Middle East—much as his father did.

Jefferson argues that my emphasis on the global realities of gender must lead away from the 'psychic' dimension and the task of building a psychosocial analysis of masculinity. If my formulation in the article 'Masculinities and Globalization' (1998) has this implication, then I must accept responsibility for a misstatement. I have never thought that masculinities (or gender relations as a whole) could be understood without close attention to psychological issues. I assume that is true of global processes of gender construction too, so that the research agenda I suggest, with a focus on very large-scale institutions, markets and mass communications, needs a psychological dimension. For instance, I would see value in studying the psychodynamics of gender among actors in global arenas such as multinational business management (if these folk will allow it!); in studying the emotional and cognitive processes involved in international threat, risk, 'defence', aggression; in studying the ways gender ideologies in global communications are selectively adopted or rejected in local contexts; in studying the relation of the individual to global society as well as local or national society (for instance, questions of alienation in relation to the global economy).

I will not comment extensively on Jefferson's psychological argument. It seems to me a valuable line of thought, but needing—like all psychoanalytic argument—to be tested in concrete case-study analyses. That is very much what Chodorow did, and for that reason I would give a good deal more credit to her treatment of gender diversity in *Femininities, Masculinities, Sexualities* (1994) than Jefferson does. I think it important that psychoanalytic arguments on gender should be historicized, as is done in relation to femininity by Nielsen and Rudberg (1994).

I would also emphasize the diversity of the psychoanalytic tradition, the value for instance of existential psychoanalysis and the Adlerian tradition, even the diversity of treatments of Oedipal relations and sexuality within classical psychoanalysis (Lewes, 1988). There is also, of course, a rich literature of non-psychoanalytic psychology which has important lines of thought on gender (e.g. Hollway, 1984). The reason for emphasizing this is that it may be a mistake to postulate one core mechanism of gender development, and derive characteristics of the gender order from it. Arguably there are multiple psychological mechanisms of affiliation or positioning within the gender order, which may gain greater or less salience in different historical circumstances—including circumstances of 'crisis' in gender relations.

At the end of the day, the biggest difference between these two articles is that Jefferson is making a serious attempt to develop a gender analysis, and Hall is not. Hall's lack of a gender analysis leaves him with nothing to say about two central problems—why there is a connection between violence and *men*, and what might be done about gendered violence. Therefore he can propose no politics of change. All he can do, at the end of his article, is to say the problems are terrible but every strategy he knows of is hopeless.

One does not need to be a woolly New Age optimist to think that violence reduction and violence prevention are possible. There are quite concrete things that can be done, and are being done, to contest gendered and gender-based violence, and this work is increasingly making use of the research on masculinities. (For examples from a range of countries see Denborough, 1996; Kaufman, 1999; Breines et al., 2000; Morrell, 2001.) The spectrum of action ranges from rape prevention to international conflict resolution and includes economic redistribution, education and disarmament. The fact that social research on masculinities has begun to make a significant contribution to this field of debate and practice is, to me, one of its most important benefits.

References

Altman, D. (2001) *Global Sex*. Chicago, IL: University of Chicago Press.

Breines, I., R. Connell and I. Eide (eds) (2000) *Male Roles, Masculinities and Violence: A Culture of Peace Approach*. Paris: UNESCO Publishing.

Buchbinder, D. (1998) *Performance Anxieties: Re-producing Masculinity*. Sydney: Allen & Unwin.

Bulbeck, C. (1998) *Re-orienting Western Feminisms*. Cambridge: Cambridge University Press.

Carrigan, T., R. Connell and J. Lee (1985) 'Toward a New Sociology of Masculinity', *Theory and Society* 14(5), 551–604.

Chodorow, N. (1994) *Femininities, Masculinities, Sexualities*. Lexington, KY: University Press of Kentucky.

Connell, R.W. (1995) *Masculinities.* Cambridge: Polity.

Connell, R.W. (1998) 'Masculinities and Globalization', *Men and Masculinities* 1(1): 3–23.

Connell, R.W. (2000) *The Men and the Boys.* Berkeley, CA: University of California Press.

Connell, R.W. (2002) *Gender.* Cambridge: Polity Press (forthcoming).

Davies, B. (1993) *Shards of Glass: Children Reading and Writing beyond Gendered Identities.* Sydney: Allen & Unwin.

Denborough, D. (1996) 'Step by Step: Developing Respectful Ways of Working with Young Men to Reduce Violence', in C. McLean et al. (eds) *Men's Ways of Being*, pp. 91–115. Boulder, CO: Westview Press.

Donaldson, M. (1991) *Time of Our Lives: Labour and Love in the Working Class.* Sydney, Allen & Unwin.

Donaldson, M. (1998) 'The Masculinity of the Hegemonic: Growing up Very Rich', *Journal of Interdisciplinary Gender Studies* 3(2): 95–112.

Ferguson, M. (1983) *Forever Feminine: Women's Magazines and the Cult of Femininity.* London: Heinemann.

Hearn, J. (1998) *The Violences of Men: How Men Talk about and How Agencies Respond to Men's Violence to Women.* London: Sage.

Hochschild, A. (1989) *The Second Shift: Working Parents and the Revolution at Home.* New York: Viking.

Hollway, W. (1984) 'Gender Difference and the Production of Subjectivity', in J. Henriques et al. *Changing the Subject: Psychology, Social Regulation and Subjectivity*, pp. 227–63. London: Methuen.

Kaufman, M. (ed.) (1999) *Men and Violence.* Special issue of *IASOM Newsletter* (International Association for Studies of Men), vol. 6.

Kimmel, M. (1987) 'Rethinking "Masculinity": New Directions in Research', in M. Kimmel (ed.) *Changing Men: New Directions in Research on Men and Masculinity*, pp. 9–24. Newbury Park, CA: Sage.

Laumann, E.O., J.H. Gagnon, R.T. Michael and S. Michaels (1994) *The Social Organization of Sexuality: Sexual Practices in the United States.* Chicago, IL: University of Chicago Press.

Lea, S. and T. Auburn (2001) 'The Social Construction of Rape in the Talk of a Convicted Rapist', *Feminism and Psychology* 11(1): 11–33.

Lewes, K. (1988) *The Psychoanalytic Theory of Male Homosexuality.* New York: Simon & Schuster.

Mac an Ghaill, M. (1994) *The Making of Men: Masculinities, Sexualities and Schooling.* Buckingham: Open University Press.

Marchand, M.H. and A.S. Runyan (eds) (2000) *Gender and Global Restructuring: Sightings, Sites and Resistances.* London: Routledge.

Messerschmidt, J.W. (1993) *Masculinities and Crime: Critique and Reconceptualization of Theory.* Lanham, MD: Rowman & Littlefield.

Morrell, R. (ed.) (2001) *Changing Men in Southern Africa.* London: Zed Books.

Naples, N. (ed.) (1998) *Community Activism and Feminist Politics: Organizing across Race, Class, and Gender.* New York: Routledge.

Nielsen, H.B. and M. Rudberg (1994) *Psychological Gender and Modernity.* Oslo: Scandinavian University Press.

Ptacek, J. (1988) 'Why do Men Batter Their Wives?', in K. Yllö and M. Bograd (eds) *Feminist Perspectives on Wife Abuse*, pp. 133–57. Newbury Park, CA: Sage.

Roper, M. (1994) *Masculinity and the British Organization Man since 1945.* Oxford: Oxford University Press.

Thorne, B. (1993) *Gender Play: Girls and Boys at School.* New Brunswick: Rutgers University Press.

Tomsen, S. (1998) 'He Had to Be a Poofter or Something': Violence, Male Honour and Heterosexual Panic', *Journal of Interdisciplinary Gender Studies* 3(2): 44–57.

Walby, S. (1997) *Gender Transformations.* London: Routledge.

Wetherell, M. and N. Edley (1999) 'Negotiating Hegemonic Masculinity: Imaginary Positions and Psycho-Discursive Practices', *Feminism and Psychology* 9(3): 335–56.

Zulehner, P.M. and R. Volz (1998) *Männer im Aufbruch: Wie Deutschlands Männer sich Selbst und wie Frauen sie Sehen.* Ostfildern: Schwabenverlag.

BOB CONNELL is Professor of Education at the University of Sydney. He is the author or co-author of 16 books, including *Class Structure in Australian History, Making the Difference, Gender and Power, Schools and Social Justice, Masculinities* and *The Men and the Boys.* His current research concerns gender equity, globalization and intellectuals.

[4]

Making bodies matter:

Adolescent masculinities, the body, and varieties of violence

JAMES W. MESSERSCHMIDT
University of Southern Maine, Portland, USA

Abstract

Previous studies of adolescent male violence have ignored, inter alia, offender agency, body, and gender. The life-history method offers a means to explore, concurrently, all three. In this article, the life histories of two white working-class adolescent male violent offenders are juxtaposed and analysed. Although both boys initially constructed culturally idealized hegemonic masculinities, bodily and sexual practices institutionalized in the school played a major role in the construction of two differing forms of masculinity (subordinate and opposition) as well as corresponding types of violence (sexual and assaultive).

Key Words

the body • hegemonic masculinity • masculinity challenges • opposition masculinity • sexuality • subordinate masculinity

In June 1993, the American Sociological Association (ASA) convened an intensive workshop of leading sociologists working on violence. The goals of the workshop were to examine existing research on the social causes of violence, identify promising research directions, and address policy issues. Three years later the ASA published the workshop report, *Social Causes of Violence: Crafting a Science Agenda*, highlighting the nature of research conducted thus far on violence and identifying priority areas for future study. In particular, the report (Levine and Rosich, 1996: 9) emphasizes that US teenagers 'have increasingly become both victims and perpetrators of violent crime' and youth violence 'is growing more rapidly than in any other subgroup.' Consequently, the workshop report calls for research on the relationships among age, gender, social class, and violence and suggests that future studies should examine different forms of violence and how 'situational or lifestyle factors' relate to them.

Arguably, examination of offender experience may help clarify many of the concerns outlined by the ASA report. I have thus tried to walk in the shoes of violent boys—talk to them in depth about their experiences—and learn what they actually did and experienced and how their lives resulted in violence. To conceptualize how age, gender, class, and social situation are related to specific type of violence, one must appreciate how adolescent male violent offenders construct and make sense of their particular world, and comprehend the ways in which they interpret their own lives and the world around them. Realistically, how can we begin to understand adolescent male violence if we do not understand what such violence means to the offender himself?

The life-history method is particularly suited to this task because it richly documents personal experiences and transformations over time. It is what Thomas and Znaniecki (1927) characterized as the 'perfect' type of sociological material. Such classics of criminology as Shaw's (1930) *The Jack Roller* and Sutherland's (1937) *The Professional Thief* illustrate 'the power of life-history data to illuminate the complex processes of criminal offending' (Sampson and Laub, 1993: 204). Indeed, the method demands a close evaluation of the meaning of social life to those who enact it, revealing *their* experiences, practices, and social world. As Agnew (1990: 271) points out, the accounts of those involved in crime 'may be the only way of obtaining accurate information on the individual's internal states and those aspects of the external situation that the individual is attending to.'

Accordingly, this article focuses on the life stories of two adolescent working-class males involved in violence: Zack and Hugh (both pseudonyms). Obviously, two case studies are not a representative sample. Therefore, my conclusions here are only suggestive. However, life-history research does not seek to gain a large and representative sample from which bold generalizations may be made; its procedure can be best described as 'stratified purposeful sampling' (Patton, 1990: 172–4). I have no reason to believe that these two boys differ significantly from the general population of boys in their social milieu. Moreover, the life histories simultaneously show that important aspects of sexual and assaultive violence by working-class teenage males have been overlooked in the past and, thus, are an extremely fertile source for further investigations and theory building.

I interviewed Zack and Hugh in 1997 as part of a larger life-history study of adolescent masculinities and varieties of violence and non-violence.

The chief questions of the larger study are: Why do some boys engage in violence and some boys do not? Why do those boys who engage in violence commit different types? The sample consists of 15 white New England small-town working-class boys, aged 15 to 18. Ten of the boys were incarcerated or receiving private counseling for sexual or assaultive violence and were categorized according to offense type: 'sex offender' (five boys who acted in a sexually violent manner against another adolescent who was at least one year younger) and 'assaultive offender' (five boys who acted in a physically violent way against another person). The remaining five boys were categorized as 'non-violent' because they had not admitted committing (nor been formally charged with committing) a sexually violent and/or assaultive act. Detained boys were identified by prison personnel who obtained informed consent prior to each interview. Boys attending private counseling were similarly identified by therapists.

Each boy voluntarily participated in confidential one-on-one tape-recorded informal conversational interviews. The conversations were fluid, allowing each boy to take the lead rather than merely to respond to topical questions. The conversations were normally completed in two meetings of two to three hours each. The goal was to grasp each boy's unique viewpoint—his personal vision of the world.

Each conversation attempted to reflect the situational accomplishment of masculinities and the eventual use of violence as a result of personal life history. As such, the interviews drew on the insights of 'structured action theory' (Messerschmidt, 1993, 1997a). Having various theoretical origins (Giddens, 1976, 1984; Connell, 1987, 1995; West and Zimmerman, 1987; West and Fenstermaker, 1995), structured action theory emphasizes the construction of gender as a situated social and interactional accomplishment. In other words, gender grows out of social practices in specific social structural settings and serves to inform such practices in reciprocal relation. Consequently, in any particular setting—whole societies or institutions or peer groups—varieties of gender are constructed in a relationship of power. Thus, the conversations investigated how both sexual and assaultive violence may be accountable practices for 'doing masculinity'—the social construction of different types of masculinities—in their particular social settings. This article reports findings on two of the 15 case studies, detailing and comparing a sex offender (Zack) and an assaultive offender (Hugh).

Previous criminological studies of sex offenders ignore adolescent males who sexually assault younger children. Those social science studies which have examined this type of sex offender ignore gender and agency (see Messerschmidt, 1997b, for a review). Moreover, although some recent criminological work notably contributes to our understanding of adolescent masculinities and crime (e.g. Collison, 1996; Hagedorn, 1998), no life-history research on adolescent masculinity and violence exists and no studies on youth violence explore why any given adolescent male engages in one type of violence rather than another. Thus, this article advances criminological literature on adolescent male sexual and assaultive violence.

The two life histories also reveal the importance of another neglected topic of contemporary criminology: the body and its relation to crime. Sociological criminology traditionally accepts a strict dichotomy between 'society' and 'biology', focusing on the former as exclusively defining the realm of criminological inquiry. To avoid any inclination to biological reductionism, sociological criminology has treated each part of this dichotomy as an unconnected intellectual domain that necessitates separate analysis. However, as becomes clear in the life stories detailed in this article, 'society' and 'biology' form a false dichotomy and must be viewed as inextricably linked. I argue for a 'body friendly criminology' that accounts for the fact that men and boys are active agents in their social relations and, therefore, takes into account the intent of social actors and how social action relates to the body as a meaningful construction in itself (see further Scott and Morgan, 1993; Shilling, 1993; Connell, 1995). Indeed, our bodies constrain or facilitate social action and, therefore, mediate and influence social practices. In short, one cannot consider human agency—and, therefore, the differing forms of violence by Zack and Hugh—without taking into account the body. However, we are getting ahead of ourselves. Let me now detail the two life histories.

Two pathways to violence

Here, then, are the life stories of Zack and Hugh, both white working-class adolescent males convicted of a violent offense. They were specifically chosen from the larger pool of 15 for several reasons. First, they differ in the type of violence each engaged in: Zack committed *sexual* violence; Hugh committed *assaultive* violence. Second, they allow analysis as to why adolescent boys may exclusively engage in one type of violence (sexual or assaultive). Finally, these two case studies are nicely juxtaposed because both Zack and Hugh grew up in the same neighborhood and attended the same school at the same time. Thus, this article is unique in reporting data as to why boys from the *same* social milieu come to engage in *different* types of violence. We begin with Zack.

Zack

Zack is a youthful 15 year old who was intrigued that I was interested in his life story. He quickly immersed himself in conversation. Zack is from a working-class town where he lives with his grandmother, aunt, uncle, and two younger female cousins (9 and 12 years old). Zack became a member of this family at the age of four, when his grandmother adopted him. His biological father disappeared when he was two. His mother is an alcoholic, unable to care for him.The adoption initially was distressing to Zack:

> She [grandmother] came to pick me up and I really didn't want to go. I was really attached to my mom and I remember just crawling under a table and latching myself to my mom's leg and not wanting to go.

Q. You were frightened of moving in with your grandmother?
A. Yeah, but my grandmother was real nice to me and she told me why I had to come—that my mom couldn't take care of me.

Zack's grandmother works as a nurse's aid and his uncle works only part time as a carpenter. His aunt does not work outside the home but does most of the household cooking and cleaning. The kids and the uncle have no assigned household chores, except 'helping out' now and then as needed. Besides reporting these explicit practices defining 'men's work' and 'women's work' at home and in the workplace, Zack's account of family interaction revealed a very close relationship with his grandmother. During Christmas she would always 'buy me a room full of toys. It was unbelievable. I really liked her a lot.' Zack also described a warm bond with his uncle. In fact, Zack's uncle was his only model of masculinity while growing up—his uncle's ideas and practices representing what masculinity 'was all about.' During the years they lived together, Zack's uncle encouraged in Zack a liking for sport, especially football. Indeed, it was this interaction with his uncle that cultivated Zack's idea of a future: 'Since I was young, I wanted to be a football player. I watched football on TV with my uncle all the time and I'd say, "Wow, look at that, that's gonna be me someday." And my uncle would say, "That's great Zack." ' Indeed, Zack stated that throughout his childhood the meaning of masculinity remained the same—to 'be strong and a good football player. That's it.'

Zack did not, however, enjoy such an amiable relationship with his aunt. In fact, she was physically and verbally abusive to Zack but not so to his two younger cousins. Zack's aunt was extremely obese and would use her size against him—slapping and pushing him, and throwing him against walls. Zack felt he could never do anything right to please his aunt and eventually concluded that he was the cause of the physical violence and verbal abuse: 'She would swear at me and say, "If you weren't such a bad kid I wouldn't have to act like this." I felt I was the problem, something about me, because she never screamed like that at my cousins, you know.'

Thus, Zack saw his aunt as having the power in the house and using it in an aggressive and tyrannical manner. His grandmother and uncle were passive members of the family who deferred to his aunt and never disciplined Zack or his cousins: 'She controlled everything. My grandmother and uncle just paid the bills and brought in the food. She was like a saint to everyone but me.' His relationship with his aunt was extremely distressing to Zack and participation at school reinforced the negative masculine self-esteem that evolved from this interaction at home.

Initially, Zack liked school and did quite well. From kindergarten to second grade Zack 'really excelled in school,' was 'doing awesome' schoolwork, and had lots of friends. However, in third grade circumstances at school began to change. By this time he had gained considerable weight and, indeed, other students considered him 'fat,' as did he himself. As Zack states: 'I was really chubby and large, and I wasn't very athletic. I dressed funny. I'd wear sweat pants and the shirts with little alligators—so I wasn't popular.' The 'cool guys' at school would consistently tease and physically assault Zack: 'They'd call me "fatty," "chubby cheeks," "wimp," and stuff like that. I got pushed down a lot and stuff. I got beat up a lot in the school yard.'

The bullying for being overweight and the constant physical assault extended through grade school and middle school. Zack did not respond physically to the bullying because he felt he would be 'beat up.' When asked if he discussed this bullying with anyone at home, Zack replied:

> Yeah, I talked with my uncle. I'd come home and say, 'People are picking on me at school,' and he'd say, 'Oh, you have to fight back or they'll keep it up.' But I was scared to fight back. So I was really confused what to do.

Throughout third and fourth grades, Zack coped with the bullying by avoiding, as much as possible, the 'popular kids' (who seemed to be doing most of the bullying). In the fifth grade, however, after again discussing the bullying with his uncle, Zack decided he would follow his uncle's advice because simply avoiding the provoking students was not working. During one major bullying incident in which he was persistently pushed around by a 'cool guy,' Zack attempted to 'fight back' physically but was beaten severely—'he pile drived me into the ground.' At the end of the 'fight' (which took place on the playground while a large group watched), several students shouted 'names at me like "fatty," "fatty can't fight," "you're a wimp," stuff like that.' I asked Zack how that made him feel and he answered: 'Like I was fat, weird, and a wimp. It really bothered me that kids at school didn't like me.'

Thus, Zack experienced embarrassment in school for poor grades, feelings of masculine inadequacy because of his physical size and shape, and a sense of masculine powerlessness because of his inability to 'do masculinity' in the way his uncle suggested—to fight back. Zack thus became even more of a loner at school, stopped discussing the bullying with his uncle, and never again attempted to respond physically to the harassment. When he came home from school, Zack would not play with other kids—'they wouldn't play with me'—and usually locked himself in his room to concentrate on video games. As Zack put it:

> I felt like I was a 'wimp' 'cause I couldn't do what other boys did. I never could in my life. I couldn't do anything. Other people always told me what to do, I never told anybody. I felt pretty crappy about myself. I didn't like myself and I couldn't really talk to my uncle about it.

Indeed, in school Zack was defined socially as *embodying* a 'subordinate masculinity;' he accepted this characterization and, consequently, life at home and school both seemed hopeless for him.

Notwithstanding, Zack did not give up entirely as he was determined to play on the middle-school football team—not only because of his love of football, but also to show people that he was 'somebody': 'It would make me feel like I was actually worth something, like other guys, you know.' However, during the summer, between fifth and sixth grades, Zack broke his wrist while attempting to 'get in shape.' He remained overweight, and although he tried out for the team in his sixth-grade year, he was soon cut from the team. Consequently, Zack felt even less secure about his masculinity and so, it seems, did his classmates: 'They continued to make fun of me, call me names and say I couldn't do nothin'.' So Zack perpetually avoided his classmates, which was not difficult because he was, in turn, rejected by most of them. According to Zack, the only classmates who would have anything to do with him was a group of boys he called 'the misfits.' Zack's interaction with the misfits took place only during school lunch: 'We'd all sit at the table, and you'd look at us and we'd all look like a bunch of misfits.' Other than the 'misfits' during lunch, Zack did not 'hang out' with other kids: 'I wasn't part of any groups.' He identified three major groups in school: 'The popular kids—the people who were good looking, athletes, had the cool clothes, and the girls. The brains, the people who did good in school. And then us.'

Despite his lack of school friends, during sixth grade Zack developed a sexual interest in girls. He learned this not from the adults at home, but through interaction at school. Because of the frequent 'sex talk' at school, Zack wanted to experience sex to be like all the other boys. Many popular boys and some of the 'misfits' had allegedly engaged in intercourse, so Zack felt extremely 'left out,' especially since he had never been able to arrange a date. Indeed, he identified himself as a 'virgin,' a status other boys—including numerous 'misfits'—had long ago surpassed. The continued rejection by girls made Zack feel discontented: 'I didn't really like myself 'cause girls didn't like me. I was fat and I just didn't seem to fit in. Like I'm the only virgin in the school.'

> Q. Did you want to fit in?
> A. Yeah. And I tried really hard. I tried to play football so the popular guys would like me. I tried to dress differently, dress like they [popular kids] did. I tried going on diets. I tried to get girls.
> Q. You wanted to be accepted into the popular crowd?
> A. Right. But they didn't want anything to do with me. My size, and I just didn't have the looks that they did, you know. The only way that you are in the popular group is that you have to be good at sports and girls have to like you. And I was bad at sports and girls hated me.

By the age of 11, then, Zack endured serious and continuous forms of bullying at school regarding his physical size and shape. Rather than accepting his body as something personal and unique, Zack attempted to 'fit in' by adopting certain situationally normative masculine practices: fighting back, playing football, dressing 'cool,' and obtaining heterosexual dates. He failed miserably at each. Moreover, this is exactly the time (at age 11) when he learns from his grandmother that no one in his family, except her, was interested in adopting him when he was four years old. As Zack states: 'My grandmother told me that my mom called everyone in my family and said, "Can you take my son?" And they all said no. And my grandmother was the only one that said yes.' Asked how that made him feel, Zack replied, 'I felt real bad about myself. I thought there must really be something wrong with me 'cause no one wants me, you know.' Consequently, all of these events add up to a serious lack of masculine resources and, therefore, lack of masculine self-esteem at home and at school: 'I wasn't happy at home and I wasn't happy at school. I couldn't do anything right and everybody thought I was a misfit. I didn't want to be a misfit and needed something to cheer me up.'

Accordingly, Zack sought to overcome his lack of masculine resources—and therefore his low masculine self-esteem—through controlling and dominating behaviors involving the use of sexual power. Unable to be masculine like the 'cool guys' and terribly degraded at home, Zack turned to an available masculine practice—expressing control and power over his youngest cousin through sexuality. It was during his sixth-grade year—a time when Zack experienced the distressing events just discussed and when he 'discovered' heterosexuality—that Zack sought out his cousin: 'I wanted to experience sex, like what other boys were doing. I wanted to do what they were talking about but I was rejected by girls at school.' I asked Zack to elaborate on why he turned to his youngest cousin:

> It was in the sixth grade. Me and my younger cousin, who was six at the time, we started to play this game Truth or Dare, and we just dared each other to do something. It started out pretty normal, just like standing on your head and stuff like that. But it just progressed into sexual stuff, until it was just sexual contact like oral sex and touching and stuff like that.'
>
> Q. Your cousin just went along with the game?
>
> A. Not the sexual stuff. She'd say, 'No, I don't really want to,' and then I'd force her into it.
>
> Q. How did you force her?
>
> A. Like I'd say, 'Oh, I'll let you play my Sega,' because I had a Sega and she used to always want to come and play.
>
> Q. Then she would agree to do what you asked?
>
> A. Yeah. It started out with her just touching over my clothing, and then it progressed to taking off each other's clothes and touching each other and stuff like that.
>
> Q. And she never questioned it?
>
> A. No, not anymore, 'cause I always let her play my Sega.

Zack sexually assaulted (fondling and oral penetration) his youngest cousin for three years (or until he was 14 and she was 9) by using the manipulation strategy described. The following dialogue reveals what the sexual violence accomplished for Zack:

Q. How did it make you feel when you were able to manipulate your cousin?
A. It made me feel real good. I just felt like finally I was in control over somebody. I forgot about being fat and ugly. She was someone looking up to me, you know. If I needed sexual contact, then I had it. I wasn't a virgin anymore.
Q. Is that why you sexually assaulted your cousin for three years?
A. Yeah. I wanted control over something in my life and this gave it to me. I finally felt like one of the guys.
Q. What were you thinking about right before you sexually assaulted your cousin?
A. I was just really down because I had a rough day at school.
Q. What do you mean by 'a rough day'?
A. Just a lot of teasing, being called names and being pushed around a lot. Not having any friends that meant anything. Kind of depressed about school. Not able to do things like everybody else. That made me sad.
Q. Then you would come home from school and play the game with your cousin?
A. Yeah. And that would cheer me up, make me feel better. Plus I would be sexually satisfied 'cause she would masturbate me and give me blow jobs and feeling like I have affection. No one ever said good things about me and I never did things that the other guys did. But now I did and it was really cool.
Q. Why did you choose your youngest cousin?
A. 'Cause I could tell that she was more accessible and just really easy to be able to take advantage of. She always aimed to please everyone else so I took advantage of that. And if I let her play Sega, she wouldn't tell anybody.
Q. Did you ever talk about this with the misfits or other kids at school?
A. No. But I could now talk about sex with them if I had to. I knew what it looked like and how it felt now, kind of thing. So I felt I fit in more.

Zack experienced traumatic and emotionally difficult interaction in the family and at school. The lack of masculine self-esteem developed at home was reinforced by his inability to be masculine at school. Consequently, the control, power, and sexual arousal associated with the sexual domination of Zack's youngest cousin provided a contextually based masculine resource where other masculine resources were unavailable—he was now a 'cool guy.' The sexual violence provided a sense of masculine accomplishment and, therefore, heightened his masculine self-esteem. However, the sense of maleness derived from this violent practice was short-lived, lasting usually only until Zack returned to school. Because the sexual violence did not resolve the still-threatening masculine situation at home and school, Zack was continually faced with a lack of masculine resources and, therefore, self-doubts—thus his constant achievement of masculinity through continually sexually assaulting his younger cousin.

Hugh

Hugh is a tall and well-built male aged 15 who was full of excitement to tell me his life story. Among Hugh's most vivid childhood memories is of his mother being killed in a car accident (when he was two); he later learned the driver of the car was his inebriated father. This accident led to Hugh and his younger sister (by one year) being adopted by their grandparents. Hugh lived with his grandparents for the next 10 years, until he was 12. According to Hugh, this event bothered him when he was a young boy—'I wanted a real mom and dad'—but eventually he 'got over it.'

Both 'Gram' and 'Gramps' (as he calls them) had factory jobs (Gram an assembly-line worker and Gramps a foreman); they were never at home when Hugh left for school in the morning. During elementary and middle school, Hugh and his sister made their own breakfasts and walked to school together. According to Hugh, the only thing the 'family' did together was camping: 'They'd like to go camping, so they took my sister and me. But they didn't like to do any of the other things I liked to do.' Hugh emphasized that the only 'other thing' the family did together was 'work on chores.' Saturday was designated 'chore day.' Hugh's chores included cleaning his room, raking leaves, mowing the lawn, shoveling snow, and helping Gramps fix things around the house. Hugh's sister cleaned her room and was responsible for doing the dishes, vacuuming, and helping Gram with the laundry. Like Zack, then, Hugh grew up among explicit practices defining 'men's work' and 'women's work' at home as well as in the labor market.

During the 10 years he lived with his grandparents, Hugh reports a very warm relationship with Gram—'It was always good with my Gram.' But he had a difficult relationship with Gramps—'We kind of had this thing. I never got along with him. I couldn't handle him being there. I always thought he was a mean guy.' For example, Gram never spanked Hugh for misbehavior but Gramps did. He was a big man and would sometimes hit Hugh with a 'switch.' The spankings 'made me hate my grandfather. He was so controlling; never let me do anything I wanted and always hit me when I did wrong.' Hugh saw his grandfather as an extremely domineering man who never allowed him to do 'kids stuff,' such as 'sleep over at other kids' houses. [He] didn't let me go to school dances. I always had to leave a note whenever I went somewhere when they were at work. If I didn't I would get hit with the switch.'

So Hugh grew up with a patriarchal grandfather who frequently wielded his power—'Gramps told everybody what to do, my Gram too'—and Hugh interpreted his home situation as 'being his slave.' Moreover, Hugh's grandfather never seemed to spend time with him—'I never had a father to play catch with, go fishing; my Gramps hated that stuff.' Hugh's initial model of masculinity, Gramps, thus emphasized manual labor inside (fixing things) and outside (factory work) the home, as well as male power in the household.

As a young boy, Hugh was also involved in fighting. He remembers Gramps emphasizing to him that 'it was okay' to participate in physical violence if Hugh was 'picked on' by bigger kids—'So I used to get in fights when I was just a little kid.' Classmates his age and close neighborhood friends never harassed Hugh. However, at school older boys frequently attempted to dominate and control him. For example, on the playground in grade school, older boys would occasionally 'try to kick us off the field because they wanted to play kick ball and I would say, "We were here first." And they would tell us to get off and I'd take a swing at them. It was always my way of solving stuff.' Hugh talked with Gramps about these confrontations with the older boys and Gramps endorsed his physically fighting back: 'That's about the only thing he was proud of me for. He would say, "Did you lick the other kid?" And I'd say, "Yeah." And he'd say, "That's my boy." '

The following dialogue reflects his classmates' response to Hugh's conduct as well as the masculine meaning and image Hugh constructed through the practice of fighting:

> Q. What did the other kids think about you fighting?
> A. Since I was a good fighter everybody my age looked up to me, you know. I wasn't afraid to fight. I liked it. I was the only one my age who fought the older kids.
> Q. How did that make you feel?
> A. Better than the others.
> Q. Why?
> A. Always, ever since I can remember, I'd say I wasn't going to let anybody push me around. I was going to be like Gramps said—a force in this world.
> Q. Did you want to be like Gramps? Was he a force?
> A. Yeah. He didn't let people push him around.
> Q. Did the other kids think of you as a force?
> A. They looked up to me as I said. Because it wasn't about beating the older kids up or them beating me up. It was that I held my own. I didn't let people walk all over me. And they thought that was cool.
> Q. Did you develop a reputation?
> A. Yeah. I became that force, you know. In the back of kids' minds it would always be like, 'Man, is this kid going to hit me?' So they didn't mess with me. I was strong and good with my fists, you know.

Although Hugh was a 'force' among his classmates, he never liked school and did not do well at schoolwork. He especially disliked teachers who were, for him, 'a form of authority.' In particular, Hugh detested being told to complete his homework. In fact, Hugh never did any homework, yet always passed to the next grade.

Early on in grade school, Hugh was bothered that teachers had more power than him. But after he discovered the physical power he could exert on the playground, he felt confident challenging a teacher's power in the classroom. In particular, when a teacher pressed Hugh to do his schoolwork, he would respond by 'acting out in class.' I asked Hugh for an example:

> The teacher told me to do my work and I'd say, 'I don't want to do my work.' And then the teacher would say I had to and then I'd throw my desk at him. I couldn't stay in class and do what I had to do. I was always getting in trouble. I was the one getting detention and stuff. I'd throw my desk and walk out sayin, 'Fuck you'.

Hugh began throwing desks while in elementary school. This continued in middle school. When I asked Hugh how it made him feel to respond that way, he stated:

> It felt good. It was a sense of retaliation, you know. I was doing something about it. And after I got out of the principal, kids would pat me on the back. They all wanted to be my friend, you know. I had a reputation of not being pushed around by teachers and I liked that. So I did it more.

Thus, Hugh physically controlled what he interpreted as a bad and meaningless social environment—throughout elementary and middle school he defined his masculinity against the school and its overall project.

At school, then, Hugh's physical presence allowed him to be part of what he called 'the tough crowd.' He hung out with other boys who, like himself, had a 'tough' reputation. Not only did they occasionally participate in physical violence on the playground—'fighting kids who got in our way'—they would also bully and torment the 'wimps' and 'nerds.' Indeed, other than 'acting out,' bullying the 'wimps,' and fighting, the only other thing Hugh liked about school was sports. In grade school and middle school, Hugh played all sports but he especially liked baseball and soccer. When he was in the fifth grade, Hugh was the middle-school MVP for soccer, ''cause I could run fast and when I learned how to handle the ball, you know—that's all it took.' As such, Hugh was accepted into the 'popular group' because of his athletic ability. However, his tough and physical presence outside the sports arena tended to marginalize him from this group—thus, his stronger attachment to the 'tough crowd.'

Not surprisingly, Hugh's hero during middle school was the professional football and baseball player Bo Jackson. Hugh owned all his baseball cards and had a poster of Bo on his bedroom wall. When I asked him why Bo Jackson, Hugh responded: ''cause he did it, you know. He did what he wanted, you know. He didn't let people push him around and he played two sports. Strong man. That's what I wanted to be like.'

It was also during his fifth and sixth grade years that Hugh experienced a sexual awakening in which he was introduced to sex through pornography Gramps kept at home (magazines were available on the coffee table). I asked Hugh if he had any sexual interaction at school and he responded that 'Lots of people had boyfriends and girlfriends but I didn't. When I was in school, I didn't care about sex, never thought of it much. Just wanted to play sports, you know, and fuck around with my friends.'

Thus, throughout elementary school and middle school Hugh was a 'cool guy' because he participated in sports and he developed a physical presence in school. He enjoyed a reputation of being tough and he was rewarded with friendship from other boys for his physicality, his degradation and subordination of the 'wimps' (which may have included Zack), and his success on the athletic field. Additionally, Hugh was looked up to by many kids for progressing through school without any effort—he 'beat the system.' In short, Hugh literally rose above many other boys in school, thereby constructing—indeed *embodying*—a specific type of in-school exemplary masculinity.

However, because of his 'acting out' in the classroom, bullying other kids, and continued fighting on the playground, Hugh eventually was not allowed to participate in school sports. Consequently, Hugh felt ill-treated and wounded by this edict, and realized his 'cool' masculinity was ended. As he put it: 'That was it for me. I hated school more and it was then I decided to leave, get out of school.' School no longer 'made sense' to his future plans. As far as Hugh was concerned, now that he was not allowed to participate in school sports he would never be another Bo Jackson—'I would probably end up like Gram and Gramps, a stupid factory worker.' Hugh soon decided he had had enough 'authority' at home and school. And the 'authoritarianism' at school and home combined with the overall meaninglessness of school—'Who needs an education to work in a factory?'—led him to drop out of school. As Hugh put it:

> I needed to do what I wanted to do. It's just that I wanted to be free of any rule, you know. I didn't want anybody telling me what to do. I'm not a girl, you know—ha, ha [laugh]. I wanted to get away from home and school rules. So I went out and met these people, and came down with them and started living their life.

When Hugh was only 12 (in seventh grade), he dropped out of school (never to return) and began to run the streets, eventually meeting some boys who were members of a gang. Hugh was attracted to the street life and the males he met there because, as he put it, 'They are like Bo Jackson, you know. They "beat the system".' He would be gone from his grandparents' home for months at a time, and then 'I'd come back home and Gramps would hassle me to go back to school, and I'd run off again.' When Hugh 'ran off' he would usually share an apartment with a member of the gang. I asked Hugh what he liked about the gang:

> They were like me. They didn't like society's rules. Even the rich people don't follow rules so why-should-we kind of thing, you know. And they have my back and stuff. If I needed it, they'd have my back. If I had a problem, they'd have my back and I had their back if they had a problem and we'd always do stuff together. We would just chill, do drugs, you know.

Hugh found a collective identity in the gang, a new venue that was more amicable and inviting because it provided a feeling of belonging in relation to school and home. However, part of membership in the gang required frequent involvement in assaultive violence. Hugh described many assaults, all of which were either individual or group. Hugh provided this example of an individual assault:

> I was at this dance club with my boys and girlfriend. There was this kid inside who was talking shit to us, talking shit to my girlfriend. So I said, 'Let's go outside' because I don't want him talking shit. And so we go outside and I say, 'Man, why you talking shit to me and my girl?' And he said nothin, just standin there given me that look, you know. And I have all my boys on my back; there were like eight, nine guys behind me, you know. And then I exploded on him. I punched him like three times, and he fell on the ground and he didn't even try to get back up. I pulled a pair of brass knuckles out of my pocket and I just started wailing on him, crushed the side of his face. I put him in the hospital.
> Q. What did he say to you when he was 'talking shit'?
> A. He called my girlfriend a 'bitch' and me a 'punk.'
> Q. So that bothered you?
> A. Yeah. She ain't a 'bitch' and I ain't a 'punk,' and I showed him who the 'punk' is.

Although Hugh had 'his boys' behind him, this was an 'individual' assault because he alone was responsible for settling the dispute physically. His boys would have participated only if the opponent had help from others. When I asked Hugh why he engaged in this physical violence, he stated:

> To hold my respect with my boys. I had all the boys behind me, hearing this kid talk shit. If I'd just left it alone, it would go into their heads that I don't deserve their respect. If I can't even hold my respect for myself how can I hold it from them?

Group violence differed. Every day, Hugh and his boys (and girls) would smoke marijuana, cocaine and/or crack and then the whole gang would either go out to a club or 'go stomping' (controlling their 'territory' through violence).

> Q. Is stomping also about holding your respect?
> A. Yeah. You do it to be one of the boys. It's loyalty to the boys and to our territory. It's holding on to what's ours, you know. We stomp to show our loyalty to each other and to show our territory.
> Q. Describe for me a stomping.
> A. My boys would be strapped [have guns]. I would be strapped. Someone would have a knife, you know. If we find dudes in our territory we jump out the car and start to beat on 'em. If people start shooting, you have to shoot back. More people get hurt, but you save yourself, you know. The more you can take out of them, the less people on your side get hurt.

For Hugh, then, both types of assaultive violence were masculine practices. Indeed, when asked what it meant to be masculine at ages 12 to 15 (the peak years of Hugh's gang involvement), Hugh responded that he and the other boys were expected to be 'strong, be able to hold your own, be able to fight, not back down when someone is in your face. It's just like not show fear. You can't show fear when you are a man.'

Although girls were also in the gang and, at times, involved in stomping (fighting the girls in the other gang), the major difference between males and females was, according to Hugh: 'We had the power. We told them what to do.' The following is an extended dialogue on gendered power in Hugh's gang:

> Q. Can you further explain that?
> A. You know, we'd all help cook and clean the apartment and shit like that, guys and girls together. But if a girl talk trash to you or if a girl was like running a mouth to you, we wouldn't have it. She'd just get slapped down till she wouldn't know where she was.
> Q. It's okay to 'slap down' girls in the gang?
> A. Oh yeah, if they get out of hand.
> Q. How often did that occur?
> A. It wasn't like every day because they knew who they were and they knew what they had to do, you know. They knew where they stood and they knew where we stood.
> Q. Is 'slapping a girl down' a form of violence?
> A. No, it's not violence because violence is not the way it should be. When you keep a girl in check, that's the way it should be. If she talks shit and you slap her down, that would not be violence.
> Q. Is it ever appropriate to have sex with a girl if she does not want to?
> A. No, that's not right. We'd bust them out if they did that. Once we heard about a kid who raped his sister, so we went and found him and broke both his arms. There was like bone coming out. We fucked him up bad. That just don't happen, you know. We don't like rapists.
> Q. When is violence against women appropriate?
> A. Women should get respect from men unless they deserve to lose that respect.
> Q. What would cause a woman to lose that respect?
> A. Like being a bitch, talking shit. But then they wouldn't get raped, you know. They'd just get slapped down and told to shut the fuck up and get out of the house.

Although Hugh learned about sex at home through Gramp's pornography and at school through the 'sex talk' of other boys, he remained a virgin until 13 when he was a member of the gang. Hugh had several girlfriends in the gang and, indeed, during these 'gang years' sexuality took on a heightened meaning in his life because, as Hugh explains, it is an extremely important part of the gang: 'To get respect from your boys you gotta have a woman. It's either have one woman all the time or have lots of women. If you can hustle the girls, hustle the money, and hold your own, that's where you get your respect.'

Q. What about homosexuality?
A. Gays aren't accepted in our group.
Q. Why not?
A. We don't like 'em. We don't think it's right. It's not natural.
Q. Did your gang ever bash gays?
A. Oh yeah, we stomp 'em all the time. We just see them walking down the street and so we stomp 'em because we don't want them in our territory.

In contrast to Zack, then, Hugh was rewarded during his first 15 years with favorable appraisal from others for his physicality—at home from Gramps, at school from other kids, in the gang from 'his boys.' Although Hugh likewise had a traumatic and emotionally difficult family life, unlike Zack he did not perceive his adoption as his responsibility and he was able to satisfy Gramp's masculine criteria of 'fighting back.' Indeed, Hugh practiced masculine power and control both at school (over other kids) and in the street. Hugh used his physical resource—and its accompanying positive masculine self-esteem—to dominate others through assaultive violence. Hugh responded physically when others attempted to challenge his masculinity ('talking shit') and physical confrontation with 'enemy warriors' was an essential criterion for active gang membership.

Masculinities, bodies, and violence

The changing constructions of masculinity exhibited by Zack and Hugh are critical to understanding the contrasting types of violence. At home, both Zack and Hugh appropriated, in different ways, a definition of masculinity that ultimately emphasized the use of *physical* violence to solve interpersonal problems. Connell (1995: 122) defines this type of proactive adoption of 'family values' as the 'moment of engagement' with hegemonic masculinity—'the moment at which the boy takes up the project of hegemonic masculinity as his own.'[1] Zack and Hugh adopted hegemonic masculinity as a project which included a *predisposition* to *physical* violence. This is of course commonplace in industrialized societies where hegemonic masculinity is strongly associated with aggressiveness and the capacity for violence. Especially in the US—with one of the highest rates of interpersonal violence of all industrialized countries—there remains a strong cultural connection between admired masculinity and violent response to threat (Campbell, 1993). Such violence is not merely glorified, as Anne Campbell (1993: 31) correctly argues, it is also so tightly tied to masculinity that 'aggression becomes central to the boy's notion of manhood.' This is particularly so in working-class and lower working-class communities (Luckenbill and Doyle, 1989; Bernard, 1990; Shover, 1996).

Zack and Hugh actively appropriated this notion of masculinity at home. Indeed, both of them committed themselves to the belief that physical violence is the appropriate means for solving interpersonal problems. Family dynamics and practices emphasized physical violence as the correct and effective masculine response to threat—a 'real man' is obligated to respond in this fashion. In short, the life histories clearly show how in family interaction Zack and Hugh actively participated in constructing physically violent predispositions.

However, despite concurrently growing up in the same neighborhood and attending the same middle school, Zack and Hugh, at approximately the same age, took different paths and committed significantly different types of violence and victimization. Zack became a *solitary offender* (he committed violence in private and was the lone offender), who specialized in sexual violence (he never committed any other type of crime), and he repeatedly victimized the same person—a much less powerful female member of his family. Hugh became a *social offender* (he committed crimes with accomplices and in public), who was versatile in his criminality (he engaged in a variety of crimes), and when he engaged in violence it was exclusively assaultive violence against both acquaintances and strangers.

What is interesting about these two life stories is not the violence per se, but the differing types of violence and contextual victimization. How did these differences evolve? Analysing agency and its relation to the body in the context of school can help answer this question.

Making bodies matter

School dynamics are the key to understanding Zack and Hugh's different life courses, each of which focuses on the body and its relation to masculine construction. Research shows that the tallest and physically strongest boys in middle school and high school are usually the most popular and are talked about admiringly by peers (and parents and teachers) for their size and athletic prowess (Thorne, 1993). These are the masculine 'cool guys' who participate in school athletics and who outside school defy adult authority by 'partying' on weekends (e.g. experimenting with drugs, alcohol, and sex) (Eckert, 1989; Foley, 1990). In the context of school, height and musculature increase self-esteem, prestige, and a more positive body image among boys (Thorne, 1993). As research on male adolescent development shows, boys are acutely aware of their pubertal changing selves and the responses of others to those changes (Petersen, 1988). Puberty is associated with a higher degree of concern about body image than are other age categories, and if a boy does not have the appropriate body shape and size this frequently leads to distress (Petersen, 1988). 'Teen' life is a world where bodies are increasingly subject to peer inspection and surveillance and physically small and less muscular boys are labeled 'wimps' and 'fags.' In middle school and high school, masculine social hierarchies develop in relation to somatic type. Such somatic differentiation affirms inequality among boys and diverse masculinities are thus constructed in relation to biological development (Canaan, 1987; Thorne, 1993). In short, the body has become increasingly crucial to self-image. Through interaction at school, adolescents 'make bodies matter' by constructing some bodies as more masculine than others.

As he reported, Zack saw himself as not 'measuring up' physically to the masculine ideal at school. Zack was defined and eventually accepted that he constituted a subordinate body and, therefore, subordinate masculinity. Zack perceived himself not only as flunking the body test—he was not tall or muscular and could not play football—but also simultaneously he was publicly degraded for his physical size and shape. For Zack, then, his body *constrained* masculine agency—he could not do the masculine practices the 'cool guys' were doing—and his somatic limitation was extremely troubling to him. Lack of bodily performance—his inability to 'fight back' when teased, lack of athletic skill, rejection by girls, and his short and overweight body—convinced Zack that he was different from the 'cool guys' at school and also inferior to them. In other words, his body did not live up to its contextual masculine expectations. As such, his body created what I call an in-school masculinity challenge.

Masculinity challenges are contextual interactions that result in masculine degradation. Masculinity challenges—such as those experienced by Zack—arise from interactional threats and insults from peers, or situationally defined masculine expectations that are not achievable. Both, in various ways, proclaim the boy subordinate in contextually defined masculine terms. Since 'doing masculinity' is an ongoing concern, masculinity challenges may (as discussed in the next section) motivate social action to correct the subordinating social situation and various forms of crime can be the result. Given that these interactions question, undermine, and/or threaten masculinity, only contextually 'appropriate' masculine practices will help overcome the challenge.

But Hugh did 'measure up' physically. He participated in school sports—he was soccer MVP one year—and constructed a physical presence in school that was revered by his classmates. He was tall, lean, and muscular for his age. When his masculinity was challenged on the playground or in the classroom, he would not physically back down to anyone, including teachers and the older and sometimes bigger boys. For Hugh, then, his body *facilitated* masculine agency—he successfully constructed himself as a 'cool guy' who was 'superior' to many other boys. Indeed, his ability to act out in class, bully those 'subordinate' to him, and physically fight when provoked, convinced Hugh of his own eminent masculine self-worth. In short, what Zack's and Hugh's life stories reveal is that a boy's masculine school existence is, in part, dependent upon *his capacity for power that he embodies*. As Chris Shilling puts it:

> This power is always an active power, a power which can be exercised on and over others. If a man's physicality is unable to convey an image of power, he is found to have little presence precisely because the social definition of men as holders of power is not reflected in his embodiment.
> (1993: 113)

To have a sense of 'presence' and masculine self-esteem, the male body must at the very least suggest the promise of forceful and vigorous physicality. In other words, the body intervenes in social interaction as a personal resource that socially symbolizes a boy's masculine identity.

In addition to physicality, the school organizes masculine difference and inequality through constructs of sexuality. Indeed, studies of school and sexuality show that to 'do' heterosexuality is an everyday dominant masculine bodily practice in middle school and high school, and that such sexual orientation is an important source of acceptable male identity (Mac an Ghaill, 1994; Martin, 1996). Particularly within male group 'sex talk' at school, 'sex' is not simply 'being heterosexual'—one must not be homosexual (Wood, 1984; Holland et al., 1993; Thorne, 1993). Adolescent boys use sexuality to establish hierarchies by constructing discourses that are heterosexual dominant/gay subordinate. One of the ways, then, to validate masculinity at school is to express and define oneself as heterosexual by both degrading homosexuality and also engaging in heterosexual practices. Moreover, boys who do not show an interest in girls, who are unable for a variety of reasons to make heterosexual contact, who lack knowledge of the female body, and/or who do not degrade homosexuality, risk being labeled 'fags' and are, therefore, publicly represented as embodying a subordinate sexuality and masculinity (Holland et al., 1993). Indeed, at school the 'cool guys' (that is the hegemonically masculine boys) are not only tall, strong, and athletic, but actively and publicly participate in heterosexuality—announced genital potency is another form of in-school bodily performance. The constitution of masculinity through heterosexual performance means that masculinity is especially challenged when such sexual performance cannot be realized.

Zack's life story shows that he observed the 'cool guys' and 'misfits' at school experiencing such heterosexual expectations, that he wanted to participate in these same sexual practices himself, but that he was unable to achieve such masculine expectations. Zack found his own sexuality through interaction with 'the guys' at school and this heterosexuality was for him an important resource for 'doing masculinity.' However, once again Zack's body constrained his agency and his eventual subordination was intensely distressing to him. Zack was constructed in school as embodying a subordinate sexuality, which itself became an added masculinity challenge to him.

Hugh had a different sexual experience in school. Although he was sexually awakened by his uncle's pornography and the 'sex talk' at school, sexuality was not important to him during middle school. For Hugh it was not necessary to be sexual publicly (until he joined the gang); his participation in sports, acting out in class, bullying the 'wimps,' and fighting on the playground were more than adequate bodily resources to effectively accomplish masculinity in the context of school. Hugh's bodily performance in other masculine areas allowed him the 'luxury' to disregard, in the particular context of school, the sexual realm.

Zack and Hugh, then, shared specific social structural space at school with others and, in the process, participated in the construction of common blocks of knowledge in which masculine ideals/practices became institutionalized. The particular criteria of dominant masculine identities in Zack and Hugh's school are embedded in the social situations and recurrent practices whereby in-school social relations are structured (Giddens, 1989). Nevertheless, differences between boys at school in part hinge on the body and, therefore, how they construct masculinity. Thus, 'cool guy' (Hugh) masculinity is sustained through its *bodily* relation to situationally defined 'wimp' (Zack) masculinity, even within the same class and school context. Boys in the same working-class school are distinguished through different constructions of the body and masculinity. Thus, constructs of 'cool guy' and 'wimp' inflect any class commonality with difference, producing power/powerlessness in relation to each other.

Constructing varieties of violence

The absence of physical and sexual masculine resources at school—along with the low masculine self-esteem developed at home—eventually assumed prominence in Zack's life, stimulating his search for practices that would enable him to 'do' masculinity in dominant fashion. In fact, the behavioral expressions activated by this lack of masculine resources could be realized only *outside* the school situation. Accordingly, Zack's body became party to a surrogate masculine practice that directed him to a course of masculine social action that was physically and sexually realizable—and which could be accomplished outside the boundaries of school. For Zack, then, the dominant masculine practices in school were not rejected. Rather, physical and sexual subordination directed him to *fixate* on a specific site, the home, and a particular form of conduct, sexual violence, where such practices could be realized. Moreover, Zack had access to a much less powerful person at home and, therefore, the means through which his body could attain physical and sexual expression. Given that Zack was removed from any type of recognized masculine status in school, the available sexual 'outlet' at home was especially seductive and captivating; it became an obsession and was a powerful and pleasurable means of doing masculinity. The choice to be sexually violent derived from a situational resource in which Zack could be dominant, powerful, and heterosexual through bodily practice.

For Hugh, school life—like family life—was circumscribed by institutionalized authoritarian routine. Neither interested in nor successful at schoolwork—'It's for "wimps" and "nerds" '—Hugh viewed school as irrelevant to his future and emasculating to his conception of masculinity. Hugh's bodily resources empowered him to implement a physically confrontational masculinity. As such, he joined with similar working-class boys in an unstructured, counterschool group that carved out a specific oppositional masculine space within the school, its overwhelming rules, and unnerving authority. Hugh's embodiment permitted him physically to resist the school and, in so doing, to construct behavior patterns—acting out, bullying, and fighting—that set him above the 'wimps' as well as the school. Hugh used his body in ways Zack could not: Hugh physically expressed himself in a manner culturally idolized in the school, thereby negating any masculine insecurities developed at home. Moreover, in joining the counterschool group, Hugh began to separate himself from the dominant masculinity and to construct an in-school opposition masculinity. Any possible remaining 'cool guy' masculine thread was especially severed when his favorite in-school masculine bodily practice was denied him (sports). Hugh thus left school and found masculine comfort in a street gang. The gang was an arena where Hugh could bodily express himself through physical confrontation. Within the collective setting of 'me and my boys,' such practices as individual and group assaultive violence were particularly attractive, providing a public ceremony of bodily domination over and humiliation of others.

Although in the family both Zack and Hugh experienced traumatic and emotionally difficult events and launched masculinities that emphasized physically standing up to threat, it was their differing abilities to fulfill such a predisposition at school—and their subsequent bodily and masculine subordination (Zack) or superordination (Hugh)—that focused their interests and behaviors in the direction of sexual violence (Zack) and assaultive violence (Hugh). For it was the social situation of the school that defined both physical and heterosexual performance as essential criteria for 'doing masculinity.' Thus, these dominant criteria—within the context of a body either able or unable to construct such criteria—directed their ultimate choices of a specific type of violence and victimization. For Zack it was private and solitary sexual violence that repeatedly victimized his younger female cousin. For Hugh it was public and social assaultive violence that chiefly victimized strangers. Furthermore, Zack was a sexual violence 'specialist' while Hugh, 'versatile' in his criminal endeavors, never engaged in sexual violence.

Conclusion

As white working-class teenage boys, Zack and Hugh produced specific and different types of masculine configurations through the use of contrasting forms of violence. These different masculinities emerged from practices that reflect different bodily resources. Hugh constructed an opposition masculinity that, though individual, occurred within the context of a collective masculine project. Zack attempted to invalidate his subordinate masculine status in school through a personal reconstruction of the self, and not as part of a shared, collective project. Zack alone constructed himself as a 'cool guy' through the private, sexual domination of his younger cousin.

Although different in these crucial ways, Zack and Hugh are similar in that their differing forms of violence rely on bodily deployment and performance. Each in his telling way exercised power over other bodies: Hugh subordinated and oppressed females ('slapping them down') and males (for 'talking shit' or invading his turf) through *assaultive* violence; Zack subordinated and oppressed his younger female cousin through *sexual* violence. In these ways, Zack and Hugh experienced their everyday world from specific bodily positions and their bodies, in turn, entered negotiated social interactions and shaped future social practices. For both, their senses of masculinity were fashioned by their bodily relations in school and their bodies—as resources for social action—constrained or facilitated possible masculine agency and subsequent practice.

Notes

I am especially grateful to Piers Beirne, Bob Connell, Tony Jefferson, and anonymous reviewers for helpful comments on an earlier draft of this article.

1. Hegemonic masculinity is the culturally idealized form of masculinity in a given historical and social setting (Connell, 1995). In any specific time and place hegemonic masculinity is extolled at the symbolic level and through practice, and is constructed in relation to 'subordinated' and 'oppositional' masculinities. Hegemonic masculinity, then, is the dominant form of masculinity in a given milieu to which other types of masculinities are subordinated or opposed. For example, in the social setting of secondary school, we are likely to find representations of hegemonic masculinity (e.g. 'cool guys' and 'jocks'), subordinated masculinity (e.g. gay boys, 'wimps,' and 'nerds'), and oppositional masculinity (e.g. 'freaks' and 'tough guys'). Ethnographies of secondary schooling in Britain, Australia, and the US consistently report such masculine relationships (see Connell, 1996 for a review) and the two life histories discussed here support this research conclusion.

References

Agnew, Robert (1990) 'The Origins of Delinquent Events: An Examination of Offender Accounts,' *Journal of Research in Crime and Delinquency* 27(3): 267–94.

Bernard, Thomas J. (1990) 'Angry Aggression among the Truly Disadvantaged,' *Criminology* 28(1): 73–96.

Campbell, Anne (1993) *Men, Women, and Aggression*. New York: Basic Books.

Canaan, Joyce (1987) 'A Comparative Analysis of Middle School and High

School Teenage Cliques,' in Gary Spindler and Laura Spindler (eds) *Interpretive Ethnography of Education*, pp. 385–406. Hillsdale, NJ: Lawrence Erlbaum Associates.

Collison, Mike (1996) 'In Search of the High: Drugs, Crime, Masculinities,' *British Journal of Criminology* 36(3): 428–44.

Connell, R.W. (1987) *Gender and Power: Society, the Person, and Sexual Politics*. Stanford, CA: Stanford University Press.

Connell, R.W. (1995) *Masculinities*. Berkeley, CA: University of California Press.

Connell, R.W. (1996) 'Teaching the Boys: New Research on Masculinity and Gender Strategies for Schools,' *Teachers College Record* 98(2): 206–35.

Eckert, Paul (1989) *Jocks and Burnouts: Social Categories and Identity in the High School*. New York: Teachers College Press, Columbia University.

Foley, Douglas E. (1990) *Learning Capitalist Culture: Deep in the Heart of Tejas*. Philadelphia, PA: University of Pennsylvania Press.

Giddens, Anthony (1976) *New Rules of Sociological Method*. New York: Basic Books.

Giddens, Anthony (1984) *The Constitution of Society*. Berkeley, CA: University of California Press.

Giddens, Anthony (1989) 'A Reply to My Critics,' in David Held and John B. Thompson (eds) *Social Theory and Modern Societies: Anthony Giddens and His Critics*, pp. 249–301. New York: Cambridge University Press.

Hagedorn, John (1998) 'Frat Boys, Bossmen, Studs, and Gentlemen,' in Lee H. Bowker (ed.) *Masculinities and Violence*, pp. 201–22. Thousand Oaks, CA: Sage.

Holland, Janet, Caroline Ramazanoglu and Sue Sharpe (1993) *Wimp or Gladiator: Contradictions in Acquiring Masculine Sexuality*. London: Tufnell Press.

Levine, Felice J. and Katherine J. Rosich (1996) *Social Causes of Violence: Crafting a Science Agenda*. Washington, DC: American Sociological Association.

Luckenbill, David. F. and David P. Doyle (1989) 'Structural Position and Violence: Developing a Cultural Explanation,' *Criminology* 27(3): 419–36.

Mac an Ghaill, Mairtin (1994) *The Making of Men: Masculinities, Sexualities, and Schooling*. Philadelphia, PA: Open University Press.

Martin, Katherine A. (1996) *Puberty, Sexuality and the Self: Boys and Girls at Adolescence*. New York: Routledge.

Messerschmidt, James W. (1993) *Masculinities and Crime: Critique and Reconceptualization of Theory*. Lanham, MD: Rowman & Littlefield.

Messerschmidt, James W. (1997a) *Crime as Structured Action: Gender, Race, Class, and Crime in the Making*. Thousand Oaks, CA: Sage.

Messerschmidt, James W. (1997b) 'Adolescent Masculinities and Sexual Violence,' paper presented at the Western Society of Criminology Annual Meeting, 27 February–2 March 1997, Honolulu, HI.

Patton, Michael Q. (1990) *Qualitative Evaluation and Research Methods*. Newbury Park, CA: Sage.

Petersen, Ann C. (1988) 'Adolescent Development,' *Annual Review of Psychology* 39: 583–607.
Sampson, Robert J. and John H. Laub (1993) *Crime in the Making: Pathways and Turning Points Through Life*. Cambridge, MA: Harvard University Press.
Scott, Sue and David Morgan (eds) (1993) *Body Matters: Essays on the Sociology of the Body*. Washington, DC: The Falmer Press.
Shaw, Clifford (1930) *The Jack Roller*. Chicago, IL: University of Chicago Press.
Shilling, Chris (1993) *The Body and Social Theory*. Newbury Park, CA: Sage.
Shover, Neal (1996) *Great Pretenders: Pursuits and Careers of Persistent Thieves*. Boulder, CO: Westview Press.
Sutherland, Edwin (1937) *The Professional Thief*. Chicago, IL: University of Chicago Press.
Thomas, William I. and Florian Znaniecki (1927, 1958) *The Polish Peasant in Europe and America*. New York: Dover.
Thorne, Barrie (1993) *Gender Play: Girls and Boys in Schools*. New Brunswick, NJ: Rutgers University Press.
West, Candace and Sarah Fenstermaker (1995) 'Doing Difference,' *Gender and Society* 9(1): 8–37.
West, Candace and Don H. Zimmerman (1987) 'Doing Gender,' *Gender and Society* 1(2): 125–51.
Wood, Julian (1984) 'Groping Towards Sexism: Boys' Sex Talk,' in Angela McRobbie and Mica Nava (eds) *Gender and Generation*, pp. 54–84. London: Macmillan.

JAMES W. MESSERSCHMIDT received his PhD from the Criminology Institute in the Department of Sociology at the University of Stockholm, Sweden. He is a Professor of Sociology in the Criminology Department at the University of Southern Maine. His research interests focus on the interrelation of gender, race, class, and crime. In addition to numerous articles and book chapters, he is the author of *The Trial of Leonard Peltier* (1983), *Capitalism, Patriarchy, and Crime: Toward a Socialist Feminist Criminology* (1986), *Masculinities and Crime: Critique and Reconceptualization of Theory* (1993), *Crime as Structured Action: Gender, Race, Class, and Crime in the Making* (1997), and *Criminology* (3rd edn), with Piers Beirne (1999).

[5]

After Dunblane: Crime, Corporeality, and the (Hetero-) Sexing of the Bodies of Men

RICHARD COLLIER*

> The human mind is the most complex and delicately balanced of all created things. Wisdom cannot foresee all the consequences of its sickness. The most that wisdom can do is shield society from some of the possible consequences . . .
>
> (Dr. Robert Runcie, Archbishop of Canterbury, speaking at the Memorial Service for the Hungerford victims 1987).[1]

> According to the experts [mass] killers, who are invariably male, are unlikely to be mentally ill but are likely to have achieved very little and, as a result, harbour grudges and resentment that can develop into violent fantasies.
>
> (*Guardian* 29 April 1996, following the murder of thirty-two people in Tasmania by Martin Bryant)

INTRODUCTION

This article is an exploration of responses to a series of murders which in recent years, in Britain and elsewhere, have become known as 'lone-gunman' or 'spree' killings.[2] The particular focus is the legal, political, criminological, and media reception to the events which took place in Dunblane, Scotland in March 1996 where sixteen children and their teacher were murdered, and seventeen others injured,[3] by the forty-three year-old man, Thomas Hamilton. The article will argue that the experience of the 'lone gunman' or 'spree

* *Newcastle Law School, University of Newcastle upon Tyne, 22–24 Windsor Terrace, Newcastle upon Tyne NE1 7RU, England*

Earlier versions of this paper were presented to the Law and Society Association Annual Meeting, Glasgow, 1996, the Socio Legal Studies Association Annual Conference, University of Southampton, 1996, the Centre for Gender and Women's Studies, University of Newcastle upon Tyne, 1996, the Law School, University of Keele, November 1996, and Kent Law School, January 1997. I would like to thank all who participated in discussion for their comments and, in particular, the anonymous reviewers for the *Journal of Law and Society* for their helpful suggestions. I am indebted to conversations with Bea Campbell on aspects of the argument.

killer' is, both in its generic construction and its practice, a gendered and distinctly masculinized phenomenon. The central aim of the article is to (re)read the spree killing in such a way as to reposition the *sexed* male body within discourses around crime. It is my intention to surface the inadequacy of simply adding 'men' or 'gender' empirically to the study of crime by investigating the epistemological implications of what it might mean to theorize the masculinity/crime relation in the light of recent approaches which have sought to dissolve the integrity of the gendered 'identity' of the subject.[4] In so doing, I wish to explore the ways in which the (sexed) bodies of men continue to be constituted as an 'absent presence' within contemporary discourses around crime and criminality. I want to surface, that is, the significance of sexual difference in engaging with the criminal(ized) bodies of men in cultural and psychical terms.[5]

The first part of the article explores the content of press discourse constructions of the 'spree killing' and, in particular, representations of the gunman Thomas Hamilton in the aftermath of the Dunblane massacre. My concern is with what has been 'seen' and 'unseen'[6] within a range of 'crimino-legal'[7] constructions of the men/crime relationship. The second part of the article explores the genealogy of this silencing of the sexed specificity of the Dunblane massacre. In investigating the gender order of the signifying complex which surrounds the phenomenon of the spree killing this article is, ultimately, about Thomas Hamilton, not as a 'monster', 'pervert' or personification of 'evil', but as a *man*.

Defining the 'spree killing': a note on Dunblane

There has over the last few years been an increasing fascination, reflected in the rapid spread of the term within diverse cultural artefacts, with the phenomenon of the 'lone gunman' or 'spree killing'. The spree killing refers to the murder of several victims over a period of minutes, hours or days in one or more different locations '. . . by an impulsive killer who appears to make little effort to evade detection . . . At completion of the sequence this type of killer is unlikely to kill again; many commit suicide or are killed in shootouts with the police'.[8] The victims of the spree killing, it has been argued, appear to have some symbolic significance for the offender and are killed in a 'frenzied' attack, whether planned in advance or on the 'spur of the moment'. Though details in each case differ, a number of recent murders have been classified as examples of the spree killing. In Britain, prior to Dunblane, the most notorious of these was the case of Michael Ryan, who shot dead sixteen people in August 1987 in Hungerford, England. Internationally, and within weeks of the Dunblane massacre, in April 1996 the twenty-eight year old Martin Bryant slaughtered thirty-five people in Tasmania[9] in the worst spree killing on record. Opinion remains divided as to whether the spree killing should be considered a separate form of multiple murder.[10] What is agreed, however, is that 'almost all mass and spree murders are male with a racial composition "that closely approximates that of the population itself".'[11]

It is not my intention, in writing of Dunblane in the detached terms of social theory,[12] to '. . . trivialise the horror felt by the majority of people' at such a crime.[13] Certainly, 'the following analysis seeks neither to inflame . . . strongly felt emotions nor to hold them up to criticism or ridicule.'[14] It seeks, rather, to develop a deeper understanding of the event by addressing what remains the most obvious, taken-for-granted, yet curiously unexplored fact about not just the murders at Dunblane but crime generally: '. . . that it is almost always committed by men'.[15] Engaging with this fact is, I shall argue, essential if '. . . we are ever going to act in a way that loosens that paralysing grip of guilt and helplessness'[16] in the face of such horrific crimes.

CRIMINO-LEGAL RESPONSES TO THE SPREE MURDER: THE PRESS DISCOURSE IN THE AFTERMATH OF DUNBLANE

On March 13 1996 Thomas Hamilton, a forty-three-year-old man, fatally shot sixteen five- and six-year-old children and their teacher in the gymnasium at Dunblane Primary School in Scotland. Seventeen others were injured before Hamilton eventually put one of the guns to his own head. How are we to begin to make sense of the press discourse around such a horrific event? There exists a rich literature[17] concerned with exploring how, as unique cultural products, newspapers and other media outlets tell us much about the social, political, and moral order of our culture and, as such, play an important role in the development of an individual's sense of self.[18] However, constructing a reading from something as diffuse and complex as the press discourse is notoriously problematic.[19] The apparently random nature of the spree killing, like the serial murder, runs counter to the general assumption that crimes have 'motives' and can be presented as a deviant form of instrumental rationality. It is, nonetheless, possible to locate a certain homogeneity to the press response. A number of themes emerge and recur within the national and international media coverage of the Dunblane massacre as a transition takes place from initial shock and incomprehension at what had happened to a growing demand for answers and explanations.

1. *The vocabulary of evil – Thomas Hamilton as 'inhuman' and 'beyond reason'*

The tone of the media reporting in the immediate aftermath of the massacre was encapsulated by the powerful and moving comments of the headmaster of Dunblane Primary School. 'Evil', he stated, 'visited us yesterday . . . We don't know why, we don't understand it, and I guess we never will.' This notion that 'only the Vocabulary of Evil could explain what happened at Dunblane'[20] set the course for the following press coverage in which Thomas

Hamilton was commonly described as an 'evil freak of nature'';[21] whilst 'Dunblane returned to God',[22] he would surely '. . . Burn in Hell'[23] – 'His evil is now where it belongs – in the fires of hell'. Notwithstanding differences between tabloid and 'quality' newspapers in their representations of crime,[24] for each the language of 'good' and 'evil' appeared initially as the only available vocabulary through which the event might be described. Just as Robert Thompson and Jon Venables, the two ten-year-old boys convicted of the murder of James Bulger in 1993, had been described as the embodiment of 'unparalleled evil and barbarity',[25] the good/evil binary here suggested a possibility, if not a firm belief, that there may be no defence to some propensities of the human condition. However, this immediately poses problems for a secularized crimino-legal sphere which demands explanation and account in terms of liberal notions of human nature. In the context of Dunblane, what was being constituted at this point as a social problem? Clearly some issues were immediately comprehensible as being 'within' understanding. By the end of the day of the massacre the questions of school security and reform of gun laws had emerged as the dominant 'social problems' raised by the case. Hamilton's maleness, in contrast, did not figure in the 'pre-existing categories for rational problem-identification and problem-solution.'[26]

The terms 'evil' and 'human wickedness' promote a construction of Hamilton as a 'monster' or 'grotesque' which is misleading in several respects. First, it rests uneasily with the very *familiarity* of the 'spree killing'. If Dunblane was exceptional in terms of the age and vulnerability of the victims, it was, none the less, readily identifiable as a generic crime. The lone gunman is a recognizable phenomenon of the late twentieth century.[27] Thomas Hamilton was placed immediately within an established frame of reference. The use of 'evil' has a second, related, consequence. The vast majority of spree killers, like offenders generally, are men. Yet the ontology of Hamilton as 'inhuman' robs both the act of the murders and the body of the murderer of its sexual specificity. Hamilton is transformed into something 'beyond human', his actions emblematic of an inhumanity beyond comprehension and understanding. This banishing of Hamilton from the social, however:

> '. . . erodes . . . responsibility for understanding and challenging the individual and social forces that have produced such an . . . event. To demonise . . . removes the [act] from the realm of social action.'[28]

The expunging of the social does not simply individualize crime. It also underwrites and legitimates feelings of despair and helplessness which are commonplace responses to particularly horrific crimes: 'We cannot even begin to grasp', it was declared, what could have driven Hamilton to act as he did '. . . and there is no point pretending we can'.[29]

Crimes, even the worst and most seemingly inexplicable, do not happen in a vacuum.[30] In order to reconfigure Thomas Hamilton as a man, it is necessary to relocate his actions by contextualizing the atrocity within the gendered social framework in which he lived and died. It is necessary, that is, to reframe the relationship between men, women, and children in such a way as to problematize the ideas of hetero-masculinity which were, I now wish to suggest, central to, and the sub-text of, press reporting of the Dunblane massacre.

2. *Sexing the social: configurations of community, class, and 'otherness'*

The ontological importance given to the 'family' as the institutional source for the preservation and reproduction of moral order has been central to the discursive construction of the social within modernity.[31] It is in the context of this social/familial frame that Thomas Hamilton was systematically represented as a 'loner.' On the one hand he appeared to have few friends. No person, no locale appeared willing to claim him as one of their own. He was, on one level, 'not acceptable'. Yet his place as an outsider to this 'social' is ambiguous. It is also clear from newspaper reports that Thomas Hamilton was *known* within the community in which he lived. The numerous testimonies to his character, his 'eccentricities' and family background belied the notion that he was a stranger in the midst of an otherwise homogenous community. There exists a tension between, on the one hand, the (readily accessible) knowledge of Hamilton (who he was, what he was 'like') and, on the other, a desire to expunge him from that community, and from the sociality more generally, through reference to his status as grotesque, 'inhuman' monster and so forth. The former places him within a broader community. The latter ensures he is rendered outside the social.

Within this process, of course, something is being said about the community of which Thomas Hamilton was deemed to be not one. In this respect, press representations of the town of Dunblane reveal much about the ways in which the discursive construction of the social has been configured through reference to crime, criminality and the ontological importance of the family referred to above. One newspaper declared:

> *it would be easier for us* if Thomas Hamilton was simply a madman who came out of nowhere. But what if [he] . . . comes out of a society which itself is showing signs of deranged and violent breakdown?[32]

This is an engagement with the social. It focuses on such issues as the role of the media in promoting crime, the availability of guns, questions of school security, and so forth. Yet, each of these conversations about 'society' stop short of any engagement with the relationship between sex, gender, and crime. What results is a 'desexing' of Hamilton's maleness by fusing two ideas; that of a phantasmatic (non-criminal) *community* secured as such by reference to a historically specific *iconography of male otherness*.

(a) A space of crime: the (non-)criminal community

To clarify: the town of Dunblane was routinely depicted, almost without exception, as a place to which crime was a stranger. It appeared at the other end of a spectrum from the communities more traditionally associated with high-profile crimes.[33] It is Britain's 'dangerous places'[34] which have come to symbolize social breakdown, moral atrophy, and increasingly, notably in the context of the 'criminal' city, crimes by and against children. Dunblane, in contrast, symbolized something very different. It did not translate into familiar representations of region and place. It was, if anything, a place 'too good to be true'. An editorial in the *Guardian* captured the general assumption being made about the conflation of space and crime. Like Hungerford, the scene of the previous spree killing by Michael Ryan in 1987, Dunblane was:

> . . . the last place where one would expect random violence to erupt: small attractive country towns with strong community ties and none of the alienation associated with larger cities. Both killers lived within the communities they devastated. Both are described as lonely, secretive, friendless people. Neither was being treated for any mental disorder. Yet both committed indiscriminate and irrational violence on a massive scale. Why?[35]

This image of (non-criminal) community is fleshed out by accounts of the minutiae of everyday life. Dunblane was a town where 'nothing ever happens', a place where '. . . if a child fell in the street, three people would rush to pick them up'.[36] Interestingly, even the children who lived in the town appeared at times to be qualitatively different from their counterparts in the criminal(ized) city.[37] *Time* magazine noted:

> . . . the names [of the children] . . . were as familiar and as evocative of middle-class Scottish family life . . . Ordinary names, pretty names, the names on teachers' attendance lists, on captions of school pictures, on programs for school pageants, on line-ups for school games.[38]

On one level this mythologizing of locale, involving a conflation of certain assumptions about family life and socio-economic privilege, is a familiar phenomenon. What results is a powerful evocation of a (crime-free) world we all, it is implied (and not just the citizens of Dunblane), have lost:

> A generation of professionals – doctors, lawyers, journalists – had dreamed of somewhere the air is so crisp you can actually smell the smoke from a chimney or from a gentle puffing biddy on the street corner; where fearsome things come in picture books; where the water of life is softly reassuring as it falls – or golden, as it washes the back of the throat. Dunblane was that dream incarnate.[39]

However, it is not simply the (well-documented) association of class, crime, and notions of 'respectability' which is being made here. The 'space' of men's crime is itself, on closer examination, bound up with assumptions which betray the centrality of the family to this construction of the social. The dominant image of the community of Dunblane itself as embodiment of comfortable, crime-free existence rests upon, and derives from, a heterosexual familial frame signified as such by virtue of the presence of *children.*[40] Dunblane is presented as a place where 'families moved' and where 'children would be safe'.

(b) Thomas Hamilton as Other: the single male outsider

It is against this background that Hamilton appears outside the parameters of the familial. He *appeared* to be of this community. In 'reality' he failed to belong – he was an outsider, an impostor. Yet the depiction of his otherness involves, simultaneously, the representation of both a familiar and unfamiliar figure. Much was made of his 'peculiar' upbringing, a knowledge juxtaposed with the 'normality' of the family life of the Dunblane children, and his sexual status as a single (unpartnered) man. The *Independent*, for example, noted that:

> Loners like Hamilton are where *benign singleness* festers and turn poisonous, where being alone creates the space in which paranoia flourishes to burst out in violence' (my emphasis).[41]

It is estimated that, by the year 2001, lone men will form the largest group of one-person households in Britain.[42] Increased social atomization has brought into focus and prompted considerable research, notably under the umbrella 'crisis of masculinity', into the ways in which distinctive communities of 'lone men' are forming. It is men who are increasingly seen to be '. . . either drifting into despair, illness or break-down, or are aggressively asserting another kind of masculine identity through law-breaking and crime.'[43] The *Guardian* noted how

> The back streets of the shabbier ends of every British town are evidence of the elaborate communities of fantasy that men create as substitutes: martial arts centres, porn shops, tattoo parlours. Plus the erotica, often spiced up with violence, on the top shelf of your neighbourhood newsagent's or video store. Plus the extraordinary ease of buying drink almost everywhere, to help you sit at home and brood on all this.[44]

This, it is implied, was the habitat of Thomas Hamilton, a world symbolically far away from, though physically cheek-by-jowl with, the non-criminal and familial community of Dunblane. Quite explicitly it was stated that 'Hamilton *did not belong* to the manicured world of Dunblane. His home was a scruffy, damp council maisonette on a joyless estate in Kent Road, Stirling, five miles away.' Nor had he '. . . enjoyed the stable, happy childhood apparent in some of the children at Dunblane primary school'.[45]

The 'horror' of the criminal(ized) urban which is said to 'pursue us even here' is symbolized not just by the failure to 'escape' from crime. Within the present reconfiguration of the familial, the figure of the single male outsider has increasingly come to appear as an embodiment of social disorder, normlessness, and dislocation. However, importantly, the inadequacy of this iconography of male otherness to *consistently* depict Hamilton as 'outside' the social becomes glaringly apparent as its very familiarity at times comes to evoke rather different images of the masculine. He is, on one level, immediately recognizable (and is recognized) as a *particular type* of man. In other contexts, other genres, he would be the 'very stuff' of pulp fiction:

> . . . unmarried, 43, a thwarted scoutmaster with an obsessive interest in guns and a habit of photographing very young boys naked from the waist up . . . a familiar but dislocated story, the kind usually set in dreary rooming houses across the Atlantic – narratives pieced together after the grisly, ground-breaking crimes that are an American genre.[46]

A rich vocabulary exists, known to adults and children alike, through which to depict his otherness. Testimonies range from the relatively benign accounts of Hamilton as a 'quiet "anorak" type',[47] a 'strange moonfaced man'[48] who lived in a 'shabby bachelor apartment',[49] to the more overtly dangerous and troubling depictions of a 'vengeful misfit'[50] , a '"Mr. Creepy" or "Weird" man'[51] who was driven by 'monsters of the psyche'.[52] It is the very familiarity of these images which betrays the contingency and fluidity of the overarching framework of hetero-masculinity which would depict him as beyond society, outwith the social. Ultimately, as only few accounts noted, Thomas Hamilton:

> . . . was not a loner at all. He was the exact opposite. He wanted to run boys clubs. He wanted to run Scout camps. He belonged to a gun club. He wrote peeved letters to everyone. He had his own business. Lots of people knew him. Some loner.[53]

Far from having distinguishing marks, the stigmata of his imputed paedophilic intent, Hamilton lived in a community unsuspected. He was *known.* Reading Hamilton as 'other' is far from straightforward when his 'normality' as a man seeps through in representations which reveal much about the dualisms through which ideas of normal masculinity have been constituted in the first place. As a man with 'two sides',[54] a 'caring son' whose apparent normality betrayed the 'darker truth' of a 'mummy's boy', a 'repressed homosexual', representations of Hamilton's otherness draw on a complex discourse of hetero-masculinity[55] which is multi-layered and open-ended.[56] Yet, once again, in this process important questions are left begging around why it should be *men* whose responses to the 'bottling up' of emotions should routinely take such violent forms. Violence is banished to the criminal space of those such as Thomas Hamilton (the world of the misfit, the loner).

Such accounts are, quite simply, inadequate. In order to develop an analysis of Hamilton's sexed specificity at the level of (social) structure and (individual) psyche it is necessary to explore further how this iconography of otherness played out in terms of notions of the spree killer as social 'failure' – and why men's reaction to that failure should so frequently be understood to take such violent and destructive forms.

CONFIGURING HETERO-MASCULINITY: THOMAS HAMILTON AS REPRESSED 'FAILED MAN'

The 'classic psychological profile' of the spree killer

Though it varies from case to case (Hungerford, Dunblane, Tasmania) a number of key features recur around the image of the lone gunman as a failed man '. . . lonely, angry, resentful and ready to snap': [57]

> The classic profile of the killer as a single, lonely and obsessive man who is unable to articulate his emotions and is desperate for some form of recognition. Very few of these people are psychotic.[58]

There is some overlap with the dominant representation of the serial murderer as a 'resentment killer' out to take revenge on society for some past trauma. Like multiple murderers and serial killers, the spree killer is not generally understood to have been 'ill', at least not in the sense of suffering from schizophrenia, manic depression, and so forth. The following comments are not atypical of those made after Dunblane:

> Where you look in terms of background is at things like isolation, whether he is a loner with a possible desire for revenge, desire for status, a desire to be famous, or infamous, a desire to be a soldier or a commando who idolises guns. [59]
>
> The Man could well be someone who people thought of as odd but not mentally ill who has killed for the sake of it. People who go on spree killings . . . bottle it up until it all explodes in catastrophe . . .They harbour resentment for a long time while on the face of it they put up with being laughed at.[60]
>
> They obviously have major problems communicating their feelings and are likely to have all sorts of anger and aggression.[61]

Each of these comments draw on an emotional framework familiar to men and women. After all, 'we all know fear, uncertainty, desire and envy'.[62] In this model, rationality and intentionality is imputed to the spree killer. He decides to take 'revenge' on a society which has somehow 'rejected' him.

Such social failures, however, have a distinctly *gendered* dimension. Within a range of popular cultural texts of the 1980s and 1990s (plays, novels, films[63]), for example, these are emotions associated with a distinctively masculine (and arguably a white, ethnically specific)[64] psychology. It is white men who are, at the present moment, increasingly presumed to be experiencing these kinds of life experiences in a particularly acute form[65]. The press discourse in the aftermath of the Dunblane massacre shared, and drew on, this more general notion of masculine failure and crisis. Hamilton was an inadequate nobody, '. . . unable to succeed in society – financially, socially, sexually, academically, in sport or in their work'. Yet within this (gendered) model the *sexed specificity* of Hamilton continues to be erased, no less powerfully than it had been within the quasi-religious binary of good/evil. The dominant psychological profile model is gendered both in terms of *cause* (what is constructed as the source of rejection and failure in the first place: sexual, social, work failure) and its *effects* (in the recourse to specifically masculinized forms of violence as response: for example, the use of guns and weapons). There is, moreover, a contradiction emerging here. On the one hand, we have seen, it was said to be 'almost impossible' to pinpoint reasons for the lone gunman's actions. Like the serial murder, the spree killing does not take place in a pre-given rationally ordered society. However, the failed man narrative introduces an emotional framework in which notions of masculine failure are not just accessible and readily understandable; it also imputes an intentionality which is deeply familiar. It can, it would seem, be understood.

Ultimately, this framework serves to normalize (if not excuse) men's criminality. It does so because it remains within the positivist and modernist crimino-legal frame which seeks causes in terms of 'maleness'; but *it does not make the sexed specificity of crime explicit.* The dualism of normal/deviant fixes Hamilton as the latter; but there is no engagement with masculine subjectivity as itself being in any sense fluid and contradictory (or that men may shift between different subject positions). It negates any analysis of what Hamilton may have *shared* with other men at the very moment that it calls upon a normative masculinity by way of explanation for his actions. The failed man model places the spree killer within an understanding of crime as a deviant form of instrumental rationality. The means-ends relation which typifies crime as a modernist discourse thus remains in place. Yet, what would happen if we were to re-frame the question asked by the model in such a way as to make sexed specificity problematic? Why should it be that *his* social failures take such spectacularly violent and destructive forms?[66] Why is it, in the vast majority of cases, *men's* anger and despair (and not women's) which manifests itself, with apparently increasing frequency, in the murder of so many 'strangers'?

In the remainder of this article I wish to present a reading of the performative strategies in and through which Thomas Hamilton, as a (sexed) subject in a specific (social) location may have sought to constitute himself as 'a man'. In highlighting the performativity of masculinity it is possible, I shall argue, to interrogate the interface between the contexts in which Hamilton lived at the level of social structure and the specificities of his own life-history.

THE FANTASIZED MASCULINE AND THE (A)SOCIAL MASCULINE: (RE)CONSTRUCTING THE SEXED BODY OF THE LONE GUNMAN

Thomas Hamilton's life, from what is known, had been dominated by two principal activities: first, an involvement in the scouting and youth club movements, and secondly, by an involvement in gun clubs. In re-reading each of these activities in terms of how masculinity is performed in specific contexts, both the youth movement and the gun club can each be seen, in different and overlapping ways, as sites for the (hetero)sexing of the male body as 'masculine'.

1. *Thomas Hamilton as surrogate father: childhood, the scouting movement, and the youth club*

The dominant, indeed exclusive, representation of childhood in the press discourse around the Dunblane massacre is one of 'spotless innocence and hope'.[67] It is an innocence captured in two images extensively reproduced in television and newspaper accounts. The first is the photograph of Class P1 of Dunblane Primary School with their teacher, Gwen Mayor. This was to become a central icon, the reference point for the construction of childhood innocence around which all other images circulated.[68] The second is a freeze-frame taken from a home video recording showing Thomas Hamilton with young boys in a gymnasium assisting them in vaulting over a wooden-horse[69]. They are disturbing, haunting, and culturally familiar. It is through our subsequent knowledge, what we now 'know', that they come to tell other, more dangerous stories: of childhood destroyed by a stranger, of evil's destruction of innocence, of a woman who lost her life attempting to protect the children in her class, of a man who sexually desired those in his charge and who should not have been allowed to get into such a position of trust, authority, and power in the first place.

Such were the dominant interpretations of these images within the press discourse. Yet if each representation is reframed in a context which renders problematic the sociality of masculinities what else comes into view? I have argued above that the representation of Hamilton as both (quasi-religious) 'evil' 'grotesque' *and* (secularized) 'social failure' divert attention from the sexed specificity of the social context in which he lived. With regard to these images this is a context in which men's presence with children is *per se* presently considered problematic in certain scenarios and situations. It is a context in which, moreover, key elements of normative hetero-masculinity are constituted, not through contact or association *with* women and children, but via a range of activities primarily located as beyond the familial sphere and which take men *away* from shared physical space with women and children. The British primary school, in many ways the embodiment of a 'feminized' social space,[70] epitomizes this gendering of institution, space, and body in terms of a hierarchical structuring of sexual difference. At issue here are more general and pervasive questions, anxieties, and concerns about cultural representations of the paternal relationship which pervade the crimino-legal in its responses to Dunblane. In the case of the press discourse, the problematic nature of this relationship was consistently effaced notwithstanding the fact that it was central to the social context of Thomas Hamilton's life and actions.[71]

Hamilton was, the psychologist Paul Britton has written, neither '. . . an altruistic youth leader nor an uncomplicated paedophile' but, rather, '. . . a person who grew to need to guide, direct and control young boys; to influence how their bodies and morals developed'.[72] In so doing he was not alone. A range of institutions have historically sought to discipline, guide, direct, and control the bodies of young boys.[73] Such disciplining has been secured historically by facilitating boys' subjection and bodily proximity to the (suitable) authority of an older man or men. In a more contemporary variant, the search for appropriate male role models for young boys is seen, at a time of widespread 'father-absence', as essential to instilling in male youth non-criminal behaviour. Far from transgressing societal norms, his concern with disciplining and rendering subject to masculine authority potentially 'wayward' male youth is in fact in keeping with the British government's understanding of young men's socialization 'into crime'.[74]

It is not, in other words, because of any concern to 'discipline' boys *per se* that Hamilton's actions are seen as problematic. The youth clubs he set up exist within a terrain 'outside' the family. They are, however, no less regulated by codes of a familial ideology which ascribes to men particular social roles and functions (as disciplinarian, authority figure, protector, and 'friend'). It was by virtue of Thomas Hamilton's imputed sexual transgression that this authority was breached. The symbolic dominance of the father-figure ideal of this authority, however, remains in place. In the freeze-frame image of a man assisting boys in the gymnasium, Thomas Hamilton encapsulates a paternal presence which is, in other contexts, deemed desirable (as being, for example, a central strategy in crime prevention). As both 'surrogate father' in the youth club and 'rogue male' in the primary school Thomas Hamilton appears the embodiment of, at the same time as he makes visible, the pervasive *absence of men* from the lives of children whether in their capacity as (biological or social) fathers or as 'caregivers' to children and welfare workers across a range of institutions and organizations.[75] The 'normality' of men's relationships with young boys is deeply contested (to be regulated, policed, and rendered subject to surveillance). Indeed, the relationship between men and children constitutes, at present, a major political conversation[76] which rests, in part, on a consciousness of men as potential threats to the safety, integrity, and autonomy and, ultimately, to the lives of children. These threats cannot be confined to the extra-familial, though it is significant how at present a whole range of stories – hitherto subjugated knowledges – are articulating the point that 'strangers' have been a significant problem in the lives of many young men in terms of sexual abuse in locations such as the youth club, the school, and the church. It is arguably *within* the parameters of the (hetero-)sexual family that the rupture between men and children is being most rigorously and pervasively experienced in late modernity/postmodernity. It is, none the less, the pervasiveness of a threat of the 'dangerous' male which more generally transcends (and in so doing disturbs) the utility of the public/private dualism as a meaningful distinction in seeking to locate the crimes of men.

As such, the representation in the press discourse of the community of Dunblane as being somehow beyond, or without, crime assumes a particular significance in terms of its relation to the familial. The dominant image of childhood was, we have seen, one of 'innocence destroyed'. The innocence of childhood secures the body of the child within a particular configuration of the social. Whereas the serial killer, it has been argued, chooses as his victims individuals or groups who can be seen to be somehow 'outside' the social (down-and-outs, hitch-hikers, and so on),[77] Thomas Hamilton chose as his victims the very subjects – children – who constituted the sociality of Dunblane as a phantasmatic community. The representation of Hamilton as a straightforward paedophile appears to restore the order of the (familial) community. It *appears* to efface the rupture caused by a breach of men's (surrogate) paternal trust. Increasingly, however, the family of modernity is being displaced as institutional source for the preservation and reproduction of moral (sexual) order. It is in this context that the problematic nature of the relationship between men and children becomes something which cannot be sutured by reference to certainties and securities evoked by essentialist representations of masculinity constituted through the concepts, categories, and binaries which have marked the gender order of modernity. That which is considered 'dangerous' about men has, it would seem, moved somewhat closer to 'home'.

2. *The cultural framework of idealized masculinity: the 'copycat' spree killer and the gun club*

> There are calls for the gun club in a basement under the House of Lords to be scrapped as an example to the nation and turned, of all things, into a créche.
>
> (*South China Morning Post*, 22 March 1996)

Alongside his involvement in youth clubs Thomas Hamilton had one other abiding interest: a fascination with handguns, many of which he had obtained over a twenty-year period. In the months following the massacre, culminating with the publication of the Cullen Report in October 1996, an at times intemperate and heated debate over the legal regulation of firearms has been rarely out of the news in Britain.[78] It was, and is, a debate in which gender is systematically silenced. Both the 'sporting' and 'lone' gunman appear routinely as de-sexed figures. The debate, it seems, has *nothing* to say of men and masculinity. Certainly, the sport of firearms shooting attracts both women and men among its participants. However, it is an activity framed by a particular gender politics and order.[79]

The above comment in the *South China Morning Post* that, 'of all things', there were calls for the gun club in a basement under the House of Lords to be 'turned . . . into a créche' appears a throwaway comment. It suggests that in Britain the debate over gun control has become far removed from 'reality'. Yet it does, albeit unintentionally, capture an important point. The fact that a decision had been made to install in the basement of Britain's second legislative chamber a gun club, as opposed to any provision for the care of children, is indicative not just of the priorities of those who made that decision. It would be misleading to suggest simply that 'times have changed'. It symbolizes the hierarchical structuring of power, resources, and access to decision-making positions in terms of sexual difference which cannot be confined to one institution (such as Parliament) or organization. In the case of the gun club this was, in terms of (empirical) membership/ involvement and prevailing ethos, a pervasively *masculinized* culture.[80] The Cullen Inquiry noted how the authorities had shown a 'tacit sympathy' towards the prevailing gun culture; the attitudes of the police and gun licensing officers had been 'coloured' by this 'official' (legitimate) gun culture.[81] Shooting remains a popular pastime amongst members of the men-dominated legislature and judiciary.[82] Notwithstanding subsequent tightening of the law regulating firearms ownership in the light of Cullen's recommendations, this broader culture highlights a tension between the purported deviance of Thomas Hamilton's involvement with firearms and the 'normality' of *other* men's actions and attitudes, a tension exemplified by the press discourse as it sought to understand the spree killer in terms of the phenomena of 'copycat' violence.[83] Had Hamilton, having witnessed the 'fame' (however fleeting) accorded to other lone gunmen in recent years, sought to kill in order to achieve his own '. . . status, a desire to be famous, or infamous . . .'?[84]

Such a question individualizes crime at the moment it negates consideration of the wider social context in which men's relationships to violence are established in particular ways. As an editorial in the *Independent* noted, 'Hamilton's story, like the story of so much violence in our society, is a tale of men and weapons, sex . . . power and revenge.'[85] The culture which encircles schools is one of incessant violence in which, it is estimated, 30 per cent of boys between the ages of fourteen and fifteen carry weapons and where a third of teenage boys and two-thirds of girls fear physical attack.[86] The broader framework which surrounded Thomas Hamilton and the school is itself encoded by representations of potency, privilege, and empowerment associated with traditionally public locations for the achievement of idealized heterosexual masculinity – locations, that is, such as the gun club (or, indeed, the office, the legislature, the sports field or the university).

3. *The 'criminal man' as social (hetero-sexed) subject*

The following encapsulates the dominant reading within the press discourse of the events in Thomas Hamilton's life in the weeks prior to the massacre (a reading with which the Cullen Report was to subsequently concur). Hamilton had forcefully resisted the term 'pervert' with which, he proclaimed, he had been unjustly labelled. In a sense he 'fought back', protesting his 'normality' to everyone from the Queen to the Ombudsman in a series of '. . . articulate but increasingly obsessive'[87] letters complaining of his 'damaged reputation.' It was only when this strategy of resistance 'failed' that he finally 'snapped'.

It is possible, I wish to suggest, to read the 'resistance' of Thomas Hamilton in a rather different way. In his account of the murder of James Bulger, *Destroying the Baby in Themselves,* David Jackson has noted how Jon Venables and Robert Thompson, the two ten-year-old boys convicted of the murder, existed '. . . for much of [the] time within the constraining framework of adult authority, regulation and surveillance.'[88] Thomas Hamilton, in relation to his work, home, family and, it seems, sexuality, may also be seen to have been a dis-empowered subject. However, unlike two ten-year-old children, as an adult male he had access to a range of institutional resources through which he might seek to establish and exercise power and control over his own (and other) lives. In seeking to carve out an identity for himself '. . . in a different framework that seemed to offer . . . some status and self-respect'[89] he turned to a range of organizations and behaviour, in and through which he might constitute claims to other sources of power, other subject positions and definitions of masculinity from those through which his 'failure' as a man was otherwise being repeatedly confirmed.

In this active renegotiation of existing frameworks of masculine identification (in the form, for example, of his participation in youth work and gun clubs) Thomas Hamilton's (sexed, specific) *male* body is connected with, and ascribed meanings through, notions of sexualized violence and potency. Far from setting him apart, this connected Thomas Hamilton to those other men and boys who on a daily basis, in Jackson's words, long to associate themselves with the power and conventionality of masculine identity '. . . because of the dominating position that heterosexual masculinity occupies in our Western culture. Practically, this means trying to *heterosexualise* and *masculinise* their . . . bodies.'[90] This is a culture pervaded by images of hypermasculine toughness, which valorizes, in multifarious ways, the male body acting on space in conjunction with the skilled use and technical knowledge of weapons, be they guns or knives. Many boys routinely carry weapons. It is not hard to envisage how images of masculine bodies, bulging muscles, and empowered actors might be enticing and seductive for those who lack, in so many other respects, any commanding presence and status in the world. Through the use of weaponry, indeed, the male body is itself transformed. Far from seeing the build-up to the massacre as one of Hamilton losing control therefore, it is to locate the offence as a means of *taking* control.[91] As Cullen himself concluded about Hamilton:

> . . . he lacked any real insight into the fact that his (own) conduct had led to the decline in his fortunes . . . he turned his fantasy into reality in order to achieve control in one final and terrible manner.'[92]

This was, however, a taking of control which was – most importantly – profoundly masculinized. To adapt and re-write Jackson's argument, this is to see the actions of Thomas Hamilton as closely connected to a '. . .

desperate struggle to become masculine . . .'.[93] Although Thomas Hamilton's killing of sixteen children and their teacher '. . . was exceptional in degree and intensity, he was not a one-off, devilish, "freak of nature". He shared many of the learnt tendencies of aggressive, heterosexual manliness that many insecure young boys and men are desperately striving for today. Although representing a heightened, extremely unusual form of these tendencies, Thomas Hamilton existed firmly within the common continuum of male violence.[94]

To recap the argument at this point: Thomas Hamilton, in trying to masculinize himself within the ideals of traditional heterosexual masculinity, can be read as attempting to forge a more commanding and potent sense of himself as a man.[95] He did this, I have argued, through his involvement in (at least) three major activities. First, in his participation in the youth clubs, in which he is constituted as (surrogate) father-figure. Secondly, in his involvement with firearms and gun clubs, in which his subjectivity is empowered (however fleetingly) through the constitution of the body as 'masculine'; and, finally, and by way of a combination of each of the above, in his ultimate invasion, re-framing, and destruction of the largely feminized space of the Primary School at Dunblane which resulted in the death of sixteen children and their teacher.

CONCLUDING REMARKS: RECONSTITUTING THE CRIMES OF MEN *AS MEN*

> What is it about our world that impels men such as Thomas Hamilton to go on random, apparently motiveless killing sprees? This is a new kind of crime, not much more than a decade old, and signs were available long before its emergence.[96]

I have argued that a number of oppositions pervade the press discourse in its constructions of Thomas Hamilton. The result is a rich iconography of masculine otherness far more complex than the initial focus on good/evil, normal/deviant binaries would suggest. As a single (unpartnered) man he is not a 'family man' for he is of no family. Yet he is understood as other *through* the family. The crisis of representation of the paternal relation which surrounds the case results from the reconfiguration taking place within postmodernity of the sociality and contingency of those oppositional categories through which hetero-masculinity has hitherto been constituted as a naturalized, essentialist phenomenon. In this process, the broader heterosexual matrix which has historically framed understandings of men's crimes and criminality itself appears as, I have suggested, a phantasmatic ideal. The representation of Thomas Hamilton's 'dangerousness' embraces a range of images, behaviours, and demeanours which cannot be confined to the 'pervert/paedophile'-'normal' binary. Nor does it fit in which any straightforward representation of Hamilton as a (self-evident) 'psychopath'.

In the suggestion that there is something new and distinct about the spree killing, that it is a 'new kind of crime', it is envisaged that crime has 'transformed itself and mutated'. Crime appears as '. . . a law unto itself, outside the law, an outlaw'.[97] Outside the law, beyond reason, a space opens up for speculation about the dark side of 'human nature' which marked so much of the media coverage of Dunblane. Yet what, I have argued, constitutes a more plausible reading of the symbolic power of Dunblane is to locate representations of Thomas Hamilton in relation to a transformation in the discursive experience of the social. With this in mind, it should not surprise that the present re-configuration of men's relationships with children (all too evident in contemporary 'law and order' debates) should also involve a reframing of hitherto self-evident 'dangerous' masculinities of men and boys. For what is at issue here is ultimately the concept of childhood itself and the way in which it relates to the idea of the social. From the child's post-Enlightenment positioning as an unequivocal source of love, the child of postmodernity has come to signify simultaneously both a 'nostalgia' for an innocence-lost[98] and, notably in the form of the criminality of male youth, destructive social breakdown and moral dislocation. Following the investment of the innocence of childhood with no less than grounding a sense of sociality at a time of intolerable and disorientating change, it is no wonder that the abuse and destruction of such innocence should then be seen to strike at the remaining vestigages of that social bond; nor, as in the aftermath of the deaths of the Dunblane children (and, indeed, James Bulger), that what should surface should be such an intense expression of collective pain at the loss of that social identity.[99] In contrast to Hamilton's embodiment of 'evil', the Dunblane children appear as permanent and dependable, the incarnation of a 'nostalgic' vision of the child which has increasingly come to preserve no less than the meta-narrative of society itself.[100]

Where does this leave the politics of masculinity, the relationship between masculinity and crime? In this article I have presented an interpretative genealogy of how the 'silencing' of masculinity is achieved in one particular context. I have taken the press coverage of Dunblane as illustrative of the broader phenomenon whereby the sociality of men's crimes *as the actions of men* is routinely effaced. This is a question traditional political discourse appears incapable of addressing, something which says much about contemporary understandings of the relation between the crimes of men and the idea of the social. Faced with the events at Dunblane even the eloquence of politicians seemed to fail: '. . . some public catastrophes', it was stated, 'are out of public reach.'[101] For others the 'pain for the grieving silenced [traditional] politics.'[102] That which was evacuated, silenced from the very outset was, I have argued, any analysis of Thomas Hamilton not as a 'lone gunman', 'spree killer' or 'monster' but *as a man.* For all the limited engagement it contains addressing Thomas Hamilton's 'character and attitudes', his 'mood' and 'psychological and psychiatric evidence', there is no trace of any such questions in the Cullen report.[103] 'Traditional' politics seemed to sense, but barely express, the feeling of the betrayal of the vulnerable which run through the crimino-legal response to Dunblane and, more generally, to crimes against children. The terms 'no evidence' and 'no action taken' were repeated constantly during the Cullen inquiry. Certain assumptions about men and crime pervade this lack of response to those mothers who made complaints about the actions of Thomas Hamilton.[104] What had happened to the knowledge which so clearly existed about his actions (and was so evident in the accounts of women and children)? How was it, in a sense, 'neutralized'? The dominant representation of the spree killer as (asocial) other fed into a valorizing of childhood innocence which, perhaps ironically, itself served to silence the voices of those children who sought to speak of, and be heard in, their testimonies of the crimes of men.

To re-configure the relationship between masculinities and crime leads, ultimately, to a transformation in how crime is imagined. It leads to a set of different questions and issues which ill-fit the traditional formulations of liberal political and crimino-legal thought (in terms, for example, of public/private, mind/body). In one sense Thomas Hamilton is a 'one-off'. Yet from such '. . . so called "aberrant" cases' much can be learnt about the crimes of men more generally. Indeed, it is arguably all the more pressing to locate the thread which links such crimes with the fantasies and actions of 'normal' men. We have yet, it appears, to be challenged by what Thomas Hamilton may have shared with other men.[105] It is precisely such questions which raise important and difficult issues about the responses to and reception of the life and death of Thomas Hamilton. To dismiss the lack of response on the part of 'the Authorities' to 'do something' about his activities as *simply* a bureaucratic failure or regulatory matter (of firearms, school security)[106] is to misread – and to negate analysis of – the pervasive masculinism of state institutions themselves in terms of their assumptions, prevailing culture and, importantly, conceptualization of whether other 'subordinated' masculinities are, or are not, perceived of as actually or potentially 'criminal'.[107] In order to develop an understanding which might 'shield society from the consequences' of men's criminality, it is necessary to 'reflexively re-configure the relationship between the social and subjectivity'.[108] Far from being a 'one-off', exceptional and not-to-be-repeated event, in (re)locating the 'lone gunman' within a broader framework of idealized masculinity, the recent instances of spree killings can be seen as highlighting, not just a failure to protect women and children from the depredations of 'psychopathic' males, but as also raising important, and disturbing, questions about the boundaries of what constitutes 'acceptable' male behaviour in the first place.

NOTES AND REFERENCES

1 Quoted in the *Guardian*, editorial, 14 March 1996.

2 These are distinct from the phenomena of 'serial killing', on which see, further, J. Stratton, 'Serial Killing and the Transformation of the Social' (1996) 13 *Theory, Culture and Society* 77–98. On non-politically motivated homicides, including the spree killing, see D. Gresswell and C. Hollin, 'Multiple Murder: A Review' (1994) 34 *Brit. J. of Criminology* 1–14.

3 A detailed account of the events can be found in the *Report of the Public Inquiry into the shootings at Dunblane Primary School on 13 March 1996* (1996; Cm. 3386; Chair, Lord Cullen) - hereafter, the Cullen report. An outline of the events can be found in 'Minutes of Mayhem that took 17 Lives: Dunblane Inquiry' *Guardian*, 30 May 1996. The details of what happened will be considered further below.

4 In relation to theorizing masculinity, see, further, S. Gutterman, 'Postmodernism and the interrogation of masculinity' in *Theorizing Masculinities*, eds. M. Kimmell and M. Kaufman (1994); D. Saco, 'Masculinity as Signs: Poststructuralist Feminist Approaches to the Study of Gender' in *Men, Masculinity and the Media*, ed. S. Craig (1992).

5 See, for example, J. Butler, *Gender Trouble* (1990); J. Butler, *Bodies that Matter* (1993); E. Grosz, *Volatile Bodies: Towards a Corporeal Feminism* (1994); M. Gatens, *Imaginary Bodies* (1996). Also J. Butler, 'Against Proper Objects', (1994) 6(2/3) *Differences: J. of Feminist Cultural Studies* 1–27; 'Gender as Performance: An Interview with Judith Butler' (1994) 67 *Radical Philosophy* 32–9 (interviewed by P. Osbourne and L. Segal). For an excellent introduction to queer legal theory see, further, C. Stychin, *Law's Desire: Sexuality and the Limits of Justice* (1995): L.J. Moran, *The (Homo)Sexuality of Law (1996).*

6 A. Young, *Imagining Crime* (1996) 112.

7 My use of 'Crimino-legal' here delineates, following Young, id., more than simply 'criminology', 'criminal justice' or 'criminal law' but, rather, '. . . all of these together with the popular discourses that are manifested in the media, cinema and advertising, in order to convey the sense that "crime" has become (been made?) a potent sign which can be exchanged among criminal justice personnel, criminologists, politicians, journalists, film-makers and, importantly, (mythical) ordinary individuals' (id., p. 2).

8 Gresswell and Hollin, op. cit., n. 2, p. 3.

9 See, for example, 'Slaughter in the Sun' *Guardian*, 29 April 1996: N. Rufford and P. Arthur, 'The Misfit Behind the Massacre' *Sunday Times*, 5 May 1995.

10 K. Busch and J. Cavanaugh, 'The Story of Multiple Murder: Preliminary Examination of the Interface Between Epistemology and Methodology' (1986) 1 *J. of Interpersonal Violence* 5–23; R. Rappaport, 'The Serial and Mass Murder: Patterns, Differentiation, Pathology' (1988) 9 *Am. J. of Forensic Psychiatry* 38–48; M. Rowlands, 'Multiple Murder: A Review of the International Literature' (1990) 1 *J. of the College of Prison Medicine* 3–7.

11 Gresswell and Hollin, op. cit., n. 2, p. 3.

12 M. King, 'The James Bulger Murder Trial: Moral Dilemmas and Social Solutions' (1995) 3 *International J. of Children's Rights* 167–87.

13 See, for example, Young, op. cit., n. 6, p. 111: '. . . personal reactions to it are as strong as they ever were . . . in writing this chapter I have had frequent bad dreams and have felt a deep sense of horror'. Also, King, id., p. 168.

14 King, id., p. 168.

15 T. Newburn and E. Stanko (eds.), *Just Boys Doing Business? Masculinity and Crime* (1994) 1.

16 D. Jackson, *Destroying the Baby in Themselves: Why did the two boys kill James Bulger?* (1995) 3.

17 See, for example, R. Ericson, P. Baranik, and J. Chan, *Visualising Deviance: A Study of News Organisation* (1987); R. Ericson, P. Baranik, and J. Chan, *Negotiating Control: A*

Study of News Sources (1989); R. Ericson, P. Baranik, and J. Chan, *Representing Order: Crime, Law and Justice in the News Media* (1991).

18 K. McEvoy, 'Newspapers and Crime: Narrative and the Construction of Identity' in *Tall Stories? Reading Law and Literature*, eds. J. Morison and C. Bell (1996).

19 See, further, A. McRobbie, *Postmodernism and Popular Culture* (1994).

20 *Time Magazine*, 25 March 1996.

21 *Daily Express*, 20 March 1996.

22 *Daily Mirror*, 20 March 1996.

23 *Sun*, 20 March 1996.

24 The 'quality' (broadsheet) press tends to seek more liberal, rational explanations in contrast to the more sensationalizing tendencies of the tabloids. Given the latter's (considerably) greater circulation, it is open to question what effect this has on the framing of public opinion. Notwithstanding these differences, each tended to share an initial depiction of Hamilton in terms of 'evil'; compare *Daily Mirror*, 20 March 1996. On the day Dunblane primary school re-opened, it was stated that 'the evil has gone.' (*Sun*, 23 March 1996).

25 Mr. Justice Moreland, summing up in the James Bulger murder trial (*Guardian*, 25 November 1993). On the Bulger case see, further, Young, op. cit., n. 6, p. 111: Jackson, op. cit., n. 16.

26 King, op. cit., n. 12, p. 167–8.

27 Features of the spree killing have been taken up in the representation of other crimes: see, for example, accounts of the apparently random knife attack by a shopworker in Birmingham, England, which left one person dead and nine injured (*Guardian*, 30 July 1996).

28 Jackson, op. cit., n. 16, p. 4.

29 Editorial comment *Daily Mirror*, 14 March 1996.

30 P. Barker, 'Loner in Our Midst' *Guardian*, 15 March 1996.

31 Stratton, op. cit., n. 2, p. 78.

32 *Guardian*, 15 March 1996.

33 Compare with the representation of community in the aftermath of the murder of James Bulger; Young, op. cit., n. 6, p. 120.

34 B. Campbell, *Goliath: Britain's Dangerous Places* (1993).

35 *Guardian*, 14 March 1996.

36 E. Fergurson, D. D. Harrison, and R.McKay, 'Dunblane: the Story That Need Never Have Been Told' *Observer*, 17 March 1996.

37 See, for example, 'Fear Rules in No Go Britain: A Report on the parts of the country most people would rather not think about - never mind live' *Independent on Sunday*, 17 April 1994.

38 *Time*, op. cit., n. 20.

39 *Observer*, op. cit., n. 36.

40 A number of reports noted how the adults who lived in Dunblane, a commuter town, tended not to be familiar with each other. The children, in contrast, *knew* each other and the primary school had come to be a focus of life in the town. It brought people, who otherwise lived very separate lives, together. As such, the mass murder of the children took on a particular resonance in its symbolic violence against the idea of a community which had seemed crime-free.

41 *Independent*, 16 March 1996. Hamilton had been brought up to believe his natural mother, to whom he was very close, was in fact his sister: see, further, Cullen report, op. cit., n. 3, para. 4.2, p. 20.

42 Barker, op. cit., n. 30.

43 Jackson, op. cit., n. 16, p. 17.

44 Barker, op. cit., n. 30.

45 Fergurson, Harrison, and McKay, op. cit., n. 36. My emphasis.

46 *Guardian*, op. cit., n. 32.

47 *Independent*, 18 March 1996.
48 *Time*, op. cit., n. 20.
49 id.
50 *Chicago Tribune*, 20 March 1996.
51 *Guardian*, op. cit., n. 35.
52 *Time*, op. cit., n. 20.
53 D. Campbell, 'He was a loner: he kept his cliches to himself' *Guardian*, 13 July 1996.
54 *Guardian*, 31 May 1996
55 id.
56 A similiar reading informs A. Young's discussion of the mothers of Jon Venables and Robert Thompson, the two boys convicted of the murder of James Bulger (Young, op., cit., n. 6, p. 125).
57 *Guardian*, 29 April 1996.
58 id.
59 Gerard Bailes, Novik Clinical Forensic Unit, quoted in G. Younge 'He Just Shot Everyone Coming In', id.
60 Ian Stephen, quoted in Younge, id.
61 Clive Meux, Senior Lecturer, Institute of Psychiatry, London, and consultant at Broadmoor Top Security Hospital, quoted in Younge, id.
62 P. Hoggett, 'A Place for Experience: A Psychoanalytic Perspective on Boundary, Identity and Culture' (1992) 10 *Environment and Planning: Society and Space* 345–56, at 345.
63 See, in particular, on the 1993 film *Falling Down*, C. Clover, 'White Noise' in *Sight and Sound*, May 1993, 6–9.
64 According to Clover (id., p. 9), the 'Average White Male' '. . . is the great unmarked or default category of western culture, the one that never needed to define itself, the standard against which other categories have calculated their difference'; 'No Travis Bickle this, *Falling Down*'s story is precisely that of *Taxi Driver* . . . its whole effect depends on seeing D-Fens [the principal character in the film, played by Michael Douglas] not as a vet descending into madness, but as a tax-paying citizen whose anger allows him to see, with preternatural clarity, the madness in the society around him' (p. 8).
65 See, further, R. Collier, '"Coming Together?": Post-Heterosexuality, Masculine Crisis and the New Men's Movement' (1996) 4 *Feminist Legal Studies* 3–48.
66 In relation to urban disorder, see Campbell, op. cit., n. 34.
67 *Time*, op. cit., n. 20.
68 Compare with representations of school photographs in the Bulger case, notably in relation to representing the innocence of James Bulger himself: Young, op. cit., n. 6, p. 116.
69 The video was to later form the basis of a BBC *Panorama* documentary on Dunblane, broadcast 16 September 1996.
70 Men remain rare in primary school teaching, except as the Head of School. Even before the emergence of high-profile debates around school security in the 1990s, following a number of murders and attacks inside and outside school grounds, the very presence of an unknown man in any school is enough to arouse suspicion.
71 In July 1973 Thomas Hamilton became a leader in the Boy Scouts movement. In 1974, at the age of twenty-one, he was subsequently dismissed as leader of a local troop for 'inappropriate behaviour.' In the intervening years he made frequent attempts to be allowed to re-enter the organization, the last in 1988: he was rebuffed on every occasion.
72 P. Britton in the *Sunday Times*, 17 March 1996. Notwithstanding that the Cullen inquiry heard from 171 witnesses unrestrained by libel laws, hard evidence linking Hamilton with sexual abuse of children remained meagre (*Guardian*, 11 July 1996).
73 See, further, A. Parker 'The Construction of Masculinity Within Boys' Physical Education' (1996) 8 *Gender and Education* 141–57.
74 The stated aims of the 'boot camps' introduced by the British government as a way of instilling military discipline for young offenders, for example, emphasize similar concerns

with the disciplining, surveillance, and regulation of male bodies. C. Murray, *The Emerging British Underclass* (1990). In the British context, see N. Dennis and G. Erdos, *Families Without Fatherhood* (1991).

75 C. Skelton, 'Sex, Male Teachers and Young Children' (1994) 6 *Gender and Education* 87–93. Also K. Pringle, *Men, Masculinities and Social Welfare* (1995).

76 A. Burgess and S. Ruxton, *Men and Their Children: Proposals for Public Policy* (1996).

77 Stratton, op. cit., n. 2, p. 82.

78 By way of an exception, see B. Campbell, 'The Problem With Arms and Men' *Guardian*, 23 July 1996.

79 On the gender politics of the gun lobby, see, further, R. Connell, 'Politics of Changing Men' (1995) 25 *Socialist Rev.* 135–59, at 146–7.

80 Note, for example, the Masonic links it was suggested Thomas Hamilton had made (*Scotsman*, 22 March 1996).

81 *Guardian*, 11 July 1996.

82 'Who Are the Judges?' (1987) 76(1) *Labour Research* 9–11.

83 For example, 'Gun Man Obsessed by Hungerford shot 17 bystanders' *Times*, 25 May 1996.

84 G. Bailes, quoted in Younge, op. cit., n. 59.

85 *Independent*, 16 March 1996.

86 The results of a survey of 24,000 teenagers in 1996 (J. Balding, *Young People: Tenth Report* (1996).

87 *Times*, 15 March 1996. On the events preceding the massacre, see Cullen report, op. cit., n. 3, ch. 5.

88 Jackson, op. cit., n. 16, p. 9.

89 id., p. 16.

90 id., p. 32.

91 See N. Eastman, 'Madness or Badness?' *Guardian*, 22 October 1996.

92 Cullen report, op. cit., n. 3, para. 5.46.

93 Jackson, op. cit., n. 16, p. 24.

94 This section re-writes, in the context of Dunblane, Jackson's analysis of the Bulger murder (id., p. 4).

95 id., p. 28.

96 Editorial, 'They Deserve Our Answers' *Independent on Sunday*, 17 March 1996.

97 Young, op. cit., n. 6, p. 6.

98 C. Jenks 'The Postmodern Child' in *Children in Families: Research and Policy*, eds. J. Brannen and M. O'Brien (1996).

99 id., p. 20.

100 id., p. 21.

101 H. Young 'Many Questions, No Answers' *Guardian*, 14 March 1996.

102 *Independent*, Editorial, 15 March 1996.

103 See, for example, paras. 5.2, 5.25–5.28, 5.37–5.49. Government strategy continues to be to regulate the body of the paedophile in quite specific ways: see the consultation paper, *Sentencing and the Supervision of Sex Offenders*, published 17 June 1996.

104 See, for example, Cullen report, op. cit., n. 3, ch. 4.

105 For a rare exception to this, in another context, see J. O'Sullivan, 'We're still in the dark over West's madness' *Independent*, 12 September 1996.

106 Which is, in effect, what the Cullen report concludes. A senior police officer subsequently resigned in the wake of the comments made on bureaucratic failings in the report.

107 It is an interesting question as to whether, had the complaints being made about Thomas Hamilton come from men, rather than women, they would have met with a similar reception in terms of identification of men's dangerousness.

108 T. Jefferson, Review (1996) 36 *Brit. J. of Criminology* 323.

Part II
The Spectrum of Masculine Crime

[6]

CULTURE, MASCULINITIES AND VIOLENCE AGAINST WOMEN

Joachim Kersten*

The visibility of male-dominated criminal violence differs substantially from culture to culture. Accordingly, a perception of masculinity and male dominated violence as monolithic categories is misleading. Australian, German, and Japanese data display significant variations in the visibility of violence against women. In the light of this, standard gender neutral explanations of comparative criminology will be reviewed. In a conceptualization of 'hegemonic masculinity' in the context of sexual assault the visibility of the rapist in Australia is interpreted as a consequence of economic and cultural crises of gender relations causing a transformation of hegemonic masculinity. At present, historical and political constellations in Germany and Japan result in the visibility of different features of male dominated violence.

Theoretical Considerations: Crime, Masculinities, and Sexual Assault

In recent social science research 'relational and, hence, fluid conceptions of masculinity' have been employed to examine '(re)presentations of gender' in the media, in film, and in television programmes (Saco 1992: 25). An interesting case in question is the analysis of an icon of American masculinity: Clint Eastwood (Smith 1994). Such studies start to deconstruct masculinities like Dirty Harry and his enemies in the streets and in the police force. The criminological mainstream, however, is still reluctant to ponder obvious traits of the gendered reality of crime, victimization, and crime control although, across cultures and (modern) times, lawbreaking is an activity related to 15–23 years old unmarried urban males (Braithwaite 1989; Renzetti and Curran 1992; Gibbons 1993). Correspondingly, crime control is a domain of males, and as such crime and crime control constitute a 'state of play' between hegemonic masculinity and subordinated masculinities (Connell 1987; Messerschmidt 1993; Kersten 1993*a*, 1995*a*, *b*).

Criminology has a record of ignoring gender. When gender was raised in theorizing, the fact that women commit fewer crimes of a violent nature than men has resulted in binary and/or essentialist notions of male and female. The criminalization of females, although an area in definite need of research (Gibbons 1993), is in logical terms not exactly a good starting point for an analysis of male over-representation. Sex ratio variations in reported crime data across cultures or time are indicative of differential treatment against females (Gibbons 1992; historically informed, Feeley and Little 1991) and no suitable basis for a theory of masculinity and crime (Cain 1989, 1990).

In mainstream criminology and sociology, antisocial or criminal practices of masculinities are traditionally located in subcultural life worlds and neglected elsewhere.

* Professor of Sociology, Hochschule für Polizei, Baden Württemberg, Germany. This is a revised version of a paper presented to the American Society of Criminology's 1993 Annual Meeting 'Violent Crime and its Victims', Phoenix, Arizona, 27–30 October 1993.

JOACHIM KERSTEN

When, in the realm of male-dominated power and control such as management, politics, military, police, justice, law, medicine, and academia, crime became a subject, gender was rarely taken into consideration. 'Hyper-masculinity' and a vague notion of 'machismo' became synonyms for ethnic and lower-class masculinities. In summary, criminology tends to employ masculinity as a taken for granted, essential category that needs no further deconstruction. As recent work demonstrates, masculinity is neither a monolithic entity (Gilmore 1990; Newburn and Stanko 1994; Polk 1994), nor part of the male 'sex role' (for a criticism of the 'role' paradigm in gender studies see Edwards 1983; Connell 1987, 1990, 1995; Saco 1992; Messerschmidt 1993). Masculinity as an abstract configuration of social orientations and practices, and masculinities as acting agents of power, domination, and the use of force have, without any doubt, ties to deviance *and* social control. This holds, particularly, in regard to violent crime *and* to violence as a result of 'protection' and punishment. In most cultures and historical times only very few of these connections between masculinity and violence can be grasped with one-dimensional assumptions about the 'annihilation of women' being 'the source of meaning and identity for men'/'all men are rapists' and the like. The 'violent heterosexual male' has served as the protagonist for substantial parts of theorizing (for a detailed critique see Messerschmidt 1993: 39–45), but to use Messerschmidt's metaphor, as the one and only *angstgestalt* he is as practical for research into variations of male-dominated crime across cultures and times as a bulldozer.

Consequently, a social science focus on gender and male over-representation means more than to 'simply . . . add another variable and stir—the variable itself needs to be studied and understood' (Menkel-Meadow and Diamond 1991: 223). The binary conceptualization of gender has led to flaws in the conceptualization of male-dominated interpersonal crime and also of female victimization. Messerschmidt (1993) conceives of specific forms of crime and violence, including robbery and sexual violence, as public representations of masculinity and as displays of particular hegemonic masculinity. Hence, constructs of masculinity are dependent on interactions in which control of the situation is paramount. In the case of street crime such control can be achieved by means of dehumanizing 'others' as victims of robbery, assault, and sexual assault. In these confrontations structural subordination of masculinities, mainly along the categories of class and race, can be momentarily reversed.

In historical studies, though without an explicit reference to gender, John Dower (1986) and Christopher Browning (1991) have described the mechanisms that lead 'ordinary men', not underclass males, into committing atrocious crimes. Masculinity then, becomes a key issue in the dehumanization of 'others', and in the actual commitment of murderous work and rape on a mass-scale level during the times of war and ethnic fighting.[1]

In more general terms, hegemonic masculinity is: ' . . . a social ascendancy achieved in a play of social forces that extends beyond contests of brute power into the organization of private life and cultural processes'. In a connection to crime and violence '"hegemony" does not refer to ascendancy based on force', but it is not irreconcilable with the use of violence (Connell 1987: 184).

In recent studies of cultural anthropology, concepts and practices of 'good' masculinity are associated with three areas of social action. These have been claimed as

[1] Ex-Yugoslavia provides terrible support for Dower's and Browning's theorizing.

essential properties of 'maleness' and as such they constitute the core of hegemonic masculinity in patriarchal societies:

—'procreation' as normative heterosexuality and as a domain of sexual domination over women;
—'protection' as practices of physical control of men as enemies and women as property of men;
—and 'provision' of goods and food for families and communities which legitimate the exclusion of women from high status areas of paid work and decision making (Gilmore 1990; see also Badinter 1992 and Connell's 1995: 32f criticism of Gilmore's comparative study).

In a context of crime, such constructs of 'good' or 'real' masculinities are subject to both the self definition of deviant 'outlaw' masculinities and to the construction of the criminal offender, and (even more pronouncedly) to the image of the 'gang' as the collective 'other'. Constructs of 'evil' masculinities make up the control discourse of hegemonic masculinity, particularly in the media, and in the institutionalized practices of the criminal justice system. There, the gestalt of the offender figures as the antithesis of legitimate, male-dominated social action and as a threat to those practices of procreation (normative heterosexuality), protection (police/military/state), and provision (breadwinning) that produce and reproduce hegemonic masculinity in a given culture at a given time.[2] Although the crime control discourse focuses on the control of lower class males with whom a display of gender as particular hegemonic masculinity may serve as the last resort to status, the above functions relate to constructs of masculinity across the borderlines of class, race, and even age. The male fixation with procreation as normative heterosexuality, with domination through control over weaker persons, mostly women and children, forms the decisive nexus to practices of sexual assault. Such practices and their control may differ due to historical, cultural, and situational causes. However:

—perpetrators of hetero- and homosexual rape are nearly always male;
—across historical times and different cultures hetero- and homosexual rape has been identified as a domain where proof of masculinity and male domination are at stake;
—rape or seduction of females (as male properties) is a traditional origin of male feuds;
—sexual assault is situated at the borderline of state control of crime and gender policies;
—forcible rape of females occurs as a collective male practice at times of war and ethnic fighting, in police stations, or in criminal subcultures (e.g. bikers, organized crime). Collective practices of sexual abuse/assault perpetrated by white (also Japanese) males of upper- and middle class origin can be seen in sex tourism.

[2] Although this discussion is concerned primarily with masculinities, it is appropriate to note that historical analyses have identified images of 'evil women' as the basis of penal practices against 'witches'. Such constructs are equally linked to the domains of hegemonic masculinity. Witches and their powers were seen as the cause of impotence in husbands (procreation); or were held responsible for the poisoning of mothers and infants (protection); or as causing the failure of mothers to breastfeed their children (provision); or as being responsible for bad harvests or weather.

These traits of sexual assault demonstrate that rape is a practice linked to specific frameworks of gender relations in which issues of hegemonic masculinity are transformed, or at stake. Rape has to do with male power but in more varied and complicated ways than the radical view has put it in early theorizing. Visibility of rape is highly selective and promotes a 'stranger-danger' perception of the crime (Kersten 1993*a*: 465f). Besides, the 'stranger-danger' rapist as an image of fear of crime is a preferred protagonist of popular culture coverage of crime. This portrayal of rape is resistant to changes in the known facts about rape. It has a powerful impact on law and order debates (Soothill 1991; Kersten 1994). Media coverage of rape is influenced by factors independent of the empirical reality of rape. The visibility of the 'stranger' as the perpetrator of rape in the media appertains to the cultural fascination/apprehension of the most fearful image of evil masculinity a society can muster in any given time and culture (Kersten 1993*a*: 466f). The following is the exploratory investigation of a proposition:

The image of the rapist as a stranger, as a public enemy and as the antithesis of hegemonic masculinity is an artifact that corresponds to specific cultural crisis of gender relations due to changes in the social and economical framework of male work, male dominated protection, and a change in gender relations of a given society.

Cross-cultural Variation in the Visibility of Sexual Assault

In this comparison the term 'visibility of sexual assault' appertains to official crime statistics, victim survey data, and media coverage of rape in three countries during the last years. Australia, Germany, and Japan as industrialized countries display substantial differences in the visibility of male-dominated assaultive crimes (see Kersten 1993*a*: 466ff; 1995*b*). Among other reasons, Australia has been selected for this comparison because of the country's high incidence of assault victimization. The situation has similarities to that of the US, but bears no link to racial discrimination or inner-city neighbourhood social disintegration.

The reported crime data demonstrate suggestive differences in all areas of violent crime, but they are most pronounced in the categories of serious assault and sexual assault. In other publications (Kersten 1991, 1993*a*, 1995*b*) the comparative data are presented in detail. In this paper a summary of the main characteristics of assault visibility in the three countries will have to suffice:

—At the end of the 1980s/early 1990s rates of reported sexual assault in the Australian states exceeded the Japanese rates of reported rape by a factor of more than 20. German rates were at about one third of the Australian rates (Dörmann in Kühne and Miyazawa 1991; Chappell 1993; Kersten 1993*a*).

—As much as a comparison of reported rates across nations is a fault-ridden (but routinely used) exercise in criminology, and does not allow for far-ranging conclusions, the long-term steady rise of the Australian rates from 5.3 reported incidents per 100,000 population in 1976/77 to more than 20 in 1991/92 is an indication of the visibility of rape in that country (National Committee 1991: 24). Rates in all areas of reported interpersonal crime have shown a substantial increase in the Australian jurisdictions, but the longitudinal growth of reported rape is steeper than that of robbery and serious assault (Mukherjee and Dagger 1992).

—In Germany the case load of reported rape has decreased by 30 per cent in the last decade. Since reunification, rates of rape have shown an increase (BKA 1994: 121). In Japan during the same time period rates of reported rape per 100,000 population have been reduced by 50 per cent. There, between 1960 and 1990 rates of reported rape have altogether decreased by 78 per cent (Dörmann in Kühne and Miyazawa 1991: 40; Research and Training Institute Ministry of Justice Japan 1993: 59; Kersten 1993*a*: 469). A decline of such size can hardly be explained by factors like 'shame culture' or 'inferiority of Japanese women'. As a result of rapid modernization, an active Japanese women's movement has, among other things, achieved a public debate about rape and *sekuhara* (sexual harassment). Why should there be a drop in the willingness to report violent crime victimization?

A substantially higher visibility of interpersonal crime in Australia is supported by the findings of recent international crime survey data (Japan Urban Security Research Institute 1990; Kühne and Miyazawa 1991; Chappell 1993). The most comprehensive survey included 16 industrialized countries. Again, serious doubts about the validity of the findings have been raised. Still, the German, Japanese, and Australian rates of sexual assault victimization data exhibit proportionate variations similar to those in the official statistics. The Australian sample displays a victimization rate in the category 'sexual attack, sexual molestation' of 7.3 per cent, the German 2.8 per cent, and the Japanese 1.4 per cent of respondents. Australia's victimization rate under the heading 'sexual incident' is the highest of all 16 participating nations.

During 1991, in the Australian press, rape and child abductions with a sexual background were much more visible than in German or Japanese papers. The influential Melbourne newspaper *The Age* had 209 reports and articles on sexual assault. These relate to cases in the state of Victoria (4 million population). Nearly ten reports were full-page features on topics of sexual abuse of children/incest, and date rape. About 50 per cent were longer than 50–100 words. During 1991, the Tokyo edition of *Asahi Shimbun* had 60 news items covering sexual assault in the Tokyo Metropolitan district (population: 14 million) and in other prefectures. Nearly all of these reports were short. In the same year *Süddeutsche Zeitung* (Munich) had 86 reports covering sexual assault, mainly cases in Munich and Bavaria (population: 11 million). This included more than ten reports about rape cases in other countries. Twenty-four articles exceeded the length of short news items.

In the late 1980s, visibility of violent attacks, among them a number of massacres where Australian amok shootists killed innocent bystanders, including many women and children, resulted in the inauguration of a National Committee on Violence.[3] During the second National Conference on Violence, the (then) director of the Australian Institute of Criminology summarized the findings of the committee's research groups:

[3] In the late 1980s in Germany a similar committee on violence ('Gewaltkommission') started work after the killing of a police officer by violent demonstrators. Sexual assault played no significant part in the report.

These . . . observations about the state of violence in the nation confirm . . . that Australia remains a society afflicted by intolerable levels of violence. Our society is also one which has long condoned this violence as a means of resolving disputes across a wide range of activities and settings (Chappell 1993: 12).

While at first the debate about violence remained at a fairly general level of gender neutral 'interpersonal' crime, the prevalence of male-dominated violence against women and children shifted the focus to domestic violence, rape, and incest. In 1991 in Australia, concerns about stranger rape were widespread and were reported to influence the everyday life behaviour of citizens (Westbury 1991: 82). Women were quoted to be afraid to use public transport or to use taxis after a series of rapes committed by taxi drivers, or to go out after dark or without male protection. A media campaign 'Violence is ugly', financed by the state government of Victoria addressed everyday life features of physical and sexual violence against women. In 1992 ABC aired a television documentary on sexual assault ('Without Consent') which caused an enormous riposte. This led to a conference of the Australian Institute of Criminology where further details of the size of the Australian rape problem were revealed[4] (Easteal 1993).

In a new edition of the first study of the history of women in Australia and the Australian women's movement (Summers 1994), the author names aspects of the culture of Australia[5] which support a notion of 'aggressive masculinism' as a cultural trait. Historical studies have seen this at the basis of Australian gender relations since the days of transportation (Saunders and Evans 1992: 101; Carmichael 1992: 107; Hughes 1987; Kersten 1995*b*).

In the light of these data, it seems appropriate to conclude that sexual assault of the type that is most likely to be reported to police or to victimization survey interviewers is much more visible in Australia than in Japan and Germany. Furthermore, despite increased awareness of rape victimization, feminist campaigns, refuge and rape crisis centre policies in all three countries, a significant increase in figures of reported rape is only visible in Australia while in the other countries under comparison rates have been stable or decreased substantially.

Overall, the percentage of Australian victims who report crimes to police is roughly the same as that of other nations (Walker 1990: 4). Given the results of recent self-report victimization data, less than 20 per cent of Australian rape victims reported the rapes they suffered. Rapes by strangers (43.5 per cent) and estranged husbands (29.2 per cent) were far more likely to be reported than those which had acquaintances and family members as perpetrators (Easteal 1993: 81). However, in official Australian data stranger-rapists figure as a minority (between 22 per cent and 40 per cent). Most reported rape crimes have perpetrators whom the victim did know before the rape occurred (Moran 1993: 45). It follows that in official data strangers are proportionally

[4] Although comparative survey data are not available, it is questionable whether the findings of an Australian survey on women's perception of men as rapists would find a similar response in Japan or Germany In the Australian data more than two thirds of female respondents (n=5,303) agree (35 per cent 'strongly') to the statement 'All kinds of men, many of them normal and respectable in other ways, are rapists' (Easteal 1993: 23).

[5] '. . . when most Australian men say to a girl they have just met at a party "Do you want a ride home?" or if they ring her and say "Do you want to go to a drive-in?" what they generally mean is "Do you want a fuck?", and any girl who takes the invitation at face value is likely to find herself landed on a lonely road and forced to walk home or else spend the evening fighting off a genuinely amazed male who refuses to believe that she did not realize the contract she had entered into' (Summers 1994: 253).

'over-reported' and acquaintances are under-reported. It also follows that victimization in Australia occurs mostly during date, acquaintance, and intra-family rapes. In official and victimization data children and young persons constitute half of the victim population (ibid. 48; Easteal 1993: 76) with family members as the most likely offenders of sexual assault against children under age 11.

Variations in the Visibility of Sexual Assault: Examples of Gender-neutral Explanations

In other work the 'routine' theories of comparative criminology have been criticized for their lack of capacity when it comes to the low crime rates in Japan (Hamilton and Sanders 1992; Braithwaite 1989; Kersten 1993*b*). For lack of space these arguments have to be summarized. With respect to Japan's internationally accredited low crime rates, in Western writing most credit goes to the effectiveness of formal crime control, i.e. policing (Bayley 1976). Japanese criminologists have raised some serious arguments against such claims by pointing out that Japanese police given their number and powers are less efficient than their American or European counterparts (Araki 1988; S. Miyazawa, 1992). Other Western studies emphasize the efficiency of informal control or a unique cultural propensity towards 'shaming' which would make crime prevention in Japan such a successful collective effort (Braithwaite 1989; see Kersten 1993*b*). They generally refer to Ruth Benedict's work (1946) about Japanese shame culture,[6] without providing further evidence to substantiate the link between the 'national character' and fewer crimes. Other authors point at the alleged co-operation between the Japanese police force and organized crime, *Yakuza* (night-time policing), and the alleged fact that at times the police turn a blind eye to underworld crime are seen as explanations for the low crime rates in Japan (van Wolferen 1989: 103).

However, in the realm of crimes with masculinity as a primary or background motivation, to a substantial degree gangsters themselves are seen to commit the crimes in question. Large proportions of the homicide rate and the rates of sexual assault and serious assault are attributed to *yakuza* members (Hoshino 1988: 35; Tamura 1992; Kersten 1993*a*). Rapes and murders of foreign sex workers appertain to 'control' practices in the underworld dominated sex industry, and are not the acts of outsiders.

Japan and Germany are generally perceived as countries with an enduring historical and political tradition of authoritarianism, i.e. a strong shared belief in authority, discipline, and order. If such assumptions would result in a higher willingness to report rape, assaults ought to be reported at a higher rate in these countries than in Australia. The German and the Japanese penal codes share a common heritage to the extent that the German 'Strafgesetzbuch' was imported into Japanese law after the Meiji modernization. Both penal laws are characterized by a high degree of codification and inquisitorial procedures. Furthermore, police numbers (in proportion to the population) are higher in Japan and Germany than in the Australian states. Police powers of investigation in Japan and Germany greatly exceed those of their Australian counterparts, while in Australia (and in Germany) defence lawyers certainly have more rights than in Japan. Police/rape victim relations are problematic in all three societies, and

[6] For a critical discussion of Benedict and Japanese 'shame culture' cf. Geertz (1988: 115–26). In a thorough study of Germany's and Japan's postwar strategies of denial and acceptance of responsibility for the atrocities of World War II, Ian Buruma (1993) firmly rejects Benedict's notion of a unique Japanese shame culture as a 'mechanical' concept, and in his book on the Western perception of Japan Shimada (1994) comes to similar conclusions.

cannot be the single reason for a lower willingness to report rape to the authorities in Japan and Germany. Germany and Japan have compulsory registration laws which—in both countries—are even more strictly policed for foreign residents. This makes it fairly easy for police to locate citizens when criminal investigations are carried out against suspects. Japan has an additional family register which increases the number of available strategies for surveillance and identification. Germany and Japan have compulsory ID card systems. In contrast, Australian states have no address registration system for their citizenry. Australian residents have no ID cards; they need a passport only if they intend to travel to overseas countries. Before the statutes were changed only a few years ago, police in Victoria had no right to take fingerprints[7] or forensic samples, if suspects did not consent.

In spite of the lower rate of police presence and with limited powers of investigation, Australian police 'clear' between 70 and 80 per cent of sexual assault, i.e. equivalent proportions of the crime are cleared in all three countries. It follows that different structural determinants of formal control in the countries under comparison are not a satisfactory explanatory device for the variations in rape visibility.

Similarly, on a routine basis variations in population density, urbanization, and climate are pointed at to explain differences in crime visibility. The urbanization of Australia, supposedly one of the highest of all industrialized countries, is routinely used as an explanation for high rates of victimization (Walker 1990: 5; Chappell 1993).[8] Compared to cities in Japan and Germany, most of the suburbs of Australian cities display a parkland scenario. Urbanized areas of Japan (e.g. Kanto or Kyoto-Osaka) or urban conglomerates in Germany (Main or Ruhrgebiet) are definitely more crowded than any of Australia's cities. Another approach sees climate (i.e. the geographical latitude of countries) as the main variable predicting the occurrence of victimization: Australians would spend less time indoors than people elsewhere (Walker 1990). However, most reported and unreported sexual assaults in Australia occur in the homes of victims or perpetrators. With most of its densely populated region having extremely hot and humid temperatures in the summer months, Japan's crime rates should at least exceed those of Germany.

Cultural coherency/'racial harmony' assumptions tend to link rising rates of violent crime with the growing number of foreign residents in each country. Given the characteristics of rape reporting, one can assume that non-nationals are over-represented in the statistics of reported sexual assault. However, in all three countries, rape is a domain of home grown, male-dominated crime. Despite an increase in crime in Australia, with regard to crimes committed by non-Australians, it has been established quite clearly that the crime rates in these sectors of the population are generally lower than those of the Australian-born population (Hazlehurst 1987). In conclusion, it seems that none of the standard macro-explanations of comparative criminology sits very comfortably with the differences in the visibility of sexual assault victimization that can be observed in the three countries.

[7] In contrast, expatriates who reside in Japan or citizens of Korean descent who live in Japan in the third generation were (at the time of writing) still being fingerprinted as a matter of routine.

[8] Australian criminologists, although discussing the very same survey data, use a definition of urbanization which appears to be in complete contradiction to that underlying the international victims' survey ranking. There Australia ranks at the bottom of the scale (JUSRI 1990: 101).

CULTURE, MASCULINITIES AND VIOLENCE

Variations in the Visibility of Sexual Assault: Explanations that Include Gender

In all three societies hegemonic masculinity is established as a hierarchy of genders, classes, and majority/minority relations; as a gender and race specific division of labour in public and private spheres; as a domination of women by men, and younger men by older men; of workers by men with status and access to power; of males, females, and children with minority status by mainstream culture, by the state and its institutions. While in all countries under comparison majority and minority women can be the subjects of sexist discrimination, both cultural majority men and women in Japan, Germany, and Australia draw substantial advantage from practices of social and racial discrimination against minority men and women.

Standard assumptions of Western sociology about the link between reported rape (as visible sexual assault) and notions of gender 'equality', ubiquity of pornography, etc. do not fit well with the variation of visibility discussed in this research. Consider findings by Baron and Straus (1990) about the impact of such factors as 'gender inequality', 'pornographic readership', 'cultural spillover', and 'social disorganization' on cross-national rape rates in the US. This comparison of cross-cultural rates of rape, although based on much more heterogeneous sets of data than the US study, comes to different conclusions. Gender equality measured in terms of job equality resulted in lower rates of rape victimization in Baron and Straus's work; the opposite is the case here: job equality (in the mechanical definition of Baron and Straus) is lowest in Japan and highest in Australia. Pornographic readership was positively linked to rape in the US; in Japan the low visibility of rape corresponds with widespread fictitious accounts of blatant sexism and pornography including rape (e.g. in *manga*), with very high distribution. Japan has a tradition of erotic illustrations (perceived as pornography in the West) and public displays of oversized genitalia during religious festivities (Bornoff 1991; Shimada 1994). Moral censorship and a Victorian tradition of prudishness is most commonplace in Australia (Dysart 1992: 52f), where rape is extremely apparent. To untangle the variation in the visibility of rape as a powerful symbol of male domination/normative heterosexuality, socio-economic and cultural factors in gender relations and in the 'state of play' between hegemonic and subordinated masculinities need to be considered. None of these issues bears any significance in the rape research by Baron and Straus.

Low rape visibility in Japan

Unsubstantiated claims about the ubiquity of rape and rapists in Japan need to be taken with care. Indeed, the most explicit critics agree that Japan's streets are safer for women than those in Western countries (Horsley and Buckley 1991: 236; Taylor 1983: 193; Condon 1991: 83; van Wolferen 1989: 194). Instead of fear of crime, these authors claim, there is a more pronounced feeling of being safe from attacks of assaulters. This may be the case for attacks originating from non-acquaintances, but is it also valid for rape and incest in the context of intimate relationships like the family, and for date rape? The official data display a significant over-representation of 'strangers': of 1,335 reported rapes (1991) only 11 had family members and 288 acquaintances as perpetrators. All other offenders were listed as strangers. Although it seems safe to conclude that acquaintance rape is dramatically under-reported, a number of factors may lead to a lower incidence of date rape and sexual assault in the family or against intimate partners. In contrast to the record of Japanese soldiers in China, Korea, and other occupied countries during the war (Buruma 1993; Dower 1986), a tradition of non-confrontational behaviour within the boundaries of the culture and within the individual's reference group is certainly a factor that contributes to a lower degree of visible physical assault in public. In spite of remarkable drinking customs among *salariimen*, public fights are rare. This may also result in fewer violent assaults on females in public. The architecture of Japanese cities and suburbs (although changing to a less favourable design—Miyazawa 1990: 229f), and the organizational set up of school, workplace, and family life seems less conducive to both forms of sexual violence, to assault in 'the dark alley', and to the indoor variety of sexual attacks that spread fear in many Western societies. It is commonplace knowledge in the West that school and work schedules for the Japanese population are demanding. Additionally, the group relatedness of most male and female social activity in educational institutions, at work and in the (scarce) leisure periods serves as a safeguard against attacks. First dates often involve pairs of young males and females. Because of the lack of privacy in the home, or the availability of other spaces, dating (and even married) couples use 'love hotels' for more intimate exchanges. Generally, seduction, which by definition borders on force, plays a less pronounced role in Japan. This may result in lower rates of date rape.

The contractual bases of the majority of marriages involve their own family and the in-laws as a control agency for assaultive behaviour. Neighbourhood control and other forms of surveillance (e.g. in parks) are more intense than in the West. The co-sleeping patterns (Lebra 1976: 140) may protect married women from unwanted sexual pursuits by a husband during the few hours he is at home at night. As the popular saying goes, the most important fact about husbands is their health and that they are *not* at home. *Salariiman* fathers tend to have only guest status in the family. Unemployment is low, and alcohol is normally consumed with workmates in pubs, not at home where there is rarely enough space to have parties. All this may protect family members from attacks which figure exceptionally high in Australian rape statistics.

Consider the different understanding of sexuality in the Japanese culture. There, sexual practices are not so much located in paradigms of love, romance, exclusive intimacy, and normative heterosexuality[9] but rather in a paradigm of health. Sexuality is conceived of as a bodily function, and there are rules for communication about sexual desires, e.g. when a room in a 'love hotel' is required. The status of Japanese women as the head of the family in all decisive areas of family finances (husbands have to hand their salaries to their wives) leads to a situation of economic autonomy which does not exist in Western countries. Such phenomena of women's financial independence and domination in everyday life affairs are rarely acknowledged when the construct of the 'miserable' and oppressed Japanese woman has to serve as the 'other' of the 'liberated' Western model of femininity (for an informed debate see Cherry 1987). In contrast, domestic violence and rape of intimates have obvious links to the economic dependency that marks the situation of most victimized (and non-victimized) women in Western countries.

[9] To the author's best knowledge attacks on homosexuals are not known in Japan. Buruma's (1984) work indicates a wider variety of gender displays in Japan, and a cultural acceptance of intermediate forms, e.g. *onnagata* actors in *kabuki*.

Messerschmidt's (1993) conceptualization of 'tough' masculinity as a public situational display and reflection of male gender, in the context of male-dominated violence, often in connection with otherwise low status and lack of resources, fits the image of members of *yakuza* underworld groupings (Buruma 1984; Gilmore 1990; Kersten 1993*b*) but not that of the average salaried member of the work force. In the life worlds of *salariimen* public displays of toughness, independence, and potency as indicators of masculinity defined as social and physical achievement are rather frowned upon. The group of males in the workplace and in the pub after work exhibits patterns of 'maternal' values: understanding, an emphasis on caring for others and on reliability, displays of emotions etc. *Karoshi,* i.e. 'death from working too much' is not so much a consequence of 'hyper competitive' orientations but rather a result of 'hyper devotion' to the firm or the boss. The Japanese cultural mainstream concept of masculinity is, in a way, another transformation of the *samurai* ethos. This makes it entirely different from the masculine 'bushman and digger' ethos of Australian nationalism. Japanese constructs of masculinity are much less homophobic and 'machismo' focused than the masculinities of frontier societies like Australia or the US, and their perpetual emphasis on 'real' manhood (for examples of frontier and gun lobby masculinities in these countries see Connell 1995). Despite their aggressive business tactics in the West, in Japan's *salariiman* culture, group acceptance and membership in successful groups are ranked much higher than a display of the individually successful tough guy (Kersten 1994*b*). If rape is correlated to feelings of power and domination over weaker objects (female or male), such individual or group orientations are more pronounced in cultures where male power in traditional domains of protection and provision are dwindling. In that regard, present day corporate Japanese members of the dominant *salariiman* culture invest much less in displays and proofs of such specific masculinity than their Australian counterparts. Japan's hegemonic status in business and finance, and the fact that provision in Japan is male-controlled, may produce less demand for displays of masculinity that subdue weaker subjects by sexually assaulting them. Japanese men are clients of the 'water trade' with its 'ejaculation' branch (prostitution). They purchase emotional and/or sexual services by women to boost their masculinity on a mass scale. The 'water trade' exploits women from Asian and other poor countries. Bornoff calls sex tourism the 'rape your neighbour' version of Japanese men's sexuality. All this may result in a lower visibility of certain rapes, namely the ones that are most likely to be reported in Australia and elsewhere in the West in Japan herself.

As the recent 'comfort women' affair (forced prostitution of women in occupied territories) and the 'sekuhara' (sexual harassment) debate have demonstrated, suspicions about official and private strategies of denial of shameful aspects of Japanese past and present are quite appropriate. It may well be that sexual assault is seriously underreported in Japan, but there is, at the same time, clear evidence that the visibility of certain types of rape as a public threat to women play no significant role in contemporary Japan. The opposite is true for Australia.

High rape visibility in Australia

The extreme visibility of Australia's 'uncontrollable and dangerous' men has to be deciphered against a background of a deep social, cultural, and economic crisis on the fifth continent which has repercussions for gender relations. The seemingly self-evident construct of an Australian 'national masculinity' with an emphasis on physical prowess and independence[10] is crumbling (Kersten 1993*a*, 1995*b*). The loss of masculine identity through the loss of traditional functions that provide legitimacy for male cultural domination produces dire needs, especially on the part of marginalized men. Among them self-hate and a need to compensate for the loss of legitimate avenues to a male status are related to crime rates. A practice that proves the remnants of strength in the male person when a weaker and despised object (female, childish, homosexual, of other ethnic or racial origin) is dehumanized and victimized can be interpreted as one of the outcomes of masculinities under pressure (Messerschmidt 1993). The rape in the dark alley (and not the one in the victim's house or car) figures as the 'other' of hegemonic masculinity on the fifth continent, and as such it becomes the focus of widespread fear and apprehension. With physical and sexual assaults as a fact of daily life, the protection of females and children can compensate for the loss in other realms of hegemonic masculinity. In Japanese culture, the physical man *as an individual* was never a model of masculinity. This relates to (rural) traditions of collective work shared by men and women, young and old. In contrast to the individual image of the boss as a 'real man' in Australia and Germany, the 'mothering' aspects of Japanese work masculinity require much less physical masculine presence. Germany and Japan no longer have large-scale farming. Farmers are part of a historical tradition of agriculture where the primary groups of the family and the village community have traditionally been more important than the physical strength of the individual farm worker. Farming, a heavily subsidized enterprise in both Germany and Japan, is not seen in masculine terms, nor is both countries' postwar advancement in high-tech electronics or automobile production in the secondary sector conceived as 'masculine'. Accordingly, there is less need to legitimize physical masculinity in both other countries. Again, in Australia the visibility of assault with force may serve the purpose of demonstrating the need for 'good' physical men who are otherwise useless in a society increasingly dependent upon the tertiary sector and tourism.

Crime and Masculinities in a Cross-cultural Perspective

This collection of evidence for cultural and economical determinants in the construction of culture-specific gender relations and masculinities has tried to find causes for the lower visibility of sexual assaultive behaviour in Japan. The argument is of a speculative nature and needs further theoretical scrutiny and empirical testing. Whatever the flaws of this approach, it looks at gender, economic, social, and cultural factors as the basis of variations in the visibility of certain male-dominated violence. Almost all gender-neutral routine theorizing of the criminological 'malestream' is hopeless when it comes to such variations of phenomena as rape, assault, and the like (Gibbons 1993). As far as this blind spot of criminology is concerned, an exploratory gender theory approach is a more promising track than the continuation of gender-blind 'business as usual'.

In other work by the author the visibility of Germany's skinheads (Kersten 1994*c*)

[10] A construct constantly celebrated in the ANZAC legend and in 'true blue' Australianness in the advertising, for example for such heterogeneous commodities as Victorian beer, federal financial institutions, and (ironically) Australian-made Toyota automobiles.

and Japanese gangsterism (Kersten 1993*b*) are interpreted as indications of a different type of crisis related to each culture's problems in politics, the work sector, and other domains of masculinity. These appertain to both nations' postwar and, particularly, Germany's post-reunification record of *verdrängung* of the responsibility of each country's military and 'elders' as hegemonic masculinity, not just the *Führer* and the *Tenno*, for the atrocities during the war and during the occupation of neighbouring countries. In such analyses, the description of the variations 'in the . . . forms of race, class and sexual orientation . . . ' (Menkel-Meadow and Diamond 1991: 225) leads to insights into the cultural and historical construction of masculinities. As far as violence and masculinities are concerned, the study of variations is more promising than the continued use of a monolithic understanding of masculinity in the tradition of binary concepts of 'male' and 'female'.

References

Araki, N. (1988), 'The Role of Police in Japanese Society', *Law and Society Review*, 22/5: 1033–6.

Badinter, E. (1992), *XY: De l'Identité Masculine*. Paris: Odile Jacob.

Baron, L., and Straus, M. (1990), *Four Theories of Rape in American Society*. New Haven: Yale University Press.

Bayley, D. H. (1976), *Forces of Order—Police Behavior in Japan and the United States*. Berkeley: University of California Press.

Benedict, R. (1946), *The Chrysanthemum and the Sword*. Tokyo: Charles E. Tuttle.

Bornoff (1991), *Pink Samurai—The Pursuit and Politics of Sex in Japan*. London: Grafton.

Braithwaite, J. (1989), *Crime, Shame and Reintegration*. Cambridge: Cambridge University Press.

Browning, C. (1991), *Ordinary Men—Reserve Police Battalion 101 and the Final Solution in Poland*. New York: Harper Collins.

Bundeskriminalamt (1994), *Polizeiliche Kriminalstatistik*. Wiesbaden: BKA.

Buruma, I. (1984), *A Japanese Mirror*. London: Jonathan Cape.

—— (1994), *The Wages of Guilt. Memories of War in Germany and Japan*. New York: Farrar Straus Giroux.

Cain, M. (1989), *Growing up Good—Policing the Behaviour of Girls in Europe*. London: Sage.

—— (1990), 'Towards Transgression: New Directions in Feminist Criminology', *International Journal of the Sociology of Law*, 18: 1–12.

Carmichael, G. (1992), 'So Many Children. Colonial and Post-Colonial Demographic Patterns', in K. Saunders and R. Evans, eds., *Gender Relations in Australia. Domination and Negotiation*, 103–43. Marricksville: Harcourt Brace Jovanovich.

Chappell, D. (1993), 'How Violent is Australian Society?' Address given at the Second National Conference on Violence, Canberra 15 June.

Cherry, K. (1987), *Womansword. What Japanese Words say about Women*. Tokyo: Kodansha.

Condon, J. (1991), *A Half Step Behind—Japanese Women Today*, newly expanded edn. Tokyo: Charles E. Tuttle.

Connell, R.W. (1987), *Gender and Power*. Sydney: George Allen and Unwin.

—— (1990), 'The State, Gender, and Sexual Politics', *Theory and Society*, 19/5: 507–44.

—— (1994), 'The Making and Remaking of Masculinities in Contemporary Societies', paper presented at the Conference: 'Reproduktion und Wandel von Männlichkeit', Munich, 27–8 September.

—— (1995), *Masculinities*. Cambridge: Polity Press.

CRAIG, S. (1992), *Men, Masculinity, and the Media*. Newbury Park: Sage.

DOWER, J. (1986), *War without Mercy—Race and Power in the Pacific War*. New York: Pantheon.

DYSART, D. (1992), 'Eroticism and Sexual Imagery in Australian Art', *Art and Australia*, 30/1: 50–3.

EASTEAL, P., ed. (1993), *Without Consent: Confronting Adult Sexual Violence*. Canberra: Australian Institute of Criminology.

EDWARDS, A. (1983), 'Sex Roles: A Problem for Sociology and for Women', *Australian and New Zealand Journal of Sociology*, 19: 385–412.

FEELEY, M., and LITTLE, D. (1991), 'The Vanishing Female: The Decline of Women in the Criminal Process, 1687–1912', *Law and Society Review*, 25/4: 719–57.

GEERTZ, C. (1986), *Works and Lives*. Cambridge: Polity Press.

GIBBONS, D. (1992), 'Talking about Crime: Observations on the Prospects for Causal Theory in Criminology', *Criminal Justice Research Bulletin*, 7/6: 1–10.

—— (1993), *Talking about Crime and Criminals*. Englewood Cliffs, NJ: Prentice Hall.

GILMORE, D. (1990), *Manhood in the Making—Cultural Concepts of Masculinity*. London: Yale University Press.

HAMILTON, V., and SANDERS, J.(1992), *Everyday Justice—Responsibility and the Individual in Japan and the United States*. New Haven/London: Yale University Press.

HAZLEHURST, K., ed. (1987), *Migration, Ethnicity and Crime in Australia*. Canberra: Australian Institute of Criminology.

HORSLEY, W., and BUCKLEY, R. (1991), *Nippon—New Superpower*. London: BBC Books.

HOSHINO, K. (1988), 'Organized Crime and its Origins in Japan', paper presented to the 40th Annual Meeting of the American Society of Criminology, Chicago.

HUGHES, R. (1987), *The Fatal Shore. A History of the Transportation of Convicts to Australia 1787–1868*. London: Pan Books.

JAPAN URBAN SECURITY RESEARCH INSTITUTE (1990), *International Forum on Crime Prevention '90*, Conference proceedings. Tokyo: JUSRI.

KERSTEN J. (1991), 'Kriminalität, Kriminalitätsangst und Männlichkeitskultur', *Kriminalsoziologische Bibliografie*, 18/4: 41–64.

—— (1992) 'Beschämung, Verantwortung, Kontrolle? Japan als Referenzpunkt kulturvergleichender Forschung zur Kriminalitätskontrolle', *Monatsschrift für Kriminologie und Strafrechtsreform*, 75/6: 342–57.

—— (1993*a*), 'Crime and Masculinities in Australia, Germany and Japan', *International Sociology*, 8/4: 461–78.

—— (1993*b*), 'Street Youths, *Bosozoku*, and *Yakuza*: Subculture Formation and Societal Reactions in Japan', *Crime and Delinquency*, 39/3: 277–95.

—— (1994*a*), 'Die Neue Unerbittlichkeit—Law and Order und gesellschaftliche Vergeltungsbedürfnisse' in H.-M. Lohmann, ed., *Extremismus der Mitte—Vom rechten Verständnis der Deutschen Nation*, 233–46. Frankfurt: Fischer Taschenbuch.

—— (1994*b*), 'Karoshi—Vom anderen Leben und Sterben in Japan', *Psychologie Heute*, 58–63.

—— (1994*c*), 'Feindbildkonstruktionen und Gewalthandlungen bei Gruppierungen junger Männer' in W. Bergmann and R. Erb, eds., *Neonazismus und Rechte Subkultur*, 125–42. Berlin: Metropol.

—— (1995*a*), 'Junge Männer und Gewalt', *Neue Kriminalpolitik*, 7/1: 22–7.

Kersten J. (1995b), *Kriminalität, Männlichkeiten und Kultur*. Berlin/New York: Walter de Gruyter (forthcoming).

Kühne, H., and Miyazawa, K. (1991), *Kriminalität und Kriminalitätsbekämpfung in Japan*. Wiesbaden: Bundeskriminalamt.

Lebra, T.S. (1976), *Japanese Patterns of Behaviour*. Honolulu: The University Press of Hawaii.

—— (1984) *Japanese Women—Constraint and Fulfillment*. Honolulu: The University Press of Hawaii.

Menkel-Meadow, C., and Diamond, S. (1991), 'The Content, Method, and Epistomology of Gender in Sociolegal Studies', *Law and Society Review*, 25/2: 221–38.

Messerschmidt, J. (1993), *Masculinities and Crime*. Lanham, MD: Rowman and Littlefield.

Miyazawa, K. (1990), 'The Changing Situation of Crime and Crime Prevention Measures', *International Forum on Crime Prevention*, Conference proceedings, 228–231. Tokyo: JUSRI.

Miyazawa, S. (1992), *Policing in Japan—A Study on Making Crime*. Albany: State University of New York Press.

Moran, A. (1993), 'Patterns of Rape: A Preliminary Queensland Study', in P. Easteal, ed. *Without Consent: Confronting Adult Sexual Violence*, 35–54. Canberra: Australian Institute of Criminology.

Mukherjee, S., and Dagger, K. (1992), *The Size of the Crime Problem in Australia*. Canberra: Australian Institute of Criminology.

National Committee on Violence (1990), *Violence: Directions for Australia*. Canberra: Australian Institute of Criminology.

Newburn, T., and Stanko, E., eds. (1994), *Just Boys doing Business? Men, Masculinities and Crime*. London/New York: Routledge and Kegan Paul.

Polk, K. (1994), *When Men Kill—Scenarios of Masculine Violence*. Cambridge, UK/New York/ Melbourne: Cambridge University Press.

Renzetti, C., and Curran, D. (1992), *Women, Men, and Society*. Boston: Allyn and Bacon.

Research and Training Institute Ministry of Justice Japan (1993) *White Paper on Crime 1992*. Tokyo: RTIMJJ.

Saco, D. (1992), 'Masculinity as Signs: Poststructuralist Feminist Approaches to the Study of Gender' in S. Craig, ed., *Men, Masculinity, and the Media*, 23–40. Newbury Park: Sage.

Saunders, K., and Evans, R., eds. (1992), *Gender Relations in Australia. Domination and Negotiation*. Marricksville: Harcourt Brace Jovanovich.

Shimada, S. (1994), *Grenzgänge—Fremdgänge. Japan und Europa im Kulturvergleich*. Frankfurt/ New York: Campus.

Smith, P. (1993), *Clint Eastwood. A Cultural Production*. London: UCL Press.

Soothill, K. (1991), 'The Changing Face of Rape?', *British Journal of Criminology*, 31/4: 383–92.

Summers A. (1994) *Damned Whores and God's Police. The Colonization of Women in Australia*, updated edn. Ringwood: Penguin.

Tamura, M. (1992), 'The Yakuza and Amphetamine Abuse in Japan', in H. Traver and M. Gaylord, eds., *Drugs, Law and the State*, 99–118. Hongkong: Hongkong University Press.

Taylor, J. (1983), *Shadows of the Rising Sun: A Critical View of the 'Japanese Miracle'*. New York: William Morrow.

van Wolferen, K. (1989), *The Enigma of Japanese Power*. London: Macmillan.

Walker, J. *et al.* (1990), 'A Comparison of Crime in Australia and Other Countries', *Trends and Issues*, 23. Canberra: Australian Institute of Criminology.

Westbury, V. (1991), 'Women Hating—An Australian Talent', *The Bulletin*, 8 October, 82.

[7]

ASSAULT ON MEN

Masculinity and Male Victimization

ELIZABETH A. STANKO* and KATHY HOBDELL†

The purpose of this paper is to present the findings of an exploratory study of how men experience criminally defined physical violence. It places men's responses explicitly within a framework that takes masculinity seriously. This paper concludes by raising theoretical issues about male recipients of violence, about ways to offer support to men who experience violence through an understanding about the context of masculinities in men's lives, and about gender and theorizing in the field of criminology.

Introduction

While official statistics indicate that men are the typical targets of physical violence (Hough and Mayhew 1983; Hough and Mayhew 1985; Gottfredson 1984; Shepherd 1990), we have little sense of the impact of such violence on men's lives. In contrast, feminist research has exposed the hidden reality of violence for women's lives (Kelly 1988; Stanko 1988) and has provided a wealth of information illustrating the impact of men's violence upon women (Stanko 1985).

The pioneering work exploring crime victims' experiences in the UK in depth began in the early 1980s. Maguire, in his study of burglary victims (Maguire 1982), interviewed nearly equal numbers of women and men. While he noted women's more severe emotional reactions, Maguire showed that men were more likely to express anger than distress or shock in response to burglary. It was women's distress, not men's anger, that was explored more fully in the text. In Shapland *et al.*'s 1985 study, men represented three-quarters of those interviewed. The authors found no differences between male and female assault victims. Neither of these studies used the social context of gender, masculinities as well as femininities, as a base from which to explore individual reactions to criminal assault. These contexts, we argue, are important for understanding individual reactions to, and providing support for, men and women experiencing assault.

Criminology's failure to explore men's particular experiences of violence is often attributed to men's reluctance to report 'weakness'. This silence is, we are led to believe, a product of men's hesitation to disclose vulnerability (see e.g. Maxfield 1984; Crawford *et al.* 1990), as in, for instance, the study of the fear of crime, where women's reported fear is the most significant, and consistent, finding (LaGrange and Ferraro 1989). The assumed reticence of men, and the unproblematical acceptance of it by researchers, turns the focus of attention in the victimization literature almost exclusively to women and their experiences of physical and sexual assault or to women's higher fear of crime (Gordon and Riger 1988; Stanko 1987; Warr 1984, 1985). Indeed, with the exception of feminist research, the bulk of criminology continues to eschew the

* Faculty of Law, Brunel University. I am grateful to Claire Corbett, Tony Jefferson and especially to Tim Newburn for commenting upon earlier drafts of this article.
† Islington Victim Support.

exploration of gender as a significant contributor to how victims respond to their experiences of crime and violence. While 'feminist methods' cannot be applied unproblematically to the study of men (Morgan 1992), they do point to the importance of taking experience, located within a gendered context, seriously.

Equally significant is how an image of the invulnerable man, embedded within criminological theory, coincides with a form of what Connell (1987) suggests is 'hegemonic masculinity'. Men who are gay, for example, have a sense of how their gayness places them in many situations of vulnerability in homophobic societies. Non-white men must negotiate their physical vulnerability because of white racism. Although many men's lives are affected by the need to evolve strategies for negotiating violence with other men, research suggests that men restrict their lives less than women do (Gordon and Riger 1988). Nevertheless, the multiple intricacies of people's lives confirm that the reality of male vulnerability is complex.

Avoiding the implications of gendered experience for the delivery of support and aid to victims itself has implications. Models of assisting victims coping with violence have very different approaches and philosophical roots, with the feminist, self-help approach of refuge and rape crisis firmly rooted in an understanding of women's experiences of physical and sexual intrusion (Dobash and Dobash 1992). According to this approach male violence, experienced by an individual woman, is not merely the result of an unfortunate encounter with an individual man, but a manifestation of men's power in general and the subordination of women (see, for example, Kelly 1988; Stanko 1985).

The victim support movement in the UK during the 1980s spoke of victim-coping as a gender-neutral phenomenon, with the lead in government-sanctioned victim support services coming mainly from care- or welfare-oriented groups of volunteers (Maguire and Corbett 1987). Only recently has Victim Support in Britain begun thinking about male victims of crime. Social psychologists, too, have speculated about victims' coping strategies, with some limited attention to gender (Resick 1985). This approach, though, focuses upon how individuals (many of whom just happen to be women) mediate the impact of violence (Burgess and Holmstrom 1974; Bulman-Janoff and Frieze 1983).

To begin a masculine-grounded approach, it is important to make explicit the assumptions about men and risk of violence which, we shall argue, influence the coping strategies of male recipients of violence, the reactions of those around them, and the theorists who generalize about violence and its effect on people of both genders.

Noted but not notable: men in theories about risk of violence

Routine activities and lifestyle theories, by far the most often advanced in explanations of exposure to violence, suggest that features of people's lives, notably their time out of the home, away from suitable guardianship, and in contact with willing offenders, influence their risk of encountering violence (Cohen and Felson 1979; Hindelang *et al.* 1978). While these theories note the powerful predictors of victimization that rest in demographic factors, such as age, race, sex, and marital status, they do not treat these factors as problematical.

Most theories about individual risk of victimization, influenced by data gathered through large-scale victim surveys such as the US Bureau of Justice Statistics' National Crime Survey (Hindelang *et al.* 1978) and the British Crime Surveys (Hough and

Mayhew 1983, 1985; Mayhew *et al.* 1989), focus on features of lifestyle and criminal opportunities to explain *young men's* higher involvement in crime and subsequent injury (Gottfredson 1984; Shepherd 1990). Even the local crime surveys conducted in Britain, especially those conducted through the co-operation of Islington Council, look at victimization through a similar lens of 'lifestyle' or routine activities theory, concentrate on the gendered dimensions of women's high levels of fear and experiences of crime, and place women's fear within a wider structural context of economic, racial, and gendered inequality (Jones *et al.* 1986; Crawford *et al.* 1990). In the second Islington survey, though, Crawford *et al.* (1990) offer no explanations for men's low levels of fear, nor do they offer any detailed analysis of why those men who do report fear, do so.

While lifestyle/routine activities theories are used to explain greater vulnerability to crime of certain categories of people, these theories fail to address the thorny issues of how power, mediated by economics, race/ethnicity, gender, age, physical ability, and so forth, influences risk of victimization, and in particular of violence (see also Stanko 1990). Feminists, for example, have argued that official statistics fail to reflect women's widespread experiences of violence at the hands of known and unknown men (Stanko 1988), and that this reflects an institutionalized bias against the recognition of many forms of violence against women. So too, women's tacit judgements about their right and ability to complain about men's violence illustrates a form of institutionalized impediment (Stanko 1985). Most of the violence men experience, especially that undergone at the hands of other men, has been excluded from the analysis of how power works in that violence, save for the practice of policing of violence against non-white and/or gay men. The state's use of violence against men, particularly working-class and marginalized men, has been documented (Jefferson 1991), yet rarely classified as criminal assault. Thus, while the explanations for women's experiences of men's violence are steeped in the analyses of the structures of patriarchy, explanations of men's experiences of criminal violence are devoid of critical commentary about the structures of men's lives, unless it be the structure of class against class.

Men's actual or potential experiences of violence, whether it be criminally defined or not (Clarkson *et al.* 1991), have not been the primary target for contemporary sociological explorations of masculinity. While in the sociological literature there has been an extended debate on why *some* men get involved in certain sorts of violence (see, for example, Dunning *et al.* 1988; Jefferson 1992; Hobbs and Robins 1991; Hobbs 1989), there is very little on differences in the *impact* of violence. In looking carefully at the combined literature on fear of crime and risk of victimization, one is left with this curious gap. Men, by and large, continue to report significantly less 'fear of crime' than women. Yet men report physical assaults to police and seek emergency medical attention for injury (Shepherd 1990); but there is no sense of how they feel about these experiences of assault. Nor do we have an understanding about how different men, with their varying relationships to and engagement with hegemonic masculinity (see Connell 1987) and with the state, respond to violent victimization. With the contradictions between risk and fear, commentators on gender and fear of crime are merely using a cultural stereotype uncritically as the basis for explanation (see LaGrange and Ferraro 1989; Maxfield 1984; Stanko 1987).

We are left in a position, in theorizing about victimization, that identifies men's lifestyles as the factor that exposes them to danger. Crime prevention advice on violence avoidance, at least for men, is non-existent. The Home Office's flagship crime prevention campaign, *Practical Ways to Crack Crime*, is silent on advice to men. Yet we know that male victims and male offenders are often one and the same individuals (Sampson and Lauritsen 1991). As we shall see later, this knowledge is also held by the police and may affect the way they treat male victims of violence. In the criminological literature, at least, there is little more than recourse to stereotypes of 'macho' reticence. Boys, we are left to sigh, will just be boys.

Men talk: an exploratory study of physical assault

The purpose of this study was to gain an understanding of the coping strategies of men who had experienced a physical assault.[1] Open-ended interviews, designed to explore how assault had affected their lives, were conducted with thirty-three men, all contacted through Islington Victim Support Scheme or through Hobdell's contacts with police and probation officers. Hobdell conducted the interviews. The interview schedule was purposefully designed to explore the men's understanding of the gendered context of their responses to assault.

The sample is by no means representative of all men who experience assault; most of the men were victims of violence *recorded* by the police. All had experienced some emotional and physical injury, and legal categories of the recorded crimes ranged from actual and grievous bodily harm, street robbery, and aggravated burglary to common assault. It included men injured in the course of their work and others injured in their own homes, outdoors, on their way to and from home, or in public places. Their assailants were mainly strangers, although customers, clients, and ex-partners' lovers were represented among the offenders. All but one of their assailants were men. Most of the assaulted were injured in what could be characterized as an 'unfair' fight (Shapland *et al.* 1985; Stanko 1990). The men who were referred to Victim Support were more likely to have been attacked by strangers, as is the case for crime against women.[2]

Nineteen of these men had more than one reported experience of violent victimization in adulthood. They were mainly white and heterosexual, although some were homosexual or bisexual, and some were from the ethnic minority communities.[3] Their ages ranged from 16 to 82, with clustering around the 20–30 age group.

The Male Frame

The men interviewed located their emotional, physical, and social responses to their victimization in relation to 'being men'. The frame of masculinity was quite apparent, and was the focus for discussion within the interviews. The men admitted a reticence around speaking of the injuries they had suffered as a result of the crimes and their feelings related to the assaults. It seemed that the occasion for the interview, however,

[1] The study was undertaken by K. Hobdell, supervised by E. Stanko in 1987–8, and funded by the Cripplegate Foundation. Hobdell conducted all the interviews.

[2] Although Victim Support has recently published a report on domestic violence (1992), many schemes are still reluctant to take on violence against women whose assailants are husbands/lovers.

[3] Racial violence on non-white men, and how non-white men experience violence within the context of masculinities and institutionalized racism, especially that of policing, is an important area for future study.

enabled men to speak about their feelings, in spite of their suggestion that such emotions were rarely allowed to surface.

Looking back on it, I wasn't really able to actually look at it in a way that would have been helpful . . . because the male bit in me said, 'You ought to be able to cope, you ought to be able to be strong enough to face aggression when necessary' . . . it's irrational. (Tom)

Men don't help their cause, do they? They've got this stone-age macho image. They go out to work . . . that's so common in the police force, because you have a macho uniform, you have macho powers and authority. Men in the police don't open up. Men in general. My male friends don't . . . But my own knowledge of men who are prepared to talk freely, it's invariably with a woman. (police officer)

The men used terms such as 'the John Wayne syndrome', 'macho-man', 'cave man', 'defender', and 'natural man' to articulate the existence of an ideal image of manhood.

I think a woman is [to be] taken care of by men and men are fighters in their own right. They [men] don't want no one to take care, they take care of themselves. They fight for their own ends like I have done. That's a natural man. (Ted)

Negotiating physical violence while growing up was a backdrop to the men's lives. Gay men, black men, able-bodied men, working-class men, or middle-class men (and men with all the various intersecting features of race–class–sexual orientation–physical ability–geographical setting–etcetera) noted the compounding factors of negotiating violence. For example, in Stanko's (1990) study, one man recalled attending secondary school in the heart of a 'National Front' neighbourhood. Potential danger for him was clearly linked with the threat of racial violence in a specific locale with a reputation for supporting white supremacy. Not all men participated in the 'rough and tumble' of childhood and adolescence. Some avoided violence; some described past physical confrontations as 'just the usual schoolyard fights', 'a few scuffles a year', 'nothing too serious, pulling punches and playground fights'. Violence between boys was also understood as a fight between a white boy and a black boy; a 'femininized' boy and an appropriately masculine boy; an Irish boy and a local, East End lad; and so forth. Here too the men noted the complexities of race, class, sexual orientation, physical ability, and particularities of geographical areas on negotiations of violence.

As Connell (1991) has noted, within some men's lives violent incidents seem to be continuous (see also Robins 1992). Thus, the 'nothing too serious' is a very relative assessment, another indication of how men contextualize experiences of violence.[4] A few spoke of seeing 'a lot of bad things happening', and a few acquired scars from fighting as 'status symbols' (see also Seidler 1991; Stanko 1990).

Some of the men grew up in households with varying amounts of domestic violence. By and large, though, all this violence from friends and kin was something the men 'just dealt with'. The men spoke about vulnerability in terms of physical strength. Danger and harm were described in terms of a physical challenge which many men assumed, on a one-to-one confrontation, they could probably handle. Many men were, however, able to describe instances when they became uneasy because they felt physically

[4] Newburn (personal communication) notes that 'the usual schoolyard fights' used to 'scare the shit out' of him. However, as a boy, he learned to remain close enough to the violence to pretend that he was not afraid of it, and so he was able to join in the general banter about what 'a good fight' it had been.

vulnerable to groups of young men, or to situations they knew to be, or according to folklore might be, dangerous. 'Bad' pubs, 'bad' sides of town, untrustworthy 'characters' could then be avoided or frequented, depending on whether one wished to participate in or avoid violence. Many men suggested that, in negotiating danger, they oriented management of danger to that of physical contests with men, by avoiding either dangerous situations or dangerous groups of men (usually young men).[5]

Masculine confrontations often involve 'character contests' (Athens 1980) or 'saving face' (Connell 1991). In other words, part of men's knowledge involves anticipating and/or avoiding masculine character contests, even if they choose actively to initiate them. Vulnerability to attack was characterized by the men interviewed here as stemming from situations where the (later) victim did not start the fight himself or where the 'rules' changed; for example, with the opponent pulling out a knife. Violence may be 'justified' when the other man or men initiate the fight (Connell 1991). This may be part of the explanation why this particular event was experienced as traumatic. One man, for example, physically confronted one of two assailants during an attempted robbery. He was slashed in the back with a Stanley knife by the other assailant, who thereby changed the rules of the 'fair' refusal to an 'unfair' encounter.

When such confrontations are not voluntary, nor 'fair', then they become transformative events, illustrations of a kind of vulnerability many men do not *consciously* consider when they think about their personal safety. This is in sharp contrast to how many women consciously negotiate their vulnerability, knowing that confrontation with even a single man can be physically, but for most, more importantly, sexually threatening (see Stanko 1990; Gordon and Riger 1988).[6] For most of the men in this study, injured outside of employment, the likelihood of *intrusive* physical violence had never worried them, even though some reported witnessing violent incidents at places they frequented, such as pubs, discos, and football matches. There seems to be an assumption, at least in terms of the crime prevention literature, that men can handle themselves in physical contests, as long as they are 'fair', or that they feel competent to spot potential trouble, thus avoiding conflict. There also seems to be a tacit understanding that the men who must encounter routine harassment and threat, because of colour, sexual orientation, and so forth, do so as part of their successful negotiation of their safety as men.

For those injured at work (police and probation officers, publicans, post office clerks), confrontations were almost 'expected'.

Everybody in this job who's walking the streets has got to expect an assault. (police officer)

You have to be in such a way [expect racial harassment] in the Post Office behind [the] counter. You have to forgive and forget. You have to be abuse-proof. In the Post Office, the customer comes first. (Jobrul)

The experience of violence considered the 'worst' was generally the one that was the most recent, or where the recipient could not control how the violence occurred, or

[5] Sexual danger is a reality for some men. Prison is the place where men acknowledge the potential threat of rape (Lockwood 1980; Wooden and Parker 1982). Recent studies of male rape victims now document the impact of sexual violence upon some men's lives (see Mezey and King 1992).

[6] It may be that one of the most disarming aspects of female offenders is that victims do not anticipate possible danger. Yet few women take advantage of their relative immunity.

because it happened 'on top of' unresolved consequences of previous trauma (Newburn 1992).

What is interesting about 'transformative violence' is how this type of violence comes to be characterized as an intrusive, potentially criminal matter.

I've seen plenty . . . situations where you've had to be tough and in control. I've had everything. I've been attacked in the bar with a knife on a few occasions . . . I've been to Court on many occasions through violence. You're prepared for it. [Yet this time] It's a different type of violence. (publican)

The male frame thus provided some measurement of what was within the bounds of what each man considered appropriate male confrontations. The men often recognized, however, the limitations of an exaggerated image of the capable man. Moreover, they sometimes questioned how other men could have been so indifferent to how the recipients might suffer from an unwarranted attack.

I can't understand it, why someone for no reason, would pick on someone and beat the shit out of them . . . I keep thinking it's to do with power, these large groups of males and they think they're strong to show power and machismo. (Frank)

The male frame was a core component in making sense of other men's behaviour, and their own reactions/responses to their being targets of other men's unprovoked violence. But men are not a homogeneous group to be referred to simplistically as thinking, experiencing, or behaving in *a* particular way. Rather, their social and psychological worlds are mediated by their age, ethnic origin, sexual orientation, religion, employment, and so on. Indeed, their understanding of, and playing out of, their masculinity is also affected in just such ways (see Connell 1987, 1991). Consequently, one might expect that just as attitudes to crime vary among men, so do reactions to criminal victimization.

The Men's Reactions to Victimization

As would be expected from previous general research on reactions to victimization (Bulman-Janoff and Frieze 1983; Kilpatrick 1985; Maguire 1982; Maguire and Corbett 1987; Shapland *et al.* 1985), the men's accounts of the effects of assault ranged from the immediate, within hours of the assault, to those lingering over weeks and months, and even extending over years. At the time of assault, the impact was generally one of shock, fear, anger, and/or disbelief. This seemed to be followed by a time in which the experience itself, and the consequences of it, were assimilated and incorporated within the context of the individual's life. For each man, the experience was unique. For some, it was one of a series of recently experienced stressful life events; for others, it was a total disruption of a reasonable life-routine. This continuum of physical and emotional reactions to assault has been noted by others (see, in particular, Shapland *et al.* 1985).

Physical effects

The body, suggests Connell (1987), is a crucial locus for men's sense of themselves as men. Physical injury transforms what may have been previously healthy and capable of defending one's space in a masculine order to the body of a 'lesser man'. Physical injury due to criminal injury is an affront as much to a masculine order of things as it is to the individual man.

The physical injuries sustained ranged from bruising to severe internal and external injuries. Five men were in intensive care and others faced varied periods in hospital. Eight men were off work for more than six weeks. Over half the men interviewed received out-patient treatment in hospital. Over half of the men reported long-term physical problems as a result of their injury. These ranged from partial paralysis to muscle wastage and loss of sensation, hearing problems, and/or headaches. Seven bore scars which were either a constant reminder of the experience or a disfigurement, and, for some, a source of discomfort and pain. Experiencing severe injury perhaps acted as a catalyst for the respondents' self-reflection.

Emotional effects

Trauma resulting from victimization is typically described as 'post-traumatic stress'. Defined as a 'normal' reaction to an event that is outside the range of usual human experience and that would be markedly distressing to almost anyone, post-traumatic stress disorder, as described in DSM-III-R (American Psychiatric Association 1987), has become the professional shorthand for many victims' responses to sudden events. What is interesting in the present context is that the men termed this transformative violence as traumatic, distinguishing it from 'normal' violence.[7] They spoke clearly and at length of the traumatic consequences of this kind of attack.

The reaction reported most consistently was that of fear. There were men who said that at the time of the assault they were in fear of their lives, convinced that they could be killed or severely mutilated. Four feared they might die as a result of their injuries and one elderly man felt that the shock of the experience might kill him. Three men were reluctant to leave hospital because it was where they felt safe. Some men experienced fear in relation to particular venues, situations which served as triggers to remind the victim of the stressful event. For example, spotting a security van parked outside a bank, being in the proximity of a mainline station, seeing someone who resembled the attacker, or being in a large crowd of people could cause a great deal of anxiety.

I'm afraid I'm not so sociable as I was . . . I won't casually talk to people like I used to . . . I've definitely changed. (Gerard)

It's anywhere there's a large group of males . . . any group of over 4 males can start me to look . . . I would be conscious that they were there. The last thing I'd do in my whole life . . . is to go to a football match. (Frank)

I never open the door to anybody. If people knock on the door at night I'm still shaking like a leaf all the time. Even when friends come . . . I don't suppose I'll ever feel safe. (Brian)

Fear, phobias, disruptions to routine sleep and social patterns, hypervigilance, and exaggerated startle responses were commonplace. These reactions are typical of 'post-

[7] There is a glaring gap in the criminological literature about how women and men make sense of 'normal' violence. Stanko's research (1990) merely raises questions about gender and interpretations of violence.

traumatic stress'. Many of the men reported also having to deal with intense feelings of anger, hatred and a desire for revenge.

I think I'm feeling more angry nowadays. I felt really hurt at first. I feel angry because I feel like I've been violated in some way. Perhaps when I've got to a more altruistic stage I'd like people to understand what it is for men to go through this sort of thing. Because I'm a big, powerful man and part of the thing is that I could kill somebody. I feel that part of being a male is learning how to control that aggression that we all have and I feel I should have a bit of support about that, simply because I didn't use what I've got. (Chris)

I lose my temper a lot, whereas before I wouldn't. I get more uptight. I'm that bit nervous about things. (Patrick)

I've become an aggressive person since this. I'm on the defensive the whole time. I feel threatened and I'm ready to jump. I know I shouldn't. That's how it is. I try not to be. (Tim)

Of the thirty-three men interviewed, ten felt this experience of victimization had radically altered their lives and to some extent their personalities. For five, this was a totally negative outcome, leaving them with feelings of anger, vulnerability, fear, and mistrust. Three men experienced severe psychological problems, two of whom were referred to psychiatric departments. There was no apparent evidence of any existing psychological disturbance in any of these three men prior to the assault.

I had the shakes terrible. Occasionally now for about half an hour, I'll get it and then it will go away again. Anywhere there's a queue I can't wait to get out. I can't bear the thought of anyone behind me. (Tim)

Those who were most severely affected all expressed strong notions about how men needed 'to fend for themselves'. Thus these men had difficulty sharing their emotional reactions to being victimized, and reconciling their intense feelings of vulnerability.

I think's that's what makes me depressed. You can't talk about it. You feel you've got to hold on to your masculine image. You feel like a sissy. (Tim)

It's the male thing, isn't it. It's just what I'm saying. You like to think you don't need help, you can work your own way. (Mike)

It's hard to admit all these things. It makes you feel that you are weak and you can't stand your ground. (James)

One man spoke of his changing emotions, and shared them with his friends:

You get depressed, very depressed. I used to make a joke of it . . . I started crying when they said I was going to lose my eye. I had quite a few emotional scenes with my friends . . . (Dave)

Humour, noted by some of the other men, could help to minimize the horror of the attack.

We've dealt with it by joking about it. (Paul)

These thirty-three men articulate the many aspects of facing traumatic events: minimizing the impact, joking about it, feeling overwhelmed and, at times, 'out of control'. Some completely changed their lives, moved out of the area, changed jobs, and others put the experience into perspective.

Much as it's been bad, I've learnt a lot. It's given me quite a lot of insight. The society that we live in creates these people . . . Men are still measured by how tough they are. When you're young, you're tough. That's how you get respected. We all suffer from that. (Dave)

It's not like the films at all, where you get beaten up by John Wayne and you get up again. There are so many images of violence for men and they all get up and they're the same. It's not true. It's a lie! (Chris)

While some men put their experiences into a perspective which allowed some reflection about their position as men, others responded by avoiding and trying to forget.

If you talk you're reminding [yourself] about the whole thing and coming in your mind the whole time and you'll just start worrying. Now you're remembering and you'll just live frightenedly . . . You have to die once, you don't have to die two times. If you start to worry, worry kills the people. (Jobrul)

To tell the truth I didn't really want to know anything about it, but I had to find out about the court. I just wanted to forget all about it, like it never happened. (Frank)

I get muzzy in the head. I try to forget it, which is not easy. I don't talk about it to anybody. I don't want anyone else to mention it to me or to anyone else either. (Walter)

By and large, the male frame provided the foundation for men's responses to assault. The range of the responses was wide, as were the consequent behavioural changes.

Behavioural effects

However the men characterized the violence to themselves, there were many changes in their habits and actions. Some took precautionary or avoidance measures, while others armed themselves for future encounters. Some chose a period of social isolation:

I was in the house the whole time. I was getting terribly depressed. I didn't want to go out, didn't want to meet people. (James)

Some became hypervigilant about their personal safety:

It means that you're always locking doors and you're being more careful than you were before . . . you're always looking behind you and any noise at all scares you. (Patrick)

For one man, the fact that he felt vulnerable was an affront to his masculinity, and his duty to protect women.

I was never frightened of anyone . . . I still have those feelings but I can't do much about it now, so I have to shut up. I've become a coward I suppose. I'm frightened to be as I was . . . If I walk out with my wife or daughters I feel I can't protect them and that's not nice. Your manhood is taken away from you. I feel if someone attacks me they will do more damage than they realize. I can't defend myself. (Ted)

These violent encounters effectively altered the men's strategies of safety. While there was a range of adjustment to this orientation to personal safety involving the reconsideration and rearrangement of precautionary behaviour, many of the men were angry that they now had to consider personal safety as *consciously* problematical. This state, they felt, was unmanly.

Ten of the thirty-three men began carrying objects as self-defence weapons, either outdoors or at home. These objects ranged from a hammer to keys or a walking stick.

I do keep myself armed with a weapon, since then, some heavy weapon that might slow down my assailant. I need that extra care. (Tim)

One man has carried an umbrella for self-protection every day since a robbery five years ago.

Others' reactions and support

Research suggests that a victim's social support network is important in helping, or hindering, a person's ability to cope with a traumatic event (Wortman 1983; Hoff 1990). Others' responses can be both positive and negative experiences for the traumatized. Social institutions, such as the police, hospital, court, or employer, can also help or hinder coming to terms with an assault. Secondary victimization (Maguire and Pointing 1988) may exacerbate the effects of crime upon a victim. These responses too show how masculinity remains in the frame of victimization. While many of the men spoke of positive support, they also spoke of unsympathetic or inappropriate responses. These came from the same types of individuals who often provided sympathetic support.

Partners, family, and friends The support most men received was of an emotional nature, generally a response of concern and empathy. For a few, it meant having people available to them to contact at any time, people who were ready to hear and to share deeply distressing and humiliating feelings of shame, hate, and fear.

Everyone was coming up to me [in hospital], a load. That was one thing about it. I had swarms of people I'd not seen for donkey's, which was really nice. I think half of it was curiosity; they'd heard different stories. (Lloyd)

Men's need for women's support was often expressed. The use of women for emotional support was common. At the same time, men often reported that this emotional sharing brought additional anxiety, either because they wished to protect the women from the harsh realities of their experiences, because they shunned the feelings of being smothered by caring, or because they felt guilt about the burden this placed on these women. For younger men, whose mothers bore the brunt of this concern, there were additional problems.

I didn't say anything because I didn't want my Mum to get worried. (Sanjay)

Me old girl was going 'Come home early, don't do anything or say anything to him' [the assailant]. I felt like I was a little kid again. It feel horrible, but at least I knew me mum cares about me. It's nice being cared for. (Ray)

A number of the married men did not want to share the intensity of their feelings with their wives, for various reasons: they felt it was weak and unmanly to talk about feelings, or they wanted to protect their wives, or felt that their feelings were too horrendous and might be damaging to them.

I didn't speak to the wife. I didn't want to tarnish her with what happened that night. I felt it was dirty . . . not only what happened, but the feelings I had. I hated [them]. (Bill)

What I don't like is the feeling I have scarred her [his wife]. However, it's brought us closer together. (police officer)

Nine men described the male support they received as promises to retaliate (see also Shapland *et al.* 1985). Men 'rallied' around to 'put things right' or 'even the score', illustrating how masculinity and its forms are collective processes (see Connell 1991). In some cases the victim perceived this as 'just letting off steam', but generally it was seen as a genuine offer. Although providing some form of comfort and assurance that the assault was 'not a fair contest', this also raised problems for some men concerned about the potential escalation of violence.

At the time I had untold amount of people saying, 'We'll find who it is for you and we'll see it out.' A lot of people were offering to sort it out for me. (Lloyd)

Some reported negative comments which reflected upon their competence as men.

They [my friends] said, 'You should have known better not to go out at that time of night.' And a doctor in casualty said 'Why didn't you give them the money?' I said I hadn't the time! (James)

My brother said, 'What's the matter, are you getting old or something? Aren't you able to take care of yourself?' I thought to myself, he could be right. It made it worse. It made your ego feel worse. (Tim)

Support of family and friends, regarded as key to coping with trauma, can be both helpful and a hindrance. These contradictions deserve more research, particularly the contribution of the male frame to how such support and assistance is received by the assaulted man.

Institutional supports Men, especially young men, are by far the most typical targets for police scrutiny (Rawlings and Stanko 1991). The men in this study characterized their treatment by the police in the context of their previous contacts with police, and with the expectation that they would be treated 'as victims'. Police responses, as might be expected, were reported as both positive and negative.

They were really friendly for a change. Their attitude towards me was nice. It surprised me. I've been searched a couple of times in the street and it's quite the opposite thing. (Frank)

They [the police] have been very good. I haven't felt a nasty attitude from them at all. They're treating it like a nasty crime, which it was, even though they know it was a 'queer-bashing'. (Paul)

Just as the police were able to provide positive support for some, they also annoyed and angered some of the men.

They [the police] were going, 'Who done it?' and I was going, 'I don't know.' They were going,

'Don't hassle us, we only want to do our work.' They were asking for about half an hour and I'm still lying on the floor!' (Ray)

It may be that police sometimes assume that many assaults involving men are just 'fair fights' gone awry. To what extent police, usually male officers, bring their own experiences/assumptions of male–male violence to bear when handling such complaints is an important area for future research. Whatever the case, police referrals to Victim Support, as Maguire and Corbett's (1987) research shows, tend to underrepresent male victims of crime.

Nineteen men had been referred to, and contacted by, their local Victim Support Scheme. All nineteen had been informed of the Criminal Injuries Compensation Board and had been offered assistance with claims forms. Some were able to ask for, and receive, emotional support.

She [the Co-ordinator] was marvellous. It was the fact that somebody outside of my own circle could care enough to come around and sort of lift me off the floor. She put new heart into me. (Basil)

Others could not find a way to ask for help.

A couple of times I was wishing [I had contacted Victim Support]. Well, I should have got in touch with you. I was wishing that I'd got another letter from you. (Mike)

Clearly, there is a need for far more research about how men accept and ask for support after experiencing violence. This support may indeed be viewed as crime prevention, since many men seem to make some reflections about violence in general. One man in Stanko's study (1990), for example, began to rethink his own participation in violence after a 'transformative violent' event.

Most of the men injured at work experienced a lack of support from their employers. They complained of the short shrift they received from employers, who after all, had some responsibility at least towards their employees who were injured at work.

The management were not good at all, I think the Head [Teacher] just saw it as an embarrassment or something that might tarnish the image of the school. (Chris)

Looking back, the help that I received through normal probation supervision was not appropriate to the fear and victimization. I felt that it increased my sense of victimization and it increased my denial. I think violence has got to be a much more open subject for people working in vulnerable professions with violent people. It's got to be an ongoing acknowledgement, included in training. (Tom)

They [the pub owners] just think of one thing, that the pub's running all right. They were more concerned with what might have been taken than about me. They never came to see me in hospital at all. You're an insurance cover for their business. You look after their money . . . it's because of their money that you get broken into. (Patrick)

Dissatisfaction with their treatment in court was also expressed by some. Six of the ten men who attended Crown Court found the experience stressful, disturbing, or disappointing.

I felt dirtied by what the person [barrister] was insinuating about my sexuality and my professional standing. He just went for everything. It made me feel sick. I was the one that was on trial. (Chris)

The thing that I resent most about the criminal justice system dealing with this was his barrister, floating the possibility that I had an extra thin skull and so it was not really [the assailant's] responsibility. My skull is normal. The unfortunate thing was he hit me on the parietal bone. I actually resent that a lot more than I resent that I'm a spastic. (Martin)

Men's needs as victims: observations of the study

Maguire (1984) suggests that victims' needs are not a fixed, objectively discernible and quantifiable entity. Needs are in some senses negotiated with the person or agency offering assistance, and the closer the relationship, the more likely they are to emerge. This study bears this out, but also implies that the negotiation is a two-way process. Gender plays a significant part in this negotiation.

If we look at what had helped these men, perhaps 'needs' become more sharply defined. First, the recognition by others with whom they came into contact that they *had* suffered an assault was a validation that this assault was *not* some mutual exchange of blows. Second, the empathy shown to them as *victims* opened the way to hear how this violence was perhaps different from other experiences of violence. Third, practical assistance came without judgements about their masculinity. Fourth, it was the positive support, especially by male 'mates' and female family and intimates, that most benefited many of the men. Fifth, there is no doubt that avoidance, humour, and minimizing were useful ways of dealing with the violence for some men.

However, for those men who felt that expression of emotion is not 'macho', there is a trap. With a need to retain their masculinity and therefore their self-esteem, they are then left to cope with intense, confusing, and at times overwhelming feelings, as they put themselves beyond the release of sharing with others.

Masculinity and Victimization

What is never questioned in the literature on crime, victimization, and fear of crime is masculinity. Not only have those studying victimization neglected masculinity, but criminologists have generally ignored the most basic of facts: men are overwhelmingly the law-breakers *and* the law-enforcers. As feminist criminologists have pointed out, this *fact* of gender does have consequences, for victims, offenders, and professionals working within the system. It surely has consequences for how police and others respond to men who are assaulted.

From this study, it appears that male victims of assault view their victimization through a male frame, the essence of which sees victimization as 'weak and helpless'. This creates difficulties for men in expressing feelings, leaving them isolated and unable to ask for support. Moreover, men seem to be able to externalize blame, as opposed to women, who have a tendency to internalize blame when victimized. Feelings of anger are quite prominent in men and dealing with their anger is often a problem for others.

We have no doubt that our understanding of victims and victimization can only be enhanced when criminologists begin to take masculinity seriously. This research, exploratory in scope, raises many questions about the processes of coping with violence, about how men negotiate violence, and how criminal justice professionals view male victims. No longer is it appropriate to dismiss men as 'naturally' reticent. Unless we probe deeper into men's lives, we will fail to advance what we know about crime and victimization.

References

ATHENS, L. (1980), *Violent Criminal Acts and Actors*. London: Routledge Kegan Paul.

AMERICAN PSYCHIATRIC ASSOCIATION (1987), *Diagnostic and Statistical Manual of Mental Disorders*. Washington, DC: APA.

BULMAN-JANOFF, R., and FRIEZE, I. (1983), 'A Theoretical Perspective for Understanding Reactions to Victimization', *Journal of Social Issues*, 39/2: 1–17.

BURGESS, A., and HOLMSTROM, L. (1974), 'Rape Trauma Syndrome', *American Journal of Psychiatry*, 131: 981–6.

CLARKSON, C., CRETNEY, A., DAVIS, G., JONES, S., and SHEPHERD, J. (1991), 'The Background, Reporting, and Criminal Prosecution of Assaults', paper delivered to the 1991 British Criminology Meeting, York.

COHEN, L., and FELSON, M. (1979), 'Social Change and Crime Rate Trends: A Routine Activity Approach', *American Sociological Review*, 44/4: 588–608.

CONNELL, R. (1987), *Gender and Power*. Stanford: Stanford University Press.

—— (1991), 'Live Fast and Die Young: The Construction of Masculinity among Young Working-Class Men on the Margin of the Labour Market', *The Australian and New Zealand Journal of Sociology*, 27/2: 141–71.

CRAWFORD, A., JONES, T., WOODHOUSE, T., and YOUNG, J. (1990), *The Second Islington Crime Survey*. London: Middlesex Polytechnic.

DOBASH, R. E., and DOBASH, R. P. (1992), *Women, Violence and Social Change*. London: Routledge.

DUNNING, E., MURPHY, P., and WILLIAMS, J. (1988), *Social Roots of Football Hooliganism*. London: Routledge.

GORDON, M., and RIGER, S. (1988), *The Female Fear*. New York: Free Press.

GOTTFREDSON, M. (1984), *Victims of Crime: Dimensions of Risk*. London: HMSO.

HINDELANG, M., GOTTFREDSON, M., and GAROFALO, J. (1978), *Victims of Personal Crime*. Cambridge, Mass.: Ballinger.

HOBBS, D. (1989), *Doing the Business*. Oxford: Oxford University Press.

HOBBS, D., and ROBINS, D. (1991), 'The Boy Done Good: Football Violence, Changes and Continuities', *Sociological Review*, 39/3: 551–81.

HOFF, L. A. (1990), *Battered Women as Survivors*. London: Routledge.

HOUGH, M., and MAYHEW, P. (1983), *The British Crime Survey*. London: HMSO.

—— (1985), *Taking Account of Crime: Key Findings from the 1984 British Crime Survey*. London: HMSO.

JEFFERSON, T. (1990), *The Case against Paramilitary Policing*. Milton Keynes: Open University Press.

—— (1992), ' "Wheelin' and Stealin' " ', *Achilles Heel*, no. 13, Summer: 10–13.

JONES, T., MACLEAN, B., and YOUNG, J. (1986), *The Islington Crime Survey*. Aldershot: Gower.

KELLY, L. (1988), *Surviving Sexual Violence*. Cambridge: Polity.

KILPATRICK, D. (1985), 'Research on Long-term Effects of Criminal Victimisation: Scientific, Service Delivery and Public Policy Perspectives', Washington DC: National Institute for Mental Health.

ASSAULT ON MEN

LAGRANGE, R., and FERRARO, K. (1989), 'Assessing Age and Gender Differences in Perceived Risk and Fear of Crime', *Criminology*, 27/4: 697–719.

LOCKWOOD, D. (1980), *Prison Sexual Violence*. New York: Elsevier.

MAGUIRE, M. (1982), *Burglary in a Dwelling*. London: Heinemann.

—— (1984), 'Victims Needs and Victim Services: Indications from Research', paper delivered to the Third International Institute on Victimology, Lisbon, Portugal.

MAGUIRE, M., and CORBETT, C. (1987), *The Effects of Crime and the Work of Victim Support Schemes*. Aldershot: Gower.

MAGUIRE, M., and POINTING, J., eds. (1988), *Victims of Crime: A New Deal?* Milton Keynes: Open University Press.

MAXFIELD, M. (1984), *Fear of Crime in England and Wales*. London: HMSO.

MAYHEW, P., DOWDS, L., and ELLIOT, D. (1989), *The 1988 British Crime Survey*. London: HMSO.

MEZEY, G., and KING, M. (1992), *Male Victims of Sexual Assault*. Oxford: Oxford University Press.

MORGAN, D. (1992), *Discovering Men*. London: Routledge.

NEWBURN, T. (1992), 'Making a Difference: Social Work after Hillsborough', report submitted to Rowntree Foundation.

RAWLINGS, P., and STANKO, E. (1991), 'Precarious Protection: Policing, Crime Prevention and Personal Safety', paper delivered to the 1991 British Criminology Conference, York.

RESICK, P. (1985), 'Reactions of Female and Male Victims of Rape or Robbery', unpublished paper, University of Missouri, St. Louis.

ROBINS, D. (1992), *Tarnished Vision*. Oxford: Oxford University Press.

SAMPSON, R., and LAURITSEN, J. (1991), 'Violent Victimisation and Offending: Individual, Situational and Community-level Risk Factors', unpublished paper, University of Missouri, St. Louis.

SEIDLER, V. (1991), *Recreating Sexual Politics*. London: Routledge.

SHAPLAND, J., WILLMORE, P., and DUFF, P. (1985), *Victims in the Criminal Justice System*. London: Routledge.

SHEPHERD, J. (1990), 'Violent Crime in Bristol: An Accident and Emergency Department Perspective', *British Journal of Criminology*, 30/3: 289–305.

STANKO, E. (1985), *Intimate Intrusions*. London: Routledge.

—— (1988), 'Hidden Violence to Women', in Maguire and Pointing, eds., *Victims of Crime: A New Deal?*: 40–6.

—— (1987), 'Typical Violence, Normal Precaution: Men, Women, and Interpersonal Violence in England, Wales, Scotland and the USA', in Hanmer and Maynard, eds., *Women, Violence and Social Control*. London: Macmillan.

—— (1990), *Everyday Violence*. London: Pandora.

VICTIM SUPPORT (1992), *Domestic Violence: Report of a National Inter-Agency Working Party*. London: Victim Support.

WARR, M. (1984), 'Fear of Victimization: Why are Women and the Elderly More Afraid?', *Social Science Quarterly*, 65: 681–702.

—— (1985), 'Fear of Rape among Urban Women', *Social Problems*, 32/3: 238–50.

WOODEN, W. S., and PARKER, J. (1982), *Men Behind Bars: Sexual Exploitation in Prison*. New York: Da Capo Press.

WORTMAN, C. (1983), 'Coping with Victimisation: Conclusions and Implications for Future Research', *Journal of Social Issues*, 39/2: 195–221.

[8]

Enacting Masculinity: Antigay Violence and Group Rape as Participatory Theater

Karen Franklin

Abstract: Two frequent types of violence by young men in groups are rapes of women and assaults on perceived gay men. This article draws on scholarship from multiple disciplines to propose a theoretical linkage between these two seemingly disparate forms of violence. It proposes that the two forms of violence serve near-identical functions for certain young men. These functions include social bonding, the celebration of power, and the public display of heterosexual masculinity through the subordination of women and men perceived as feminine. In other words, group rape of women and violence against homosexuals are parallel forms of cultural theater, with the victims serving as interchangeable dramatic props. This argument is advanced through an examination of a 2003 case in which athletes from Mepham High School in Long Island, New York, sexually assaulted their younger teammates during a week-long summer training camp.

Key words: gang rape; gay-bashing; violent offenders; sex offending; social norms

At a summer football camp in August 2003, a group of upper class boys from Mepham High School in Long Island, New York, assaulted several younger teammates over a period of days (Pingel, 2004). Three younger boys were singled out for especially brutal treatment, including anal rape with broomsticks and other objects. None of the boys told their coaches what had happened; their ordeals only came to light because one boy needed medical treatment after he returned home. The three main offenders were lightly punished: one was sent to a juvenile boot camp, another went to a juvenile detention facility, and a third went home on probation.

The victims in this case were not female, nor were they—to public knowledge—sexual minority. However, this incident links aspects of both antigay violence and the group rape of girls and women. Indeed, this incident is an example of the functional overlap between different forms of violence committed by young men in groups. Specifically, it is argued here that young men in certain social environments choose victims who symbolize the feminine "other," whether they be girls, women, gay men,[1] or—as in this case—younger and weaker males.

This article posits that the commonplace nature of antigay violence and group rape in modern Western societies is because both are ideal ways for young men to visibly demonstrate their masculinity, which includes heterosexuality as a central element. Compared with other types of violent crime, these crimes are especially likely to involve young males who

1. This article does not address violence against lesbians, which has overlaps with both violence against gay men and violence against women more generally (Franklin, 1997). The limited empirical research suggests that assaults on perceived lesbians are often an escalation of anti-woman attacks (Tallmer, 1984; von Schulthess, 1992). Pharr (1988) argues that any woman who opposes male dominance and control, regardless of sexual orientation, may be labeled a lesbian and attacked. The 2003 murder of 15-year-old Sakia Gunn in Newark, New Jersey (Wang, 2003), is a recent example of this phenomenon.

Correspondence concerning this article should be addressed to Karen Franklin, P.O. Box 1084, El Cerrito, CA 94530. E-mail: mail@karenfranklin.com are strangers or only casual acquaintances to the victim, and victims who are outnumbered. In addition, most offenders in both categories are never apprehended or prosecuted. In both forms of group violence, young men ritualistically enact an exaggerated version of the gender-role norms expected of men in hypermasculine social environments. Their victims serve as almost interchangeable dramatic props in this performance art, in that both females and gay men symbolize the nonmasculine "other."

The article starts by outlining a few relevant aspects of group violence before describing general features of antigay violence and group rape. It then examines the Long Island case as an example of the almost interchangeable nature of victims in youthful male group violence in the service of masculine identity development.

Group Violence

Because a large proportion of violence is committed by individuals who normally obey the law (Mawson, 1987; see also Baron & Richardson, 1994), scholars are increasingly focusing on situational contributors to violence, for example intoxication and conditions of anonymity that decrease the likelihood of being caught. This situational focus is particularly useful in studying youth violence. There is increasing research support for the idea that violence is a young man's game, something that most men mature out of by their late 20s (Maruna, 2001; Mawson, 1987). As they mature and assume adult roles and responsibilities, men typically shift their allegiances from their teenage friends to their families, partners, children, and careers (Sampson & Laub, 1993).

As this research implies, an important contributor to youthful violence is the influence of the group on individual behavior. Members of crowds frequently behave in ways that contradict their individual values; research into juvenile delinquency has largely adopted this explanation of crime perpetrated by youth as the outcome of group processes. Highly influential was Matza's (1964) notion of *drift*, in which young people participate in criminal acts without fully intending to do so and without necessarily possessing values that condone crime. The result is collective action over which the individual feels little control. In such situations, each person comes to believe that the other members of the group are more committed to carrying out the act than they really are.

Even when motives are consciously formulated in a premeditated way, in collective actions there is often a large gap between the original motives and the extent of actual destruction, through a process of *behavioral contagion*, in which things go further than was intended (Polansky, Lippitt, & Redl, 1950). Social psychologists have identified several group processes that may contribute to violence, including *diffusion of responsibility* and *deindividuation*, or a temporary loss of one's self-awareness in the spirit of the group.

For youth peer groups, violence serves several social functions. One function is the garnering of social status by individuals who are cut off from other means of achieving it. Another function is to increase group solidarity and cohesion through cooperative enterprise; this in turn is desired because it bolsters interpersonal social support. In a study of convicted robbers, for example, Cordilia (1986) found that about one in five were "situation-casual offenders" for whom group factors overrode monetary gain as a motive. These men's motives included cooperation, companionship, and strengthening of group cohesion through play and adventure.

Antigay Violence

The emergence of the homosexual as a distinct social category (D'Emilio, 1986; Katz, 1976) created a new symbol for men to contrast themselves against. Homosexuality was perceived primarily as deviant *gender identity*, as opposed to sexual attraction, and thus was shorthand for effeminate men and masculine women who rejected socially proscribed sex roles (Marshall, 1981). The fear of being labeled a "sissy" or "fag" put pressure on all men to conform to a narrow standard of gender behavior. Over the past century, as heterosexuality became an increasingly integral component of masculine identity (Herek, 1986), young men could demonstrate their masculinity not only through sexual conquest of women, but also through the public denigration of perceived homosexuals.

Newspaper accounts and anecdotal evidence

suggest that antigay violence has been widespread in the United States at least as far back as the 1930s, when homosexuals began to emerge as a visible minority. Although accurate data are difficult to obtain (Franklin, 2002),[2] victimization surveys have consistently revealed high levels of harassment and violence against gay men and lesbians. Berrill's (1992) overview, summarizing two dozen national, regional, and local victimization surveys, remains perhaps the most comprehensive. Overall, 80% of sexual minority respondents reported verbal harassment, 44% reported threats of violence, 33% were chased or followed, 25% described being pelted with objects, 17% were physically assaulted, 13% were spat upon, and 9% were assaulted with objects or weapons. Settings include streets and other public venues, private residences, schools, and workplaces.

Surveys of teenagers and young adults suggest that targeting of individuals perceived to be sexual minorities is so commonplace as to be socially normative. For example, 91% of sexual minority youth in a national survey (Gay Lesbian & Straight Education Network, 2001) reported hearing frequent antigay comments at school. About 14% of the youths reported being punched or kicked because of their sexuality, and another 28% reported being shoved, pushed, or otherwise physically harassed (see Human Rights Watch, 2001; Russell, Franz, & Driscoll, 2001). Assailants are typically in their teens and early 20s, and come from all races and economic classes (e.g., Comstock, 1991; Patton, 2003).

In a survey of community college students in the San Francisco Bay Area (Franklin, 2000), 18% of young men reported that they had physically assaulted perceived gay men or lesbians, and another 32% acknowledged antigay name-calling. Many of these assailants were not vehement in their antigay attitudes, instead citing negative societal stereotypes about homosexuality as justifications for their assaults. Key stereotypes cited were that gay people violate gender norms and that they are sexually predatory. In interviews with juvenile offenders in Australia, Van de Ven (1995) found these same stereotypes used to justify antigay assaults.

Research into attitudes toward gay men and lesbians supports the prospect that heterosexism—the ideological system that stigmatizes nonheterosexual forms of behavior and identity—is but one component of the broader ideologies of sexuality and gender, and that homosexuality violates not only sexual taboos but gender norms as well. For example, gay men and lesbians who conform to heterosexual gender norms are more accepted than those who do not (Millham & Weinberger, 1977). Thus negative reactions to gay people as well as to heterosexuals who deviate from sex-role norms is more of a learned form of social control of deviance than a defensive reaction to perceived personal threat.

In a series of empirical explorations, Herek (1987) found that attitudes toward gay people served different psychological and social functions for different individuals. Each of the three symbolic functions identified by Herek allows individuals to define themselves by using homosexuals as abstract symbols of who they are *not*. In the "value-expressive" function, antigay bias helps individuals affirm their identities by expressing personal values, such as being a good Christian. In the "social-expressive" function, individuals win membership in a social group by denigrating homosexuals as outsiders. In the "defensive" function, an individual might attack homosexuals to reduce anxiety caused by internal psychological conflicts.

Franklin (2000) extended Herek's research from attitudes to behaviors. Surveying 500 young adults, she

2. One reason that data are unreliable is because sexual minority victims—like rape victims—often do not report attacks. Historically, antigay assaults were rarely reported due to the belief that attackers would go unpunished, and fear of secondary victimization by police. Even with the advent of modern hate crime laws and a generally more favorable environment for gay hate crime victims, underreporting remains prevalent. For example, in the years 2002-2003 between 53% and 60% of individuals who reported antigay victimization to gay community anti-violence groups did not file police reports (Patton, 2003). Of those who did report assaults to police, police refused to accept a report in an estimated 15% to 20% of cases. Further, police often fail to classify incidents as antigay hate crimes, or to report them to the Federal Bureau of Investigation under the voluntary guidelines of the Hate Crimes Statistics Act of 1990 (Franklin, 2002). Another problem is that victimization data rely largely upon convenience samples within the gay community, and thus exclude closeted sexual minorities as well as heterosexuals who are mistakenly perceived as gay, an estimated 10% of victims (Patton, 2003).

found four primary motivations for antigay assaults. The first of these was *antigay ideology*, in which assailants saw themselves as enforcing societal norms against gender-deviant behavior. The second was perceived *self-defense*, in which respondents described themselves as victims of homosexual aggression or flirtation.

The final two motivations were primarily group-related in nature, and support the idea that much antigay assault is aimed at demonstrating masculinity—e.g., toughness and heterosexuality—to peers. *Peer dynamics* assailants reported assaulting gays in order to prove their toughness and heterosexuality and to live up to their friends' expectations. They tended to lament the harm to their victims, but minimized their own roles and freedom of choice. *Thrill-seekers* said they wanted to feel strong, have fun, and alleviate boredom. They tended to minimize the level of harm done and to depict incidents as amusing.

Given the peer-related functions of antigay violence, it is not surprising that a large percentage of such assaults are committed by young men in groups. In Franklin's (2000) survey, about three-quarters of the young adults who admitted antigay assaults said they did so within a group context. Just more than half of assailants reported being in groups of three or more, and another 20% were in pairs. In contrast, their gay victims were typically alone. About a third of incidents reported to gay community anti-violence projects involve multiple assailants (Patton, 2003). In 2002, the most recent year for which data were available, 72% of these group attacks involved two to three offenders, and 28% involved four or more offenders.

If antigay violence is a vehicle for young males to demonstrate their toughness and heterosexuality to their peers, group rape is an even more direct means of achieving the same goal. Both forms of violence have the additional advantages of offering little risk of injury, and providing direct and corroborated evidence—unlike second-hand accounts of sexual conquests—of one's masculine virility.

Group Rape[3]

Despite its prevalence, group rape is rarely examined as a distinct phenomenon; indeed, it has been called the most understudied of all serious criminal offenses (Geis, 1971). As the literature on rape proliferates, the past few decades have seen only a handful of scholarly publications on group rape or its motivations (e.g., Blanchard, 1959; Ehrhart & Sandler, 1986; Geis, 1971; Gidycz & Koss, 1990; Groth & Birnbaum, 1979; Hamilton, 1979; Holmstrom & Burgess, 1980; O'Sullivan, 1991, 1998; Rozee-Koker & Polk, 1986; Sanday, 1990). This is in contrast to the attention on the phenomenon in the popular news media,[4] as well as in popular language, through such terms as *running trains*, and *gang banging*.

Like antigay violence, the rape of women is widespread. The percentage of surveyed women reporting rape or attempted rape varies from a low of 14.5% to a high of 54%, with most studies indicating a lifetime prevalence rate of about one in four women (Koss, 1998; Sanday, 2003). The percentages are higher in certain settings, such as the U.S. military (Nelson, 2002).

Not only do large percentages of women report being sexually assaulted, but large percentages of men report committing sexual assaults.[5] In one recent survey (Knight, 2003), 38% of blue-collar men and 15% of male college students admitted having sex with a

3. In this article, the terms *group rape* and *gang rape* are used interchangeably to define multiple-assailant rape, that is, a rape involving two or more assailants. Some authors (e.g., Groth, 1979; O'Sullivan, 1998) further distinguish between *pair rapes* and rapes involving three or more assailants.

4. In one recent year, for example, Scotland Yard detectives described a wave of gang rapes by young teenage males (Burrell, 2002); a special task force was established in the Boston area after a rash of gang rapes (Farmer, 2002); 20 adolescents went on trial in Paris for gang raping a 15-year-old girl ("Twenty accused," 2002); and members of an elite university club in Japan admitted a string of gang rapes ("Members of Japanese," 2003).

5. This article limits itself to male-on-female sexual assault. Male-on-male sexual assault is an underreported and understudied phenomenon (Groth & Burgess, 1980; Scarce, 1997), which has sufficient distinctions that it merits separate analysis. In a study of group rapes by Groth (1979), 10% of the victims were male. There is evidence that sexual assault victimization is more common among gay than heterosexual men (Duncan, 1990).

woman whom they knew did not want to have sex. In another study (Hall, Teten, & Sue, 2003), 38% of European American men and 33% of Asian American men acknowledged sexual coercion of women. In yet another study (Koss, 1998), 25% of men acknowledged sexual aggression, with 4.4% admitting rape. Similarly, in three surveys of U.S. Navy recruits, between 10% and 12% reported committing rape before joining the military (Merrill, 2001). In a study by Malamuth (1981), 35% of male college students indicated they might rape a woman if they could be assured of not getting caught. In circumstances of protracted warfare, rape and group rape become endemic, often as a weapon of warfare (Koss, Heise, & Russo, 1997).

The precise percentage of rapes committed by multiple assailants is unknown, but it is probably somewhere between 10% and 33%. At the low end, U.S. government crime victimization data suggest that one out of 10 sexual assaults involves multiple offenders (Greenfeld, 1997). A somewhat higher figure comes from a survey by Koss (1998), in which 16% of the men who admitted raping women said they acted in concert with other men. Based on a survey of the literature, Rozee-Koker and Polk (1986) estimate that about one-third of reported rapes were perpetrated by multiple offenders, with a whopping three-fourths of all rape offenders being group rapists. About 41% of self-identified date rapists in a study by Kanin (1985) reported participating in group rapes. In a 1965 study by Amir (as cited in Geis, 1971), 43% of reported rapes in Philadelphia involved multiple offenders, with 71% of reported rapists being group rape offenders. Finally, Mosher and Anderson (as cited in Muehlenhard & Schrag, 1991) found that 10% of a sample of college men reported waiting their turn in line with other men to share a "party girl."

The victim in group rape—like that in antigay violence—is reduced to nothing more than a dramatic prop through which the assailants simultaneously prove their heterosexuality and bond with each other through the sharing of fear and danger. The performance aspect is central, as group rapists ritualistically take turns, converse about taking turns, watch each other, and engage in simultaneous sex with victims. The symbolic status of the victim is suggested by the fact that she is typically a stranger, or at most a casual acquaintance, to the assailants. Whereas more than 80% of women know their attacker in single-assailant rapes, more than three-quarters of group rapists are strangers (Greenfeld, 1997).

Similar to the ideological function of antigay violence, another function of group rape is as an exercise of social control, with "the deployment of the penis as a concrete symbol of masculine social power and dominance" (Sanday, 1990, p. 10). In her in-depth interviews with convicted rapists, Scully (1990) identified *revenge-punishment* as a recurrent theme. This punishment may be directed against a particular woman or against the entire female sex. Just as antigay violence is used to punish individuals who deviate from societally proscribed gender roles, group rape is used to punish women who are perceived as violating gender norms for females, such as by being promiscuous or outside of male control.

Connected with this function of social control and punishment is the exhibition of aggression. Multiple-assailant rapes often involve more violence, threats of violence, and weapons than do individual rapes, with the amount of aggression and degradation often increasing as an attack progresses (Gidycz & Koss, 1990; Groth & Birnbaum, 1979; Mawson, 1987; Rozee-Koker & Polk, 1986; Scully, 1990). This aggression can be seen as essential to proving toughness and bravery, that is, masculinity. It may also be a group expression of male contempt for women and feminity. The current popularity of *bukkake*, a symbolic group rape in which multiple men—up to 75 at a time—degrade a woman by squirting semen on her face attests to the prevalence of such contempt. A Google search for this term in March 2004 met with 3.4 million hits, with web sites that glory in the degradation and objectification of women.

The Mepham High School Case

The parallels between antigay violence and group rape of women can best be understood if one conceives of the victim in each case as fundamentally a symbolic prop, a vehicle for a dramatic production performed by young men for each other's consumption. The main goal of the drama is to visibly demonstrate one's masculine prowess to peers. On an ideological level, the production also serves to graphically prove masculine power and feminine weakness. This lens enables us to see the similarities not only between antigay violence and group rape, but also the overlaps with other, superficially dissimilar forms of male group aggression. The case of the Mepham High School football team is one such example.

Between August 22 and August 27, 2003, the 68 football players of Mepham High School in Long Island, New York, attended a training camp in Wayne County, Pennsylvania. They were chaperoned by five adult coaches. During the weeklong camp, a group of three upperclass boys, ages 15, 16, and 17, repeatedly assaulted certain younger players, singling out three younger boys for the worst abuse.

According to a subsequent Grand Jury investigation report (Pingel, 2004), the assaults began on the first night of camp, when one of the young victims was taped to his bed. The boy was then forced to go to an adjoining cabin and put powder and gel in the hair of another underclassman. The next day, two assailants held down a boy while a third assailant sodomized him with a broomstick. This was done in front of other players, who laughed and joked about it. The broomstick assault was repeated the day after that. This time, the assailants applied duct tape to the victim's pubic area, buttocks, legs, and eyebrows, inflicting severe pain by pulling off the hair on these parts of his body. Again, other players witnessed the assault.

In all, three younger players were sodomized with objects, including broomsticks, pine cones, and—in one case —a golf ball that was inserted into a boy's anus and rammed in further with a broomstick. Two players endured these assaults on multiple occasions, and were also forced to assault each other in front of the other players. For example, they were forced to put Mineral Ice on their testicles and then alternately kick each other in the groin. Another time, an assailant made one victim place a banana in his boxer shorts, after which the boy's friend was forced to eat the banana out of the shorts. Following this, a player was forced to lie naked with a potato chip on his buttocks, while another player ate the chip from that location. A victim was forced to make "degrading racial epithets" to an African American player. The younger players were also beaten with plastic bags of ice on their bare backs. Two of the victims later required medical treatment, including rectal surgery in one case (Henican, 2003).

This case is an example of a not-unusual phenomenon in which the bullying of younger, weaker boys takes on a sexualized and/or antigay flavor; indeed, there is significant overlap among so-called hazings, group rapes, and antigay assaults. For example, a study (see Chase, 2001) of antigay violence in Washington State schools chronicled eight gang rapes of boys and girls that were motivated by the victims' suspected homosexuality. In addition, several of the killers in a rash of school shootings in the 1990s throughout the country had been persistently harassed as gay.

The Mepham case bears resemblance to both antigay assault and group rape in its ritualized enactment of masculine power. Older, physically stronger, and more prestigious players engaged in a public display of masculinity, celebrating their strength by violently emasculating their weaker—that is, less manly—teammates. The theatrical element is evident in the requirement of an audience; the laughing approval of this audience provided visible endorsement of the upperclassmen's gendered entitlement. That vilification of the feminine was a core component is illustrated by the emasculation of the victims, through forcing them to assume the female role in simulated sexual acts as well as through the depilation ritual in which one boy was feminized through painful removal of his body hair.

This case illustrates both the heterosexist and misogynistic components of masculinity ideology. The boys were younger and weaker; therefore, they were treated like women or gay men. Masculinity ideology requires boys to be strong and tough, lest they be reduced to the status of women and dominated by other men. Thus, other players did nothing to intervene or to inform their coaches of what was transpiring in the cabins, either out of a belief that the victims deserved punishment for being weak, or out of fear of the consequences to themselves. Far better to be a ringside spectator than to play the role of victim in this drama.

Leaders and Followers

In the Mepham case, all participants were not equal. The lead actor was a 16-year-old boy with a long disciplinary record for threatening teachers and assaulting schoolmates. This is frequently the case in antigay assaults and group rapes, in which a more delinquent leader plans the act and is the first to throw a punch or have intercourse with the victim. In a study by Groth and Birnbaum (1979) of 30 multiple-assailant rapes, in most cases one man was the identifiable leader. The leader hatched the plan and was the first to sexually assault the victim; leaders were more likely to have previous convictions for solo rapes.

Interviews with assailants suggest that the instigator often acts out of a need to prove his leadership—and by implication his masculinity—to the others (Franklin, 1997, 1998). The followers provide the leader with the courage to commit the assault. They, in turn, are often emotionally dependent on the leader, and they may feel enormous pressure to live up to his expectations.

In interviews with a group of boys who had engaged in a series of egg- and orange-throwing incidents targeting gay men, Weissman (1978) found this difference between the motivations of the group's acknowledged leader and his followers. The leader described feeling a need to prove himself to the group: "Sometimes you're forced into doing something to prove yourself to others" (p. 12). A follower, in contrast, described it as "like a game of chicken—someone dared you to do something and there was no backing down....It was a symbol of prestige" (p. 10). Each boy described feeling covertly reluctant but not wanting to express fear; afterwards, the boys reported feeling very close to each other.

The division of participants is crucial to understanding male group aggression. In masculinist, assault-prone environments, men fall into one of three categories: *dominators*, *dominated*, and *followers* (Sanday, 2003). Followers feel like they must go along with the dominators, lest they be branded as nonmasculine, risk expulsion from the group, or, in extreme cases, become victims themselves. With so much riding on their participation, many find it hard to decline. As a member of the Cincinnati Bengals who was implicated in a 1990 rape by a dozen other players explained, "It was very hard for you to say, 'Nah, no, no,' because you're going to get ragged about it. You're going to get teased" (Benedict, 1998, p. 46).

Participants in antigay assaults and group rapes usually recall feeling positive emotions at the time. During the assault, there is a drug-like high produced by the excitement and danger. Afterwards, there is a feeling of closeness and camaraderie, a sense of bonding produced by communal transgression. But there may also be an enormous, collective sigh of relief, in that they have survived this public test with their masculinity intact.

In other words, underneath the experienced veneer of camaraderie and warmth is a desperate struggle to achieve dominance, maintain status, or even to get through the ordeal with one's masculinity intact.[6] This competition for status or survival is not directly acknowledged. Rather, it is camouflaged by the ostensible goal of debasing a weaker, more feminine outsider.

This brings up a potential difference between assaults on younger or weaker boys and antigay assaults or group rapes. Unlike females or gay males, some heterosexual male victims have the prospect of being rewarded for enduring the abuse by an opportunity to join the dominant group in the future. This was presumably true in the Mepham case, involving younger members of the football team; it is also true in fraternity hazings. However, dominant boys often target outsiders who have no prospect, or desire, to join the bullies. These include not only females and gay males, but also racial minorities, individuals with physical or mental handicaps, and anyone else outside the assailants' clique.

6. At times, the competitive nature of the sport is more obvious. Groth and Birnbaum (1979) quote a group rapist as describing how, "after we had her, we asked her who was best" (p. 116). In other cases, young men engage in contests to see how many women they can conquer. For example, a group of white suburban athletes in Lakewood, California, who dubbed themselves the "Spur Posse," competed for the highest number of sexual conquests, with the high scorer accumulating 66 points by the time of their arrests (O'Toole, 1997).

A Climate of Abuse

According to the Grand Jury investigation report, the Mepham assaults resulted from the failure of high school officials to intervene in multiple, prior incidents. The report described "a custom or history of hazing" at the school, which included regular beatings of younger players by dominant jocks. Authorities had not adequately intervened in prior incidents of violence by athletes at the school, such as a 1995 incident in which a boy was beaten, stripped, and held upside down while his head was plunged into a urinal (Vitello, 2003). The regularity, and seeming normality, of abuse at the school may explain why numerous classmates witnessed and/or knew of assaults, but closed ranks and did not report them (Henican, 2003).

A social climate in which certain dominant males are tacitly permitted to harass and assault females and weaker males is a common ingredient in environments with high rates of group rape and antigay violence. This climate was a striking backdrop to two notorious crimes of recent years—the 1989 gang rape of a mentally retarded girl in Glen Ridge, New Jersey, and the 1999 school shooting massacre in Littleton, Colorado.

In the Glen Ridge rape case, a group of athletes lured a mentally retarded girl to their basement hangout and sexually assaulted her, forcing her to orally copulate them and then raping her with a broom handle and a bat. This case resembled Mepham in several striking ways in addition to the use of objects as symbolic penises. The assailants were athletes, members of the football, baseball, and wrestling teams. A large group of boys was present, with some as spectators and others—the dominators of the group—as lead actors. The instigators had disciplinary records for prior abuse of schoolmates and others. Teachers and school administrators had not intervened against their rampant sexual harassment, which included pinning girls against lockers and grinding their bodies against them, or pulling out their penises and masturbating at girls in class (Lefkowitz, 1997). One of the group's favorite activities was so-called *voyeuring*, in which one boy would stage a sexual act with a girl while the other boys covertly watched; the boys bragged at school about these activities, and even passed around a videotape of one such dramatic production.

This was similar to the atmosphere at Columbine High School that so enraged outsiders Eric Harris and Dylan Klebold, whose shooting rampage killed 13 and wounded 21. Like at Glen Ridge and Mepham, athletes at Columbine reigned supreme. The state wrestling champion, the leader of a clique of athlete bullies and the symbol of injustice for the school shooters, was allowed to park his $100,000 Hummer all day in a 15-minute parking space. The school indulged athletes' rampant sexual and racial bullying and physical abuse of others, including Harris and Klebold (Adams & Russakoff, 1999). For example, a sports coach did nothing when the athletes targeted a Jewish boy in gym class, singing songs about Hitler when he made a basket, pinning him to the ground and doing "body twisters" that left him bruised all over, and threatening to set him on fire. Like at Glen Ridge, the abuse was so severe that some students feared going to school.

Where there is rampant sexual harassment of girls and women, there is usually antigay harassment as well. This was true at Columbine High School, where Harris and Klebold had endured repeated antigay harassment by the jocks, and persistent rumors that they were a gay couple. It was also true at many of the other schools where shootings erupted in the past decade.[7]

Masculine Environments and the Antifeminity Norm

In all of these cases, the ringleaders were athletes. The folkloric notion that athletes tend to be more sexually aggressive than other men has been borne out by research (Benedict, 1998; O'Toole, 1997). Higher rates of rape are concentrated among the more aggressive team sports, such as football and basketball,

7. Barry Loukaitis, who killed a teacher and two students in Washington state, had been taunted by school jocks as a "faggot." Luke Woodham in Mississippi, who killed two students and wounded seven others, was often called "gay" by classmates. Michael Carneal, who killed three fellow students and wounded five in Kentucky, was labeled as "gay" in the school newspaper. Charles Williams in Santee, California, who shot at 15 students and adults and killed two, had been derided as "a skinny faggot" (Chase, 2001; "Deadly lessons," 2000; see also Newman, Fox, Harding, Mehta, & Roth, 2004).

and in particular revenue-producing sports. Benedict (1998) argues that sexual violence is not an inherent aspect of athletics. Rather, sports stars are more likely to commit sexual assaults because of their sense of entitlement and superiority. This certainly appears to be the case at Mepham, Glen Ridge, and Columbine high schools, where athletes were regarded as above the law. Benedict further argues that sexual coercion within sports is due to how masculine identity is defined within certain sports environments.

This argument can be extended to other environments as well. Not surprisingly, a central feature of masculine subcultures with high rates of group rape are *social norms* that condone sexual coercion (O'Toole, 1997). Social norms provide rules for individual behavior within a given social context; they help us determine what is socially correct, based on what other people think is correct (Cialdini, 1988). It is commonsensical that when men associate with other men who endorse sexual or antigay violence, they will be more likely to find such violence acceptable. Indeed, in a study of fraternities with high versus low levels of violence toward women, Boswell and Spade (1999) found that social norms vary by context; men from the more sexually egalitarian fraternities became more abusive toward women when attending parties at the misogynist houses.

Environments with social norms supportive of antigay violence and group rape include certain fraternities, military forces, street gangs, police departments, rock groups, and sports teams. Fraternities are a prevalent site of group rapes. For example, of 50 group rapes on college campuses documented in one study (Ehrhart & Sandler, 1986; see also Martin & Hummer, 1989), "the great majority" were at fraternity parties; a number involved college athletes. And both group rape and antigay violence are endemic in the U.S. military, which Nelson (2002) describes as a training ground for institutionalized misogyny. Women and gays are the butts of frequent jokes and crude songs, such as a rewrite of the popular "Candyman" song entitled "the S and M man," which celebrates gang rape and intercourse with dead women. Among Navy recruits, there is competition to demonstrate sexual prowess and conquest of women through anal intercourse, known as "earning one's brown wings."

Explaining the hostility toward women and gay men in these environments is their shared preoccupation with *masculinity*, or the extrusion of all things feminine. Although most of us know masculinity when we see it, it is not so easily defined. Indeed, an emerging body of scholarship has taken on the task of exploring the multiple masculinities in modern culture (e.g., Bowker, 1998; Connell, 1995; Kimmel, 1997; Rotundo, 1993; Sabo, Jupers, & London, 2001). Masculinity has been described as "terrifyingly fragile" (Kaufman, 1997) because it exists only in men's minds, as an ideology or a set of behaviors. In other words, it is not biologically endowed; it exists only in contrast to its supposed opposite, "femininity."

McCarthy (1994) traces modern notions of masculinity back to the European and American expansionism of the mid-nineteenth century and the consequent emergence of social Darwinism, which repopularized medieval "warrior values and myths" regarding physical courage, strength, and honor in order to justify colonial domination of "inferior" peoples. Under this version of masculinity, men measure themselves against the standard of the successful "Marketplace Man," who wields economic and social power over others (Kimmel, 1997). Since few men can achieve this ideal, most spend their lives in relentless pursuit of masculinity, constantly fearing exposure as frauds. Indeed, Kimmel argues that *fear* is the overriding emotion driving men's behaviors—fear of being dominated, of being seen as weak, of being humiliated. In one study, for example, when women and men were asked what they most feared, women reported a fear of being raped and murdered, whereas men confessed that their greatest fear was being laughed at (Noble, 1992, as cited in Kimmel, 1997, p. 235).

The unrelenting drive to prove their manhood leads males to frantically distance themselves from all things considered feminine. Empirical evidence of this antifemininity norm as a fundamental component of masculinity crystallized in the mid-1980s. Thompson and Pleck (1986; see also Brannon & Juni, 1984) analyzed young men's descriptions of stereotypical male attributes and identified three primary components: (a) gaining status and respect, (b) self-reliance and toughness, and (c) avoidance of femininity.

Although attributes of masculinity vary depending upon economic class and race, masculine signifiers in childhood include toughness, fighting ability, and skill at boys' games, whereas in adulthood they include heterosexual prowess, confident bodily comportment, and occupational achievement. It is during the developmental stage in which they are striving to establish their masculine identity that young men are most likely to engage in exaggerated public demonstrations of masculinity. This is also the age in which men share the highest allegiance with other men, and are most likely to be focused on all-male activities and environments, making the respect and acceptance of other men of critical importance.

Men's prisons provide a classic example of how men in hypermasculine environments demonstrate their masculinity through dominating, or feminizing, others. Stripped of all social power except their status as men, prisoners can lose this too if they are perceived as weak or passive—that is, feminine. Through rape, "the ultimate humiliation," a man is symbolically emasculated and redefined as "female," becoming the property of his conqueror (Rideau & Wikberg, 1992, p. 75; Sabo, Jupers, & London, 2001). That the defense of masculinity is central to this ritual is suggested by prison rapists' stated motivations, such as "We're going to take your manhood" or "We're going to make a girl out of you" (Roskey, 1988, pp. 52-53). The irony of male-on-male rape as a way to demonstrate heterosexual prowess suggests that masculinity is less about sexual behavior than personal identity.

Masculine subcultures with high rates of group rape share a core set of social norms, values, and practices. According to O'Sullivan (1998), these include: (a) women being viewed as a threatening "other"; (b) heterosexual sex without intimacy (men who are tender with women are ridiculed as "pussy-whipped"); (c) pervasive homophobia; (d) a sense of entitlement due to their group prestige; (e) cooperation combined with competition, especially competition to perform risky acts; (f) cultural practices of misogyny, such as songs and jokes glorifying sexual violence; (g) sharing of sexuality, for example through mandatory reporting of sexual experiences and through voyeuring, or watching each other have sex; and (h) hazing as a common practice.

In a study of college date rapists, Kanin (1985) found that rapists were much more likely than a control group to be immersed in a "hypererotic male culture" that condoned sexual aggression against "deviant" women, such as "teasers" and "loose" women. These date rapists were much more likely than the controls (41% versus 7%) to have engaged in "gang-bangs."

Similarly, Boswell and Spade (1999) found that fraternity houses where women felt at risk of rape had a misogynistic atmosphere in which men and women mingled less, more alcohol was consumed, the volume of the music was higher, and men engaged in more crude behaviors, sexual innuendo, and cursing. Interestingly, the researchers noted that the women's bathrooms in these houses were filthy, signifying the members' outspoken contempt for women. The members of these houses were more likely to play varsity athletics, and less likely to have steady girlfriends.

Homoeroticism and Homophobia

Linking antigay violence and group rape may seem counterintuitive, because of their different relationships to sex and sexuality. The one is visibly sexual, with obvious homoeroticism; the other is nonerotic. One is manifestly antigay; the other is not necessarily concerned with homosexuality at all. But these superficial differences exist on a continuum, and should not mask the fact that both forms of violence are aimed primarily at publicly demonstrating masculinity and heterosexuality.

The homoeroticism of group rape was pointed out in one of the first scholarly treatments of group rape, by Blanchard (1959), who commented that "the idea of 'sharing the girl among us fellows,' congregating around a common sexual object, and being sexually stimulated together as a group certainly have their homosexual implications" (p. 259). Similarly, in her ethnographic study of fraternity culture, Sanday (1990) commented on the obvious homoeroticism in the widespread practice of "pulling train": "A group of men watch each other having sex with a woman who may be unconscious. One might well ask why the woman is even necessary for the sexual acts these men stage for one another" (p. 12).

Sanday goes further in describing the preoccupation with homosexuality, and playing out of homosexual feelings, that she observed in fraternity culture. For example, in a common ritual known as the "circle dance," the "brothers" circle around, arm in arm and sometimes naked, going faster and faster until they lose control and fall down atop each other; brothers periodically step into the middle of the circle and mime sexual and/or lewd acts, including homosexual intercourse. Similarly, she found the brothers to be preoccupied with oral sex, which one fraternity man acknowledged as containing "more homoerotic potential" than heterosexual intercourse (p. 123).

The reframing of a homoerotic activity as a demonstration of heterosexuality is doubly ironic in that men who do *not* participate are accused of being gay. Indeed, one way men in hypermasculine environments reassure themselves of their heterosexuality—and masculinity—is through constant antigay banter and harassment. In recent years, fraternities have sported slogans such as "Drink Beer, Kill Queers" and "Club Faggots, Not Seals" on T-shirts, on rubber stamps for partygoers' hands, and on their buses (Nardi & Bolton, 1991, p. 355; National Gay and Lesbian Task Force, 1992, p. 20).

Some rape scholars (e.g., Groth & Birnbaum, 1979; O'Sullivan, 1991) dispute the notion that group rape is homoerotic, saying it is less about sexual desire than about power, domination, and male bonding. Indeed, for many men the experience is strikingly nonerotic; men often do not ejaculate, and they frequently use objects in place of penises (O'Sullivan, 1991). In these contexts, like in some acts of individual rape, the penis is used as a symbol of male power, to conquer, degrade, and feminize.

Rather than being a homoerotic experience, the rape may be experienced by participants as a dramatic contest in which one's peers evaluate one's sexual, or masculine, prowess. Journalist Nathan McCall (1994), in a candid first-person account of "running trains" as a teenage boy, recalls feeling a mixture of fear, guilt, and performance anxiety:

> All the fellas were there and everybody was anxious to show everybody else how cool and worldly he was....I wasn't about to let it be said that I was scared of pussy. I took a deep breath and tried to relax and free my mind. I knew I couldn't get an erection if I wasn't relaxed. That would be even more embarrassing. I didn't want to pull my meat out unless I had an erection. It would look small. Somebody might see it, shriveled up and tiny, and start laughing....I placed myself into her wetness and moved my body, pretending to grind hard. After a few miserable minutes, I got up and signaled for the next man to take his turn....Somebody whispered, "That shit is *good*, ain't it?" I said, "Yeah, man. That shit is good."....I felt sorry for Vanessa....I think some of the other guys felt sorry, too. But the guilt was short-lived. It was eclipsed in no time by the victory celebration....We burst into cheers and slapped five with each other like we'd played on the winning baseball team. (pp. 48-49)

For McCall (1994) and his crew, the train was not about sexual gratification but about homosocial bonding. "Even though it involved sex, it didn't seem to be about sex at all....[It] marked our real coming together as a gang. It certified us as a group of hanging partners who would do anything and everything together" (p. 49).

The absence of eroticism is even more apparent in the Mepham case. Although the victims were anally raped with objects, and many of the dramatic scenes that the victims were forced to perform featured simulated homosexual acts, there is no hint of sexual arousal or gratification. Rather, anal rape and other simulated sexual acts were used to emasculate and degrade. This is not uncommon. O'Sullivan (1998) reports on two sexual assaults by groups of athletes on weaker teammates, as well as several cases of wrestlers sexually assaulting defeated opponents as part of post-match victory celebrations. In addition, she reports an incident in which a group of fraternity men sodomized a gay man who had walked by their house holding hands with another man, thus punishing him for violating cultural norms against visible displays of homosexuality.

Thus, both group rapes and antigay violence are not only public demonstrations of masculine dominance, they are celebratory dramas. Typically, the atmosphere is one of recreation and fun. The group is reveling in its shared power. This can be true whether the men hail from the social elite, as in the case of fraternity brothers, or from less privileged backgrounds, as in McCall's previously described account. Although young men may experience temporary powerlessness due to their age, or more long-term powerlessness due to their economic class and/or race, they still maintain relative superiority due to their sex. Group rape and antigay violence are two methods of demonstrating this male power over individuals with less social power.

Although antigay violence is nonerotic, it remains a public dramatization of sexuality. Whereas group rape is ostensibly an enactment of heterosexuality, in that the actors perform sexually with females, gay-bashers are proclaiming their sexuality in contradistinction to homosexuality. Thus, the two forms of violence are opposite sides of the same coin—the public enactment of heterosexual masculinity. This explains why one rarely encounters misogyny or heterosexism in the absence of the other.

Conclusion

This article has argued that antigay violence and the group rape of women serve similar functions and are committed under similar environmental conditions. Both forms of violence are used not only to demonstrate masculinity to peers, but also to punish gender role violations and to enforce gender subordination—in the one case against women who violate the strictures for female sexuality, and in the other against men who violate norms for gendered behavior.

The article posits that aggression against both women and perceived gay men is socially normative in certain male groups. Indeed, it is the group—and not any one individual in isolation—that commits the assault. Violence against women and gay men is prevalent within misogynistic and heterosexist environments that condone or even glorify violence. In the absence of societal animus and contempt for women and gay people, young men would not find these types of behaviors acceptable, and such assaults would not be excused by authority figures as "boys will be boys."

This analysis suggests that group violence against those who symbolize the feminine "other" will decrease as the hypermasculine ideal becomes less central to heterosexual male identity. This may not be as impossible a goal as one might think. Merely altering potential assailants' perceptions of gay people and women from value-laden symbols of differentness to real persons may reduce the incidence of violence (Herek, 1990). This has been demonstrated in the case of antigay harassment, which is rampant on most high school campuses today (Franklin, 2000; Human Rights Watch, 2001). Systematic programs to train teachers and educate students, particularly under the guidance of charismatic leaders, have dramatically improved the safety of gay students in certain schools (e.g., Farrell, 1998; Szalacha, 2001). Similarly, in their study of high- and low-risk fraternities, Boswell and Spade (1999) found one of the central differences to be the degree to which men and women mingled socially, as opposed to connecting solely around sex. On an anecdotal note, Lefkowitz (1997) pointed out that the athletes in the Glen Ridge case who declined to participate in the rape, leaving the scene as it began to unfold, were those who had sisters and strong women in their lives.

Short of larger and more long-range changes, this article points to the utility of distinguishing between a drama's lead actors and its bit players. The leaders need to be identified early in their transgressive careers; in cases such as those discussed here, subsequent violence could have been avoided if authorities had intervened earlier. Followers, on the other hand, may be reached through educational efforts and reduction of their dependency and sense of peer pressure to conform to the group.

Antigay violence and group rape are typically studied in different forums. Researchers interested in antigay violence tend to be affiliated with the anti-hate crimes movement. Group rape, in contrast, is rarely studied as a distinct entity; the few researchers who have focused on it hail from the feminist, anti-rape, and anti-domestic violence camp. It is hoped that a focus on the commonalities between the two types of youthful male group violence will encourage overlapping research and prevention efforts. ◆

References

Adams, L., & Russakoff, D. (1999, June 12). Dissecting Columbine's cult of the athlete. *Washington Post*, p. A1.

Baron, R.A., & Richardson, D.R. (1994). *Human aggression* (2nd ed.). New York: Plenum.

Benedict, J.R. (1998). *Athletes and acquaintance rape.* Thousand Oaks, CA: Sage.

Berrill, K.T. (1992). Anti-gay violence and victimization in the United States: An overview. In G.M. Herek & K.T. Berrill (Eds.), *Hate crimes: Confronting violence against lesbians and gay men* (pp. 19-45). Newbury Park, CA: Sage.

Blanchard, W.H. (1959). The group process in gang rape. *Journal of Social Psychology, 49,* 259-266.

Boswell, A.A., & Spade, J.Z. (1999). Fraternities and collegiate rape culture: Why are some fraternities more dangerous places for women? In L.A. Peplau, S.C. DeBro, R.C. Veniegas, & P.L. Taylor (Eds.), *Gender, culture, and ethnicity: Current research about women and men* (pp. 269-283). Mountain View, CA: Mayfield Publishing Co.

Bowker, L.H. (1998). *Masculinities and violence.* Thousand Oaks, CA: Sage.

Brannon, R., & Juni, S. (1984). A scale for measuring attitudes about masculinity. *Psychological Documents, 14,* 6-7.

Burrell, I. (2002, March 28). Yard warns of attacks by teenage rape gangs. *London Independent,* p. 13.

Chase, A. (2001). Violent reaction: What do teen killers have in common? *In These Times,* pp. 16-28.

Cialdini, R.B. (1988). *Influence: Science and practice* (2nd ed.). Glenview, IL: Scott, Foresman & Co.

Comstock, G.D. (1991). *Violence against lesbians and gay men.* New York: Columbia University Press.

Connell, R.W. (1995). *Masculinities.* Berkeley, CA: University of California Press.

Cordilia, A.T. (1986). Robbery arising out of a group drinking-context. In A. Campbell & J.J. Gibbs (Eds.), *Violent transactions: The limits of personality* (pp. 167-180). Oxford, England: Basil Blackwell.

Deadly lessons: School shooters tell why. (2000, October 15-16.) *Chicago Sun Times.* Retrieved January 26, 2004, from http://www.suntimes .com/shoot

D'Emilio, J. (1986). Making and unmaking minorities: The tensions between gay politics and history. *Review of Law and Social Change, 14,* 915-922.

Duncan, D.F. (1990). Prevalence of sexual assault victimization among heterosexual and gay/lesbian university students. *Psychological Reports, 66,* 65-66.

Ehrhart, J.K., & Sandler, B.R. (1986). Party rape. *Response to the Victimization of Women and Children, 9,* 2-5.

Farmer, T. (2002, Oct. 30). Task force formed following alleged rapes. *Boston Herald,* p. 3.

Farrell, J.M. (1998, September 10). Dade schools get "A" for safety of gay kids. *Miami Herald.* Retrieved September 10, 1998, from www.miami.com/mld/ miamiherald/

Franklin, K. (1997). *Hate crime or rite of passage? Assailant motivations in antigay violence.* Unpublished doctoral dissertation, California School of Professional Psychology, Berkeley/ Alameda.

Franklin, K. (1998). Unassuming motivations: Contextualizing the narratives of antigay assailants. In G.M. Herek (Ed.), *Stigma and sexual orientation: Understanding prejudice against lesbians, gay men, and bisexuals* (pp. 1-23). Thousand Oaks, CA: Sage Publications.

Franklin, K. (2000). Antigay behaviors among young adults: Prevalence, patterns, and motivators in a noncriminal population. *Journal of Interpersonal Violence, 15,* 339-362.

Franklin, K. (2002). Good intentions: The enforcement of hate crime penalty-enhancement statutes. *American Behavioral Scientist, 46,* 154-172.

Gay Lesbian & Straight Education Network. (2001). *The 2001 national school climate survey: Lesbian, gay, bisexual and transgender students and their experiences in school.* New York: Author.

Geis, G. (1971). Group sexual assaults. *Medical Aspects of Human Sexuality, 5,* 101-113.

Gidycz, C.A., & Koss, M.P. (1990). A comparison of group and individual sexual assault victims. *Psychology of Women Quarterly, 14,* 325-342.

Greenfeld, L.A. (1997). *Sex offenses and offenders: An analysis of data on rape and sexual assault.* Washington, D.C.: U.S. Department of Justice, Bureau of Justice Statistics.

Groth, A.N., & Birnbaum, H.J. (1979). *Men who rape: The psychology of the offender.* New York: Plenum.

Groth, A.N., & Burgess, R.N. (1980). Male rape: Offenders and victims. *American Journal of*

Psychiatry, 137, 806-810.

Hall, G.C.N., Teten, A.L., & Sue, S. (2003). The cultural context of sexual aggression: Asian American and European American perpetrators. In R. A. Prentky, E. S. Janus, & M. C. Soto (Eds.), *Sexually coercive behavior: Understanding and management* (pp. 131-143). New York: New York Academy of Sciences.

Hamilton, J.W. (1979). Single case study: Multiple group rape: Psychosocial considerations. *Journal of Nervous & Mental Disease, 167*, 128-130.

Henican, E. (2003, September 19). One school's wall of silence. *Newsday*, p. A2.

Herek, G.M. (1986). On heterosexual masculinity: Some psychical consequences of the social construction of gender and sexuality. *American Behavioral Scientist, 29*, 563-577.

Herek, G.M. (1987). Can functions be measured? A new perspective on the functional approach to attitudes. *Social Psychology Quarterly, 50*, 285-303.

Herek, G.M. (1990). The context of anti-gay violence: Notes on cultural and psychological heterosexism. *Journal of Interpersonal Violence, 5*, 316-333.

Holmstrom, L.L., & Burgess, A.W. (1980). Sexual behavior of assailants during reported rape. *Archives of Sexual Behavior, 9*, 427-439.

Human Rights Watch. (2001). *Hatred in the hallways: Violence and discrimination against lesbian, gay, bisexual, and transgender students in U.S. schools*. New York: Author.

Kanin, E.J. (1985). Date rapists: Differential socialization and relative deprivation. *Archives of Sexual Behavior, 14*, 219-231.

Katz, J. (1976). *Gay American history: Lesbians and gay men in the U.S.A.* New York: Avon.

Kaufman, M. (1997). The construction of masculinity and the triad of men's violence. In L. L. O'Toole & J. R. Schiffman (Eds.), *Gender violence: Interdisciplinary perspectives* (pp. 30-51). New York: New York University Press.

Kimmel, M.S. (1997). Masculinity as homophobia: Fear, shame, and silence in the construction of gender identity. In M. Gergen & S. Davis (Eds.), *Toward a new psychology of gender: A reader* (pp. 223-242). New York: Routledge.

Knight, R. (2003, October). *Assessing the underlying constructs of a rapist typology using the MASA*. Paper presented at the meeting of the Association for the Treatment of Sexual Abusers, St. Louis, MO.

Koss, M.P. (1998). Hidden rape: Sexual aggression and victimization in a national sample of students in higher education. In M. E. Odem & J. Clay-Warner (Eds.), *Confronting rape and sexual assault* (pp. 51-69). Wilmington, DE: Scholarly Resources Inc.

Koss, M.P., Heise, L., & Russo, N.F. (1997). The global health burden of rape. In L. L. O'Toole & J. R. Schiffman (Eds.), *Gender violence: Interdisciplinary perspectives* (pp. 223-241). New York: New York University Press.

Lefkowitz, B. (1997). *Our guys: The Glen Ridge rape and the secret life of the perfect suburb*. New York: Vintage Books.

Malamuth, N.M. (1981). Rape proclivity among males. *Journal of Social Issues, 37*, 138-157.

Marshall, J. (1981). Pansies, perverts and macho men: Changing conceptions of male homosexuality. In K. Plummer (Ed.), *The making of the modern homosexual* (pp. 133-154). London: Hutchinson.

Martin, P.Y., & Hummer, R.A. (1989). Fraternities and rape on campus. *Gender and Society, 3*, 457-473.

Maruna, S. (2001). *Making good: How ex-convicts reform and rebuild their lives*. Washington, D.C.: American Psychological Association.

Matza, D. (1964). *Delinquency and drift*. New York: Wiley.

Mawson, A.R. (1987). *Transient criminality: A model of stress-induced crime*. New York: Praeger.

McCall, N. (1994). *Makes me wanna holler: A young black man in America*. New York: Vintage Books.

McCarthy, B. (1994). Warrior values: A socio-historical survey. In J. Archer (Ed.), *Male violence* (pp. 105-120). London: Routledge.

Members of Japanese university party group admit gang rapes. (2003, Sept. 17). *Agence France Press*. Retrieved December 2, 2003, from Lexis/Nexis database.

Merrill, L. (2001). Childhood abuse and premilitary sexual assault in male Navy recruits. *Journal of Consulting & Clinical Psychology, 69*, 252-261.

Millham, J., & Weinberger, L.E. (1977). Sexual

preference, sex role appropriateness, and restriction of social access. *Journal of Homosexuality, 2,* 343-357.

Muehlenhard, C.L., & Schrag, J.L. (1991). Nonviolent sexual coercion. In A. Parrot & L. Bechhofer (Eds.), *Acquaintance rape: The hidden crime.* New York: John Wiley & Sons.

Nardi, P.M., & Bolton, R. (1991). Gay-bashing: Violence and aggression against gay men and lesbians. In R. Baenninger (Ed.), *Targets of violence and aggression* (pp. 349-400). Amsterdam: Elsevier Science.

National Gay and Lesbian Task Force. (1992). *Anti-gay/lesbian violence, victimization & defamation in 1991.* Washington, D.C.: Author.

Nelson, T.S. (2002). *For love of country: Confronting rape and sexual harassment in the U.S. military.* New York: Haworth Press.

Newman, K.S., Fox, C., Harding, D., Mehta, J., & Roth, W. (2004). *Rampage: The social roots of school shootings.* New York: Basic Books.

O'Sullivan, C.S. (1991). Acquaintance gang rape on campus. In A. Parrot & L. Bechhofer (Eds.), *Acquaintance rape: The hidden crime* (pp. 140-156). New York: John Wiley & Sons.

O'Sullivan, C.S. (1998). Ladykillers: Similarities and divergences of masculinities in gang rape and wife battery. In L. H. Bowker (Ed.), *Masculinities and violence* (pp. 82-110). Thousand Oaks, CA: Sage.

O'Toole, L.L. (1997). Subcultural theory of rape revisited. In L. L. O'Toole & J. R. Schiffman (Eds.), *Gender violence: Interdisciplinary perspectives* (pp. 215-222). New York: New York University Press.

Patton, C. (2003). *2003 Preliminary report, national coalition of anti-violence programs.* Available from National Coalition of Anti-Violence Programs, 240 West 35th Street, Suite 200, New York, NY 10001.

Pharr, S. (1988). *Homophobia: A weapon of sexism.* Inverness, CA: Chardon Press.

Pingel, F. (2004, March 10). Text of grand jury report. *Newsday.* Retrieved March 11, 2004, from www.newsday.com

Polansky, N., Lippitt, R., & Redl, F. (1950). An investigation of behavioral contagion in groups. *Human Relations, 3*(4), 319-348.

Rideau, W., & Wikberg, R. (1992). *Life sentences: Rage and survival behind bars.* New York: Times Books.

Roskey, M.L. (1988). *Ideology in instances of anti-gay violence.* Unpublished doctoral dissertation, University of California, Irvine.

Rotundo, E.A. (1993). *American manhood: Transformations in masculinity from the revolution to the modern era.* New York: Basic Books.

Rozee-Koker, P., & Polk, G.C. (1986). The social psychology of group rape. *Sexual Coercion & Assault, 1,* 57-65.

Russell, S.T., Franz, B.T., & Driscoll, A.K. (2001). Same-sex romantic attraction and experiences of violence in adolescence. *American Journal of Public Health, 91,* 903-906.

Sabo, D., Jupers, T.A., & London, W. (2001). *Prison masculinities.* Philadelphia: Temple University Press.

Sampson, R.J., & Laub, J.H. (1993). *Crime in the making: Pathways and turning points through life.* Cambridge, MA: Harvard University Press.

Sanday, P. (1990). *Fraternity gang rape: Sex, brotherhood, and privilege on campus.* New York: New York University Press.

Sanday, P. (2003). Rape-free versus rape-prone: How culture makes a difference. In C. B. Travis (Ed.), *Evolution, gender, and rape* (pp. 337-362). Cambridge, MA: MIT Press.

Scarce, M. (1997). *Male on male rape: The hidden toll of stigma and shame.* New York: Plenum.

Scully, D. (1990). *Understanding sexual violence: A study of convicted rapists.* Boston: Unwin Hyman.

Szalacha, L.A. (2001). *The sexual diversity climate of Massachusetts' secondary schools and the success of the safe schools program for gay and lesbian students.* Unpublished doctoral dissertation, Harvard University.

Tallmer, A. (1984). Anti-lesbian violence. *Task Force Report* (p. 4). Washington, D.C.: National Gay Task Force.

Thompson, E.H., & Pleck, J.H. (1986). The structure of male role norms. *American Behavioral Scientist, 29,* 531-543.

Twenty accused in suburban Paris gang-rape trial. (2002, Sept. 16). *Agence France Press*. Retrieved December 2, 2003, from Lexis/Nexis database.

Van de Ven, P. (1995). Talking with juvenile offenders about gay males and lesbians: Implications for combating homophobia. *Adolescence, 30,* 19-42.

Vitello, P. (2003, October 28). Masquerade at Mepham. *Newsday*, p. A8.

von Schulthess, B. (1992). Violence in the streets: Anti-lesbian assault and harassment in San Francisco. In G. M. Herek & K. T. Berrill (Eds.), *Hate crimes: Confronting violence against lesbians and gay men* (pp. 65-75). Newbury Park, CA: Sage.

Wang, K. (2003, October 5). Rights group begins where life ended. *Star-Ledger* (Newark, NJ), p. 16.

Weissman, E. (1978, August). Kids who attack gays. *Christopher Street*, pp. 9-13.

[9]

"Men are expected to enjoy, or at least not shirk, adventures ranging from street fights, to heavy drug use binges, to commission of acquisitive felonies."

SITUATIONAL CONSTRUCTION OF MASCULINITY AMONG MALE STREET THIEVES

HEITH COPES
University of Alabama–Birmingham
ANDY HOCHSTETLER
Iowa State University

HEITH COPES is an assistant professor in the Department of Justice Sciences at the University of Alabama–Birmingham. His primary research interest is on criminal decision making. His current research focuses on the motivations and fears of carjackers.

ANDY HOCHSTETLER is an assistant professor in sociology at Iowa State University. His articles appear in social science journals including Criminology; Social Problems; Crime, Law and Social Change; Deviant Behavior; *and* Journal of Criminal Justice. *His current interest is variation in the experience of incarceration and effects on reintegration and recidivism.*

Increasingly, theorists recognize that the influence of masculinity on decision making is situationally contingent and embedded in interactions. Using interviews with ninety-four male street thieves, the authors describe the situations that bring constructions of masculinity into the foreground of street crime. In certain situations, men are likely to engage in criminal behavior as a mechanism for constructing their masculinity. The authors find that hanging with criminally capable associates and partying are critically significant for understanding when masculine concerns bear on criminal decision making. In these situations, copresent others interpret inappropriate actions or responses as definitive signs of weakness, passivity, and failure in the struggle to be a man. They also examine how age and criminal experience shape conceptions of masculinity and the style of their enactment.

Keywords: *masculinities; crime; criminal decision making; situational*

Recently, criminologists have devoted increased attention to crime-antecedent events (Athens 1997; Groves and Lynch 1990; Katz 1988). Out of an apparent concern for the state of existing decision-making research, many researchers began studying the situations that lead to crime. These critics noted that examining criminal decisions as the outcome of an economic calculus provided a misguided understanding of the choice process (Shover and Honaker 1992). Criminal decisions are embedded within a framework of events and an outlook that tremendously slants economic calculation. To understand criminal decisions, it is necessary to understand the perspective of the actors making decisions, their interpretations of events, and their material and expressive goals (Katz 1988; Jacobs and Wright 1999; Shover 1996). How the offender wishes to be seen by others is of great importance in the development of many crimes. In certain circumstances, the malefactor views committing crime as altogether appropriate, if not righteous (Katz 1988).

Researchers interested in masculinity endorse this recent focus on underlying social considerations in specific criminal choices and how they play out in real criminal situations. If we argue that crime is the situational accomplishment of gendered expectations, then the means for

AUTHORS' NOTE: The authors contributed equally to research and writing. We thank the editors of the journal and the anonymous reviewers for their comments on an earlier version of this article. *Direct all correspondence to Heith Copes, Department of Justice Sciences, University of Alabama–Birmingham, 901 South 15th Street, Birmingham, AL 35294.*

achieving these expectations are theoretically critical links between masculinity as structure and masculine action (Jefferson 1997). As Messerschmidt (1993) stated,

> Because masculinity is a behavioral response to the particular conditions and situations in which men participate, different types of masculinity exist in the school, the youth group, the street, the family, and the workplace. In other words, men do masculinity according to the social situation in which they find themselves. (pp. 83-84)

Those young men who prove their manhood by fighting in the streets or in bars might not call on physical violence in their homes or at work. Despite admonitions against the neglect of situated action, surprisingly few studies have focused specifically on the accounts ordinary offenders give of their decisions and the role that masculine considerations plays in their choices (Jefferson 1997, 538; Miller 1998).

In this article, we examine the typical arrangement of events and interactions before street thefts are committed with an eye toward identifying obvious and less than obvious masculine themes. We pay special attention to antecedent situations that appear to be particularly criminogenic for street thefts committed by males. Understanding theft by men is important since it is these acts that encompass much of what we understand about criminal decision making, and it is these acts that largely compose the "crime problem." Analysts have argued, more or less implicitly, that street crimes emanate from a subcultural venue where the connection between emphasized forms of masculinity and crime is easy to see. However, even for common crimes, the mechanisms and details of interaction that connect beliefs and ideals are underexamined. As a result, it would be easy to inaccurately conclude that offenders draw on uniform, trans-situational, masculine repertoires and to neglect how environments and interactions shape the ideals decision makers reference (Jefferson 1997). Recognizing that the work of previous investigators subsumes our findings, we attempt to paint a picture of masculinity, interaction, and the foreground of criminal decision making with slightly more detailed strokes than used in the past. As part of our analysis, we specify how conceptions for evaluating worth among men in the lower tiers of the working class are valuable for interpreting stylistic differences between crimes of older thieves as compared to those of younger thieves.

SITUATIONAL ACCOUNTABILITY AND MASCULINITY

Two empirical discoveries reinvigorated interest in how situational interaction contributes to crime. First, investigators confirmed that offending is associated with lifestyles that include drinking, drug use, and congregation with other offenders and is likely to occur in domains where these activities occur (Agnew and Peterson 1989; Felson 2002; Kennedy and Baron 1993; Sacco and Kennedy 2002). Second, research showed clearly that many offenders give their crimes little forethought and that criminal choices are often improvisational and spontaneous (Bennet and Wright 1984; Feeney 1986; Wright and Rossi 1986). These discoveries led criminologists to recognize that certain situations are imbued with meanings that contribute to criminal potential and to look more closely at the situations where crimes develop (Birkbeck and Lafree 1993). Many of the resultant ethnographies and qualitative studies speak to the situational construction of masculinity and its place in criminal decision making.

Beynon (2002, 54) pointed out that investigators interested in situational interaction often study masculinities indirectly without specific reference to gender. To reinforce the point, he noted that researchers of youth culture and delinquency for many years have focused on gendered interactional norms without acknowledging specifically that this is what they are doing. Indeed, the same can be said of many criminological investigations of the offender's perspective. For example, when Cordilia (1986) interviewed sixty-seven imprisoned male robbers, she found that thefts often arise out of a "group drinking context." Her participants reported that their crimes originated out of spontaneous interaction within a drinking group. She described the situational establishment of a fatalistic, competitive, and reckless outlook among groups of impoverished, intoxicated men that causes offenders to "focus on the proximate rewards of group cohesion" at the expense of more careful consideration of their choices (p. 170). Similarly, Shover (1996) contended that evaluation of risk can easily be neglected in company that "celebrates and affirms values of spontaneity, independence, and resourcefulness" (p. 233). The aforementioned researchers imply that offenders' concerns about acting masculine and their gendered character projects guide many interactions preceding crime. Several researchers note specifically that crime can be interpreted as an endeavor that proves one's adherence to a particular form of masculinity and as an effort to get a reputation as an adherent (Collison 1996, 441; Jackson 1995, 28; Messerschmidt 1993; Hobbs 1994; Katz 1988).

The concept of situational accountability is critical to linking constructions of masculinity to criminal behavior (Fenstermaker, West, and Zimmerman 1991; Messerschmidt 1993, 1997). Actors realize that others hold them accountable to behavioral dictates consistent with immediate circumstances. Thus, "they construct their actions in relation to how they might be interpreted by others in the particular social context in which they occur" (Messerschmidt 1993, 79). Actors demonstrate that they are appropriately masculine or feminine by performing behaviors that others easily interpret within an evaluative framework. This framework is localized, immediate, and attributed to present company, albeit nested in cultural and subcultural ideals. It is widely acknowledged that masculinity is a "situational accomplishment" (Kersten 1996) and "has the capacity for rapid modification" (Beynon 2002, 10). It is lived experience in specific spaces (Westwood 1990), a presentation of self "which is negotiated implicitly or explicitly over a whole range of situations" and interactions (Morgan 1992, 47). Therefore, understanding the influence of masculinity on any given phenomenon requires close attention to commonality in immediate circumstances and in the ideals referenced by participants.

There are slight differences in the masculine values attributed to street criminals by researchers, and there is ongoing discussion of regional and temporal variation in offenders' constructions of self (Bottcher 2001; Collier 1998; Winlow 2001). However, descriptions of street offenders' lifestyles and broad ideals are largely the same, and most everyone seems to agree that crime is especially likely to occur in situations that impugn or threaten character constructions based on claims of dangerousness, criminal know-how, or criminal capability (Athens 1997; Katz 1988; Messerschmidt 2000; Shover 1996, 107). Despite this fact, investigators give more attention to the subcultural value system among street thieves than to how this system affects unfolding situations that lead to crime and intracategory variation in how offenders try to establish character and act masculine in specific social situations. Our analysis focuses on social situations and settings that evoke a particular masculinity through implied and overt interpersonal challenges and manly competitions. These definitive situations make masculine claims salient and constrain available repertoires.

Offenders understand that others will interpret inappropriate action in these settings as failure in the "struggle to be masculine" (Jackson 1995, 24).

METHOD

For this study, we draw on data from semistructured interviews with ninety-four men under community supervision in a southern metropolitan area between 1998 and 2000. All were on probation or parole at the time of the interviews for robbery, burglary, or motor vehicle theft. The state department of correction granted us access to files of men under community supervision. We used information from these files to identify and contact suitable participants to interview. They contained addresses and phone numbers, if available, of offenders who had committed the crimes of interest. We contacted nearly three hundred men and invited them to participate. The ninety-four participants represent those who consented to be interviewed. We paid participants $15 for a one- to two-hour interview.

Our sample is one of men who had formal contact with the criminal justice system and not one of free-ranging offenders. Critics have voiced their concerns over the potential shortcomings of research based on samples derived from criminal justice sources (Cromwell, Olson, and Avary 1991; Glassner and Carpenter 1985). Despite these criticisms, there is little doubt that investigations of street crime using samples of known offenders have produced detailed, accurate, and useful data on a variety of topics (e.g., Athens 1997; Maruna 2000; Rengert and Wasilchick 2000; Shover 1996). There is little reason, moreover, to believe that the results of these studies contradict or are inconsistent with what has been learned from studies using active offenders, especially when discussing their interpretations of their lives and behaviors. Even when confined to prison, an offender "carries his interpretations with him" (Sutherland 1973, 50).

We conducted interviews in places that were convenient for respondents. Interview locations included probation and parole offices after their regular appointments, their homes, local libraries, or other quiet places. In a few instances, we conducted interviews in areas that were not ideal settings for interviews, including parks, cars, and taverns. We constructed an initial interview guide to provide uniform coverage of topics, but we allowed offenders the opportunity to talk about events that they thought were important in shaping their criminal decisions. Interviews focused on offenders' motivations to commit crime, the target selection process, perceived risks and rewards of participating in crime, and techniques and skills used to accomplish the tasks. We also asked offenders about their families, relationships, occupations, criminal histories, patterns of drug use, and other aspects of their lives, with a particular emphasis on the time surrounding their most recent period of criminal activity. Substantial attention was devoted to understanding the lifestyle of offenders, how they saw themselves, and how they selected other members of their social circles at the time of their offenses. This lifestyle section of the interview provided significant insight into what offenders valued among their male peers.

Interviews followed a loose structure and concentrated on the immediate life circumstances and events preceding a "typical" felony theft that the respondent could recall. Through probing for recollections of conversations and activities that precede theft and events that occur during and immediately after it, we had participants recount the process of a felony theft in as much detail as possible. Obviously, offenders located the events that they described within a larger lifestyle and extended course of events including repeat offending. Nevertheless, the most fruitful request we made was to have the offender think of one of his typical crimes and then to describe in as much detail as possible all of the events leading up to the incident. Participants described what they were thinking about, what kinds of conversations they were having with co-offenders, and what happened during and after they completed the offense. We tape-recorded and transcribed interviews. We then analyzed the interviews with a software package designed to code and organize textual data.

Although reflecting a wider range of criminal experience, the offenders we interviewed are very much like those in other investigations of street crime (Jacobs 1999; Shover 1996; Wright and Decker 1994, 1997). The offenders in the sample varied from criminal novices to persistent offenders. Some had no previous arrests, and others had lengthy rap sheets that reflected years of persistent offending. Crimes in offenders' records ranged in severity from minor drug possession or driving under the influence to rape, kidnapping, and murder. Even among those who had few convictions, most admitted that they committed multiple thefts. Admission of dozens of felony thefts was not rare. This level of criminal activity is common among persistent thieves—a category that clearly captures at least 25 percent of the men we interviewed. Thirty-one of our participants had been imprisoned more than once for felony theft. The mean age at the time of the interview was thirty-one. Only eighteen (19 percent) of the offenders were married, while sixty-five (69 percent) were single. Eleven had previously been married (12 percent). These men typically were poor and uneducated. Approximately 60 percent of them did not have steady jobs at the time of the offense, and almost all of those who did occupied the lowest rungs of the labor market. Racial minorities made up half of the sample. As mentioned earlier, the sample consists entirely of men. While this is a limitation of the research, it also allows for efficiency in presentation and analysis since women are likely to have different influences on their decision making, and masculinity may have a distinct influence on female offenders' decisions (Miller 1998).

MASCULINITY IN THE FOREGROUND: JUMPING IN OR PUSSING OUT

To describe how certain social situations bring masculine concerns to the foreground, it is necessary to briefly review the masculine ideals held by those in our sample. Many masculine concerns are intertwined with other values associated with street culture that have been documented by decades of ethnographic research on street criminals. This line of research informs us that among street offenders, it is important to appear (1) autonomous, (2) capable of providing for oneself, and (3) action oriented (Anderson 1999; Cohen 1955; Gibbs and Shelley 1982; Jacobs and Wright 1999; MacCleod 1987; Miller 1958; Shover 1996; Wright and Decker 1997). Offenders contrast their lifestyles with those of hesitant, passive, and compliant persons who settle for mundane existences and dependence on others (Akerstrom 1985). This outlook, long thought to be criminogenic, is linked to conceptions of masculinity and can be construed as a universally available avenue of achievement that allows the offender to interpret failures at work and domesticity as achievement of freedom (Jefferson 1994; Messerschmidt 1993, 1997; Simpson and Ellis 1995). Their ideals are masculine because they draw on general ideals of manhood and are contrasted with traits symbolically attributed to women in patriarchal society and even more so in the harshly patriarchal worldview of the street offender.

Nearly all investigations of street offenders' lifestyles show that they have an exaggerated desire for autonomy. They typically resent authority, external control, and restrictions associated with conventional work-a-day living and domesticity; that is, "to be cool, one must not be under anyone else's thumb" (Jacobs 1999, 33). Many active offenders cannot envision themselves in workplaces or relationships that require subordination, discipline to authority, or interference with their habits and parties (Akerstrom 1999; Irwin 1970; Shover 1996; Sutherland 1937). As part of their particular visions of autonomy, street offenders place a great deal of importance on appearing to be independently capable of providing for their needs (Maruna 2000). They spend money in ways that emphasize ostentatiously their seemingly effortless ability to provide for themselves and those around them even at the cost of empty pockets in the morning. Like most males, street offenders emphasize what Brittan (1989) colorfully called the "heroic hunter as breadwinner" (p. 77) as a masculine ideal (Kersten 1996). However, they approximate successful achievement of the goal by wanton partying and conspicuous consumption meant to demonstrate independence from the restraints of relationships and routine financial concerns. In some ways, their pursuits resemble vacations taken by young working men (Collison 1996).

In further demonstration of their adherence of a value system emphasizing unrestricted freedom, many street offenders associate manly behavior with risk taking and subsequently admire those who do the same. A measure of impulsivity and a "devil-may-care" attitude are respectable in street offenders' social surroundings. Men are expected to enjoy, or at least not shirk, adventures ranging from street fights, to heavy drug use binges, to commission of acquisitive felonies. Those who cannot keep up are quickly labeled *punks*, *pussies*, *bitches*, or other similar terms intended to highlight subjectivity and the inability to face trying situations head-on.

Offenders, like most everyone else, are not committed to a singular view of masculinity and are tolerant of diverse ideals and means of achieving them. Most offenders have long-term goals that in some ways conflict with their desire for the forms of autonomy and action they are seeking during periods of active offending. At the same time, they are notably intolerant of those who play at the notion of masculinity outlined above but are unable to back up their claims in defining situations. Once a criminal identity is claimed, it must be backed up or the actor risks losing credibility in the few venues where his style and abilities are taken seriously (Katz 1988). Offenders use any number of insults, most with feminine connotations, to describe cowardly pretenders who provoke or help create situations that they cannot handle.

These masculine ideals are not inherently criminogenic, as they can be realized in a number of ways not involving crime. They are, however, conducive to crime in certain social situations. Specifically, these values lend themselves to criminal behavior when men find or place themselves in situations where they are partying or hanging out. Here, crime becomes a mechanism of gender construction because the situation has clarified the salience of a particular vision of masculinity. In these social settings, men often engage in grandiose talking, which frequently involves boasting that relies on cultural stereotypes of masculinity and femininity. The likelihood of having one's identity challenged is significantly increased when circumstances clearly evoke the particular form of masculinity admired on the streets or when one is already showing off. For instance, being at a party without offerings, being unwilling to jump into a criminal and potentially dangerous situation, or being unable or unwilling to back up boasts undermines masculine claims. Similarly, posturing oneself as one of the boys in a crowd that defines itself as criminally capable often results in situations where one is expected to act.

We argue that street thieves use constructions of gender to create and interpret criminal opportunity and to generate compliance from indecisive or wavering co-offenders, especially when partying or hanging out. In certain social spaces, offenders often have a heightened sensitivity to being labeled as anything but masculine. They are aware that those they encounter while partying or hanging out are likely to endorse the same focal concerns. Reference to the importance of autonomy, provision, or action inevitably occurs in these situations. In many cases, interaction is scripted intentionally by at least one actor who is firmly set on a criminal outcome or who is creating a scene suitable for demonstrating his ostensible familiarity and experience with crime or street life. In other words, some men use situational scripts quite consciously to entice or coerce others to join them in criminal adventures and to enhance the value of their own actions in maintaining a desired social and self-image.

PARTYING AND HANGING WITH THE BOYS

Offenders' descriptions of their lifestyles left little doubt that participation in hedonistic parties preceding crime was interpreted among their peers as a worthwhile endeavor, if not the only way for a man to live life to its fullest. If there is one phrase that describes typical events that precede decisions to commit acquisitive street crime, it is "desperate partying" (Wright and Decker 1997, 35). By partying, offenders unambiguously mean the use of drugs and alcohol for prolonged periods. Some of the parties were milder than others, but most were exceptionally "wild" or "hard" even by the standards of regular drug users. By the time they committed their crimes, some groups had been partying for days, a feat attributable in part to a taste for drugs that interfere with sleep. Offenders who fail to invest fully in the party by moderating drug use or attempting to leave early may be taunted playfully but with a clear message. On trying to leave a party to get some sleep, one offender recalled that he decided to stay only after his friend asked antagonistically, "You need a nap? What are you, an eight-year-old girl or something?" Another robber recalled that he rode along on a crime purely out of a sense of obligation to the people with whom he had indulged in a lengthy binge. Having already committed to the party, leaving when supplies are soon to be replenished would be awkward:

> [We were] snorting dope all night. They were going to do this [crime], but I had to go to work in the morning. I know I've got to go to bed. I didn't even do any of the drugs we got out of it; I had to leave. Everybody else is going, so I go. Can you believe that seven of us piled in a car to go and do this?

A thief who was well connected with fences explains that in the context of certain parties, criminal opportunity is sure to be seized by eager recruits: "I just take anybody, whoever, along. Somebody's gonna go when you are around a bunch of dope and the stuff [merchandise] is already sold." Another offender explains that attendance at certain parties is key to identifying the criminally motivated or those who can be easily motivated:

> And then the next time I would go somewhere I would take somebody else. I mean these people just hang out. They ain't got nothing to do; they just want some dope probably . . . just something to do. I would just take them along.

Partying implies the presence and consumption of drugs and alcohol. But many offenders do not have a constant supply of illicit drugs on hand. Street thieves sometimes "hang with their boys" without indulging in illicit intoxicants, often while milling around and waiting for an opportunity to get high. Offenders frequently congregate on street corners, in bars, or at someone's house where the types of parties that interest them occur regularly. One reason that participation in offenders' social gatherings implies criminal capability is that those assumed to have criminal experience and ability frequent these settings. Our point is that the mere choice of attending these gatherings contributes greatly to criminal potential, and it is not just the activities likely to occur in these settings that contribute to criminal definitions of the situation. The spaces impart meaning, and the presence of known and reputed thieves sends a message that those present are tolerant of criminal activity and potentially willing to participate. Several of the offenders whom we interviewed had local reputations for their criminal prowess or experiences. These men could safely assume that the people willing to go "riding around" with them were also open to criminal opportunities.

In many cases, a novice offender's perception of opportunity is rooted in the presence of people assumed to be more capable of crime. The point is not lost on inexperienced offenders that criminal motivation, whether acquiescence or eagerness, for crime began when they came into the presence of someone they knew or suspected to be criminally active, criminally capable, or intent on offending. In hindsight, they often comment that these inspirational co-offenders "seemed to know what they were doing." From the perspective of the other side of the interaction, an experienced burglar notes that an established criminal reputation turns others' heads toward criminal opportunities: "They know if they come with me, they going to get some money." Merely to be in the presence of seasoned offenders forms the basis of a claim of criminal ability and opens eyes to criminal possibilities. To the extent that street crime results from masculine claims, the claim of association with the criminally capable is essential. Established thieves have proven to others in their social world that they are appropriately masculine. To hang with people of this caliber establishes one's own identity and reputation; therefore, younger men often position themselves socially around the more experienced so that they can profit by association.

In addition to the importance of proper reciprocation and carrying through on a line of action commensurate with partying activities, it is important to many young street offenders to be viewed as dependable and loyal in risky situations (Cohen 1955; Shover 1996). If one is partying and cannot continue to "hang" with the rest of the group or cannot provide for his share of the drugs, then his worth is threatened. This individual is at risk of being perceived as weak and passive, or as "having no heart." This threat occurs not only in the mind of the individual offender but is also expressed by other group members. The desire to live up to a masculine self-image then becomes a strong component in the decision to engage in antecedent activities and street crime.

CRIMINAL DELIBERATION: BUCKING UP HEADS

Certain settings are criminogenic due to the potential of challenges and confrontations of one's masculine persona. In the presence of people who are already engaged in risky behavior or are known to be active offenders, events or statements that might otherwise be ambiguous impart meanings that are clear to all. Offenders often discuss crime using ambiguous language. The phrase *making money* or discussions of the need to make money initiated many of the criminal deliberations described to us. It is the setting that gives meaning to the phrase, and everyone knows that nothing legal is being proposed. Once everyone is "on the same page," offenders often rely on conversational posturing and one-upsmanship to build confidence and move their group toward crime (Cromwell, Olson, and Avary 1991; Hochstetler and Copes 2003). Tales of past criminal successes, exaggerations of expected rewards of an offense, diminishing the potential risks, and encouraging statements like "we can do this" or "there ain't nothing to it" are elements of these challenges. These conversations create such an optimistic tone that hesitation by those who have claimed to be criminally capable is laughable. As one offender said,

> When you get like that and you get around a couple of your partners and they like ,yeah, we going to do this. You like, alright let's do it. That's just how it is. You buck each other's head up. And then when you around

> them you ain't going to coward out. There on the spot, you might as well do it. So there it is.

Most criminologists who have considered offenders' conversations as an important element of crime construction have focused on conversations after they turn to planning (Cromwell, Olson, and Avary 1991; Feeney 1986). By this point, the scene is set. Criminal deliberation and planning do not emerge from a blank conversational slate but from earlier conversations and events in which at least one offender has made claims of criminal capability or ability. Often, these claims are made in an indirect manner that evokes the masculine themes of being a provider and an adventurer. By conversationally posing as one who has what it takes to commit a crime, offenders cause others to reference appropriate cultural tool kits (Swindler 1986). An experienced thief explains how his inexperienced partner initiated their crime:

> One thing led to another and everybody is talking about robbing and stealing and stuff like that. The other guys knowed that I was pretty well off into criminal activities. And so, maybe one thing led to another and I was just cutting up with the dude. Then he got kinda serious about it and I said, "Well hell, if you're serious let's go for it."

Making claims during conversations designed to impress can easily be taken as an interpersonal challenge and often instigates more direct challenges. A car thief remembers the turn in the conversation that preceded his crime.

> One night me and two of my partners was sitting on the levy smoking weed. For some strange reason my little partner Chip was like, "So-and-so went on a car lot the other night and you know those little boxes they had the keys in the boxes on the window." I'm like, "They don't have the damn keys in the window. Stop tripping!" [He said,] "Man, I'm telling you." So, we end up going to a car dealership. . . . I am just really being nosy to see if they are lying, to call their bluff. And we break one of the boxes and he was right, they had keys in it.

For individual offenders already committed to completing a crime or for whom crime is routine, masculine posturing is opportunity. A young burglar recalls the last minutes of his group's criminal deliberation and how his friend encouraged the crime by questioning the extent of the young man's nerve:

> [He would] just go on and say all kind of stuff, like say you're getting scared and say your momma had more nerve than you did. [He would say] stuff to more or less make you mad so that your temper and you just would get out and do it anyways.

These overt challenges are best understood as metaphorical devices that raise the question, "Are you really with us, or have you only been acting criminally capable?" Overt references to gender typically appear at this stage and can be seen as one form of "talking it up," a phrase that captures the general encouraging tone of criminal conversations directly before engaging a target (Cromwell, Olson, and Avary 1991; Hochstetler and Copes 2003; Shover 1996; Tunnell 1992).

> I was worrying about what they going to say, that I ain't got the balls enough to go do this. I said, man I got to do this or they are going to look down upon me. I said the hell with it, I'm just going ahead and doing it. I had to do it or they would clown [make fun of] me.

Last-minute chatter keeps masculine claims salient and is intended to shore up allegiance and to ensure commitment to a dangerous situation. Emasculating insults bring the subtext of masculine ideals already present in less overt posturing and risky antecedent situations to the surface. One offender recalls the taunts he received prior to a crime he committed: "They had started trying to buck my head up to do some things. [They said things] like, 'Ah man, you wouldn't do this, you a pussy.' "

AGE AND SITUATED MASCULINITY

We have mentioned that gendered ideals are used to generate compliance and to interpret the presence of criminal opportunities in specific social settings, particularly partying and hanging out. The masculine themes that are called on and the way offenders use these themes are not the same for all. A significant body of research shows that masculine identities vary by social position, or as Messerschmidt (1993) contended, "boys will be boys differently" (p. 87). Our interviews reveal that thieves construct their behavioral ideals in ways that are appropriate for their ages and that their ages influence the structure of the situations where they conduct themselves and their crimes.

To understand how masculinity shapes crime, it is necessary to examine various forms of situations and subtle variation in what men are trying to accomplish in them. Age and criminal experience play prominent parts in this variation. Obviously, it is difficult to distinguish the unique effects of age and criminal experience in a sample of convicted street thieves, since most have lengthy criminal records for men their ages. There are also exceptions to statements about the relationship between age and offending style, which add further complexity. Young men with tremendous criminal experience and who are thoroughly socialized into entrepreneurial criminal subcultures often approach crime much like older men, for example. Some older men, usually those who are extremely intoxicated, commit thefts that are in the usual style of juveniles. Nevertheless, the older men and younger men in our sample conducted the situations preceding their offenses differently. In addition, their degree of reliance on different conceptions of masculinity varied. Older men were apt to define their actions in opposition to the passive acceptance of a mundane and humble daily existence and in opposition to juvenile styles of acting out. Younger men, almost singularly, focused on distinguishing themselves from cautious and weak qualities stereotypically attributed to women.

As can be seen in prison narratives across the decades, older offenders have always worried over the dishonorable and foolish behavior of upcoming generations of offenders in ways that mirror the concerns of conventional elders (Irwin 1970). This mature concern, in part, reflects the fact that the action-adventurer role, as carried out by young men, is a distasteful mark of immaturity among aging men. Older offenders believe that the young often lose sight of the purpose of crime, which is to remain free to do as they please over an extended period. In their view, youths do not understand that the trick to successful crime is to always be on the lookout for criminal opportunities having either low risk or high potential for return and for the appropriate time to seize them. Criminologists have recognized for decades that older offenders have more clearly defined materialistic motivations than do their younger counterparts. This explains, in part, why older men are more likely to offend alone and to commit property crimes with less purely expressive motives than younger offenders (Ezre 1987). As one older offender said,

> Everybody steals cars for different reasons. Now to a teenage kid, he might steal a car just to joyride, and the police may chase him, and he may end up killing himself or killing somebody. But to a mature person, if they stole a car, they going to steal it for two reasons. They either going to steal to fix up their car or they going to steal it to sell to somebody else.

When older and younger thieves offend together, older offenders encourage their young accomplices to act like men by staying "calm, cool, and collected." As a rule, older thieves have little tolerance for those who panic or those whose disregard for risk shows while "on the job." One aging habitual thief recalls stealing with a young accomplice:

> Nervous people make me nervous and accidents happen when people are nervous and frustrated. It's a bad thing to say, but I was good at what I done. I have busted someone in the head that I was with for trashing a place. . . . What good does that do you?

When young men encounter older men, especially older men with extensive criminal experience, they are generally impressed and often aim to borrow the style of their elders. Extremely experienced offenders usually acknowledge that at some point in their careers they acquired a criminal maturity beyond their years by emulating older thieves (Shover 1996). A robber explains his admiration of his partner in their early offenses together: "He had experience. He knew what the hell he was going in there for. He knew what the hell the deal was. He was someone I looked up to."

Although desperation and drug use sometimes cloud their judgment, older offenders typically have enough experience to know how to be temporarily successful at crime. They are "streetwise" (Anderson 1999; Westwood 1990). They pride themselves on having the patience to wait for the right moment, a trait they do not believe younger men and men of the younger generations possess. They often keep dozens of possible targets or promising locales under casual surveillance until a convenient chance arises. When they are ready to offend, older offenders arrange their social circumstances with more clearly defined criminal intent than youthful offenders do. For older men, crime often is the desired outcome of the day, and they seek out circumstances that make it possible.

Older offenders' crimes tend to be "put together" by someone. Often, one offender has a specific crime in mind, or simply a desire to offend, and assembles others whom he assumes will also be motivated for and capable of the crime. Since co-offenders were assembled because they are known or thought to be candidates for recruitment, these men probably are beyond being impressed by blind bravery. In seasoned offenders' groups, there is little to gain by emphasizing willingness to commit crime or showing off one's ability to take risks. Posturing as a deliberate, seasoned thief and willing provider rather than an adventurer is more appropriate for crimes hatched in circumstances preceding older men's crimes than in those that erupt instantaneously in the street and are more common among the young. Among older men, conversations before crime are more practical, involving slightly more planning, somewhat realistic estimates of the expected take, and a plan for disposal of stolen items and subsequent acquisition of drugs. The tone of the conversation is little different from any time these men get together and rarely has the same degree of the nervous, giddy quality of deliberations that precede young offenders' crimes. For offenders who know that all present are familiar with crime, little needs to be said, and conversation on the way to the scene of the crime is minimal or composed of small talk.

At the scene of the offense, older men tend to concentrate on staying cool under pressure, and when they show off, they emphasize the ability to do so. In a few cases, for example, older burglars stopped to smoke a joint or eat a sandwich during an offense. Others prided themselves on how nonchalantly they could commit felonies without drawing attention even though the crimes occurred in public settings. The rush of crime is to be controlled and usually is enjoyed fully by older men only when they have returned to safety.

While the crimes of older men are likely to arise from intentional settings and play predominantly on the provider and autonomy ideals, younger men's crimes are relatively spontaneous, and their form is shaped by the desire for action and to avoid being seen as passive or cowardly. Young men spend more leisure time in each other's company than older ones. Therefore, they usually need not assemble a crew for theft. Young offending groups, especially those that have not stolen together many times, typically do not congregate with their sights firmly set on offending. They recognize that they are assembling for action and that places where the action is have the potential for crime.

But even when hanging out in open-air drug markets or driving around aimlessly at midday while drinking with other unemployed young men, crime remains a possibility and not a clearly articulated objective. Younger offenders often think that their crimes "happened" with little volition when circumstances seemed to demand immediate action. As one young offender describes, "I just got wrapped up with a stolen car." This young man claimed to be unaware of his friend's intention to steal a car, and before he could back out, it was "too late." He added, "It wasn't something planned—it just happened."

For young men, the appearance of a target often sparks criminal motivation and strikes everyone simultaneously. In fact, young men often see the appearance of a target in the presence of their peers and onlookers as a challenge to the front of bravery and ability to take risks that they have presented. Many robberies have occurred because someone confronts or insults a group of young men in the streets or has the gall to treat them as if they were incapable of crime. A young, homeless robber remembered that his brutal robbery began when another young man had the audacity to show that he was carrying valuables in a setting where he should have known better: "I ain't going to be played for a punk like that."

When conversations precede youths' crimes, they often focus on whether a crime should be done at all and on determining who has the courage to go through with it. Dares and overt challenges are common. When young thieves are "called out," they believe that they have little choice but to go through with a criminal act. They must act regardless of fear, and if they show signs of hesitation, whether in the form of excessive questions or delays, the power of their adventurous displays is diminished. Recalling his youthful days of joyriding in stolen cars, an offender stated,

> I had a friend named Craig. He used to brag, "Man I can get them [cars] in five minutes, man." And I would say, "Yeah, but you get nervous. I don't. I bet I can get that before you." It was something like . . . we would just be walking around town or around the courthouse, you know. I would say, "Get it." He was like, "Check if nobody is looking." I would say, "I told you, you was nervous." I'd get in there, start it, and take off.

In these conversations, youths play off each other in an exploration of willingness to offend. This banter helps assure them that they have support and an appreciative audience for crime. In the face of such challenges, eager young thieves seem determined to demonstrate unpredictability, risk taking, and fearlessness.

> We were driving down the road after leaving the club; we noticed a guy walking. I was like, "man we should rob him." They were like, "Yeah man. What, you going to do it?" I said, "Look, you don't know me." Everything I done did in the past, how's he going to sit there and call me a pussy. He don't know what I'm [capable of] doing.

The way in which they show off and the inherent excitement of dangerous events often cause youths to commit theft with a flare that distinguishes them from older men's thefts. Youthful offenders embrace, and sometimes attempt to intensify, the rush that results from crime. In retrospect, they often are surprised by the extent to which they "got carried away" and let their better judgment fall under the influence of the excitement of showing off. Fights turn to robberies where violence far exceeds what was necessary to steal. Burglaries result in needless destruction of property. Stolen cars are driven dangerously and in ways that attract attention. Stolen guns are shot from cars. The thrill of it all sometimes results in rowdy celebrations before an escape has been achieved. In part, these actions are the reckless mistakes of immaturity. They can also be interpreted as attempts to accomplish the image that youthful men value. In their view, hard men flaunt risk taking and take it to levels that will impress even other risk takers.

Variation in situational structures where crimes occur is an important reason for differences in how younger and older men carry out their crimes. Most thieves precede their offenses with parties, big talk, and social exchanges. But the parties, talk, and posturing of younger and older thieves are different. These differences speak to respectable behavior as one ages in the unsuccessful life trajectory of the type lived by most thieves. Although older offenders continue to conspicuously display the proceeds of crime, they are much less concerned with their friends' evaluations of their readiness, toughness, or "badness."

DISCUSSION

Offenders' views of what it means to be a man influence action within a context that leaves few outlets available. For a number of reasons, they cannot provide a financially or socially stable existence for their dependents; they cannot be players in the stock market, business world, or even the factory. They cannot indulge in real luxury. Thus, these men seek adventurous situations that lend themselves to demonstrations of willingness and eagerness to break the law, tempt danger, and spend criminal rewards. In demonstrations of autonomy and action, they jump to the forefront of criminal deliberation and crime commission and often look forward to the opportunity for doing so.

Masculinities may have infinite personal forms that are channeled and formed by cultural, social, and organizational positions. People construct gender based on the situation that confronts them. We have examined how male offenders use their interpretations of the expectations attributed to men in their social world to symbolically frame lines of action when considering a particular offense. Offenders, who already heavily invest in masculine fronts that emphasize their unrestricted lifestyles and freedom from concerns, turn masculine posturing up a notch in appropriate circumstances. To participate in heavy drinking and drug use, to engage in conversations that imply criminal ability, and to join in social networks and groups where potential for crime is high are to evoke masculine cultural norms of the variety discussed here. If there is any set of actions that lead to street crime, it is these instances of showing off.

Description of "moment-to-moment accomplishment" of "what is and what is not proper to the categories woman and man" is recognized in a way that is intuitive with both the analyst's and reader's understandings of their culture (Coleman 1990, 186). The disreputable young men who occupy the bottom of the socioeconomic ladder and are responsible for most street crime probably do not have the same conventions and attitudes toward women as middle-class college professors. For them, to act like a woman is to be a passive subordinate or a punk. Such a reputation can be bothersome in a world where intimidation games are common and the threat of violence lies just below the surface of many interactions. Even within this world, however, offenders are cued toward criminal trajectories of behavior by situational actions and words that evoke subcultural themes of the taker and the taken or the "players and the punks" in current street lexicon. The interactions that precede many crimes are exchanges of subtle and overt social signals that remind participants of their place and the expectations of manhood. Indeed, it seems that in many crime groups, self-interested actors are quite consciously and apparently playing on others' masculinities, insecurities, and claims to simultaneously achieve a criminal objective and enhance their own status as criminally capable.

One aim of this article was to contribute to the theoretical understanding of criminal decision making. Our findings have implications for at least three theoretical issues. First, they imply that constructions of gender are important symbolic frames for determining appropriate situational behavior and as such are a relevant part of criminal decision making. Gender metaphors enter the minds of offenders as they deliberate over crime and encourage offenders to follow through on a criminal course. Criminal decision-making research has often concentrated on easily operationalized perceptions of risk and rewards, but psychosocial variables influencing constructions of opportunity and decisions often escape empirical research. For example, current models of decision making fail to address the cognitive process that might explain why men typically are greater risk takers than women in experimental studies, an oversight that should be clear to decision-making researchers.

Second, our finding that older men construct the situations preceding crime in a style that differs from that of young men suggests that constructions of masculinity may be important for understanding variation in the subjective rewards and costs of crime. Most men age out of crime and the desire to be action oriented. Even the aging thieves whom we interviewed no longer sought to be seen as impulsive action-adventurers. As men age, they no longer rely on impulsiveness and action as a way to frame their identities, and as such, threats centered on these themes no longer provoke them to engage in crime. If understanding of criminal decision making is to advance, we must recognize that seemingly equivalent outcomes do not necessarily result from equivalent goals in what offenders are trying to accomplish. The intersection of life history, identity, cognitive schemes, and situations is as important for understanding criminal decisions as is simple utilitarian calculus of risk and reward of crime.

Finally, our findings show that settings determine the scripts that offenders draw on when choosing crime. Criminologists have emphasized the importance of the settings in which offenders place themselves for decades, especially in the lifestyle and routine activity perspectives (Cohen and Felson 1979; Hindelang, Gottfredson, and Garafolo 1978). Routine activities studies have demonstrated, mainly by examining the temporal and spatial correlates of crime, that crime is likely to occur in some settings much more than others and that these settings are characterized by motivated offenders and the presence of suitable targets (Cohen and Felson 1979). Lifestyle studies expanded on this notion by showing that victimization and offending can be predicted by lifestyles that place people in public, high-risk settings for crime. However, insufficient attention has been given to how certain settings and activities trigger cognitive frames that make offending seem reasonable to some people. Why is it that crime is likely to occur in certain bars at certain hours of the evening? Our analysis would suggest that it is not only the selection of the locale but the meaning that the locale has for participants and their expectations. Motivated offenders do not just bump into suitable targets and react. They build a frame of interpretation within the confines of the setting and the dictates of their lifestyle that makes the target suitable. Masculinities come into play within this interaction of offenders, audience, and environments. Ethnographers can contribute greatly to understanding the details of how gendered lifestyles and objectives enacted in environments affect the choice to offend.

REFERENCES

Agnew, Robert, and David Peterson. 1989. Leisure and delinquency. *Social Problems* 36:332-50.

Akerstrom, Malin. 1985. *Crooks and squares: Lifestyles of thieves in comparison to conventional people.* New Brunswick, NJ: Transaction.

———. 1999. Looking at the squares: Comparisons with the Square Johns. In *In their own words: Criminals on crime*, edited by Paul Cromwell, 23-32. Los Angeles: Roxbury.

Anderson, Elijah. 1999. *Code of the street: Decency, violence and the moral life of the inner city.* New York: Norton.

Athens, Lonnie H. 1997. *Violent criminal acts and actors revisited.* Chicago: University of Chicago Press.

Bennet, Trevor, and Richard Wright. 1984. *Burglars on burglary.* Hampshire, UK: Gower.

Beynon, John. 2002. *Masculinities and culture.* Philadelphia: Open University Press.

Birkbeck, Christopher A., and Gary Lafree. 1993. The situational analysis of crime and deviance. *Annual Review of Sociology* 19:113-37.

Bottcher, Jean. 2001. Social practices of gender: How gender relates to delinquency in the everyday lives of high risk youths. *Criminology* 39:893-932.

Brittan, Arthur. 1989. *Masculinity and power.* New York: Basil Blackwell.

Cohen, Albert. 1955. *Delinquent boys*. New York: Free Press.

Cohen, Lawrence, and Marcus Felson. 1979. Social change and crime rate trends: A routine activity approach. *American Sociological Review* 44:588-608.

Coleman, Will. 1990. Doing masculinity/doing theory. In *Men, masculinities and social theory*, edited by Jeff Hearn and David Morgan, 186-202. London: Unwin Hyman.

Collier, Richard. 1998. *Masculinities, crime and criminology*. London: Sage.

Collison, Mike. 1996. In search of the high life: Drugs, crime, masculinities and consumption. *British Journal of Criminology* 36:428-44.

Cordilia, Ann T. 1986. Robbery arising out of a group-drinking context. In *Violent transactions*, edited by Anne Campbell and John J. Gibbs. New York: Blackwell.

Cromwell, Paul, James Olson, and D'Aunn Wester Avary. 1991. *Breaking and entering: An ethnographic analysis of burglary*. Newbury Park, CA: Sage.

Ezre, Edna. 1987. Situational or planned crime and the criminal career. In *From boy to man, from delinquency to crime*, edited by Marvin E. Wolfgang, Terrance P. Thornberry, and Robert M. Figlio. Chicago: University of Chicago Press.

Feeney, Floyd. 1986. Robbers as decision-makers. In *The reasoning criminal: Rational choice perspectives on offending*, edited by Derek B. Cornish and Ronald V. Clarke, 53-71. New York: Springer-Verlag.

Felson, Marcus. 2002. *Crime and everyday life*. 3d ed. Thousand Oaks, CA: Pine Forge Press.

Fenstermaker, Sarah, Candace West, and Don H. Zimmerman. 1991. Gender inequality: New conceptual terrain. In *Gender, family and economy*, edited by Rae Lesser Blumberg. Newbury Park, CA: Sage.

Gibbs, John J., and Peggy L. Shelley. 1982. Life in the fastlane: A retrospective view by commercial thieves. *Journal of Research in Crime and Delinquency* 49:299-328.

Glassner, Barry, and Cheryl Carpenter. 1985. The feasibility of an ethnographic study of adult property offenders. Report prepared for the National Institute of Justice.

Groves, W. Byron, and Michael Lynch. 1990. Reconciling structural and subjective approaches to the study of crime. *Journal of Research in Crime and Delinquency* 27:348-75.

Hindelang, Michael, M. Gottfredson, and J. Garafolo. 1978. *Victims of personal crime: An empirical foundation for a theory of personal victimization*. Cambridge, MA: Ballinger.

Hobbs, Dick. 1994. Mannish boys. In *Just boys doing business? Men, masculinities and crime*, edited by Tim Newburn and Elizabeth A. Stanko. New York: Routledge.

Hochstetler, Andy, and Heith Copes. 2003. Managing fear to commit felony theft. In *In their own words: Criminals on crime*, 3d ed., edited by Paul Cromwell, 87-98. Los Angeles: Roxbury.

Irwin, John. 1970. *The felon*. Berkeley: University of California Press.

Jackson, David. 1995. *Destroying the baby in themselves: Why did the two boys kill James Bulger?* Nottingham, UK: Mushroom Publications.

Jacobs, Bruce. 1999. *Dealing crack: The social world of streetcorner selling*. Boston: Northeastern University Press.

Jacobs, Bruce, and Richard Wright. 1999. Stick-up, street culture, and offender motivation. *Criminology* 37:149-74.

Jefferson, Tony. 1994. Theorizing masculine subjectivity. In *Just boys doing business? Men, masculinities and crime*, edited by Tim Newburn and Elizabeth A. Stanko. New York: Routledge.

———. 1997. Masculinities and crime. In *The Oxford handbook of criminology*, 2d ed., edited by Mike Maguire, Rod Morgan, and Robert Reiner. Oxford, UK: Oxford University Press.

Katz, Jack. 1988. *Seductions of crime*. New York: Basic Books.

Kennedy, Leslie W., and Stephen W. Baron. 1993. Routine activities and a subculture of violence: A study of violence on the street. *Journal of Research in Crime and Delinquency* 30:88-122.

Kersten, Joachim. 1996. Culture, masculinities and violence against women. *British Journal of Criminology* 36:381-95.

MacCleod, Jay. 1987. *Ain't no makin' it: Leveled aspirations in a low-income neighborhood.* Boulder, CO: Westview.

Maruna, Shadd. 2000. *Making good: How ex-convicts reform and rebuild their lives.* Washington, DC: American Psychological Association.

Messerschmidt, James W. 1993. *Masculinities and crime: Critique and reconceptualization of theory.* Lanham, MD: Rowman and Littlefield.

———. 1997. *Crime as structured action: Gender, race, class and crime in the making.* Thousand Oaks, CA: Sage.

———. 2000. Becoming "real men": Adolescent masculinity challenges and sexual violence. *Men and Masculinities* 2:286-307.

Miller, Jody. 1998. Up it up: Gender and the accomplishment of street robbery. *Criminology* 36:37-66.

Miller, Walter. 1958. Lower-class culture as a generating milieu of gang delinquency. *Journal of Social Issues* 14:5-19.

Morgan, David H. J. 1992. *Discovering men*. London: Routledge.

Rengert, George, and John Wasilchick. 2000. *Suburban burglary: A tale of two suburbs*. 2d ed. Springfield, IL: Charles C Thomas.

Sacco, Vincent, and Leslie Kennedy. 2002. *The criminal event: Perspectives in space and time.* Belmont, CA: Wadsworth.

Shover, Neal. 1996. *Great pretenders: Pursuits and careers of persistent thieves*. Boulder, CO: Westview.

Shover, Neal, and David Honaker. 1992. The socially bounded decision making of persistent property offenders. *Howard Journal of Criminal Justice* 31:276-93.

Simpson, Sally S., and Lori Ellis. 1995. Doing gender: Sorting out the caste and crime conundrum. *Criminology* 33:47-77.

Sutherland, Edwin. 1937. *The professional thief.* Chicago: University of Chicago Press.

———. 1973. *On analyzing crime*, edited by K. Schuessler. Chicago: University of Chicago Press.

Swindler, Ann. 1986. Culture in action: Symbols and strategies. *American Sociological Review* 51:273-86.

Tunnell, Kenneth. 1992. *Choosing crime: The criminal calculus of property offenders*. Chicago: Nelson Hall.

Westwood, Sallie. 1990. Racism, black masculinity and the politics of space. In *Men, masculinities and social theory*, edited by Jeff Hearn and David Morgan. London: Unwin Hyman.

Winlow, Simon. 2001. *Badfellas: Crime, tradition and new masculinities*. Oxford, UK: Berg.

Wright, James D., and Peter H. Rossi. 1986. *Armed and considered dangerous*. Hawthorne, NY: Aldine de Gruyter.

Wright, Richard T., and Scott Decker. 1994. *Burglars on the job: Street life and residential break-ins*. Boston: Northeastern University Press.

———. 1997. *Armed robbers in action: Stickups and street culture*. Boston: Northeastern University Press.

[10]

MANAGING TO KILL: MASCULINITIES AND THE SPACE SHUTTLE CHALLENGER EXPLOSION

JAMES W. MESSERSCHMIDT
University of Southern Maine

It has been ten years since the Space Shuttle Challenger exploded in midair, just 73 seconds into flight, killing all seven crew members. The Presidential Commission (1986) investigating the explosion concluded that the loss of Challenger was due to a failure in the joint between two segments of the right Solid Rocket Booster (SRB). O-rings—intended to prevent hot gases from escaping through the joint during the propellant burn of the rocket engine—failed to seal properly because of the extremely cold temperature at launch time (29 degrees F). More specifically, the cold temperature impaired O-ring resiliency, allowing the hot gases to escape, ignite, and within seconds penetrate the External Tank.[1]

The Presidential Commission (1986) further concluded that problems with the O-ring design were well-documented, and therefore well-known, by both government (NASA) and corporate (Morton Thiokol, Inc.) officials years before that fateful day. Indeed, the Commission concluded that the explosion was "rooted in history" and that a "flawed decision-making process" led to the launch (p. 82).

In addition to the Presidential Commission, criminological investigations of the explosion have appeared in recent years, focusing primarily on the organizational context within which the "flawed decision" to launch was reached (Kramer, 1992; Vaughan, 1989, 1994). This article contributes to this evolving reexamination of the explosion by considering the fact, which previous investigations ignore, that those involved in the decision to launch Challenger were *all* men; my interest is in the gendered character of the events

I am especially grateful to Pat Carlen, Carol Cohn, Bob Connell, Walter DeKeseredy, Tony Jefferson, Mark Maier, Barbara Perry, Dianne Sadoff, and Diane Vaughan for helpful comments on earlier drafts of this paper.

Address correspondence to the author at the Department of Criminology, University of Southern Maine, Portland, ME 04103.

and decisions leading to the Challenger explosion. Indeed, such an investigation opens a window to corporate decision-making, generating new insights into corporate masculinities and corporate crime.[2]

Maier's (1993) account is the sole examination of the explosion that considers gender; unfortunately it relies on David and Brannon's (1976) outdated sex-role theory. Although I have criticized sex-role theory elsewhere (Messerschmidt, 1993), it should be pointed out that such analysis ultimately homogenizes men by reducing all masculinities to one normative standard type, and is therefore unable to account for human agency and the social construction of differing masculinities.

Gender is conceptualized here not in this traditional sociological sense, but rather as an active, behavior-based, situational accomplishment (Messerschmidt, 1993; Thorne, 1993; Connell, 1987, 1995a; West & Fenstermaker, 1993; West & Zimmerman, 1987). Conceptualizing gender in terms of social situation and structured action permits a deeper formulation, not only of what has been visible, but what previously has been hidden—such as masculinit*ies* (Connell, 1995a; Messerschmidt, 1993). This newly emerging feminist perspective, outlined below, is used to examine the relationship between the differentiation of corporate masculinities (managers vs. engineers) and the Space Shuttle Challenger explosion.

GENDER AS STRUCTURED ACTION[3]

West and Zimmerman (1987) argue that in Western industrialized societies there exist but two "sex categories," and that individuals are assigned at birth to one or the other. Moreover, in all social situations we attempt to adorn ourselves with culturally appropriate "female" or "male" fashion and in every interaction we consistently engage in gender attribution, identifying and categorizing people by appropriate sex category while simultaneously categorizing ourselves to others (see also Kessler and McKenna, 1978).

Nevertheless, as West and Zimmerman (1987) argue, *gender* entails considerably more than the social signs of a sex category. Rather, gender involves a situated accomplishment: "the activity of managing situated conduct in light of normative conceptions, attitudes, and activities appropriate to one's sex category" (p. 127). And because gender is the outcome of social practices in specific settings, it serves to inform such practices in reciprocal relation. Thus, while sex category defines social identification as woman or man, gender systematically corroborates that identification through social interaction: we coordinate our activities to "do" gender in situational ways.

Crucial to conceptualization of gender as situated accomplishment is the notion of "accountability." Because individuals realize their behavior is accountable to others, they configure and orchestrate their actions in relation to how they might be interpreted by others in the particular social context in which they occur. In other words, in their daily activities individuals attempt to become socially identified as female or male. Accountability thus "allows individuals to conduct their activities in relation to their circumstances" (West & Fenstermaker, 1993, p. 156) and thereby highlights the possibility that gender varies by social situation and circumstance. Within every interaction, then, we encourage and expect others to attribute a particular sex category to us. We facilitate the ongoing task of accountability by demonstrating we are "male" or "female" through concocted behaviors that may be interpreted as such. In this way, we do masculinity or femininity differently, depending upon the social situation and the social circumstances we encounter. Thus, "doing gender" renders social action accountable in terms of normative conceptions, attitudes, and activities appropriate to one's sex category in the specific social situation in which one acts.

In this view, then, masculinity is accomplished systematically, not imposed on men or settled beforehand. Although early in life we develop relatively fixed individual identities as a member of one sex category, masculinity is never a static or a finished product. Rather, men construct masculinities in specific social situations. In other words, men participate in self-regulating conduct whereby they monitor their own and other's gendered conduct.

Although masculinity is "made," so to speak, through the unification of self-regulated practices, these practices do not occur in a vacuum. Instead, they are influenced by the social structural constraints we experience. Following Connell (1987, 1995a), and outlined elsewhere (Messerschmidt, 1993), three specific social structures—gender division of labor, gender relations of power, and sexuality—underlie relations between women and men. These social structures are not external to social actors, nor simply and solely constraining. On the contrary, structure is realized only through social action and social action requires structure as its condition. Moreover, women and men do gender in specific social situations, thereby reproducing and sometimes changing social structures. And given that men reproduce masculine ideals in socially structured specific practices, there are a variety of ways to do masculinity. Although masculinity is always individual and personal, specific forms of masculinity are available, encouraged, and permitted, depending upon one's social situation, class, race, and sexual orientation. Accordingly, masculinity must be viewed as *structured action*—what men do under specific social structural constraints.

In this way, then, social relations (such as class, race, and gender) link each of us in a common relationship to others: we share structural space. Consequently, common or shared blocks of knowledge evolve through interaction in which particular masculine ideals and activities play a part. Through such interaction, masculinity is institutionalized, permitting men to draw on such existing, but previously formed, masculine ways of thinking and acting to construct a masculine identity for specific settings. The particular criteria of masculine identities are embedded in the social situations and recurrent practices whereby social relations are structured (Giddens, 1989).

We must thus recognize, first, that men are positioned differently throughout society and that, therefore, they share with other men the construction of masculinities peculiar to their position in society. We must accept also that socially organized power relations among men are constructed historically on the bases of class, race, sexual preference, and specific social situations; that is, in specific contexts (such as organizations) some men have greater power than other men. In this sense, then, masculinity can be understood only as a relational construct.

Connell's (1987, 1995a) notion of "hegemonic masculinity" is relevant here. Hegemonic masculinity is the culturally idealized form of masculinity in a given historical setting. It is culturally honored, glorified, and extolled at the symbolic level in the mass media. In Western industrialized societies, hegemonic masculinity is characterized by work in the paid labor market, the subordination of women, and heterosexism. Hegemonic masculinity, as the culturally dominant ideal, influences but does not determine masculine behavior. As Thorne (1993) notes: "Individuals and groups develop varied forms of accommodation, reinterpretation, and resistance to ideologically hegemonic patterns" (p. 106). Although men attempt to express hegemonic masculinity through speech, dress, physical appearance, activities, and relationships with others, these social signs of masculinity accommodate to the specific context of one's actions and are self-regulated within that context. Thus, masculinity is based on a social construct that reflects unique circumstances and relationships—a social construction that is renegotiated in each particular context. In other words, social actors self-regulate their behavior and make specific choices in specific contexts. As Connell (1987) points out, everyday masculine practices draw on the cultural ideals of hegemonic masculinity but they do not necessarily correspond to actual masculinities as they are lived. What most men support is not necessarily what they are. In this way, then, men construct varieties of masculinities through specific practices. By emphasizing diversity in gender constructions, a more fluid and situated approach to gender is realized.

Taking this approach permits us to conceptualize gender and crime in new ways, ways that enable us to explore how and in what respects masculinity is constituted in certain settings at certain times, and how that construct relates to crime. For example, as discussed earlier, work in the paid labor market is central to hegemonic masculinity and, therefore, to the lives of most men. Indeed, "the job" is a major basis of identity and what it means to be a man. For criminology, however, the association among masculinity, work and crime historically has been explored only in the case of *unemployed* men engaged in street crime. And routinely at issue here is not the unemployed male's relationship to work per se but, rather, his limited or lack of access to the paid labor market. What is missing in the criminological and gender studies literature is a full consideration of gender and crime within the context of work and, especially, in the setting of white-collar work. This article attempts to fill that void by examining the relationship between masculinity and crime involving male managers and engineers in a particular corporate organizational setting.

The focus of the remaining sections, then, explores the differentiation of corporate masculinities by observing the work and product of their construction in a specific setting and through certain practices. I examine such masculinities not in terms of relations between women and men, but as they are reproduced among men in corporations. A review of the empirical evidence on the Space Shuttle Challenger explosion, with an eye to the social context in which both gender and corporate crime are accomplished, reveals that gender is a critical structural tool in corporations. Indeed, the definition and interpretation of the boundaries between masculinities, and thus the hierarchical separation of some men from other men, are critical organizational bases in corporate bureaucracies. Accordingly, the specific masculine meanings constructed through particular occupations and the ways in which corporate crime is related to those meanings and occupations must be analyzed thoroughly. As such, I argue that only through an analysis of corporate masculinities can we make coherent sense of the Space Shuttle Challenger explosion.[4]

Although men are always doing masculinity, the significance of masculine accomplishment is socially situated and, thus, is an intermittant matter. That is, certain occasions present themselves as more intimidating for demonstrating and affirming masculinity. In such settings, sex category is particularly salient; it is, as Morgan (1992) puts it, "more or less explicitly put on the line" (p. 47)—a time when doing masculinity requires extra effort. Under such conditions in corporations, corporate crime may be invoked as a practice for doing masculinity and distinquishing masculinities from one another. The Space Shuttle Challenger explosion provides an excellent case study of how in the same social situation, one type of masculinity (manager) was constructed through the commission of corporate crime, while contemporaneously another type of masculinity (engineer) was constructed through resisting that crime.

RISKY TECHNOLOGY

The National Aeronautics and Space Administration (NASA) had long been interested in frequent, economical access to space and, in 1970, the White House declared that funding on the order of previous NASA projects—such as Gemini and Apollo—was no longer possible (President's Commission, 1986). Thus, to obtain funding from Congress, NASA had to guarantee a program with low development costs and dependable routine operations. To accomplish this, NASA proposed a Space Shuttle that would be both reusable and cost-effective in design.[5] Moreover, the Shuttle was to be economically self-sufficient through satellite launchings and commercially supported in-flight research. It was in the increasingly austere fiscal environment of the early 1970s, then, that the Shuttle was born.

Morton Thiokol, Inc. (MTI) was selected on November 20, 1973 to receive the NASA contract to design and build the SRBs. Not surprisingly, costs were the primary concern of NASA's selection board.[6] Although the board noted several problems with the MTI proposal, they were deemed "technical in nature" and "the costs to correct did not negate the MTI cost advantage." Furthermore, the dual O-ring feature was especially noteworthy to the selection board.[7] Thus, a cost-plus-award-fee contract, worth approximately $800 million, was awarded to MTI (President's Commission, 1986).

However, from the beginning there were problems with MTI's dual O-ring design, all of which were well-documented by both NASA and MTI.[8] Despite consistent evidence of the hazardous nature of the O-ring design, Shuttle missions were not halted to correct the anomalies. In fact, as the President's Commission points out, with the landing of the fourth test flight, "the orbital flight test program came to an end [and remarkably] NASA declared the Space Shuttle 'operational'" (p. 5). Initially, managers and engineers at both NASA's Marshall Space Flight Center in Huntsville, Alabama (which has authoritative responsibility for the Orbiter's main engine, the External Tank, and the Solid Rocket Booster) and at MTI incessantly rationalized that after some initial erosion, the O-rings would ultimately seal intact; if the primary O-ring failed to seal the joint, the secondary O-ring would act as a back-up. Flight after flight was approved by both organizational managers and engineers, "accepting the possibility of some O-ring erosion due to hot gas impingement" and the belief that redundancy would prevail (President's Commission, 1986, p. 132).[9]

By January 24, 1985, however, when the 15th Shuttle flight was launched, the temperature of the O-rings at launch was 53 degrees F, the coldest launch temperature to that date. On that flight, O-ring erosion occurred in both SRBs as well as in both primary and secondary O-rings. Accordingly, several MTI *engineers* became much more concerned and reported to Marshall that this launch occurred during the "worst case temperature change in Florida history" and that "low temperature enhanced the probability of erosion" (President's Commission, 1986, p. 136). Although previously MTI engineers felt the possibility existed for significant reduction of the erosion problem and a belief in redundancy, the results of this flight clearly indicated the anomalies needed to be corrected immediately. As Roger Boisjoly, the leading engineering specialist at MTI, stated in a letter to MTI management:

> This letter is written to insure that management is fully aware of the seriousness of the current O-ring erosion problem in the SRB joints from an engineering standpoint. . . .It is my honest and very real fear that if we do not take immediate action to dedicate a team to solve the problem, with

> the field joint having the number one priority, then we stand in jeopardy of losing a flight along with all the launch pad facilities. (Boisjoly, 1987, p. 4)[10]

However, MTI management was not forthcoming with the resources necessary to solve the O-ring problem. As Boisjoly goes on to point out: "the MTI management style would not let anything compete or interfere with the production and shipping of boosters" (p. 1).

Thus, by 1985, the O-ring erosion problem had been well-documented at Marshall and MTI, yet the management of both organizations ignored engineer concerns and labeled the problem an "acceptable risk" rather than suspending Shuttle missions until the problem was fixed. Additionally, in that same year NASA published a projection calling for 24 flights per year by 1990.

Arguably, NASA was under pressure throughout the early- to mid-1980s to meet both customer commitments and Congressional approval—which meant not only launch a certain number of flights per year but launch them on time. Indeed, as the President's Commission (1986) concludes:

> From the inception of the Shuttle, NASA had been advertising a vehicle that would make space operations "routine and economical." The greater the annual number of flights, the greater the degree of routinization and economy, so heavy emphasis was placed on the schedule. (p. 164)

Within this context, Marshall managers responded to the O-ring problem not by cancelling flights and fixing the problem (since delays were to be avoided), but by proceeding full speed ahead. As the President's Commission (1986, p. 152) put it, in the face of "unrelenting pressure to meet the demands of an accelerating flight schedule," these managers considered the faulty seal "nonserious" and an "acceptable risk." The result was a pattern of risk-taking practices by Marshall managers.

While Marshall managers faced the imperative of a routine and economical flight schedule, MTI faced far-reaching contract negotiations with NASA and competition from other aerospace suppliers/manufacturers. As McConnell (1987) argues, negotiations between NASA and MTI regarding the second phase of the lucrative Shuttle SRB contract were intensely troubling for MTI throughout much of 1985:

> In the 1970s contract, Thiokol was assigned the production of the first thirty-seven sets of boosters. Given the increased flight schedule, that number would be used by the end of 1986. Therefore, Thiokol was actively negotiating for the second-phase contract that would cover the next sixty sets of boosters, a procurement award worth a billion dollars. However, other aerospace companies had been lobbying Congress for at least two years to force NASA to break Morton Thiokol's monopoly on producing

> the SRB's. In the fall of 1985 Thiokol's management was acutely aware of this lobbying effort, which Congressional staff members called a "full-court press," by Thiokol's competitors. (pp. 180-181)

Indeed, by winter of 1985 NASA initiated competitive bidding on the pending contract renewal—"thus seriously threatening for the first time Thiokol's thirteen year monopoly" (President's Commission, 1986, p. 60). Consequently, MTI managers were not in the position to irritate their most prominent customer by suspending Shuttle flights until a new O-ring design was developed. So they, in the manner of their counterparts at Marshall, accepted escalating risk. In short, both Marshall and MTI management came to accept the O-ring problem as "unavoidable and an acceptable flight risk" (President's Commission, 1986, p. 148).

THE LAUNCH DECISION

On January 27, 1986, NASA scrubbed the scheduled flight due to high crosswinds at the launch site and rescheduled Challenger for the following morning (President's Commission, 1986, p. 17). By the early afternoon of January 27, 1986, MTI engineers became increasingly concerned over the predicted low temperature of 29 degrees F for the rescheduled launch time, especially in light of the near disaster one year earlier at 53 degrees F. This concern led ultimately to a teleconference between Marshall and MTI officials on the issue of temperature. Data regarding the effect of low temperature on the O-rings and the joint seal were presented by MTI engineers along with an opinion that launch should be delayed until the temperature was at least 53 degrees F. Marshall requested that MTI prepare and telefax a more formal presentation to both Marshall and Kennedy Space Center officials (in Florida) for a full-fledged teleconference later that evening.

At approximately 8:45pm EST, the second teleconference commenced. The telefax presented a history of the O-ring erosion in the SRB joints of previous flights. Roger Boisjoly, the leading engineering specialist at MTI, expressed deep concern about launching at such low temperature. Boisjoly argued that the Shuttle should not be launched below a temperature of 53 degrees F because such temperature would result in the O-rings becoming less resilient and, therefore, incapable of sealing the joint before hot gases ignited to cause an explosion. As Boisjoly stated to the President's Commission, it would be "like trying to shove a brick into a crack versus a sponge" (p. 89). Indeed, by now both MTI management and engineers agreed that the Shuttle should not launch until temperatures reached at least 53 degrees F. Notwithstanding, Marshall managers "were not pleased" with MTI's conclusions and recommendations (p. 90).

Marshall challenged MTI's data and conclusions primarily by accusing

MTI of trying to establish new launch-commit criteria based on a 53-degree F standard. Eventually, Lawrence Mulloy, SRB manager at Kennedy, responded to MTI's concern about temperature by stating: "My God, Thiokol, when do you want me to launch, next April?" (p. 96). Mulloy insisted that MTI's position was irrationally qualitative, based simply on experience rather than rational, quantifiable, evidence. A further exchange between MTI and NASA representatives continued for quite sometime, with MTI maintaining that launch should not occur outside the 53 degree F data base. George Hardy, deputy director of science and engineering at Marshall, responded by stating: "I'm appalled at your recommendation" (p. 94).

Thus, MTI found themselves on the defensive and experienced formidable coaxing to reverse their no-launch recommendation. MTI was placed in a social situation where they had to demonstrate convincingly it was *not* safe to launch, whereas in all previous pre-flight conferences MTI was required to verify it was safe to launch. In other words, they had to prove the launch would fail![11]

Eventually the debate reached an impasse. Overwhelmed at having to prove that the joint would fail, MTI management sought a five-minute off-line recess to reevaluate the effect of temperature on the O-rings. The caucus (lasting at least thirty minutes) began with Jerry Mason, senior vice president at MTI, stating to the three managers around him, "we have to make a management decision" (p. 92). Assuming that management was about to consider reversing the earlier no-launch decision, the MTI engineers (especially Roger Boisjoly and Arnie Thompson) attempted a last-minute explanation of the effects of low temperature on O-ring resiliency. Boisjoly explained this attempt to the President's Commission:

> Arnie actually got up from his position which was down the table, and walked up the table and put a quarter pad down in front of the management folks, and tried to sketch out once again what his concern was with the joint, and when he realized he wasn't getting through, he just stopped.
>
> I tried one more time with the photos. I grabbed the photos, and I went up and discussed the photos once again and tried to make the point that it was my opinion from actual observations that temperature was indeed a discriminator and we should not ignore the physical evidence that we had observed. . . .I also stopped when it was apparent that I couldn't get anybody to listen. (pp. 92-93)

In short, these two engineers ardently tried to stop management from reversing their earlier unanimous no-launch decision.

During this exchange, it was clear that three of the four managers supported a launch, but that Bob Lund, vice president of engineering, remained committed to the earlier no-launch decision. After some further discussion of the data, with Lund remaining the sole holdout among the managers, Mason turned to Lund and instructed him "to take off his engineering hat and put on his management hat" (p. 93). The managers then agreed they had to make a management decision, as Mason states, "in order to conclude what we needed to conclude" (p. 1383). At this point the engineers were excluded from the decision-making process and a final management review was conducted by the four managers only. The MTI managers, then, with Lund concurring, decided to reverse the decision of the engineers and approve the launch for the next morning. As the President's Commission put it:

> At approximately 11pm EST, the Thiokol/NASA teleconference resumed, the Thiokol management stating that they had reassessed the problem, that the temperature effects were a concern, but that the data were admittedly inconclusive. Kilminster read the rationale recommending launch and stated that that was Morton Thiokol's recommendation. (p. 96)

MANAGING TO KILL

How can we begin to understand the fact that, in the face of a strong possibility of risk to human life, MTI engineers recognized this threat and argued against the launch whereas MTI managers yielded to Marshall pressure and voted unanimously to launch?[12] It is now well-established in the sociological literature that gender is embedded in corporations and that gender is accomplished through concrete corporate activities, resulting not only in gender divisions (e.g., gender divisions of labor; "male" and "female" jobs) but, also, in situationally specific gendered images, symbols, and practices (Acker, 1992). More specifically, corporations often are defined through metaphors of masculinity. As Joan Acker puts it:

> Today, organizations are lean, mean, aggressive, goal oriented, efficient, and competitive but rarely empathetic, supportive, kind and caring. Organizational participants actively create these images in their efforts to construct organizational cultures that contribute to competitive success. (p. 253)

The gendering of corporations involves a presentation of self as a gendered member of the corporation and, for the corporate manager, this means specific practices, such as rationality, instrumentalism, careerism, decisiveness, productivism, and risk-taking, that help the corporation be successful (Kerfoot & Knights, 1993). Indeed, as we have known for almost twenty years, corporate-managerial masculinity is measured by success in reaching corporate goals;

accordingly, managerial gendered practices align themselves with corporate needs (Acker, 1990; Kanter, 1977; Tolson, 1977).

MTI managers, like other corporate managers, pursued such gendered practices to assist MTI in attaining its goals. Like other corporate managers, MTI managers consistently faced economic pressures that focus on the present and the near future: "the *next* milestone, the *next* contract, and the *next* stockholders' report are 'real' near-terms subjects that a manager must always address" (Dubinskas, 1988, p. 195). As indicated, the immediate situational goal of MTI was to preserve a lucrative government contract. Given the social situation of uncertainty in reaching this goal caused by the O-ring problem, rather than "hang tough" and continue to oppose the launch, MTI management engaged in risk-taking behavior to achieve their corporate objective. MTI managers rationalized giving greater weight to the advantage of risk-taking practices over halting Shuttle flights until the O-ring problem could be fixed. They chose the risk-taking path as more likely to advance both their individual masculine performance (gender) as well as corporate success (social class).[13]

When managers talk about "what is at stake" in their jobs, the answer invariably is "the growth of the organization" and, hence, their ultimate status (Dubinskas, 1988, p.199). Interviews with corporate managers show that they regard a manager who fails to take risks as one who should not be in the business of managing, and that risk-taking is especially warranted when faced with possible failure to meet corporate goals (March & Shapira, 1987). To be sure, for managers faced with such uncertainty in meeting goals, "the desire to reach the target focuses attention in a way that leads generally to risk-taking. In this case, the opportunities for gain receive attention, rather than the dangers" (p. 1413). Thus, we should not be surprised that the MTI managers reversed the decision of the engineers and approved the launch. Indeed, prestige accompanies the advocacy of such risk-taking and advocates of risk are perceived as especially capable managers, particularly when successful on the previous occasion (p. 1414).[14]

In this context, then, for MTI managers risk-taking became the situational defining feature of managerial masculinity. Risk-taking is widely documented as a masculine practice, where risk-ladened social situations are responded to more often by men/boys than women/girls as a challenge, an opportunity to "prove" ones worth and demonstrate prowess to others (Arch, 1993).[15] The MTI managers were no different from many other men confronted with a risk-ladened situation; risk-taking for them was, simultaneously, doing masculinity. What is different is that this risk taking masculine practice was specific to the particular social situation of this corporation. Clearly, the unique social conditions surrounding Challenger flights—preserving a lucrative government contract—created a context for MTI managers to push the limits of SRB technology. Because these managers had to demonstrate that the SRBs could survive a rigorous flight schedule, rather than acknowledge design flaws, they demonstrated corporate-managerial competence by supporting the necessity for remaining on schedule. Thus risk-taking became an available resource for achieving corporate goals because they "got away with it last time." As one member of the President's Commission (1986) observed:

> [The Shuttle] flies [with O-ring erosion] and nothing happens. Then it is suggested, therefore, that the risk is no longer so high for the next flights. We can lower our standards a little bit because we got away with it last time. (p. 148)

In other words, because flight after flight was "successful" (an explosion did not occur), this rationalized further risk-taking. Having survived the challenge, MTI managers became increasingly comfortable continuing the risk-taking behavior; thus, risk-taking became a practice not only for securing corporate goals but for solving the gender accountability problem at "the job." Risk-taking was not solely a practice for demonstrating corporate loyalty, but simultaneously for rendering such action accountable in terms of the normative conceptions and activities appropriate to the male sex category in this corporation. Because threats to profitmaking are concurrent threats to corporate-manager masculine accomplishment, risk-taking is an acceptable means of resolving both problems: risk-taking is a resource in this particular setting for accomplishing profit (class) and masculinity (gender). Accordingly, risk-taking was normalized among MTI management, permitting these men to draw on previously formed risk-taking behavior as a resource for doing masculinity. In short, managerial risk-taking became an institutionalized practice, a masculine resolution to the spectacle of technological uncertainty.

Thus, MTI managers gave Marshall the green light to launch in order to, as the President's Commission stated: "accommodate a major customer" (p. 104). Indeed, throughout "the first three weeks of January 1986, NASA and Thiokol conducted negotiations over a one-billion-dollar contract," and extremely important contract discussions were scheduled for January 28th—"the day after Thiokol managers made their recommendation to proceed with the launch, the day the Challenger was destroyed" (McConnell, 1987, p. 60). In this context, agreeing to take the risk demonstrated not only loyalty to the corporation but, simultaneously, provided MTI managers with a resource for doing masculinity—and, simultaneously, corporate crime—in that specific social setting.

Moreover, the attraction to risk-taking by these corporate-managers had as much to do with the social action itself as with what it produced in terms of corporate goals. The validation of manager effectiveness at MTI was one's proclivity to "go to the limit" in bringing a flight to "successful" fruition (President's Commission, 1986, p. 110). Each victorious challenge reconfirmed for others one's identity as an accomplished, proficient manager. Fervently effectuating risk-taking social practices provided these managers with the opportunity to exercise diligent control over the situation and bring it to a triumphant conclusion. This is consistent with other research on corporate-manager masculinity, which indicates that such managers are ranked "in terms of their capacity to display attributes of control over the definition of the reality of events" and are "constantly preoccupied with purposive action in the drive to be 'in control'" (Kerfoot & Knights, 1993, p. 671-672). Thus, every successful launch was taken as proof that one was "in control" and, therefore, possessed "the right stuff" to be a *man*(ager).[16] Indeed, the "enterprise of winning" by overcoming danger is for managers "life consuming" and results in "an inward turned competitiveness, focused on the self, creating, in fact, an instrumentality of the personal" (Donaldson, 1993, p. 665). As Kerfoot and Knights (1993) argue, at the level of embodied experience, this corporate-manager masculinity results:

> in the position whereby individuals feel "driven" for no discernable reason, other than as a part of what it means, and how it feels, to subscribe to an ideal of competence, and where the display of vulnerability is to threaten the image of that competence. (p. 672)

This translates into the denial or suppression of emotionality, fear, and uncertainty and, therefore, in the social situation of the off-line caucus, it should not be surprising to find MTI managers unanimously supporting launch; to do otherwise would mean exhibiting fear and uncertainty. These corporate-managers displayed, as Kanter (1977) put it in her discussion of managerial masculinity, "a capacity to set aside personal, emotional considerations in the interests of task accomplishments" (p. 22). Indeed, MTI managers disregarded (at least publicly) during the entire teleconference and off-line caucus the fact that human beings were on Challenger. The task was to "get Challenger up" and all factors antagonistic to that goal, including human life, were deemed irrelevant. This masculine discourse on the part of MTI managers is similar to the "technostrategic" discourse outlined by Cohn (1987, 1995) in her important research on nuclear defense intellectuals. Cohn (1995) found that during professional meetings these men systematically suppressed:

> the emotional, the concrete, the particular, the human bodies and their vulnerability, human lives and their subjectivity—all of which are marked as feminine in the binary dichotomies of gender discourse. In other words, gender discourse informs and shapes nuclear and national security discourse. (pp. 134-135)

Similarly, MTI managers eschewed any discussion of human beings (the flight crew) and their vulnerability to the risky technology. And clearly, it was the masculine discourse which generated this *indifference* to the human consequences of managerial decisions. In short, being more attentive to the survival of their lucrative contract rather than the survival of human beings was a means of "doing masculinity" and, as a result, corporate crime.[17]

The decision to launch by MTI managers can be understood, then, in terms of its captivating and enticing masculine appeal—a social practice that had become normalized in MTI managerial relationships. And because masculinity is constantly renegotiated and "made," voting to launch (and, therefore, changing their earlier no-launch position) was an acceptable (that is accountable) practice for its making in that particular social situation; a practice that "allowed" these managers to live up to a particular masculine ideal.

It is tempting to end the analysis here simply by reasoning that risk-taking masculinity "gave rise" to this corporate crime. Although this conclusion is attractive and not without substance, it disregards the diversity of masculinities actually constructed in corporations and thus their relation to corporate crime. Consequently, we must consider the varieties of masculinities at MTI, not just one type. Indeed, analyzing masculinities places us in a position to address why some men at MTI (engineers), despite the institutionalized and heavy emphasis on risk-taking, ardently opposed the launch. It is to the engineers that we now turn.

RESISTING LAUNCH

"Of all the major professions," Wajcman (1991) writes, "engineering contains the smallest proportion of females" and, like management, "projects a heavily masculine image" (p. 145). However, corporate managers validate masculinity by success at securing corporate economic goals while engineers are concerned primarily with technical competence/achievements and tend to devalue economic goals (Cockburn & Ormrod, 1993; Vaughan, 1989). Indeed, managers and engineers "identify themselves as being in—and 'from'—different 'worlds'" (Dubinskas, 1988, p. 185). Consequently, both managers and engineers weave gendered distinctions into their everyday understanding of "the job," and thus construct masculinity differently.

The relationship between "technical competence" and the social construction of gender difference is well-documented in the literature; as Cockburn (1985) puts it: "femininity is incompatible with technological competence; to feel technically competent is to feel manly" (p. 12). Nevertheless, to argue that technical competence is "manly" is not to infer only one type of technical masculinity. Indeed, working class and middle class men construct masculinity differently, depending upon their relation to technology in the workplace. For working-class men, the work environment of the shop floor is given significance by associating manual work with a physically strong and active type of masculinity. In other words, the masculinity of the shop floor stresses the presentation and celebration of physical prowess (Clatterbaugh, 1990; Cockburn, 1983, 1985; Willis, 1979).

Professional engineers, however, do not claim physical prowess but construct masculinity through their possession of abstruse and "expert" technical knowledge (Wajcman, 1991). As Cockburn (1985) shows, for professional engineers "intellectuality and analytical power are appropriated for masculinity" (p. 196). Wajcman (1991) further points out that this knowledge bestows masculine power on engineers: "in relation to other men and women who lack this expertise, in terms of the material rewards this skill brings, and even in terms of their popular portrayal as 'heroes' at the frontiers of technological progress" (p. 144). Thus, technical competence is a key source of masculine power among men and "doing engineering" is simultaneously "doing" a particular type of technically competent masculinity. Indeed, being in control of the very latest technology (such as the Space Shuttle Challenger) "signifies being involved in directing the future" and so is a highly esteemed activity, whereas mastery over other kinds of technology (such as machines on the shop floor) does not accord the same status or power (pp. 144-45). Professional engineering not only increases for engineers "their sense of the greatness of their sex," but additionally inculcates "a sense of being special" among the technically competent (Cockburn, 1985, p. 172).

Clearly, then, a major part of engineer masculinity is to be in command of the particular technology and, therefore, to know the limits of that technology. Consequently, engineers (relative to managers) place very high priority on quality and safety (Starbuck & Milliken, 1988). Indeed, Cockburn (1985) stresses the emotional investment engineers lodge in "their" technology:

> In the main these men identify themselves with technology and identify technology with masculinity. . . . Engineers identify so closely with the technology with which they are involved that many will choose their employment less by the salary it offers than by the complexity of the technology it opens up to them.

Anticipating Cockburn twenty years earlier, Florman (1976) emphasized the sensual pleasures secured from "doing engineering" and most recently, Hacker (1989) speaks of a "masculine eroticization of engineering" in which technological innovation is realized as exhilarating and a source of intense pleasure and arousal.

Given this emotional charge, engineers have a direct interest in the technology succeeding as planned and, concurrently, technological success delivers a virile status upon engineers, thereby ensuring a claim to "engineer masculinity" (Wajcman, 1991). As a result, risk-taking is *not* the appealing masculine practice to engineers it is to managers. Indeed, for engineers, inasmuch as technical failure threatens their masculinity, it should not be surprising that MTI engineers would exhibit greater caution regarding O-ring capability and argue against launch.

Thus, while managers see themselves as "realists" struggling with immediate economic crises that sometimes demand risk-taking, engineers attempt to protect their work from myopic managers and are more inclined to disdain risk-taking (Dubinskas, 1988, p. 201). Indeed, these strikingly different practices were accomplished situationally during the off-line caucus and brilliantly illustrate the relational character of masculinities. They demonstrate how the definition of masculinity is not only the collective work of a group of people, in this case corporate managers and engineers, but is constructed differently through social interaction. Both groups exhibit the different ways masculinity is defined and sustained, and how this proprietary masculinity relates to their definition of work-related issues; managers and engineers actively confront the work situation and shape practices for solving problems. Yet they do this in distinctly different ways, and it is this contrasting social action that is central to the production of different masculinities. From essentially similar starting points, class, race, and gender privilege as well as engagement in "mental labor," two divergent masculinities are produced. Both groups of men pick up the theme of hegemonic masculinity regarding the importance of work in the paid labor market (and clearly both have benefited from the subordination of women), yet they rework that hegemonic theme in situationally specific ways.

Additionally, the *relationship* between these masculinities is in part the basis of MTI organization. As with other male dominated organizations, such as the military—general/soldier (Connell, 1995b) and the police—office cop/street cop (Messerschmidt, 1993), it is the relationship between engineer and manager masculinities—technically competent but subordinate to managerial authority on the one hand, dominating and economically competent on the other—that is in part the foundation of MTI organization. Yet as indicated, this relationship is far from one of simple complementarity but rather is embedded in a power hierarchy.[18] At MTI a difference in corporate masculinities was constructed in practice by the asymmetry of power between managers and engineers. "Decisions" were ultimately in the hands of management, yet as we have seen, the power to manage is not always easily exercised. Engineers can and do wield the weapon of "technical competence," at least to some degree, to make their collective voice heard. During the off-line caucus, two MTI engineers attempted to protect "their technology" by challenging managerial authority. There was a contest of masculinities in which both managers and engineers were attempting to control the SRB technology. Nevertheless, there are limits to oppositional practices by the less powerful, as noted by the engineers themselves. For example, Boisjoly stated to the President's Commission: "I had my say, and I never take any management right to take the input of an engineer and then make a decision based upon that input, and I truly believe that" (President's Commission, 1986, p. 1421). Similarly, Brian Russell, another MTI engineer told the Commission (p. 1487): "It was a management decision at the vice president's level, and they had heard all they could hear, and I felt there was nothing more to say."[19]

What these statements reveal is that power is a relationship that structures social interaction between men in the corporation. By engaging in practices that reproduce the division of labor and power, managers and engineers are not only doing their job and, therefore, reproducing corporate organization, they are also constructing masculinities. Both managers and engineers are acknowledging through practice that the lopsided power relationships are indeed "fair."

In addition, the comment by Jerry Mason to Bob Lund during the off-line caucus—to take off your "engineering hat" and put on your "management hat"—is key to understanding the social construction of, and relationship between, masculinities. Lund was vice president of engineering, making him both an engineer and a manager. Initially, Lund put on his engineering hat and argued against launch. However, once he entered the social situation of the off-line caucus, Lund followed instructions, put on his "management hat," and concurred with the other managers to approve launch.

What this reveals is that through the exchange of "hats," Lund reestablished a corporate-manager masculinity that had been diminished by his earlier opposition to launch. The problem for Lund was to produce configurations of behavior that could be seen by others as normative. Yet, as the social setting changed—from outside to inside the caucus—so did the conceptualization of what is normative masculine behavior. In short, Lund formed different types of masculinity that could be assessed and approved in both social settings as normal.

The case of Lund demonstrates how we maintain different gender identities that may be emphasized or avoided, depending upon the social setting. Men construct their gendered action in relation to how such actions might be interpreted by others (that is, their accountability) in the particular social context in which they occur. Given the power relation prevalent in the off-line caucus, Lund did masculinity differently because the setting and the available resources changed.[20]

Overall, the disparate degree of power among men significantly impacts the varieties of masculinities constructed, and therefore support for, or rejection of, the launch as a resource for doing masculinity. Engineers were able to oppose the launch because such a practice was, in this particular situation, a resource for doing gender; attempting to prevent the launch was an accountable practice for doing engineer masculinity. Thus, MTI managers (including Lund) advocated an unsafe launch, whereas engineers resisted such a launch, because of different masculine meanings attaching to the particular practice.

CONCLUSION

Gender is one of the most significant ways we make sense of our daily work environment, and work in the paid labor market is a crucial condition for the construction of masculinities. Both managers and engineers construct masculinity at the workplace, but the way in which they do so reveals a fundamental difference. This diversity is strikingly apparent in support for or rejection of the Challenger launch. Indeed, as Morgan (1992) argues, the kind of work determines "the material out of which certain masculinities are shaped" (p. 86). The corporation sets limits for the type of masculinities that might be constructed and one's position in the corporate division of labor and power determines the resources available for masculine practices. The Challenger illustration reveals how the corporate division of labor and power is constituted by social action and, in turn, provides resources for doing masculinity. In this way social structures both constrain and enable social action and, therefore, masculinities and corporate crime. In short, the data on the Space Shuttle Challenger explosion provides empirical support for structured action theory and, therefore, how in the same social situation, one type of masculinity (manager) was constructed through the commission of corporate crime, while contemporaneously another type of masculinity (engineer) was constructed through resisting that crime.

Thus, managers and engineers experience their corporate world from a specific position in the organization and, accordingly, construct masculinity in a uniquely appropriate way. Indeed, conceptualizing the Challenger explosion from a structured action perspective demonstrates that we are able now to explore sociologically which males commit which crimes in which social situations. In other words, why some men in corporations "manage to kill" while other men do not.

END NOTES

1. The report of the Presidential Commission provides the most thorough documentation of the events and decisions that led to the launch, and serves here as the primary data on the explosion.

2. I agree with Sellin (1938) who long ago criticized criminologists for limiting their investigations to violations of the law. For Sellin, such a definition of crime disregards a fundamental criterion of science: "the scientist must have the freedom to define his/[her] own terms" (p. 23). In other words, criminologists should not be restricted in their research simply to violations of legal precedents. Consequently, although no one involved in the decision to launch Challenger was criminalized by the state, following Beirne and Messerschmidt (1995), I label this act "corporate crime" because it conforms to the following definition: "Corporate crime is any illegal and/or socially injurious act of intent or indifference, that occurs for the purpose of furthering corporate goals, and that physically and/or economically abuses individuals in the United States and/or abroad." As I show in this article, although the deaths of the seven crew members were not intentional, it clearly was a socially injurious act of indifference that occurred for the purpose for furthering corporate goals.

3. The content of this section is a summary of the perspective spelled out in Messerschmidt (1993) on pages 61–86.

4. This does not mean other social relations—such as class and race—are insignificant. Indeed, gender, class, and race relations perpetually constrain and enable social action and determine social position and, thus, we are always, to a certain extent, "doing" gender, class, and race. Nevertheless, the *salience* of each for influencing crime vary from one situation to another. That is, in one situation gender and race may both be important for actuating crime while in another gender may only be relevant. As I show below, in the particular social setting of the Challenger launch decision, both gender and class (but not race) were highly salient to this behavior.

5. As McConnell (1987) states: "They decided that the strap-on fuel boosters would be equipped with large parachute to carry them to a soft water landing one hundred miles downrange from the launch site after their fuel was spent. The huge external tank would be sacrificed after use. But the orbiter would glide back to a shuttle landing field near its launch site, be mated with a new fuel tank and refurbished solid boosters, and be ready for flight again within two weeks" (p. 40).

6. A December 12, 1973, NASA selection board report stated (cited in President's Commission, 1986): "Thiokol's cost advantages were substantial and consistent throughout all areas evaluated. . . .The Thiokol motor case joints utilized dual O-rings and test ports between seals, enabling a simple leak check without pressurizing the entire motor. This innovative design feature increased reliability and decreased operations at the launch site, indicating good attention to low cost (design, development, testing and engineering) and production. . . .Thiokol could do a more economical job than any of the other proposers in both the development and the production phases of the program" (p. 120).

7. MTI engineers based their SRB design on the Air Force's Titan III model. However, since the Titan had experienced occasional erosion of its single O-ring design, MTI engineers adopted a second, presumably redundant O-ring arrangement into each joint, to hypothetically make the Challenger safer.

8. Early tests performed between 1977 and 1980 showed that during the initial period of launch, pressure surge "joint rotation" occurred, causing the secondary O-ring to become completely disengaged from its sealing surface (President's Commission, 1986). Moreover, the orbital test flight series, which consisted of four flights from April 1981 to July 1982, repeatedly evinced O-ring erosion caused by "joint rotation." For example, after the third test flight, inspection revealed "that joint rotation caused the loss of the secondary O-ring as a backup seal" which could ultimately result in a "loss of mission vehicle and crew due to metal erosion, burn through, and probable case burst resulting in fire and deflagration" (pp. 125-26).

9. Vaughan (1994) provides an interesting discussion of how managers and engineers jointly defined the SRB joints an "acceptable risk." However, she fails to acknowledge and analyze the engineers changing position, especially the necessity of fixing the erosion problem prior to future flights. I examine this turnabout below.

10. The President's Commission (1986) would subsequently agree with Boisjoly, stating that the O-ring erosion history presented to MTI management by the engineers "was sufficiently detailed to require corrective action prior to the next flight" (p. 148).

11. As Bob Lund (President's Commission, 1986), vice president of engineering at MTI stated in testimony to the President's Commission: "We have dealt with Marshall for a long time and have always been in the position of defending our position that we were ready to fly. . . .[now] we had to prove to them we *weren't* ready" (pp. 1456-1457). And as Roger Boisjoly (President's Commission, 1986) put it: "This was a meeting where the determination was to launch, and it was up to us to prove beyond a shadow of a doubt that it was not safe to do so. This is in total reversal to what the position usually is in a pre-flight conversation" (p. 1421).

12. Due to space limitations I concentrate my analysis in the remaining sections exclusively on the corporate (MTI) decision to launch.

13. Although all the major MTI managerial decision-makers were caucasian, the social construction of "whiteness" was not the salient feature to this situation as gender and class. In other words, class and gender were directly threatened by the O-ring problem but not race. Moreover, this socially injurious act conforms to the definition of corporate crime outlined earlier (see endnote 2) since the decision to launch helped further MTI's corporate goal of preserving a lucrative contract.

14. The importance of risk-taking in the corporate-managerial world was recently highlighted in a book on women managers. According to Driscoll and Goldberg (1993), to gain entry to the masculine corporate-managerial "club," "women would do well to become risk-takers" because "risk-taking pays off . . . the greater the risk, the greater the reward" (p. 46).

15. The sociology of risk literature has shockingly ignored this important link with gender. See, for example, Short and Clarke (1992) and Luhman (1993).

16. It should therefore not be surprising to find that interview data of corporate managers shows that they "care about their reputations for risk-taking and are eager to expound on their sentiments about the deficiencies of others" (March and Shapira, 1987, p. 1413).

17. Bob Lund, vice president of engineering at MTI, stated the following to the President's Commission (1986) when asked why he initially opposed launch: "You know this program has people on it, and so I am very concerned about that, and I want to make sure that if there is any hint of a problem, that we are not extending that" (p. 1459). However, he is the only person to acknowledge such a concern to the Commission, there is *no* evidence he announced this concern at any time during the launch decision process and, finally, he eventually voted—with the other managers—to launch Challenger. Thus, although MTI managers did not intend harm to the seven crew members, they clearly were indifferent to the human consequences of their actions and, therefore, committed corporate crime (see the definition of corporate crime in endnote 2). Moreover, I must stress that it was the gendered interaction and discourse within the particular social situation of the teleconference and off-line caucus that generated this indifference.

18. Due to space limitations, I am able to consider only power relations at MTI. However, we also observe power relations between managers of the two organizations. MTI's reversal from a no-launch to a launch decision clearly must be understood in terms of its relatively powerless position vis-a-vis Marshall. That is, MTI must be responsive to its major customer or potentially suffer dire economic consequences. Marshall managers, by reason of their powerful position, had the resources to pressure MTI to prove it was unsafe to launch. Consequently, a full understanding of the power dynamics involved in this event—something clearly beyond the scope of this paper—must consider this relationship between the "men at Marshall" and the "men at MTI."

19. This comment by Brian Russell indicates that the two engineers, Roger Boisjoly and Arnie Thompson, who challenged the authority of management during the off-line caucus were acting as spoke persons for the other eight engineers.

20. Lund simply was not "jumping" from one masculinity to another. To "do" manager masculinity in this setting required Lund to actively demasculinize what had previously been an acceptable masculine practice for him (opposing the launch). When asked by the President's Commission (1986) why he changed his mind when he changed his hat, Lund responded by supporting Mulloy's gendered dichotomy discussed above: irrational/qualitative (wimpish) vs. rational/quantitative (masculine). In short, by supporting the launch, Lund was able to patently separate himself from what the particular situation of the caucus defined as "wimpish" and, therefore, be assessed as normatively masculine.

REFERENCES

Acker, J. (1992). Gendering organizational theory. In A.J. Mills and P. Tancred (Eds.), *Gendering organizational analysis* (pp. 248-260). Newbury Park, CA: Sage.

Acker, J. (1990). Hierarchies, jobs, bodies: A theory of gendered organizations. *Gender and Society*, 4(2), 139-158.

Arch, E. C. (1993). Risk-taking: A Motivational basis for sex differences. *Psychological Reports*, *73*, 3-11.

Beirne, P., & Messerschmidt, J. W. (1995). *Criminology* (2nd ed.). San Diego, CA: Harcourt Brace.

Boisjoly, R. M. (1987, December 13-18). *Ethical decisions: Morton Thiokol and the Space Shuttle Challenger disaster*. Paper presented at the Annual Meeting of the American Society of Mechanical Engineers, Boston.

Clatterbaugh, K. (1990). *Contemporary perspectives on masculinity*. Boulder, CO: Westview Press.

Cockburn, C. (1983). *Brothers: Male dominance and technological change*. London: Pluto Press.

Cockburn, C. (1985). *Machinery of dominance: Women, men and technical knowhow*. London: Pluto Press.

Cockburn, C., & Ormrod, S. (1993). *Gender and technology in the making*. Newbury Park, CA: Sage.

Cohn, C. (1987). Sex and death in the rational world of defense intellectuals. *Signs*, *12*(4), 687-718.

Cohn, C. (1995). Wars, wimps, and women: Talking gender and thinking war. In M. S. Kimmel & M. A. Messner (Eds.), *Men's lives* (pp. 131-143). Boston: Allyn and Bacon.

Connell, R. W. (1987). *Gender and power: Society, the person and sexual politics*. Stanford, CA: Stanford University Press.

Connell, R. W. (1995a). *Masculinities*. Berkeley, CA: University of California Press.

Connell, R. W. (1995b). Masculinity, violence, and war. In M. S. Kimmel & M. A. Messner (Eds.), *Men's lives* (pp. 125-130). Boston: Allyn and Bacon.

David, D. S., & Brannon, R. (1976). *The forty-nine percent majority: The male sex role*. Reading, MA: Addison-Wesley.

Donaldson, M. (1993). What is hegemonic masculinity? *Theory and Society*, *22*, 643-657.

Driscoll, D. M., & Goldberg, C. R. (1993). *Members of the club: The coming of age of executive women*. New York: The Free Press.

Dubinskas, F. A. (1988). Janus organizations: Scientists and managers in genetic engineering firms. In F. A. Dubinskas (Ed.), *Making time: Ethnographies of high technology organizations* (pp. 170-232). Philadelphia: Temple University Press.

Florman, S. C. (1976). *The existential pleasures of engineering*. New York: St. Martin's.

Giddens, A. (1989). A reply to my critics. In D. Held & J. B. Thompson (Eds.), *Social theory of modern societies: Anthony Giddens and his critics* (pp. 249-301). New York: Cambridge University Press.

Hacker, S. (1989). *Pleasure, power and technology: Some tales of gender, engineering, and the cooperative workplace*. Boston: Unwin Hyman.

Kanter, R. M. (1977). *Men and women of the corporation*. New York: Basic Books.

Kerfoot, D., & Knights, D. (1993). Management, masculinity and manipulation: From paternalism to corporate strategy in financial services in Britain. *Journal of Management Studies*, *30*(4), 659-677.

Kessler, S., & McKenna, W. (1978). *Gender: An ethnomethodological approach*. New York: John Wiley.

Kramer, R. C. (1992). The Space Shuttle Challenger explosion: A case study of state-corporate crime. In K. Schlegel & D. Weisburg (Eds.), *White-collar crime reconsidered*. (pp. 214-243). Boston: Northeastern University Press.

Luhman, N. (1993). *Risk: A sociological theory*. New York: Aldine.

Maier, M. (1993). "Am I the only one who wants to launch?": Corporate masculinity and the Space Shuttle "Challenger" Disaster." *masculinities*, *1*(1-2), 34-45.

March, J. G., & Shapira, Z. (1987). Managerial perspectives on risk and risk taking. *Management Science*, *33*(11), 1404-1418.

McConnell, M. (1987). *Challenger: A major malfunction*. Garden City, NY: Doubleday.

Messerschmidt, J. W. (1993). *Masculinities and crime: Critique and reconceptualization of theory*. Lanham, MD: Rowman and Littlefield.

Morgan, D. H. J. (1992). *Discovering men*. New York: Routledge.

President's Commission. (1986). *Report of the Presidential Commission on the Space Shuttle Challenger accident*. Washington, D.C.: U. S. Government Printing Office.

Sellin, T. (1938). *Culture conflict and crime*. New York: Social Science Research Council.

Short, J. F., & Clarke, L. (Eds.) (1992). *Organizations, uncertainties, and risk*. Boulder, CO: Westview Press.

Starbuck, W. H., & Milliken, F. J. (1988). Challenger: Fine-tuning the odds until something breaks. *Journal of Management Studies*, *25*(4), 319-340.

Thorne, B. (1993). *Gender play: Girls and boys in schools*. New Brunswick, NJ: Rutgers University Press.

Tolson, A. (1977). *The limits of masculinity*. New York: Harper and Row.

Vaughan, D. (1989). Regulating risk: Implications of the Challenger accident. *Law and Policy*, *11*(3), 330-349.

Vaughan, D. (1994, August 5-9). *Risk, work group culture, and the normalization of deviance: NASA and the Space Shuttle Challenger*. Paper presented at the Annual Meetings of the American Sociological Association, Los Angeles.

Wajcman, J. (1991). *Feminism confronts technology*. University Park, PA: Pennsylvania State University Press.

West, C., & Fenstermaker, S. (1993). Power, inequality and the accomplishment of gender: An ethnomethodological view. In P. England (Ed.), *Theory on gender/feminism on theory*. (pp. 151-174). New York: Aldine.

West, C., & Zimmerman, D. H. (1987). Doing gender. *Gender and Society*, *1*(2), 125-151.

Willis, P. E. (1979). Shop floor culture, masculinity and the wage form. In J. Clarke, C. Critcher, & R. Johnson (Eds.), *Working class culture*. (pp. 185-198). London: Hutchinson.

[11]

Criminal careers, desistance and subjectivity:

Interpreting men's narratives of change

DAVID GADD AND STEPHEN FARRALL
Keele University, UK

Abstract

This article analyses the life-stories told by two men who appeared to be desisting from crime. At the time of their respective interviews, both men had reduced the frequency and intensity of their offending behaviours, although neither man had completely stopped offending. Using these men's life-stories, the authors endorse Shadd Maruna's argument that the study of criminal careers and desistance needs to embrace a more adequately psychosocial conception of subjectivity. However, in contrast to the cognitive approach preferred by Maruna, the authors seek to demonstrate that an interpretive approach to narrative material, sensitive to the possibility of unconscious motivations, better explains some of the contradictions evident in desisters' life-stories, especially in relation to the heavily gendered issue of family formation. The authors draw particularly on the psychoanalytic work of Tony Jefferson to make their argument.

Key Words

criminal careers • desistance • masculinities • psychosocial • subjectivity • violence

Introduction

Criminology has witnessed a growth of interest in the later stages of criminal careers, especially those stages associated with desistance from crime (Sampson and Laub, 1993; Shover, 1996; Maruna, 2001). It would appear that men's offending tends to peak at age 18 before sharply reducing (Holden, 1986; Barclay, 1990). By the age of 25, the majority of those who have embarked on criminal careers have desisted, although men whose offending is far more entrenched typically do not desist until they are much older (Farrington, 1997).

Of course ageing does not in and of itself 'cause' desistance. Rather, 'age' is an 'index' of other processes that have some bearing on involvement in crime, such as the amount of time a person is likely to have been enmeshed in social networks and their psychological development and maturation (Smith, 2002: 702; cf. Gottfredson and Hirschi, 1990). The findings of criminal careers research illustrate this point well. Male offenders typically cease to offend at about the same time they embark on the processes associated with family formation and (re)enter stable employment (Farrall and Bowling, 1999; Laub and Sampson, 2001; Farrall, 2002). Both employment and family formation are events in the life-course that happen more frequently at certain ages than others. Leaving the city where they had grown up was associated with reductions in subsequent offending (self-reported and officially recorded) for the cohort of research subjects who partook of the Cambridge Study in Delinquent Development[1] (Osborn, 1980). Likewise, the disintegration of peer groups—another event that happens at certain points in the life-course more often than others—also anticipated desistance from delinquency in several other cohort studies (Knight and West, 1975: 49; Cromwell et al., 1991: 83; Warr, 1998).

However, desistance is not just about objective transformations in offenders' circumstances, but also a range of subjective phenomena. Unsurprisingly, research has found that shifts in identity—for example becoming a parent or role model, or recognizing old-age is imminent (Meisenhelder, 1982; Shover, 1983: 210; Burnett, 1992; Hughes, 1997; Maruna, 1997, 2001)—and feeling shame at one's past behaviours (Leibrich, 1993: 204, 1996) are often associated with desistance. The fear of serious assault or death are also reasons ex-offenders—especially serious and persistent street criminals—often give for desisting (Cusson and Pinsonneault, 1986: 74; Sommers et al., 1994: 138–40; Maruna, 1997: 78; Hughes, 1998: 147). In addition, the desire to avoid further offending is a recurring theme in some ex-offenders' accounts of change (West, 1978; Shover, 1983; Shover and Thompson, 1992; Moffitt, 1993; Sommers et al., 1994; Pezzin, 1995), not least because desistance—like recovering from alcoholism—involves an unending state of *going* straight, with few of its practitioners ever fully satisfied that they have recovered, reformed or *gone* straight (Maruna, 2001). The experience of punishment sometimes belatedly induces this desire to reform. For example, Cusson and Pinsonneault's (1986) in-depth interviews with ex-robbers document how some offenders grow tired of doing time in prison, especially when the prospect of longer sentences becomes a reality.

In short, before desistance begins, offenders typically re-evaluate their lives (Shover, 1983: 213; Cromwell et al., 1991: 83; Leibrich, 1993: 56–7). Some researchers view this re-evaluation process as something akin to 'burn-out' (Burnett, 1992; Hughes, 1998). Others, like Shover and Thompson, prefer the rational choice notion that: 'the probability of desistance from criminal participation increases as expectations for achieving friends, money, autonomy and happiness via crime decrease' (1992: 97). But in contrast to this theoretically simple explanation, ex-offenders themselves frequently offer contradictory and conflicting rationalizations for desistance (Burnett, 2004). Rarely have researchers attempted to move beyond these rationalizations to provide a more interpretive psychosocial understanding of the processes involved. For example, the birth of children, the faith of significant others and the desire to make amends are themes that recur in many narratives of reform (Denzin, 1987; Brown, 1991; Devlin and Turney, 1999; Farrall, 2002). Yet how these stories connect to the conflicts and tensions many offenders experience in becoming parents and partners remains under-researched and under-theorized.

Narrative and life-course perspectives

The life-course perspective has been defined as the study of 'pathways through the age differentiated life span', and as a form of study particularly concentrating on the 'expectations and options that impinge on decision processes and the course of events that give shape to life stages, transitions and turning points' (Elder, 1985: 17, quoted in Sampson and Laub, 1993: 8). The concepts most central to this perspective are the notions of 'trajectory' and 'transition'. The concept 'trajectory' refers to a line of development over the life-course (such as an employment career), whereas the concept of 'transition' refers to events (e.g. first job or promotions) that interrupt a trajectory. Hence, Sampson and Laub summarize the life-course perspective as focusing upon 'the duration, timing and ordering of major social events and their consequences for later social development' (1993: 8).

As Sampson and Laub note (1990: 610), criminology has been slow to appreciate the importance of the life-course for understanding criminal careers—although this has begun to change in the decade since they made this observation (e.g. Sampson and Laub, 1993; Farrall, 2002). One of the attractions for us of the life-course perspective is its more direct concern with the wider contexts of offending behaviour (Laub and Sampson, 2001: 44). The onset of offending has been related to psychological problems in childhood, most notoriously, in David Farrington's insistence that:

> People graduate from hyperactivity at age two to cruelty to animals at age six, shoplifting at ten, burglary at fifteen, robbery at twenty, and eventually spouse assault, child abuse and neglect, alcohol abuse, and employment and later health problems later on in life.
>
> (Farrington, 2002: 658)

Farrington adds:

> The antisocial child tends to become the antisocial teenager and then the antisocial adult, just as the antisocial adult then tends to produce another antisocial child.
>
> (Farrington, 2002: 658)

Yet Sampson and Laub (1993) demonstrate that this kind of trajectory is far from inevitable. In their analysis of the Gluecks' data-set (comprising the life-circumstances of 500 delinquents and 500 non-delinquents entering their teens in the 1940s and 1950s), Sampson and Laub highlight the influence of social relationships in accounting for continuity *and* change in individual criminal careers. In Sampson and Laub's view, employment and marriage have the potential to lock individuals into relationships that confer extensive sets of obligations and expectations. These obligations and expectations are capable of generating forms of crime-inhibiting 'social capital' that cultivate informal control through an interlocking network of social bonds.

However, the problem for this kind of large-scale research is disentangling the meaning social relationships hold for those persisting with, or desisting from, crime. While social bonding can inhibit crime, involvement in offending can have a profoundly negative effect upon an individual's future social relationships. As Thornberry explains: 'Serious and prolonged involvement in delinquent behaviour is likely to adversely influence social relations with family and peers, belief systems, and the success and timing of transitions to adult roles and the life course' (Thornberry, 1997: 4). Conversely, we know that some criminal careers are launched, and even accelerated, by the support of family members and friends who are well integrated within criminal networks (Hobbs, 1988, 1995). Unfortunately, much criminal careers research proceeds as if the meaning of these all-important social relationships can be simply read off from evidence of their presence. A notable exception is found in Shadd Maruna's (2001) seminal study of ex-offenders' 'self-concepts' and 'personal strategies' *Making Good.*

In *Making Good*, Maruna demonstrated the important role that narratives play in structuring offenders' and ex-offenders' understandings of themselves and their relationships. Maruna used content analysis to identify different 'mindsets' exhibited by 20 career criminals (i.e. offenders who thought they would persist with crime for the foreseeable future), and by 30 desisters who expressed a desire to change and had (probably) not been involved in criminal activities over the previous 2–3 years. Although not particularly different in terms of their quantifiable social background (educational qualifications, criminal records, drug and alcohol usage), scores on standard personality tests, expressions of self-righteousness and 'adventurous, rebellious and independent' desires (2001: 59), Maruna found that his persistent offenders were more likely than his desisters to see themselves as either determined by unpleasant pasts (i.e. unhappy childhoods) or as victims of circumstance. Persisters were also more likely to believe they would only be able to change their ways if they happened upon some 'lucky strike' or mythical 'big score'.

Conversely, desisters tended to ground their stories more in biographical details (perhaps to make their transformations seem more credible), more often perceived themselves as beneficiaries of some outside force (i.e. the faith of a significant other) that had helped them to break 'the cycle', seemed more satisfied with their lot and tended to consider themselves empowered to 'give something back' to society. Desisters tended not to blame themselves for their past misdemeanours, differentiating their 'real', 'changed' responsible selves from the 'fake', 'determined' and troubling selves manifested during their offending careers. Unlike persisters, desisters typically claimed to have *made something good* from the difficulties they had lived through; they often equated redemption with achieving some higher moral purpose. Typically, desisters positioned themselves as 'super-fathers', 'role models' for others in trouble, or 'wounded healers' investing in the next generation. In fact, Maruna found that his desisters routinely expressed an 'inflated, almost missionary sense of purpose in life' (2001: 9), a tendency evidenced in the autobiographies of other reformed offenders (Devlin and Turney, 1999).

Hence, unlike much other criminal careers research, Maruna's study reveals the *emotional* depth of experience that underpins the process of desistance. He also reveals how the change process is inextricably related to each individual's capacity to position themselves *through their narratives* as heroic transgressors successfully struggling against the tide of social pressures favourable to the commission of crime. As we argue later, both insights can be reconciled with theoretical observations taken from Tony Jefferson's work on the much-debated subject of masculinities and crime.

Criminal careers and the turn to masculinities

To date, criminologists engaged with critical debates about gender and sexuality have struggled to incorporate the phenomenon of desistance into their analyses. In the early 1990s, feminist criminology drew attention to the behavioural similarities between those men and boys labelled 'criminal' and the politicians and police officers who routinely condemn criminal behaviours (Campbell, 1993; Walklate, 1995). In attempts to theorize the power relations that differentiate male law-breakers from law enforcers, some work on masculinities began to conceptualize crimes—especially violent crime—as a relatively 'everyday' means for 'accomplishing' masculinity for impoverished and marginalized young men (Messerschmidt, 1993, 1997). At this point, the feminist critique of men's abusive behaviour in the private sphere might have prompted a more thorough-going criminological analysis of men's involvement in parenting but this is still sadly lacking (Collier, 1998).

All this might lead one to conclude that the scope for theoretical convergence between life-course researchers and masculinity theorists is very slight. For critical gender theorists, men's symbolic and material dependence on the nuclear family is heavily implicated in the self-same social relationships and structures that routinely reproduce patterns of male delinquency and sexual inequalities more generally (Connell, 1995: ch. 5). However, this point has largely escaped the attentions of those exploring desistance from crime. When male ex-offenders cite their investments in stable 'nuclear' families as catalysts for positive life-changes, few criminal careers researchers have queried whether such investments are mutually beneficial to the various family members involved. Likewise, the assumption—routinely made in criminal careers research—that desistance is associated with family formation ignores the extent of violence and abuse *within* heterosexual families (but see Quigley and Leonard, 1996: 355).

To date, the best empirical work on masculinities has tended to draw heavily on Bob Connell's (1987, 1995, 2002) attempts to retain an understanding of gender that is sensitive to multiple structures of inequality, global and local imbalances of power, but still conversant with the range of troubling dilemmas and contradictions many men experience in their everyday attempts to negotiate interpersonal relationships. Some exemplary work within the sociologies of youth (e.g. Frosh et al., 2002) and education (Mac an Ghail, 1994), as well as within social psychology (Edley and Wetherell, 1999) has drawn on Connell's insights to demonstrate: (a) why so many boys become complicit with oppressive practices that contradict their own understandings of what is otherwise fair or desirable; and (b) how these contradictions can create modest opportunities for young people to resist the reproduction of sexism, racism and homophobia. The scope for similar work aimed at making sense of criminal careers and their termination seems vast here. For example, is it that masculine identities are so *fluid* that they can easily be socially renegotiated or reconstructed (Edley and Wetherell, 1999), or do the historically embedded structures that foster power differentials *among* men, as well as *between* men and women, largely determine the life-trajectories of those already involved in crime (Connell, 2002; Hall, 2002)? Are desisters the sons of feckless and/or abusive fathers trying hard to do things differently to their predecessors (Lupton and Barclay, 1997; cf. Farrington, 1996), or are they yesterday's absent fathers filled with regrets? Does the issue of individual motivation matter, or are those who change typically those who 'got lucky' and/or who moved away from the social contexts and circumstances that caused their offending in the first place (Parker, 1976)?

Unfortunately, critical work on masculinity within criminology has yet to broach these questions. Within criminology, it remains hotly contested whether Connell's notion of a 'gender order'—in which certain masculinities are subordinated and marginalized in relation to a 'hegemonic position'—necessarily aids criminological explanation. Jim Messerschmidt's (1993, 1995, 1997, 1999, 2000) attempts to reconcile Connell's insight with the ethnomethodological notion of 'gender as situational accomplishment' has been at the heart of this controversy. While most masculinity theorists in criminology would agree with Messerschmidt that the best theoretical insights are likely to be gleaned from in-depth case analyses, biographical research and ethnographies, Messerschmidt's insistence on interpreting these materials through his own structured action theory is increasingly contested. Among the critiques that have been levelled at Messerschmidt's approach are accusations of tautology (Walklate, 1995) and observations that this approach reproduces a dualistic conception of gender that fails to shake off all the problems associated with earlier work on 'sex differences' (Miller, 2002). Others have argued that Messerschmidt's approach embodies the same social determinism as Mertonian strain theory (Jefferson, 1997a; Hood-Williams, 2001) and that his work overstates the social acceptability of domestic violence, underplaying the very reasons why such abuses so often remain 'domestic secrets' (Gadd, 2000a, 2003a). Some critics have felt that Messerschmidt understates the contradictions that perpetrators have to negotiate in order to depict their abusive behaviour as masculinity accomplishing (Strange, 2003). Other scholars detect a more complex relationship between male violence and a global economy (especially a night-time economy) that capitalizes on both young people's (highly gendered and sexualized) desires and some working-class men's historically rooted capacity to cultivate a posture of physical hardness (Hobbs et al., 2002).

Anticipating many of these criticisms and bringing them together in his work over the last 10 years, Jefferson (1994, 1997a, 2002) has argued the case for a fuller conception of masculine subjectivity than structured action theory can offer. As we shall explain, in trying to theorize the tensions many men experience in becoming masculine, Jefferson has produced a model of subjectivity that could also illuminate the psychosocial dimensions of experience that come into play when career criminals narrate their experiences of change. Central to Jefferson's (1994) argument is the necessity of understanding masculinity in a way that men will recognize, and hence the importance of paying attention to the relationship between social and psychic processes that are often in tension with each other. For the purpose of conciseness, three elements of Jefferson's thinking are outlined here: *discursive positions*, *defended subjects* and *identification*.

Let us deal with 'discursive positions' first. Crucial to Jefferson's attempts to overcome essentialist notions of masculinity and femininity is the notion that people choose, however consciously or unconsciously, to invest in a range of different, often contradictory, discursive (and hence historically constituted) positions. This idea—borrowed from the early work of Wendy Hollway (1989)—opens up the possibility of a more complex understanding of 'the social' (with all its gendered, raced and classed inflexions) and its negotiation by individuals looking to make sense of their experiences in a world in which some frames of reference are more empowering than others. In his analyses of Mike Tyson, for example, Jefferson explains how the very masculine discourses of 'hardness', and later 'aggressive heterosexuality', empowered a young black man growing up in the contexts of an institutionally racist society, a multiplely disadvantaged neighbourhood, and a less than harmonious household. Needless to say, most of the other discourses available to Tyson at that time were either disempowering (for example, racist and colonial discourses that position blacks as inferior) or provided fewer positions from which he could defend himself so easily (for example, feminist discourses of sex equality). Hence, we could argue that power motivated Tyson's choice of discursive investments, implicating him in the reproduction of a certain form of highly racialized masculinity.

This notion that social discourses offer up defensible positions to vulnerable subjects brings us to Jefferson's second conceptual insight. Crucial to Jefferson's attempts to theorize subjectivity more adequately are his efforts to reconcile psychoanalytic—specifically Kleinian concepts—with this poststructuralist, sociological understanding of the nature of the 'discursive'. In both his work on masculinity and fear of crime (Hollway and Jefferson, 2000), Jefferson uses Klein's notion that people depend upon psychic defence mechanisms to fend off feelings of anxiety to theorize an essential conflicted, but also, biographically unique 'inner world'. For example, Jefferson (1996) describes the transformation in Tyson—from a lisping 'little fairy boy' to a 'compleat destroyer'—in terms of the boxer's discovery of his capacity to 'split off' from his feelings of physical vulnerability, and project them violently onto others where they could then be safely attacked. Perhaps the most graphic example of this was Tyson's desire to force the noses of his opponents into the back of their skulls. Elsewhere Jefferson (1997b, 1998) has also endeavoured to capture Tyson's deep-seated insecurities about being unattractive to women and the relevance of these insecurities to Tyson's rape of a young beauty queen named Desiree Washington.

Throughout this work, Jefferson argues that the defence mechanisms of splitting and projection enabled the young schoolboy Tyson—that is, they gave him the psychological resources necessary—to identify with those aggressors who had badly bullied him. It is this question of how the processes of *identification* contribute to the establishment of relatively stable, but often partly permeable *identities*, that constitutes the theoretical problematic which Jefferson (1998, 2002, forthcoming) has posed to criminologists and gender theorists alike. Jefferson has argued that in order to further extrapolate the relationship between the psychic and the social we must grapple with the psychic dimensions of 'identification'—the processes through which identity is constantly formed, revised, consolidated and (importantly) undermined—in relation to others, real and imagined. This notion of identification is the terrain that engages with the question of how it is that people actually come to embody ideas and ideals (often manifested in the discursive positions they take up) and hence the limits and possibilities for psychological change, given the significance of relationships formed in childhood to this process.[2] This takes us back full circle to the question of the kind of identity-work that was going on when Maruna's desisters narrated their stories of change. Why was the idea of investing in the next generation so important to these men and how did it relate to their own upbringings?

Summary and methodological implications

In the analysis section of this article, we posit a preliminary answer to this question through detailed discussion of two men's life-stories. But let us first recap. Simplifying our observations, we have made three major points thus far. First, the 'risk-based' criminal careers literature is so preoccupied with statistical prerogatives that it often makes generalizations that are either vague or not typical of any particular case existing in reality. Second, the life-course perspective, while drawing our attention to the contingencies of work and family life, has failed to spot the gendered nature of men's places within these spheres, and is hence often devoid of an analysis of power, wider social consequences and the complexity of meaning that social and personal relationships have for the people in question. Third and last, much of criminology's masculinities literature draws such a close affinity between gender and crime that it is difficult to see how criminal men can be anything but offenders unless the resources at their disposal change radically. Bringing together insights from Hollway (1989), Jefferson (1997a) and Maruna (2001), our hypothesis is that how and why male offenders change depends on their cathectic investments in, and attachments to, certain social configurations—relationships, institutions and social discourses—and on the corroborating experiences of recognition and empowerment (or otherwise misrecognition and disempowerment) that result from each individual's positioning in these configurations. Where we depart from Maruna, and draw upon Hollway and Jefferson, is in our contention that getting at this psychosocial interface, where structure and agency intersect, is not necessarily best achieved using content analysis; a method unavoidably preoccupied with *manifest* meanings. On this point we are in greater agreement with Hollway and Jefferson (2000) who argue that to get at this psychosocial interface requires a form of in-depth case analysis that is sensitive to the *latent* or *unconscious* meanings of respondents' narratives, including all the absences, contradictions and avoidances intrinsic to them.

Large-scale studies that disaggregate data about individuals into variables that can be used to make generalizations about 'the typical case' are of limited value when one is aiming to make sense of phenomena that are partly biographically contingent. As Hollway and Jefferson explain in relation to the 'fear of crime' debate:

> One person's unique defensive structures cannot be simply read off from their social, demographic characteristics . . . We are all more or less 'irrational' subjects. The point is to explain the relationship between the rational and irrational in human behaviour; not to stop when we have reached the limits of the 'rational' . . . The lessons for the limits of generalisability may be similarly hard but equally necessary: unless the individual case is kept in mind at each stage of the analysis, similar demographic profiles will either produce spurious, misleading generalisations or so many exceptions to the rule that the (generalising) point of the exercise all but disappears under them . . . This is not a plea to prioritise the individual case study over studies designed to produce generalisable findings, but is a strong reminder that generalisations that have not taken account of biographical as well as demographic data are unlikely to prove very useful basis upon which to advance either academic or public policy debates.
>
> (Hollway and Jefferson, 2000: 127–8)

To our minds, the parallels between the rational subject assumed in much of the literature on the fear of crime and the risk-exposed subject assumed in much of the criminal careers literature render Hollway and Jefferson's argument persuasive in this latter context. Furthermore, because case analysis is so labour-intensive, we also agree with Hollway and Jefferson that the cases chosen should be selected on theoretical grounds. In the next part of this article we seek to illustrate the kind of in-depth case analysis we are advocating. Our case studies are selected principally on the basis that they are theoretically interesting. Both of our research subjects had:

- been repeatedly involved in relatively serious forms of crime in their younger years;
- at certain points in their lives, reproduced a cycle of 'anti-socialness', one being the son of a violent father who had become violent himself, and the other the son of an absent father who had abandoned his own child in adult life;
- showed some signs of being in the process of desisting from crime; and
- not been reconvicted for criminal offences within the past three years according to official sources.

Dan[3]

At the time when he was interviewed, in 1998, Dan was a 34-year-old unemployed labourer who had (until relatively recently) lived on a council estate located in a city in the north of England. Dan lived with his wife and four children, two of whom were his own. Dan and his wife had continued to live together despite a trial separation, the length of which was not entirely clear.[4]

Dan's criminal career began in his mid-teens when, he claimed, he 'started to rebel'. This 'rebellion' took the form of truancy, solvent abuse and burglary—initially stealing tools from garden sheds, but later breaking into shops and dwellings. Dan was sentenced to 3 months in a detention centre for burglary when he was 15 years old. He was sentenced to 5 years for aggravated burglary, grievous bodily harm and carrying offensive weapons when he was 18, having assaulted the occupant of a house he was burgling. Dan's last criminal conviction was for shoplifting at age 23—an offence he attributed to the loss of income incurred when 'the prostitute' whose earnings he lived off 'got caught'.

Nevertheless, Dan had been both a cannabis user and a perpetrator of domestic abuse since his teens. Indeed, Dan was interviewed because he had referred himself to an anti-violence counselling programme. At the time of interview, Dan had been receiving one-to-one counselling for six months, was attending a groupwork programme for batterers and was going to RELATE[5] with his partner. In addition to his 'domestic violence', Dan still occasionally got into fights in the street with men in his neighbourhood.

During his two interviews, Dan did not discuss why he had given up burglary and shoplifting, only the factors he felt pre-empted his entrance into crime. Dan blamed his father for his own criminality:

> Many a night he would come home from work and his tea would go up wall . . . He'd be beating my mum up. I'd jump on his back to stop him. And that is when I'd get attacked . . . I grew up through that. As I got to a teenager I started to rebel . . . Ended up going to prison. Urm, which at that time I didn't think about it, but when I reflect on it, that were an escape. That were the only way I could get away from him.

Although Dan's dad was the kind of man who would have a 'laugh and joke' with his son's 'mates', at home he exhibited a cruel 'sadistic streak'. Not only did Dan's father routinely abuse and humiliate Dan's mother,[6] but he also abused the family pets[7] and would 'punish' Dan for aggravating him by punching, kicking and beating him with the buckle end of his belt. If Dan got assaulted by other boys, his father would call him by girls' names. For reasons unbeknown, Dan's father had once tried to force Dan to put a knife into an electric socket, risking electrocution.

Dan used the examples of the abuse he had suffered to blame his father for the break-up of his own marriage with 'Jenny':

> I thought to myself, 'If it weren't for him being the way he were towards me then I wouldn't be the sort of person that I am' . . . And also he were making excuses, saying it were the beer that were the reason he were violent towards me mum and what have you. And I'm like saying, 'What about me? Why were you violent towards me'. [He said,] 'I've never touched you. Never laid a finger on you.' Totally denied it to me face. And like I were just gobsmacked. I just couldn't believe it. And I just said to me wife [Jenny], 'That's it. I just don't want to know him. He can't admit what he has done to me. As far as I'm concerned he's dead.'

Dan implicated his father's brutal behaviour in his decision to address his own domestic violence. In stark contrast to the pride he took in the fights he had with men, Dan had felt uncomfortable talking about his violence against women since the very first time he had perpetrated this kind of assault:

> Something happened one day. We [Dan—aged 18—and his first girlfriend] were arguing about something. She said something to me and I just grabbed her by the throat. I was strangling her. Literally strangling her. She couldn't breath. Her eyes were popping out her head. And like I pushed her away and thought, 'Flipping heck! What am I doing like?' And that is when it started. That were the first time I were violent towards one [a woman]. I'd been violent before in fights with lads and what have you.

Despite this discomfort, Dan had abused nearly all of the women he 'dated' subsequently. This abuse included locking his partners in rooms, preventing them from leaving the house, punches to the face, damaging property and threatening to kill himself. Since he had started receiving counselling, Dan's physical assaults on Jenny had reduced in both their frequency and intensity. However, Dan freely admitted that there were still 'odd outbreaks of violence and mental abuse on both sides':

> Because there were a lot of frustration . . . where my wife was involved, because she's asking me to 'stop this, stop that, stop hitting me, stop mentally abusing me', but she wouldn't give me the same thing.

Furthermore:

> There has been odd times when I have stopped her going to sleep at night because we'd been arguing or I've tried to stop her going out, but then thought better off it and said, 'All right. If you want to go, go.'

Three years prior to his interviews (with Gadd) Dan had broken Jenny's wrist by slamming a door against it while she was holding their baby daughter. On a subsequent occasion Jenny had 'inadvertently' sliced a knife through Dan's fingers during an argument, and Dan had 'barricaded' them both in the house to stop Jenny visiting her new lover. On this occasion, the police arrested Dan, but—as on the other occasions when Dan had been arrested for assaulting his wife—he was released the next day without charge.

Although Dan had started being violent to Jenny six months into their relationship, it was when he broke her wrist that their relationship changed most.

> And that were the end of the relationship as it had been . . . She were no longer telling me she loved me . . . Sex life practically disappeared. Urm, and this went on for about two years. Basically it were a nightmare, worse time I have had in years.

During their trial separation, Jenny embarked on a relationship with another man who lived nearby. Nevertheless, this relationship ended when the man failed to intervene when he saw Dan assaulting Jenny. It was then that Jenny decided to give her and Dan's relationship 'another go', concluding that her lover was 'full of shit'.

By this point Dan had already 'disowned' his dad. Dan's father had been diagnosed with a 'personality disorder' following his arrest for another particularly vicious attack on Dan's mother. This chain of events made Dan increasingly conscious of the similarities between himself and his father: both men had been alcoholics, both had a history of suicide attempts, both had been to prison and both had been reluctant to admit that they had 'got a problem' with violence.

Jenny had also drawn Dan's attention to the similarities between him and her eldest son, Jason (Dan's stepson). After witnessing Jason 'slamming doors when he doesn't get his own way, storming off upstairs, stamping his feet', Dan reached the conclusion that:

> I have got to be the one to break that chain. Because I don't want my son to grow up like I grew up. Even though I'm not violent towards me children urm it's still going to have an effect on them.[8]

In fact, Dan seemed excited by the prospect that Jason would disown his biological father:

> There's been these empty promises—'I'll come and see you every week. And I'm going to buy you this, get you that . . .' And plus the fact that his dad has been in and out of prison. Urm. And he's like not so much said that he's disowned his dad, but he's [Pause] . . . Me wife's been saying for years, 'One day he'll realize what his dad is really like' . . . And we think that time has come . . .

When Jenny and he got back together, Dan started to receive counselling for his violence, his doctor making a referral when Dan renewed his prescription of anti-depressants. Dan freely admitted that the changes he had made were modest and far from absolute:

> Well at the moment I feel things are improving. Me and Jenny are talking a lot more now. Getting on better. And even though Jenny says there haven't been changes, basically she only says that when we are arguing. When we are not arguing she does agree that I have made certain changes. And I think if I can get over my jealousy, which is the main problem at the moment, I think we'll be all right. I think we'll get on fine.

In fact, Jenny had recently arranged for Dan to work with her in the pub so that he did not 'feel excluded'. Dan hoped that one day he and Jenny would own their own pub: no doubt an exciting prospect for a couple who were often too poor to put petrol in their car.

Nevertheless, despite his changing attitude towards domestic violence, Dan retained a strong investment in being tough but measured, a firm but fair disciplinarian. For example, Dan felt Jenny was 'too soft where the kids are concerned' (this attribution of passivity contrasting starkly with the 'woman possessed' he said Jenny was when she was angry), but Dan also believed he had earned the 'respect' of local children for breaking the ribs and leg of a man whose wife had physically assaulted Jenny on a previous occasion.

> I mean it were like we took so much shit for so long from people on that street. And then all of a sudden, after that happened it were like everybody were fine with us. And we did earn respect from beating two people up sort of thing. But that's the sort of place, culture we live in now.

A follow-up contact with the anti-violence counselling service revealed that Dan completed 54 counselling sessions, staying with the service for a further 6 months after Gadd had interviewed him. Self-report data gathered by an external assessor during Dan's time in counselling suggested he did reduce his violent and controlling behaviours while he was on the programme. A search of the Offenders' Index[9] revealed that Dan had not been convicted of an offence since the time of interview.

Anthony

Anthony was 29 years old on the first occasion that he was interviewed in 1998, as part of a project exploring the impact of probation supervision on the lives of probationers. Anthony lived in a commuter town in the south of England. He changed addresses over the course of the research. He resided with his sister at the time of the first interview; he was on his own when interviewed for the second time; and he lived with his new girlfriend when interviewed on a third and final occasion. At the time of the first and second interviews, Anthony was serving a 12-month probation order with the condition that he attend an anger management course. The probation order was Anthony's sentence for having caused actual bodily harm to a co-worker in the factory where he worked.

Like Dan's, Anthony's criminal career began in his teens. When he was 16, Anthony apparently confessed to the police that he had undertaken 30 dwelling burglaries. On this occasion, Anthony had asked the police to take 102 other charges into account. Checks of official records (the Offenders' Index and Police National Computer) did not yield details of all these offences, but did suggest an offending profile consistent with Anthony's own description of his criminal career. Between 1986 and 1997 Anthony was convicted 29 times for offences including burglary, criminal damage, affray, possession of offensive weapons, common assault, theft, actual bodily harm (ABH) and various motoring offences. Although Anthony had only served one custodial sentence (for burglary), he had been fined several times, served two periods of community service and had been conditionally discharged once.

The ABH for which Anthony received probation entailed his head-butting a co-worker who had derided his appearance. Although the co-worker's comments 'started as banter', Anthony reacted violently, assaulting the co-worker and breaking this person's two front teeth. As a result, Anthony was sacked. Anthony claimed that at the time of this assault, he was 'stressed' because of moving from the home he shared with his wife and daughter. He also said that he hated his work, describing his workplace as like 'a concentration camp'. Anthony regularly drank heavily with friends, used cannabis, amphetamines, ecstasy and cocaine (although not 'dirty drugs' like 'smack' and 'crack') and got into fights in the pubs and clubs he frequented. Interestingly, though, Anthony was avoiding ('like the plague') hanging around with a long-term 'mate' whom he described as 'dangerous' and a 'nutcase', 'all right' when he was sober but a 'bully boy' who lashed out at anyone when drunk.

Between interviews one and two, much of Anthony's social life revolved around using and transporting drugs, and seeking out one-night stands with women whom he described as 'not bad looking . . . all right, but . . . slappers'. Although there was no evidence to suggest that Anthony was regularly violent towards women in the same way as Dan, Anthony had to stop himself (on at least one occasion) from hitting one of his girlfriends. Anthony said he had been tempted to hit his girlfriend in retaliation after she had 'slapped' him 'round the face' for staying out all night. Instead, Anthony restrained himself.

When his relationship with his wife broke down, Anthony left the home he shared with her and his child to live with his sister.[10] At the time of Farrall's first interview with him, Anthony was clearly aggrieved that his wife had started divorce proceedings and was dating another man. While he claimed to be enjoying his new-found 'independence', Anthony wanted 'revenge' for the break-up of his marriage. When he discovered his wife was dating another man, Anthony said he:

> was angry and . . . wanted to kill him. And I wanted to kill her. I did say once that I'd shoot her, me and my daughter. That's how bad I was at one stage. But as it's worn off, I've got more placid if you know what I mean. I've calmed down a bit.

However, Anthony's self-purported placidity was highly contingent. Although he did not know what his wife's new partner looked like, Anthony had told his wife:

> 'Don't bring him anyway near me. If I see you in town with him—I will.' Cos inside I know I will . . . It's inside you, you know what I mean? You can't stop that. And I'm not going to go stalking him or anything . . . It's just that if I see him in a pub or in the street, I'll hit him . . . I will . . . It's a matter of principle. When I split up with my wife, within six weeks, she was seeing him. As far as I know, she could have been seeing him beforehand. But she swears blind she weren't. But I still got that doubt. It will always be there—until I actually get it out, get it out of my system, actually give him a kicking, it will always be there.

Anthony considered many of the hypothetical scenarios (i.e. cognitive reasoning exercises) he was asked to undertake on the anger management programme he was attending as 'stupid' and 'completely crap'. But he valued his probation officer's capacity to listen: 'Like if I got a problem or anything or if I want to get something off my chest, I can tell him about it. He's like a calming influence.'

Indeed, Anthony's drug use was not entirely unconnected to the problems he needed to offload. Sometimes he would smoke 'spliff after spliff after spliff', knowing 'it always seems to make people more talkative'. He also realized that many of the times when he was feeling 'angry . . . just wanting . . . revenge', he was typically: 'pissed up or stoned or doing a lot of pills or . . . whizz. That screws your head—it don't give you a chance to think cos your head's all messed up anyway.'

Anthony's own daughter continued to live with his ex-wife after their separation. Although Anthony anticipated that he would never have permanent custody of his daughter, he believed he and his daughter would both benefit from being together: 'The only person I want now is my daughter—and I want her permanently, but I'll never get her permanently. That's the only person I need to help—myself and her.' Indeed, at the time of the second interview nine months later, it seemed that Anthony had not completely ruled out the prospect of a reconciliation with his wife despite valuing his new-found 'independence'.

During this second interview Anthony also revealed that he was spending more time with his father, who had been diagnosed with cancer of the pancreas. Although Anthony said he had become 'close' to his father, it was his mother who brought him up.[11] Anthony remembered that when he was a child his father was 'in the pub . . . all the time. He was a womanizer and that.' Anthony revealed little more about his father, but jested 'I'm getting like him'.

At his third interview seven months later, Anthony reported that his wife had remarried and was expecting another child. On this occasion, Anthony was actually in breach of his probation order, having stopped attending:

> Once I knew I'd lost me job, and was in debt to my rent, I just thought 'fuck it, fuck everything'. Move away from the area . . . just forget everything, forget the anger management, forget probation, and just move on. I don't think I need it anymore, personally speaking.

Although unemployed, Anthony said he was 'not really looking for work'. After 'five years on two shitty jobs', he said he wanted 'about a year off'. Nevertheless, Anthony claimed his offending had reduced and his drinking and drug use had diminished. Anthony had not been in a fight for about six months. His explanation of why he reduced his offending behaviour centred almost exclusively on the impact of his partner 'Cleo'.

When Anthony first met Cleo at a nightclub he had felt quite protective towards her.

> We'd had a couple of pills and that, she had a pill that night as well. We were both out of our face—good Es—and she was losing the plot, so I had to keep an eye on her.

But since they had moved in together Anthony had come to perceive Cleo as a crucial stabilizing influence on him.

> SF: So, what would you say has been the thing that has enabled you to stay out of trouble?
>
> A: Stability with Cleo, I reckon. Having a girlfriend. Living with her. She keeps you level headed, you get angry about something, you've got someone there to sit you down and say, 'Don't worry about it. Calm down' . . . When you're on your tod you just brew on it, don't you? . . . [A]nd usually let it out on the wrong person . . . [In the past, I'd] go and get pissed up and get a bit depressed, and then you go and see someone or someone says the wrong word and you end up fighting. But now I am not depressed at all, I wake up most mornings happy. I don't need drink to get to sleep at night or anything like that no more.

Anthony claimed he generally put Cleo 'first', before his friends (although 'most of them' were 'inside' prison), and that he had been able to take on a 'father figure' role in relation to Cleo's children. The probation office from which Anthony was supervised had no further contact with him after this interview was conducted. A search of the Offenders' Index suggested that Anthony had not been arrested or reconvicted in the three years since this third interview.

Narratives, subjectivity and change

What are we to make of Dan and Anthony's stories? Perhaps the best place to start is to ask how sure we can be that these men actually desisted. Checks with practitioners who had contacts with these men and searches of official records did not undermine these men's claims that they had reduced their offending. Yet we cannot know for sure whether these men actually stopped offending or simply avoided detection by the criminal justice system. This is a serious problem not only with our research but with the vast majority of research into criminal careers, 'what works' style evaluations and with criminological research more generally (Farrall, 2002; Rumgay, 2003). The nature of criminological enquiry invariably leaves researchers dependent on an uneasy mixture of self-reports, practitioners' impressions and reconviction records. The central lesson to be learned here is that all hard and fast claims about criminal careers need to be treated with considerable caution, regardless of who makes them or the paradigms employed; the reliability of criminological data of this kind is hardly ever as assured as criminologists would like.[12]

On the basis of the available evidence though, we feel reasonably confident in claiming that burglary and theft were no longer part of Dan's and Anthony's everyday lives. Still, while both men appeared to be desisting from violent crime, the way in which their lives were organized *and* the ways in which they conceived their relationships did not preclude possibilities for the commission of further assaults. What if Anthony had seen Cleo with an old boyfriend whilst out nightclubbing? What if Dan's incorrigible jealousy resurfaced the next time a customer flirted with Jenny in the pub where she worked? We cannot know for sure what happened, or will happen, next. But given that there are relatively few career criminals who undergo complete transformations of self (Jennings, 1990; Maruna and Farrall, 2004), or otherwise radical or religious conversions, the kind of modest, precarious and by all accounts ambiguous change depicted in Dan's and Anthony's interviews may be quite typical of men in the later stages of desistance—a view with which other scholars seem to concur (Foote and Frank, 1999). As Maruna cautions: '[M]ost of the persisters one finds do not seem to really persist, most of the desisters do not really seem to desist, and, honestly, it is getting harder than ever to find any "innocents"' (2001: 43).

Part of the problem is that criminal careers scholars' preoccupation with behaviour that transgresses the law obscures as much as it clarifies when it comes to making sense of changes in the lives of career criminals. As feminist research with victims of domestic violence has repeatedly shown (e.g. Kelly, 1988; Dobash et al., 1996), perpetrators often deploy a continuum of controlling and frightening behaviours, only a small minority of which can be easily defined as criminal. This was clearly the case with Dan, and had almost certainly been the case with Anthony around the time when his ex-wife started dating another man. More broadly, the problem is that the tidy relationship between offending behaviour and 'propensity' assumed in so much of the criminal careers literature simply does not exist.

The obsessive jealousy that both Dan and Anthony displayed on different occasions illustrates the important role of contingency—that is, unexpected changes in the life-course—in what happens, or does not happen, with regards to future crimes. Hence, both case studies illustrate the shortcomings of the kind of criminal careers research that assumes readily calculable risks and probabilities. The respective sons of abusive and absent fathers, both Dan and Anthony had become like their dads. However, while it had taken many years and some very troubled relationships for both men to become conscious of these similarities, both had tried to resist reproducing their father's mistakes. Expressed in the terminology of the life-course perspective, we could say that both men's criminal careers were characterized by trajectories that commenced with the early onset of delinquency, developed into relatively heavy involvement in property crime and substance abuse, and culminated in occasional acts of violent crime in adult life, interspersed with regular recreational drug use and convictions. These trajectories were punctuated by transitions—such as leaving home, settling down and separation, finding and losing jobs, having children and step-parenting and (through different means) coming to understand their fathers' mistakes—that eventually established a pathway towards desistance.

Yet, in response to those who prefer the life-course perspective, we would argue that an understanding of how and why some of these transitions fostered desistance—while others sparked more persistent or different forms of offending—is a matter that can only be resolved through engagement with the specifics of the cases. One cannot simply extrapolate that involvement in tightly knit families or paid employment produces the kinds of social capital that reduces offending. To the contrary, the closeness of Dan's family networks could be cited as a factor that enabled both his own and his father's violence to proceed without sustained criminal justice intervention. Likewise Anthony's employment in a menial factory job—a job he likened to working in 'a concentration camp'—seems to have added to his frustration, and was, in fact, the scene of the assault for which he was put on probation. One way of interpreting these empirical disjunctions from the life-course perspective would be to point out that the meaning and experience of both manual employment and family life for men living in the 1990s was qualitatively different to those brought up between 1930 and 1950. This is a point Sampson and Laub (1993: 254) themselves concede. To the extent that there was continuity in these men's lives, this was at least in part forged in the telling. This point takes us to the narrative and discursive elements of Maruna's and Jefferson's work.

Like many of Maruna's desisters, Dan commenced his story with a rather deterministic account of his behaviour as a youth. Dan claimed that at certain points in his life his participation in crime, his violence towards women and his separation from his wife were all 'caused' by his father's abusiveness. Given his father's violence, Dan's juvenile 'rebellion' was, in his view, almost inevitable and imprisonment was 'an escape'. This deterministic account of Dan's past contrasted starkly with his more free-willed account of his recent struggles to acknowledge that he had 'a problem' and muster the commitment needed to do something about it by seeking help from various counselling agencies, disowning his father and attempting 'to break the cycle'. This disowning of his father seemed further reinforced by Dan's hope that his stepson would not make the same mistake (what Maruna refers to as a 'generative script'). Dan did not want Jason to turn out as he had and was pleased to see his son acknowledging that his biological father was unreliable.

A similar narrative structure is evident in Anthony's account. When Anthony was first interviewed, he described himself as compelled to violence by the stress of his marital break-up. His head was all 'messed up', both by the large amounts of elicit drugs and alcohol he was consuming, and because of intense feelings of bitterness and jealousy he was experiencing. Fifteen months later, a generative narrative was exhibited in Anthony's third interview when he mentioned his desire to have custody of his daughter, an arrangement Anthony assumed would 'help' them both. Anthony then identified his partner's capacity to keep him 'level headed' as a force that secured changes within himself. Anthony claimed that he stopped Cleo from 'losing the plot', and that she exerted a 'calming influence' on him.

While both these men's stories are biographically unique, what gives them a familiar feel is the structure of meaning on which they draw. If we follow Jefferson's point that these meanings are embedded in a wider network of social discourses in which people choose—not always freely—to invest, then it is relatively easy to spot how masculinity was being performed in both of these men's lives and in the telling of their stories. Dan's story is that of a troubled youth *hardened* by the actions of an uncaring, alcoholic and abusive father. The discourse of 'rebellion' deployed here feels a little forced, burglaries hardly being acts of defiance, and imprisonment offering little freedom from the fear and abuse Dan sought to escape at home. But the discursive movement from 'rebellious but troubled youth' to 'local hard man' and then to 'protecting, but fallible family man' makes it easy for us to conceive how Dan was able to accommodate changes in his offending behaviour (for better and worse) without undergoing any radical transformation of self.

Throughout his interviews, Dan constructed his violence towards women in a way that suggested it merited little justification. Indeed Dan's wife, Jenny, seemed to have endorsed Dan's desire to be respected as a local 'hard man' despite being at the brunt of his domestic violence. Dan apparently provided Jenny and their children with the kind of protection other men on their estate could not offer; hence Jenny's decision to leave her new boyfriend who stood by and watched her get hit. As a father, Dan had constructed himself as a firm disciplinarian—a counterbalance to his wife's 'softness' and craziness ('a woman possessed')—at least until the parallels between himself and his own father became too apparent. Thereafter, Dan positioned himself as a moral guardian to his children; despite having got things wrong, Dan would (heroically) break the 'cycle' (of violence), enabling his children to benefit from his mistakes.

Anthony's recollections were no less 'masculinity accomplishing'. His disclosures in his first interview centred heavily on his new-found freedom, post-separation. Casual sex, heavy drinking and the occasional pub fight were all part of this bachelor's 'high-life'. Like Dan, Anthony was also aggrieved at being jilted but the discourse of revenge—against his wife's new partner—provided him with one (not an entirely convincing) way of rationalizing his predicament in identifiably macho terms without conceding the moral 'high ground' (Katz, 1988). Although there were no doubt many occasions when his public violence seemed like 'mindless aggression' to others, in his discursive reconstructions Anthony (like Dan) reconstructed his violence towards other men as justified and purposive, the meeting of perceived threats with appropriate levels of force (Hobbs, 1995). Despite his convictions for violence and his murderous feelings towards his ex-wife's new boyfriend, the discourse of revenge Anthony invested in enabled him to distinguish himself from his 'nutcase' friend who would 'lash out' at anyone when drunk. Subsequently tapping into a heavily heterosexualized discourse, as routinely reproduced in romantic fiction (McRobbie, 1991; Walkerdine, 1994) as it is in criminal careers research literature, Anthony identified 'the love of a *good* woman' as his path to salvation. Here, Anthony reproduced the commonplace 'to have and to hold' discourse Hollway (1989) identified in her classic study about how couples negotiate feelings of vulnerability. This discourse conveys the dynamics of Anthony's and Cleo's mutual interdependence—his protectiveness in return for her 'calming influence'—as well as his (macho, sexist) desire to distinguish her from the sexually promiscuous 'slappers' he used to date.

Continuity in the life-course can thus be achieved by male career criminals (at least in part) through investments in heavily gendered discourses (youthful rebelliousness, hardness, compulsive promiscuity, protector and provider, disciplinarian). These discourses establish meaning through differentiation. This differentiation entails the evocation of certain stereotypes of women ('possessed', 'soft', 'loose', unfaithful, devious) and men (nutcases, absent fathers, child abusers, alcoholics and wimps). But, as Jefferson reminds us, if we want to grasp these men's experiences of masculinity, as opposed to just the logic of their social constructions, we have to resist the temptation to reduce their psychological worlds to the sum of social discourses. Moreover, an analysis of social discourses does not help us to make sense entirely of both men's tendencies to engage in behaviours that defy rational, instrumental explanation. Why, for example, did Anthony want to kill a man he had never seen—a man who may not have met his ex-wife until after she and Anthony had separated? And what does Anthony's additional revelation that he wanted to shoot his wife and his daughter tell us about his feelings at that time? Likewise, what was Dan trying to achieve by barricading himself and his wife in their house? Why had he attempted suicide on several occasions? Could he not see that however much his neighbours congratulated him for taking on other men on his estate, his violence towards his wife would require a much more complicated set of justifications and was hardly ever likely to be publicly endorsed as evidence of a fair fight, hard won?

Examples like these illustrate the incapacity of social discourses to completely contain or condition the psychological worlds inhabited by our respondents (see also Frosh, 1994). Neither of these men readily verbalized what it was they were so troubled by when their partners left, yet the powerful (sometimes murderous) fantasies that came into play when this happened suggest to us considerable feelings of emotional dependency and humiliation that could not be readily admitted. It is not possible to make sense of these sorts of thoughts and feelings from a simple rational choice or social learning perspective. Indeed, this kind of emotional complexity is too readily obscured when the dictates of methodology focus exclusively on the relationship between social scripts and cognitive reasoning.

One does not have to dig too deep to envisage a connection between the various manifestations of 'hardness' Dan and Anthony engaged in, their self-destructive behaviours and addictions and the uncomfortable thoughts and feelings that they preferred not to confront. Many of the stories these men told conveyed the defensive quality of their thinking and behaviour. Both claimed not to be bothered about things that persistently preoccupied them; both blamed others for their own behaviour; and both used drink and drugs to alleviate their psychological turmoil so that they literally did not have to *think*. Many of these defences took on a macho sexist quality. For example, it seems relatively plausible that when Dan referred to his wife as a 'woman possessed' and when Anthony differentiated himself from his 'nutcase' mate, something of the mental disarray both men sometimes found themselves enduring (and probably were accused off) was being split off and located elsewhere, in other people where it could be safely attacked. Both men routinely disavowed their self-evident *emotional* and *financial* dependency on their partners by positioning themselves as 'protectors'—a phenomenon which we might argue is all the more common, given the way in which changes in the global economy over the last 20 years have reduced the opportunities for many men in the West to accrue the sense of self-respect and achievement their fathers gleaned from paid employment (Minsky, 1998: 148).

However, there are also places in both of these men's narratives where the psychodynamics alluded to exceed the explanatory contours of the term 'defended subject', and approximate the clinical usage of the concept of 'defence mechanisms'. An insight drawn from one of the first—and too often forgotten—psychoanalytic criminologists Edward Glover (1960: 318) is helpful here. Glover was a keen advocate of the Freudian idea that the enactment of violent behaviour could be considered a 'symptom equivalent' to psychosis—a behaviour that actually spared the individual from experiencing psychotic mental symptoms. Without wishing to deny the relevance of sexism and power in explaining these men's behaviours, it is difficult to imagine the time when Dan barricaded himself in his house to stop his wife leaving, or the time when Anthony was seeking revenge on a man whom he had never met, without some reference to some form of psychotic state, or manic denial of reality. The reality of both situations was that both men's partners wanted to leave them. Anthony's response was to displace his hurt feelings onto a fantasy of his wife's new partner upon whom he could exact revenge. At its most horrifying, Anthony's desire to transcend the extreme sense of humiliation he felt about this was expressed in his fantasy of triumphantly exterminating his ex-wife's new partner, and *then* shooting his wife and daughter. Similarly, Dan's barricading himself might be interpreted as the enactment of his psychic denial of the fact that his wife actually preferred another man's company; the physical barricading reflecting a failure of psychical containment. Dan's behaviour smacked of desperation as much as male power. He fantasized that his wife would wish to stay with him if only he could physically contain them both within their house. In many respects typical of the behaviour of abusive men, and not entirely inconsistent with the discourses of 'protector' in which Dan and

Anthony invest, this kind of behaviour can be viewed psychoanalytically as a form of 'acting out' (see also Cordess and Hyatt-Williams, 1996) that might have spared its actors from the full force of the psychic symptoms they were unable (or unwilling) to tolerate.

This is not to suggest that our interviewees were psychotics. As Stan Cohen (2001) has argued, denial—like splitting, projection and displacement—is a relatively common manifestation of the desire to be innocent of troubling recognitions. It thus permeates western culture and politics at all levels. But how and why some people act out their denials with much greater frequency and intensity than others is a question which has yet to be fully answered. Developing theories and concepts capable of suturing complex psychic phenomena with their cultural moorings and behavioural manifestations is not an easy task (Evans, 2000; Hall, 2000). But it strikes us that in order to develop the life-course perspective within criminology, it will be necessary to entertain an age-graded understanding of defensiveness that entails a theoretical understanding of the form 'troubling recognitions' are likely to take as people mature. Here we have only provided a cursory outline of the social and psychic dynamics intrinsic to the pattern of continuity and change exhibited in Dan and Anthony's recent pasts. Self-evidently a richer understanding of these men's earlier years would have necessitated a much grander research strategy than we appreciated at the time we undertook our interviews. But we feel confident in claiming that it is almost impossible to make sense of either Dan's or Anthony's involvement in crime without first taking account of how their various anxieties and fears were shaped by a host of contradictory and lofty *social* expectations: social expectations about the appropriateness of fighting back, hiding vulnerable feelings, controlling public and private spaces, about what 'good' wives and mothers do and (perhaps more ambiguously) about the role and responsibilities of 'good' fathers and husbands.

Our view is that men's own experiences of trying to live up to these kinds of expectations is a task that criminal careers research must broach if it is to deliver a meaningful and critical understanding of pathways in and out of crime. It seems self-evident that both Dan's and Anthony's own and their father's failures to deliver anything approaching what might—for lack of a more commonly used expression—be called 'good enough fathering' (Kraemer, 1995; Frosh, 1997) is implicated in both men's involvement in crime and the forms of change they embrace. Yet to analyse this phenomenon further would entail exploring the whole issue of identification that Jefferson has put so squarely on the agenda. Even the most basic of psychoanalytic ideas appear to have more to offer in terms of understanding these men's childhoods than can be gleaned from most of the literatures on masculinities and crime and criminal careers and desistance. For example, in her book *Psychoanalysis and Culture*, Ros Minsky explains that:

> in Freud's theory, the symbolic father seems to stand for the following ideas: we cannot remain permanently in a merged state of being with our mother,

> dominated by phantasies, without destroying the possibility of 'growing up' in the sense of having satisfying, relatively unmerged relationships with other people; we can never achieve a state of wholeness, perfection and complete fulfilment because other people can never be entirely predictable so we have to learn to tolerate frustration; we have to submit to the law and authority of culture to the extent that we cannot have incestuous relationships with our parents and, in normal circumstances, we should not murder those people who stand between us and our desires.
>
> (1998: 135)

Conversely:

> Klein's work suggests that the child may experience a violent father as expressing not only his (the father's) own destructive feelings but also, through projection, those of the child so the father's violence is denied. This may then set up a pattern of denial of feelings which have been split off so that later, as an adult, violent behaviour may suddenly erupt from nowhere because ordinary expressions of anger have been denied.
>
> (1998: 139)

> [I]f the actual father leaves permanently, or is absent for long periods, the child is likely to idealize him, sometimes to conceal its anger with the father from itself. Since idealization is unrealistic because it obscures the real person with phantasy, this may affect the child's future relationships with partners who may be idealized at first but later denigrated. If the child feels very angry with an abandoning father this may set up frightening phantasies of being attacked by the father in the form of burglars, thieves, rapists and other nightmare attackers . . . Sometimes when fathers leave, the child feels that this is its fault, that it is the direct result of its own destructive impulses with the result that more reparative, creative phantasies are unable to develop subsequently.
>
> (1998: 149)

Hence, there is much in both classic Freudian and Kleinian theory to alert us to the potentially complex patterns of development men like Anthony and Dan would have encountered. Both were men who had struggled to 'tolerate frustration' and who suffered murderous thoughts. Hence, there may be merit in the Freudian notion that the sons of emotionally and/or physically absent and/or abusive fathers are likely to be prone to developing super-ego problems (Hood-Williams, 2001). However, both men's denials of feelings that suddenly erupted into violence, as if from nowhere, their tendencies to idealize and then denigrate partners, their fears of being attacked or humiliated by other men, their belated recognition of how their fathers treated their mothers, and their struggles to make reparation for harms caused, render the Kleinian arguments equally persuasive. Unfortunately, the kind of therapeutic and observational work that would be needed to support or refute these kinds of hypotheses exceeds the limits of acceptable criminological methodologies. We have no way of knowing if the adolescent Dan perceived his father as a violent thug or identified with him as a relatively invulnerable figure, a source of protection in contrast to his heavily victimized and vulnerable mother. We know not whether Dan admired, envied or resented his father's capacity to laugh and joke with his mates in public, despite his private brutality. Likewise, we do not know if Anthony had always been aware of his father's absence during his childhood, nor what he imagined his absent father to be like.

These questions may be better left to clinically trained researchers. Nevertheless, what criminologists might be able to contribute to an understanding of the relationship between (social) gender and (psychic) identification is a greater understanding of the nature of development in adult life: a greater recognition that people have the capacity to develop different patterns of identification and to reconfigure their 'object relations' post-adolescence. Such a recognition would entail greater sensitivity to those transitional periods when generational differences most matter. These moments almost certainly include making a life with a partner and having children. But they also include those moments when children force adults to rethink their childhood assumptions (Kraemer, 1995) because the tables are turned, and moments when adults come to accommodate an understanding of their parents' mortality (Diamond, 1998). Elements of both these phenomena appear in our case studies and constitute, as we argue, transitional moments in these two men's lives as fathers, partners and offenders.

These moments present both positive and negative possibilities for change. For example, Dan's disowning his father might be interpreted as a form of psychic separation, facilitated by his growing consciousness of the contradictions in his life and their embeddedness in father–son similarities. Likewise, we might speculate that Anthony's belated attempts to become close to his (chronically ill) father helped him internalize some form of paternal identification grounded more in reality and less in fantasy. In both Kleinian and Freudian terms a less fantastical paternal identification would probably reduce Anthony's tendency to idealize and denigrate, and hence diminish his more murderous, triumphalist fantasies. Yet, all of these possibilities are highly contingent. Without Dan and Anthony first developing the capacity to acknowledge the many points of identification between themselves and their fathers, the kind of 'disowning' that could have taken place might have culminated in further violent denials, and hence parts of the self being repeatedly split off, with deleterious consequence for both the men and others close to them (Gadd, 2002).

Conclusion

Applying Jefferson's model of subjectivity to the cases of two men's criminal careers has taken us down a theoretically complex road towards a psychosocial criminology many criminologists would themselves prefer to avoid (Jefferson, 2002). Nevertheless, Jefferson's approach enables us to theorize why some desisters (like Maruna's) invest so enthusiastically in their tales of reform and what emotional functions these investments might have. Moreover, as we have illustrated, thinking through what desisters are actually doing within a more gender-sensitive framework is an important, albeit difficult, task. More generally, we have shown that answers to the question 'why do people stop offending?' are unlikely to be evident in the surface-data we gather about criminal careers. The latent or unconscious meanings embedded in offenders' narratives are as important as the actual words, narratives or discourses used. These unconscious meanings can only be 'got at' through in-depth interpretive work.

Moreover, criminologists working in this field must live with the uncertainty of neither knowing exactly how much crime their respondents have been involved in, nor exactly how offenders feel when they rationalize their behaviour with a whole gamut of techniques of neutralization. Those 'turning points' in criminal careers identified in aggregate data may well be methodological effects that only appear so salient because of *absences* in the information gathered. Therefore, criminal careers researchers need to think through what the risk and protective factors they routinely cite—(un)employment, (in)adequate parenting, marriage and divorce, social exclusion and inclusion, drug use and abstinence—mean to their research subjects, as well as how these correlate with rates of offending at aggregate levels. Our data support Sampson and Laub's (1993) contention that the lives of ex-offenders exhibit both continuity and change. However, creating an adequately psychosocial criminology involves more than adding back the psychological into the social (Jefferson, 2002). Such a discipline would strive to conceptualize both how people position themselves in relation to social events and psychological problems, and how defences against psychological pain (for example, loneliness, fear, depression) get reproduced, repackaged and rebranded in certain social discourses (of 'hardness', 'compulsive heterosexuality' and the 'protective family man'). While the concepts of 'transition' and 'trajectory' may be useful at an aggregate level, the meanings that produce continuity and change depend upon continually shifting pyscho*dynamics* that are to some extent biographically unique, and have the potential to disrupt, expedite and/or hinder changes in the social arena. As C. Wright Mills once observed:

> Know that many personal troubles cannot be solved merely as troubles, but must be understood in terms of public issues . . . Know that the *human meaning* of public issues *must* be *revealed by relating them to personal troubles and to the problems of individual life.*
>
> (1959: 226, emphasis added)

Of course, the public problem of crime is inseparable from the private troubles endured by many individuals. In men's accounts of violence, the private troubles of drink and drug abuse, infidelity, sexual jealousy, together with absent, emotionally unavailable and abusive fathers, are often turned into public issues. Yet theoretical work in this field often fails to move beyond a social learning and/or rational choice model of subjectivity. As the two cases we have discussed demonstrate, these models of subjectivity simply do not capture the complex processes of identification and dis-identification through which male offenders differentiate themselves from negative cultural stereotypes of men (e.g. feckless fathers, alcoholics, wife-beaters and wimps) and from men they themselves appear most like (e.g. fathers and their partners' former spouses). Without concerted attempts to understand the subjective realities inhabited by those with these personal troubles, the *human meaning* of criminal behaviour will always escape us.

Notes

The authors would like to thank Lynn Chancer, Tony Jefferson and anonymous reviewers for comments on earlier drafts of this article, and Ben Bowling, Richard Collier and Shadd Maruna for their observations about the case material discussed herein.

1 Similar findings were made by Sampson and Laub (1993: 217) and Jamieson et al. (1999: 133) using other data-sets.

2 Most recently this has taken Jefferson's work into the field of child development, and specifically into an engagement with Jessica Benjamin's (1998) idea that how gender development pans out depends heavily on how we negotiate (physically as well as in fantasy) our desire to be both like our parental figures and desirable to these parental figures. But, as the late John Hood-Williams (2001) observed, the issue of identification remains a puzzle to psychoanalysts of all persuasions, which we should not rush to resolve in order to satisfy the more normotic concerns of sociological criminology.

3 Pseudonyms are used in all instances. 'Dan' was interviewed twice by Gadd for his study of male identities and partner abuse. Gadd's methodology was heavily influenced by Hollway and Jefferson's (2000) work and deployed their free association narrative interview method in interviews with 8 men who were seeking counselling to help them stop being violent to their partners, and nine practitioners working for a project that helps violent men to change. See Gadd (2000b, 2002, 2003b) for further details of the methodology used. 'Anthony' was interviewed three times by Farrall for his study of the impact of probation supervision on the lives and offending trajectories of 200 men and women. See Farrall (2002) for further details of the methodologies employed.

4 Dan explained:

> We actually split up for three months. Urm. We were still living in the same house. Had separate beds. Urm, urr, and that were because of my violence and urm mental abuse. Urm, so it took us a long time to get through that and I think we are just about coming through it now. And this were like. Well, to be honest, it's

been going on for about three years. This bad patch has like stretched out for like three years.

5 A national service which offers couple-counselling.
6 Dan had seen his father dragging his mother round the street, having first ripped off her clothes.
7 Once nailing their cat to his mother-in-law's front door so she would have to open it.
8 However, Dan's subsequent disclosures cast doubt upon his assertion that he was not violent towards his children. When explaining how Jason's truanting continued to be 'a major source of conflict', Dan said: 'I've laid off. I don't chastise him *any more*. Basically I let him do what he wants. Because if I say anything to him, me and him end up arguing.'
9 The Offenders' Index is a Home Office-funded database which contains information about the criminal histories of over 6 million offenders convicted of standard list offences since 1963. It was created purely for research purposes and is widely used by those researching the criminal careers of British offenders.
10 Anthony described his younger sister as 'like a mother' to him. His sister had put him up despite her own problems with 'depression'.
11 Anthony talked less extensively about his family of origin than Dan, partly because of the different focus of the research projects for which the two men were interviewed.
12 These problems are not resolved when the case material in question is backed up by conviction data, as masculinity theorists have recently discovered. An analysis of masculinity in the Central Park jogger rape case was a centrepiece of Jim Messerschmidt's (1993) *Masculinities and Crime*. Now that someone else has confessed to the crime, and the original suspects' convictions have been quashed, the theoretical basis upon which that work was premised is undeniably weaker (Jefferson, forthcoming).

References

Barclay, G. (1990) 'The Peak Age of Known Offending by Males', *Home Office Research Bulletin* 28: 20–3.

Benjamin, J. (1998) *Shadow of the Other: Intersubjectivity and Gender in Psychoanalysis*. London: Routledge.

Brown, J. (1991) 'The Professional Ex-', *Sociological Quarterly* 32(2): 219–30.

Burnett, R. (1992) *The Dynamics of Recidivism*. Oxford, UK: Centre for Criminological Research, University of Oxford.

Burnett, R. (2004, forthcoming) 'To Reoffend or to Not Reoffend? The Ambivalence of Offenders', in S. Maruna and R. Immarigeon (eds) *After Crime and Punishment*. Cullompton, Devon: Willan Publishing.

Campbell, B. (1993) *Goliath*. London: Methuen.

Cohen, S. (2001) *States of Denial: Knowing about Atrocities and Suffering*. Cambridge: Polity Press.

Collier, R. (1998) *Masculinities, Crime and Criminology*. London: Sage Publications.

Connell, R.W. (1987) *Gender and Power Society: The Person and Sexual Politics*. Cambridge: Polity Press.

Connell, R.W. (1995) *Masculinities*. Cambridge: Polity Press.

Connell, R.W. (2002) 'On Hegemonic Masculinity: Response to Jefferson and Hall', *Theoretical Criminology* 6(1): 89–100.

Cordess, C. and A. Hyatt-Williams (1996) 'The Criminal Act and Acting Out', in C. Cordess and M. Cox (eds) *Forensic Psychotherapy, Volume 1: Mainly Theory*, pp. 9–12. London: Jessica Kingsley Press.

Cromwell, P., J. Olson and D. Avary (1991) *Breaking and Entering*. London: Sage Publications.

Cusson, M. and P. Pinsonneault (1986) 'The Decision to Give Up Crime', in D. Cornish and R. Clarke (eds) *The Reasoning Criminal*, pp. 72–82. New York: Springer-Verlag.

Denzin, N. (1987) *The Recovering Alcoholic*. Newbury Park, CA: Sage Publications.

Devlin, A. and B. Turney (eds) (1999) *Going Straight*. Winchester: Waterside Press.

Diamond, M. (1998) 'Fathers with Sons: Psychoanalytic Perspectives on "Good Enough" Fathering throughout the Life Cycle', *Gender and Psychoanalysis* 3(3): 248–99.

Dobash, R., R. Dobash, K. Cavanagh and R. Lewis (1996) 'Re-education Programmes for Violent Men: An Evaluation', *Research Findings No. 46*. London: Home Office Research & Statistics Directorate.

Edley, N. and M. Wetherell (1999) 'Imagined Futures: Young Men's Talk about Fatherhood and Domestic Life', *British Journal of Social Psychology* 38(2): 131–94.

Elder, G.H. (1985) 'Preface', in G.H. Elder (ed.) *Life-Course Dynamics*, pp. 15–20. Ithaca, NY: Cornell University Press.

Evans, J. (2000) 'Introduction: Psychoanalysis and Psychosocial Relations', in P. du Gay, J. Evans and P. Redman *Identity: A Reader*, pp. 121–9. London: Sage Publications.

Farrall, S. (2002) *Rethinking What Works with Offenders: Probation, Social Context and Desistance from Crime*. Cullompton, Devon: Willan Press.

Farrall, S. and B. Bowling (1999) 'Structuration, Human Development and Desistance from Crime', *British Journal of Criminology* 39(2): 253–68.

Farrington, D. (1996) 'Criminological Psychology: Individual and Family Factors in Explanation and Prevention of Offending', in C.R. Hollin (ed.) *Working with Offenders*, pp. 3–39. Wiley: Chichester.

Farrington, D.P. (1997) 'Human Development and Criminal Careers', in M. Maguire, R. Morgan and R. Reiner (eds) *The Oxford Handbook of Criminology*, 2nd edn, pp. 511–84. Oxford: Clarendon Press.

Farrington, D. (2002) 'Developmental Criminology and Risk-Focussed Crime Prevention', in M. Maguire, R. Morgan and R. Reiner (eds) *The Oxford Handbook of Criminology*, 3rd edn, pp. 657–701. Oxford: Oxford University Press.

Foote, C.E. and A.W. Frank (1999) 'Foucault and Therapy: The Disciplining of Grief', in A.S. Chambon, A. Irving and L. Epstein (eds) *Reading Foucault for Social Work*, pp. 157–87. New York: Columbia University Press.

Frosh, S. (1994) *Sexual Difference: Masculinity and Psychoanalysis*. London: Routledge.

Frosh, S. (1997) 'Fathers' Ambivalence (Too)', in W. Hollway and B. Featherstone (eds) *Mothering and Ambivalence*, pp. 37–53. London: Routledge.

Frosh, S., A. Phoenix and R. Pattman (2002) *Young Masculinities*. Basingstoke: Palgrave.

Gadd, D. (2000a) 'Masculinities, Violence and Defended Psychosocial Subjects', *Theoretical Criminology* 4(4): 429–49.

Gadd, D. (2000b) 'Deconstructing Male Violence: A Qualitative Study of Male Workers and Clients on an Anti-Violence Programme', unpublished PhD dissertation, Keele University, Staffs.

Gadd, D. (2002) Masculinities and Violence against Female Partners', *Social and Legal Studies* 11(1): 61–80.

Gadd, D. (2003a) 'Reading between the Lines: Subjectivity and Men's Violence', *Men and Masculinities* 5(4): 333–54.

Gadd, D. (2003b) 'Making Sense of Interviewee–Interviewer Dynamics in Narratives about Violence in Intimate Relationships', *International Journal of Social Research Methodology* 6(1): 1–19.

Glover, E. (1960) 'Psychoanalysis and Criminology: A Political Survey', in E. Glover *The Roots of Crime*, pp. 314–24. London: Imago.

Gottfredson, M. and T. Hirschi (1990) *A General Theory of Crime*. Stanford, CA: Stanford University Press.

Hall, S. (2000) 'Who Needs "Identity"?', in P. du Gay, J. Evans and P. Redman (2000) *Identity: A Reader*, pp. 15–30. London: Sage Publications.

Hall, S. (2002) 'Daubing the Drudges of Fury: Men, Violence and the Piety of the "Hegemonic Masculinity" Thesis', *Theoretical Criminology* 6(1): 35–62.

Hobbs, D. (1988) *Doing the Business: Entrepreneurship, the Working Class, and Detectives in the East End of London*. Oxford: Clarendon Press.

Hobbs, D. (1995) *Bad Business: Professional Crime in Modern Britain*. Oxford: Oxford University Press.

Hobbs, D., P. Hadfield, S. Lister and S. Winlow (2002) '"Door Lore": The Art and Economics of Intimidation', *British Journal of Criminology* 42(2): 352–70.

Holden, C. (1986) 'Growing Focus on Criminal Careers', *Science* 233: 1377–8.

Hollway, W. (1989) *Subjectivity and Method in Psychology*. London: Sage Publications.

Hollway, W. and T. Jefferson (2000) *Doing Qualitative Research Differently:*

Free Association, Narrative and the Interview Method. London: Sage Publications.

Hood-Williams, J. (2001) 'Gender, Masculinities and Crime: From Structures to Psyches', *Theoretical Criminology* 5(1): 37–60.

Hughes, M. (1997) 'An Exploratory Study of Young Adult Black and Latino Males and the Factors Facilitating Their Decisions to Make Positive Behavioural Changes', *Smith College Studies in Social Work* 67(3): 401–14.

Hughes, M. (1998) 'Turning Points in the Lives of Young Inner-City Men Forgoing Destructive Criminal Behaviours: A Qualitative Study', *Social Work Research* 22(3): 143–51.

Jamieson, J., G. McIvor and C. Murray (1999) *Understanding Offending among Young People*. Edinburgh: The Stationery Office.

Jefferson, T. (1994) 'Theorising Masculine Subjectivity', in T. Newburn and E.A. Stanko (eds) *Just Boys Doing Business*, pp. 10–31. London: Routledge.

Jefferson, T. (1996) 'From "Little Fairy Boy" to the "Compleat Destroyer": Subjectivity and Transformation in the Biography of Mike Tyson', in M. Mac an Ghail (ed.) *Understanding Masculinities: Social Relations and Cultural Arenas*, pp. 153–67. Buckingham: Open University Press.

Jefferson, T. (1997a) 'Masculinities and Crime', in M. Maguire, R. Morgan and R. Reiner (eds) *The Oxford Handbook of Criminology*, 2nd edn, pp. 535–58. Oxford: Clarendon Press.

Jefferson, T. (1997b) 'The Tyson Rape Trial: The Law, Feminism and Emotional "Truth"', *Social and Legal Studies* 6(2): 281–301.

Jefferson, T. (1998) 'Muscle, "Hard Men" and "Iron" Mike Tyson: Reflections on Desire, Anxiety and the Embodiment of Masculinity', *Body and Society* 4(1): 103–18.

Jefferson, T. (2002) 'For a Psychosocial Criminology', in K. Carrington and R. Hogg (eds) *The Future of Critical Criminology*, pp. 145–67. Cullompton, Devon: Willan.

Jefferson, T. (forthcoming) 'Gender and Crime', in P. Essed, A. Kobayashi and D.T. Goldberg (eds) *A Companion to Gender Studies*. Malden, MA: Blackwell.

Jennings, J.L. (1990) 'Preventing Relapse versus "Stopping" Domestic Violence: Do We Expect Too Much Too Soon from Battering Men?', *Journal of Family Violence* 5(1): 3–61.

Katz, J. (1988) *Seductions of Crime*. New York: Basic Books.

Kelly, L. (1988) *Surviving Sexual Violence*. Cambridge: Polity Press.

Knight, B.J. and D.J. West (1975) 'Temporary and Continuing Delinquency', *British Journal Of Criminology* 15(1): 43–50.

Kraemer, S. (1995) 'What Are Fathers For?', in C. Burck and B. Speed (eds) *Gender, Power and Relationships*, pp. 203–17. London: Routledge.

Laub, J.H. and R.J. Sampson (2001) 'Understanding Desistance from Crime', in M. Tonry (ed.) *Crime and Justice: An Annual Review of Research*, vol. 26, pp. 1–69. Chicago, IL: University of Chicago.

Leibrich, J. (1993) *Straight to the Point: Angles On Giving Up Crime*. Otago, New Zealand: University of Otago Press.

Leibrich, J. (1996) 'The Role of Shame in Going Straight: A Study of Former Offenders', in B. Galaway and J. Hudson (eds) *Restorative Justice*, pp. 283–302. Monsey, NJ: Criminal Justice Press.

Lupton, D. and L. Barclay (1997) *Constructing Fatherhood*. London: Sage Publications.

Mac an Ghaill, M. (1994) *The Making of Men*. Buckingham: Open University Press.

Maruna, S. (1997) 'Going Straight: Desistance from Crime and Life Narratives of Reform', *The Narrative Study of Lives* 5: 59–93.

Maruna, S. (2001) *Making Good*. Washington, DC: APA Press.

Maruna, S. and S. Farrall (2004, forthcoming) 'Desistance from Crime: A Theoretical Reformulation', Special Issue of *Kölner Zeitschrift für Soziologie und Sozialpsychologie*. Eds, D. Obermitter and S. Karstedt.

McRobbie, A. (1991) *Feminism and Youth Culture: From "Jackie" to "Just Seventeen"*. Basingstoke: Macmillan.

Messerschmidt, J. (1993) *Masculinities and Crime*. Maryland: Rowman & Littlefield.

Messerschmidt, J.W. (1995) 'From Patriarchy to Gender: Feminist Theory, Criminology and the Challenge of Diversity', in N. Rafter and F. Heidensohn (eds) *International Feminist Perspectives*, pp. 167–88. Buckingham: Open University Press.

Messerschmidt, J.W. (1997) *Crime as Structured Action*. London: Sage Publications.

Messerschmidt, J.W. (1999) 'Making Bodies Matter: Adolescent Masculinities, the Body, and Varieties of Violence', *Theoretical Criminology* 3(2): 197–220.

Messerschmidt, J.W. (2000) *Nine Lives: Adolescent Masculinities, the Body, and Violence*. Boulder, CO: Westview Press.

Meisenhelder, T. (1982) 'Becoming Normal: Certification as a Stage in Exiting from Crime', *Deviant Behaviour* 3: 137–53.

Miller, J. (2002) 'The Strengths and Limits of "Doing Gender" for Understanding Street Crime', *Theoretical Criminology* 6(4): 433–60.

Mills, C.W. (1959) *The Sociological Imagination*. New York: Oxford University Press.

Minsky, R. (1998) *Psychoanalysis and Culture*. Cambridge: Polity Press.

Moffitt, T. (1993) '"Life-Course Persistent" and "Adolescent-Limited" Antisocial Behaviour: A Developmental Taxonomy', *Psychological Review* 100(4): 674–701.

Osborn, S.G. (1980) 'Moving Home, Leaving London and Delinquent Trends', *British Journal of Criminology* 20(1): 54–61.

Parker, H. (1976) 'Boys Will Be Men: Brief Adolescence in a Down-Town Neighbourhood', in G. Mungham and G. Pearson (eds) *Working Class Youth Culture*, pp. 41–4. London: Routledge.

Pezzin, L.E. (1995) 'Earning Prospects, Matching Effects and the Decision to

Terminate a Criminal Career', *Journal of Quantitative Criminology* 11(1): 29–50.

Quigley, B.M. and K.E. Leonard (1996) 'Desistance of Husband Aggression in the Early Years of Marriage', *Violence and Victims* 11(4): 355–70.

Rumgay, J. (2003) 'Drug Treatment and Offender Rehabilitation: Reflections on Evidence, Effectiveness and Exclusion', *Probation Journal* 50(1): 41–51.

Sampson, R. and J. Laub (1990) 'Crime and Desistance over the Life Course: The Salience of Adult Social Bonds', *American Sociological Review* 55(5): 610–27.

Sampson, R. and J. Laub (1993) *Crime in the Making*. London: Harvard University Press.

Shover, N. (1983) 'The Later Stages of Ordinary Property Offender Careers', *Social Problems* 31(2): 208–18.

Shover, N. (1996) *Great Pretenders*. Oxford: Westview.

Shover, N. and C. Thompson (1992) 'Age, Differential Expectations and Crime Desistance', *Criminology* 30(1): 89–104.

Smith, D. (2002) 'Crime and the Life-Course', in M. Maguire, R. Morgan and R. Reiner (eds) *The Oxford Handbook of Criminology*, 3rd edn, pp. 702–45. Oxford: Clarendon Press.

Sommers, I., D.R. Baskin and J. Fagan (1994) 'Getting Out of the Life: Crime Desistance by Female Street Offenders', *Deviant Behaviour* 15(2): 125–49.

Strange, C. (2003) 'Masculinities, Intimate Femicide and the Death Penalty in Australia, 1890–1920', *British Journal of Criminology* 43(2): 310–39.

Thornberry, T. (1997) 'Introduction: Some Advantages of Developmental and Life-Course Perspectives for the Study of Crime and Delinquency', in T. Thornberry (ed.) *Developmental Theories of Crime and Delinquency*, pp. 1–10. London: Transaction Press.

Walkerdine, V. (1994) 'Femininity as Performance', in L. Stone (ed.) *The Education Feminism Reader*, pp. 57–69. New York: Routledge.

Walklate, S. (1995) *Gender and Crime: An Introduction*. London: Prentice Hall.

Warr, M. (1998) 'Life-Course Transitions and Desistance from Crime', *Criminology* 36(2): 183–215.

West, G.W. (1978) 'The Short Term Careers of Serious Thieves', *Canadian Journal of Criminology* 20(2): 169–90.

DAVID GADD is a Lecturer in Criminology at Keele University. He has previously published articles on the topics of masculinities, domestic violence and psychoanalysis. David is currently working on an ESRC-funded research project, with Bill Dixon, Tony Jefferson and Ian Loader, addressing the issue of racist violence and harassment in North Staffordshire.

STEPHEN FARRALL is a Research Fellow in the Department of Criminology at Keele University. He has published over 20 articles in academic journals. One of his most recent publications is *Rethinking What Works with*

Offenders: Probation, Social Context and Desistance from Crime (2002, Willan Publishing). Stephen is currently retracing participants from this sample for a further follow-up study funded by the Leverhulme Trust. He is also co-editing a (2004) Special Edition of the *Howard Journal of Criminal Justice* on desistance and criminal policy with Shadd Maruna.

Part III
Cultural And Ethnographic Analyses

[12]

MASCULINITY AND HEROISM IN THE HOLLYWOOD 'BLOCKBUSTER'

The Culture Industry and Contemporary Images of Crime and Law Enforcement

RICHARD SPARKS*

This article considers the connections between masculinity and heroic agency in certain versions of popular film. It proposes that how films dignify and celebrate the suffering and striving of their leading men may be quite centrally indicative of durable sensibilities regarding the qualities and virtues seen as defining manliness; and, moreover, that some of the more drastic reaffirmations of rugged masculinity in recent films starring Schwarzennegger, Stallone, and others are in reaction against instabilities in current notions of masculine gender identities. It is in such aspects of representation, and in what they suggest about the appeal of such films to their audiences, that we should now locate discussions of the social influences of screen 'violence'.

Linguists speak of terms as displaying 'marked' or 'unmarked' forms. Until very recently 'he' was in general use as an unmarked personal pronoun: one had to mark departures from a presumed male reader or company of male subjects. Nouns too have marked and unmarked forms. The unmarked cases of 'nurse', 'nanny', and 'secretary' would seem to be feminine, as in a different vein is 'prostitute': they can all be qualified by adding the prefix 'male-', but otherwise they take feminine pronouns automatically. By contrast the unmarked cases of 'prisoner', 'criminal', 'defendant', 'offender', and 'delinquent' (not to mention those of 'judge', 'detective', 'Superintendent', and so on) remain masculine. If this is so, what follows for the understanding of the positions of crime and law enforcement in popular culture from the initial realization that the unmarked case of all the following terms is masculine: 'hero', 'villain', 'cop', 'killer', 'psycho', 'hood', 'private eye', 'con', 'gangster'? And surely more abstract terms are also gendered in their unmarked forms: 'heroism', 'violence', 'action'?

It has by now been pointed out many times that criminology traditionally fails to consider fully the implications of the unmarked gender of its key topics and terms (so often in fact that one might dare to hope that it were no longer true). The doings of boys and men have been so overwhelmingly at the forefront of the discipline's concerns that it has neglected to note clearly just how centrally their boyishness or manhood is constitutive of the activity itself. Something of this sort has also long been true of discussions of media 'violence', in a number of respects. First, we have rarely spoken with sufficient clarity about the startlingly evident fact that historically the heroic agents of popular film and television have, predominantly, been men. Secondly, in discussions of the 'effects' of media 'violence' there is the largely unexamined, but no less overwhelming, point that really it is the 'effects' on the behaviour of males (and more particularly boys) that underlies the social anxiety and animates the research. It is

* Professor of Criminology, Keele University.

perhaps only in respect of pornography that the gendered nature both of representation and reception has been fully and clearly discussed, but even there the sophisticated analysis of the 'performance' of sexuality and the invocation of desire through conventions of depiction is a fairly recent development (see Kappeler 1986). In short, the heroism, the villainy, the action, and the violence are in a certain sense invisible for as long as the masculinities on which they rely remain unmarked and unremarkable.

There are a number of avenues along which the examination of masculinities in the popular media might fruitfully be taken forward by criminologists. This paper is intended as a preliminary exposition of some of these. In particular it seeks to indicate some points of possible connection between certain fields of research (criminology and film/media studies) that often go on very separately. Among the questions that seem to me to be germane (and around which the essay is organized) are the following:

(1) What are the sources of the recurrent appeal of masculine heroic figures in film and television and what sorts of significance do they embody for their audiences?
(2) Has the nature of the heroic agents portrayed in popular narratives changed recently in terms of the masculinities that they display (or else via the extension of traditionally male kinds of prowess or resourcefulness to female characters?) If so, to what sorts of cultural transformations of sensibility do such changes respond?
(3) How might a nuanced approach to the question of masculinity in the media revise or illuminate the enormous but generally rather repetitious and inconclusive debate on the 'effects' of media 'violence'?

Let us raise this last point briefly first—and return to it later—as it has the most obvious bearing on some traditional criminological concerns. It has often been noted that both 'lay' and official concern over media violence have a prominent but rather intermittent presence in public debate. The screen violence question is a scab often picked at, but not constantly so nor with consistent intensity. In earlier work I observed that the volume of social research on screen violence has similarly varied: its quantity has a way of tracking barometrically the raisings and lowerings of the temperature of political debate (and its consequences for the flow of research funding) (see Sparks 1992: 19–21; see also Rowland 1983). The easiest way to cope with this sort of phenomenon would be to file it under the heading of 'moral panics'. This certainly has some *prima facie* plausibility given the kinds of moral enterprise and political opportunism that precede and attend each such episode of clucking concern. On further reflection, however, it is a stance that now seems at best only partially helpful. The notion of moral panic is a rather heavily descriptive and processual one. It sensitizes us to the fact that a moment of heightened moral anxiety occurs but does not in and of itself illuminate what is substantively at stake in the rhetorics that encircle a given issue *nor* just why that issue should attract a particular kind of attention at some particular time. It is also, famously, a largely agnostic idea which asserts (or silently assumes) that the level and kind of concern evinced over an issue is unwarranted.

This last point is generally much less clearly decidable than the moral panic notion presupposes, as the debates about the fear of crime most amply demonstrate (Hale 1994). Moreover, an expression of concern resembles a moral panic only for so long as it remains trapped within the grooves of received ideas, reiterating familiar strains of moralizing disapproval. It is much less clear that screen violence has no case to answer when one rethinks it not as a miasmic source of cultural decadence, nor yet in terms of a positivist attempt to quantify and catalogue behavioural 'effects' (the so-called 'bullet theory' version of media studies—see Hodge and Tripp 1986: 194), but rather in terms of the transmission and reproduction of hegemonic masculinity. This is not entirely a new argument, but it remains more provocative than the rest of the even older old arguments, and I return to some of its implications in conclusion below.

Nevertheless, moral panic theory might well have enjoyed another outing during 1993–4 when, in the aftermath of the grisly murders of James Bulger and Suzanne Capper, press attention again focused with some eagerness on the malign effects of screen violence, and more particularly on the ready availability of unsuitable home videos to children and young teenagers. Some newspapers (the *Daily Mirror* perhaps in particular) went into campaigning mode; radio phone-ins and television chat programmes were held. The House of Commons Home Affairs Committee took evidence and produced a report (Home Affairs Committee 1994). Little that could be described as new research was forthcoming, although one much-quoted review and synthesis of existing work firmly took the view that behavioural 'effects' of viewing violence had been adequately demonstrated (Newson 1994). In short, the perspectives remained recognizably similar, but the centre of gravity of the debate appeared to move decisively in the direction of a consensus of respectable opinion that screen violence had been shown to be harmful.

There was, however, one small but provocative piece of research which raised some new questions. Hagell and Newburn's study *Young Offenders and the Media* (1994) undertook a systematic comparison between the viewing habits and preferences of a sample of known young offenders and those of a cohort of young people who were not so identified. The study revealed rather few differences in the media use of the two groups. Those which did exist seemed to flow from differences in the use of daily time rather than differential involvement with or attachment to any particular set of images, violent or otherwise. Moreover, when asked to name their favourite actors or screen heroes the responses of the delinquent and non-delinquent boys were hard to tell apart. To the extent that clear favourites emerged they were largely the same—Arnold Schwarzenegger and Jean-Claude van Damme reigned supreme. Hagell and Newburn provide a somewhat lengthier list for the young offenders than for the other boys, but it continues pretty much in the same vein—Bruce Willis, Sylvester Stallone, Bruce Lee, and so on.

None of this should surprise us unduly. Certainly there is no reason from the point of view of studies of masculine gender identities (Brittan 1989; Segal 1990) to presuppose that young offenders should be any more attached to images of heroic manhood (or for that matter more misogynist) than their more ostensibly conforming peers. The point is rather that the imagery is somewhat pervasive: it is what the young men have in common rather than what differentiates them. We cannot therefore address the question of the cultural salience of those depictions or of the violences that they include primarily by trying to discriminate between law-abiding and law-breaking men and boys. We must first attend to their wider prevalence and more general attraction.

Squaring-up: The Constant Hero

Readers who begin from an interest in laws and law-breaking (in short criminologists) often find much of the work that exists on screen violence very unconvincing. The experimental 'effects' tradition (with its endlessly ingenious manipulations of 'aggressiveness') has rarely been able to argue credibly that its concerns have any clear external referent or criteria of validity (for judicious overviews see Noble 1975; Hodge and Tripp 1986). The literature is enormous. Yet it remains rather poorly integrated into larger criminological or sociological debate. Television researchers have rarely gone to great pains to show how their concerns intersect with the kinds of familial, ecological, or economic dynamics that interest other students of crime. Conversely, perhaps indeed disappointingly, no currently important criminological position numbers the assimilation of screen imagery in any very prominent place among its explanatory resources. There is a stand-off. Some students of the media attribute to them a uniquely important and central role in socialization and indoctrination. Criminologists, by contrast, characteristically treat the popular media as if they were wallpaper, ever-present but inert (or else allude to them as a kind of 'indexical' explanation, the one we resort to when all else fails).

Other starting points are, however, possible. Film theorists, for example, generally eschew the kinds of questions about causality that so preoccupy public debate about the media in favour of questions about *how* the media operate. How is a visual image made interpretable as meaningful or pleasurable? How is a sequence of images made into a followable narrative? How do certain images of men and women become established as especially alluring, desirable, worthy of admiration, heroic?

Simplifying freely we may say that film theory has two primary strands in its approaches to these sorts of questions, both of which are of some importance in seeking to develop an account of the prevalence of images of heroic masculinity in popular film and television. The first is an approach to cinematic (and latterly televisual) *form* (in the influential views of Christian Metz (1974) for example). That body of work is concerned to discover how the film is constructed to provide a meaningful 'text' and to identify the units of meaning (or 'syntagms') that compose it. This tradition stresses the continuities between narrative structure in film and in earlier popular or folk forms. Such approaches, commonly drawing upon the folklorism of Vladimir Propp (1968), tend to emphasize that the infinite variety of possible real stories is woven from a restricted stock. They suggest that there is an underlying 'morphology' whose basic elements include the various ways in which heroes undergo tests, overcome obstacles, gain and lose confederates and finally emerge triumphant. In short, one can argue that a notion of heroic overcoming through struggle is embedded very deep in our sense of what is a well-formed story. On its own this formalism often seems 'thin'. It is not that nothing real is identified (see for example, Eco's (1979) witty and provocative extension of a formalist approach to the James Bond sequence of stories). But there is a danger of over-asserting the universalism of the forms and hence of courting a certain lack of historicity or sensitivity to contexts of reception. Moreover, formalism risks telling us what we already know (e.g. that heroes are mostly male) while leaving on one side what to many will seem a more basic and prior set of questions: Why do we enjoy heroic narratives? To what aspects of ourselves do they speak? Just *why* is the agonistic hero so generally and pervasively male?

Here we come to the second major strand in academic film theory, namely an approach to the dynamics of *address* and *reception* (perhaps most celebratedly in the views of Laura Mulvey (1975)). Within film theory the answers to the kind of motivational questions outlined above are often proposed within a version of psychoanalysis. For Mulvey, in a view subsequently much revised and extended by others (e.g. Neale 1983), the heart of the appeal of narrative cinema is provided by an imagery of desire, identification, and pleasure in looking. In particular Mulvey focuses on the narcissisitic identification of the male spectator with images of mastery and omnipotence:

As the spectator identifies with the main male protagonist, he projects his look on to that of his like, his screen surrogate, so that the power of the male protagonist as he controls events coincides with the active power of the erotic look, both giving a satisfying sense of omnipotence . . . (Mulvey 1975: 12)

If this view is correct the depiction of heroic manhood (which is first and foremost a question of men looking at representations of men in a certain way) is a pivotal dimension of mainstream cinema and television. Mulvey and others have been at pains to show that this 'economy' of charged and emotive looking does not presuppose a singular male image. Rather there is an array of possible masculinities in various postures of omnipotence and vulnerability, mastery and suffering. To some of these the spectator relates as to an ego-ideal; in other cases the look is complicated by masochistic or sadistic desires. Moreover, heroes can occupy a variety of positions in relation to social institutions: they may be integral or marginal figures, upholders or opponents of secular authority and so on.

Thus even in a genre such as the Western (so often traduced as simple-minded and two-dimensional) considerable variation is possible, by playing upon the ambivalences that the basic narrative components provide. One of the central oppositions structuring the Western in Mulvey's view is between the societal reintegration of the hero through marriage or his exclusion through departure (*The Searchers*, *Shane*) or death (*The Man Who Shot Liberty Valance*, *Ride the High Country*). What then can we infer about the nature of heroism from the frequency of the latter two alternatives? In many cases the Western hero is simply unassimilable. He is too primordial; he lives too much by violence and is too fundamentally alone to find a place in any scheme of social convention. The moments which frame the narrative of *The Searchers* offer perhaps the definitive case. In the first moment of the film we look out through an opening door on to a desert landscape, beautiful but inhospitable, across which a figure approaches towards us. In the last moment the door closes as the same figure Ethan Edwards (John Wayne) recedes into the distance and Ethan is left to 'wander between the winds' like his 'savage' enemy the native American whom he so closely resembles (Bingham 1994: 68). One of the main aims of the Western is to dignify its heroes by imposing tragic fates upon them, and at the same time to create a foundation myth centring upon their acts of renunciation. That is, as Jane Tompkins (1992: 37) points out, there is an implicit rejection of a feminized civility in favour of a reunion with wild nature. (Indeed Tompkins regards the whole moral structure of the Western as providing pretexts for male violence, a point to which we return below.)

The point is that, with few exceptions, the Western is one genre in which narrative form and visual iconography combine in order painstakingly and deliberately to imbue male heroism with grandeur. In the hands of its most accomplished directors (Howard Hawks, Anthony Mann, John Ford) this is carefully established in relation to the elemental spaciousness of the barely populated landscape—a deliberate attempt to lift the narrative away from mere social or historical contexts. Similarly the choreography of the genre's climaxes—the convention of the shoot-out most especially—exists to establish the heroes' liminality and their transcendence through battle. If the Western is a reactionary genre it is so *because of* the artistry that is devoted to poeticizing the struggles of its male heroes.

Police and private eye movies are more sociologically complex genres than the Western. In striving less for a notion of the elemental they also permit a far wider scope and variety of masculinities, in and against a more varied array of settings and narrative problems. In this respect they attain the status of 'myth' only in a far looser and more modern sense than Westerns do. They are for these reasons far more often constrained by reality principles, and more concerned to situate their heroes in circumstances that invite recognition (in Hodge and Tripp's (1986: 116) terminology their 'modal fit' with the viewer's interpretive schemes is much closer). Yet their concern to dignify the hero is often no less acute, and frequently the sketching in of a more plausibly secular and constraining (and frequently corrupt) social world is similarly devoted to allowing the hero to distinguish himself—to demonstrate his integrity, his prowess, his lonely probity. In these respects these films are generally not less lovingly devoted to their heroes than Westerns are. In particular they begin from and extend many of the same assumptions about the discomfort of the heroic male in respect of the norms and institutions that inhibit his autonomy and curb his freedom of action.

Accordingly urban crime films attribute to their heroes a somewhat more extensive (but not essentially dissimilar) set of orientations towards law and institutions than Westerns. These include being external to the law (*The Fugitive*), or marginally connected to it as a private investigator (Humphrey Bogart as Philip Marlowe), or within the institution but still insubordinately individualistic (everything from *Dirty Harry* to *Beverley Hills Cop*), or inside but actively opposing a surrounding corruption (*Serpico*, *Brubaker*).

At one time (Sparks 1992; in common with others such as Gitlin 1979 and Clarke 1986) I took the view that placing heroes in such positions had *principally* to do with an embedded scepticism that Hollywood and the TV networks attributed to their audiences about the legitimacy or competence of secular legal institutions: the hero stood out in relief because the ordinary realm of criminal justice was ineffective, or corrupt, or bureaucratic, and so on. I thought, that is to say, that these versions of heroism primarily addressed our *political* frustrations. Clearly this view has some merit, and the contemporary cinema is replete with such imageries which can wear either a sophisticated and disillusioned scepticism (*Chinatown*) or a reactionary populism (*Dirty Harry*) as their preferred attitude. I have come to suspect, however, that such tropes are somewhat secondary to the more primary logic of the heroic narrative as such; or at least that the order of priority between the story as an opportunity for heroic display, and the psycho-social conditions which lead us as audience to respond to a hero of a certain type, is muddier and more complex than I formerly knew. The main business of many movies is just the evocation of an heroic masculinity whose principles of absolute individuation, solitude, probity, and personal resourcefulness themselves *demand* the social marginality of the principal figure, much as their Western antecedents did. Raymond Chandler, who knew something about heroism in crime fiction, was quite clear in his view that the prime concern of the detective story was with the hero himself:

Down these mean streets a man must go who is neither tarnished nor afraid. The detective in this kind of story must be such a man. He is the hero. He is everything. He must be a complete man and a common man, and yet an unusual man. He must be, to use a rather weathered phrase, a man of honour, by instinct and inevitability, without thought of it, and certainly without saying it. (Chandler 1944, quoted in Mandel 1984: 35)

Perhaps the source of my earlier emphasis—one which is shared with other commentators—was to read popular crime narratives too much from within the disciplinary horizon of criminology, as if films were documents of a more prosaic kind than in fact they are. The outcome would be to misidentify their ostensible 'topics' as the real sources of their pleasure or appeal. Of course to refocus the issue of heroism around the question of masculinities does not foreclose the possibility of such 'political' readings but only complicates them. It requires us to recognize, for example, that the hero is inherently an overcoded image: he bears meanings about justice, morality, and law, and about being a man, in the same layered iconography.

Consider in this vein the much-discussed example of 'Dirty' Harry Callahan, in the various screen incarnations that Clint Eastwood has given him. Following Eco, Bingham (1994) notes that the successive 'Harry' films reiterate features or 'moves' from the first. They play upon the themes and variations of an already known scenario. Bingham shows that like musicals such films permit moments of departure from narrative while the star does a 'number', except that in Harry's case the 'number' involves pointing guns at people rather than tap-dancing. So, 'Harry' films commonly begin with a set piece, prior to and separate from the main plot, which reintroduces the star and gives him his menacing/wish-fulfilling tag line for the movie ('Do you feel lucky?' 'Make my day', and so on) before pitching him into the serious business of the identification and elimination of his arch opponent. Bingham summarizes the purport of these films thus:

The films find aberrant, out-of-control villains of a primal, unfathomable evil. While the threat of these killers would seem to call for a strong authoritarian power, the films deny any suggestion of police-state control . . . by celebrating the authority of the individual. The films vest vigilante power in an 'official hero'. (he belongs to the police force) who defies the authority of which he is ostensibly a part. This paradox—an authority figure rebelling against authority—allows the films to avoid actually advocating authoritarian repression, although they condense a wish for it. (Bingham 1994: 184–5)

All of this makes Harry, in Bingham's view, not an anti-hero but an anti-Establishment hero. The hero is defined by his singular capacity for action, and he must free himself from any constraint that inhibits this. He is in this sense a 'primal man' (Bingham 1994: 186), an observation that has led some critics to view *Dirty Harry* as a 'disguised Western' (Ray 1985). In the 'Harry' films, it seems, nothing *social* or institutional can compete with the hero as the source and justification of authority—a tendency which led Pauline Kael to comment on *Dirty Harry*, 'this action genre has always had a certain fascist potential, and now it has finally surfaced' (Kael 1972).

It is of course unwise to centre an account of a genre (let alone a gender) around the agenda of its most extreme instances. Cop and private eye movies have shown themselves to be capable of all manner of inflections, some severely revisionist and disillusioned (*Chinatown, Prince of the City*), others knowingly humorous (*Beverley Hills Cop*) and some featuring versions of masculinity decidedly less overbearing than that of Dirty Harry (*Sea of Love*, for example). Even the brief two decades since the moment of *Dirty Harry* have witnessed a much intensified focus on the plasticity of sexual identities. This has given rise to the proposition that masculinity these days is no longer 'performed' unproblematically: it is either reasserted with some vehemence (a 'backlash' phenomenon) or else vested with a certain irony (Bingham 1994: 232; Holmlund 1993: 214). Let us then briefly consider some of the vagaries of masculinity in the contemporary cinema.

Acting Out: Male Heroes and the 'Blockbuster'

If masculinity has in any sense become a more openly problematic and contested notion in recent times, how (if at all) has this been registered in popular film and television, and with what consequences? We need not look for revolutionary developments here. The homology between masculine prowess and conventions of heroism is too deeply embedded for that; and in any case if some form of 'crisis of masculinity' can indeed be discerned, some of its cultural manifestations are at least as likely to wear a snarlingly retrogressive face as they are merrily to assimilate ideologies of 'new' manhood. Moreover, questions of gender do not stand in isolation from surrounding cultural preoccupations. If the purposes of the action film include the visualization of a certain form of order (cf. Ericson *et al.* 1991: 4)—the challenges it undergoes, the means of its restoration or repair—then the demands made upon the hero as an agent of retribution or restoration and the evocation of the world that he inhabits necessarily stand in a dialectically intimate relation to one another. And if those surrounding conditions come to be depicted as more and more chaotic, lawless, and disorderly, then the response called forth from the hero's saving presence becomes only the more intense. Moreover, if an equation is drawn (whether explicitly in political discourse, or implicitly in fiction) between the anomic condition of the world and the subversion of the masculine order and its ideals, then the stage is set for an especially vigorous re-assertion of heroic potency and virility (cf. Theweleit 1987).

This does not contradict the view already noted that masculinity has become an increasingly self-conscious 'performance' (or in some versions a 'masquerade' (Holmlund 1993)) rather than a tradition that anyone can comfortably inhabit. Frederic Jameson's remarks on 'pastiche' are perhaps pertinent. Jameson argues that the mere fact that a tradition has become uprooted or exhausted does not mean that it cannot be recycled: rather the reverse because 'the producers of culture have nowhere to turn but the past—the imitation of dead styles . . . ' (Jameson 1984: 65), but with the addition of a certain 'blank irony'. Perhaps what we see in the contemporary Hollywood 'blockbuster' is the reactionary face of postmodern pastiche. In this it would closely recall Giddens's definition of fundamentalism as the attempt to invoke traditional categories under post-traditional conditions (1994: 84–6).

One of the ways into these issues that has found most favour with film theorists is through the star images or *personae* of Hollywood's leading men. In particular the films and careers of Mel Gibson, Sylvester Stallone, Arnold Schwarzenegger, and Bruce Willis have received much commentary (see Cohan and Hark 1993). One of the most striking features of most of these stars (not to mention their near peers such as Kurt

Russell and Dolf Lundgren) is their evident, indeed exaggerated, muscularity. Many stars of earlier periods (John Wayne perhaps most obviously) have presented emphatically and heftily masculine figures but with few exceptions (Kirk Douglas in *Spartacus*) the detail and definition of their physique has not been dwelt upon so lingeringly. Stallone and Schwarzenegger are not just male heroes: their pumped up bodies signify (nay, yell) 'Masculinity' as if these days one *showed* masculinity by presenting it in excess—a prototypical, warrior essence (see Creed 1987; Tasker 1993).

There are certain other features that have also been attributed to a number of major recent Hollywood action movies:

1. In line with Jameson's expectations, what we may be observing is really a more drastic performative reenactment of what went before. We see masculinity 'hyperbolized' (Bingham 1994: 232) in the ultra-physiques of Schwarzenegger or Stallone; or else we have the 'hyper-masculine' close-to-the-edge dangerousness of the Mel Gibson character in the *Lethal Weapon* films (Fuchs 1993).

2. By the same token certain common motifs from earlier movies are also prone to being recycled and amended. Principal among these are perhaps images of male friendship and pair-bonding. 'Buddy' movies are nothing new, but some commentators see in recent films an intensification of the emotional and erotic charge of these relationships, one consequence of which is that women are 'ejected' from some of these narratives altogether. The cultural 'togetherness' that is preferred is that of the cross-racial male pair (*48 Hours*; *Lethal Weapon*) (see Fuchs 1993; Holmlund 1993).

3. Men do emote, but within a narrow compass. The primary emotions that they evince include grief (for lost love or slain partners) and rage (for the same reasons). Consider the moments in *Black Rain* for example when Nick (Michael Douglas) broods over his murdered partner's possessions and lastly carefully unwraps his gun: it is the emotional palette of the revenger's tale. Heroes suffer, and they *care*. They undergo grief, loss, and physical pain (on the prevalence of torture imagery in blockbusters see Holmlund 1993; Tasker 1993). There are variations, of course. Male pairs can embody different dimensions of masculine virtue, as with the domesticity of Murtaugh versus the isolation of Riggs in the *Lethal Weapon* films. Moreover there are attempts to present a cuddlier, less severe image of manly strength, for example Arnold Schwarzenegger's undercover assignment as an infant school teacher in the absurd *Kindergarten Cop*.

4. There is a potent strain of anti-establishment feeling in almost all blockbusters. In some cases authority figures are explicitly villainous (*Lock Up*) or have used and abandoned the hero (*Rambo*) or are uselessly incompetent and obstructive (*Die Hard*). In each case the hero is singularly alone and thrown back on his own resources. In several instances such images are overlain by strongly dystopian images of the near future which either pit struggling humans against implacable machines (*Terminator*, *Blade Runner*) or heroize the machines themselves (*Terminator II*, *Robocop*) by subverting the human/machine distinction. Even where a movie takes place in the present (*Die Hard*) it invokes its most fearful aspects (terrorism). Many of these films seem to imply the failure of politics as such: there is a vacuum into which the hero must step, motivated not by profession, duty, or patriotism but rather by his purely personal and familial bonds, or by a still more basic instinct for survival (Tasker 1993).

5. The concluding passages of most of these films are exceedingly spectacular, not to

say cataclysmic. They are marked by explosions, vast pile-ups, fires, deaths of the wicked, and miraculous escapes of the virtuous (in *Total Recall* Arnie provides Mars with a breathable atmosphere). They are replete, therefore, with signifiers of unreality (even though the effects and stunts have to be convincing as never before). What are we to make of this? And what has it to do with the question of 'violence'?

Conclusion: Further Thoughts on Heroism, Men, and Violence

It has often been suggested that heroic fictions presuppose some sort of failure of social arrangements—or their violent disruption by a figuratively or literally alien force—in a way that makes redemptive intervention from without necessary. It is a moot point whether we tell ourselves such stories *in order* to ratify our desire for heroes or whether we feel the need for heroes when we already find the world alien and hostile. Arguably what we see in some recent Hollywood cinema is a magnification of these antique starting points. Much mainstream cinema offers us scenes from the apocalypse as a way of introducing, justifying, and winning our support for the hero. The social world evoked in *Robocop* or *Total Recall* is dangerous, lonely, chaotic, and deeply hostile, littered with industrial ruins and seething masses of anomic humanity. In many such movies narrative problems have been pared down to their manichean essentials (and as such are marketable and followable anywhere in the world). Identification and rejection are uncomplicated—heroes are outcasts unsullied by attachments or institutional connections, yet they remain 'of the people' and their painstakingly crafted physiques recall in imagination the hardness of men's physical labour.

To say that these figures address male fantasies is to state the obvious. What is more difficult and more interesting is to say how they do this and with what consequences. The tone of some of the 'screen violence' debate has shifted lately. It has become less complacently agnostic on the importance of the issues, but at the same time less certain and more cautious on questions of proof and the status of the evidence (Hodge and Tripp 1986). Yet we find it no easier now than before to specify what happens when we view or how this relates to the transmission or acquisition of any attitude or outlook.

The term 'violence' of course resists codification (Barthes 1985). Violence in stories has no separate, independently definable existence (see Hall 1976). It is embedded in narrative, imbued with meaning, invested with aesthetic concerns, laden with moralities. It is simply not helpful to seek to isolate the question of violence from the regimes of representation in which it occurs. But this does not betoken any lesser concern. For instance, the mere fact that what happens in many Hollywood movies is consciously and deliberately marked as 'fantasy' does not in and of itself deny it any emotive or suasive force. As Rosalind Coward (1987: 26–7) has pointed out:

> Nobody can persuade me that the way in which this culture currently deals with violence and aggression is anything other than deeply destructive and dangerous. [These fantasies] also often present violence as something integral to masculinity . . . For feminists the whole question of the relationship between fantasy and reality has always been a much more pressing political question than for most men.

To put the matter another way, one thing that the debate on screen violence and masculinity can learn from developments for example in the study of pornography is that one can develop a sophisticated grasp of how the genre works (as a form of signification) without lapsing into agnosticism about its moral and political implications (see Kappeler 1986; Itzin 1993). The study of screen violence is perhaps on the point of breaking with its traditional dependence on notions of 'pseudo-mechanical rather than semiotic causality' (Hodge and Tripp 1986: 201).

Let us remind ourselves, therefore (though we should not need reminders), that images that are cognitively 'unreal' can nevertheless remain psychically and emotionally terribly powerful. We know more and more clearly now from studies of audience reception that screen images are multiply interpreted, often in ways that resist or query their 'preferred reading' (see for example Schlesinger *et al.* 1992); but the more perplexing issue is what happens when we do view with pleasure and involvement, allow ourselves to be enraptured, and so on. As Hodge and Tripp soberly note, even in fantastical images, 'an image of violence is still an image of violence, and viewers who enjoy it are still endorsing those impulses in themselves' (1986: 117). For these reasons the moral structure of the narrative—its commitments, its endorsements—is crucial to any understanding of its possible 'effects'. What happens so that we actively want our heroes to act forcefully? For Tompkins this is

> The entire purpose of the pattern . . . to get the audience to the point where it can't wait till the hero lets loose with his six-shooters . . . Vengeance, by the time it arrives, feels biologically necessary . . . This is the moment of moral ecstasy. The hero is *so right* (that is, so wronged) that he can kill with impunity. (Tompkins 1992: 228–9)

These then are not quantitative issues about how much 'violence' one witnesses. They are *filmic* issues about narrative structure and point of view and other aspects of *mise en scène*. As Bingham comments on the controversial rape scene in *High Plains Drifter*, which he sees as being validated and endorsed within the film, can we not envisage a spectator who would be appalled by the scene? To which the answer is 'of course . . . but the film was clearly not made for such a spectator' (1994: 166).

Finally, there is an often overlooked strand within contemporary criminology that has gone to some pains to explore those aspects of crime that have principally to do with fun, excitement, risk-taking, and pleasure. This perspective is perhaps most fully developed by Katz (1988), whose emphasis lies on the experiential 'foreground' of law breaking—the forbidden pleasures that lie beyond its 'invitational edge'. For Katz some of these have to do with often momentary experiences of 'dizziness', underlain by a will towards 'transcendence'. Similarly, Cusson (1982) stresses that action, excitement, and play as aspects of delinquency are experienced as ends in themselves, undertaken for the sheer thrill of the sensation of living intensely.

I have no intention of pronouncing on whether the demand for action as its own reward is exclusively or predominantly male. But it does seem that when undertaken by men and boys its imaginative scripts are peopled with images of proud, undaunted, courageous, romantic masculinities. Meanwhile, for most of us men—seduced into conformity rather than crime—that realm of transcendence and of heroized masculinity is available vicariously. Most of us are not risk-takers most of the time; but we do like sensation and arousal and the frisson of imagined fear. We take our 'edgework' (Lyng 1990) at second hand. And, moreover, the kinds of 'dizziness' that we so enjoy (Mel Gibson's 'crazy' performance in *Lethal Weapon*, for instance) are legitimated and given permission by being attached principally to heroic law enforcers. Those of us who continue to involve ourselves in what one of my female students so aptly described as 'just dodgy blokes' films' could fruitfully reflect on what aspects of our own identity are satisfied (or at least gratified) by Hollywood's muscular masculinities. Whether such stories ever do 'script' the activities of those who really do take the more dangerous paths is still uncertain. But it remains open to us to ask a question parallel to Katz's 'what are people trying to do when they commit a crime?': 'what is it that we do when we view?'

References

Barthes, R. (1985), 'On the Subject of Violence', in *The Grain of the Voice*. London: Jonathan Cape.

Bingham, D. (1994), *Acting Male*. New Brunswick, NJ: Rutgers University Press.

Brittan, A. (1989), *Masculinity and Power*. Oxford: Blackwell.

Chandler, R. (1944), 'The Simple Art of Murder', *Atlantic Monthly*, December.

Clarke, A. (1986), 'This is not the Boy Scouts: Television Police Series and Images of Law and Order', in T. Bennett, C. Mercer, and J. Woollacott, eds., *Popular Culture and Social Relations*. Milton Keynes: Open University Press.

Cohan, S., and Hark, I. R. (1993), eds., *Screening the Male*. London: Routledge.

Coward, R. (1987), 'Violent Screen Play', *Marxism Today*, December, 24–7.

Creed, B. (1987), 'From Here to Modernity: Feminism and Postmodernism', *Screen*, 28/2: 47–67.

Cusson, M. (1982), *Why Delinquency?* University of Toronto Press.

Eco, U. (1979), *The Role of the Reader*. London: Hutchinson.

Ericson, R. V., Baranek, P., and Chan, J. (1991), *Representing Order*. Buckingham: Open University Press.

Fuchs, C. (1993), 'The Buddy Politic', in S. Cohan and I. R. Hark, eds., *Screening the Male*. London: Routledge.

Giddens, A. (1994), *Beyond Left and Right*. Cambridge: Polity Press.

Gitlin, T. (1979), 'Prime-time Ideology: The Hegemonic Process in Television Entertainment', *Social Problems*, 26: 251–66.

Hagell, A., and Newburn, T. (1994), *Young Offenders and the Media*. London: Policy Studies Institute.

Hale, C. (1994), *Fear of Crime: A Review of the Literature*. Canterbury Business School: University of Kent.

Hall, S. (1976), 'Violence in the Media', in N. Tutt, ed., *Violence*. London: HMSO.

Hodge, R., and Tripp, D. (1986), *Children and Television*. Cambridge: Polity Press.

Holmlund, C. (1993), 'Masculinity as Multiple Masquerade', in S. Cohan and I. R. Hark, eds., *Screening the Male*. London: Routledge.

Home Affairs Committee (1994), *Fourth Report: Video Violence and Young Offenders*. London: HMSO.

Itzin, C. (1993), ed., *Pornography: Women, Violence and Civil Liberties*. Oxford: Oxford University Press.

Jameson, F. (1984), 'Postmodernism—Or the Cultural Logic of Late Capitalism', *New Left Review*, 146: 53–92.

Kael, P. (1972), *Deeper Into Movies*. Boston: Little Brown.

Kappeler, S. (1986), *The Pornography of Representation*. Cambridge: Polity Press.

Katz, J. (1988), *Seductions of Crime*. New York: Basic Books.

LYNG, S. (1990), 'Edgework: A Social Psychological Analysis of Voluntary Risk-taking', *American Journal of Sociology*, 95/4: 851–86.
MANDEL, E. (1984), *Delightful Murder*. London: Pluto Press.
METZ, C. (1974), *Film Language*. Oxford University Press.
MULVEY, L. (1975), 'Visual Pleasure and Narrative Cinema', *Screen*, 16/3: 6–18.
NEALE, S. (1983), 'Masculinity as Spectacle', *Screen*, 24/6.
NEWSON, E. (1994), *Video Violence and the Protection of Children*. University of Nottingham.
NOBLE, G. (1975), *Children in Front of the Small Screen*. London: Constable.
PROPP, V. (1968), *Morphology of the Folk-Tale*. Austin,TX: University of Texas Press.
RAY, R. B. (1985), *A Certain Tendency in the Hollywood Cinema 1930–80*. Princeton University Press.
ROWLAND, W. (1983), *The Politics of TV Violence*. London: Sage.
SCHLESINGER, P., DOBASH R. E., DOBASH, R. P., and WEAVER, C. K. (1992), *Women Viewing Violence*. London: British Film Institute.
SEGAL, L. (1990), *Slow Motion*. London: Virago.
SPARKS, R. (1992), *Television and the Drama of Crime*. Buckingham: Open University Press.
TASKER, Y. (1993), 'Dumb Movies for Dumb People', in S. Cohan and I. R. Hark, eds., *Screening the Male*. London: Routledge.
THEWELEIT, K. (1987), *Male Fantasies*. Cambridge: Polity Press.
TOMPKINS, J. (1992), *West of Everything: The Inner Life of Westerns*. Oxford: Oxford University Press.

[13]

IN SEARCH OF THE HIGH LIFE

Drugs, Crime, Masculinities and Consumption

MIKE COLLISON*

Contemporary social theory draws our attention again to the role of consumption in the construction of the self. The project of constructing self-identity through consumption increasingly relies on global rather than parochial images and traditions, and often proceeds via mimicry. In this paper the biographical narratives of a group of young male offenders are used to explore some of the problems and possibilities of growing up male on the margins of civil society. It is suggested that drug use, drug dealing, and 'normal' crime serve as important cultural and emotive resources for scripting a particular, and powerful, masculine identity on the street. Thus, some conventional themes in delinquency theory are recast in the terms of modern social theory and cultural studies.

. . . now its violence for me, its a better buzz, when I haven't had a fight right, its like you feel angry, when you've had a fight you feel good . . . street fighting, you just stab with a bottle or anything, dirty is street fighting, you've got to watch your shoulder all the time, that's what your mates are there for, to watch your back so you're safe . . . getting like America isn't it? (20-year old)[1]

In this paper I want to re-tell some stories about self, daily life, crime, and drug use in the city, or on one of its satellite estates. These autobiographical narratives were recorded recently in a male young offenders prison[2] but they do not simply reveal a male account of life at a time variously described in social theory as postmodern, late modern, advanced liberal, and reflexive (Bauman 1992; Beck 1992; Giddens 1984, 1991; Lash 1994; O'Malley 1994). What they do reveal is some of the pleasures and pains of youth in general, and underclass[3] male youth in Britain specifically. The richly textured stories of these young men capture a profound contradictory and exclusionary tendency in modern society at the end of the century. For, while it is the case that one cannot now speak sensibly of a singular and reductive masculinity, but rather of a range of possible masculinities (Jefferson 1994), it remains to ask what form of masculine identity is open to the young men of the (ex) working class now described as an 'underclass' (Lash 1994: 134).

* Department of Criminology, University of Keele.
The author would like to thank Pat Carlen and Tony Jefferson for their helpful comments on an earlier draft of this paper.

[1] Most of the sample were poly-drug users, but their use was not indiscriminate. Having experimented with most drugs locally available the majority went on to choose a particular combination of drugs which seemed to fit in with their daily activities and their sense of desired self. Thus, drugs combine in a drug-style. There is also an emotive, rather than motivational, symmetry between drug-style and crime-style; amphetamines and car crime, temazepam and violence, cocaine and street robbery, and so on. Space precludes detailed description of each offender's drug and crime pattern.

[2] The fieldwork prompting these observations was made possible by an Economic and Social Research Council award (R00023 4371) and the energetic support of the Governor, staff and inmates of Stoke Heath Young Offenders Institution.

[3] I use underclass here, not in Charles Murray's sense (1990), but to describe a class 'structurally downwardly mobile from the working class' incorporating 'much of information society's "excluded third"' (Lash 1994: 130).

Full details of the crime, drug, treatment, and punishment biographies of the 80 young men (aged 17 to 21) interviewed may be found elsewhere (Collison 1994*a*, *b*). For the moment it is only necessary to record that: the majority had grown up in or around the city; they had mostly begun crime in their pre- or early teens; drug use figured centrally and excessively in the lives of 59 per cent of the sample; the clear drug preference was for either cannabis (in expensive quantities) and/or the 'dance drugs' (amphetamine, MDMA, LSD), and use cohered in a drug-style; even the 15 per cent of the sample regularly consuming heroin made sure that they were 'here' (Katz 1988: 82) for their peers by controlling the sedative effects of the drug with cocaine/crack, amphetamine (usually by injection), and temazepam; and 74 per cent of the 72 ever drug users began their crime careers before, or at the same time as, their first involvement with drugs (cf. Parker *et al.* 1988; Burr 1987). Rather 'brutally', these young men's crime ('graft' work) and drug careers peaked in their mid-teens (Hirschi 1969; Braithwaite 1989).

The paper draws on familiar, and not so familiar, themes in recent social theory and cultural studies in order to explore some features of male forms of delinquent lifestyle at the limits of order and on the edge of chaos (Katz 1988; Lyng 1990). Here I shall be looking, tentatively and all too briefly, at the contemporary priority given to consumption, communication, leisure, and agency in social relations, a promise of the good life which contrasts with an actual 'tough, solid, resistant and harsh' (Bauman 1992: 155) daily life which is peopled by, for the lucky, a 'MacDonalds proletariat' (Lash 1994: 120). If postmodern consumer society is classless someone has forgotten to convince those at the bottom. Put another way, a central tension of 'reflexive modernity' is that between the 'cult of the self' (of narcissism and nihilism) and forms of new or merely persisting structural exclusions (Lasch 1995). Enigmatically, the young men grasped the structuring of their lives in a throw-away phrase: 'its down to me innit?' Accounts of daily life in the literal, metaphoric, or mimetic ghetto describe the ways biography and lifestyle are (re)invented in forms which reproduce structural exclusion (from the school, the labour market, the family, etc.), an exclusion which is (mis)recognized as almost purely volitional (Giddens 1984; see also Katz 1988: 216). These narratives are those of 'reflexivity losers' (Lash 1994: 127).

The argument will be that one situational resolution (or, more properly, a set of linked resolutions) of this central tension instantiates as predatory male street crime, excessive drug use, and normatively inappropriate leisure. There is a level of ontological security and trust to be found on the street which obviates some of the uncertainties and insecurities of being male on the margins of civil society. Following the sensible lead of both social theorists and young offenders the remaining discussion focuses on consumption, risk, and economy in more detail, before finally considering the meaning of 'growing up to be mad'.

Consumption

The contemporary urban flaneurs, or strollers, play with and celebrate the artificiality, randomness and superficiality of the fantastic melange of fictions and strange values which are to be found in the fashions and popular cultures of cities . . . a . . . decontextualization of tradition and a raiding of all cultural forms to draw out quotations from the imaginary side of life are found among the young 'de-centred subjects' who enjoy the experimentation and play with fashion and the stylization of life as they stroll through the 'no-place' postmodern urban spaces. (Featherstone 1991: 24, 65)

Born, or 'thrown' (Lash 1994: 161), into a competitive and highly individualistic consumer society, and barely recollecting any different narrative organization of social relations, young people in general increasingly speak of their relations to one another via the language of consumption (as every parent laments) (Bauman 1992: 49). They are modern 'flaneurs' watching others while watching themselves strolling the Shopping Mall of youth fashion(s) and the 'Disneylands' of pharmacology in search of various heightened experiences and extravagant pleasures (Benjamin 1982; Featherstone 1987; Smart 1992).[4] The city, especially, is a place of 'cultural disorder and stylistic eclecticism' (Featherstone 1991: 103) where one finds 'consuming displays, displays of consuming, consuming of signs, signs of consuming' (Lefebvre 1971, quoted in Featherstone 1991: 103–4). In some limited sense, and out on the street or in the club/marquee, the cognitive and aesthetic wisdom of modern youth is profoundly postmodern in its agnosticism—anything and everything goes: down one's throat, up one's nose, and still for a significant minority in some areas, in one's veins. But the signs (of consumption) have not been emptied of all their meaning, nor their communicative force. Young people might 'munch' or 'snack' on the images but something important is at stake (Bauman 1992: 155; see also Baudrillard 1983).

There is a pressure to spend: on the social level, the pressure of symbolic rivalry, for the needs of self-construction through acquisition (mostly in commodity form) of distinction and difference, of the search for social approval through lifestyle and symbolic membership . . . (Bauman 1992: 50).

Unnecessary consumption (where wants become needs) is not new to modern society but various writers have drawn attention to an accelerated trend in the latter half of the twentieth century towards the reflexive construction of self-identity through responsible consumption. To consume is to expose oneself to risk—both in the global environmental sense meant by Ulrich Beck (1992), and, more usefully here, as an individual looked on and judged by others (Bauman 1992; Giddens 1991; but see Warde 1994).

. . . got a little taste for champagne . . . I know it weren't the taste, it was the thought of, know what I mean? People seeing me drinking it . . . (21-year old)

or,

. . . I'd see me mates walking around with all these fashionable clothes . . . if you haven't got them you're a tramp, if one of me mates is walking around in a snide (here meaning cheap imitation—author) pair of trackies I say you're a tramp . . . (18-year old)

or,

. . . I speak through my clothes. (Eco 1973, quoted in Hebdidge 1979: 100)

[4] Drugs may offer something of the Disneyland experience of whimsical and wistful plays about past, present, and future—without actually having to go there—and, in this sense, may be a good example of what Baudrillard means by 'hypersimulation' (Baudrillard 1983). But the world is not all like this, as the paper argues. Baudrillard's problem, according to Zygmunt Bauman, is that he thinks that it is—'he is dead serious' (Bauman 1992: 152).

IN SEARCH OF THE HIGH LIFE

The disciplinary project of 'simple modernity' (Lash 1994)—to instil obedience and self-control, to 'subordinate the body to reason' (O'Malley 1994: 4), to recognize one's place in a class and gender—has been replaced by a variety of projects surrounding the 'cult of the self' (O'Malley 1994: 7; Rose 1989). Consumption is not merely of clothes, or drugs, or cars, or music, but of styles and stylizations (images) of life—an everyday aesthetics (Willis 1990). The young men interviewed wanted to be 'super-consumers' (Cusson 1983: 55; Katz 1988: 215) in this respect and drew from, embellished, parodied, and fragmented the subcultural 'traditions' of New York, Los Angeles, and Milan (the global community) rather than those lost to '(ex) working class males' in the de-industrialized British city (Lash 1994: 134; Hebdidge 1979; Hobbs 1989; see also Davis 1988). They were inventing a possible lifestyle in the routine practices of daily life as a 'narrative of self-identity' drawing on both local and global experience (Giddens 1991: 81)—'I was living for going out' (20-year old). (And going out was living.)

Money is obviously a key, as is street taste:

. . . like yer parents don't buy you enough clothes when you're that age . . . they didn't know what I wanted . . . Nikes, Adidas, Reebok, you know top range . . . the fashion n that . . . if you've got a pair of Nicks trainers (cheap imitations—author) you get the piss taken out of you . . . you had to get Reeboks . . . I got used to the idea they couldn't afford it. (18-year old)

Long-term aspirations are almost always modest and cognizant of the actors' structural location in a place with no future (Merton 1968: 190). Yet, the 'eternal present' of ego (Beck 1992: 135) demands a style of consumption that fends off peer disgrace. Although most young offenders will cite money as a primal motivation for crime (excitement or 'buzz' being the other), this is not simple avarice but, rather, registers the intense importance of Labels for the self—and pride:

. . . seen people were living their own lives . . . they had the things they wanted . . . they were going to clubs as well, to me that looked good . . . when you can earn money there, buy a car there, its a kind of street respect that people end up giving you . . . I were at that age when you go, well, lads go through that change . . . (19-year old)

If the motivation were simple avarice then crime is a spectacularly inefficient longer-term solution (Katz 1988: 216–17):

. . . we got £4,500 so were a big wedge, that lasted us about five week, it went nowhere, bought clothes and everything with it, but we was mad . . . (18-year old).

Drugs as commodities provide a useful, but not the only, illustration here. For most of the 1980s heroin use was increasing rapidly in Britain and typically sedimented in particular housing areas within, or 'orbiting' around, the inner city (Burr 1987; Parker *et al.* 1988; Pearson 1987*a*; South 1994). The 'new users' of heroin ('skag', 'smack', 'brown') were predominantly lower class young males in their late teens or early twenties who 'could handle it' (Dorn and South 1989; Pearson 1987*b*). Using addict notifications to the Home Office as a rough yet ready guide, between 20 per cent and 27 per cent of opiate users are female (Home Office 1994; Giggs 1991). Aside from all the simple psychic use-value wrapped in a bag, and ignoring the money exchange-value for the moment, heroin could be a source of male (street) cultural capital:

Heroin use was not the organizing theme in his life; it was only one of several seductive ways of staying in the action . . . even the hustling heroin addict may experience his drug use as part of a larger fascination to test his mettle. (Katz 1988: 207; see also Preble and Casey 1969)

A common wisdom among the heroin users, often sifted from their experience of older siblings on 'brown', was that 'you go down on it if you don't take it right'. So long as you did take it right heroin could remain a culturally, as well as pharmacologically, powerful drug. Yet, as style (rather than addiction), heroin use does not always appeal across time, space, and as we have seen, gender. Here is a new wisdom:

I've seen too many people go down on it (heroin—author) . . . seen people who were there one minute (pause) next minute down (pause) selling their own clothes to you . . . I know to stay away from it . . . me mates, one minute they've gone from being alright lads knowing the score (pause) shivering little shits now, haven't got a clue, aren't making money, aren't going out grafting . . . they're the lowest of the low. (21-year old)

Tastes change, as they seem to have done in the 1990s for drug commodities. Now, anything up to 10 per cent of the 16 to 19 age group across class, gender, race, and geography are 'munching' their way through many 'Disneylands' by taking MDMA ('Ecstasy') and LSD, and then 'chilling out' on cannabis (Mott and Mirrlees-Black 1993; Leitner *et al.* 1993; Pearson *et al.* 1991). A much larger number just 'chill out'. Like many other commodities these drugs are easily purchased and easily consumed. Access to their pleasures requires little effort, and their effects can be intense, transient, and prompt repeat consumption. Further, these stimulating and hallucinating commodities are currently central to the appropriate (lifestyle) consumption and appreciation of others. Anecdotal evidence from youth workers, leisure professionals, the media, and police suggests that up to 70 per cent of contemporary young 'rave'/ 'house'/'club' goers take drugs.

. . . I couldn't be straight in a rave . . . I had to be on something to experience the feeling . . . when I'm in a nightclub and I'm straight I feel paranoia to dance . . . people looking at me, but if I'm on something . . . (19-year old)

I will say more on the question of anxiety (self-doubt), ontological security, and neo-tribalism suggested by this narrative later. But for now the simple point is that drugs are rapidly becoming a normal part of weekend leisure-life and enable it to succeed:

. . . I was always told that you're not actually *there* until you take the drug . . . so I tried it one time . . . the music was different, the surroundings n that, than when I was *normal minded*. (19-year old) (my emphasis)

Indications are that this spectacular consumption reveals an emerging gender equality (Leitner *et al.* 1993; Parker 1993). Forever-young males and females are incorporating illicit drug consumption as part of their 'recreational repertoire' (Parker 1993: 2). For the majority, narratives of self may be scripted and embellished at the weekend because on Monday, back in the other 'lifestyle sectors' of work/school/family (Giddens 1991: 83), the task of fashioning an individuated biography through the competitive yet standardizing (over-socializing) education and labour markets returns (Beck 1992: 135). The successful, and reflexive, actor must be accomplished at moving between lifestyle sectors—at keeping a diverse narrative of self going (Giddens 1991: 54).

If pleasure is the 'sine qua non of leisure activity', and if drug use is now a 'normal aspect of a commodified society' (Mugford and O'Malley 1991: 29; see Urry 1988), then some equalizing up of traditional gender difference is to be expected, because these drugs (and their imagery) are not marketed in simply (masculine) gendered ways, nor in traditionally gendered places (on the street corner). This much may be speculative, but I would want to suggest that excessive (and poly) use stretching out across inappropriate time and space is more likely a consequence of a particular masculine narrative of self-identity that weaves together symbiotically crime and drug use on the edge of, or satisfyingly beyond, reason (Katz 1988; Walters 1994). In other words, some young men wake up to find themselves incompetent at moving between lifestyle sectors (having already been excluded from a number of them—see below). Uncommonly then, leisure and 'graft' stretch out through the week in apparent chaos yet function as important sources of credibility and respect. This was a situation common to the young men interviewed and their street peers.

The causal power of peer group affiliation forms part of the common sense of criminology as it does for criminal justice professionals (Braithwaite 1989). It is always an older peer group which figures in the fears and anxieties of parents, probation officers, magistrates, and politicians, and in the prison reflections of offenders themselves. The stories of drug experimentation tell of 'this group of lads' who seemed to be doing more enticing things:

> . . . if you've grown up with drugs around you you're going to take drugs, cos like you wanna know what its like, cannabis to glue to gas t' glue all at the same time, then it was amphetamine, cannabis and glue, after that it was smack, cannabis and E's and acid, amphet it just like speeds you up, you feel on top of the world, you feel faster than you are, feel above everybody . . . (20-year old)

Three points. First, as suggested above recent surveys of youth clearly reveal that large numbers of adolescents encounter drugs in their daily lives at school and at play, but some locations are saturated with them. In these locales drugs take on the shape of an ordinary everyday commodity with a currently modest exchange-value, yet spectacular use-value. As crime opportunities present themselves largely within the physical spaces bounding every day routines (see Bottoms 1994; Felson 1994), so too do drug-consuming opportunities. Locations are likely to be gendered in specific ways. Secondly, captured in the phrase 'speeds you up', is the sense of pace at which modern youth life must be lived (in various spheres)—and its competitiveness. Thirdly, the need for action—to be 'above everybody'—concocts a recipe of (male) excess. This is not to deny that some drug taking is designed around the need for a protective cocoon of security and the reduction of anxiety (Giddens 1991: 19–20)—cannabis and heroin have a similarity here. But for young men like these drugs provided a handy 'pharmacological filofax' for an action oriented and powerfully executed daily life on the street and in the club (and in between, in the shop, house, car, or face of another).

MIKE COLLISON

Risk

Much has been said about risk in modern society, the risks of modern society and the Risk Society (Beck 1992; Giddens 1991; O'Malley 1992; Warde 1994).[5] Predominantly, the concern has been with prudential risk reduction or aversion, whether privately or publicly. Here I want to play with the obvious idea that young people like taking risks (Plant and Plant 1992: 115) before looking at a significant loss for many young offenders (males and females)—of the family or of care.

Risk calculation and risk taking are not just related to critical moments in the biography—risk is a common part of adolescent life rather than the unusual prompt for momentous decisions. Risk taking is about achieving and displaying 'independence, identity and maturity' (Jack 1989, quoted in Plant and Plant 1992: 115). For individual risk behaviours such as smoking, drinking, drug taking, fast driving, unprotected sex and so on, the vitality of adolescence underpins two common attitudes to risk; either the expertly known risk does not apply in my case, or, the risk is a future, and therefore, unknowable one (and cannot be, nor needs to be for the present, guarded against). It is fortuna. There is, of course, another attitude—the experts have got it wrong. All adolescents more or less seek to push it to the edge. But, certain kinds of risk taking are more typical of what one might call 'hegemonic masculinity' (Jefferson 1994: 12). Persistent predatory street crime is one of them; another, as intimated above, forms itself into that heady mix of crime and excessive drug use.

What I like is action. I like risking my skin, it puts some value on it. I know you will think I'm nuts, but danger makes me high. (Mesrine 1977, quoted in Cusson 1983: 35)

. . . everyone's bound to have a dabble when they're younger aren't they? . . . experiment, boredom, it can be a bit of excitement . . . like drugs it (crime-author) opened new doors, the adrenalin running n that . . . I was living on the edge all of a sudden. (19-year old)

Burgling a house is an activity laced with excitement (the 'buzz' of crime) but it is also laden with risk: legal apprehension, assault by the homeowner, or later in these accounts, the police; or even later and back on the street, of failure in front of one's male peers.

. . . I always used to leave the room they was sleeping in till last . . . they never used to hear me for some reason, I never used to hear myself . . . it was scary and it was exciting . . . (20-year old)

Few young offenders stop long to calculate the risks but rather trust in a mystical invincibility, hope for a run of good luck or fate, simply do it, and sometimes use drugs to situationally erase risk:

. . . trips make you want to go out and do cars. (18-year old)

I've screwed a place and like I've been straight but the thing is . . . if you're straight you think if they come home or . . . if the police come, but if you're smashed you just don't think . . . just think ah fuck it. (20-year old)

[5] As an illustration there are 14 index entries for risk in a recent collection of thoughts on reflexive modernity (Beck *et al.* 1994).

What is being said here? Two things, at least, it seems to me. First, that playing with probability is deeply and intrinsically satisfying (see Hagan 1988: 152–3). Criminology always knew this but repetitively and scientifically repressed it. Secondly, and allegorically, drugs used in this way provide a level of security from risk to an always vulnerable male self.

Some young men like taking temazepam with alcohol—it is a crazy cocktail: 'you blank out, that's what made me take more, I liked the things that it made me do' (20-year old). One of the options open afterwards is to say convincingly to a partner 'I am not (violent) like that'.[6]

Why liberate the body (passion) from reason? Intentional risk taking immediately juxtaposes 'an ordered sense of self and environment (to) a disordered self and environment' (Lyng 1990: 857). The stories of young male car thieves dwell briefly on the rational rhythms of a necessary economy (take a car, sell a car, take another . . .) but at length on the satisfactions of chaos and getting a chase from 'pure' (lots of) police cars: 'a good feeling inside getting chased by the police' (18-year old) (cf. Campbell 1993; Parker 1973). Stephen Lyng calls edgework an 'experiential anarchy' where 'participants often describe the experience as being much more real than the circumstances of everyday existence' (Lyng 1990: 861, 864).

> . . . like what I really want to do like to occupy my time, I'd like to go jump out of planes like that, that's exciting to me, I couldn't afford things like that . . . so I just pinch cars, get chases, do burglaries and enjoy myself that way . . . (19-year old)

Edgework represents a sometimes spontaneous search for a dramatic self within a world of alienation and over-socialization (Lyng 1990: 870). Being on the edge, or over it—beyond reason and in passion—is momentarily to grasp a spiritual and romantic utopia.

If this is so then it sheds some light on the particular stories about 'Raves' or 'House Parties'. These seemingly (at least recently to legislators) chaotic events are condensed sites of youth leisure (Redhead 1993). There is an element of neo-tribalism in them in so far as they draw participants momentarily and emotionally together from across the traditional segmentations of class, gender, race, and geography. Also, rather than incoherence or threat, most party-goers recount feelings of ontological security and succour together with a reduction of anxiety (based on trust) which is achieved through the co-presence of strangers who might spontaneously embrace one another, and will not be drunk/violent on alcohol (see Bauman 1992: 136–7; Giddens 1984; Goffman 1967). Most significantly, the young men talked to did not generally go to the party with a predatory sexual intent/desire, and also did not take their present partner, they went to have a good time in 'ecstasy, empathy, and affectual immediacy' (Featherstone 1991: 101).

A (street) powerful and predatory masculinity could take time out from anxiety by stepping outside daily life and its routines with the help of drugs (Giddens 1991: 37). Sometimes this could be a big step, with the weekend beginning on Thursday to only finish in the early hours of Monday. The short remainder of the week was then left to the task of crime, and maintaining credibility and respect up front.

[6] This can be thought as a 'technique of neutralization' (Sykes and Matza 1970: 295–6), or 'vocabulary of motive' (Mills 1972: 447), or less prosaically, as explaining action by the phrase 'out of his fuck'n head' (Matza 1964: 76).

Having said that risk behaviour is a common part of adolescent life (although it is gendered in particular ways (Plant and Plant 1992; Hagan 1988)) and an essential part, or focal concern, of street life for underclass young males (cf. Millar 1958), it is important also to stress its routine features. What comes across so clearly in biographical narratives such as these is that extreme (by any rational calculus) risk both defies reason and is presented as disarmingly ordinary. While daily life is reflexively monitored, it comes as something of a package imbricated with a whole number of discursively isolable risks. But they are not thought of in this way, and daily life would be impossible if they were. One simply does life, does crime, does drugs, does the male (street) thing. The good life means being 'on your toes'.

'On your toes' sometimes has a literal meaning for young people. Well over half the young men had been brought up within a two-parent family but repetitively talked of family discord and violence, especially in their relationships with successive stepfathers ('the boyfriend'), and periodic exclusion from home. Family sagas weaved together intense rivalry with stepfathers/boyfriends over the affections of, and in protection of, the Mother; resistance to authority (again especially that of the non-biological Father); and the simultaneous rejection/loss of family:

. . . it was always me mum and me and me sister, then someone else comes along and bosses you about . . . who's he to do that? . . . I started being a little bastard . . . (19-year old)

. . . me Mum like . . . the worry I've caused her . . . I don't want to go losing me Mum . . . I think the world of me Mum . . . (18-year old)

These are tough young men talking.[7]

Having been excluded, or by excluding themselves, they then led an itinerant lifestyle in the spaces between family and state, periodically interrupted by intervention of the latter. Of particular relevance in Britain (see Carlen 1988) is the fact that 32 out of the 80 young men had experienced residential (the majority) or non-residential professional child care because of crime, truancy, or being beyond parental control. Despite some good experiences of care, more typical is this view of loss: 'nobody cares in care' (20-year old). The loss of natural or institutional family life is compensated for in the present (but not in the longer-term) by peers:

. . . me Mum was a bad alcoholic, me Dad put us in short term care, they signed it to long term care . . . *me mates are me family now* . . . (20-year old) (my emphasis)

Economy

So far I have been playing mostly in the foreground of crime, drugs, and masculinities. Now we can brusquely step into the background (Katz 1988: 311–12). I am going to use economy here in a broad sense to include those normative processes and structures, like schooling and like youth recreation, designed to effect an entrée into legitimate labour, consumption, and leisure, but which routinely close the door after the young person has bolted.

[7] Some young men had already embarked, intentionally or unintentionally, on (re)creating their own families, displaying immense concern for their own children's future, yet they were incapable of envisaging and enacting family life.

IN SEARCH OF THE HIGH LIFE

The subsiding of social structures in reflexive modernity is especially felt by the underclass. In the ghetto there is a general emptying-out of social structures, of the institutions of socio-economic and cultural regulation . . . The result is not individualization but anomie, and a deficit of regulation. The result is the gang-bonding of young males and racial violence. This of course applies not only to the urban minority ghettos but to the white ghettos of Britain's council estates in Liverpool, Glasgow and Newcastle where working-class fathers breed underclass sons. (Lash 1984: 130–1)

Scott Lash's account of reflexive modernity, a modernity characterized by information and communication (rather than production) industries and in which human agency is progressively freed from structure (Freisetzung), rightly draws attention to the existence of reflexivity losers who represent the downside (underclass) to reflexivity winners—'the (new) new middle classes' (Lash 1994: 127–35). These reflexivity losers have not been freed from structure and their ability to self-construct their own life narratives, through material and cultural consumption for example, is strictly limited (Lash 1994: 120).

Schooling is a passport to success yet is repetitively denied to young men like these, as they deny it. Nearly all those interviewed admitted some school truancy with just less than half being persistently absent from the classroom once they entered secondary education. There were two immediate reasons for 'wagging' or 'sacking' school (see Carlen *et al.* 1992; Willis 1977): disengagement with school and its project, and enchantment by the rich life outside.

. . . couldn't cope with school, teachers always gave me a hard time, but I gave the teachers a hard time . . . (20-year old)

. . . I'm not fucking thick, but it just didn't interest me. When I was in school, I was the kind of person who just used to disrupt a class, if I was in a class I'd disrupt it, I don't know what it was with me. I'd always be getting sent home, always getting detention, always be getting suspended . . . (21-year old)

Clearly the truants here resisted authority, a common sentiment among young offenders being that they feel injustice in being told what to do by anyone in authority. The impact of pedagogic authority is, in the first moment, experienced as a repressive fate in the pre-modern sense, that is as predestiny or fortuna, something to be resigned to because it 'always happens to lads like us' (Giddens 1991: 109; cf. Matza 1964: 188). In the second moment, pedagogic authority is experienced as the shaming of a reflexive, and hence modern, self (Braithwaite 1989)—'shame eats at the roots of trust more corrosively than guilt' (Giddens 1991: 65). The young man defiantly saying 'I'm not thick' provides one example of the response to shame while another, in saying 'I could wag it and just wander around the school . . . they just didn't seem to be interested' (20-year old), suggests a more pervasive feeling of indifference to self on the part of the other. There are two classic responses to this situation: to rebel and risk formal exclusion—the 'other side of shame is pride' (Giddens 1991: 66)—or to leave the context where self is in doubt, to simply drop out.

Not all offenders are truants nor truants offenders and, despite a prevailing political rhetoric, much juvenile crime takes place outside school hours or occurs in school (Cusson 1983; Felson 1994). However, the second immediate reason for truanting given by interviewees directly links to the context of crime and hedonistic consumption. Life beyond the school gates was simply more exciting and real. Here, it was not so much the school which failed, and would fail in the future, to keep these young men in, but the seductions and doubt of adolescent life outside which drew them out:

. . . a few of the lads from my school came from . . . (area) . . . bringing cars to school, used to get in the back of them . . . I were buzzing off it . . . (19-year old)

Seduction and male doubt are combined:

I'd be going to school and me mate would come up, 'you're not goin to school?, you dickhead, . . . you pussy', and you'd go 'who you calling pussy? . . . come on I'll go and nick a car'. (19-year old)

In 'sacking' school, for whatever immediate reason and however reflexively, these young men reproduced the educational conditions of their own inequality and scholastic failure. Meanwhile other structures had been emptying out.

De-industrialization and the haemorrhaging away of the sectoral economy (Davis 1988: 48), and particularly the youth economy, has created (as well as all those jobs in information intensive firms located in the urban hinterlands) 'junk jobs' on the one hand and, on the other, 'large armies of unemployed, especially among young males' (Lash 1994: 120). Unlike Paul Willis's working-class pupils 'learning to labour' some underclass young males are learning to 'graft', or do nothing (Willis 1977). For, in the current economic climate in Britain many of the traditional, and male, manual industrial jobs have disappeared as they have in much of Europe, and especially Eastern Europe (Beck 1992; Lash 1994). Capital has gone off-shore. In 1993 the national youth unemployment rate for 16 to 19 year olds was 22 per cent for males and 16 per cent for females (*Social Trends 1994* (1994)). In those urban districts devastated by de-industrialization local rates of youth unemployment can be considerably greater than these aggregate figures suggest and, among street peer groups, the subculturally shared experience may be of full and enduring joblessness. Of course, this reality is routinely masked in Britain by statistical procedures and by increasing numbers of 16 to 18 year olds staying on in school merely to avoid having to do one of the youth training schemes on offer at low wages and with little future of a 'real' job (AMA 1993; Campbell 1993). Lash further argues that to be excluded from information intensive structures in this way is to be excluded from citizenship and is 'effectively both political and cultural exclusion from civil society' (Lash 1994: 133).

I've tried to get loads of jobs, I've had jobs then you get made redundant and so on, they just don't last, I don't really want to get a job, who does want to work? . . . I reckon I'd be wasting me time, people with A levels can't get jobs these days . . . (20-year old)

Instrumentally, the low wages, or no wages at all, become an effective situational explanation for doing crime; 'not worth working all week for £30 when I could go out and make that in about ten minutes' (19-year old). Earlier in their teenage years it was not poverty which directly prompted crime—although most came from families on welfare—rather it was the premature desire to be financially independent from their parent(s) and control something of their lives.

The majority of the sample came from socio-economically deprived city locales with few civic amenities and those that had been built, for example youth clubs, had often been destroyed by the disenchanted 'lads' themselves. These were areas where there was:

. . . nothing to do, it was like hanging round on street corners, then a youth club got built and like that was the main place everyone started going there, we was all made up . . . we all got barred from there, you were back on the streets again . . . just robbin again. (18-year old)

. . . playground opened a few years ago . . . all destroyed now . . . when we was younger, it was us that really started it off, you know, destroying it, with nowt to do. (18-year old)

But lives are not all grim and desperate (Hagan 1988: 152). These were areas where 'you've gotta be street-wise to survive' (20-year old), and where housing policy (Bottoms 1994; Mannheim 1965) had forgotten, or never known, cultural transmission theory: 'no nice people on my estate . . . full of criminals' (20-year old). But the areas were simultaneously places which were lively, exciting, and seductive: 'there's a lot of things happening, car thieves, lot of drug dealing, lot of this that and the other, prostitution . . . ' (20-year old). As they were normal, 'I can only say normal because I've never really lived anywhere else rather than (pause) other than the ghetto, always lived in the ghetto' (18-year old).

Why are such areas currently exciting and seductive? I want to glance now at what might replace absent structures and roles: drugs.[8] Expendable male youth have 'regrouped around the one social organization that seems to give them clout: the street gang' (Davis 1988: 52). If (predominately) male youth have only momentarily and stylistically done so on Britain's street corners, nevertheless, the cultural significance and messages of incipient 'turf wars' over drugs, and more traditional symbolic battles across urban estates, requires some thought in relation to reflexive modernization. For, if the (re)creation of self through consumption realizes an 'I' freed from communal ties and the cultural traditions of a lost male working class, then the male-bonded street community of drug dealing and video stealing may represent a fragment of the 'revenge of the repressed "We"' (Lash 1994: 111). Other (different) fragments are to be found on some football terraces, in racist attacks, and in neo-Nazi movements across Europe.

Drug crime is overwhelmingly male (just over 90 per cent of all offenders: Home Office 1994). It is characteristic of poor urban communities. Why? Drugs and drug economies are repetitively thought about as other. Local communities in the industrial world are corrupted by outsiders—Mafiosi, Yardies, Colombians, Triads, or, less poetically, existing criminal organizations. Thus, drug economies are represented in public discourse as 'alien' conditions precipitating the repeat victimization of naive and impressionable young drug users and the wider community of the respectable poor (HM Government 1994).

Rather than being 'alien', drugs (and all the crimes associated with them) form a crucial part of the irregular economy in poor communities (Auld *et al.* 1986; cf. Hobbs 1989). So much so in some American and emerging British neighbourhoods that one can speak of a 'counter economy' (Davis 1988: 49). Ian Taylor cogently argues that the expansion of drug demand and supply must be understood within the framework of the global and local political economy of the 1980s and 1990s (Taylor 1992: 188). As

[8] A fuller discussion of community and drug economies may be found in my book on drug law enforcement (Collison 1995).

local drug economies emerge, organized in the early 1980s around heroin and latterly (and variously) around crack, cocaine, amphetamine (again), and LSD in Britain, they then have the potential for becoming part of the economic infrastructure and alternative gendered opportunity structure of marginalized communities (cf. Maher and Curtis 1992; Waldorf 1993). They replace the absent structures.

Like 'normal' crime, drug and drug related crime can become embedded in certain areas (Hope 1994), thus, the relationship between drugs and the cultural economies of the inner city should also be central to this analysis. Drugs carry symbolic power (Wilson 1990: 530). Learning from America a deeper analysis:

> . . . would clearly have to encompass key features of contemporary American culture including its accelerated work ethic, the loss of a clear sense of individual meaning and identity sometimes discussed as the problem of 'narcissism', and the declining sense of a connecting teleology or purpose to social life itself. (Taylor 1992: 188).

For young underclass men the promised land is there on TV but here it 'stinks' (Messerschmidt 1986: 61). In contrast, the drug economy provides young men with a realistic chance of 'fast living' (Johnson *et al.* 1990: 11). In Britain some youths might reasonably ask 'how else do you get a BMW, a vodaphone and a gun?' (see Taylor 1993). Drug crime, like normal acquisitive crime, creates a space for the acting out and embellishing of predatory forms of masculinity (Hagan 1988: 152–3). Street level drug dealing, whether round the corner or in film—and the one is frequently suffused with the other—promises action and status success (cultural rather than simply material):

> I were in with the lads, in with the guys, I was in with everybody . . . it just got to me head, all the black guys, and the Asian guys . . . I thought yea I'm one of the lads here why sack it? (18-year old)

In view of the analysis above it should come as no surprise to find that 36 of the sample (45 per cent) had played a central or peripheral role in drug distribution networks, although only four of these had been convicted of a drug supply offence—this crime pays, unless careless enough to poach others customers, or to default on debt.

Growing Up to Be Mad

'Mad' is a common street term. It carries a meaning of prestige much like the word 'bad' in America, but more often it is used directly to capture a self (or situation) which pushes it further than others; does more crime, breaks more rules, uses more violence, is more wrong. The mad joy-rider, street-fighter, thief, drug user, leisure-worker makes a statement in chaotic deviance which both signifies difference from normative orders and over-socialization, and belonging within a peer group. 'Sad' may be used tragically to describe the intrusions of mundane reason into daily life: getting arrested, excluded (from school, the home), addicted, going honest, and worse, wearing cheap 'imitation' clothes.

Symbolically, a masculine self identity was fashioned around money, consumption, toughness, and respect, as it has always been on the street. But there is a significant new dimension to male street culture (and for youth culture in general) touched on above:

The alleged absence of role models . . . came not from the absence of men and masculinities in their lives—the lads were surrounded by a macho propaganda more potent in its penetration of young men's hearts and minds than at any other time in history—they were soaked in globally transmitted images and ideologies of butch and brutal solutions to life's difficulties. (Campbell 1993: 323)

A favourite film of many interviewees was New Jack City.

Without fully rehearsing a well-known argument, the world of work, and for the traditional working-class youth a world of physically demanding labour, provides many cogent images of masculinity—as does the world of the (violent) family and the world of (male) play on the street and in the pub (see Campbell 1993; Messerschmidt 1993). Think now of a situation where there is no work, or where the work is no longer physically demanding and supportive of community, where families and their role examples are increasingly dislocated by divorce, desertion, and single parenthood, and where much of legitimate play has been sanitized of its violence (the rules and organization of modern football being just one example).

Denied the economic and social power of legitimate work, limited though it might be, and having become incompetent at moving easily between lifestyle sectors, these young men played with, and at, their video fantasies (only half in jest) set against the grainy screen of the local street. It is important to be one of the 'lads'. This project drew less from fast disappearing local cultural traditions and structures than from the 'traditions' of the global community and the structures of drugs. If the argument here is robust then forms of predatory and excessive lifestyle among some young underclass males can be grasped, not as direct and simple responses to poverty, nor as consequences of a lack of socialization (quite the reverse in some respects), but as on-going attempts to both 'munch' the image and fill the 'no place' of structure and identity—to get a reputation as mad.

I have intentionally let the young men do their own talking rather than, perhaps unnecessarily, always draw the connections between narrative and theory. But, hopefully the paper has illustrated the way that critical new forms of social analysis can bear on some pretty old concerns of criminology. In this spirit I will let a young violent offender close more eloquently than theory could:

. . . depends how mad you are, some people are scared of you, they think you've got a lot of power . . . no-one will talk to me the wrong way . . . I feel like I've got a name for meself . . .

References

Association of Metropolitan Authorities (1993), *School Leaver Destinations*. London: AMA.

Auld, J., Dorn, N., and South, N. (1986), 'Irregular Work, Irregular Pleasures: Heroin in the 1980s', in R. Matthews and J. Young, eds., *Confronting Crime*, 166–87. London: Sage.

Baudrillard, J. (1983), *Simulations*. New York: Semiotext.

Bauman, Z. (1992), *Intimations of Modernity*. London: Routledge.

Beck, U. (1992), *Risk Society: Towards a New Modernity*. London: Sage.

Beck, U., Giddens, A., and Lash, S. (1994), *Reflexive Modernization*. Cambridge: Polity Press.

Benjamin, W. (1982), *Das Passagen-Werk*. Frankfurt: Suhrkamp.

Bottoms, A. E. (1994), 'Environmental Criminology', in M. Maguire, R. Morgan, and R. Reiner, eds., *The Oxford Handbook of Criminology*, 585–656. Oxford: Oxford University Press.
Braithwaite, J. (1989), *Crime, Shame and Reintegration*. Cambridge: Cambridge University Press.
Burr, A. (1987), 'Chasing the Dragon', *British Journal of Criminology*, 27/4: 333–57.
Campbell, B. (1993), *Goliath: Britain's Dangerous Places*. London: Methuen.
Carlen, P. (1988), *Women, Crime and Poverty*. Buckingham: Open University Press.
Carlen, P., Gleeson, D., and Wardhaugh, J. (1992), *Truancy, The Politics of Compulsory Schooling*. Buckingham: Open University Press.
Collison, M. (1994*a*), 'Drugs and Delinquency: A Non-Treatment Paradigm?', *Probation Journal*, 41/4: 203–7.
—— (1994*b*), *Crime, Drug and Treatment Careers*. Swindon: ESRC.
—— (1995), *Police, Drugs and Community*. London: Free Association Books.
Cusson, M. (1983), *Why Delinquency?* Toronto: University of Toronto Press.
Davis, M. (1988), 'Los Angeles: Civil Liberties between the Hammer and the Rock', *New Left Review*, 170: 37–60.
Dorn, N., and South, N. (1989), 'Communication, Education, Drugs and HIV', in J. Strang and G. Stimpson, eds., *Aids and Drug Misuse*. London: Routledge.
Featherstone, M. (1987), 'Lifestyle and Consumer Culture', *Theory, Culture and Society*, 4: 55–70.
—— (1991), *Consumer Culture and Postmodernism*. London: Sage.
Felson, M. (1994), *Crime and Everyday Life*. Thousand Oaks: Pine Forge Press.
Giddens, A. (1984), *The Constitution of Society*. Cambridge: Polity Press.
—— (1991), *Modernity and Self-Identity*. Cambridge: Polity Press.
Giggs, J. (1991), 'The Epidemiology of Contemporary Drug Abuse', in D. Whynes and P. Bean, eds., *Policing and Prescribing*, London: Macmillan.
Goffman, E. (1967), *Behaviour in Public Places*. New York: Free Press.
Hagan, J. (1988), *Structural Criminology*. Cambridge: Polity Press.
Hebdidge, D. (1979), *Subculture: the Meaning of Style*. London: Methuen.
Hirschi, T. (1969), *Causes of Delinquency*. Berkeley: University of California Press.
HM Government (1994), *Tackling Drugs Together*. London: HMSO.
Hobbs, D. (1989), *Doing the Business: Entrepreneurship, the Working Class and Detectives in the East End of London*. Oxford: Oxford University Press.
Home Office (1994), *Statistics of Drug Seizures and Offenders Dealt With, United Kingdom, 1993: Statistical Bulletin*. London: HMSO.
Hope, T. (1994), 'Communities, Crime and Inequality in England and Wales', paper to the Cropwood Conference, Cambridge, September.
Jefferson, T. (1994), 'Theorising Masculine Subjectivity', in T. Newburn and E. A. Stanko, eds., *Just Boys Doing Business?*, 10–31. London: Routledge.
Johnson, B. D., Williams, T., Deik, A., and Sanabria, H. (1990), 'Drug Abuse in the Inner City: Impact on Hard-Drug Users and the Community', in M. Tonry and J. Q. Wilson, eds, *Drugs and Crime*. Chicago: Chicago University Press.
Katz, J. (1988), *Seductions of Crime*. New York: Basic Books.
Lasch, C. (1995), *The Revolt of the Elites and the Betrayal of Democracy*. New York: W. W. Norton and Co.
Lash, S. (1994), 'Reflexivity and its Doubles: Structure, Aesthetics, Community', in U. Beck, A. Giddens, and S. Lash, *Reflexive Modernization*. Cambridge: Polity Press.

LEITNER, M., SHAPLAND, J., and WILES, P. (1993), *Drug Usage and Drugs Prevention: The Views and Habits of the General Public*. London: Home Office.

LYNG, S. (1990), 'Edgework: A Social Psychological Analysis of Voluntary Risk Taking', *American Journal of Sociology*, 95/4: 851–86.

MAHER, L., and CURTIS, R. (1992), 'Women on the Edge of Crime: Crack Cocaine and the Changing Contexts of Street-Level Sex Work in New York City', *Crime, Law and Social Change*, 18: 221–58.

MANNHEIM, H. (1965), *Comparative Criminology*. London: Routledge and Kegan Paul.

MATZA, D. (1964), *Delinquency and Drift*. New York: John Wiley and Sons Inc.

MERTON R. (1968), *Social Theory and Social Structure*. New York: Free Press.

MESSERSCHMIDT, J. (1986), *Capitalism, Patriarchy, and Crime*. New Jersey: Rowman and Littlefield.

—— (1993), *Masculinities and Crime*. Lanham, MD: Rowman and Littlefield.

MILLAR, W. B. (1958), 'Lower Class Culture as a Generating Milieu of Gang Delinquency', *Journal of Social Issues*, 14: 5–9.

MILLS, C. WRIGHT (1972), 'Situated Actions and Vocabularies of Motive', in I. L. Horowitz, ed., *Power, Politics and People*. Oxford: Oxford University Press.

MOTT, J. and MIRRLEES-BLACK, C. (1993), *Self-Reported Drug Misuse in England and Wales*. London: Home Office.

MUGFORD, S., and O'MALLEY, P. (1991), 'Heroin Policy and Deficit Models', *Crime, Law and Social Change*, 15: 19–36.

MURRAY, C. (1990), *The Emerging British Underclass*. London: IEA.

O'MALLEY, P. (1992), 'Risk, Power and Crime Prevention', *Economy and Society*, 21/3: 252–75.

—— (1994), 'Penalising Crime in Advanced Liberalism', paper to the American Society of Criminology, Miami.

PARKER, H., NEWCOMBE, R., and BAKX, K. (1988), *Living with Heroin*. Milton Keynes: Open University Press.

PARKER, H. (1973), 'The Joys of Joy-Riding', *New Society*, 3 January.

—— (1993), '"Pick and Mix": Alcohol, Drugs and the 1990s Adolescent', paper to the British Criminology Conference, Cardiff.

PEARSON, G. (1987*a*), 'Social Deprivation, Unemployment and Patterns of Heroin Use', in N. Dorn and N. South, eds., *A Land Fit for Heroin: Drug Policies, Prevention and Practice*. London: Macmillan.

—— (1987*b*), *The New Heroin Users*. Oxford: Basil Blackwell.

PEARSON, G., DITTON, J., NEWCOMBE, R., and GILMAN, M. (1991), 'MDMA/Ecstasy: New Wave of Drug Use', *Drug Misuse in Britain: National Audit of Drug Misuse Statistics*, London: ISDD.

PLANT, M., and PLANT, M. (1992), *Risk-Takers: Alcohol, Drugs, Sex and Youth*. London: Tavistock.

PREBLE, E., and CASEY, J. J. (1969), 'Taking Care of Business: The Heroin User's Life on the Street', *International Journal of Addiction*, 4/1: 1–25.

REDHEAD, S., ed. (1993), *Rave Off*. Aldershot: Avebury.

ROSE, N. (1989), *Governing the Soul: The Shaping of the Private Self*. London: Routledge.

SMART, B. (1992), *Modern Conditions and Postmodern Controversies*. London: Routledge.

Social Trends 1994 (1994). London: HMSO.

SOUTH, N. (1994), 'Drugs, Control, Crime, and Criminological Studies', in M. Maguire, R. Morgan, and R. Reiner, eds., *The Oxford Handbook of Criminology*, 393–440. Oxford: Oxford University Press.

SYKES, G. M., and MATZA, D. (1970), 'Techniques of Delinquency', in M. E. Wolfgang, L. Savitz, and N. Johnston, eds., *The Sociology of Crime and Delinquency*, 292–9. New York: Wiley.

TAYLOR, I. (1992), 'The International Drug Trade and Money-Laundering: Border Controls and Other Issues', *European Sociological Review*, 8/2: 181–93.

—— (1993), 'When Drugs Make the Running', *The Guardian*, 22 October.

URRY, J. (1988), 'Cultural Change and Contemporary Holiday-Making', *Theory, Culture and Society*, 5: 35–55.

WALDORF, D. (1993), 'Don't Be Your Own Best Customer: Drug Use of San Francisco Gang Drug Sellers', *Crime, Law and Social Change*, 19: 1–15.

WALTERS, G. D. (1994), *Drugs and Crime in Lifestyle Perspective*. London: Sage.

WARDE, A. (1994), 'Consumption, Identity-Formation and Uncertainty', *Sociology*, 28/4: 877–98.

WILLIS, P. (1977), *Learning to Labour*. Farnborough: Saxon House.

—— (1990), *Common Culture*. Milton Keynes: Open University Press.

WILSON, J. Q. (1990), 'Drugs and Crime', in M. Tonry and J. Q. Wilson, eds., *Drugs and Crime*. Chicago: University of Chicago Press.

[14]

IN SEARCH OF MASCULINITY

Violence, Respect and Sexuality among Puerto Rican Crack Dealers in East Harlem

PHILIPPE BOURGOIS*

Based on ethnographic fieldwork conducted while residing next to a crack house in El Barrio, New York, for almost five years, this article analyses how the social and economic marginalization of second- and third-generation Puerto Rican immigrants in the inner city has polarized violence and sexuality against women and children, both within the family and on the street. Traditional working-class patriarchy has been thrown into crisis by the restructuring of the global economy and the expansion of women's rights. Unable to replicate the rural-based models of masculinity and family structure of their grandfathers' generation, a growing cohort of marginalized men in the de-industrialized urban economy takes refuge in the drug economy and celebrates a misogynist, predatory street culture that normalizes gang rape, sexual conquest, and paternal abandonment. Marginalized men lash out against the women and children they can no longer support economically nor control patriarchally.

For several decades young African-American and latino men in the inner cities of the United States have been killed at considerably higher rates than soldiers in the line of fire during World War II. More inner-city African-American and latino men are under supervision by the criminal justice system than are enrolled in higher education (Mauer 1992). Although accurate figures for Puerto Rican males on the US mainland are usually not disaggregated in census statistics, their levels of violence and institutional incarceration probably parallel those of urbanized African-Americans. Policy advocates and community leaders specifically identify young, inner-city Puerto Rican men—the focus of this article—as being in a state of crisis (Pérez and Cruz 1994).

Public discussion of the problems faced by poor men of colour tend to fuel polemical, moralistic debates that blame the psychological deficiencies of pathological individuals or the social pathology of 'subcultures' (cf. *New York Times Magazine* 1994). US politicians and the media in the 1990s have largely responded with traditional 'family value' crusades. Individualist, blame-the-victim, and ethnocentric analyses of poverty and social marginalization are standard fare in the United States where social theory in the post-World War II decades has been traumatized by a McCarthyist terror of political economy and an 'all-American' tendency towards cultural essentialism or

* Research Fellow, San Francisco Urban Institute and Associate Professor of Anthropology, San Francisco State University.

The author would like to thank the following institutions for their generous support for this project: the Harry Frank Guggenheim Foundation, the Russell Sage Foundation, the Wenner-Gren Foundation for Anthropological Research, the Social Science Research Council, the San Francisco Urban Institute and the College of Behavioral and Social Sciences of San Francisco State University, the US Census Bureau, and the National Institute on Drug Abuse.

even biological determinist/racist interpretations of social inequality (see the critiques by Katz 1986 and the special issue of *Critique of Anthropology* 1993). Building on conservative interpretations of Oscar Lewis's (1966) culture of poverty concept, and Daniel Moynihan's denunciation of the black family (Rainwater and Yancey 1967), analyses of intrapersonal violence tend to be dominated by psychologists and social workers who focus on the inter-generational transmission of abuse within a therapeutic analytic framework. With notable exceptions (Feldman 1991; Sluka 1990), the growing literature by anthropologists on violence neglects the problems of the industrialized world. Instead anthropologists pursue their 'predilection for the exotic' by conducting participant-observation studies on the margins of the world economy, leaving little room for dialogue with other disciplines (see bibliographical review by Ferguson 1988).

Progressive, culturally sensitive critiques of the ethnocentrism and class-bias inherent in most discussions of African-American families notwithstanding (Burton 1991; Jarrett 1994; Stack 1975), paternal abandonment and domestic violence among the inner-city poor in the United States is a serious problem. To reach any understanding of why such large numbers of poor men are killing one another and are abandoning or abusing their progeny in the United States, one must set the debate in its larger social structural and political ideological contexts. Most obviously, the restructuring of the global economy has decimated the employment opportunities of the entry-level working class. This results directly in an exacerbation of the material crisis in the reproduction of the conjugal and even the extended family in the United States. As a matter of fact, the US Census Bureau's normally dry, impersonal statistical summaries uncharacteristically used the adjective 'alarming' in a 1994 report to describe the over 100 per cent increase in family poverty rates for young workers during the 1980s and early 1990s (DeParle 1994: A8). Parallel to these economic shifts, public sector services for the working poor have broken down in the context of an explicitly political hostility to the fate of the marginal (Wacquant 1995). Predictably, this has been accompanied by a rise in urban racial segregation and a polarization of cultural hostility across class and ethnic lines (Tonry 1995).

Working-class Patriarchy in Flux in East Harlem

The escalation of social marginalization in the United States has had grave consequences for how poor men 'do masculinity' (Messerschmidt 1993) as they take refuge in the underground economy and increase their levels of domestic and interpersonal violence. Traditional working-class patriarchy has been thrown into a prolonged material and ideological crisis as increasingly large numbers of men are unable to reproduce what some theorists, building on Gramsci (1991), have called 'hegemonic masculinity' (Connell 1987; Messerschmidt 1993). Fewer and fewer men are able to find stable, unionized jobs that pay them a family wage with family benefits as factories relocate overseas in search of inexpensive labour. Unable to provide economically for their conjugal unit, they lose the material legitimation for demanding autocratic 'respect' and domineering control over their wives and children.

At the same time that working-class patriarchy has been undermined economically by the restructuring of the global economy, women of all social classes have entered the labour force in increasing numbers since World War II. Furthermore, major cultural and political movements have mobilized women across the globe. As feminist women of colour have noted, this women's movement has been dominated by an anglo-centric middle-class bias which defines emancipation in terms of individual rights and upward economic mobility (Acosta-Belén 1993; Mohanty 1984; see also Jaggar 1983). Nevertheless, throughout most sectors of US society, there has been an ideological dislocation in post-World War II forms of patriarchal social organization. Of course, the reorganization of family arrangements, the restructuring of gendered labour markets, and the transformation of ideologies around sexuality has been a highly uneven and political process. Furthermore, the fundamental ideologies that enforce male domination remain in place. Like patriarchal Luddites, resisting change, men often attempt to reassert their declining level of patriarchal control over women and children through violence.

In the Puerto Rican case, the change in power relations has been further polarized since World War II by a massive rurál to urban migration set in a hostile cultural context. The Puerto Rican experience is dramatic by world standards because of the island's colonial relationship to the United States (Meléndez and Meléndez 1993; Rivera-Batiz and Santiago 1994). Few peoples in recent history have experienced such rapid economic changes; such a diasporic emigration; or have suffered such intense social marginalization and cultural denigration (Bonilla and Campos 1986; Dietz 1986; Rodríguez 1989). A Puerto Rican case study, consequently, allows for a detailed examination of how major historical changes affect men and women differently. Puerto Ricans in the United States reveal the centrality of gender and sexual category alongside class and ethnicity in the social pressure cooker that historical experiences of domination and resistance always render so dynamic and painful.

Second-generation inner-city Puerto Rican men who participate in the underground economy offer a particularly poignant example of how social suffering is complexly gendered. For these reasons, when I lived with my family in East Harlem, New York during the late 1980s through the early 1990s in order to study street-level crack dealers, gender power relations—and specifically the relationship between interpersonal violence and masculine struggles for dignity—emerged as a central research focus (Bourgois 1995*a*). In these pages I will explore how inner-city Puerto Rican men, who are confined to the margins of a nation that is explicitly hostile to their culture and no longer requires their labour power, reconstruct their notions of masculine dignity around interpersonal violence, economic parasitism, and sexual domination. Increasingly large proportions of frustrated, desperate men have taken refuge in a street culture of resistance that roots its material base and its ideological appeal in the growing drug economy, which offers a concrete alternative to exclusion from the legal economy and its anglo-centric culture. Through my ethnographic dialogues I hope to show that rather than being mere pawns of larger social structural and ideological forces, drug dealers who participate in street culture are active agents seeking dignity—even if violently and self-destructively. What might be 'explained' as individual psycho-pathology or dismissed as some kind of cultural essentialist machismo (see discussions by Paredes 1971 and Ramírez 1993) needs to be contextualized in history and understood as the expression of contradictory struggles for power and meaning.

IN SEARCH OF MASCULINITY

The Historical Context

In the decades following World War II between one third and one half of Puerto Rico's population migrated to New York City in search of employment in factory sweatshops (Bonilla and Campos 1986; Bose 1986). They arrived at precisely the historical moment when these kinds of manufacturing jobs were leaving the industrialized countries as multinational corporations have increasingly sought out lower labour costs and more pliant governments throughout the Third World (Rodríguez 1989; Bourgois 1995*b*; Sassen 1991). This sets the stage for the dramatic changes in family structure and male power roles among second- and third-generation East Harlem residents. Coming primarily from the poorest sectors of society, and often arriving directly from sugar plantations, marginal family farms, or decaying coffee haciendas, definitions of masculinity among Puerto Rican immigrants are embedded in interpersonal webs of 'respeto [respect]' defined around gender, age, kinship, and community status. Puerto Ricans still often refer to the long-since urbanized descendants of immigrants from the countryside as 'jibaros', a term that is loosely definable as 'hillbillies' or 'country bumpkins'. In the classic 'traditional' setting of the family farm, the worth of the autocratic pater familias hinged most immediately on the larger community's perception of the respect accorded to him by his wife and her abundant children. Several generations later on the inner-city street, the idealized legacies of the hierarchies and prestiges that were formerly rooted in the rural family and in the personal hierarchies of small farming or plantation communities have been redefined into an explicitly misogynist and sexually violent street culture. The traditional search for respect has been radically transformed into a fear of disrespect. Unemployed or drug dealing/addicted men find themselves flitting homeless from one sexual relationship to another, without the protection of a family or an economically viable community.

Vivid memories of a rural patriarchy repeatedly surface in the idealized childhood reminiscences of the mothers of the crack dealers I befriended:

> Mrs Ortiz: What I liked best about life in Puerto Rico was that we kept all our traditions. And in my village, everyone was either an Uncle, or an Aunt. And when you walked by someone older, you had to ask for their blessing. It was respect.
>
> In those days children were respectful. There was a lot of respect in those days. My father was very strict. When a visitor came, my father only spoke to us with his eyes, because children were not supposed to be in the room. He would just look at us, and that meant we had to disappear; we had to go to our room. We weren't allowed to be in the same room as the older folks.
>
> I tried to teach my children a little of what my father had taught me.

Mrs Ortiz's son, Primo, the manager of the crackhouse where I spent much of my time, can no longer 'speak' to his children 'with his eyes' and expect to have his commands immediately obeyed. A man's oppressive power in his home in rural Puerto Rico was predicated upon his being able to work hard and provide materially for his wife and children. He was supposed to co-ordinate the labour power of his wife and children around the agricultural cycles and intermittent wage labour opportunities of the precarious semi-subsistence rural economy. In inner-city New York, the increasingly large cohort of male high school dropouts who are excluded from the new service sector jobs that require a minimal education and which entail public subservience to anglo-dominated professional office culture have lost the material basis for the patriarchal family prerogative of rural Puerto Rico. Former modalities of male respect can no longer be achieved through a conjugal household or an extended kin-based community. Instead, the unemployed or drug dealing man lashes out at the women and children he can no longer support or control effectively. The memory of his grandfather's former power hangs heavily upon him as he harks back to a patriarchal 'jibaro' past he can no longer reproduce.

The Polarization of Domestic Violence

This was the case for Primo's father when he lost his job at a garment factory and became 'a nasty alcoholic (*borrachón sucio*)'. Primo's earliest memories of his father are of him beating up his mother. Worse yet, all the subsequent men in Primo's mother's life offered the growing boy a similarly brutal masculine model defined around physically victimizing women.

Primo: When I was a kid I never really liked'ed nobody to be with my mother. I didn't like any of her men, because I didn't like it when they would have fits, and hit her; get wild and beat her down.

There was this one guy when I was still a little kid in the seventies, named Luis, who was dating my mother. He would hurt her, just to hurt her.

One time he got wild on my mom . . . I was sleeping, and woke'd up.

My mother called the cops, and the mother-fucker grabbed a knife. My heart stopped. That was the only time I got up and came through for my mother. I stood in between after he had made a coupla swings.

Primo reproduced this cycle of brutality 15 years later when he too beat up his girlfriend in front of her children. Powerlessly struggling with his inability to hold a steady job and earn respect through economic faithfulness to his household, he had pursued the street male role of gigolo, and was living off a woman named Candy, who was one of the few female sellers in the crack dealing network I befriended. Primo pretended publicly to enjoy 'free loading (*cacheteando*)' on Candy's generosity and love for him. In fact, in private retrospective conversations Primo admitted that he was also in love. After several months of the patriarchal role reversal of being economically supported by a woman and forced to satisfy her sexual desires upon demand, however, he attempted to recoup his personal sense of male respect by the only means immediately at his disposal: public physical violence. Years later in crackhouse conversations, he emphasized his outrage over how his sense of masculinity was 'dissed' (disrespected) by Candy's violation of domestic roles:

Primo: That woman 'dissed' me. She was making so, fucking, much money. That bitch was making even more than I knew about. That bitch was no good. It was like the kids were all living without their mother. The kids were taking care of themselves. Her baby, Lillian, was less than a year old. Hell! Junior was the mother. He was changing the diapers.

And sometimes I felt sorry and shit, so I would do it. I was there, changing the diapers and she wasn't around!

Worse yet, Candy inverted patriarchal sexuality:

Primo: Plus, you see, like, when she would come home, she used to get in a mood, or something, and I didn't wanna BOTHER . . . It was fucked up, because she had grabbed a knife. (distant gunshots)

Upon leaving Candy's household following a violent break-up, Primo returned to full-time crack dealing. On slow nights he would provide me and the crackhouse lookout, Caesar, with detailed accounts of the final fight that ended his economically and sexually dependent relationship with Candy. The fight began when Primo refused to make love to Candy. This prompted her to accuse him of having outside girlfriends. It was almost as if Primo used the tape-recorded conversations in the crackhouse as therapy to resolve the confusion generated by the gender taboos that he had broken when he lived off Candy. He also needed to bond with his male friends in the crackhouse by celebrating his ability to triumph over a misbehaving woman. His description climaxed with how he managed to disarm Candy, in order to beat her more severely in front of her children:

Primo: As soon as she put the gun down—I don't remember exactly where she put it, but I saw her take out the clip—I went, 'Fucking Bitch!' (swinging both fists). And I mushed her.

I was pissed man. I shouted, 'Come on, Bitch! I'm not playing with you anymore.'

Philippe: What about the kids?

Primo: The kids were there in the room all nervous, I guess they were crying . . . Put it this way: the children knew their mother was wrong, but I was hitting their mother, and they wanted to jump on me. When I saw their faces, I knew that I had to be prepared for them, too. I was ready to like, block their swings.

Vulnerable Males

In contrast to the legitimation that Primo constructs for his violence against Candy, Primo condemns his own father's violence toward his mother and sisters. He explicitly sees his father as a failure; he was never able to respect him as a patriarchally socialized child should:

Primo: My father's a sick man now. He's got diabetes. He's a chronic drinker; and when he gets drunk he gets violent. So its like he's no fucking good, so why be with him? That's why my mother had to say, 'Hike!' (grinning abruptly and jerking his thumb over his shoulder like a sports umpire calling an out)

And every time I would see my father, once they were separated—'cause they were never divorced—it was every other week. And he was just like not correct. Always with a beer in his hand. Always drunk and crying. We were kids. We were thinking 'Fuck you. I don't care'. He used to buy us candy. And we used to be chillin' with our candy. And then he used to come to me, and ask, 'Is your mother with anybody?' I don't remember my answers but I probably used to say 'yes', or whatever. He was drunk and stupid.

Maybe he regretted the things that he did. And he could have been better off. I don't remember really too hard. And then he collapses, shakes. I used to hate that.

This particular detail of Primo's father collapsing in a shaking fit of jealousy when his son tells him about his estranged wife's new lover refers to a Puerto Rican psychosomatic medical condition known as *ataque de nervios* (Lewis-Fernandez 1992; Guarnaccia *et al.* 1989). These 'nervous attacks' usually afflict women, and are associated with jealousy, abuse, and/or failure in love. The fact that Primo's father might engage in such a feminine expression of angry vulnerability in front of his children and close friends illustrates the sense of male impotence he must have felt as a failed labour migrant in the United States. He would respond by beating up the nearest vulnerable female, whose respect he was no longer capable of commanding.

Primo: Then he used to start off fighting with my sister, the oldest one. Later, she would hit me.

Ultimately Primo recognizes that he too is a failure as a man. He specifically identifies this in biological terms as a 'male thing'. In Primo's poignant description of how several generations of men in his immediate lineage have all been crushed, one can discern the gender-specific experience of social marginalization in the Puerto Rican diaspora:

Primo: I tell you Felipe, I gotta check myself out. 'Cause like I was telling my mother, in my family, it goes like this: all the men are bugged . . . My mother's oldest brother is bugged. He stands in the window talking to himself . . . My mother's other brother—another uncle of mine—he just walks along like a zombie, and he don't look at nobody. I'm his nephew and his godson. He writes some script, it look like shorthand, but it is absolutely no fucking shorthand. He writes in his notebook and scribble scrabble on the notebook. But the guy has his job. He keeps his job. He keeps his place, but he is out of his mind . . . If you look at him walking down the street, he look like a bum. He just walks straight, looking down. He's bugged . . . I remember when he wasn't bugged. He and my mother went to Puerto Rico, when he wasn't bugged. You know, I tell my mother I got a feeling that all the people in my family, I mean all the guys, are gonna snap one day in the future. I think about myself in the future and I'm gonna be bugged . . . But for some reason, somehow, my grandfather wasn't bugged. My grandfather passed away, he wasn't bugged, he just died.

Significantly, none of Primo's sisters—he had no brothers—were involved in the underground economy or even participated in street culture's violence. They all either worked full-time at entry-level jobs in the service sector (i.e. managing a McDonald's, attending customers in a clothes boutique, and working as a nurse's aide in East Harlem's municipal hospital) or were married in long-term relationships raising young children. Primo's pride in his sisters' success illustrates, not only how rigidly women's roles are defined, but also, once again, how differently women are affected by the experience of growing up poor in the inner city.

Primo: You know my mom's good! She raised up three beautiful daughters that didn't fuck up . . . Maybe they got married early and bullshit, but there's nothing about drugs in the streets. They know what's good and wrong. My sisters ain't violent. They not in the street—none a' that.

Conjugal Stability and Legal Employment

In contrast to their often bravado behaviour and explicitly misogynist diatribes, most of the two dozen crack dealers who I befriended admitted to aspiring to an ideal-type, middle-class, nuclear family. In fact, many had actually lived in stable households with the mothers of their children for significant periods of time. This usually occurred during their periods of stable, legal employment. The complex interrelationship between joblessness, personal pathology, family instability, and structural vulnerability in the labour market came up frequently in our conversations. The following account of the relationship between employment and drug use in Primo's life illustrates the interaction between personality and social structure in the construction of masculine subjectivities.

Primo: I was 19 when I had my kid. He was born in '83, on May 20-something. We were teenagers going steady—me and Sandra. I had found a job and stayed steady with her. We got a crib, and I was making good money . . . I was a good nigga', boy. Every penny that I used to get was for my hobby, which was radio CB-ing. She got pregnant. We didn't really want it. But then I told her, 'I'm just as responsible as you are, so if you keep it, I'll take the consequences.' So she kept it. It's too bad. But that's all right . . . And I wasn't selling drugs or doing nothing. I was a goodie, goodie. I had money in the bank, I had money in the house. Sandra never suffered. She was big, and pregnant, and fat . . . When Papito was born I was working at US Litho. I was a good nigga'. I had good hours. I was working from 4:00 to 12:00 at nights . . . I was a hard worker, I was into that overtime. Whatever they give me, I gonna work. I want to bring money to the house . . . This is how I stopped sniffing (cocaine): one day, my son wanted to play with me. I was in the rocking chair, and I didn't want to play with him. It was like, 'Leave-me-alone' type shit. And I was thinking about it, and I realized it. I noticed my son was growing up. Plus I bled one time . . . I said, 'Nah, this can't be.' This ain't me, 'cause I'm always lovable with my kids, singing songs, little school songs that I learned when I was a kid in school . . . I used to sit in a rocking chair, reading him his ABCs and numbers, just to keep his mind busy. You got to read to your kids when they're little, like even when they're only months old, so that they always got things in their brain . . . Then at work they changed my hours to 2:00 a.m. to 10:00 a.m. I said, 'I can't handle them hours; I have a family.' . . . I used to fall asleep on the job; 'cause I had my son. And this girl, Sandra, my son's mother, had found work off the books. And as she was leaving, I was coming in, and my son was on top of me. He wanted to play. He already slept, you know, so I couldn't sleep . . . And that's when I started fucking up. That's when I started smoking 'woolies' (marijuana cigarettes laced with crack), and I was drinking a little. I was staying up all day, and then I didn't want to go to work . . . Man, it's like, oh, God! I used to come from work; I didn't know whether to go to sleep, or hang out and sleep later. And my son, was there, wide awake; he was two, and wanted to play with me. So they fired me because I was falling asleep on the job. They said, 'We have to let you go because you have a family, and I know you want to be with your family, because you have these hours, and we can't switch you back to the daylight hours. We need somebody for these hours, where you don't seem to fit in.' . . . They were firing everybody; just looking for reasons. It was like business was bad . . . After that I went AWOL smoking crack.

Primo acutely felt his failure as a father—and as a man:

You know, Felipe? Now my son is 6 years old. It gets me sad when I think about shit like that . . . It's like, I'm not there for 'im. Just like my father was never there for me . . . And my son loved being with me. Sometimes I was always fixing something in the apartment. So this kid, he used to grab the tools, and just start hammering things, like, look at me, and start trying to do the same thing. I love that shit . . . That's why I used to cry a lot when I first left my son. It was only a couple months after they fired me at US Litho . . . I used to go to the bathroom and cry like a bitch. 'Cause I knew I was leaving soon and that meant: no more kid . . . But you know what, man! I believe in . . . I believe that when you're with someone, and you have a child, you should make the fucking best of it, whether you're doing good or not. You gotta make a commitment; like a family thing, like old-fashioned.

Philippe: What the hell are you talking about?!

Primo: It always seems like I'm full of shit when I say things like that, 'cause I don't support my kid, but that's because, I . . . right now, I'm not supporting my son, but . . . Matter of fact, you know last weekend, when we were talking one time about the last time we had cried, that's the last time I teared, was last weekend. I was thinking about my little nigga'. I was supposed to keep him for the weekend, but I called too late. I fucked up. It was a hassle. (Perking up again) Matter of fact, I remember my father once saying to my mother that he used to cry, because he misses me, because I'm his only son. Now I feel bad, 'cause a few days away from today, it's Papito's birthday, and I'm not gonna give him anything. I don't got the money.

Philippe: You wouldn't rather have those 25 dollars you just paid for the dope (heroin) and the perico (cocaine), to spend on your son's birthday present instead?

Primo (sniffing from a packet of heroin): Well . . . I'll definitely get him a present. I love that nigga'.

Stable legal employment for both spouses is crucial for enabling young men to begin defining masculinity around sharing in the material and emotional reproduction of children. The problem is that most of the legal jobs available to high school drop-outs in New York City are not only poorly remunerated but are also considered to be feminizing. This is because the service sector, specifically office support services in the finance, real estate, and insurance (FIRE) industries, have been the fastest growing employers since the 1970s. Most of the supervisors at the lowest levels of the service sector are women, and street culture castigates males who are publicly subordinated across gender lines. Typically, in their angrier memories of disrespect at work, many of the male crack dealers refer to their female bosses in explicitly sexist language, often insulting their body parts, and dismissing them with street slang and sexualized curses. They often describe their female supervisors as having male sexual organs and they describe themselves and the other men around them at work as being effeminate.

Caesar: I lasted in the mail room for like eight months at this advertising agency that works with pharmaceutical shit. They used to trust me . . . But I had a prejudiced boss. She was a fucking ho' (prostitute). She was white. I had to take a lot of shit from that fat, ugly bitch, and be a wimp . . . I didn't like it but I kept on working, because 'Fuck it!', you don't want to fuck up the relationship. So you just be a punk . . . Oh my God! I hated that head supervisor. That bitch was REALLY nasty. She got her rocks off on firing people, man. You can see that on her face, boy. She made this one fucking guy that worked with me cry—and beg for his job back . . .

The changing high-tech, office service jobs of the post-industrial, globally-linked economy offers few opportunities for young men from the inner city who have dropped out of high school. Not only do young men have difficulty politely taking orders from women, but they often consider it to be downright emasculating to have to run and fetch coffee for their work-place superiors and, worse yet, to have to deliver their services with a cheerful smile. Consequently, even when they endure in their positions as messengers, copy machine operators, or mail room clerks they tend to develop reputations for having 'bad attitudes'; this further limits their opportunities for upward mobility in office place hierarchies.

Primo never bought Papito, his 7-year-old son, a birthday present. In fact, he did not even go to visit him that week. Coincidentally, during these same days my preteenage neighbours, Manny and Angel, forced me to witness on my tenement stoop the flip side of the father/son generation gap. Eyes sparkling, Angel told me proudly, 'I'm going to see my father this weekend.' His little brother Manny immediately responded with his eyes dull and sad, 'I'm not gonna see my father; he's in jail.' As if by script, just moments later we saw another little boy, my neighbour's 3-year-old son nicknamed Papo, shrieking with delight. A 20-year-old man swaggered up almost embarrassedly to hug the little boy, mumbling affectionately '*Ay mi hijo* (Oh my son) God bless you!' The mother watched, revealing no emotion. Papo's father had just been allowed out of prison for the afternoon on a drug rehabilitation/work-release arrangement. An hour or so later, little Papo was screeching again, but this time in anguish. His father had to leave in a hurry to report back to prison before dusk. The superintendent of our tenement later explained to me that Papo's father was the person who had burglarized Papo's mother's apartment two-and-a-half years ago when Papo was only 6 months old. Papo's father had known the apartment was empty because he was supposed to be meeting his infant son in the park at the time. His new girlfriend served as look-out while he stole the VCR and television from out of his son's apartment.

Investing in Promiscuity

Sexual conquest and promiscuity represent another important forum for redefining masculine dignity in street culture that is related to the imperative to glorify one's economic parasitism on the mothers, lovers, wives, and children one can no longer support (Anderson 1989; De la Cancela 1986). Primo's look-out, Caesar, was most adamant in celebrating sexually his inability to maintain a family. Unable to reproduce the patriarchal aspirations of his grandfather's generation within the context of a nuclear family and an extended kin-based community, he concentrated his male energies into macho one-upmanship and sexual belt-notching. He worked hard at exaggerating his sexual promiscuity and hard heartedness:

Caesar: We's just like those green sea turtles that be in the Galapagos. Those turtles get out of the shell, and they run to the sea, and they never know who their parents was . . . They go through their whole life. Then they bone somebody or they get bone't. They have kids and they never see them . . . I don't feel guilty about the kids I got thrown around out there, because I have no heart Felipe. I'll fuck anybody, anytime. Besides these bitches is crazy nowadays.

Primo also sexualized his notion of male power. One late night after finishing his shift at the crackhouse, I accompanied Primo to visit a social club to drink bootleg liquor. Swigging from his drink and giggling, Primo waved at three women who were playing pool together. Feigning an old-fashioned Puerto Rican rural accent, he said in Spanish, 'Look how well my women get along with each other (*Mira como mis mujeres se llevan bien*).'

At the time Primo was under pressure from his probation officer to find a job. A New York City Narcotics Circuit judge had given him a two-to-four-year suspended sentence for selling crack to an undercover agent. One of the conditions for his supervised freedom was that he find legal employment. As he plotted which one of 'his women' he was going to spend the night with, I purposefully reminded him that he had to call the employment office early the next morning if he did not want to be sent to prison. Primo simply changed the unpleasant subject and took refuge in his sexual promiscuity.

Primo, (sombrely): Oh shit, Felipe, you're right! But you know what? (chuckling) Out of all these bitches hanging around, I take that one (pointing to Maria) . . . (sombrely again) This has happened to me before. One day in front of the Game Room, I saw a legion of girls on the corner (chuckling again). Like a herd of girls talking to each other. And when I looked, I said, 'God damn! I had all of them.' It was my ex-wife Sandra, Candy, Maria, Jaycee, and I think some other girl that I don't remember.

Philippe: How'd that make you feel—good?

Primo: No. It felt'ed weird. (Noticing Caesar eavesdropping eagerly through the blasting music) No, it felt'ed good, then weird . . . I'm telling you Felipe, I got a golden dick. All my cousins be that way (slapping Caesar five). We all got golden dicks.

Gang Rape

Toward the end of my residence in East Harlem several of the crack dealers with whom I had developed my closest relationships admitted to having been gang rapists in their adolescence. The gang literature in the United States, written primarily by criminologists and sociologists only occasionally mentions rape (Campbell 1991; Huff 1990). It is usually presented as an initiation ritual and it is sometimes noted that this violent act serves to bond the boys homoerotically and misogynistically (Bourgois 1995*a*: ch. 5). Participating in gang rape is one of the ways youths achieve their manhood.

All these ritualized dimensions—coming of age, mutual bonding, and ritual initiation—apply to the accounts of adolescent gang rape provided by the crack dealers. Primo, for example, had difficulties becoming sexually aroused when his companions would begin to rape one of the girls in their network. He felt humiliated and excluded when they sent him home for being 'too little' to join in their sexual violence.

Primo: Back in those days I was younger. My dick wouldn't stand up. It was like nasty to me; I wasn't down with it. I can't handle that. So they be goin' upstairs with a girl, and of course they already knew that I'm not going to be down with it, so they ask me (in a hostile voice), 'What'cha gonna do man? Go home or what?' . . . So fuck it, the best thing I could do is break out. 'See you guys tomorrow'; or else, I just wait downstairs in the bar, or something.

Primo gained acceptance from the older boys that he admired by becoming an active accomplice in their gang rapes.

Primo: I wasn't really with it, but I used to act wild too, because the bitch is gonna have to pass through the wild thing. And sometimes, it could be me acting stupid with a bat or something, so that she has got to stay in the room with whoever is there . . . Sometimes the older guys, they would play the nice role for awhile with the girl, but once they get that piece of pussy, she gets dished. It's like psshhht, pssht (making slapping motions). She gets beat down: 'I own you now, bitch.' That was back in the days. Nobody is with that shit no more. Pussy is too easy to get nowadays.

In addition to emphasizing the ritual dimension to adolescent gang rape and its particular frequency in the youth gang context, it is important to understand public rape within the same context that I have presented domestic violence. Gang rape is an extension into the public domain of males trying to reassert the anachronistic patriarchal power relations of previous generations that have been undermined by shifts in gender power relations. As girls increasingly carve out more autonomous roles in public male-dominated settings, boys lash out violently. They legitimatize their sexual violence against young teenage girls, claiming that they are 'teaching them a lesson'. As a matter of fact, the street expression for gang rape is 'to run a train on a bitch'. Sometimes the expression is modified into 'training a bitch', as if the assaulted person were a dog being taught a lesson, or a new trick. Primo, who was aware of my horror and anger over his accounts of gang rape, often argued with me to try to make me—and any future reader of these tape recorded dialogues—understand the street's dichotomy between worthy and unworthy rape victims:

Primo: Put it this way, Felipe, these bitches were young, dumb, and full-a-cum. If they are hanging out too much, and they start seeing that we are wild, and if they are still hanging out, then we know that we can take them.

Philippe: That is some sick shit you're saying. You motherfuckers were nothin' but a bunch of perverts.

Primo (frustrated): I mean look at their attitude; if they hang out too long, believe me, then they know what's happening. If the girl is gonna hang then she's gonna get dicked. I mean these bitches, they would just keep hanging out, and hanging out. They be coming back to the bar everyday, so then we know that they really want a dick . . . They would take the bitch aside, because we had her *confianza* (trust). By then it was easy to force her into doing it with all of us . . . Besides the bitch get smacked, or something, if she don't.

Philippe: That's rape, man. Don't you understand?

Primo: I mean the way I remember it (speaking directly into my tape-recorder), I was so fucking young. I looked at it like, most likely, whoever never came back to hang out at the club, passed through some trauma, and it's gonna be hidden within their life, for the rest of their life, and they're never goin'a hang again. Instead they go home, and chill the fuck out, and keep a dark secret for the rest of their life. (Looking at me defensively) I used to feel sorry, sometimes too, for them . . . But some bitches was more suitable, and used to just come back and hang. 'Cause I guess it was like they was on the streets, and they passed through their first shit, and now fuck it: '*Voy a hangear*' (I'm going to hang out).

Philippe (interrupting): Come on, man, get real! Nobody likes going through that shit.

Primo (speaking slowly): Well . . . It was their decision, Felipe. I mean, the first time, maybe they weren't into it. Sometimes there be tears in their eyes. They didn't want to be forced.

Caesar (laughing at Primo's confusion and my anger, grabbing the tape-recorder from me): But they were forced; but they liked'ed it; and they come back for more; 'cause they're with it. They just get used to the fact: 'We own you now bitch!'

Philippe: You motherfuckers are sick! (Loud gunshots in the nearby background followed by the sound of someone running).

Primo (running to peek through the door at the noises outside): No! You gotta understand Felipe, even when they say no, they're loving it.

Despite their rationalization of their violence against women as patriarchal justice, they ultimately considered the women they abused to be a reflection of their own sense of internalized worthlessness.

Primo: We used to talk between each other, that these women are living fucked up, because they want to hang out with us . . . And what the fuck we got to offer? Nothing! We used to wonder.

Caesar: We don't be doing nothing! Bitch be stupid to go with a nigga' like us.

Individual Responsibility and Social Structural Victimization

It is impossible to present ethnographic dialogues on experiences of oppression and social marginalization without conjuring negative images that risk re-enforcing racial- and class-based stereotypes. An open, uncensored discussion of masculinity in street culture risks creating a forum for the public humiliation of the poor and powerless. Chicano cultural critics have long since noted how anglo perceptions of latino machismo reflect deep-seated historical prejudices (Paredes 1971). This is exacerbated by the fact that ethnocentric assumptions are so unconsciously ingrained in the public 'common sense' that descriptions of extreme social misery and brutality such as those presented in these pages are interpreted as a cultural reflection of a particular ethnic community—in this case Puerto Rican immigrants in the United States. Obviously, such an 'airing-of-dirty-laundry' interpretation runs counter to the theoretical and political arguments of this article, which are opposed to cultural essentialist explanations for human action. The same applies to any interpretation that claims women on the street and in the household have provoked male violence against themselves because of their demands for greater rights. That kind of blame-the-victim perspective not only glorifies the stability of previous patriarchal status quos, but also overly individualizes the long-term macro-structural transformations in gender relations that are occurring across the globe. As has been the case historically for all major power shifts between antagonistic groups, the complicated process whereby women are carving out a new public space for themselves is rife with contradictory outcomes and human pain.

As I noted in the opening pages, this is exacerbated by the fact that the fundamental status quo that enforce male domination have not been altered. As many feminist theorists have long since noted, many of the struggles and achievements of women in the past decades have been framed in terms of individual rights that ultimately largely mirror or invert patriarchal models of 'empowerment' (Butler and Scott 1992; Jaggar 1983). On another theoretical plane part of the problem with understanding experiences of oppression and resistance—whether masculine or not—is that, as Jefferson (1994) notes, the relationship between personality and society is poorly understood. Agency/structure relationships are usually presented in dualistic terms—if addressed at all (see theoretical critique by Giddens 1991). Sexuality, family organization, gender-power relationships, and the cultural construction of intimacy are crucial issues affecting the minute details of our daily quality of life. In many respects they remain taboo subjects for ethnographers who are under an unconscious mandate to present positive images of the people who they study and live with. Quantitative survey researchers have never had any direct access to these complex dimensions of daily life since most people conceal their intimate experiences of violence, sexuality, substance abuse, etc. from even their closest friends—let alone outside interviewers or survey researchers.

There is no definitive solution to the complex problems inherent in the politics of representation of intimate ethnographic conversations across racial and class-based lines. The men in these pages often behave in cruel and violent ways, not only against the women and children in their lives but also against themselves. Despite the risks of writing this difficult material for outsiders to read, however, I feel that if I failed to confront it—especially the most painful dimensions of misogyny and sexual violence in street culture and in individual action—I would be colluding in the sexist status quo. While all of the crack dealers are victims from a social structural perspective, they are also agents of destruction in their daily lives. They wreak havoc on their loved ones and on their larger community. Of course, from an analytical perspective the particularly brutal forms that masculinity has assumed on the streets of inner city USA—where crime rates, murder rates, and incarceration rates are the highest in the entire industrialized world—is ultimately a reflection, not just on the political economic model of the United States but rather of the fundamental lack of basic human rights among the socially marginal in the United States—most notably the lack of individual freedom, access to health care, shelter, education, and public safety by inner-city residents. The polarization of formerly rural-based patriarchal masculine subjectivities toward greater public violence, widespread sexual abuse, and overt economic parasisitism on inner-city streets are merely symptomatic expressions of these basic political and cultural inequities. Behind the most gruesome of the crackhouse conversations evoked in these pages lies the massive public and private sector breakdown that has occurred since World War II in most US inner cities, and the de facto apartheid ideology that legitimates a public 'common sense' tolerating rising levels of immiseration among the working-poor.

References

Acosta-Belén, E. (1993), 'Defining a Common Ground: The Theoretical Meeting of Women's, Ethnic, and Area Studies', in E. and C. E. Bose, eds., *Researching Women in Latin America and the Caribbean*, 175–86. Boulder, CO: Westview Press.

PHILIPPE BOURGOIS

ANDERSON, E. (1989), 'Sex Codes and Family Life Among Poor Inner-City Youths', *The Annals of the American Academy of Political and Social Science*, 501: 59–78.

BACA ZINN, M. (1989), 'Family, Race, and Poverty in the Eighties', *Signs: Journal of Women in Culture and Society*, 14: 856–74.

BONILLA, F., and CAMPOS, R. (1986), *Industry and Idleness*. New York: Centro de Estudios Puertoriqueños, Hunter College.

BOSE, C. E. (1986). 'Puerto Rican Women in the United States: An Overview', in E. Acosta-Belén, ed., *The Puerto Rican Woman: Perspectives on Culture, History, and Society*, 2nd edn, 147–69. New York: Praeger.

BOURGOIS, P. (1995*a*), *In Search of Respect: Selling Crack in El Barrio*. New York: Cambridge University Press.

—— (1995*b*), 'The Political Economy of Resistance and Self-Destruction in the Crack Economy: An Ethnographic Perspective', *Annals of the New York Academy of Sciences*, 719: 97–118. Special Issue, 'The Anthropology of Lower Income Urban Enclaves: The Case of East Harlem', ed. J. Freidenberg.

BURTON, L. (1991), 'Caring for Children', *The American Enterprise*, 2/3: 34–7.

BUTLER, J., and SCOTT, J., eds. (1992), *Feminists Theorize the Political*. New York: Routledge.

CAMPBELL, A. (1991), *The Girls in the Gang*, 2nd edn. Cambridge, MA: Basil Blackwell.

CONNELL, R. W. (1987), *Gender and Power*. Stanford, CA: Stanford University Press.

COOK-LYNN, E. (1989), 'The Broken Cord', review, *Wicazo Sa*, 5/2: 42–5.

Critique of Anthropology (1993), Special issue on US inner-city poverty and the 'underclass debate', 13/3.

DE LA CANCELA, V. (1986), 'A Critical Analysis of Puerto Rican Machismo: Implications for Clinical Practice', *Psychotherapy*, 23/2: 291–96.

DEPARLE, J. (1994), 'Sharp Increase Along the Borders of Poverty', *New York Times*, 31 March, A8.

DIETZ, J. L. (1986), *Economic History of Puerto Rico: Institutional Change and Capitalist Development*. Princeton: Princeton University Press.

DORRIS, M. (1989), *The Broken Cord: A Family's Ongoing Struggle with Fetal Alcohol Syndrome*. New York: Harper and Rowe.

FELDMAN, A. (1991), *Formations of Violence: The Narrative of the Body and Political Terror in Northern Ireland*. Chicago: University of Chicago Press.

FERGUSON, B., with FARRAGHER, L. (1988), *The Anthropology of War: A Bibliography*. New York: H. F. Guggenheim Foundation.

GIDDENS, A. (1991), *Modernity and Self-Identity: Self and Society in the Late Modern Age*. Cambridge: Polity Press.

GRAMSCI, A. (1971), *Selections from the Prison Notebooks*. London: Lawrence and Wishart.

GUARNACCIA, P. J., DE LA CANCELA, V., and CARRILLO, E. (1989), 'The Multiple Meaning of Ataques de Nervios in the Latino Community'. *Medical Anthropology*, 11: 47–62.

HUFF, C. R., ed. (1990), *Gangs in America*. Newbury Park, CA: Sage.

HUNT, R. C. (1971) 'Components of Relationships in the Family: A Mexican Village', in F. L. K. Hsu, ed., *Kinship and Culture*, 106–43. Chicago: Aldine.

JAGGAR, A. (1983), *Feminist Politics and Human Nature*. Sussex: The Harvester Press.

JARRET, R. L. (1994), 'Living Poor: Family Life Among Single Parent African-American Women', *Social Problems*, 41/1: 30–49.

JEFFERSON, T. (1994), 'Theorising Masculine Subjectivity', in T. Newburn and E. Stanko, eds., *Just Boys Doing Business? Men, Masculinities, and Crime*, 10–31. London: Routledge.

Katz, M. (1986), *In the Shadow of the Poorhouse: A Social History of Welfare in America*. New York: Basic Books.

Lewis, O. (1966), *La Vida: A Puerto Rican Family in the Culture of Poverty—San Juan and New York*. New York: Random House.

Lewis-Fernández, R. (1992). 'Ataques de Nervios or Panic Attacks: An Embodied Contestation of Puerto Rican Ethnicity', paper prepared for AAA session on 'Healing, Bodily Practices, and Caribbean Ethnicity', San Francisco, 2 December.

Malveaux, J. (1987), 'The Political Economy of Black Women', in M. Davis, M. Marable, F. Pfeil, and M. Sprinker, eds., *The Year Left 2: An American Socialist Yearbook*, 52–73. London: Verso.

Mauer, M. (1992), 'Americans Behind Bars: One Year Later', The Sentencing Project, Washington, DC.

Meléndez, E., and Meléndez, E., eds. (1993), *Colonial Dilemma: Critical Perspectives on Contemporary Puerto Rico*. Boston: South End Press.

Messerschmidt, J. W. (1993), *Masculinities and Crime: Critique and Reconceptualization of Theory*. Lanham, MD: Rowman and Littlefield, Inc.

Mohanty, C. T. (1984), 'Under Western Eyes: Feminist Scholarship and Colonial Discourses', *Boundary 2*, XII/3, XIII/1: 333–58.

New York Times Magazine (1994), 'Who Will Help the Black Man? A Symposium Moderated by Bob Herbert', 4 December, 72–7, 90, 92–3, 109–10.

Paredes, A. (1971), 'The United States, Mexico, and Machismo', *Journal of the Folklore Institute*, 8/1:17–37.

Pérez, S., and Cruz, S. (1994), *Speaking out Loud: Conversations with Young Puerto Rican Men*. National Council of La Raza: Washington, DC.

Pollitt, K. (1990), 'A New Assault on Feminism', *The Nation*, March, 408–17.

Rainwater, L., and Yancey, W., eds. (1967) *The Moynihan Report and the Politics of Controversy*. Boston: MIT Press.

Ramírez, R. (1993) *Dime Capitán: Reflexiones sobre la Masculinidad*. San Juán: Huracán Ediciones.

Rapp, R. (1987), 'Urban Kinship in Contemporary America: Families, Classes and Ideology', in Leith Mullings, ed., *Cities of the United States: Studies in Urban Anthropology*, 219–43. New York: Columbia University Press.

Rivera-Batiz, F. L. and Santiago, C. (1994), 'The Labour Market and Socioeconomic Performance of the Puerto Rican Population in the United States 1980–1990', monograph prepared for The National Puerto Rican Coalition, Washington, DC.

Rodríguez, C. E. (1989), *Puerto Ricans: Born in the USA*. Winchester, MA: Unwin Hyman.

Sassen, S. (1991), *The Global City*. Princeton: Princeton University Press.

Singer, M., Valentin, F., Baer, H., and Jia, Z. (1992), 'Why Does Juán Garcia Have a Drinking Problem? The Perspective of Critical Medical Anthropology', *Medical Anthropology*, 14: 77–108.

Sluka, J. A. (1990), 'Participant Observation in Violent Social Contexts', *Human Organization*, 49/2: 114–26.

Stack, C. (1975), *All Our Kin: Strategies for Survival in a Black Community*. New York: Harper.

Tonry, M. (1995), *Malign Neglect—Race, Crime, and Punishment in America*. New York: Oxford University Press.

Wacquant, L. (1995), 'The New Urban Colour Line: The State and Fate of the Ghetto in Postfordist America', in C. J. Calhoun, ed., *Social Theory and the Politics of Identity*. New York: Basil Blackwell.

[15]

'Boozers and Bouncers': Masculine Conflict, Disengagement and the Contemporary Governance of Drinking-Related Violence and Disorder

Stephen Tomsen
University of Newcastle/University of Sydney, Australia

The links between crime, violence and male offending are now more deeply researched in a growing international literature that understands much antisocial and criminal behaviour as a social resource for the attainment and protection of masculine identities. Nevertheless, the tie between masculinity and nonoffending has been much less explored. This focus group study of understandings of public drinking-related conflict and violence among young male drinkers and security officers in a combined urban and rural district of New South Wales illustrates the significance and complexity of these links. Masculine concerns inform a readiness for involvement with conflict and its enjoyment through the prominence of issues of social status, gender policing, honour and carnival during different social occasions. But this must be understood in relation to the different masculinity 'projects' (Connell, 1995) that contrast security officers with an idealised professional self-image and the majority of drinkers, from a more violent minority. A surprisingly common pattern of 'respectable' masculine subjectivity informs disengagement from serious violence. This is often characterised by an exaggerated view of the rational male self as safe and in control of most social interaction in dangerous public contexts. The pitfalls of this may even be enhanced by the new influence of campaigns around 'risky' public drinking that aim to instill ideals of responsible self-governance.

Much traditional criminological discourse had a deep-rooted obsession with the study and control of 'dangerous' forms of masculinity (particularly working-class male delinquency), but rarely tackled the relation between criminality and the socially varied attainment of male status and power. In the last two decades, analyses of crime have problematised the disproportionate involvement of men in crime and violence and explored the creation and reproduction of male identities in different illegal activities (Collier, 1998; Jefferson, 1996; Naffine, 1997). Despite the flaws of reductionist views about male criminality that fail to incorporate the multiple effects of different social structures, this wider research shift can be received as a positive advance in understanding crime (Messerschmidt, 1997).

In particular, ethnographic studies of criminal activities that incorporate detailed analyses of actors' views and the masculine meanings of crime in relation to both local groups and wider cultures and social structures point beyond glib generalisations about the maleness of crime (Bourgeois, 1996; Collins et al., 2000; Winlow, 2001). This work illustrates a continuing challenge in the need to explain the relations of male criminality to official forms of masculinity including those that are reproduced in the criminal justice system, and also how the interplay between these reflects power relations between different men (Tomsen, 1996). As well as this, researchers are pressed to reconcile these findings against the phenomenon of a widespread masculine *disengagement* from direct involvement in crime and violence. A superficial interpretation of these accounts can reify participation in crime (especially violent crime) as a principal social means of establishing masculinity. The need to explain both participation in violence and disengagement in a way that respects individual agency and situational diversity has already been argued (Athens, 1989). From the vantage point offered by the new literature on masculinity, researchers must again ask why it is the case that even most socially disadvantaged men just occasionally, rarely or never engage in these behaviours with their masculine identities remaining unthreatened? Furthermore, what models of masculinity inform these decisions to disengage and what views generated within male groups support this process?

An ethnographic approach is well suited to explaining the phenomenon of drinking violence and the mixed relations that different men have to it (see Monaghan, 2002, and Hobbs et al., 2003, for important recent British examples). Young men figure prominently in drinking-related incidents as offenders and as the perpetrators or victims of assault. The general link between intoxication and violent activity by young men has been widely confirmed in quantitative studies, although the exact nature and dynamics of any causal link still elude researchers. Pharmacological approaches fail to explain how aggression, violence and drinking are closely related to periods of extended social interaction and the striking high level of young male involvement in these activities (Collins, 1989; Fagan, 1990; Marsh & Kibby, 1992). Anthropological evidence suggests a high level of variation in alcohol-related aggression across cultures (McAndrew & Edgerton, 1969). Knowledge about the social context of violence and efficacy of measures taken to regulate it has been deepened by recent observational monitoring of the situational variables in drinking 'hot spots' with assault and disorder (Wells, Graham, & West, 1998). Australian researchers have been at the forefront of this (Homel, Tomsen, & Thommeny, 1991, 1992; Homel & Clark, 1994; Homel et. al. 1997; Lang et. al., 1995). But the underlying link between masculine identity and the contexts of public drinking could be fully studied by a local analysis of drinking-related violence as it is subjectively experienced and interpreted by its human participants.

Models explaining violence between males often stress the significance of the protection and attainment of honour in social interaction (Archer, 1994; Felson & Steadman, 1983; Polk, 1994). These need to be assessed against the frameworks for understanding aggressive and violent incidents that are held in local contexts and evidence about the personal and peer group value of masculine involvement with heavy drinking, violence and risk-taking. A previous account of a Sydney-based study has also signalled the importance of rule-breaking and masculine protest as part of group episodes of drinking violence and brawling and the frequent power contents emerging between patrons and staff in venues (Tomsen, 1997). In line with this, the issue of gendered interaction with private security and staff has been explored by overseas researchers in relation to the significance of a perceived injustice or masculine grievance in drinking settings (Wells, Graham, & West, 1998). Yet the relative weight of the factors suggested by these different explanatory models is still unknown, especially in relation to the significant contemporary changes that are being made to the regulation of public drinking. Major New South Wales developments to curb excessive drinking and related disorder and violence in the last decade have included drinker education, server-intervention, staff antiviolence training, and the regulation and the monitoring and prevention of violence and disorder via local liquor accord measures. These strategies have involved close cooperation between local police, council and planning authorities, venue managers and staff, security firms and drinkers themselves with important outcomes for conflict and violence resulting from this.

Aims and Methods

Specific aims of this project were to uncover features in the interaction of young male drinkers and security, examine whether masculine conflict was ameliorated by the enhanced regulatory changes in local public drinking environments since the 1990s, and to assess views about such changes and their efficacy. A wider goal was to offer research evidence about the nature of the causal link between male drinking and public disorder and violence from a social actor perspective.

This research comprised a study of the links between social constructions of masculinity (as the collective male attainment of an empowered gender identity [Connell, 1995]), violence and disorder in public-drinking contexts in the Newcastle/Hunter region. Focus groups were conducted at local venues in 2002. Data were generated from discussions with 30 young men in these group situations. Participants comprised a nonrandom sample of men who drank regularly in local venues and a smaller number of security officers and venue staff who were employed in these locations. The 20 security officers who participated in focus groups were recruited from a mix of local firms. Their regular work was spread around Newcastle, the Hunter, Central Coast and Sydney regions and comprised a mix of licensed and nonlicensed entertainment venues and events.[1]

Drinkers were recruited via advertising and contacts in licensed venues in Newcastle's inner city and the wider Newcastle and Hunter regions. These included a circle of mates attending university/tertiary studies together, friends from a local soccer team, and a less respectable group from the Maitland/Hunter region with limited education, marginal employment and histories of trouble with police and authorities. Their style of 'disrespectable' working class protest masculinity was apparent in coarse and sometimes distinct language (e.g., more swearing and language such as 'flogging' as a term for assault), overt sexism, racism and disrespect for authority. They also revealed greater risk-taking behaviour such as extremely heavy drinking with no concern for health effects, disorderly actions leading to criminal charges and involvement in fights even when outnumbered and against the odds.[2] All of the participants were aged between 18 and 25 years. Seven were in full-time employment, and an equal number in part-time work. Ten were full or part-time students and six were unemployed.

Interview questions and focus group topics concerned aspects of male identity, drinking histories and styles and the subjective experience of drinking and intoxication, especially in peer groups. Additionally, participants were asked about perceptions of threat in public space and drinking contexts, the contrast between scenarios of violence and nonviolence, and the drinker's own interpretations of the causes and pattern of aggressive and physically violent encounters. These groups explored aspects of the interactions young men have with each other and security staff in local public-drinking venues. Drinkers were questioned in detail about their views of the apparent effects of antiviolence education and strategies and regulatory mechanisms adopted in drinking environments. Focus groups of six to 10 participants were conducted late in the afternoon in licensed clubs in Newcastle and Maitland.

Drinking

As participants were recruited in local venues or from groups known to go to them, it follows that all participants frequented licensed premises as part of their regular social activity. Most visited a number of venues regularly and they would usually visit more than one on a night out. Group drinking varied from two or three times a week to as little as once a month. Participants typically engaged in this activity a few times a week and especially on weekends. Students tended to drink more when they were on holidays. As an entire night of social drinking could cost well over $100 each, this also depended on the amount of money available and this factor was most significant for the unemployed or part-time workers. Participants often cut the expense by sharing cartons at home or by drinking beer in a less expensive suburban hotel or licensed club in the early evening before they moved on to city venues and nightclubs. Some spoke positively about the attractions of cheap drink hours ('happy hours'), which have not fully disappeared from city venues, and referred to occasions promoted and known as 'students' nights' with discount prices. Quite contradictorily, the majority of participants voiced positive support for server-intervention measures that could deter general levels of drunkenness in venues.

For some, a night out could mean only having three or four drinks. Most also described sessions of much heavier drinking that happen every few weeks or more. But for others, these occasions were more typical. Heavy drinking was described as each person consuming a whole bottle of spirits, being very hung-over and unable to recall details of the night before. This was associated with group 'shouting' and long occasions ending late in the city. The most extreme understanding of heavy drinking (from a member of the Maitland/Hunter group) was a complete loss of consciousness: 'In all honesty, I don't reckon you have a problem until you hit rock bottom. You know — pass out.'

Drinking was seen as an important aspect of a young man's social life and enjoyed in periods of 'time-out' from a routine existence. This comprised patterns of difficult work and study, or, for some, the boredom of unemployment. Drinking was used as a means to deal with 'bad days' even if the results were a part of a chance process:

> Let off some steam — getting a break. Especially after a stress day — when you have had a fight with your girlfriend or something like [that]. I just want to go out and get wasted.
>
> Sometimes but you go out and you have had the worst day and you get drunk and you meet someone after your first drink and the whole day changes and it is good — but you don't always go out angry and stay angry. Sometimes you can go out angry and end up happy as. Sometimes you can go out happy as and end up with your front teeth broken.

A further important element of this release was the opportunity to socialise with male friends and the mateship this affirmed. Drinking is valued as a social lubricant that promotes mixing with less tension when with friends and occasionally meeting girls. It was also said to be valuable for reducing the level of inhibition among intoxicated girls and creating opportunities for sex:

> It is more social. I wouldn't talk to chicks if I didn't drink. I can't socialise without alcohol — I just freeze and get self-conscious.
>
> I am a pretty ugly bloke and it is real hard to get a chick. So you shout them a couple of beers until they are seeing double vision and they are going, 'You are hot, you are gorgeous — you are going home with me'.

Violence, Conflict and Safety

Most stated they did not like late night venues with 'seedy old people' who are 'looking for fights' though on some 'big nights' attendance at these locations can happen. They also agreed they did not like clubs with a rough image and made overall attempts to avoid conflicts with security, other drinkers and people encountered during a night out ('You just smile and then cruise', 'We just keep away'). A few directly denied feeling unsafe during these occasions. But groups of male friends were also very conscious of the need to look out for each other when drinking in public and at night. Other remarks suggested caution about locations and people's behaviour, such as avoiding certain streets and malls at night, avoiding some of the very late venues with adverse reputations and watching carefully if 'hassled' by a large group in a venue. Similarly, there was a general reluctance to be out alone:

> Go out alone? Yes, I would because I know I would meet up with somebody in town. Generally, I wouldn't walk like in the CBD by myself, because you don't know what dickhead is going to smack you up. I had a broken nose by being in a club by myself.

It was argued that potential aggressors could be anticipated because of their appearance and actions. Involvement in conflicts was also understood in a discourse of personal agency that positioned these patrons as being completely in control of unfolding events. At the same time, it implied that victims are to be blamed for their own treatment:

> You can just pick up the vibe. You can just get the feeling in you. You can feel they are talking about you or looking at you. You can feel someone looking at you and you look at them and they are just staring at you.
>
> You do learn a lot of lessons when you are out so nobody can teach you what is going to happen the night that you go out. You may get in a fight or you may not. You may have trouble with a security guard or not. It all comes down to you. At the end of the night it is your choice that you end up in the gutter or you are walking out the door with a smile on your face with two chicks under your arm.

This impression was contradicted by comments and accounts that suggested many conflicts were difficult to foresee, such as disputes due to closeness and bumping in dark and crowded venues. Despite the view of control and personal agency in events, some fights were seen as happening rapidly and without intention and the drinkers felt they had no chance to avoid them or conciliate. Even the most placid of the young drinkers, who displayed a generally relaxed attitude towards insults from others, described how they had all at some time been involved in situations that they could not restrain. This was due to the frequent unpredictability of other people as much as it was due to their own occasional boisterousness:

> ... you might just have intentions of going out just to hang out with your mates and then you are put on a table with another group right next to you and you are going to have to put up like a big wall if you are not going to have any contact at all. I am not saying that is going to be a problem straightaway. It is that personal space thing. Some people are really cool with it and some people are definitely not. Also, when there is a table next to you and you get up and you are a bit drunk and you accidentally knock em it depends on their reaction, because if you go 'sorry mate didn't mean to' it is their reaction then. The ball's in their court.
>
> Sometimes you can't help it. They come up and grab you and it is on. And you, and you don't know what's happening to you.
>
> The other night at ... we were sitting at the window and this huge guy walked past and I said 'How are you doing?' And he called me a couple of words I didn't approve of. And so I yelled out the window something back to him and sat down. Next thing this hand comes through the window and lifted me up by the neck. Eventually it took four security guards to hold him down.

The majority of the drinkers in the focus groups professed a relaxed attitude towards insults from other people and believed that violence should never be actively looked for, although it sometimes cannot be avoided, such as when either they or a friend have been physically attacked. Nevertheless, this outlook sometimes led to involvement in serious brawling that was described with evident pleasure and appreciated for its suspension of normal orderly social patterns. Enjoyable time-out can entail disorder and violence (Tomsen, 1997). The accounts of such occasions also reflect a continuing pattern of enthusiastic watching and talking about informal violence among men. For example, one drinker and his mates excitedly described a dispute with venue staff in the middle of a crowded street where they had intervened to protect a friend from victimisation. This may have been intended to resolve the matter. It did, however, develop enough to involve a range of other patrons and security staff from nearby venues who had a limited knowledge of the origins, nature of the dispute or different allegiances, as both onlookers and participants: '... oh mate it was good. It was just like a big day out. You had an idea who is on whose side, sort of thing. I was just too drunk and confused and punched on.'

The major causes of venue violence cited in these groups included intoxication, as certain people are 'idiots when they get drunk' or 'bad drunks'.[3] Some other factors were aggressive and unbalanced personalities (some people are just 'na na') and mixing drink with illicit drugs such as speed and heroin. Participants also referred to conflicts between security and drunken patrons, the presence of rough or old people, football teams and racially/ethnically distinct groups, crowded space, territoriality in suburban areas and towns and arguments over females and late-night transport. Most agreed that local venues and streets had become safer due to practices such as refusing entry or service to intoxicated patrons. Nevertheless, some said it was still easy to get entry or a drink in a busy venue 'as long as you are standing up straight' (see Briscoe & Donnelly, 2002, for survey results that match this pattern). A few believed that there is no way to further manage aggressive human behaviour. But practical suggestions concerned addressing long lines at venues, the design of crowded premises that caused conflicts over the desire to rest outside, and absurd charges for water that seem intended to ensure most people consume alcohol or reflected a management suspicion about illicit drug-taking among patrons.

Honour and Male Disputes

A few participants at the start of one focus group spoke very critically about the possibility that they were invited to join because all young men were seen by social researchers as a particular problem with regard to drinking and disorder. They argued this had to be balanced by a consideration of the problems of older drinkers and the actions of aggressive females, such as the harassment and assault of single girls by groups of women. But this argument was confounded when the link with masculinity was conceived in an essentialist way, with involvement in disputes seen as the natural result of young men socialising and drinking:

> I reckon it is just alcohol and male testosterone. It is just really how young men act. You go to the club and you see a fight and you will see 10 fights between males under 25. You will rarely see two 40-year-olds out the front having it on.

Less essentialist but socially grounded connections with masculinity were implied in talk about men who claim and acquire social status from involvement in fights. Drinkers can be 'showing off to their mates' and 'if there are a few chicks around they all puff up and try and show that they are better'. Some disputes also had the quality of gender policing among men. Males who construed the different actions or appearance of others as insufficiently masculine could react with violence. For example, one group participant spoke of the frequent problems set off by his formal dance training. He enjoyed displaying this skill in different venues and fights often resulted, especially when this impressed girls:

> I reckon the thing is the macho/masculine dudes being cool sitting in the corner with a cigarette in their mouth and they see the bloke over there dancing with eight chicks. He goes, 'I will go show that little poofter'.

Protecting a sense of honour in public encounters was another regular but not inevitable factor determining the pattern of conflict. Some drinkers felt compelled to be involved in disputes in the face of a serious direct insult:

> I suppose someone could be seen as a wimp if they back away from a fight even though this guy has done a really bad thing to you. You don't want to fight because you don't want to get into trouble or something like that. And you back away and maybe lose some respect from your friends. I don't know anyone who would do that.

The circumstances of 'a really bad thing' are contrasted with less important slights and disputes that do not compel the retaliation more aggressive males are seen to be drawn into. For most, there is a preference to avoid fights over minor matters. These drinkers weigh up an insult or challenge against other considerations about continuing on with a good night out that a serious fight would probably bring to a quick end and the physical risk of any involvement in violence:

> Like most of us are pretty calm when it comes to things like that. You probably walk away. Try and talk to the bloke. Whereas some wouldn't bother — they would just throw a punch.
>
> The ability to step back, look at the bigger picture, and be aware of the repercussions of your actions. And how big the guy is.

Members of the Maitland/Hunter group were distinct from this general drinker pattern of uncommon violence and restraint. They made many comments that could have been attempts to shock the focus group moderator, but they also did not appear to need to engage in a contrived masculine performance. These young men had significantly higher rates of drinking and less restraint when the money was available. They expressed less moderation over trivial disputes and were more inclined to get into conflicts and fights, on some nights feeling more 'aggressive' and inclined to 'look for it', and this fight-seeking was preferably done in the city where this would have fewer implications than if done locally.

Furthermore, they were less concerned about the times when they were themselves assaulted by patrons or 'secas' ('they are lethal — they are just out looking for fights too') or ended the night in a police cell. In an unexpected paradox, these participants did not agree about any direct relationship between heavy drinking, aggression and what the moderator called 'masculinity', at the same time as their own actions epitomised this relationship. In denying this link, they appeared to understand 'masculinity' as meaning some exceptional and premeditated social display aimed at claiming male status. For them, heavy drinking and less predictable violence were viewed as the natural consequences of belonging to the male sex even when the social attainment of male status is apparent as a factor:

> Nine times out of 10 I have had a fight in the pub — I wake up and I know that I shouldn't have done it. But at the height of it all you think I can knock this cunt out, and you walk around saying to people 'Who is the man?' And they are all like 'You the man', 'You the man'.

Similarly, intimidation of smaller and weaker males was viewed as part of a natural male pattern and little care was expressed about the possible negative consequences of engaging in bullying. These more violent participants denied that occasionally being badly bashed by police, security or other drinkers ever had the effect of restraining their own inclinations towards violence. In fact, they instead implied that past episodes of victimisation merely taught them to be more cunning when involved in disputes. This also confirmed their view that victimisation is part of a natural male order and best compensated for by a successful assault on somebody else:

> If you look at someone and you know you've got it over them, you are going to put it on them. I do it if I run out of money. I walk up to somebody and take his beer from under his nose and say 'thanks mate'. If you know you can do it you are gonna do it. At the end of the night you are walking away and you see four blokes coming to you and it is because of what happened earlier.
>
> Flattening never teaches a lesson. I have copped many a flogging. I don't think that I have ever learned a lesson from a flogging. What it teaches you is 'Move faster, you little prick'.

Conflict With Security

Most participants had experienced some excessive force from security officers who were working as 'bouncers'. A few young men were openly hostile and viewed security as bullies who victimise smaller or intoxicated opponents. They described their interactions with security in the language of masculine rivalry over physical attributes. The body is a fundamental site of engagement that signals both covert and overt power among men, and this is sharply so in the context of public drinking:

> There are arrogant dickheads on the steroids with dicks this big [drinker makes a small gap between his fingers].
>
> I have been physically hit by a 'bouncer' and I did not like it and it was a pain in the arse because he was like this tall and about this wide [stretches his arms up and out] and look how big I am. It is obvious he was pushing steroids.

One Maitland participant related in a disturbingly matter-of-fact tone how he attacked other venue patrons and was then violently assaulted by 'secas' in a local venue:

> They kicked me fair in the neck, right here. It was good. It stung. I was trying to breathe. It was, like, getting caught. I could breathe so far and then it was getting stuck and I couldn't breathe no more.

Several complained about how security amplify their immediate power over patrons with arbitrary decisions. They suggested security make inconsistent judgments about venue entry and favour young girls, who are asked fewer questions about their age, as a higher number of female patrons will give a positive image to the venue. By contrast, they place young males under greater physical scrutiny:

> Every time you go out. Bouncers suck. They kick you out. You wait in line to get in somewhere for ages, and as you go to get in you stumble a bit — 'Right, too drunk'.
>
> Sometimes you have a bit of a problem getting into places. They just look at you or don't really like you or something like that ... you have to straighten up. It's an art.

Security officers can at different times be concerned about intoxication, a potential for disturbance that is construed subjectively from some loud activity or simply because 'they don't like you'. They suggested that security ignore incidents that happen close to or outside venues such as street fights broken up by friends and onlookers. Participants also related instances of abuse of power such as security keeping a patron's personal identity card without reason or overlooking acts of aggression or misbehaviour from their own friends.

One young man described how he was the victim of an unprovoked attack from the mate of security officers and was then thrown out for bleeding (like several others involved in fights or accidents). He was left to fend for himself before friends drove him to a hospital:

> The night that I got my broken nose, I was on the ground, got up off the ground and sat on the seat and was sitting there spitting the blood off. And I was there for about 30 seconds ... and they walked up to me and said 'out'. So I had to walk outside with a broken nose pissing out blood. I found a napkin on the ground and put it to my face. That is what I had to find. The club was not worrying about me; they were just worried about the blood on the floor.

Another participant, who worked as a barman in a licensed venue, complained that plenty of security officers are still unfamiliar with the laws surrounding their work or the real extent of their powers to intervene and use force or physically restrain patrons.

These negative remarks were contradicted by comments that suggested only a minority of security officers were a problem for drinkers, or that security are a mixed blessing whose presence gives a general feeling of safety for most patrons: 'A lot of the time security holds stuff together ... you take the security away and every establishment will not be safe.'

This ambiguity was mirrored in the views that security hold about drinkers. Both security officers and drinkers framed interactions with each other through a concern with signals of respect and disrespect. Officers suggested that most of the patrons they deal with were not aggressive and behaved well, but there was a regular uncertainty about relations with drinkers. It was suggested that only a minority was really difficult and even that 'everybody' liked security staff except for the 'people who hate us'. Issues of masculinity shaped fights between drinkers and attacks on male security guards ('When they are drunk a lot of them get "small man syndrome"'). Furthermore, a sizeable number of drinkers undermined their sense of authority by showing a greater degree of open respect for a venue licensee or manager or with open insults. For example, some drinkers referred to security as 'plastic cops'.

Discussion of these interactions reflected how these episodes were experienced as insulting or emasculating in an occupation with a very fragile sense of professionalism and limited social status, but which emulates elements of the official masculinity of public policing (tough, team-focused, disciplined and controlled). This issue signalled a further dimension in the experience and protection of male honour in these locations and its importance for the security officers' own sense of worth. Yet like the majority of drinkers, all of the officers insisted that they had a restrained response to disrespectful gestures and remarks. They claimed that there was no direct link between these and outbreaks of violence and that the current industry need was for 'good communicators'.[4] In fact, any deployment of a sudden and unpredictable response to such problems did not fit the wider ideals of constant scrutiny and close supervision of masses of patrons.

Discussion

In this study, participants often understood violence as an essential force. Aggression and conflict while drinking were conceived as typical of young groups of men or even due to the combined chemical effect of alcohol and male hormones. This view was held persistently by some and shared between drinkers and security officers. In line with this essentialism, the connection with masculinity was suggested implicitly rather than directly in accounts of interactions and incidents and appeared to reflect a belief in its unremarkable natural quality. But this information also signalled the elemental role of gendered identities in the origins and meanings of drinking-related conflict and violence. These do not shape human action in a uniform and deterministic way. This varies by context and the forms of different individual and collective masculinities that are generated socially: evidence about male drinkers and security officers reflect how these are embedded in peer group and occupational identities and the oppositions between them. Both drinkers and the majority of security officers construct rival masculinities around public drinking and its regulation. This typically occurs in situations that impose a surface order on groups of people without resort to open violence in a mutual relation of power, submission and evasion.

Participants related episodes where men engage in violence to impress women and mates or spoke about the public masculine status and enhanced self-image that they could acquire by successfully victimising other males. A few occasions suggested the significance of some aggressors wanting to punish what they saw as unconventional male behaviour.[5] Patrons who react violently to trivial insults reflect the ongoing importance of the attainment and protection of male honour, but a commitment to quick and full retaliation was not typical. Among most, this honour was only seriously threatened by backing down in the face of a major insult or attack. The need to respond had to be balanced against the physical risk of injury and the other likely effects of involvement. Even without serious consequences, participation in violence has a nuisance value that these young men were well aware of. It often effectively ended a good night out. Intoxicated and aggressive men who respond violently to minor affronts are ridiculed and laughed about in accounts of the actions of others. A much broader range of security officers and drinkers were drawn to watching, talking and joking about violence than the actual numbers willing to readily participate in it. A controlled masculine style marked the young Newcastle men, whose everyday work and study routines were counterbalanced by regular occasions of rowdy group drinking.

Members of the Maitland/Hunter group engaged in more regular aggressive heavy drinking and risk-taking activity, in keeping with a form of masculine protest characteristic of young men with marginal social status, restricted work prospects and minor criminal histories. These males felt a compelling need to respond to all minor insults and a few of them made use of these as opportunities for involvement in violence. Most disturbingly, the more violent participants had no evident sense of outrage about their own victimization, such as in very serious attacks from security guards they had provoked. The experiences and actions of several suggest a steady progression of brutalisation, belligerence and violent performance, with public drinking venues as an arena for key moments in a dangerous 'violentisation' process (Athens, 1989). Some also consciously set off conflicts with security, staff or other drinkers as part of their own developed practice of social disruption and appreciation of violence as a key element in a fragmented night shaped around risk-taking, disorder and unpredictability.

But the majority understood themselves as men who are self-controlled and without need to react violently unless compelled by self-defence. Within a recurrent discourse of the ideal masculine subject as both reasoning and agentive, they held contradictory views about whether or not violence could be avoided as a matter of choice and most appeared to overstate the extent to which individuals could consciously avoid fights. Paradoxically, this reasoning masculine subjectivity can also coexist with evident concerns about safety. Although some denied feeling unsafe, other remarks and actions suggested a sharp public sense of dangerous people and places.

A similar respect for a rational masculine subjectivity was reflected in the security officers' idealised view of their own controlled professionalism. In their accounts of mutual conflicts, both drinkers and security in turn constructed each other as being irrational and volatile actors who were illegitimately masculine and therefore not meriting respect. This restrained pattern contrasts with the more aggressive style of protest masculinity that remains among a minority of socially marginal drinkers. It also differs from the masculine pleasure of occasional carnivalesque outbreaks of uncontrolled group disorder and violence that break up normal expectations about social interaction. These occasions are still valued by many less regularly violent patrons (and possibly less openly by some security) in the increasingly regulated and normalised environments of contemporary public leisure.[6]

Conclusion

The link between crime and male offending is now being explored internationally in a new research approach that eschews essentialism and understands crime as a resource for the social achievement of masculinity. The most theoretically sophisticated of these accounts stress the complex effects of social structure and agency that can shape both offending and nonoffending (Connell, 1995; Jefferson, 1996; Messerschmidt, 1997). This study demonstrates the dynamic nature of this crime and masculinity link and how it differently shapes views about safety, danger and violence held by drinkers and security officers working in drinking venues. These views are constructed around the protection of social status, the informal policing of public gender and the occasional attractions of carnivalesque disorder. Matters of honour and social respect can be especially significant to male drinkers and security officers and vitally shape the interaction between them, but this research suggests major variations in the significance of honour and how this is linked to different individual and group masculinities in varying social circumstances.

Study results included an unexpected stress on safety and a belief that in many circumstances a controlled withdrawal from conflicts could reflect and shore up a respectable masculine identity. This belief balances some of the general attraction of recreational violence that is part of everyday masculinities. Of course, this is partly possible as the social contexts of mens' collective drinking offer a range of other behaviour, including homo-social bonding, high rates of consumption, loudness and minor rule-breaking, that establish masculine identities. Nevertheless, this signals a general need to explain masculine disengagement from conflict and violence and its relation to various complementary and rival ways that masculinity is pursued, particularly as 'projects' of collective social action (Connell, 1995). The latter were reflected in the different patterns of conflict among the drinkers and security officers studied. The more overtly aggressive group of marginalised young men was inclined to retaliatory violence with less interest in the negative consequences. This clearly contrasted the situation of most drinkers and security officers who construct a form of reasoned masculine identity for themselves, and in so doing reconcile withdrawal from conflict with maleness and redefine much violence as unpleasurable.

The extent of this ethic of restraint could suggest the effectiveness of an internalised pattern of risk-management and social governance linked to contemporary public health campaigns that include promotion of responsible drinking and drug use by specifically targeting young people as agents of self-regulation (Moore, 2002; Petersen & Lupton, 1996). But a continuing historical difference in responses to social conflict among 'respectable' and 'disrespectable' working-class men seems to be reflected here. In this study, the persisting influence of this dichotomy was more obvious than a postindustrial masculine crisis shaping patterns of drinking-related violence and its regulation by private security that has been suggested in similar contemporary research (Hobbs et al. 2003; Monaghan, 2002; Winlow, 2001). There was scant evidence that even 'respectable' participants adopted such messages about responsible drinking as being relevant to their own persistent heavy drinking or real likelihood of unavoidable victimisation in some contexts. Any intention to avoid or minimise violent and dangerous confrontations with other males is an outcome that should be lauded, and it appears that many young men have learnt to moderate their own involvement in such incidents. Nevertheless, it is noteworthy that these campaigns do much less to challenge a view of masculine self-agency that gives an exaggerated impression about individual capacities to avoid violence, control risk and remain safe across a range of public contexts.

Endnotes

1 A full analysis of these security officer focus groups is forthcoming.

2 One learnt about the potential danger of drinking and illegal drugs from his drug-dealing mother ('I was always around home invasions and robberies and shit — she was a bad alcoholic'). This comment referred to the chances of being physically victimised when drunk or stoned rather than long-term negative outcomes.

3 Some comments generalised about this to suggest that all drinkers are potentially violent due to the effects of alcohol: 'Anybody can have one too many and once you have too many it don't matter who you are you are going to try and fight someone.' This appeared to be an instance of deviance disavowal by a regularly violent drinker.

4 There is no doubt that this claim was partly motivated by an occupational interest in distancing contemporary events from the adverse historical reputation of security in licensed venues. At the conclusion of one focus group (and as a tape recorder loudly clicked off) officers returned to talking about the critical need for an implied physical threat in their work. A very experienced male officer summed up discussion by noting that 'there is always that intimidation factor in this job'. Hobbs et al. (2003) also concluded that actual violence and the credible threat of violence remain as vital elements in contemporary bouncing.

5 The practice of masculine gender policing in and around night-time drinking locations in Newcastle also takes the form of assaults directed at gay/homosexual men who fail to hide their sexual identities or are regarded by assailants as too flamboyant in appearance or behaviour (George, 2005). For New South Wales examples of the policing of male public identity in antihomosexual homicides, see Tomsen (2002).

6 It is likely that the greater regulation and use of surveillance in licensed venues and urban public space is linked to the recent Australian phenomenon of disorderly youth 'swarming' at private suburban parties (Toohey, 2003).

Acknowledgments

This research was generously supported by funds from New South Wales Health and the Crime Prevention Division of the New South Wales Attorney-General's Department. Focus groups were organised by Key Insights (a Newcastle social research consultancy) and completed with assistance from Shane Homan and Donna Russo. I give particular thanks to Ken Polk for help with references and to Bob Connell and James Messerschmidt for their comments on a draft of this article.

References

Acher, J. (1994). Violence between men. In Archer, J. (Ed.), *Male violence*. London: Routledge.

Athens, L. (1989). *The creation of dangerous violent criminals*. London: Routledge.

Bourgeois, P. (1996). *In search of respect: Selling crack in El Barrio*. Cambridge, UK: Cambridge University Press.

Briscoe, S., & Donnelly, N. (2001). *Assaults on licensed premises in inner-urban areas*. Alcohol Studies Bulletin, No. 2. Sydney, Australia: New South Wales Bureau of Crime Statistics and Research.

Briscoe, S., & Donnelly, N. (2002). *Young adult's experience of responsible service practice in New South Wales*. Alcohol Studies Bulletin, No. 3. Sydney, Australia: New South Wales Bureau of Crime Statistics and Research.

Collier, R. (1998). *Masculinities, crime and criminology*. London: Sage.

Collins, J. (1989). Alcohol and interpersonal violence: Less than meets the eye. In N. Weiner & M. Wolfgang (Eds.), *Pathways to criminal violence* (pp. 49–67). Newbury Park, CA: Sage.

Collins, J., Noble, G., Poynting, S., & Tabar, P. (2000). *Kebabs, kids, cops and crime: Ethnicity and crime in Australia*. Sydney, Australia: Pluto Press.

Connell, R.W. (1995). *Masculinities*. St. Leonards, Australia: Allen and Unwin.

Fagan, J. (1990). Intoxication and aggression. In M. Tonry & J.Q. Wilson (Eds.), *Crime and justice: A review of research on drugs and crime* (vol. 13; pp. 241–320). Chicago: Chicago University Press.

Felson, R., & Steadman, H. (1983). Situations and processes leading to criminal violence. *Criminology*, *21*, 59.

George, A. (2005). Gay citizenship and the policing of anti-gay violence in New South Wales. Unpublished doctoral dissertation, University of Newcastle, Australia.

Hobbs, D., Hadfield, P., Lister, S., & Winlow, S. (2003). *Bouncers: Violence and governance in the night-time economy*. Oxford, UK: Oxford University Press.

Homel, R., Tomsen S., & Thommeny, J. (1991). The problem of violence on licensed premises: The Sydney study. In T. Stockwell, E. Lang, & P. Rydon (Eds.), *The licensed drinking environment: Current research in Australia and New Zealand* (pp. 33–40). Melbourne, Australia: National Centre for Research into the Prevention of Drug Abuse.

Homel, R., Tomsen, S., & Thommeny, J. (1992). Public drinking and violence: Not just an alcohol problem. *Journal of Drug Issues*, *22*, 679–697.

Homel, R., & Clark, J. (1994). The prediction and prevention of violence in pubs and clubs. *Crime Prevention Studies*, 3, 1–46.

Homel, R., Hauritz, M., Wortley, R., McIlwain, G., & Carvolth, R. (1997). Preventing alcohol-related crime through community action: The Surfers Paradise Safety Action Project. *Crime Prevention Studies*, 7, 35–90.

Lang, E., Stockwell, T., Rydon, P., & Lockwood, A. (1995). Drinking settings and problems of intoxication. *Addiction Research*, 3, 141–149.

Marsh, P., & Kibby, K. (1992). *Drinking and public disorder*. London: Portman Group.

Messerschmidt, J. (1997). *Crime as structured action: Gender, race, class and crime in the making*. Thousand Oaks, CA: Sage.

Monaghan, L. (2002). Regulating unruly bodies: Work tasks, conflict and violence in Britain's night-time economy. *The British Journal of Sociology*, *53*(3), 403–429.

Moore, D. (2002). Opening up the cul-de-sac of youth drug studies: A contribution to the establishment of some alternative truths. *Contemporary Drug Problems*, *29*(1), 13–63.

Naffine, N. (1997). *Feminism and criminology*. St. Leonards, Australia: Allen and Unwin.

Petersen, A., & Lupton, D. (1996). *The new public health: Health and self in the age of risk*. St. Leonards, Australia: Allen and Unwin.

Polk, K. (1994). *When men kill: Scenarios of masculine violence*. Melbourne, Australia: Cambridge University Press.

Stockwell, T., Lang, E., & Rydon, P. (1993). High risk drinking settings: The association of serving and promotional practices with harmful drinking. *Addiction*, 88, 1519–1526.

Toohey, P. (2003, July 12–13). Party animals. *The Weekend Australian Magazine*, 16–19.

Tomsen, S., Homel, R., & Thommeny, J. (1990). The causes of public violence: Situational and other factors in drinking-related assaults. In D. Chappell et al. (Eds.), *Australian violence: Contemporary perspectives* (pp. 177–194). Canberra, Australia: Australian Institute of Criminology.

Tomsen, S. (1996). Ruling men? Some comments on masculinity and juvenile justice. *The Australian and New Zealand Journal of Criminology*, *29*, 191–194.

Tomsen, S. (1997). A top night: Social protest, masculinity and the culture of drinking violence. *The British Journal of Criminology*, *37*(1), 90–102.

Tomsen, S. (2002). *Hatred, murder and male honour: Anti-homosexual homicides in New South Wales, 1980–2000*. Research and Public Policy Series No 43. Canberra, Australia: Australian Institute of Criminology.

Wells, S., Graham, K., & West, P. (1998). 'The good, the bad, and the ugly': Responses by security staff to aggressive incidents in public drinking settings. *Journal of Drug Issues*, *28*, 817–836.

Winlow, S. (2001). *Badfellas: Crime, tradition and new masculinities*. Oxford, UK: Berg.

[16]

Hard men, shop boys and others: embodying competence in a masculinist occupation

Lee F. Monaghan

Abstract

Emerging studies on private security work in Britain's night-time economy explore important sociological themes such as masculinities and violence. Contributing rich ethnography to this literature, and in furthering an embodied sociology, this paper describes the gendered construction of competency among 'bouncers' or door supervisors within the context of their potentially violent work. Centrally, it explores the door supervisors' variable bodily capital (comprising body build and acquired techniques of the body) alongside normative limits to their violence. Here physicality is central to the practicalities of doorwork, risk management and the embodiment of dominant and subordinate masculinities. Within doorwork culture, embodied typifications such as 'hard men', 'shop boys' and others (eg, 'bullies' and 'nutters') are related to assessments of possible violence against doorstaff, the delineation of (flexible) boundaries for their own (in)appropriate violence against 'problematic' customers and the construction of competent identity. Besides contributing empirical data to the literature this paper underscores the integrative potential of embodiment for social scientists *and* urges policy makers to appreciate the degree to which (potential) violence is embodied in the night-time economy.

Embodying social studies of masculinities and violence

There is an important and growing body of social scientific literature on masculinities and violence (eg, Cavanagh *et al.*, 2001; Tomsen, 1997). Recent contributions, following a 'somatic turn' and a burgeoning literature on the social aspects of the human body (Shilling, 1993), are also beginning to explore embodiment as an integral component of male coded violence and the performance of plural masculinities (eg, Messerschmidt, 1999). Concrete studies of fairly precise areas of social life, including research on 'bouncers' or nightclub and pub security staff, similarly forge links between the sociologies of masculinities, violence and the body (Winlow, 2001). Here attention is given to the ways in which physicality and violent bodily potential – attributes associated with traditional working-class masculinities – have been transformed into marketable assets in Britain's fast expanding liminal night-time economy (Hobbs *et al.*, 2000). Contributing substantively to this literature, this paper provides detailed ethnographic insights into the social construction of competency among doorstaff in Southwest Britain. Formally, this participant observational study also supports arguments for an 'embodied sociology' (Williams and Bendelow, 1998) which is grounded in the inescapable corporeality and emotional vicissitudes of everyday and everynight social life.

Embodiment, as cogently argued by Williams and Bendelow (1998), has been neglected as an explicit theme within social theory. This is now being redressed but, as stated by Wacquant (1995), what is surprising is that in all this extant theorising there is relatively little empirical work on the concrete incorporating practices and sometimes messy empirical realities of actual flesh and blood bodies (see, for example, Vol. 49, No. 3 of *The Sociological Review*). Recent and emerging ethnographic research on nightclub and pub security work has the potential to help redress this lacuna (Monaghan, 2002). Drawing parallels with qualitative research on 'bouncers' undertaken by Hobbs and colleagues (eg, Hobbs *et al.*, 2002; Lister *et al.*, 2000; Winlow *et al.*, 2001), and referencing other social scientific work on the body, masculinities and violence (eg, Athens, 1997; Connell, 1995; Elias, 2000; Mauss, 1973), this paper furthers efforts to bring 'lived bodies' (Williams and Bendelow, 1998) into social theory.

After outlining the research, this paper describes how the door supervisors' 'bodily capital' (Wacquant, 1995) – comprising body build and acquired techniques of the body (Mauss, 1973) – is implicated in hierarchical in-group relations, typifications and gendered selfhood. Within this potentially hazardous occupation, bodies categorised through shared vocabularies of body idiom (Goffman, 1959) are thoroughly implicated in discourses and practices pertaining to male-coded violence. And, because biology is never determinate of the social (Shilling, 1993), working bodies designated as 'female' may also figure in constructions of dominant/violent masculinity. The remainder of the paper then explores the degree to which physical violence by and to bodies is normalised and routinised bodily labour among doorstaff in their risk environment. Following Winlow *et al.* (2001: 538), attention focuses upon the ways in which the precise boundaries of legitimate violence (representing markers for occupational competence and gender identity) are variable and debated within the door supervisors' embodied habitus.

The research: an embodied ethnography

While contact with certain key informants and research sites persist, most of this participant observational study was undertaken between 1997 and 2001 in seven city-centre licensed premises in Southwest Britain. Contingencies and personal circumstances interrupted fieldwork (no data were recorded in 1998, for example), but social access and re-entry was always facilitated given my links with a head doorman (who informally recruited doorstaff) and my ethnographic immersion in bodybuilding gyms (Monaghan, 2001). Indeed, commercial gyms, often serving as informal recruitment sites for doorstaff, were invaluable in allowing me to get into this subterranean occupation.

As a reflexive ethnographer I know my male gender, relative youth (under 30 during the main study period) and bodily capital (muscular, weighing approximately 16 ½ stone at six-foot), represented resources for getting in and getting on with this study. Certainly, I personally possess a non-violent self-image (*cf.* Athens, 1997) but my embodied social history consisting of lifting weights and boxing – practices contributing to my own habitus, cultural capital and dispositions (*cf.* Bourdieu, 1984) – rendered me willing and able to assume an active membership role (Adler and Adler, 1987). Similar to Winlow (2001), this meant I became a 'bouncer' in order to study their world. And, while I never intentionally concealed my academic interests, I was primarily seen as a doorman by fieldwork contacts. Noting this is important because 'the social role of the participant observer and the images which respondents have of him [*sic*] have a decisive influence on the character of the data collected' (Vidich, 1955: 354).

I use pseudonyms when referring to licensed premises and their inhabitants, and I have changed certain background details to preserve anonymity. These establishments varied in their size, customer capacity, appearance, mood, opening times and number of doorstaff employed. Uncle Sam's, for example, was a 'super-pub' that closed before midnight, held up to 2,000 people and employed approximately ten doorstaff at the weekend. Sunshine, a club with longer opening times, employed six doorstaff at the weekend and catered for up to 1,000 customers. Although there was variability between these premises, all catered for a predominantly young, white, heterosexual clientele. Time spent at each site varied, ranging from one night to fourteen months. All but one site was located in the same city, employing a network of doormen and a few doorwomen who often knew or knew of each other. (The ratio of doormen to doorwomen was in the region of 10:1.) Although sampling was largely opportunistic, capitalising upon links and clustered employment opportunities within a specific urban locale, fieldwork was undertaken on a time-sampling basis at various sites thereby enhancing theoretical representativeness. Reference to ethnography conducted elsewhere in Britain (Hobbs *et al.*, 2002; Winlow, 2001) and published insider accounts (eg, Thompson, 2000), also lends greater external validity to knowledge claims made in this study.

Regarding the characteristics of doorstaff – a misnomer in that working 'on the doors' often entails working away from building access points – most contacts were young men of working-class origin (*cf.* Winlow, 2001: 98). Ages ranged from 19 to 45. Most were in their late twenties/early thirties and white, though some were of ethnic minority status (eg, Middle Eastern, African, Afro-Caribbean). Fieldwork stints, consisting of between one and five working visits per week, ranging between three and fourteen hours per shift, brought me into contact with over 60 doormen. And while many contacts were fleeting (in an occupation with a high staff turnover), others were more prolonged and sustained. All contacts presented, in accord with hegemonic masculinity (Connell, 1995), an image of heterosexuality, including the few doorwomen with whom I regularly talked (N = 5). While a significant minority of contacts were 'officially' unemployed (especially younger doormen working midweek in one popular nightclub with a late license), most combined part-time doorwork with full-time employment in the formal economy. (Similarly, see Thompson, 2000, on the often secondary nature of doorwork.) Occupations included: tax inspector, salesman, carpenter, scaffolder, gym owner, trainee accountant, office clerk, karate instructor, chef, mechanic and aircraft engineer.

A grounded theory approach (Glaser and Strauss, 1967) was adopted during concurrent data generation and analysis. Word processed files, containing ethnographic observations written as soon as possible after fieldwork, were read and re-read. This lead to the identification of emergent themes and the development of a flexible coding scheme which, in turn, strategically informed subsequent fieldwork visits. Importantly, the coding scheme also served as a basis for indexing segments of data which were stored in computer generated text files and readily accessed for systematic grounded analysis (Weaver and Atkinson, 1994).

Bodily capital

Similar to other manual workers labouring under conditions of deskilling and casualization (Connell, 1995: 55), door supervisors are largely defined in relation to their potentially forceful bodies. The physical body is their economic asset. For these predominantly male workers, bodily capital may be transformed into other forms of capital such as income and masculine validating recognition (*cf.* Wacquant, 1995). Their bodily capital comprises two main dimensions: body build (size, weight, height and general appearance of the physique) and techniques of the body (Mauss, 1973) such as fighting potential and an ability physically to control violent situations. Both dimensions are intimately related to gendered, working-class constructions of occupational competency (Winlow, 2001) in a night-time economy that encourages drunken hedonism among customers of licensed premises (Hobbs *et al.*, 2000; similarly, see Tomsen, 1997). Certainly, not all doorstaff possess exemplary masculine bodies. Nonetheless, bodily capital is extremely salient in relation to in-group typifications, relations and the forging of masculine identities in their risk environment.

Before data reporting and analysis the partiality of this account should be stressed. Certainly, competence in doorwork culture comprises other physical *and* cognitive dimensions which are relevant for a non-dualist embodied sociology (Williams and Bendelow, 1998). Local knowledge, concentration, an ability to read minute changes in a situation and anticipate potential threats are all important. Other unexplored aspects include the many ways in which door supervisors' exterior bodies are moulded and presented for purposes of territoriality (Lyman and Scott, 1967). Much could be said about 'insulation' (comprising distinct uniforms, use of the body and facial idiom to indicate impenetrability) at the entrances to urban licensed premises. Moreover, while this paper describes aspects of occupational competence (specifically, body build and fighting ability) an important sub-text is that hardness is *mental* as well as physical (*cf.* Jefferson, 1998). While this theme is broached below, exigencies of space prohibit detailed commentary. Nonetheless, it should be recognised that negative sanctions are likely for doorstaff failing to police themselves for signs of emotional weakness. Similarly, given historical civilising processes (Elias, 2000) and mass CCCTV surveillance, the unrestrained expression of raw male-coded emotions (aggression, anger and hate) may incur negative sanctions within and outside of this group. Reduction of an individual's status in masculine hierarchies is the most obvious social risk, sometimes resulting in instant dismissal and unemployment.

Body build

Tomsen (1997), in researching assaults in pubs, states that aspects of popular leisure entail social protest and resistance to middle class morality: for many drinkers, especially young, working-class males, violence provides a liberating sense of release, group pleasure and carnival. Unsurprisingly, managers of popular drinking establishments therefore employ 'bouncers' or doorstaff to supervise and possibly eject patrons (Tomsen, 1997: 100). In minimising security costs these managers typically eschew large door teams in favour of large doormen who derive their authority from the sheer physicality of their bodies (Hobbs *et al.*, 2002). Congruently, given a general perception among doorstaff that occupational hazards are attenuated in smaller security teams, body build represents an imaginary, if not real, resource for minimising the risk of violence to themselves. In this risk environment, bodily size (with its implicit suggestion of violence) is symbolically significant. The majority of workers constituting competent door teams in Southwest Britain were physically large men:

> Fred, a well respected head doorman, will be providing security at a new, large club, and has been consulted by the door agency manager about clothes for his door team: 'He wanted to know what size jackets to get. I mean, we need twenty jackets! I told him not to go pissing about getting lots of different sizes. It's too much messing about. Just get the big ones, 52 inches, like we've got here. A couple of small ones for the women. And if they're too big it's tough. Most of the boys are lumpers [big] anyway. If

he got a few 44 inches they'd fit people like Martin, but if he leaves then were stuck with these [smaller] jackets aren't we?' (Friday 17th September 1999: Sunshine.)

Within doorwork culture, 'common norms [. . .] encourage people to develop their bodies in a manner which symbolises the *social* value placed on individual identities' (Shilling, 2001: 333–4). In an occupation that values the construction and projection of a forceful masculine identity, certain doormen are more highly respected and paid given the sheer physicality of their bodies. Undoubtedly, the displayed sizeable body must also be an effective performative body; big men should also be hard men (Winlow, 2001). Yet, the symbolic centrality of *individual body build* was clear even among doorstaff according significance to other social dimensions such as worker solidarity. Below the intersection of risk and body build was immediately cited followed by reference to teamwork:

> A large group of large 'off duty' doormen were in the club drinking. They introduced themselves to several doormen working tonight: 'Our club is being refurbished, so we've all come out for a good drink. There's fifteen of us but we're not out for any trouble. We get enough of that at work!' As they drank, danced and chatted among themselves, a working doorman approached me: 'Fucking hell! If they had any trouble nobody would stand a chance. Look at the size of them all. And you can see they gel well together, they'd work well as a team. They'd flatten anyone who kicked off'. (Saturday 28th October 2000: Uncle Sam's.)

Body build, which figures in embodied constructions of plural masculinities and the emotional vicissitudes of doorwork culture, is also underscored in the following light-hearted exchange. Here, Fred, the head doorman at Sunshine who obtained work elsewhere, suggests Big K should replace him. However, this 'promotion' was problematic for Big K who, in using his own body as a narrative resource, was wary about working with incompetent doorstaff. For this large doorman, body build was prioritised, comprising height, weight, muscle and body shape:

Big K [with a smile] to Fred:	'That's fucking good isn't it! "Here be head doorman, but I'm taking all the boys with me. Find your own!" It's no good saying "be head doorman" if I've got to find my own boys. And I don't want just anybody here with me either. I don't want any Muppets'.
Fred:	'Well, Odd Job said he'd stay here'.
Big K.:	'I want some big boys here, some huge big fuckers'.
Fred:	'Yeah, well, there's Odd Job and there's Mark there'.
Big K [joking]:	'I said big fuckers. Not a couple of short arses. I want huge fuckers, 6′10″ and 25 stone!' [Mark and Odd Job,

	while muscular, are not very tall. Neither took offence with Big K.]
Fred:	'Well, there's Toby. You know Toby don't you? He's big'. [About 6′4″ and at least 20 stone.]
Big K:	'You must be joking. I don't want them big out here [signalling a large stomach with his hand], I want them big like this [pointing to his chest and shoulders]'. (Friday 17th September 1999: Sunshine.)

Analytically, it is clear that 'bodily norms not only enable individuals to recognise and label others [. . .] but to grade them hierarchically, and stigmatise them in a manner which facilitates discrimination (Goffman, 1963, 1968)' (Shilling, 2001: 337). Such bodily processes, which, in doorwork culture, often revolve around body build, are highly gendered. In the social study of masculinities attention is drawn to the ways in which men exercise power not only over women, but also among themselves. Following Connell (1995) it is important to recognise the plurality of masculinities *and* intra-gender relations that effectively include and exclude different kinds of masculinity. In short, hierarchies exist between men embodying superordinate and subordinate masculinities and the body is the primary vehicle in negotiating this perilous landscape (Courtenay, 2000: 1391).

Empirically, it is apparent that 'competent' doorstaff – typically, men who are tall and muscular – are contrasted physically with others who are subordinate in gendered hierarchies. The previous excerpt, for example, makes brief reference to so-called 'Muppets': a disparaging term used locally to discredit security personnel who do not 'measure up' to the job. So-called 'Muppets' usually have experience providing security at the minimum wage in retail establishments such as burger bars, supermarkets and corner shops; or, from the perspective of experienced nightclub doorstaff, 'Muppets' physically look like they should be working in these 'safer' environments. Sometimes called 'Burger King Bouncers', 'Spar Bouncers' or 'Shop Boys', these types are subordinated and marginalised in doorwork culture. Discrimination against these non-imposing bodies, as indicated below, may also be compounded given competition over security contracts:

> During the early stages of the 'take over' of Presentations the door agency had difficulty recruiting doormen. According to the agency manager no other door agencies in the area were willing to supply men through fear of repercussions. (The owner of the previous door agency was, by all accounts, widely feared.) Only one 'agency' in the city would supply workers: an agency reportedly supplying security staff to supermarkets. Because this firm was not part of the nightclub security scene it was rumoured among several doormen that they were unaware of the potential danger. However, several doormen had deep reservations about these 'extra members' ability to provide effective 'back up'. Most were younger than the established

> doormen (early 20s as opposed to late 20s, 30s), and many were boyish in appearance. Tom described them as 'Shop Boys', and used other derogatory labels: 'Well, with the Tesco tearaways there we'll be all right if we have any shop lifters. Look at them. They're a right bunch of Muppets!' [. . .] We met Bill, one of the door agency managers, in the car park. After being greeted by him, Tom enquired: 'Are the Tesco tearaways here again tonight?' Bill laughed: 'Tesco tearaways?' Mark, another doorman, enquired: 'somebody said that they are only being paid something stupid like £3.60 an hour by their agency'. Bill, disconcerted by this, replied: 'I hope not. They're taking the same risks as you. They should be getting the same'. Oliver, another doorman who was part of the 'in-group', then said: 'Well yeah, I suppose, because if the other doormen [who were displaced following the take over] come here they'll go straight for them. They stand out a mile. They shouldn't be here for their own safety really'. Two days later, older, more experienced 'nightclub' doormen who travelled in from another city replaced the 'Shop Boys'. (Thursday 22nd July 1999: Presentations.)

The accomplishment of dominant masculinity via the impugnment of another person's 'inferior' bodily capital, may be independent of biological sex; 'masculinity can be and is performed by women' (Cheng, 1996; cited by Whitehead, 1999: 59). During this study, several women worked as door supervisor and while they often embodied attributes associated with hegemonic masculinity (competence, force, assertiveness) their real material bodies seldom matched the physical proportions of their male colleagues. Nevertheless, doorwomen are employed in licensed premises because they often effectively regulate female customers. Interestingly, physically smaller doorwomen, similar to doormen, also focused upon body build when discussing and estimating the competency of female colleagues:

> Lisa and Kara, who normally work on Saturday night at Uncle Sam's, were unavailable. Hence, Fred temporarily recruited another doorwoman. This woman looked anorexic, prompting Mark, a doorman, to say to me: 'She's only good as a watcher, an extra pair of eyes to spot trouble. She couldn't do anything if there was any trouble'. Later I talked to Rosy who was also working at Uncle Sam's. She was more disparaging. With an expression of disbelief, this athletically muscular doorwoman said to me: 'What the hell is Fred thinking of? What can she do? She's a twig!' (Saturday 2nd September 2000: Uncle Sam's.)

In a masculinist occupation that values strong working bodies, bodily capital is significant within and across sexual divisions. However, muscle mass – which is often taken as emblematic of masculinity – may also be considered an impediment. The following narrative, which caricatures a 'muscle-bound' male steroid abuser, underscores the earlier point that sizeable bodies must also be fit for action. Interestingly, this 'elitist orientation' is also evidenced among other groups participating in risk or 'edgework' practices that demand an embodied 'ability to maintain control over a situation that verges on complete chaos' (Lyng, 1990: 859). The in-group claim that doorstaff should possess technically competent bodies is explored in greater detail below:

> Tom described a local doorman who weighs about 25 stone and is a heavy user of steroids. After talking disparagingly about his 'excessive' steroid regimen, he scoffed at the man's poor diet and general fitness: 'When they have a food break at work he has six doughnuts with a protein drink! That's what he's like. Once all the doormen were called to a fight. Ten minutes later when it was all over, he appeared puffing and panting. He couldn't get off the window ledge in the fire escape. He was in there having his break, heard the call on the radio, but got stuck. They couldn't put him on the front doors either because if there was trouble in the club, by the time he'd ran upstairs it'd all be over'. (Friday 30th July 1999: Presentations.)

Techniques of the body

Britain's night-time economy is a potentially violent domain wherein doorstaff 'derive an economic rent from their potential to utilise pragmatic violence as a mode of social control' (Lister *et al.*, 2000: 384). In this occupation violent ability is therefore of ultimate social significance (Hobbs *et al.*, 2002). Drawing from anthropology, violent ability may be described as a 'technique of the body' (Mauss, 1973) which, far from being natural or biologically determined, is socially acquired. For doorstaff such bodily capital is instrumental in regulating potentially 'unruly' customers (Monaghan, 2002), minimising the physical risks of doorwork and constructing a sense of competency. Physically smaller doorstaff, in particular, underscored their diligently acquired bodily techniques during informal ethnographic interviews:

> Jack is not a particularly big man. He is approximately 5′7″ and weighs no more than 13 ½ stone. We talked about bodybuilding and steroids. Jack lifts weights but has no intention of 'bulking up' by taking steroids. Reflecting upon his build, he said: 'People sometimes say to me "what if you were working and there was some 6′5″ guy who started a fight?" I just say: "good, it'd work to my advantage because I'd be a lot faster than him"'. Jack claimed he kept his body weight down because of his martial arts, adding he would simply become too slow if, in his terms, 'I was all puffed up'. (Saturday 6th May 2000: Uncle Sam's.)

Doorwomen, in also attempting to dignify their 'dirty work' through an emphasis upon the heroic (Waddington, 1999: 299), similarly stressed the importance of their own body techniques. Such talk, in combination with observed physical enactments, negated any suggestion that they were the 'weaker sex' and at a physical disadvantage in a risk environment. Here, as above, body techniques comprising an 'education in composure' are 'congruent with the needs of a specialised society' (Shilling, 2001: 334) and are implicated in the presentation of self:

> Kara denied the risks of doorwork were magnified because of her sex and slight build: 'I don't think because I'm a woman or because of my size I'm more at risk. I think my size gives me speed, and I can use that with my agility to sort out situations much more effectively'. Later Dez and Kara talked about their involvement in martial arts. Dez described the particular style of Karate he is trained in: 'There's none of this high kicking and flying through the air business. You don't need any of that when you can [tongue in cheek] just poke them in the eyes and knee them in the bollocks'. Kara laughed: 'Yeah, as a woman I just go for a man's weak points. I just aim low all the time'. (Uncle Sam's.)

Martial artists possess a repertoire of violent conduct – 'a panoply of "traditionally efficacious acts" ' (Wacquant, 1995: 88) – that is potentially useful for nightclub security work. However, techniques used to inflict severe bodily injury (eg, broken limbs) are clearly of limited value (Thompson, 2000: 32). The unacceptability, if not impracticality, of potentially fatal fighting techniques is underscored when those possessing them appear to relish the prospect of inflicting grievous bodily harm. Violence has 'real human costs' (Tomsen, 1997: 100) and victimisation is not always trivialised among doorstaff who may otherwise present themselves as heroic and solidly masculine. Worker typifications – specifically, the labelling of certain doorstaff as 'nutters' or 'psychos' – indicate that the bodily execution of fighting techniques is circumscribed within this stratified occupation.

Appropriately performed bodily techniques, which are constitutive of the forceful, gendered and occupationally competent body, are acquired not only through martial arts but also through the experience of providing security in licensed premises. Competency, comprising an ability physically to control carnivalesque bodies in commercial space, is acquired through gendered social learning processes and is attributed to those successfully presenting their own bodies as confident and self-assured:

> While at the gym Mark and Martin [doormen] talked with Kay (female gym instructor) and her female friend. Unsurprisingly, because the gym serves as a recruiting ground for doorstaff, both women know most of the doormen at Uncle Sam's. During conversation discussion centred on Winnie, a new recruit to doorwork. Kay informed us that Winnie was 'quite upset' on Sunday; he complained to her that he knew Fred (head doorman) only had him working at Uncle Sam's 'because he can't get the boys that he really wants'. There was an element of truth in this, but Mark, sensitive

> about not disparaging Winnie, commented: 'Well, I wouldn't go that far. All right, it'd be ideal to just have super hard doormen working there but you can't always have the ideal. And in all fairness, the more that he works there, the more that his confidence increases each time. So, you know, he will tell people that they have got to drink up. One fella, I was showing him the door at the end of the night, and he was pissed and getting a bit shirty [aggressive]. Winnie was stood there with me. I pushed this bloke to Winnie and he could have gone 'what?' [lifting his hands up in the air and looking flustered] but he took him out. All right, he took him out like this [at arm's length] and ended up in the street. But he's willing to have a go'. (Saturday 18th March 2000: The Gym.)

In summary, the embodiment of competence and force within Britain's night-time economy is constitutive of masculine and occupational identity among doormen and a few doorwomen. Bodies, which are sizeable and/or versed in forceful action, fulfil occupational imperatives and are central in the construction, presentation and performance of a situationally 'appropriate' (authoritative, dominant) gendered self. Body build, specialised fighting ability and/or apprenticeships into the bodily habits of doorwork are economically valued and are implicated in the social construction of occupational competence. Of course, the skilful deployment of physical violence is the ultimate validation of the worker's social, cultural and economic worth: doorstaff must be willing and able to put themselves into an embodied stream of violent conduct. Yet, as suggested by the typification 'nutter', their violence and talk of such violence also occurs within and constitutes normative limits. Again, in furthering an 'embodied sociology' (Williams and Bendelow, 1998), the following makes bodies explicit when exploring shared and individual boundaries for the competent door supervisors' violence.

Embodiment, (in)appropriate violence and competency

While violence is normalised and routinised bodily labour among doorstaff, such action is circumscribed. Discourses and the performance of fighting skills are culturally bounded albeit within an enacted environment wherein the *precise boundaries* of violence (eg, when to use it, against whom, what level is appropriate) are irresolvable (Winlow *et al.*, 2001: 538). In short, there are general, though, as suggested below, highly permeable and individualised *bodily limits* beyond which violence (once instigated) should not be used by competent doorstaff:

> Several doormen recounted a past violent incident where Barry, a doorman who was also present in the discussion, reportedly stamped on somebody's head. Garet disagreed with kicking people when they were down: 'If you can't finish 'em off with them [looking at his two fists] then you shouldn't

bother'. Barry dissented: 'Nah. Fuck 'em. I'll do anything. I'll bite their nose or ears off if I have to, even take their eyes out'. Garet had different views. Barry justified his position: I used to think like you [Garet]. Once I hit this fella to the floor and he was going "no, I've had enough, that's it". So, I left him alone like. He got up and whacked me over the back of the head. No. That's never gonna happen again. No way, no chance. I'll finish 'em off whatever way I can. I don't give a fuck now. It's either you or them'. Clayton, an older doorman renowned for his fighting ability, caught the last part of this conversation. He made an interesting comment about moderating his violence:

Clayton: 'I'm very reluctant to use my right hand. I'll always use my left 'cause I had a very scary experience. Very scary. I was fighting with this bloke and I hit him there [pointing to Garet's chest]. I broke eight of his ribs with my right hand. He went back and hit his head against a stone wall and was knocked unconscious. He was in intensive care after that. I was OK in that the police were looking for a white man. They were told a white man did it [Clayton is black]. But, no. Now on I use my left'.

Oxo interjected: 'Yeah, it'd be on your conscience if he died'. (Monday 18th November 1997: Murphy's.)

Expressed Ideas concerning the (in)appropriateness of doorstaff violence are contingent, varying between and among these workers doing plural masculinities. Such talk, which may be related to risk management, masculine hierarchies and competency, is also thoroughly embodied. Other studies on violent masculine cultures such as football hooligans (King, 2001) and the police (Hunt, 1996) highlight similar processes but the bodies in such work have something of an 'absent presence' (Shilling, 1993). Bodies, however, matter (Messerschmidt, 1999). Physical bodies, which are topical for doorstaff qua expressive bodies during interaction rituals (Collins, 2000; cited by King, 2001: 577), are divided and classified according to their perceived ability to inflict and absorb punishment. Vulnerable parts of the victim's body (eg, the head, nose, ears or eyes) may be out of bounds for security staff using (un)acceptable parts of their own dominating bodies (eg, the feet, teeth or right hand) at one time, only later to be reviewed given changing circumstances, experiences and definitions of the situation.[1]

Other micro-interactionist studies exploring shifting orientations to physical violence, or rather, the appropriateness of violence from the perspectives of socially located actors, are valuable but they again need to make gendered bodies explicit. Violent careers and acts, following Athens (1997), for example, may be related to the self-images actors possess, their generalized others and interpretations of the situation (eg, the need to defend oneself from attack, deal with a frustrating situation or somebody deemed malicious) but such definitions and associated actions are also embodied and related to constructions of masculinity which are enumerated in Britain's night-time economy.

The doorman below, forming what Athens (1997) terms a malefic interpretation, takes pleasure from his 'appropriate' violence against a *malicious*[2] customer and, in describing this, asserts his own masculinity, i.e. economic worth and bodily ability to practice 'territoriality' (Lyman and Scott, 1967). As suggested, there is also an embodied, situated sensuality to 'excessive' violence construed as legitimate on commercial grounds (Winlow, 2001):

> Bar staff shouldn't have to take any abuse off customers. Last week when I was working a man threw a bottle at one of the bar staff. Well, two of us dragged him out. We flew down the stairs, hitting his head against the wall as we turned the corners. (He laughs.) It was on camera but we said to the club manager that we were going down so fast that we couldn't turn him properly. And when we got him outside we gave him a couple of digs over a car bonnet. (Wednesday 2nd February 2000: Uncle Sam's.)

For vigilant working bodies, the need physically to defend oneself and others, practice 'turf defence' (remove transgressors) in response to territorial encroachment (Lyman and Scott, 1967) and maintain gendered/occupational authority over disrespectful customers taking 'time out' from 'normal social rules' (Tomsen, 1997: 100), render their (indeterminate levels of) violence appropriate. Analytically, it should, of course, be recognised that such occupationally legitimated violence may largely become habituated with occupational group norms, becoming taken-for-granted and part of the natural facts of life (Schutz, 1970). And, if such violence is inextricably bounded by everynight normal life, it may require little or no reflection; it may simply be done. As above, CCTV surveillance may not necessarily check violent trajectories and actions among doorstaff routinely dealing with and in violence. However, if doorstaff wish to avoid instant dismissal and/or police arrest, their *witnessed* violence must remain reasonable and accountable to non-group members. Accounting practices – or 'remedial work' intended by violent actors to obfuscate their culpability in the events described (Cavanagh *et al.*, 2001) – may be relatively unproblematic for experienced doorstaff (*cf.* Lister *et al.*, 2000: 395) but discernible parameters delineate the appropriateness of their pragmatic *and* retributive violence: it is spatially contingent, dependent upon different social audiences and enactments of the 'mindful' body. Absence of witnesses in back-stage regions (Goffman, 1959), for example, render fire escapes and alleys behind clubs more 'appropriate' settings for the 'competent' door supervisors' wilful violence (*cf.* Lister *et al.*, 2000: 396). If executed on the dance floor, however, the normalised violence reported above would be much more questionable and questioned.

The appropriateness of doorstaff violence is clearly multi-faceted. Such action is, however, also intimately related to the bodily, affectual dimensions of group belonging. Following Mellor and Shilling's (1996) corporeal re-reading of classical social theory, bodily co-presence in a tightly bounded group promotes sensual solidarities, effervescent sociality and bloody revenge against 'others' who assault the collective body. Fieldwork observations and published insider accounts (Thompson, 2000) confirm this. That said, embodied survival ties are not always realised among fragmented and individualised workers displaying cool loyalties, and instant dismissal is likely for those eschewing 'appropriate' (yet unspecified levels of) violence in front stage regions (Goffman, 1959). Elsewhere in Britain such workers are typified as 'empty shirts' (Winlow *et al.*, 2001), suggesting they are *dis-embodied* in contrast to competent security staff:

> A few weeks ago Butty, a doorman working at a nearby club, was violently attacked on the front door by a gang of drunken men. Today I talked to Winnie who recounted the events, the severity of Butty's injuries and other information: 'They threw a metal post at him and cut an artery in his head'. I asked whether Butty had since returned to work? Winnie said he had, despite needing hospital treatment; however, four other doormen were 'sacked' because 'the lot of them ran inside the club while Butty was being battered on the front door'. My informant and I knew that violent intervention by these other doorstaff was not simply accepted, it was unequivocally expected. (Saturday 22nd July 2000: Supermarket.)

Doorstaff are often stereotyped as 'licensed thugs' and, in Tomsen's (1997) study, are deemed responsible for the majority of serious injuries inflicted on drinkers. No doubt, the door supervisors' willingness to use violence may be compounded by in-group concerns over the generation and protection of male honour (Tomsen, 1997: 95) as well as preserving the physical integrity of their own flesh and blood bodies. However, occupational norms establishing the appropriateness of *non*-violence also emerged during this ethnography. Again, bodies, read through shared vocabularies of body idiom (Goffman, 1959), are implicated in the construction of these group-based norms. Drunken customers exhibiting a loss of self-control, sometimes becoming grotesque, leaky, carnivalesque bodies (Bakhtin, 1968), for example, are often problematic (embarrassing, irritating, corporeally polluting) for others but this does not in and of itself render them legitimate targets for the majority of doorstaff I talked with. Some of my contacts, in enacting the 'civilised body' (Elias, 2000) or conformist models or masculinity, privately disparaged others for using force indiscriminately against intoxicated bodies. Others were condemned for routinely using unnecessary violence against physically smaller, non-threatening customers. Similar to football hooligans who forge definitions of correct conduct in an honour based culture (King, 2001), doorstaff denigrated 'unmanly' colleagues for attacking unequals. They were, in their terms, 'bullies' who 'take liberties' and who thus should not be working the doors.

Nonetheless, violence, or the possibility of violence, constitutes the door supervisors' working environment irrespective of the predominant individual types found within these communities. Similar to the police, doorstaff may wish to avoid trouble (*cf.* Waddington, 1999: 294) but conflict occurs within and around licensed premises for many reasons and takes many forms. Unruly customers and potential customers sometimes argue and fight among themselves, they become confrontational with security staff who are charged with various regulatory work tasks (eg, stopping fights, screening entrants, keeping doorways clear, asking people to leave at the end of the night) and, in the absence of a 'restraining judgement' (Athens, 1997), violence ensues (Monaghan, 2002). In this context, doorstaff violence and talk of such violence – rather than being wholly negative – is functional. Not only is violence practical in various situations, talk about violence constitutes subjective social identities and delimits embodied group and personal boundaries. Occupational discourses of violence, similar to discourses of risk in athletic subcultures (Monaghan, 2001), are constitutive of socially competent bodies and identities. Consider the following extract where a doorman impugns the masculinity of two violent colleagues and, in so doing, makes claims in respect of his own position in gendered hierarchies. The inappropriateness of certain bodies (and body parts) for the competent door supervisor's violence, the failure to form restraining judgements and an observed inability to physically dominate 'when it counts' all figure in his construction and presentation of self:

> Wayne and Tom talked about the recent violent episode which resulted in Odd Job and Barney being arrested and charged with Actual Bodily Harm. Wayne then disparaged these two men: '. . . Barney is just head shot. He's a nutter. Earlier that night he kicked this boy in the head when he was out of it on the floor. There was no need for it. I'm not against giving someone a kicking if they're fighting or if they go for one of the boys, but you don't just do it for no reason like that. Odd Job is a lump, but he only throws his weight about with boys who are smaller than him. He's a bully. Barney will go for people as big as him, but he's mad. [. . .] Odd Job is a liability. He goes throwing his weight around with smaller boys. There's this boy who comes in here, a lumper [big] he is and he has quite a few friends who are a lot smaller than him. If Odd Job hit one of this fella's friends he would batter Odd Job and we'd have a handful getting him out. There's nothing to Odd Job. I worked at Lion's Bar once and there was a call at Sunshine [violent incident in club next door] so we went round to help. Now, you don't go down if you're punched around the eye. Odd Job, who was working at Sunshine, went down on the floor though after a punch to the eye'. (Saturday 11th March 2000: Uncle Sam's.)

Such disparaging 'body talk' always relates to third parties. 'Bullies', 'nutters' and those unable to 'take a punch', similar to 'shop boys' and 'Muppets', represent 'other' types who are contrasted with the competent narrator. For my contacts, violence personally executed was rarely considered inappropriate (unwarranted and/or excessive) in the particular circumstances encountered or recounted. However, a small minority of doorstaff – representing negative or deviant cases – relished using force which their colleagues considered wholly inappropriate. Their dominating styles of body use, it seems, emerged not specifically for the collective good but primarily to reinforce their own fragile sense of masculinity. These individuals, as 'self-image promoters' (Toch, 1969), 'habitually precipitate[d] violent situations in which they [could] demonstrate their power, courage and importance' (Horowitz and Schwartz, 1974: 240). Sid, for example, a young inexperienced doorman, reportedly took 'sleepers' (i.e. drunken customers who had fallen asleep) out of one club in a headlock. To my surprise, Sid, rather than being embarrassed, proudly confirmed this when I asked him about it. Because his means were primarily self-serving and ill suited to collectively valued ends he was privately disparaged by several other doormen.

One may question why such behaviour towards non-threatening bodies is tolerated among competent doorstaff. Attention to social context is informative; specifically, the occupational imperative to impose authority and order in licensed premises and the constant possibility that doorstaff will be assaulted by more able, recalcitrant bodies. As noted by Tomsen (1997: 95), bloody violence against 'bouncers' is no mere abstraction in public drinking venues. Here door supervisors who are disparaged by their peers for their inappropriate violence may redeem themselves. One doorman, after agreeing with a colleague's statement that Sid 'needs a good battering, he thinks he's invincible but he's not' said: 'The one good thing about Sid is that if it kicks off he's there right away. He's not afraid to get stuck in' (Friday 30th July 1999: Presentations). Within this risk environment, some head doormen will even actively recruit deviant types such as 'nutters' given their violent reputation. Their unrestrained violence may, in premises populated by strong, boisterous bodies, represent an asset rather than a total liability:

> Fred wanted extra doormen for a new club. Talking to several other doormen, he asked about potential recruits: 'Aye, Odd Job, what about Barney?' Odd Job raised his eyebrows: 'Yeah? I was working with him at this one club, and he picked up one of them things [pointing to a metal post used to cordon off queues] and threw it at somebody!' Fred, aware of Barney's reputation for fighting, added tongue in cheek: 'Well, I'll put him in a corner somewhere quite, and chain him to a fire extinguisher so he can't go off causing trouble. Anyway, we need a few people like him. This new club is a sports bar. There'll be loads of Rugby boys [i.e. physically large and potentially unruly men] drinking in there'. (Saturday 4th September 1999: Sunshine.)

Though, even for Fred, there were limits. For example, Fred described Sid as a 'bully boy' and vowed never to employ him. Fred kept his word even though there were occasions when he desperately needed more doormen and

Sid had enquired about work. And, after employing Barney for several weeks, Fred dismissed him following a witnessed violent assault on a customer. After this very public incident, which resulted in Barney's arrest, Fred said: 'He's mad. He's a time bomb waiting to go off' (Friday 11th February 2000: Uncle Sam's).

Finally, it may be assumed that doorstaff with criminal records for violence have, by definition, acted inappropriately thus rendering them unsuitable for nightclub security work. Certainly, the public police and local licensing authorities take this view, seeking to limit employment opportunities for doorstaff with prior convictions. However, some doorstaff claim that 'you constantly have to step outside the law to do the job' (Thompson, 200: 113) and convictions are actually indicative of valuable doorwork experience. In the extract below, Kara claims authoritative attempts to ban doormen with violent criminal records will have certain unintended consequences vis-à-vis the efficient policing of busy urban nightclubs. Here conformist models of masculinity (comprising diplomacy, non-physicality, obedience to the law) are noted and rejected using occupational typifications, viz. 'glass collector types' who are subordinate to 'good, old time doormen' possessing the requisite bodily capital:

> Kara claimed many of the experienced and well-known doormen in the city are finding it increasingly difficult to renew their licenses following objections from the police. According to Kara this is resulting in the necessary recruitment of less able types:
>
> Kara: 'The police are getting all the good, old time, doormen that way, see. They're slowly getting rid of all the good ones by kicking up a fuss when their licenses are due. They object to the licensing committee saying they've got records for violence. But they're bound to have records. Working on the doors is a lot easier today than it was in the past. There was a hell of a lot more trouble years ago. Before it was an eye for an eye, and so, that's why these doormen have got records'.
>
> Dez: 'I remember. I worked this one place, my first club, and these guys were whipping out pipes and using them. I was wondering where they got them. We went into the toilet and saw they had ripped them off the wall'.
>
> Kara: 'Exactly. That's what it used to be like. Now you can't even touch somebody without fear of arrest. And the police want these glass collector types working the door. You can have one or two working like that but you also need guys like Jordan and Gus who used to work here. They can talk to people but they can also punch. They can't work here now because they're unlicensed. So, you get the glass collectors in and before the police know it they'll be called out every five minutes. They won't be able to cope. It'll be a nightmare for them. They'll be like [tongue in cheek] phoning up all the

good, old time, doormen saying "we want you back!" Crazy'. (Thursday 9th March 2000: Uncle Sam's.)

In summary, economic and socio-cultural factors legitimate the sometimes injurious use of violence by doorstaff in their risk environment. Such violence, which may become habituated for doorstaff as part of their everynight routines (Schutz, 1970), may certainly lie outside formal legal boundaries delimiting reasonable force. However, while violence is normalised and routinised bodily labour among doorstaff, it is also circumscribed. Occupational boundaries for violence, dependent upon socially located emotional/mindful bodies, body parts and shared vocabularies of body idiom (Goffman, 1959), are permeable and flexible but they delineate limits of acceptability. No doubt, those routinely transgressing widely shared boundaries – 'nutters' such as Barney or 'bullies' such as Sid – have some commercial utility: both doormen possessed the requisite bodily capital and were willing to risk their bodies in performance. Nonetheless, they, and other third parties representing negative role models, were also considered a liability. Unrestrained violence (eg, stamping on people's heads), non-violence in situations requiring force (eg, protecting a colleague), illegal public assaults (eg, retributive violence inside licensed premises rather than backstage regions) and the selection of inappropriate targets (eg, forcefully ejecting non-violent bodies) increased the social and physical risks of doorwork for the perpetrators and sometimes their colleagues. Correspondingly, their competency or suitability to doorwork was questioned which, in turn, had real material effects. Sid and Barney, for example, were unable to secure regular work in establishments I researched. However, this did not prevent them from seeking and obtaining doorwork elsewhere.

Conclusion

Contributing empirically to recent studies on 'bouncers' (Hobbs *et al.*, 2002; Winlow, 2001), and in furthering an embodied sociology (Williams and Bendelow, 1998), this ethnography explored constructions of competency among doorstaff in Southwest Britain. As discussed, potentially violent working-class masculinity is routinely invoked, embodied and enacted by doorstaff in their contexts of nightly life. For these workers, their gendered bodies and capacities are their economic asset (Connell, 1995: 55). Dimensions of masculinity enumerated and valorised in urban licensed premises include body build (muscle, size, shape, height and weight), techniques of the body (fighting ability) and a willingness to risk one's body in performance. In a masculinist occupation, the bodily suggestion of forceful action is also significant for doorwomen presenting themselves as physically competent and controlling.

Such aspects of masculinity, constructed in and through embodied, hierarchical relationships, may not be realised by all doorstaff all of the time but they are important vehicles of gendered power (Connell, 1997; cited by Mooney, 1998: 757). Within their risk environment, constructions of situationally dominant masculinity, tempered at times with enactments of the consciously restrained 'civilised body' (Elias, 2000), are positively valued. Occupational typifications such as 'hard men', 'shop boys' and others (eg, 'nutters' and 'bullies') reflect these gendered bodily preferences, constituting a hierarchy between plural masculinities. Sociologically, it is therefore necessary to recognise (certainly, at least in the context of doorwork) the degree to which corporeality is an integral component of gendered identities, power relations and (potentially) violent social action (Winlow, 2001: 97–159). A sociological ethnography of doorwork, similar to the new critical study of masculinities and violence, must make bodies explicit. This was also clear when exploring occupational boundaries for legitimate violence, the appropriateness of which is dependent upon socially located emotional/mindful bodies, body parts and shared vocabularies of body idiom (Goffman, 1959). While other studies of masculine cultures also describe the normative emergence of cultural limits to violence (eg, Hunt, 1996), the bodies in such work are often marginalised thereby obscuring sociological understanding of *physical* violence (Messerschmidt, 1999).

Empirical sociologists are increasingly recognising the centrality of the body (Nettlton and Watson, 1998). Previously neglected in mainstream sociology, there is now a burgeoning interest in the social significance of bodies. For contributors such as Williams and Bendelow (1998) and Shilling (2001), it is also necessary to go further by developing an embodied sociology. Hopefully the present ethnography supports this larger theoretical endeavour where 'sociologists – as embodied practitioners and living, thinking, feeling agents – put minds back into bodies, bodies back into society, and society back into the body' (Williams and Bendelow, 1998: 212). An embodied ethnography of doorwork, similar to other emerging body studies, underscores the sociological significance of lived bodies. If the social lives and breathes, if society is embodied, then bodies are far more than a peripheral adjunct to sociology.

In drawing this paper to a close, two final points. First it is worth underscoring the possibilities of cross-fertilisation which an embodied and empirically grounded sociology promises. Within a very limited social sphere such as the one described above, productive links may be forged between social scientists interested in work, employment and organisations; criminology and deviance; health and illness; the risk society and gender studies. It is here that analytic focus on the body, and what it means to be an embodied subject, may serve as an integrating component that unites social scientists with traditionally disparate analytic interests and research agendas (Williams and Bendelow, 1998).

Moreover, such corporeal studies may prompt those concerned with recommending and developing social policy to understand the complexity of the issues confronting them. As noted, the search for profit means that managers of licensed premises typically favour large doormen over large door teams (Hobbs *et al.*, 2002). Congruently, doorstaff, who risk being assaulted while working, have a general preference for colleagues possessing the requisite bodily capital. Ethnography makes clear that risk management and economies of scale in the nightclub security industry take a specifically *embodied* form. For those interested in practical recommendations, it should therefore be stressed that the night-time economy – co-constituted by effervescent, carnivalesque bodies – is a risk environment for both doorstaff and their charges. Risk of bodily injury, among those at work and play, is no mere abstraction in urban licensed premises. This, of course, begs the question: 'what can be done?'

From a social policy perspective, specific strategies have already been proposed within the literature for reducing the risk of assault *by bouncers against customers*. Lister *et al.* (2000) suggest that more detailed and formalised signing in-books (completed by doorstaff at the start of their shift) alongside police photographic databases may be useful vis-à-vis the identification of violent bouncers, better prosecution rates and thus the upholding of the deterrence capacity of the criminal law. However, such 'one sided' strategies, which entail targeting and excluding 'problematic' doorstaff, will ultimately be of limited value. As noted elsewhere by Hobbs and colleagues, wider macro-social influences – including the political, economy, which compress alcohol and leisure consumption into particular times and spaces – invariably shape everynight situations wherein violence is commonplace (Hobbs *et al.*, 2000). The quasi-liminality of the weekend, the proliferation of drinking venues promoting a sense of abandon and the attractions of violence for drinkers (Tomsen, 1997) invariably increase the economic and cultural value of doorstaff acting as entrepreneurs in potentially violent 'bodily capital' (Wacquant, 1995). These, and other issues amenable (although by no means exclusive) to an embodied sociology, indicate that effectively tackling violence in the night-time economy will not be straightforward. Certainly, given present economic and socio-cultural conditions, 'inappropriate' (levels of) violence will continue despite informal occupational sanctions among doorstaff and more formal mechanisms of exclusion.

Newcastle University

Received 8 January 2001
Finally accepted 15 March 2002

Acknowledgements

I wish to thank the two anonymous referees and the editorial team of *The Sociological Review* for commenting upon an earlier version of this paper. Thanks also to Dick Hobbs, Simon Winlow, Phil Hadfield and Stuart Lister for keeping me informed about their recent ESRC research on 'bouncers' and violence in Britain's night-time economy.

Lee F. Monaghan

Notes

1 Certainly, as with policė (canteen) subculture (Waddington, 1999), expressive in-group talk among doorstaff may bear little relation to how they routinely behave while 'on the job'. For example, while some 'bouncers' *may* resort to biting problematic customers, I have never observed such action. Yet, such 'body talk' is oriented to the practicalities of this risky occupation, reflecting very real concerns about the problematic nature of their sometimes violent work and the degree to which their own violence may be deemed appropriate in a context of physical and legal insecurity.

2 As with police officers (Waddington, 1999: 301), if doorstaff can persuade themselves (and others) 'that those against whom coercive authority is exercised are contemptible, no moral dilemmas are experienced – the [privately] policed section of the population "deserve it".'

References

Athens, L., (1997), *Violent Criminal Acts and Actors Revisited*, Chicago: University of Illinois Press.

Bourdieu, P., (1984), *Distinction: A Social Critique of Judgement and Taste*, London: Routledge.

Cavanagh, K., Dobash, R.E., Dobash, R.P. and Lewis, R., (2001), '"Remedial Work": Men's Strategic Responses to their Violence against Intimate Female Partners', *Sociology*, 35(3): 695–714.

Connell, R., (1995), *Masculinities*, Cambridge: Polity.

Courtenay, W., (2000), 'Constructions of Masculinity and their influence on Men's Well-Being: A Theory of Gender and Health', *Social Science & Medicine*, 50 (10): 1385–1401.

Elias, N., ([1939] 2000), *The Civilizing Process: Sociogenetic and Psychogenetic Investigations*. (revised edition) Oxford: Blackwell Publishers.

Glaser, B. and Strauss, A. (1967), *The Discovery of Grounded Theory*, Chicago: Aldine.

Hobbs, D., Lister, S., Hadfield, P., Winlow, S. and Hall, S., (2000), 'Receiving Shadows: Governance and Liminality in the Night-Time Economy', *British Journal of Sociology*, 51 (4): 701–717.

Hobbs, D., Hadfield, P., Lister, S. and Widow, S., (2002), 'Door Lore: The Art and Economics of Intimidation', *British Journal of Criminology*, 42: 353–370.

Horowitz, R. and Schwartz, G (1974), 'Honor, Normative Ambiguity and Gang Violence', *American Sociological Review*, 39 (2): 238–251.

Hunt, J., (1996), 'Normal Force', in Rubington, E. and Weinberg, M. (eds) *Deviance: The Interactionsit Perspective* (6th edition), Needham Heights, MA: Simon & Schuster.

Jefferson, T., (1998), 'Muscle, Hard Men and Iron Mike Tyson: Reflections on Desire, Anxiety and the Embodiment of Masculinity', *Body & Society*, 4 (1): 77–98.

King, A., (2001), 'Violent Pasts: Collective Memory and Football Hooliganism', *The Sociological Review*, 49 (4): 568–585.

Lister, S., Hobbs, D., Hall, S. and Winlow, S., (2000), 'Violence in the Night-Time Economy; Bouncers: The Reporting, Recording and Prosecution of Assaults', *Policing and Society*, 10: 383–402.

Lyman, S. and Scott, M., (1967), 'Territoriality: A Neglected Sociological Dimension', *Social Problems*, 15: 235–249.

Lyng, S., (1990), 'Edgework: A Social Psychological Analysis of Voluntary Risk Taking', *American Journal of Sociology*, 95 (4): 851–886.

Mauss, M., ([1934] 1973), Techniques of the Body', *Economy and Society*, 2 (1): 70–88.

Messerschmidt, J., (1999), 'Making Bodies Matter: Adolescent Masculinities, the Body, and Varieties of Violence', *Theoretical Criminology*, 3 (2): 197–220.

Monaghan, L., (2001), *Bodybuilding, Drugs and Risk*, London: Routledge.

Monaghan, L., (2002), 'Regulating "Unruly" Bodies: Work Tasks, Conflict and Violence in Britain's Night-Time Economy', *British Journal of Sociology*, 53 (3): 403–429.

Mooney, K., (1998), '"Ducktails, Flick-Knives and Pugnacity": Subcultural and Hegemonic Masculinities in South Africa, 1948–1960'. *Journal of South African Studies*, 24 (4): 753–774.

Nettleton, S. and Watson, J., (eds), (1998), *The Body in Everyday Life*, London: Routledge.

Shilling, C., (1993), *The Body and Social Theory*, London: Sage.

Shilling, C., (2001), 'Embodiment, Experience and Theory: In Defence of the Sociological Tradition', *The Sociological Review*, 49 (3): 327–344.

Schutz, A., (1970), *Reflections on the Problem of Relevance*, New Haven: Yale University Press.

Toch, H., (1969), *Violent Men*, Chicago: Aldine.

Tomsen, S., (1997), 'A Top Night: Social Protest, Masculinity and the Culture of Drinking Violence', *British Journal of Criminology*, 37 (1): 90–102.

Vidich, A., (1955), 'Participant Observation and the Collection and Interpretation of Data', *American Journal of Sociology*, 60: 354–360.

Wacquant, L., (1995), 'Pugs at Work: Bodily Capital and Bodily Labour Among Professional Boxers', *Body & Society*, 1 (1): 65–93.

Waddington, P., (1999), 'Police (Canteen) Sub-Culture', *British Journal of Criminology*, 39 (2): 287–309.

Weaver, A. and Atkinson, P., (1994), *Micro-Computing and Data Analysis*, Aldershot: Avebury.

Whitehead, S., (1999), 'Review Article: Hegemonic Masculinity Revisited', *Gender, Work and Organization*, 6 (1): 58–62.

Williams, S. and Bendelow, G., (1998), *The Lived Body: Sociological Themes, Embodied Issues*, London: Routledge.

Winlow, S., (2001), *Badfellas: Crime, Tradition and New Masculinities*, Oxford: Berg.

[17]

'Ducktails, Flick-knives and Pugnacity': Subcultural and Hegemonic Masculinities in South Africa, 1948–1960

KATIE MOONEY

(Department of History, University of the Witwatersrand)

The Ducktails were a white youth gang subculture which emerged within post Second World War South Africa. They were rebellious, hedonistic, apolitical and displayed little respect for the law, education or work. Collectively their identity was shaped by specific racial, class and gender elements. Within gender studies, femininity has been at the forefront whereas investigations into masculinities have rarely featured. This article contributes towards a better understanding of masculinity and particularly white masculine identities within an historical context. Particular attention is given to the way male members of the subculture constructed, sustained and practised their masculinity. Specifically, this article argues that Ducktail masculinity was not static or homogeneous but was rather multifarious, embracing characteristics such as image, territoriality, loyalty, pugnacity, competitiveness, virility and homophobia. This sets the context for an exploration of the relationship of conformity, conflict and control that emerged between Ducktail masculinity and other more accepted and dominant masculinities.

Background

The Ducktail subculture emerged in a period characterised by far reaching changes in South African society.[1] The Depression years followed by the Second World War profoundly disrupted the lives of black and white South Africans alike. This article, however, focuses on whites. Tens of thousands of people migrated from the countryside to the towns; 200,000 white soldiers were conscripted into the army and women entered industrial employment on an unprecedented scale.[2] Family life was severely dislocated. Following their victory in 1948 the National Party government wrestled with these and other problems through a programme of social engineering whereby they extended government regulation and control in most spheres of South African life. The rise of the National Party to power afforded white South Africans, and in particular Afrikaans-speaking whites, a more privileged position in the labour market and in the wider social, cultural and political spheres. The post-war decade also witnessed the expansion of contradictory expressions of popular culture such as fashion, music (especially rock-'n-roll), film and entertainment facilities

---

1 All interviews cited were conducted by the author between 1996 and 1997. Interviewees were selected according to the responses received from a letter requesting information on the subject which was placed in *Bike SA* (a local motorcycling magazine). Additional information was drawn from government documents and press cuttings.

2 Berger estimates that a total of 300,000 men were conscripted into the army and nearly two-thirds of them were white. See I. Berger, *Threads of Solidarity: Women in South African Industry, 1900–1980* (Indiana, Indiana University Press, 1992), pp. 132–133.

aimed at youths.[3] In this context, youths became more visible as a social category modelling themselves on new international subcultural styles.

The term 'ducktail' was originally used to denote a hairstyle; where all the hair is swept back with Brylcreem and moulded into a point (reminiscent of a duck's tail) at the back. Usually a quiff was pulled down onto the forehead which was accompanied, in most cases, with side-burns. 'Ducktail', with its subcultural connotations, was first used by the press in the early 1950s. This does not mean that the subculture only emerged at that point. Rather, Ducktail gangs formed the core of the subcultural movement and their origins can be traced back to the late 1940s. By 1958 they were a widespread phenomenon, their presence felt in all the major urban centres including Johannesburg, Pretoria, Cape Town, Durban, Port Elizabeth, East London, Bloemfontein and Kimberley.

As a subculture they were hedonistic, convivial, rebellious, apolitical and had little respect for the law, education or work. Generally, the Ducktails were involved in both social and 'anti-social' activities. Their social activities were propelled by their pursuit of pleasure and entertainment. They frequented the cinema, bioscope-cafes, roadhouses, 'sessions', dance halls, billiard rooms, bars, public parks and experimented with *dagga* (marijuana) and alcohol. Some of the Ducktails – mostly the male members – were involved in quasi-criminal and criminal activities such as those reported by flat dwellers in Mooi Street, Johannesburg to a journalist from *The Star*. According to one female resident:

> The menace to the public of young men roaming the city streets by night and by day, selling liquor to natives, smoking dagga, and accosting and assaulting passers-by, had become completely out of hand. These young men were the White *tsotsis* of Johannesburg, the products of broken homes, the sons of mothers who thought only of having a good time. They were hardly out of school before they became members of liquor and dagga gangs operating in the heart of the city. Another female flat dweller stated that, 'Words cannot describe the things which go on in and around Plein Street. Liquor is sold to Natives almost openly by long-haired, smartly dressed youths'.[4]

In general their 'anti-social' activities involved gate crashing, vandalism, the temporary theft of cars for the purposes of joy-riding, the assault of innocent bystanders, inter-gang street fighting, petty crime, involvement in the illicit liquor and *dagga* trade, the molesting of girls and women and assaulting African and homosexual men. They were usually armed with knuckle-dusters, bicycle chains, flick-knives and clubs when engaging in these violent and illicit dealings.

There were different levels of belonging in the subculture, which took diffuse and distilled forms and which could at times become conflated. For some, the Ducktail era was characterised by knuckle-dusters and bicycle chains, quiffs and Brylcreem, bioscopes and sessions, confrontations with the police and petty crime, whilst for others it represented weekend *jolls*, rock-'n-roll and jiving, 'stovepipe' trousers and 'fifty-yard' petticoats[5]. For the majority of Ducktails it was a fashion movement, a fad similar to the Zoot Suits, Hippies, Beatniks, the Mods and Rockers, Skinheads, Punks and the present day 'Ravers'. The latter group of Ducktails did not present a real danger[6] to 'conventional' society and engaged predominantly with the stylistic elements of the subculture. The former group ignited very real concerns and fears in public opinion due to their aggressive and violent

3 For an outline of the expansion of the youth consumer industry in America, see P. Wicke, *Rock Music: Culture, Aesthetics and Sociology* (Cambridge, Cambridge University Press, 1990), pp. 28–73.

4 *The Star*, 28 July 1954.

5 A 'fifty-yard petticoat' consisted of a few layers of net which were stiffened in sugar water.

6 Danger here refers to physical and verbal abuse, assault and crime.

behaviour, which was attached to the subculture as a whole.[7] Numerous social groups can therefore be identified within the subculture as a broader phenomenon. These can be divided into the more organised quasi-criminal gang and the more loosely based 'group of friends'.[8]

Subcultural Masculinities

Youth culture has been the major focus of subcultural studies and as a general rule, it has been those subcultures considered to be 'deviant' which have attracted the most attention. In recent decades, controversy has arisen over how precisely to define subcultures. Nevertheless, most scholars would agree that subcultures are relatively small informal groups with a common set of interests which serve to unify the members whilst simultaneously differentiating them from wider and usually more 'mainstream' social groups. A youth subculture is one in which both age and generation play a definitive role in the membership and composition of the subculture.[9]

Comparatively the study of youth[10] culture in South Africa is a grossly under-researched area, with Glaser's work being the outstanding exception.[11] Despite the dearth of analysis on South African youth cultures specifically, a framework for their examination can be developed by building on a few key studies which have emerged from predominantly American and British investigations. Mention has to be made of the influential work of scholars based in the Centre for Contemporary Cultural Studies (CCCS) at the University of Birmingham. The CCCS was responsible for transforming the way in which subcultures were studied through its prioritisation of class, which at times is infused with concern about ethnicity and gender.[12]

Although there are various strengths in the CCCS analysis of subcultures, a number of shortcomings are encountered when it is applied to the South African situation. One of the major problems is the class analysis of consciousness, ideology and identity. Many would now agree that consciousness is more complex than the CCCS scholars have allowed and comprises numerous different features besides class. Race, gender, ethnicity, social background, generation, space, occupational status together with class contribute not only to the individual's 'layers of consciousness'[13] but also to the construction of identities. In fact, identity as a concept plays a minimal role in the CCCS approach. This is highly problematic because the narrow class analysis creates an impression of overall homogeneity, which underplays the diversity and internal contradictions in identities and within the subculture under analysis.

In South Africa, race is a key feature shaping youth identities. Surprisingly little has been written on *white* youth culture and even less on white racial identities in South Africa.

---

7 This is by no means a fixed division. Membership is probably viewed more accurately on a spectrum ranging from involvement on the periphery to direct participation in all aspects of the movement. The subculture itself comprised an aggregation of many different social groups.

8 The term 'group of friends' is borrowed from Bertolini's classification of Italian male youths in the 1960s. Cited in S. P. Stella's '"Rebels without a cause": Male Youth in Italy around 1960', *History Workshop Journal*, 38 (1994), pp. 168–169.

9 By age I mean a person's actual age (for example, fifteen years old). Generation refers to a specific period in a life cycle (for example, adolescence or adulthood).

10 'Youth' have featured in South African studies but youth culture has often been neglected. There is a good deal of educational, anthropological and historical literature on youth. See for example, M. Cross, 'Culture and Identity in South African Education, 1880–1990' (PhD, University of the Witwatersrand, 1994) and D. Everatt and E. Sisulu (eds), *Black Youth in Crisis: Facing the Future* (Johannesburg, Ravan, 1992).

11 C. Glaser, 'Anti-Social Bandits: Juvenile Delinquency and the *Tsotsi* Youth Gang Subculture on the Witwatersrand, 1935–1960' (MA thesis, University of the Witwatersrand, 1990).

12 See D. Hebdige and A. McRobbie and Garber's work in S. Hall and T. Jefferson (eds), *Resistance Through Rituals: Youth Subcultures in Post-War Britain* (London, Hutchinson, 1976).

13 Term borrowed from B. Bozzoli, *Women of Phokeng: Consciousness, Life Strategy, and Migrancy in South Africa, 1900—1983* (Johannesburg, Ravan, 1991), p. 303.

Studies on race have become synonymous with explorations of black racial identities. Cuso Fusco warns that racial identities 'are not only Black, Latino, Asian, Native American and so on; they are also white. To ignore white ethnicity is to redouble its hegemony by naturalising it'.[14] Much can be learnt about race from recent work produced by US labour historians and their exploration of the intersection between race and class. Wellman, for example, makes an important contribution in his call for the need to account for the '*process* through which whiteness gets invented'[15] so that the 'spaces in which alternative identities to whiteness could be learned, where multidimensional and fluid self-conception which *challenged* whiteness could be constructed'[16] are revealed. He also stresses the dynamic nature of the 'construction of whiteness' which has 'multiple meanings. It is a dynamic construction, produced by interaction between groups and ideas'.[17] In the South African context state, churches and schools all played a role in shaping white identity.

A major strength of subcultural studies is its documentation of masculinity in history. The study of masculinities has, until recently,[18] been a relatively neglected area within 'gender studies', which has had the tendency to focus exclusively on women and their oppression.[19] However, as stated above, in subcultural studies masculinity appears as an analytical category. Ironically, most work on subcultures can be criticised for its tendency to exclude girls and their roles from consideration, but this is a topic for another paper.

Although masculinity has featured in subcultural studies it has been presented in a static manner. Very little can therefore be learnt about the actual *construction and practice* of masculinity. Glaser's work is an exception to this general trend. His work is also a major contribution towards historicising subcultural masculine identities. He alerts us to the fact that masculinity is not only historically specific but it is also socially and culturally specific:

> Masculinity is, of course, a shifting concept. Male prestige and status are defined in different ways from culture to culture and from era to era. In middle-class culture, for instance, professional skills, intellect and earning capacity are emphasised, whereas physical skill and strength tend to be emphasised in working-class culture. Common to all versions of masculinity, however, is male assertiveness and fierce inter-male competitiveness alongside relatively passive, domestically oriented females. Most forms of masculinity also involve a need to control and be 'in control', whether intellectually or physically.[20]

Subcultural analysts need to go beyond simply mentioning that subcultures are vehicles for the expression of masculinity and begin to show how these masculine identities are formulated, sustained and practised whilst revealing how they conflict and co-exist with other forms of masculinity which exist at the same historical conjuncture.

Throughout this paper, it will be shown that the Ducktails' masculinity is neither static nor homogeneous but rather is 'internally divided, and embod[ies] a state of tension between contradictory desires or practices'.[21] Despite these tensions and contradictions,

---

14 Cited in D. Roediger, *Towards the Abolition of Whiteness: Essays on Race, Politics and Working Class History* (New York, Verso, 1992), p. 12.

15 D. Wellman, 'Red Baiters, Race Traitors, and Working Class Heroes: Whites, Contestation and Union Identity', Paper 28, Racializing Class, Classifying Race—A Conference on Labour and Difference in Africa, USA and Britain, St. Antony's College, University of Oxford, 11–13 July 1997, p. 2.

16 *Ibid.*, p. 2.

17 *Ibid.*, pp. 11–12.

18 The first colloquium devoted to Masculinities in Southern Africa was held in July 1997 at the University of Natal, Durban, where the initial draft of this paper was presented.

19 For an outline of recent studies on masculinity see R. W. Connell, 'The Big Picture: Masculinities in Recent World History', *Theory and Society*, 22 (1993), pp. 597–619.

20 C. Glaser, 'The Mark of Zorro: Sexuality and Gender Relations in the *Tsotsi* Subculture on the Witwatersrand', *African Studies*, 51, 1 (1992), p. 51.

21 R. W. Connell, 'Men in the World: Masculinities and Globalization', Colloquium on Masculinities in Southern Africa, University of Natal, Durban, 2–4 July 1997, p. 2.

points of convergence – which cut across class, ethnic, social and generational divides – are present. Masculine identities in the Ducktail subculture generally comprised a combination of definitive characteristics including: image (a preoccupation with appearance including dress, hairstyle, attitude and language); race (assaulting of members of the African community and the promotion of whiteness); territoriality (the defence of space, excursions into rival groups' territory, gate crashing and vandalism); individual and group competitiveness (pugnacity, fighting ability, conflicts over girls, and motorbike and car racing); and finally sexuality (an emphasis on virility, the objectification of girls and homophobia). Each of these elements were important in ensuring the acceptance of a member within the subculture. Ducktail masculinity both conflicted with and conformed to accepted masculinist values in white communities. As R. W. Connell explains:

> Different cultures, and different periods of history, construct gender differently. In multicultural societies there are likely to be multiple definitions of masculinity. Equally important, more than one kind of masculinity can be found within a given cultural setting or institution. ... These multiple masculinities exist in definite social relations, often relations of hierarchy and exclusion. There is generally a dominant or hegemonic form of masculinity, the vehicle of gendered power, which need not be (probably often is not) the most common form of masculinity.[22]

Although certain strands of the Ducktails' masculine identity were drawn from both the hegemonic and parent cultures within which they were subjoined (for example, their assertion of dominance over women and racism) certain elements, such as their promiscuity and hedonism, contrasted sharply with dominant masculine identities that were founded on sobriety, respectability, obedience to the law, Christianity, upward social mobility and discipline. Attempts were made by government officials and community and religious leaders to create a more conformist masculinity for Ducktails. This was attempted through religious campaigns, the extension of boys' clubs, organised sports and the promotion of military discipline. Each of these will be referred to in the course of this article.

Image, Style and Argot

For all members entry into the subculture was largely dependent on projecting the correct image. This included the adoption of a particular dress style accompanied by familiarity with the slang – 'Rub and Tub' – and attendance and participation in most of the subcultural activities, specifically the social ones, such as frequenting the bioscope, tea rooms, billiard rooms, roadhouses and 'sessions'.[23] As a subculture, the Ducktails were collectively committed to 'style, music, leisure and consumption'. Style, therefore, is not simply the embodiment of a 'subculture's identity' at the level of appearances but it also

> performs the function of defining the group's boundaries more sharply in relation to both its members and all outsiders, a function which has particular consequences for the group's continued existence.[24]

The Ducktails' collective style[25] was clearly visible in their dress and hairstyle code. The predominant fashion for boys consisted of mostly white, and in the late 1950s, brightly coloured, shirts (with shoestring ties) which were usually rolled up at the elbow. These were

22 Connell, 'Men in the World', p. 2.

23 'Sessions' were organised dances usually held at community centres.

24 Clarke, 'Style', in S. Hall and T. Jefferson, *Resistance through Rituals*, p. 182.

25 Here, style has been discussed in general terms but style was differentiated according to the different types of Ducktails; this was especially so for the mobile and pedestrian Ducktails. The latter either wore long jackets or no jackets at all, whilst the former wore leather jackets (out of necessity due to riding motorbikes).

worn with 'stovepipe trousers' and a comb in the back pocket. Over this, they sported either a leather jacket or a duffel coat. White or brightly coloured socks were a stylistic imperative and were accompanied with crepe-soled shoes or 'Jarmans' which were studded on the sole with horseshoes or drawing pins. Accessories included wide, leather, studded belts with big buckles and in some cases thick chains and gold or silver rings. Tattoos of daggers, hearts, or the words 'love' and 'mother' spelt across the knuckles were favoured.

A great deal of time was spent on dressing up and sculpting the hair. Usually it took patience and care to put on stovepipes (between 12 and 14 inches in circumference). Attaining the perfect 'D-A'[26] at the back required considerable effort and plenty of Brylcreem, La Pabros, and even sugar water to maintain this effect. Combs were used frequently to keep the hair in place. This was especially so for those Ducktails who rode motorbikes. For example, as expressed by Mike Malony (a Boksburg Ducktail) when referring to the sessions:

> It was very important to make the proper entrance to these events. We'd arrive on five or six bikes and sit and rev the motors a few times before cutting the engines. This let everybody know that the bad guys had arrived, and we'd gather outside before walking through the door. Three paces through the door you'd stop, check out the scene, and comb your hair to show you had come on the bikes.[27]

Their preoccupation with appearance reflects their need to project the correct image and their version of male sexuality. In this instance their masculinity was defined in terms of looking physically attractive for girls, whilst functioning as a symbol of membership in the subculture. In essence, the new clothing styles were a 'fashionable sort of go out, dressed up for the girls kind of thing'.[28]

School-going Ducktails sported parts of ducktail attire on school premises during school hours. According to Andre, who practised the stylistic dimension of the subculture:

> At Boys' High in Pretoria you could hear the guys walking with Jarmans and the principal used to write letters and threaten the guys. It was part and parcel of the whole thing, you took your flannels to the Indian tailor who tightened them to fourteen inches – so you couldn't get your feet into them with your shoes on. ... The *squares* had 22 inch bell bottoms ... we used to put on white socks with Jarman shoes (which were forbidden at school but worn anyway) and we would deliberately walk in the corridors or go to the toilet during the period, just to hear the 'click', 'click' everybody used to look ... the school ties were quite wide and we used to take them to the Indian tailor in downtown Marabastad, in Boom Street, and the guy halved the tie into a square. The fashion at that stage was one-inch (maximum) thick ties so the school tie was cut and the collar was cut away – the further up the better. Our combs were in our pockets to fix up the style but usually you had special stuff which was put on after the Brylcreem so when you do your *kuif* [quiff] it became very hard so the wind couldn't blow your *kuif* around.[29]

Challenges to authority were therefore launched at the level of style. Such forms of rebellion signify the importance of the body as 'a primary site of identity construction; style and appearance signify consciousness in relation to social environments and institutions as well as relation to peers'.[30]

---

26 'D-A' is an abbreviation of 'duck's arse'. The hair was carefully moulded with two flicks which met at the back reminiscent of a duck's tail.

27 M. Malony, 'Dance a Little Bit to the Bop, to the Bop', in *The Master Link Magazine of the Classic Motorcycle Club* (April 1997).

28 Interview, Lynton Johnson, Kempton Park, 6 March 1997.

29 Interview, Andre, Pretoria, 7 November 1996.

30 N. Lesko, 'The Curriculum of the Body: Lessons Learned from a Catholic High School' in L. G. Roman, L. K. Christian-Smith and E. Elsworth (eds), *Becoming Feminine: The Politics of Popular Culture* (London, Falmer, 1988), p. 123.

Argot also set one of the boundaries of entry into the subculture. The Ducktails adopted a syncretic type of slang, which was loosely based on old Cockney rhyming slang ('Rub and Tub'). It was an amalgamation of Afrikaans, American and British slang, as the words of the following song show:

> Standing on the corner in my ones and twos [shoes],
> Down came a joller, singing the blues.
> He clocked [looked] to the left, he clocked to the right,
> And out came the dagga [marijuana] as he asked for a light,
> Singing ducktail boogie ...
> Jolling on the corner with my razor and chain;
> Down came the ore [police], one took my name,
> He grabbed me by the collar of my charcoal float [shirt],
> Then out came my razor as I slit his throat,
> Singing ducktail boogie ... [31]

Ducktail argot served to define the boundaries of the subculture more sharply, and it allowed for the exclusion of outsiders, as they could not understand its connotations. The slang also reinforced the multi-ethnic composition of the Ducktail subculture. This language 'like other languages, mirrors the culture of its speakers'.[32] Their slang both reflected and re-informed masculine identities, being replete with sexual innuendoes and allusion to violence and crime. For example, *canned goods* meant a virgin; *goosies* meant a girl; *clean up* referred to fighting; a *rort* was usually a group fight; a *clink* or *cooler* was a prison; *scale a jammie* meant to steal a car, *charras* denoted Indians, and *bunny boys* or *queers* referred to homosexual men.[33]

For both the male and female members of the subculture, style and slang were taken and adapted from the popular world of film and music. Screen performers exerted enormous influence. The bioscope was attended at least once a week. Those actors who played roles in Western and gangster films were most favoured. The string tie, for example, was taken directly from cowboy films. The ducktail persona is epitomised in the characters that were played by James Dean in *Rebel without a Cause* (1955), Marlon Brando in *The Wild One* (1954) and Elvis Presley in *Jailhouse Rock*. Films and music also played a small but significant part in the ideological construction of masculinity. Characters played by Marlon Brando, for example, prioritised fighting ability and violence, which was central to ducktail masculine identities. However, films not only provided 'numerous macho role models for boys'[34] but they also captured the essence of their subculture's hedonism, conviviality and quest for adventure, excitement, and fun. Furthermore, it was here at the bioscope that the Ducktails were informed of the latest trends in fashion, ideology and popular culture. Presley was the greatest draw. *Jailhouse Rock*

> brought all the *manne* out. Unless you rocked up three hours before and stood in a huge queue, you missed out. The street outside the cinema was packed with bikes, at least a hundred, parked at right angles to the kerb, which was full of people. The press was there, taking photos for tomorrow's papers. The atmosphere inside was charged with excitement.[35]

---

31 L. F. Freed, *Crime in South Africa: an Integralistic Approach* (Johannesburg, Juta, 1963), p. 105. Most of the people I interviewed were familiar with the song. Freed, a key player in the creation of a moral panic concerning Ducktails and youth crime, was a lecturer in Psychiatry and Social Medicine at the University of the Witwatersrand when *Crime in South Africa* was published.

32 S. Mokwena, 'The Era of the Jackrollers: Contextualising the Rise of Youth Gangs in Soweto', Seminar Paper No 7, Project for the Study of Violence, Department of Psychology, University of the Witwatersrand (1991), p. 10.

33 Slang was obtained from interviews, press cuttings and from L. F. Freed, *Crime in South Africa.*

34 Glaser, 'The Mark of Zorro', p. 52.

35 Malony, 'Dance a Little Bit to the Bop, to the Bop', p. 11.

Not only were films watched but younger boys exchanged comics at the bioscope. Lynton Johnson reminisces of his early high school days:

> A tikkie was two and half cents and you only needed two tikkies to get into the bioscope ... Princess Bioscope was one of the ones that you went to if you were a Saturday morning bioscope freak, you watched all the trailers and you didn't miss an episode and you sang along. We swapped comics – *Superman, Dagwood and Blondie* not so much *Archie* and all the others that they made the big fuss about later on. The conventional *Mickey Mouse* and Classics (a printer group) they printed all the classic stories Robinson Crusoe and all those they were around. There were a couple of the hot *Flash Gordons* because he was also a part of the weekly serial that you watched in black and white of all these strange happenings that went on with Flash Gordon. ...War stories in a dozen and one forms where the west always won, they were against the Japanese. ... British comics like *Desperate Dan* and *Beano* they were still coming in and you could get them on a reasonably regular basis by about the mid 1950s. The American comics were the collectibles those were the ones that you swapped. Disney's comics were around along with photo-stories. Comic swapping was quite an important part of a Saturday morning and it was in the queues that this was happening while you were waiting to go in. Frequently older Ducktails stole the more valuable comics from us.[36]

Comics also played a significant role in the construction of a masculinist subculture. These were read most avidly by boys on the edge of puberty but remained popular among older boys and young men imprinting themselves deeply on their notions of masculinity. The majority of prized comics were 'super-hero' comics where the main character embodies physical strength and competitive performance. Women were generally absent in comics except for the purpose of 'romance'. These comics – like films and other forms of media – disseminated gender images which for boys stressed the need for them to be assertive, successful, to acquire physical strength, to compete with each other and to exert male dominance over girls, young women, 'weaker' boys and young men.

Likewise the new rock-'n-roll artists, such as Bill Haley and the Comets, Eddie Cochran, Little Richard, Chubby Checker, Chuck Berry and Elvis Presley made a huge impact on youths. This is seen in not only the purchase but also the collection of records and through the raucous rock-'n-roll sessions that were held. The media and in particular radio played a role in keeping South African youths up to date with both international and local music developments:[37]

> we had our hit parade, request programmes ... there were bilingual programmes ... It wasn't long after anything was a hit over there that it became a hit over here along with who sung it. Pictures of them in the music shop were available; the pin-ups on the walls were very much part of how a room would look.[38]

Parts of their style were directly taken from these new brands of entertainers. In particular, they emulated Elvis Presley and his characteristic mannerisms: overt aggressiveness and gyrating hips which offended most of the adult generation, sideburns and prominent quiff. Mike Malony, when reminiscing about Elvis, maintains that

> it's amazing now that one person could stir up such a frenzy of emotion, but nothing like this had happened before. We'd had Frank Sinatra in America, but he was an old man now. Johnny 'Cry Baby' Ray had had people fainting at his shows, but the Elvis phenomenon was our first taste of mass hysteria. When he came on the screen, half the girls in the audience screamed

36 Interview, Lynton Johnson, Kempton Park, 6 March 1997.

37 There was, however, a limited amount of local music; it was mainly Afrikaans but there were a few odd groups around, for example, 'Four Jacks and a Jill', 'Dickie Louder and the Blue Jeans', Micky Most, Billy Forest's projects and Mike Shannon and the Dianas, all of which usually played at roadhouses. Interview, Lynton Johnson, Kempton Park, 6 March 1997 and interview, John Burkes, Sandton, 17 November 1997.

38 Interview, Lynton Johnson, Kempton Park, 6 March 1997.

and the guys cheered. He represented the non-conformist rebel we felt we were. And what's more he looked the part, dark, brooding and a loner, misunderstood and dangerous.[39]

Music acted as a unifying force within the Ducktail subculture as it fundamentally guided the movement as a whole and it was a topic with which all members were familiar. Rock-'n-roll, as noted by Brake, 'is a celebration of macho male sexuality, which has a traditional notion of women's place'. Additionally rock-'n-roll with its 'raw, sexual energy ... seemed to promise a future time of freedom of movement and a stunning explosion of our own bottled up desires'.[40] Despite rock-'n-roll's roots in black rhythm and blues, it propelled youth subcultures in the 1950s with young white rebellious males being the aesthetic role models.

Racism and its Intersection with Masculinity

Virtually all Ducktails were white. At times, their racial consciousness intersected with their masculinity in the form of vicious racist assaults carried out on members of the black, coloured and Indian communities. Interactions with blacks, however, could be peaceful if business was being transacted or if an activity was consensual. For example, members of the 'coloured' band that played at the rock-'n-roll sessions in Durban 'were treated as friends and, an important sign of acceptance, dagga was smoked with them'.[41] Ducktails mixed socially with African youths at shebeens. As Freed noted with panic,

> White Ducktails in jeans and colourful shirts have been known to take their 'quacktail' tarts to brothels in African areas. Here they meet the African tsotsis dressed in zoot suits, and their black molls dressed in 'Suzie Wong' skirts. They are sometimes joined by Indian boys and girls from Fordsburg. Kwela music or rock-'n-roll records are played, to liven up the party, and when brandy is taken and 'giggleweed' smoked, the colour line in sex is speedily forgotten. We were informed that this experience was supposed to represent a 'new sort of thrill for the degenerates of both sections of the population'.[42]

Multi-racial interaction as described above was a rarity, firstly because it was becoming increasingly difficult to engage in inter-racial mixing due to far reaching apartheid legislation, and secondly as a result of the prevalent notions of racism and white superiority. The 1950s was a period in which urban planning and restructuring was a pivotal aim of the government. As Mabin and Smit note:

> The scale of urban expansion in the fifties and sixties surpassed anything which had preceded the period. While significant densification took place through high rise residential and commercial building, a hallmark of the period lay in the suburban boom ... fairly strict policing of racial reservation of land created space for middle class, white suburbanisation ... .[43]

Urban segregation and racial zoning was extended and entrenched through amendments to the Natives (Urban Areas) Act in 1952, through the enforcement of the 'section ten' provisions and especially through the consolidation of the Group Areas Act in 1957 and 1966.[44] Accompanying this the government launched an intensive slum clearance programme in the 1950s to remove 'black spots' in the cities.

39 Malony, 'Dance a Little Bit to the Bop, to the Bop', p. 10.

40 D. Jackson, *Unmasking Masculinity, a Critical Autobiography* (London, Unwin Hyman 1990), p. 201.

41 Z. M. Huithwaite, 'The Problem of the "Ducktail" in the Greyville Area of Durban' (MA, University of Natal, 1961), p. 120.

42 Freed, *Crime in South Africa*, p. 83.

43 A. Mabin and D. Smit, 'Reconstructing South Africa's Cities 1900–2000: a Prospectus (Or, A Cautionary Tale)', Programme for Planning Research, Occasional Paper Series, Number 3, presented at African Studies Seminar (1992), p. 25.

44 T. R. H. Davenport, *South Africa: A Modern History* (London, Macmillan, 1992), p. 538.

In the context of increasing racial segregation, discrimination and notions of perceived white superiority, overt aggression and hostility was directed at Africans. For example, the *Rand Daily Mail* reported that

> In 1958 Feb 22, one such clash occurred outside the Johannesburg City Hall in which several people including policemen, were injured .... Trouble had broken out earlier in the evening between Ducktails who were attending a rock 'n roll session in Selbourne Hall and Indians who were giving a song and dress display in the City Hall. A fight was said to have broken out over an Indian girl. Two policemen on duty at the rock 'n roll session intervened, but were attacked by Ducktails and severely assaulted ... Later, when the Indian display ended and Indians stepped out of the City Hall, Ducktails attacked them. Police stepped in to protect the Indians, and dispersed the Ducktails with baton charges. Thirteen Ducktails were subsequently arrested.[45]

Africans that became the Ducktails' victims were assaulted in white residential areas and in this instance 'neighbourhood sentiment tend[ed] to fuse together with racial antagonisms'.[46] In Britain, Teddy Boys carried out racist assaults in large measures due to their frustrated class positions but this was not the case in South Africa. Rather these assaults need to be placed within the context of South Africa's history of overt racism. Racism was not peculiar to the Ducktails but rather permeated the identities of most white South Africans. The unprovoked assaulting of African people was not confined to youths alone. One needs only to consult the local press and in particular the *Rand Daily Mail* to find regular references to instances of white men (over forty and fifty) carrying out brutal assaults on Africans. As with the youths these assaults were committed publicly and for no apparent reason. From this it is clear that racial antagonism played a crucial role in the development of Ducktail masculinity. Le Roux notes of the 1950s and 1960s:

> Racial stereotypes which we acquired at home were mostly reinforced at school ... the attitudes of our teachers, preachers, parents and friends left us in no doubt that Africans were very different from whites and had to be treated as a separate, inferior group ... beliefs of racial superiority were fostered by most.[47]

These outbursts were due to the prevailing racism in which black people were perceived as inferior citizens. The significance of their racism lies in what is revealed about the socialisation process,[48] which portrayed white South Africans as members of a superior race and Africans as dehumanised objects of assault. Lynton Johnson when discussing the racism of the Ducktails maintains that:

> We were all swept over with the same broom. We all grew up basically blind. There were those who obviously didn't grow up that way and they became the exiles ... we all lived in fear and dread of having a black stay on our property after hours and having a black in your home for a meal was something you didn't do however well you got on with your buddy at work who wasn't really your buddy because you didn't want anyone calling you a 'kaffirboet'.[49]

Ducktails were extremely race conscious. They conformed politically to the hegemonic racist paradigm of the state through their aggressive acceptance of dominant social expectations and prejudices which dehumanised members of the African community.

This overt violence expressed through the assaulting of innocent people was not

45 *Rand Daily Mail*, 22 February 1958.

46 R. E. Park, 'The City: Suggestions for the Investigation of Human Behaviour', in K. Gelder and S. Thornton (eds), *The Subcultures Reader* (London, Routledge, 1997), p. 18.

47 Cited in T. D. Moodie, *The Rise of Afrikanerdom: Power, Apartheid and the Afrikaner Civil Religion* (Berkeley, University of California Press, 1975), p. 198.

48 More research needs to be undertaken to probe into the psychological dimension which underpinned racial violence.

49 Interview, Lynton Johnson, Kempton Park, 6 March 1997.

confined exclusively to the African population. Attacks on white people were not uncommon. The residents in Mooi plaza complained that it was common for them to suffer broken jaws at the hands of these youths. Anybody, including children, who inhibited their actions could be, and was often, attacked. Freed alleges that

> a group of 200 defenceless children, while returning from a swimming gala at Ellis Park, was attacked for no apparent reason by a gang of young thugs, brandishing knives and knuckle-dusters, at the intersection of Claim and Bok streets. The gangsters were urged on by ducktail girls, shouting: 'Smash them! *Donder* them!'[50]

On this particular occasion, the Ducktails appear to have also been expressing their antagonism to what was considered to be respectable white youths who conformed to the ideals of school and education.

Territoriality and Pugnacity

The more involved members of the subculture arranged themselves into gangs, which more often than not were involved in 'anti-social', quasi-criminal and criminal activities. The gangs were quite rigidly organised with an identifiable leader and hierarchical structure. It must be emphasised, however, that not all Ducktails were organised into gangs. Working class boys were more likely to belong, but affiliation cut across class lines. Membership was more common for those who were closer to the city centre and who had stronger neighbourhood and community ties. For example, in a survey of 100 youths in Hillbrow, Engelbrecht found that 53 per cent belonged to gangs and that 65 per cent carried dangerous weapons, which included bicycle chains, knuckle dusters, flick-knives, rubber pipes and revolvers.[51]

Gangs were usually organised according to geographical location and territory, both of which were central to their identities. They generally took their names from the areas in which the members resided. There was a 'Jeppe Gang', a 'Fordsburg Deep Gang', a 'North End Gang' and the 'Primrose Boys' in Germiston to name but a few. The leader of the gang usually possessed great physical strength and good fighting skills. Entry into the gang was based on physical prowess, pugnacity and willingness to participate in all activities. Rufus, a Johannesburg duckie, contends that

> The leader would always be the stronger guy in the group, maybe a year older or he would have a reputation for boxing and he would be the predominant guy in the club ... it would take a good few slaps before you were allowed into the group. It depends how quick you could prove yourself you could work yourself in the first night if you got into a *raut* [fight] and you cleaned the other *oke* up and you were smaller than the other *oke* they would accept you readily.[52]

Gangs generally comprised between 10 and 20 members. Central to the gang was a strong bond of friendship and fierce loyalty, which included not only the defence of each other but also of the gang's territory. Defence of territory was a major activity of the gang and many fights were initiated due to territorial 'invasions'. According to a Primrose Ducktail, Bones:

50 Freed, *Crime in South Africa*, p. 98.

51 G. K. Engelbrecht was senior lecturer in Sociology at the University of the Witwatersrand and organised a team to research crime in Johannesburg. His study was based on his observations and analysis of youth crime in South Africa in the 1950s. His work must be approached tentatively due to its contemporary sociological nature which renders it analytically weak at times. However, it is useful due to the wealth of descriptive detail of youth in the 1950s which he provides. G. K. Engelbrecht, '*Jeugmisdaadareas en aanverwante verskynsels*' (PhD, University of the Witwatersrand, 1964), p. 201.

52 Interview, Prop, Fred and Rufus, Boksburg, 11 September 1996.

> You couldn't have ten *okes* from Germiston go to the south or vice versa 'cos you're gonna have trouble ... Jeppe, Troyeville, all those areas you couldn't go there.[53]

Cinemas and dance halls often proved focal points of conflict. Freed maintains:

> Gang warfare not infrequently breaks out in the southern suburbs. As many as twenty men from rival gangs have been observed in battle outside a cinema in Rosettenville. These men belonged to the South Hills and Rosettenville gangs, and met at the cinema by challenge. Terrified women and children in the cinema queue shrieked when the gangs started fighting in the foyer.[54]

Invading another group's territory was a major pastime for most Ducktails. For example:

> The best *jol* was to ride to another town and pull up outside a session where a lot of bikes were parked. We'd sit on the bikes revving the motors and watching the door. The local *jollers* would burst through the entrance, see that we were from Boksburg and go for their bikes. We waited until they'd almost got started, drop the clutches and thunder off into the night. Thundering down Main Reef Road at midnight ... pursued by ten irate Germiston Ducktails is not the sort of thing you tell your mother about. Fortunately, we never got caught ... .[55]

Territoriality pervaded the whole movement, sometimes expanding to a regional scale. In certain instances Ducktails from the East Rand would group together in defence of their territory against Ducktails from the South Rand. At the same time, Ducktails within the East and South Rand would fight with each other. Argot as well as dancing style was influenced by geographical location. For example, in Johannesburg a road was referred to as a 'drag' whereas in Durban it was a 'gully'.[56]

Due to their close geographical proximity, members spent a lot of time together relaxing, socialising and indulging in 'anti-social' activities. They practised a unique blend of camaraderie and competition, which was both supportive and conflictual. Within the gang, there was a strong sense of 'brotherhood' which was founded on notions of strong loyalty, aggression, toughness and fighting, each of which can be seen as the ritualistic expression of masculinity. Most activities that were undertaken were as a group. This included gate crashing, vandalism, 'borrowing' of cars and assault. There was a great deal of generosity and mutual assistance within gang and friendship networks. For example, members would assist each other with transport, with the purchase of alcohol and *dagga* and they would help out if one of the members were homeless. It was also quite common for members to rotate a work schedule. For example, a group of three Ducktails would take turns in working for a few months. According to S. G. Norman (a Johannesburg businessman who organised employment for some Ducktails):

> Three live together in a room, which they rent for three rands. A work schedule gets drawn up. Number one will work from January to April and support his two friends. Then he will retire. Number two will then accordingly work until the end of August and will support the other two. Thereafter number three gets his turn to work.[57]

For many Ducktails, however, regular work was anathema. As one Southern suburb Ducktail confided to one of Engelbrecht's students, after the formal interview had been conducted:

> They told us that they were out of work because they could not find jobs. When they got to know us better they explained that they did not work because they did not want to .... They

53 Interview, Bones, Kempton Park, 22 April 1997.
54 Freed, *Crime in South Africa*, p. 98.
55 Malony, 'Dance a Little Bit to the Bop, to the Bop', p. 11.
56 Interview, Bill Crauser, Kensington, 22 July 1997.
57 *Die Huisgenoot*, 'Die Eendsterte kry 'n Peetpa', 27 July 1958 (this and all other translations were completed by the author).

said that there were ways and means of obtaining money, but they refused to enlighten us. During the day they just loafed around and sometimes went to the bioscope.[58]

This aspect of their masculine identity was in stark contrast to the dominant masculinity, which prized men as the breadwinners and providers. The racial nature of South African capitalism accorded Ducktails the privilege to reject work. The National Party's labour policies contained job reservation provisions (the Colour Bar Act of 1926 which was extended through amendments to the Industrial Conciliation Act of 1956 and 1959).The Ducktails could thus afford not to work or to engage in employment for limited periods of time.[59]

Besides dividing the workload, Ducktails mutually assisted one another in most of their 'anti-social' undertakings. Gatecrashing parties was a popular pastime and was a means to prove one's 'manhood' and bravery to other members. If Ducktail gangs heard of a party or other social event, regardless of any connections between themselves and the hosts, they would gatecrash the party, vandalise their property and other possessions, and fight anyone who got in their way. They were usually armed with flick-knives, knuckle-dusters and clubs during these excursions.

The gangs which gatecrashed parties came from both within and outside the neighbourhood. According to Freed, the situation got so bad that the principal of a Turffontein school called in the police to stand in at school dances. Gatecrashing was a favourite activity and in 1956, 'about 50 "ducktail boys" and their girlfriends "gatecrashed" a church function for children held in Yeoville'.[60] In another instance approximately fifty Ducktails invaded a party being given by R. S. Harpur of Saxonwold on 11 January 1958.[61] Due to the lack of clubs and dance halls many house parties were held which were frequently gatecrashed by Ducktails without any links to the hosts:

> I remember my sister, who is younger than me, had a party once, in the garage and I knew there would be problems. I said to my *old lady* it's looking for trouble but she gave the party. I was round the corner and my younger *boetie* came round and told me that the *okes* were taking over. I walked in the house and guys were helping themselves to drinks and *chow* [food], the bedrooms were all occupied ... and I got my *old man's* pistol and I loaded it, put it in my back pocket and said the party is over ... there was about twenty guys, they were Primrose guys and I didn't go to Primrose for about a year and half.[62]

In addition to showing little respect for private property, some Ducktails vandalised public property – another group activity. They expressed their right to control public property within their territory by frequently damaging signs, public telephones, and parks. For example, at Rhodes Park in Kensington, a gang was responsible for destroying newly planted flowers and for smashing globes in the little open-air theatre.[63] The smashing of bars and vandalism in the cinema houses was also quite common:

> they were slashing seats in the movies, razor blades with bubble gum were stuck to the screen to try and slice it ... they were also known to put razor blades in the slides which children played on.[64]

Displaying the courage to vandalise property informed inter-male competitiveness. A more common expression of competitiveness was articulated through racing. They took part in

58 Engelbrecht, '*Jeugmisdaadareas*', p. 142.

59 Davenport points out that that there was a white labour shortage in the 1960s. Davenport, *South Africa: A Modern History*, p. 512.

60 *Rand Daily Mail*, 'Teenage Vice Talks to be Opened in Pretoria Tomorrow', 25 February 1956.

61 CAD, VWN, 747, SW109, part III. Letter of complaint from R.S. Harpur to John Cope (MP for Saxonwold), dated 20 January 1958.

62 Interview, Bones, Kempton Park, 22 April 1997.

63 *The Star*, 28 February 1955.

64 Interview, Lynton Johnson, Kempton Park, 6 March 1997.

'joy-rides' which usually involved 'borrowing' someone's car and either racing through the city or playing chicken, often without a driver's licence. In fact, between 1945 and 1954 offences against the Driver's Licence Legislation (code 087) amounted to 50 per cent of all crime committed by white 'juvenile adults'.[65] A similar type of 'theft for use'[66] was common practice amongst Italian youths or *teppismo* (hooligans) in the 1960s. Stella contends that

> The teppista who got hold of one [car] without taking definitive possession was driven to steal it by a range of impulses of desire, not by the simple taste for theft. The car was in fact a means to an end, although not an economical one: the uses made of it (driving, looking at it, showing it off, feeling it, speeding, getting into it with friends or a girl) satisfied desires of exhibitionism, collective fun, temporary enjoyment of someone else's property, and sexual power. You can do anything with a car; it is the means to omnipotence; for these young people, it took the symbolic place of money.[67]

Tolson argues that groups of boys and young men 'devote themselves to the testing of masculine prowess – in fights, arguments, explorations of the local neighbourhood – and there is also a complex boyhood culture of mutual challenge'.[68] Racing through the streets and playing 'chicken' was a common form of competition and of 'devilment' between Ducktails:

> these dark games that you played called chicken were like in the James Dean movie and it's the cars over the cliff, they were not quite that serious but you would play anything where you could see if you could best the next guy [69]

The desire for speed was expressed by most young Ducktails, more so for the bikers and owners of cars. Having access to transport in the form of a motorbike or a car was a necessity for the majority of Ducktails.[70] British bikes such as Triumphs, BSAs and AJSs were favoured although Italian bikes such as Ducatis were also popular.[71] The younger Ducktails also rode 50 cc motorcycles such as Pegasos and Zundapps but the need to obtain a faster and more powerful motorbike was important. Mike Malony (who was riding a 50 cc Pegaso) explains what he felt after riding pillion on a BSA Golden Flash (650 cc) for the first time,

> After the power of the Pegaso, the BSA gave me a new perspective on speed. Doing 90 miles per hour in a 1948 Dodge, my Dad's car, was one thing. Perched on a hot 650 behind a slightly crazy *breker* was quite another. We got to La Conga in about a quarter of the time it took me on the Pegaso. We got off the bike blinking away the tears, no one wore helmets or goggles, and Spike introduced me to the *manne*.[72]

Going into another group's territory usually resulted in races between rival groups who were either in cars or on motorbikes. A typical example is the race that occurred outside the Casbah roadhouse in Brakpan between Mike Malony and his four friends from Boksburg who were riding bikes (BSA Golden Flash, 350 Gold Star, Matchless and Ducati)

65 J.D.Venter, *The Incidence of Juvenile Crime in South Africa. An Analysis of the Problem based on Available Information*, Research Series, No. 2 (Johannesburg, National Bureau of Educational and Social Research, 1964), p. 20.

66 Stella, 'Rebels without a Cause', pp. 164–165.

67 *Ibid.*, p. 170.

68 A. Tolson, *The Limits of Masculinity* (London, Tavistock, 1977), p. 32.

69 Interview, Lynton Johnson, Kempton Park, 6 March 1997.

70 Transport was not a necessary prerequisite for entry into the subculture. Within a group of friends transport would be arranged either in a car or as a pillion on a motorbike.

71 Harley Davidsons were not favoured for two reasons. Firstly, after the Second World War the production of Harleys was suspended and secondly, members of the police force rode Harleys from the Second World War. They increased in popularity from the 1960s onwards.

72 M. Malony, 'Bert's Club and Where Things Started to Go Bad', *The Master Link—Magazine of the Classic Motorcycle Club*, March 1997, p. 24.

and the Brakpan 'Hot Rod Gang' with their V-8 Studebaker Hawk and 57 Chevie. As Mike Malony describes:

> We pulled up about three bays away and these *jollers* in the *voemies* [cars] started checking us out *skeef*. Naturally we started *tuning* them about how slow the *jammies* [cars] were and before too long, Spike [who was riding a BSA] was lined up next to the hawk in the street, engines revving, pointing to the circle at Mandy's engineering. Eddie waved Spike's white scarf and with white smoke pouring from the Stud's rear tyres, they rocketed off towards the circle .... As they disappeared into the night we could see that Spike was falling behind. We heard the roar of the V8 motor off in the distance, some squealing tyres and Spike's headlight emerged about ten yards ahead of the Studebaker ... Spike was a bike's length ahead. Back at the roadhouse, the *oke* with the hawk was tuning how he'd actually won as his car was faster. When Johnnie stepped up, a head shorter and 60 pounds lighter, and *moered* [hit] this *oke* on the side of the jaw. He went down without a sound and all hell broke loose.[73]

Although racing challenges were usually confined to rival groups of Ducktails, they could also be extended to include traffic officers,

> Riding away from the *ore* [police] was no problem, their cars were too slow and couldn't handle like our bikes. Speed cops were a bit harder but their bikes were heavy and too well maintained. They were mostly single carb 650 Triumphs or heavy 500cc BMWs ... and they didn't chase far.[74]

An even more common means of competition was displaying the willingness to fight and the ability to exert violence. Violence was a central part of the process of masculine identification and 'violent practices are a part of the social processes that produce masculinity within a male-dominated society'.[75] Most commonly of all, the Ducktails assaulted each other especially in the streets outside bioscopes, cafes, roadhouses and dance halls. In Port Elizabeth, for example:

> another favourite meeting place was a place called the Red Windmill, it's still there but it's changed very much. In those days it was way out of town and if you pitched up to the Red Windmill late at night you could more or less assure yourself that there would be a fight or there would be a race, playing chicken was very popular.[76]

The majority of fights, however, occurred at the sessions and outside dance halls. In one case seven fights – involving 80 boys – broke out at a dance that was held in the Benoni City Hall in 1949. Fighting was thus both a means of proving a member's 'manliness' and an assertion of dominance over physically 'weaker' boys. These fights were usually instigated over territorial disputes and girls. In one case a boy was assaulted because 'the young man's partner refused to dance with one of the drunk youths'.[77] Girls were perceived, by boys, as sexual objects and possessions to be won through fighting. In such cases the model of masculinity that Ducktails adopted had an underlying form of sexism in which women were perceived, either consciously or not, as anonymous objects to possess, as rewards after 'battle'. Violence was a central aspect of gang activity. It not only represented the symbolic reassertion of power but was also a measure of one's 'manhood' and status within the gang.

73 M. Malony, 'Hot Rod Gang' (unpublished), 30 May 1997, pp. 2—3.
74 *Ibid.*, p. 1.
75 D. Jackson, *Unmasking Masculinity, a Critical Autobiography* (London, Unwin Hyman, 1990), p. 188.
76 Interview, Mike Milroy, Kempton Park, 10 April 1997.
77 *Benoni City Times en Oosrandse Nuus*, 'Hooligans Terrorise Dancers', 25 February 1949.

Heterosexuality and Homophobia

A discussion of masculinity – and particularly heterosexuality – should include one of femininity as the two gender roles inform one another. It is important to unravel the power relations which emerged between males and females. Like most other elements of their masculinity, the Ducktails' expression of sexuality was contradictory and varied. Tracing the development of sexuality and expressions thereof is a complicated process, largely because it is a relatively hidden practice. Further, discussions on sexuality attempt to explore 'the most intimate and unconscious areas of experience'[78] which cannot always be reached adequately through research methods such as interviews and informal discussions.[79]

Gender relations between male and female members were ambiguous. At times, there was equality, yet at other times girls occupied a subordinate position. Unravelling gender relations in the context of youth is complicated further due to the development of sexual feelings, which generally is dependent on age, puberty and experience. For example, from interviews, it is clear that the younger boys were not as sexually active. In fact, it seems that they had very little interest in girls. Lynton Johnson remembers that boys

> grew up for longer being curious, being shy, definitely a question broadly speaking of fools rushing in where angels fear to tread, for a long while you were an angel and when the opportunity came round you sort of rushed in like a fool with a certain element ... you know like that scene in *Grease* where girls giggling here and the guys were all boasting there but both of them were sort of too scared to get together. I think that was quite typical. The parties were often quite separated and you in fact were happier with your buddies ... there was a very low key promiscuity in fact even as kids you sort of raised your eyebrows if you heard that one of your mates had had sex and he would be sort of inclined with the sort of reverence with which you treated him to sort of enlarge on the reality of it all to a little bit more tainted picture ... holding hands was quite ordinary but French kissing then you were really serious, fondling of any kind was something that you relayed to everybody you could find because you felt that you had really crossed the threshold, 'going steady' that was a big word then it really meant so much.[80]

Courtship, 'going steady' and expressing romantic feelings played a pivotal role in the development of some relationships. The 1950s was an age of experimentation and generated overt acts of sexuality such as embracing and kissing in public. At the cinema the Ducktails occupied the back rows. As Lynton Johnson explains,

> That was my first experience of free out in the open sexuality, condoms were around they were called French Letters – 'Frenchies' – you flipped a half crown and slapped down on the counter in the right shops and they would hand it over the counter in little round tins. As little guys it was 'Wow' look if you found a tin at the back of the movie house, which meant that big things had gone on.[81]

The sexual display of Ducktails defied the conservative conventions of parents and was met with harsh disapproval by wider society and in particular the press.

> It was not uncommon to find the Ducktails and their molls locked in passionate embraces in full view of passers-by. Some of the teenage girls, we were informed, had no parents or else did not know where they were. They just went about with the boys, and the boys changed their partners as often as their fancy dictated.[82]

Males and females alike had their own agendas for exploring their sexual identities. The

78 Tolson, *The Limits of Masculinity*, p. 18.

79 When dealing with sexuality in various discussions it seems that at times my age and gender affected the discussions.

80 Interview, Lynton Johnson, Kempton Park, 6 March 1997.

81 *Ibid.* 'Smooching' in the back rows of the cinema is mentioned in most interviews and in completed questionnaires.

82 Freed, *Crime in South Africa*, p. 75.

1950s marked the beginning of a sexual revolution visible through youth's overt sexual expressions. This conflicted sharply with their parents and conventional members of society who prioritised monogamy, marriage and privacy in sexual and romantic feelings. In the 1950s, sexuality was repressive as it was considered to be a social taboo that should be preserved for one's spouse after marriage. However, the Ducktails mostly rejected sexual norms through their promiscuity and opposition to monogamy. There was a certain amount of sexual freedom and choice.

For some males considerable status was attached to having a girlfriend or at least to proving their virility:

> Having a girlfriend was important but I wouldn't say it was a necessity, if you go to a party you had to have a 'squeeze' ... you had to bop and jive ... .[83]

For these males, overt sexuality as subcultural opposition faded into a conventional sexuality. For them, promiscuity had little allure because they preferred monogamous relationships. A power struggle over girls occurred between some males. At times, females were viewed by males as rewards after battle. Clashes of this kind occurred on both an individual and on a group basis. For example, in 1952 Angelo Peter Kondos (age 19) was sentenced to a £30 fine or three months' hard labour for assault with intent to do grievous bodily harm. The charge arose out of a stabbing at the Benoni Town Hall at a dance. Allegedly, the accused was interfering with the victim's girlfriend, which led to the stabbing of Charles Thomas Sayers in the shoulder.[84] The protection of masculine prestige demanded defending a girlfriend's 'honour', and being willing to do so violently.

At other times, little interest in the acquisition of a girlfriend was displayed. This was particularly so for the more organised gangs like the Greyville Ducktails in Durban. Huithwaite notes that

> A certain amount of ardent petting was noticed at some rock 'n roll sessions, but no more than one might find amongst any group of young people. Sex represents a secondary activity and appears to be considered as a threat to the solidarity of the gang .... Although individual members were interested in women, their activities often remained clandestine due to gang disapproval.[85]

However, as stated earlier, this was not the case for the bulk of Ducktails who placed a great deal of emphasis on sex and on their own sexual stimulation; for example 'bikers' were known to

> have the pockets cut out of their pants and they would never wear underpants and the girls used to you know ride like that and obviously fondle, that's what used to go on.[86]

In this particular instance, girls were perceived as objects for their sexual pleasure, which girls were obliged to perform in return for a ride on the back their motorbike. The 'objectification' of women was not simply confined to the Ducktails but it was also part of the masculine identity held by certain junior police officials. As General van der Merwe recollects:

> during my time in the police college on off days we got into the streets and we had confrontation with the Ducktails because in those times we had to go on the streets in uniform with the short hair so you're completely the opposite of the other guys. But we were looking

---

83 Interview, Bones, Kempton Park, 22 April 1997.
84 *Benoni City Times*, 'Sequel to Dance Fight', 1952.
85 Huithwaite, 'The Problem of the Ducktail in the Greyville Area of Durban', p. 90.
86 Interview, Mike Milroy, Kempton Park, 10 April 1997.

for trouble because some of those Sheilas were very nice looking ladies and we *chaffed* them and you looked for trouble. But we were tough cops you must remember, so there was no hesitation to get into a fight especially with Ducktails we said, 'No let's see who's the winner', but it was not criminality we didn't stick a knife in, you gave the guy a black eye shake his hand and take their Sheila and there you go.[87]

The objectification of girls was more evident in the Ducktails' display of collective chauvinism in the form of molestation and sexual harassment, which took place on the streets where girls were quite vulnerable. As noted by Connell, 'the street is the setting for much intimidation of women, from low-level harassment like wolf-whistling to physical manhandling and rape .... The street then is a zone of occupation by men' in which young men 'are the most intimidating and dangerous'.[88] On the street, sexual harassment can be seen as a form of entertainment which some Ducktails indulged in on a regular basis; allegedly they

gather several times a day near different commercial colleges in the Eloff Street area between De Villiers and Bree Streets and in the Plein Street area between Eloff and Hoek Streets. Here they wait for college girls to come out for their tea and lunch breaks in order to molest them with indecent suggestions. Some of the Ducktails, on whom we kept observation, were quite obviously under the influence of dagga and drink. Their shirts were hanging out of their trousers; they whistled after the girls, and touched their buttocks as they passed, and, in some cases, seized them in their arms and forcibly kissed them.[89]

Similarly, in Bezuidenhout Valley 'white youth gangs' terrorised girls at Gunnion pass (which provided a short cut to Kensington) where they grabbed unaccompanied girls and exposed themselves to them. This was one activity in which the sheilas were not present. The arrogant and chauvinistic current within the Ducktail's masculinity is highlighted through such actions. In effect, the Ducktails were enforcing their 'sexual hegemony'[90] over women through intimidation and denigration.

Sexual harassment was not confined to girls but extended to homosexual men as well. Violent, unprovoked assaults and other atrocities were carried out on homosexual men, the bulk of which were carefully planned well in advance. Allegedly

Another favourite pastime was 'moffie bashing', 'bunny bashing'. If you knew a guy was gay you would go out of your way .... Joubert Park at the station was one meeting place for 'moffies' you would go there and then go to their flat with them, beat them and scale their stuff.[91]

This was not confined to the Rand but was also common in Durban. Huithwaite contends that some of the members of the Greyville Ducktails

spoke of having 'girl friends' who were wealthy homosexual men. Often they were unscrupulous towards these people, accepting meals, presents and money from them and then refusing any sexual favours. One member said, 'We just have what we can out of them, the best wines and food, and then, if they try to touch us, we punch them up'.[92]

The worst of these reported homophobic attacks occurred in Hillbrow where there was an incident in which a gang of Ducktails

hunted down a group of *queers*, they went to City Deep [to the abattoir] and they got hold of a few pig's tails, they shave it so it's only got a bit of hair on it – now with the pig's tail all

87 Interview, Lt. General Dries van der Merwe, Pretoria, 7 November 1996.
88 R. W. Connell, *Gender and Power: Society, the Person and Sexual Politics* (Cambridge, Polity Press, 1987), p. 133.
89 Freed, *Crime in South Africa*, p. 97.
90 Glaser, 'The Mark of Zorro', p. 59.
91 Interview, Bones, Kempton Park, 22 April 1997.
92 Huithwaite, 'The Problem of the "Ducktail" in the Greyville Area of Durban', p. 91.

the hair lies one way – They went into Hillbrow that night and they hunted down the *queers* and each *queer* they found they grabbed and took one of these tails and they rammed it up their backside and they couldn't pull it out, it goes in one way and you couldn't get it out .... The Duckies were very anti-*queer* ... one of the boys ended up in Hillbrow hospital and the tail had to be cut out.[93]

Homophobia was an integral part of Ducktail masculinity but it is uncertain whether violent attacks were regularly committed. The social environment in which Ducktails operated was heterosexist and explicitly homophobic.[94] In 1939, L. F. Freed wrote a report on the incidence of homosexuality amongst youths in Johannesburg. He depicted homosexuality as a dangerous and widespread 'social evil'. Efforts were made by the office of the probation service to 'combat this perversion – or perversity – in cases where it became manifest'. Freed felt that 'a social aberration of this nature, that strikes at the very root of the moral stability of the younger generation, should at all costs be eradicated'.[95] Homophobia, as argued by Segal, 'is not primarily an instrument for oppressing a sexual minority; it is, rather, a powerful tool for regulating the entire spectrum of male relations'.[96] Homophobic acts were accepted and frequently endorsed by Ducktails and wider society. In this instance their activities were far from subcultural but rather conformed to mainstream culture's prejudice.

'The Struggle for Dominance between Masculine Forms

Ducktail masculinity did not only conform to notions of manhood embedded within mainstream white masculine identities[97] but also conflicted with and opposed them. As shown in the earlier examples, proneness to violence and pugnacity was central to masculine identities in the subculture. This hostility and disruptive presence usually resulted in violent confrontations with the armed forces, particularly the South African Police (SAP). The flying squad and police were frequently called in to control Ducktail activities. Their overt aggression was also a symbolic expression of opposition to authorities. The *RDM* reported that in 1958:

Ducktails standing on the balcony of the Selbourne Hall in the City Hall building hurled empty beer bottles into a mass of fighting police and Ducktails in the street below. Police fired some 20 shots into the air as a warning .... As the rock 'n roll session ended, Ducktails were seen trying to snatch money from the woman cashier at the door, and the two policemen intervened. A group of jeering Ducktails attacked them again. One Ducktail jabbed a policeman in the face with a fistful of knives and forks. Ghost squad police who had attended the session in plain clothes called out the flying squad. As nine squad cars pulled up outside the City Hall, Ducktails on the balcony answered with another hail of bottles .... The Ducktails, however, rushed down and attacked the police in a body. In a free-for-all that developed, police used their batons, while the Ducktails countered with knuckle-dusters and bottles.[98]

At times members of the armed forces (trainees for the airforce, new army recruits and training police officers) would group together to take 'revenge' on the Ducktails. According

93 Rufus maintains that he was not involved in this; it was something that he had heard about.

94 M. Brake, *Comparative Youth Culture: the Sociology of Youth Cultures and Subcultures in America, Britain and Canada* (London, Routledge, 1985), p. 152.

95 Historical Papers, University of the Witwatersrand, A1212/ck, 'Report on Homosexuality in Johannesburg' by L.F. Freed, 23/2/1939.

96 Cited in L. Segal, *Slow Motion: Changing Masculinities, Changing Men* (London, Virago Press, 1990), pp. 16–17.

97 Due to the lack of research into white masculinities in South African historiography, all the various forms of masculinity which prevailed in the 1950s have not been outlined.

98 *Rand Daily Mail*, 22 February 1958.

to Colonel N, one such incident occurred during 1957 in front of the Café Riche in Church Street, Pretoria, when a new army recruit

> ... was confronted by a mob of these Ducktails. They slapped his hat from his head and when he bent down to pick it up he was kicked in the face .... When he came back he obviously had to go and report that he was sick ... the officer commanding the army gymnasium ... phoned the officer commanding the airforce and they decided to let the gym trainees all have a pass for that Thursday evening ... the instructors were also told to go .... The Ben Schoeman highway wasn't there it was still the old Jo'burg road. At the ISCOR headquarters there was a circle called the *Wawiel* circle (the Wagon Wheel circle) and the army youngsters, the army gym people, who couldn't go to the gym and didn't have transport they sat there waiting because they knew that reinforcements would come from Johannesburg by motorbike. They had chains over the road and as soon as the motorbikes came they just pulled the chains up and they caught them and gave them a good hiding and the rest of the people went in to town and every Ducktail with a bit of long hair was confronted and his hair was cut and sometimes with scissors or clippers and even knives and they cleaned up the Ducktails .... Basically, after that a bloke in uniform could walk in Pretoria without being harassed but before that, it was a no go area for anybody alone in uniform.[99]

The officials not only sought 'revenge' but also to make the Ducktails conform through the symbolical cutting of their 'long' hair. These attacks on uniformed members of the armed forces by Ducktails and vice versa symbolised a struggle for dominance between two different types of masculinity. The Ducktails were effectively rejecting a disciplined, militaristic form of 'ultra-masculinity'[100] for their own aggressive 'machismo' identity. These events also reveal an affinity between Ducktails and their Hollywood heroes, both of whom resisted control by the authorities.

A motivation for these attacks was that increased military discipline was being espoused as a solution to combat 'Ducktailism' and to force recalcitrant boys to conform with wider and more socially acceptable forms of masculinity. In rejecting this, the Ducktails were opposing the common view that military discipline makes 'men out of boys'. The government's proposals for military discipline also promoted a particular form of violence and fighting technique which involved placing boys in an intense military training programme. Boys would be trained to fight in a very specific and controlled style, which was in contradiction to their uncontrolled street fighting method. In particular, numerous calls were made for the revival of the Special Services Battalion, which would not only 'give boys schooling and military training and make skilled workers of them'[101] but would also produce 'some very fine specimens of manhood'.[102] In 1956, H. J. Venter (head of the Department of Criminology at Pretoria University) contended firstly that South Africa should experiment with an unofficial junior police force, and secondly recommended that 'compulsory full-time military training from one to two years for all boys' be enforced.[103] The most common solution to controlling rebellious youths was military discipline,[104] which can be seen as an attempt to generate respect for adults and to enforce the notion of 'man as protector'. Solutions such as compulsory military training also served to 'enforce male conformity to manhood ideals ... boys have to be encouraged – sometimes actually

99 Interview, Col. N, Pretoria, 24 July 1997.

100 J. Cock, *Colonels and Cadres, War and Gender in South Africa* (Oxford, Oxford University Press, 1991), p. 58.

101 *Rand Daily Mail*, 'Juvenile Problems Discussed by Sixty Organisations', 26 June 1955.

102 *Cape Argus*, 'S.S.B. wanted to fight delinquency', 7 August 1959.

103 *Pretoria News*, 'Junior Police Force, National Service to Beat Youth Crime', 6 April 1956.

104 Through the 1957 Defence Act, white males between the ages of 17 and 65 were liable for service in the South African Defence Force. K. Satchwell, 'The Power to Defend: An Analysis of Various Aspects of the Defence Act', in J. Cock and L. Nathan (eds) *War and Society: The Militarisation of South Africa* (Cape Town, David Philip, 1989), p. 41. It must be noted, however, that initially conscription was randomly based. It was only in the 1970s that full conscription was implemented.

forced – by social sanctions to undertake efforts toward a culturally defined manhood, which by themselves they might not do'.[105]

Besides promoting military discipline, conformist members of the community made strenuous efforts to control leisure time. By 1952, almost every town on the Rand, with the exception of Benoni, had a boys' club whose aim was 'to give healthy entertainment to youths who might otherwise be wandering round the streets, and do a lot of mischief'.[106] In Johannesburg alone, there was seven such clubs. To join these clubs was effectively to cease being a Ducktail.

In addition, sporting activities[107] like boxing were promoted in an attempt to redefine Ducktail masculinity. For example in 1954, a Resident's Protection Association was formed in the Southern suburbs with the aims of keeping 'hooligans' off the streets. Mr Ferdinand Webb (organiser of the association) stipulated that members of the association would raise funds to extend the facilities of the three boxing clubs in the area and to introduce youths to social and sporting activities.[108] Alongside this were calls for campaigns to popularise existing services for youths such as Boy Scouts, Voortrekkers, Girl Guides and Church Lads' Brigades.[109] The Ducktails opposed organised sports and leisure activities, which made the attempts at popularising existing leisure activities futile. These attempts were aimed at recalcitrant youths in order to re-socialise them into the dominant, and what were considered more appropriate, values and norms founded on Christian principles, sporting ability, sobriety and a respect for work, education and upward social mobility.

In a sense, the Ducktails were a subversive force (through their hedonism, sexuality, anti-work ethic and disrespect for the law and education) which the government sought to contain. Ironically, however, for all their opposition to conformist and mainstream culture, they only took their rebellion so far and remained commited to the dominant ideals of patriarchy, homophobia and racism. In the words of Clarke:

> Even where youth sub-cultures have seemed most distinctive, different, stylistically marked out from adults and other peer-group members of their 'parent' culture, they develop certain distinctive outlooks, which have been, clearly, structured by the parent culture. We might think here of the recurrent organisation around collective activities ('group mindedness'); or on the stress on 'territoriality' (to be seen in both the Teddy Boys and the Skinheads); or the particular conceptions of masculinity and of male dominance (reproduced in all post-war youth sub-cultures).[110]

Conclusion

The attempts by government officials, religious leaders and community leaders to transform the Ducktails' masculinity were generally futile. Collectively the Ducktails rejected what was considered to be more socially acceptable and conventional forms of masculinity for their own brand, which emphasised competitiveness, physical strength, fighting ability, loyalty, virility and heterosexuality. At the same time, however, they were aggressively conformist to mainstream culture's prejudices including racism and homophobia. For males the expression and practice of masculinity was crucial in securing their membership in the

105 D. Gilmore, *Manhood in the Making: Cultural Concepts of Masculinity* (New Haven, Yale University Press, 1990), p. 25.

106 *Benoni City Times*, 'Strong Man needed for Boys' Club Here', 1952.

107 Sport was central to white South African culture in the 1950s but the Ducktails displayed no interest in organised sports as it interfered with their own agenda.

108 *Rand Daily Mail*, 'Youth Clubs to Combat S. Suburbs Gangsterism', 19 February 1954.

109 CAD, VWN, 747, SW109/4, vol. II, Report on the Church's recommendations to the Conference on Juvenile Delinquency, 1956.

110 Clarke, 'Subcultures, Cultures and Class' in *Resistance through Rituals*, p. 53.

movement. Although there were differentiations and internal contradictions, the symbolic assertion of the Ducktails' masculinity is most clearly reflected in their constant need to prove their pugnacity and to dominate physically weaker boys and innocent members of the community. The world of popular film and music of the 1950s formulated and fuelled not only the male members' masculine beliefs but also wider elements within the Ducktail subculture as a whole. Certain components of their identity were more salient than others but this saliency shifted depending on the context and circumstances. Due to the contradictory practices of masculinity within the Ducktail subculture, and culture more widely, it is clear that there were in existence multiple masculine forms which were 'always cut across by, and enmeshed within, other, differing relations of power – class, age, skill, ethnicity, sexual orientation, and so on'.[111]

Katie Mooney
Department of History, University of the Witwatersrand, Private Bag 3, Wits, Johannesburg 2050, South Africa

111 Segal, *Slow Motion: Changing Masculinities, Changing Men*, 1990, p. xi.

Part IV
Criminal Justice Settings

[18]

'There Oughtta Be a Law Against Bitches': Masculinity Lessons in Police Academy Training

Anastasia Prokos* and Irene Padavic

This article draws on participant observation in a law enforcement academy to demonstrate how a hidden curriculum encourages aspects of hegemonic masculinity among recruits. Academy training teaches female and male recruits that masculinity is an essential requirement for the practice of policing and that women do not belong. By watching and learning from instructors and each other, male students developed a form of masculinity that (1) excluded women students and exaggerated differences between them and men; and (2) denigrated women in general. Thus, the masculinity that is characteristic of police forces and is partly responsible for women's low representation on them is not produced exclusively on the job, but is taught in police academies as a subtext of professional socialization.

Keywords: masculinity, police, gender, work culture, sexual harassment, hidden curriculum

> Law enforcement training instructors often showed us episodes of the television show *COPS* as a teaching tool. In one episode, the cops arrested a shirtless man after his girlfriend had called the police. Angry at being arrested, the man yelled out, 'There oughtta be a law against bitches!' Our classroom exploded in laughter. For the remaining four months of training, when students wanted to joke about something a woman trainee had done or about women in general, they would exclaim, 'There oughtta be a law against bitches.' I estimate that I heard the phrase 25 times or more. To me, it came to epitomize the way many men recruits felt about women becoming police officers with them; women simply did not belong. (Excerpt from field notes)

Introduction

Recent theories of gender in organizations focus on the logic and processes that sustain the gender status quo (Acker, 1990, 1999a; Connell, 1987; Scott, 1986). More specifically, gender operates in organizations through several interacting processes: the construction of divisions along gender lines, the construction of symbols that reinforce those divisions, interactions between groups that produce gendered social structures, and, as outcomes of these processes, the production of gendered components of individual identity and of a gendered frame for understanding other social structures (Acker, 1990; see also Scott, 1986). Workplaces are a key site of such operations, where a seemingly gender-neutral organizational logic embeds gendered assumptions and practices deeply into the fabric of modern work.

Workers, not just work organizations, are complicit in gender creation, as ethnographic research shows, although asymmetries of power between women and men mean that they do not necessarily contribute equally to the definition of gender that prevails in a situation (Barrett, 1996; Britton, 1997; Chetkovich, 1997; Collinson, 1992; Collinson and Collinson, 1989; DiTomaso, 1989; Leidner, 1991; P. Martin, 1996, 2001; Ogasawara, 1998; Pierce, 1995; Williams, 1995; Willis, 1977). P. Martin (1998a, p. 324) explains the importance of 'framing men as agents who actively create gender hierarchy at work' (see also Collinson and Hearn, 1996; P. Martin, 2001), and Collinson and Hearn (1994, p. 5) speak of the need to 'make "men" and "masculinity" explicit [and] to talk of men's power'. Yet, as Reskin (2000) notes, much gendering is based on unconscious tendencies and need not be motivated by hostility (see also Jackman, 1994; Scott, 1990).

This article investigates a cultural practice — the creation of masculinity in police academy training — that may be implicated in a structural outcome — the low representation of women on US police forces (13.3% in 1997; National Center for Women in Policing, 1999). Police academy training represents recruits' first formal encounter with a police organization and is the first step in their professional socialization. We argue that in addition to the formal curriculum, which covers the procedures, policies, and practices of being an officer, police academies also teach the lessons of an informal 'hidden curriculum' (Bowles and Gintis, 1976; K. Martin, 1998) about masculinity. This curriculum, taught obliquely by teachers and students, instructs students about the particular form of masculinity that is lauded in police culture, the relationship between extreme masculinity and police work, and the nature of the groups that fall 'inside' and 'outside' of the culture of policing.

Because much research has shown that masculinity construction is largely an enterprise undertaken by men, why do we examine how the presence of women affects masculinity construction? In the masculinity-construction drama through which men must show to themselves, and to other men, that they conform to the dictates of appropriate masculinity, women are usually regarded as mere bit players. It is other men, not women, who put their imprimatur on appropriate masculinity (Bird, 1996, pp. 127–8; Cockburn, 1991). According to Kimmel (1994, p. 129), 'We test ourselves, perform heroic feats, take enormous risks, all because we want other men to grant us our manhood.' However, we argue that women's presence can reveal much. Masculinity is rendered most visible in situations where it is challenged, as when men face unemployment, enter traditionally female occupations (Brandth, 1998; Morgan, 1992; Williams, 1995), or, as in this case, when women enter jobs that traditionally had been used to confirm masculinity (Cockburn, 1991; Gerson and Peiss, 1985; Padavic, 1991). Thus, rather than showing that masculinity exists, we believe that studying what happens when women enter police academy training may provide insights into the *process* of masculinity construction.

While men may prefer single-sex work groups (see P. Martin, 2001), they are not always possible, and in such cases women's presence can further the masculine project in two ways. First, women can be used as a foil, allowing masculinity to be defined by what it is not. As Gamson (1997, p. 181) noted, the process of establishing a collective identity requires difference. Merely highlighting commonalities is not enough; marking off 'who we are not' is equally necessary (Barrett, 1996). As we show below, academy women became tools in the construction of boundaries that delineated who was 'in' and who was 'out' (P. Martin, 2001), in large part by making much of gender differences or creating them when they were not there. Second, women's presence can be used to elevate men's status. Devaluing women is equally as important a task as demarcating them as 'other'. As Cockburn (1988, p. 223) pointed out, the masculine identity concerns that men partly resolve by highlighting differences between the sexes inevitably produce inequality. More generally, Reskin (1988) argued that differentiation is the basis for devaluation in hierarchical systems. In this research we show that men students and instructors reinforced notions that men were superior to women in the police academy, on police forces, and in society more generally.

This is not to imply that men are the only institutional actors. A companion piece (Prokos, n.d.) shows that women did not respond uniformly to academy training. Women's responses ranged from capitalizing on stereotypical femininity, to trying to fit in with the masculine culture of the organization, to rejecting ideas about policing that equated competence with masculinity. Other researchers have documented policewomen's attitudes, identity construction, and the tension women police face between femininity and the dictates of police work (e.g. Brewer, 1991; Coffey, Brown and Savage, 1992; S. Martin, 1980). Thus, while women are more than foils or victims, the data analyzed here center on men's, not women's, actions.

Masculinity and policing

Masculinity is a social construction reproduced through everyday interactions. Its quality as a social construction rather than as a property of individual men can be seen in this definition by Kerfoot and Knights (1996, p. 86): 'the socially generated consensus of what it means to be a man, to be "manly" or to display such behaviour at any one time'. Multiple forms of masculinity exist because men (and women) construct masculinity in particular social and historical contexts. In contemporary Western society, however, 'hegemonic masculinity' (Connell, 1995) is the dominant form for reinforcing men's power on the cultural and collective levels. Although hegemonic masculinity takes different forms (Burris, 1996; P. Martin, 1998b), it is generally defined through work in the paid labor force, subordination of women, heterosexism, uncontrollable sexuality, authority, control, competitive individualism, independence, aggressiveness, and capacity for violence (Connell, 1995; Messerschmidt, 1996).

Hegemonic masculinity is a central defining concept in the culture of police work in the United States. Male police officers have drawn on images of a 'masculine cop' to enhance their sense of masculinity and to resist women's growing presence (Martin and Jurik, 1996). Hunt (1984, 1990) contended that the policeman's symbolic world is one of opposing qualities directly related to gender. Male officers equate women with feminine moral virtue, the domestic realm, social service, formal rules, administration, cleanliness, and emotions. In contrast, they equate men and masculinity with guns, crimefighting, a combative personality, resistance to management, fights, weapons, and a desire to work in high crime areas (Hunt, 1990). Thus, it is no surprise that many male police officers strongly believe that women are incapable of being good police officers.

Police officers — both managers and rank-and-file officers — share a myth of policing as action-filled, exciting, adventurous, and dangerous (Brown *et al.*, 1993). The reality of police work, however, involves much tedium and paperwork and relatively little crime fighting or violence. Regardless of the reality, male police officers cling to the image of police officers as crime fighters and downplay the femininely labeled aspects of the job, such as paperwork and social service (Hunt, 1990). Women's presence and competent performance of the masculine aspects of the job mean that the job can no longer be enlisted straightforwardly in the project of confirming masculinity. Another factor that influences male supervisors' and co-workers' responses to women cops is fear of exposure. Because women are both 'outsiders' and stereotyped as moral, male supervisors anticipate that women will expose corruption, and male rank-and-file officers anticipate that women will expose excessive violence or extramarital (or on-duty) sex (Hunt, 1990).

The first line of defense when women attempt to gain a foothold in a male preserve, thus challenging its masculine status, is to try to stop the invasion. Indeed, research shows many examples of resistance from superiors and co-workers to women's presence on police forces. Unduly harsh treatment from supervisors is common. For example, one trainer forbade a woman trainee from going to the bathroom or talking to other officers while on patrol for the first three months of her training (Heidensohn, 1992), and another sent a female officer out alone to patrol a high-crime area after she complained of unfair treatment (Feinman, 1994). Rank-and-file officers have resisted and demeaned women co-workers through their use of language and through sexual harassment. The offensive use of profanity (Morash and Haarr, 1995), the use of anti-women remarks, refusal to speak to women altogether (Balkin, 1988), and the use of affectionate terms of address such as 'hon' and 'sweetheart' (Martin and Jurik, 1996) are common. Innuendoes about women officers' sexuality, typically by referring to them as 'whores' or 'dykes', are widespread (Heidensohn, 1992; Hunt, 1984, 1990). Finally, male co-workers sexually harass women on and off duty. 'Women find sex magazines, dildos, and vibrators in their lockers and mailboxes; they encounter betting pools on who will be the first to have sex with a new female officer' (Martin and Jurik, 1996, p. 38). If this first line of defense does not succeed in eliminating women from the occupation, women's threat to the masculine character of the job can be mitigated if they can be segregated into the non-masculine, paperwork-dominated, aspects of the job, thus preserving the masculine character of the crime-fighting policeman (Hunt, 1990). If segregation is not possible, a third alternative is to use women's presence to confirm the masculine nature of the job by showing women to be unfit for it.

These elements of resistance on the part of supervisors and co-workers may have developed spontaneously in police departments. It is possible, however, that officer training programs sowed the seeds of these resistance behaviors, a possibility that we investigate here. If so, then the culture of masculinity encouraged by academy training (and further encouraged on police forces) can limit opportunities of women officers and help explain the persistent under-representation of women cops.

The hidden curriculum

In its general form, the term 'hidden curriculum' refers to the lessons schools teach students that go beyond the explicit curriculum (Bowles and Gintis, 1976). This concept originated among scholars examining the role of the schools in reproducing social class across generations. They found that schools endorse orientations that correspond to the needs of employers, such as the importance and naturalness of hierarchy and obedience (Bowles and Gintis, 1976; Giroux and Purpel, 1983). Gender scholars have recently applied the idea of a hidden curriculum to the reproduction of gender inequality (Addelston and Stirratt, 1996; K. Martin, 1998). They have pointed out that hidden curricula are crucial to the construction of gender, as schools teach and enforce what it means to be masculine and feminine and how to behave masculinely and femininely. Although research on police academy training has shown that recruits learn unrecognized and unintentional lessons during academy training (Harris, 1973), the gendered dimension of such lessons is unknown.

The setting

Certification is the first step toward establishing a law enforcement career in the United States. Police academies teach the nuts and bolts of being a police officer: here recruits practise shooting, defensive tactics, patrol-car driving, and first aid, as well as learn about state and federal law, investigations, and patrolling. Most instructors are sworn police officers from local and state law enforcement agencies, and most students and instructors are men (S. Martin, 1994; Martin and Jurik, 1996; Pike, 1992).

Because this research investigates only one academy, which is located in a rural county in the southeastern USA, the findings may not be generalizable to urban academies or to ones in other regions. Despite the academy's rural location, however, its students came from a nearby mid-sized city and almost all had graduated from one of the city's two universities; thus the student body is not exceptional on the rural/urban dimension. Residents of the south tend to hold more conservative gender attitudes (although they have become more liberal over time, see Rice and Coates, 1995), and thus we cannot make claims about the national representativeness of this study. We note, however, that while geographically limited ethnographic research cannot be considered definitive, it can add to our understanding by illustrating the processes by which women and men students learn about masculinity on police forces.

Methodology

This research is based on participant observation the first author conducted in 1997 while enrolled in a law enforcement training academy program lasting five months. She is a white woman, 27 years old at the time of the research. The other 30 students were mostly white men in their early twenties who held bachelor's degrees. There were four other women in the class, all white, and three African-American men. Of the more than 40 instructors who taught classes at various times, about 12% were women, one of whom was African-American. The academy course met eight hours a day, five days a week. Most students paid the $1000 tuition themselves, but a few were sponsored by a local police department.

Because this article is based on the participant observation of the first author, we hereinafter use the first-person voice to describe her experiences. The data for this research include notes and observations I made during my training at the academy. These data consist of short comments I wrote in the margins of my class notebooks and notes that I took after hours, often talking into a tape recorder during the commute home. I transcribed over 100 pages of such field notes. Additional data include class notes on the formal curriculum taught in lectures, as well as over 500 pages of academy-provided materials.

I used the grounded theory method to analyze the data and generate theory. The goal of grounded theory is to use data to develop theory rather than to test existing theory (Glaser and Strauss, 1967). When using grounded theory, the processes of data collection, coding, and analysis are simultaneous (Glaser and Strauss, 1967), and for much of the project this was the case. However, some of the coding was completed after the academy ended. Data analysis proceeded from coding, to developing conceptual categories based on the codes, to defining the conceptual categories, and finally to clarifying the links between the conceptual categories.

After passing the written and oral board entrance exams, an ethical dilemma arose concerning whether or not to inform other participants and school administrators of my intent to conduct participant observation research. This is the same dilemma many researchers face in doing participant observation (Diamond, 1992; Punch, 1986; Van Maanen, 1983). It became clear that making the research agenda known would jeopardize my chances of acceptance into the academy and would substantially alter my treatment by administrators, instructors, and other students, even if I were admitted. Thus, I did not reveal my identity as a researcher. The academy administration was aware that I was a graduate student in sociology and that I planned to finish my PhD. Many of the students knew that I had a master's degree (in fact, my nickname at the beginning of training was 'Masters') and that I planned to study women in law enforcement. Because the administration and other students were unaware that I was observing academy training, I rarely took field notes when I could be observed.

As a woman observing mostly male recruits, my experiences were probably different from those a man would have had. While my female status enabled my access to a wealth of data, it forced me to decide how I would handle mistreatment (Warren, 1988). As a woman in policing, there is a tension between being accepted by the group and proving that one is capable of performing police work. Acceptance often required acting in a stereotypically feminine way, yet acting capably usually contradicted such behavior (see S. Martin, 1980, for an explanation of how this occurs 'on the job' for women police). This is, in fact, the central tension women faced in the police academy: trying to negotiate acceptance as a woman and as a cop at the same time. My solution was to challenge men's behavior toward me when it implied that I was unqualified, but to not challenge their opinions about and treatment of other women.

Results

The explicit curriculum and the hidden curriculum at the police academy stood in stark contrast to one another. The explicit curriculum was gender-neutral; the hidden curriculum was riddled with gendered lessons. The ostensibly gender-neutral curriculum of the academy had as its stated goal the production of professional and competent police officers, regardless of gender. The student policy manual was scrupulously gender-neutral. The use of gender-neutral pronouns, for example, was consistent throughout the manual, as were all sections describing personal grooming (e.g. 'trainee will present a neat and clean appearance') except in rare cases (e.g. 'sideburns will not extend past the center of the ear') that were directed to one sex only. Finally, the manual stated that, 'No sexual, racial, ethnic, or religious slurs will be tolerated. Any violation will result in your dismissal from the academy.' Field notes from the first day corroborate this message by noting the instructor's repeated avowal that inappropriate sexual or racial language was inexcusable.

Despite the gender-neutral formal curriculum, hegemonic masculinity continually reappeared in the hidden curriculum, inserted by male instructors and students via their treatment of each other and of women. The first two sections, below, describe how gender boundary-setting occurred in the police academy. The second two sections show how most men students and instructors conceptualized themselves — and men more generally — as not only different from but better than women. Table 1 summarizes these elements of the hidden curriculum.

Treating women as outsiders

Men in police academy training treated women students as outsiders by using gendered language, eliminating them from classroom examples, and excluding them from bonding experiences. Women learned that they were not considered members of the 'in-group', which was defined by masculinity. Men also learned that women were outsiders in policing and that there are no repercussions for treating them as such.

Instructors' use of gendered language was pervasive. Specifically, instructors used the male pronoun when referring to students or to law enforcement officers generally. The academy's director delivered a lecture in

Table 1: The hidden curriculum in law enforcement training

	Lessons for men	Lessons for women
Treating women as outsiders	Social and physical boundaries can be created through language that excludes women, through the assumption that cops are men, through bonding with other recruits around activities that exclude women.	Instructors and other students assume cops are men. Women are virtually ignored in curriculum and are excluded from social groups.
Exaggerating gender differences	Women and men are very different and this matters more than other differences between people. If women are strong, they are like men, which is inappropriate. 'Feminine' women are incapable of the physical demands of police work.	Women and men are very different and this matters more than other differences between people. Women are the ones who are different, men are the norm, so women will be treated differently.
Denigrating and objectifying women	Women are sexual objects. Women and women's issues (such as women's victimization) are not as valuable, good, or important as men or men's issues.	The place of women in the criminal justice system is as victims and as objects of men's fantasies and ridicule.
Resisting powerful women	Women in positions of power do not need to be taken seriously.	Women asserting authority will not be taken seriously by male police officers.

which he referred to us as 'gentlemen' and 'guys'. Only twice did he catch himself and add 'and ladies', a term with more connotations of sex-appropriate behavior than the term 'women'. Instructors' use of 'guys' when addressing us was normative. Regardless of the speaker's intent, people tend to picture men when hearing the words 'man' and 'he' (Richardson, 1993). Certainly women and men students learned that the normative cop was a man.

It sometimes seemed that female police officers did not exist in the instructors' worlds. For example, when instructing class members about how to perform searches, an instructor demonstrated a search on a male student and showed how men searching a woman would do things somewhat differently in order to insure that her sexual privacy was not illegally invaded. (He made clear that the impetus behind such concern was fear of a lawsuit.) Yet, he never mentioned how women officers should search men suspects to similarly insure privacy. Clearly, he assumed that his audience of students was men, thus disregarding the women students.

Women instructors, too, perpetuated women's outsider status. One female instructor of 'employment skills' taught about appropriate attire for an interview, explaining that men should wear suits unless the interview were with a small, casual, department, in which case they might wear khaki pants, a nice shirt, and a tie. She spoke at length about how to determine which departments were casual. She mentioned that women, too, should wear suits and asked an already employed female student what she had worn to her interview, and that ended the discussion of women's interview attire. The instructor provided no details about how women should dress for different types of departments or what type of suit they should wear, leaving women recruits to ponder alone the relative merits of skirted and trouser suits. While attire is a minor issue, of course, the lesson that men's issues take precedence, even when a woman is directing the discussion, is not minor.

Police department recruiters hoping to hire new graduates gave periodic presentations, and they, too, pitched their material to a male audience. For example, one set of recruiters outlined the physical standards for male employees and completely ignored the female standard. Thus, students learned that 25-year-old men were required to run a mile and a half in approximately 12 minutes in order to be hired by a police department; no mention was made of the requirement for women. Other recruiters mentioned salary and benefit structures, but none mentioned parental leave or efforts to better integrate women. Students had opportunities to ask questions, but issues of specific interest to women recruits were not part of any recruiter's prepared presentation and were never asked in discussion.

Many men students acted as if the classroom were a male preserve by creating bonding experiences that excluded women. For example, one group of about ten men occasionally engaged in 'farting contests' and frank discussions about their sex lives. These discussions or activities usually terminated when a woman approached the group. In explaining why a loud and lively group of men tended to grow quiet when a woman approached, men students said things like, 'We can't talk about that now because there are ladies in the room', or 'That's not fit conversation in front of the ladies'. As Kanter (1977) pointed out over 20 years ago, such 'boundary heightening' remarks remind women that they are outsiders who are not welcome as full group members.

The glorification of violent masculinity further served to knit together men and exclude women. Male students frequently got together after class in one another's homes or in bars to watch football games on television; women were not invited. On one occasion, a man brought a videotaped football game into the classroom and showed it during the lunch break; the female students remained silent and did crossword puzzles. While watching, the students debated referee calls and argued over which team was better. These disputes led to alliances over teams, further intensifying the female exclusionary ties built around football.

Physical fighting was a theme dwelled on by students and instructors alike during downtimes. In one instance, the women and men students were sitting around in the gymnasium waiting for the next activity when the head physical training instructor joined us to reminisce about his younger days as a police officer and the fights he would get into. In one story, he had left the scene, only to return minutes later to assist the uniformed officers who had shown up to break up the fight that he had precipitated! Much laughing on the part of the students ensued. Other of his stories similarly glorified bar fights and associated them with being a police officer. The link that men created between masculinity and violence in its vicarious form (football) and in its instantiated form (bar-room brawls) emphasized their commonalities as men and women's difference.

In sum, male instructors and students participated in constructing an ideology in which the term 'woman cop' was oxymoronic. Through language and bonding experiences it became clear that the 'in-group', in addition to other characteristics (such as whiteness, youth, and heterosexuality), was exclusively male. Thus, women and men learned that women are outsiders in the police world, and that women police officers can be ignored as exceptions who must learn to adjust to the existing environment.

Exaggerating gender differences

Male instructors and students exaggerated differences between themselves and the women they encountered and claimed that women's differences made them inferior to men. Students of both sexes learned that women and men by nature are very different and that gender differences supersede other differences, such as those stemming from race, ethnicity, or social class. In addition, men learned that women are rarely as physically strong as men and that those who are strong are 'like men', and thus not feminine. Women learned that women are treated differently at the academy, further serving to demonstrate that they are not entirely welcome in this environment, or at least not welcome as equals.

The 'human diversity' instructor conducted class exercises that entailed physically segregating students by sex, race, geographic region, and whether or not recruits had a family member in law enforcement. This resulted in one group of white women (seen as a sex group), one group of black men (seen as a race group), and four groups of white men (a southern group, a northern group, a state-regional group, and a group with family members in law enforcement). A categorization problem arose for students whose characteristics spanned categories: which group should they align with? The instructor's solution was that sex and race 'trumped' the other categories: women and African-Americans were supposed to stay in 'their' sex or race groups even if they had family in law enforcement or identified with a region. While the ostensible point of the exercise was to make students aware of race and gender issues, the unintended effect of the hidden curriculum was to reify differences.

Another example of categorizing people in a way that reified sex differences occurred in defensive tactics class, where instructors paired women with women and men with men, purportedly to match similar-sized people. The matching of men was unproblematic: instructors suggested that men pair with men of similar size but did not suggest specific pairs. However, because we had an odd number of women, the last woman in line had to be paired with a larger man. Although at 5′9″ I was larger than all of the women (and several of the men), I had already been paired with a woman. Yet if size, not gender, were the guiding criterion, the instructor would have reassigned me to partner with the man. The assignments seemed, for women at least, to be based less on size than on gender.

Instructors highlighted sex differences between recruits in several other ways. The 'human diversity' instructor showed an ABC-network video hosted by conservative media personality John Stossel that stressed the biological imperative of gender differences. The 'communication' instructor taught us that women and men communicate entirely differently, with women seeking emotional connectedness and men seeking solutions. Another instructor explained that while a few women were quite strong, such exceptions were 'not really like women at all'. Once he had tried to arrest a 250-pound woman whom he had mistakenly 'treated like a lady'. He explained, with great animation, that the woman almost escaped because he had been unprepared for her strength and fighting ability. His distinction between 'real women' (who were 'ladies' and physically weak) and 'strong women' (perpetrators who are unwomanly, and indeed, scary: 'they can kick you so that you won't be able to have children') put female recruits in a double bind: to be feminine they need to sacrifice strength; to be a cop they need to sacrifice femininity.

Some instructors treated women and men differently based on the stereotype that women were not naturally gifted at fighting. One instructor aggressively 'picked on' women in the physical training class. Class members practiced techniques wherein they close their eyes and await the 'attack', which they fend off with the new tactic being taught. The instructor moved around the room to replace the attacking student, yet he only attacked women students. When I asked him why, he said that, in fact, he had attacked men but I simply had not seen him. (I am confident in my claim.) Because it is much more difficult to successfully perform defensive tactics against an experienced attacker, women students ended up appearing less competent (to themselves, to other students, and to the instructor) than men students, who only had to defend themselves against fellow inexperienced students. Women also experienced the opposite problem of not having enough instructor attention; another instructor demonstrated defensive tactics only on men.

Students, too, emphasized gender differences, claiming that partnering with a woman could be life-threatening (see also Charles, 1981). During obstacle-course training, for example, students had to pull a 150-pound dummy approximately 25 yards. Equal proportions of men and women had trouble with the dummy drag, as it was near the end of the physically exhausting obstacle course. Yet a student complained after the exercise that he would not want a woman to be his partner because she would never be able to drag him in an emergency. No other students publicly disagreed with him, and none of the instructors present intervened in the conversation.

Male students often treated women as if they were fragile. In physical training class, we practiced punching in pairs with protective pads. Each time, the same two or three men would very gently punch the pads women held, barely grazing the pad. These men would resume punching normally when they were switched to a male partner. Fellow students' treatment of me similarly assumed female fragility, even though I did not act in any stereotypically feminine ways. Our class president took me aside to ascertain whether I could stand up to the remarks of several male recruits who had 'gone too far' in talking about their sex lives and bodily functions in my presence. In doing so, he assumed both that I was offended (which, as a 'lady', I should have been) and that I needed help in confronting other students. Another insisted on trying to give me gun-shooting advice, even though I had both an instructor and a female student acting as coaches. While these men may have thought they were being helpful, such help was predicated on men's lack of respect for women's abilities and reified the notion of female weakness.

Male students and instructors emphasizing gender differences and acting on stereotypes of women's fragility can damage women's progress in policing. Students and instructors perpetuated the idea that women are not as qualified for police jobs as are men because they are different and inferior. Women recruits learned that they would be treated differently from male recruits at the academy and that men viewed them as intrinsically less capable and less qualified. Men learned that women are fundamentally different and thus are inadequate as police officers. They also learned some of the rudiments of appropriate masculinity by virtue of seeing it contrasted with a caricature of femininity.

Denigrating and objectifying women

We now turn to the evidence supporting the claim that masculinity is constructed not simply through lessons about what is masculine and what is not; in addition, men and women are taught that being male is better than being female. Men learned to disparage women by verbally denigrating and objectifying them (as in the comment 'there oughtta be a law against bitches'), and women students learned that such behavior is condoned by the institution they seek to enter. Men students belittled women and things associated with women — such as class material on domestic violence and rape — in addition to objectifying them. Women students learned that the expected role of women in the criminal justice system is as victims and as objects of male workers' fantasies and ridicule.

Male students' denigration of women occurred at the most basic level in their use of language. They called fellow male students 'pussies' when they failed to act appropriately manly. Besides its crudity, this expression equates femaleness with weakness, reinforcing other lessons about women's not belonging. Similarly, when students were cleaning the training room once, a man called out to the male broom-pushers, 'Why are you all sweeping? That's women's work!' This statement had the effect of insulting the men and women and delineating sharp boundaries around which tasks were masculine and which were not.

Another way that training denigrated and objectified women was through the presentation of women in training films and men's response to them. The class watched a recently made video about driving emergency vehicles in which a male officer daydreamed of a beautiful woman in a negligee when he was supposed to be concentrating on the road. The scene looked like it could have come from a pornographic film: the woman on the screen was on all fours crawling toward the camera while she licked her lips. As the class watched the film, many of the men chanted things like 'ohhh, baby' and 'hot mama'. In another instance, male students, with the instructor's unwitting complicity, dismissed the importance of crimes against women. The instructor left the room after activating the VCR to show a training film about domestic violence. Many class members ignored the film and talked loudly, often evaluating the appearance of the women in the film, particularly the women victims, saying things like 'hubba hubba' and 'ooh, she's cute!' When a woman who did not meet their standards of attractiveness appeared on the video, many men made fun of her appearance, groaning and calling out, 'she's ugly'. In this way, male students indicated their disregard for the material by ignoring the films when they were not busy rating actresses' beauty. Their actions also implied that women's appearance is more important than violence against them, indicating that to some extent they did not object to violence against women. The instructor's absence allowed the men to demean women and disregard the importance of crimes against women.

Instructors chose films that degraded and objectified women, and men students learned from such course material and from fellow students' reactions that objectification of women was acceptable. They also learned that women are not as important or valuable as men. Male students also drew on negative images of women to insult one another during training. Thus, men's interactions with each other, along with training materials and men's responses to the materials, reconstructed stereotypes about women. Women recruits learned from these lessons of the hidden curriculum that men in the criminal justice system are likely to view women as victims and sexual objects who are subject to ridicule and contempt.

Resisting powerful women's authority

The academy taught male recruits that they need not treat women in positions of power or authority with the same respect or seriousness as they accord men. Several male students resisted women instructors' institutional power by 'acting out' and by openly questioning their authority. On one occasion, a woman instructor started a video about victims of burglary, robbery, domestic violence, and rape and left the room. She had explained that we were to watch all four segments of the video, but at the end of the first segment, one of the male students turned off the VCR. The male students laughed and joked about how we did not have to do anything at all since the instructor wasn't present. It is unclear whether the men's rebellion was directed at the woman instructor, the subject matter, or both. Nonetheless, it was clear that these men did not accept the authority of this woman instructor. In another instance, almost all the men (and most of the women) laughed disrespectfully at a woman instructor-trainee who had demonstrated a physical technique incorrectly. Students also talked among themselves during female instructors' lectures more often and more loudly than during male instructors' lectures. A female instructor's lecture on 'employment skills' was repeatedly interrupted by rowdiness, until finally a female student complained to the administration.

The disrespect accorded women instructors spilled over onto treatment of female students. On the firing range, we lined up in rows, with each student coaching the shooter in front as we rotated through the shooting position. When it was my turn to coach a male student, he listened to my comments, and explained that he would not do as I suggested because he had a shooting style he liked and did not intend to change. When instructors later gave him the same advice, he obeyed. Of course, he also might have rejected advice from a male student, but I overheard no instances of this in any of the range practices.

In sum, students treated female instructors with less courtesy and respect. Male students learned that they need not accept women as superiors, or perhaps even as equals. Female students learned that male police officers may not listen to them or accept their advice were they to be in positions of authority or even equality. Because women cops will be in situations where it is crucial to relay information to men officers who then may not take it seriously, this lack of respect may give rise to second thoughts for women would-be officers.

Conclusion

While there may be no law against women (or bitches) entering the police academy, the hidden curriculum there taught recruits that dominant masculinity is necessary to performing their duties as cops. Women's presence at the academy facilitated these lessons by indicating the boundaries surrounding masculinity (accomplished through differentiation) and by highlighting masculinity's superiority over things not-masculine. Specifically, male students learned that it is acceptable to exclude women, that women are naturally very different from men and thus can be treated differently, that denigrating and objectifying women is commonplace and expected, and that they can disregard women in authority. For each of these lessons, male recruits learned accompanying strategies for excluding and antagonizing women, strategies that effectively communicated to women that they were not welcome as equals.

Three decades of research have indicated the informal barriers that male co-workers and supervisors establish to counter the threat of women's entry into traditionally male occupations (Gruber and Bjorn, 1982; Cockburn, 1988; Swerdlow, 1989; Gruber, 1998). Some male resistance stems from women's disruption of male bonding and the equation of masculine men with masculine work. We have extended understanding of the resistance process by showing that women's presence can, in fact, further the project of masculinity construction, and we offer evidence from the training grounds of one of the most masculine professions. In police academy training male students and instructors used the presence of women to aid in their construction of divisions along gender lines. As Acker (1990, 1999b) explained, the construction of such divisions sustains the gender status quo of organizations.

Why is men's domination of this particular occupation so resistant to change when women have successfully entered other formerly male domains, such as law? Perhaps the comparison of police work to other legal-system occupations is ill conceived. Men's resistance to women in policing is probably more similar to military men's resistance to women, since both involve a particular type of masculinity defined by men's control of violence. Men have always maintained a monopoly on organized violence (Connell, 1987, p. 107, 1995; Enloe, 1989; Messerschmidt, 1993; see also Barrett, 1996). In general, most militaries and police — and the individuals who control them, such as judges and general — are men. The exclusion of women from the means of organized violence, including instruction in the use of weapons and military technique is not accidental (Connell, 1987, p. 107, 1995). Indeed, as Enloe (1989, p. 6) noted, '[S]ocial processes and structures ... have been created and sustained over the generations — sometimes coercively — to keep most women out of any political position with influence over state force.' Control over institutionalized violence is a core component of men's authority in western cultures (Connell, 1987). Thus, while police culture, like the culture of many other male-dominated occupations, defines itself through masculinity, it is perhaps the association not only with masculinity, but also with violence, that leads men to resist women in policing.

Directions for future research

Women are not the only group used to help construct masculinity in police academies and departments. The culture of masculinity in these sites has traditionally excluded some men, particularly those who do not fit the requirements of hegemonic masculinity (see Bird, 1996; Acker, 1999b). Hegemonic masculinity is constructed in relation to other masculinities as well as in relation to femininity (Connell, 1995). For this reason, the presence of men who do not conform to hegemonic masculinity may threaten some men's association of masculine identity and police work. How is masculinity constructed in relation to other men as well as women? Specifically, on what criteria do men judge other men for police group membership? The construction of masculinity is complex, and understanding how men construct it in relation to other men may offer insights into their hostility towards women's presence.

Our findings are limited to the experiences and treatment of white women in one academy. These limitations point to the importance of gathering data from multiple programs and types of departments, thus permitting investigation into the crucial question of which organizational characteristics lead to less hostile training environments for women. Similar research unpacking the relationship between notions of race and ethnicity to notions of masculinity (Cose, 1995) and how various organizational practices can mediate the treatment of people of color in academies and on police forces is also crucial. Understanding the nature of the barriers faced by women, minorities, and other groups who are 'outsiders' to hegemonic masculinity is the first step in fighting for their inclusion in a politically crucial occupational niche.

Acknowledgements

We are grateful for the comments of Patricia Yancey Martin, Jan Thomas, David Quadagno, the Tallahassee Chapter of Sociologists for Women in Society, the Henry A. Murray Research Center and the Radcliffe Institute for Advanced Study, and anonymous reviewers from *Gender, Work and Organization*.

References

Acker, J. (1990) Hierarchies, jobs, bodies: a theory of gendered organizations. *Gender & Society*, 4,2, 139–58.

Acker, J. (1999a) Rewriting class, race, and gender: problems in feminist rethinking. In Feree, M.M., Lorber, J. and Hess, B.B. (eds) *Revisioning Gender*. Thousand Oaks, CA: Sage.

Acker, J. (1999b) Gender and organization. In Chafetz, J. (ed.) *Handbook of the Sociology of Gender*. New York: Kluwer Academic/Plenum Publishers.

Addelston, J. and Stirratt, M. (1996) The last bastion of masculinity: gender politics at The Citadel. In Cheng, C. (ed.) *Masculinities in Organizations*. Thousand Oaks, CA: Sage.

Balkin, J. (1988) Why policemen don't like policewomen. *Journal of Police Science and Administration*, 16,1, 29–38.

Barrett, F.J. (1996) The organizational culture of hegemonic masculinity: the case of the US Navy. *Gender, Work, and Organization*, 3,3, 129–42.

Bird, S. (1996) Welcome to the men's club: homosociality and the maintenance of hegemonic masculinity. *Gender & Society*, 10,2, 120–32.

Bowles, S. and Gintis, H. (1976) *Schooling in Capitalist America*. New York: Basic Books.

Brandth, B. (1998) Masculinity and childcare: the reconstruction of fathering. *Sociological Review*, 46,2, 293–314.

Brewer, J.D. (1991) Hercules, Hippolyte and the Amazons — or policewomen in the RUC. *British Journal of Sociology*, 42,2, 231–47.

Britton, D.M. (1997) Gendered organizational logic: policy and practice in men's and women's prisons. *Gender & Society*, 11,6, 796–818.

Brown, J., Maidmont, A. and Bull, R. (1993) Appropriate skill-task matching or gender bias in deployment of male and female police officers? *Policing and Society*, 3,2, 121–36.

Burris, B.H. (1996) Technocracy, patriarchy and management. In Collinson, D.L. and Hearn, J. (eds) *Men as Managers, Managers as Men*. London: Sage.

Charles, M.T. (1981) The performance and socialization of female recruits in the Michigan State Police Training Academy. *Journal of Police Science and Administration*, 9,2, 209–23.

Chetkovich, C. (1997) *Real Heat: Gender and Race in the Urban Fire Service*. New Brunswick, NJ: Rutgers University Press.

Cockburn, C. (1988) *Machinery of Dominance: Women, Men and Technical Know-How*. Boston: Northeastern University Press.

Cockburn, C. (1991) *In the Way of Women: Men's Resistance to Sex Equality in Organizations*. Ithaca, NY: ILR Press.

Coffey, S., Brown, J. and Savage, S. (1992) Policewomen's career aspirations: some reflections on the role and capabilities of women in policing in Britain. *Police Studies*, 15,1, 13–19.
Collinson, D.L. (1992) *Managing the Shopfloor: Subjectivity, Masculinity and Workplace Culture*. New York: Walter de Gruyter.
Collinson, D.L. and Collinson, M. (1989) Sexuality in the workplace: the domination of men's sexuality. In Hearn, J., Sheppard, D., Tancred-Sheriff, P. and Burrell, G. (eds) *The Sexuality of Organization*. London: Sage.
Collinson, D.L. and Hearn, J. (1994) Naming men as men: implications for work, organization, and management. *Gender, Work, and Organization*, 1,1, 2–22.
Collinson, D.L. and Hearn, J. (1996) Breaking the silence: on men, masculinities, and managements. In Collinson, D.L. and Hearn, J. (eds) *Men as Managers, Managers as Men*. London: Sage.
Connell, R.W. (1987) *Gender and Power*. Stanford, CA: Stanford University Press.
Connell, R.W. (1995) *Masculinities*. Berkeley, CA: University of California Press.
Cose, E. (1995) *A Man's World: How Real is Male Privilege and How High is its Price?* New York: HarperCollins.
Diamond, T. (1992) *Making Gray Gold: Narratives of Nursing Home Care*. Chicago: University of Chicago Press.
DiTomaso, N. (1989) Sexuality in the workplace: discrimination and harassment. In Hearn, J., Sheppard, D., Tancred-Sheriff, P. and Burrell, G. (eds) *The Sexuality of Organization*. London: Sage.
Enloe, C. (1989) *Bananas, Beaches, and Bases: Making Feminist Sense of International Politics*. Berkeley, CA: University of California Press.
Feinman, C. (1994) *Women in the Criminal Justice System*, 3rd edn. Westport, CT: Praeger.
Gamson, J. (1997) Messages of exclusion: gender, movements, and symbolic boundaries. *Gender & Society*, 11,2, 178–99.
Gerson, J. and Peiss, K. (1985) Boundaries, negotiation, consciousness: reconceptualizing gender relations. *Social Problems*, 32,4, 317–31.
Giroux, H. and Purpel, D. (1983) *The Hidden Curriculum and Moral Education*. Berkeley, CA: McCutchan.
Glaser, B.G. and Strauss, A.L. (1967) *The Discovery of Grounded Theory: Strategies for Qualitative Research*. Chicago: Aldine Publishing Co.
Gruber, J. (1998) The impact of male work environments and organizational policies on women's experiences of sexual harassment. *Gender & Society*, 12,3, 301–20.
Gruber, J. and Bjorn, L. (1982) Blue-collar blues: the sexual harassment of women autoworkers. *Work and Occupations*, 9,3, 271–98.
Harris, R. (1973) *The Police Academy: An Inside View*. New York: John Wiley & Sons.
Heidensohn, F. (1992) *Women in Control? The Role of Women in Law Enforcement*. Oxford: Clarendon Press.
Hunt, J. (1984) The development of rapport through the negotiation of gender in field work among police. *Human Organization*, 43,4, 283–96.
Hunt, J. (1990) The logic of sexism among police. *Women and Criminal Justice*, 1,2, 3–30.
Jackman, M. (1994) *The Velvet Glove: Paternalism and Conflict in Gender, Class, and Race Relations*. Berkeley, CA: University of California Press.
Kanter, R.M. (1977) *Men and Women of the Corporation*. New York: Basic Books.
Kerfoot, D. and Knights, D. (1996) 'The best is yet to come?': the quest for embodiment in managerial work. In Collinson, D.L. and Hearn, J. (eds) *Men as Managers, Managers as Men*. London: Sage.
Kimmel, M. (1994) Masculinity as homophobia: fear, shame, and silence in the construction of gender identity. In Brod, H. and Kaufman, M. (eds) *Theorizing Masculinities*. Thousand Oaks, CA: Sage.

Leidner, R. (1991) Serving hamburgers and selling insurance: gender, work, and identity in interactive service jobs. *Gender & Society*, 5,2, 154–78.
Martin, K. (1998) Becoming a gendered body: practices of preschools. *American Sociological Review*, 63,4, 494–511.
Martin, P.Y. (1996) Gendering and evaluating dynamics: men, masculinities, and managements. In Collinson, D.L. and Hearn, J. (eds) *Men as Managers, Managers as Men*. Thousand Oaks, CA: Sage.
Martin, P.Y. (1998a) Gender and organizations. In Myers, K.A., Anderson, C.D. and Risman, B.J. (eds) *Feminist Foundations: Towards Transforming Sociology*. Newbury Park, CA: Sage.
Martin, P.Y. (1998b) Why can't a man be more like a woman? Reflections on Connell's *Masculinities*. *Gender & Society*, 12,4, 472–4.
Martin, P.Y. (2001) 'Mobilizing masculinities': women's experience of men at work. *Organization*, 8 (forthcoming).
Martin, S.E. (1980) *Breaking and Entering*. Berkeley, CA: University of California Press.
Martin, S.E. (1994) 'Outsider within' the station house: the impact of race and gender on black women police. *Social Problems*, 41,3, 383–400.
Martin, S.E. and Jurik, N.C. (1996) *Doing Justice, Doing Gender*. Thousand Oaks, CA: Sage.
Messerschmidt, J. (1993) *Masculinities and Crime: Critique and Reconceptualization of Theory*. Lanham, MD: Rowman and Littlefield.
Messerschmidt, J. (1996) Managing to kill: masculinities and the space shuttle *Challenger* explosion. In Cheng, C. (ed.) *Masculinities in Organizations*. Thousand Oaks, CA: Sage.
Morash, M. and Haarr, M. (1995) Gender, workplace problems, and stress in policing. *Justice Quarterly*, 12,1, 113–40.
Morgan, D. (1992) *Discovering Men*. London: Routledge.
National Center for Women in Policing (1999) Equality denied: the status of women in policing, 1997. http://www.feminist.org/police/status.html
Ogasawara, Y. (1998) *Office Ladies and Salaried Men: Power, Gender and Work in Japanese Companies*. Berkeley, CA: University of California Press.
Padavic, I. (1991) The re-creation of gender in a male workplace. *Symbolic Interaction*, 14,3, 279–94.
Pierce, J. (1995) *Gender Trials: Emotional Lives in Contemporary Law Firms*. Berkeley, CA: University of California Press.
Pike, D.L. (1992) Women in police academy training: some aspects of organizational response. In Moyer, I.L. (ed.) *The Changing Roles of Women in the Criminal Justice System: Offenders, Victims, and Professionals*, 2nd edn. Prospect Heights, IL: Waveland Press, Inc.
Prokos, A. (n.d.) Tough cops and reasoned responses: the making of women and men police officers. Unpublished manuscript.
Punch, M. (1986) *The Politics and Ethics of Fieldwork*. Beverly Hills, CA: Sage.
Reskin, B. (1988) Bringing the men back in: sex differentiation and the devaluation of women's work. *Gender & Society*, 2,1, 58–81.
Reskin, B. (2000) The proximate causes of employment discrimination. *Contemporary Sociology*, 29,2, 319–29.
Rice, T.W. and Coates, D.L. (1995) Gender role attitudes in the southern United States. *Gender & Society*, 9,6, 744–56.
Richardson, L. (1993) Gender stereotyping in the English language. In Richardson, L. and Taylor, V. (eds) *Feminist Frontiers III*. New York: Random House.
Scott, J.C. (1990) *Domination and the Arts of Resistance: Hidden Transcripts*. New Haven, CT: Yale University Press.

Scott, J.W. (1986) Gender: a useful category of historical analysis. *American Historical Review*, 91, 1053–75.
Swerdlow, M. (1989) Men's accommodations to women entering a nontraditional occupation: a case of rapid transit operatives. *Gender & Society*, 3,3, 373–87.
Van Maanen, J. (1983) The moral fix: on the ethics of fieldwork. In Emerson, R. (ed.) *Contemporary Field Research: A Collection of Readings*. Boston: Little, Brown.
Warren, C.A.B. (1988) *Gender Issues in Field Research*. Newbury Park, CA: Sage.
Williams, C. (1995) *Still a Man's World: Men Who Do 'Women's Work'*. Berkeley, CA: University of California Press.
Willis, P. (1977) *Learning to Labour*. Farnborough: Saxon House.

[19]

Men Behind Bars

*"Doing" Masculinity as an Adaptation to Imprisonment

YVONNE JEWKES
University of Hull

This article, which is part of a wider ethnographic study of constructions of self in the mediated world of men's prisons, explores "manliness" as the prison coping strategy par excellence. That masculinity is likely to become more extreme in men's prisons is unsurprising, but the origins and nature of the "hypermasculine" culture and the precise means by which hierarchies of domination are created and maintained have yet to be thoroughly explored. Indeed, although men constitute the vast majority of prisoners worldwide, most studies treat the gender of their subjects as incidental and assume that in men's prisons, the normal rules of patriarchy do not apply. However, as this article demonstrates, the notion of patriarchy, although in need of refinement, is not irrelevant to the predominantly male environment, and it is now widely accepted that men can be its victims as well as its perpetrators.

Key words: prisoners; identity; self; hypermasculinity; fratriarchy; power

THE "PAINS OF IMPRISONMENT": IMPORTED OR INTRINSIC?

Prisoners are overwhelmingly young, male, unemployed, and drawn from the lower working classes. Explanations of why groups of people who face structural discrimination do not take collective action to improve the conditions of their lives but seemingly collude in their subordination by accepting the restricted life choices available to them is a complex area of analysis, but much of the so-called prison importation literature (e.g. Irwin and Cressey 1962) suggests that the forms and codes of overtly masculine behavior that characterize working-class cultures are implicated in the replication and perpetuation of imprisonment. To put it succinctly, criminal behavior in society may be regarded (at least to a significant degree) as a learned response to the imperatives of masculine hegemony, while in prisons, masculinity may be

---

Author's Note: *This article draws on materials that appear in Jewkes (2002)* Captive Audience: Media, Masculinity and Power in Prisons. *Thanks go to the anonymous reviewers whose comments on an earlier draft of this article were very valuable.* *Correspondence regarding this article may be sent to Dr. Yvonne Jewkes at the Centre for Criminology and Criminal Justice, CASS, University of Hull, Hull, HU6 7RX, UK; e-mail: Y.Jewkes@hull.ac.uk.*

seen as a learned response to the imperatives of the criminal inmate culture. Charlesworth (2000) provides an exposition of the spiral of self-destruction that culture can engender in a phenomenological account of the lives of working-class men in a town in northern England. Among the factors he highlights as being integral to the reproduction of disadvantage are the presentation of a heavily managed "front," indicating a potential capacity for aggression that must be constantly maintained in the face of systemic disrespect and stigmatization; lives lived in the context of circumscribed horizons and minimal expectations; and an inability to look beyond government institutions to broader structures of inequality when apportioning blame for the pain and degradation routinely suffered. But while inmates clearly import with them into prison a recognizable set of experiences, belief systems, and moral standpoints (arguably far wider than that which Charlesworth suggests), the experience of confinement nonetheless unites them, to some degree, in a shared experience of and response to pain and deprivation (Grapendaal 1990).

One of the earliest and most influential commentaries on prison societies is Gresham Sykes's (1958) *The Society of Captives*. Sykes observes that prisoners have to endure various structural deprivations—the "pains of imprisonment"—including losses of liberty, autonomy, security, goods and services, and heterosexual relations. For Sykes and his acolytes (*The Society of Captives* was recently "top-ranked book in prison studies"; Reisig 2001), these deprivations go significantly beyond simple discomfort, threatening the inmates' psychological well-being and attacking their sense of self-worth. Sykes's conceptualization of the structural deprivations inherent in totalitarian systems of power bears some similarities to Goffman's concept of "total institutions." For Goffman, the transition from the outside community to the world within the prison institution involves a symbolic significance that goes well beyond the passage from a "free" world to a "closed" environment. Described as a "civil death" (Goffman 1961a, 25), entry into the total institution involves being subjected to a series of social and psychological attacks that undermine the sense of self:

> The recruit . . . comes into the establishment with a conception of himself made possible by certain stable social arrangements in his home world. Upon entrance, he is immediately stripped of the support provided by these arrangements . . . [and] he begins a series of abasements, degradations, humiliations and profanations of self. His self is systematically, if often unintentionally, mortified. (Goffman 1961b, 23)

The assaults on individuals' sense of self and self-worth highlighted by these two writers remind us that however familiar some aspects of the prison culture are to some inmates, their ability to adapt to the rigors of confinement will be at least as related to their present predicament as they are to the possible influences of life before prison (Sykes 1958). The remainder of this article will draw on ethnographic data from an empirical study of four men's prisons of various security classifications in the English Midlands. It will first explore the notion of patriarchy in relation to predominantly male environments. It will then argue that the ability of men to survive their prison sentences in this climate of mortification and brutality may depend on two factors: first, they must negotiate their position within a prison hierarchy that is based on excessive displays of manliness, constructing a public identity that allows them to "fit in" with the dominant culture; and secondly, they must be able to simultaneously maintain and nurture a private, interior (and usually non-"macho") sense of self.

PATRIARCHY, FRATRIARCHY, AND HIERARCHY IN PRISONS

> You definitely have to wear a mask in prison—if you don't you're going to get eaten away. When I came in I was green. I thought I was quite streetwise on the outside, but no. You have to act tough. There's always the threat of violence. (Simon)[1]

Of all the "pains" associated with imprisonment, the fear for personal safety, which is engendered in every direction between inmates and staff, is arguably the overriding feature of life in most institutions (Scraton, Sim, and Skidmore 1991). For most inmates, peer group respect, individual status, and access to scarce resources all rest on a reputation for aggressiveness and physical strength. As in any organization, a climate of fear is bound to lead to the exploitation of weaker individuals by more powerful ones, and in prison, the illusion of power seems, on the surface at least, to resemble traditional patterns of patriarchy, with vulnerable prisoners, such as sex offenders, being routinely objectified, intimidated, and subjected to violence. Despite its wide usage, however, patriarchy has become corrupted in the wake of the feminist women's movement and has become a kind of shorthand ascription that grossly oversimplifies the structures of gender (Connell 1987). Patriarchy is now popularly used to describe what might more properly be termed *androcracy*—that is, rule by men (Remy 1990).

One way of overcoming the ambiguities inherent in the term *patriarchy* (the rule of the fathers) is to consider, instead, the merits of *fratriarchy* (the rule of the brothers), a mode of male domination that shares some of the origins of patriarchy yet is, nonetheless, concerned with a very different set of values, which seem more appropriate in an analysis of a predominantly male environment. Although not in common usage, the term *fratriarchy* is used by some gender theorists (e.g., Remy 1990; Brod 1990) to account for the disjunction between the facts of public male power and feelings of individual male powerlessness. It thus explains how, within a broadly patriarchal society in which the oppression and subjugation of women is well documented, superordinate notions of masculinity serve to weaken—for want of a better word, "feminize"—the authority of some men. Where patriarchy is a father-to-son transmission of authority and is therefore intergenerational, the dimension of temporal continuity is rendered more problematic in the intragenerational relationships of the brotherhood:

> As opposed to the patriarch, who embodied many levels and kinds of authority in his single person, the brothers stand in uneasy relationships with each other, engaged in sibling rivalry while trying to keep the power of the family of man as a whole intact. (Brod 1990, 133)

Furthermore, while the brothers may share the desires of the patriarch in matters of paternity and parenting, it is a concern largely fuelled by self-interest. Gilmore (1990, 223) states that the three core elements of manhood are impregnating women, providing for one's dependants, and protecting one's kin. While these codes of behavior are undoubtedly characteristic of men across the socioeconomic strata, it is arguable that in the lower working classes these ideals are transmuted according to the demands of association with other men and the freedom to do as one pleases and have a good time. As such, even men who marry and/or have children may permanently remain psychologically trapped in the fraternal fellowship, eschewing all responsibilities and thriving on the conflict and aggression characteristic of most male associations. As Remy (1990) demonstrates in the parlance of the 1970s, this generally amounts to "causing a bit of bovver" (p. 45).

Remy uses the term "men's hut"[2] as a metaphor for the public institutions where men go primarily to associate with other men: "This is . . . where those males who have earned the right to call themselves *men*, or are in the process of attaining this emblem of privilege, gather" (Remy 1990, 45). Men's huts for the middle-classes are institutions such as golf clubs, gentlemen's clubs, and Freemasons lodges, while working-class manifestations include pubs and betting shops. Male bonding has also, of course, found its expression in a highly visible form in political arenas, including the Houses of Parliament and extreme right-wing movements. The interesting aspect of men's huts, from the perspective of unequal power relations among men, is that they emphatically exclude not only women but also those males who have not yet earned the right to call themselves men. This form of "social closure" operates through a number of mechanisms, including exclusion of those who have not yet passed the requisite rites of passage, those who are either too old or too young to be fully respected by their peers, and those who are not versed in the special language, or the "argot," that frequently characterizes these groups. In all these respects, prison societies can be said to resemble men's huts and can be seen as a continuation of practices adopted in the working-class world of manual labor, where male ascendancy over other men on the basis of age, authority, and peer group credentials is frequently evident (Willis 1977). Apprenticeships and probationary training periods are commonly remembered as a humiliating induction into masculinity as well as trade. Yet, once the training has been successfully completed, the apprentices are generally accepted as "brothers" (Cockburn 1986). Similarly, the new prison inmate will frequently have to undergo a period of testing, involving some kind of initiation, which may entail physical assertions of strength. Young-offenders institutes are particularly notorious for the bullying that takes place on induction, but in all custodial settings, if the victim succeeds in defending himself and asserting his autonomy, he will often be accepted, at least by some sections of the prison fraternity:

> I was proud entering Wormwood Scrubs at fifteen. Before that, I was in a remand home at the age of twelve. It gave me status going to the Scrubs. . . . We'd gone thieving and had lookouts and everything. We thought we were the real thing, we felt like big men. Once inside you had to go through "recepo-bashing"—a kind of initiation where you were beaten by your "friends" to within an inch of your life. I won the fight . . . beat up three out of the four [assailants]. That made me "The Chap." (Jim)

Such brutality confirms Bowker's (1977, xi) assertion that what prisoners inflict on each other is often far worse than anything staff do to them, but, as Jim's quote indicates, it is often only those who pass such barbaric tests of manliness who gain the advantage of solidarity. Male bonding in prison, as in other predominately male spheres, reaffirms masculine hegemony not only by excluding women but also by preying on weaker men.

MASCULINITY AS PERFORMANCE

All forms of masculinity inevitably involve a certain degree of putting on a "manly front," and it therefore seems reasonable to consider the outward manifestation of all masculinities as presentation or performance. This dramaturgical conception of self, made famous by Goffman (1959), is taken up by Andrew Tolson, who gives the dramatic motif a class-based edge, arguing that the working-class boy "expresses himself, not so much in an inner competitive struggle for achievement, as through a collective toughness, a masculine 'performance' recognised and approved by his 'mates'" (Tolson 1977, 43). Although it is not being suggested here that middle-class boys do not share this need to live up to certain idealized representations of masculinity to gain the respect of their peers (based predominantly on educational and sporting achievement, perhaps), the concern here is with lower class males for whom masculinity is a kind of ritualized dramatic enactment, a generally mundane and predictable display, punctuated by sporadic bursts of excitement.

In his classic study of street-corner culture, Corrigan (1975) testifies to the intense activity that is involved in the common pursuit of "doing nothing," echoing other commentators' observations concerning passing time in prison. Occasionally, confrontations or "contests of honor" between rival gangs have to be fought and won to preserve a masculine reputation (Newburn and Stanko 1994). Contests are usually fought over territory, and a dominant feature of the working class is the intense loyalty to the locality; districts, neighborhoods, streets, and even smaller "patches" than that are closely marked by gangs and guarded, "often to apparent absurdity" (Tolson 1977, 42). Such locales arguably constitute a place where the powerful construct and exercise their power, but the weak create their own "spaces" within those places, making them temporarily their own as they occupy and move through them (De Certeau 1984). De Certeau uses the language of warfare, arguing that subordinates are like guerrillas, appropriating space as a means of resistance. This metaphor seems particularly apt in relation to the spaces connecting the different areas of prisons. Wing corridors are often called "the streets" by inmates, and it is in these long, narrow corridors, which are frequently beyond the direct sight of staff, that groups of inmates congregate during association time to replicate some of the activities that might be encountered among such groups of young men on the real streets outside:

> In here is like the street, like a rough council estate. We're all streetwise. You have to keep your street credibility, maintain an image. You get a lot of talk and bravado. It's exactly the same as on the outside. (John)

Given the opportunities these locations provide for inmates to mingle out of sight of any authorities, it may not be just banter that is exchanged in these corridors. However, an important aspect of the lower working-class male's existence is the ability to "talk up" his physical prowess. Even if an individual rarely has the need to engage in actual combat, he must impress his audience with his repertoire of stories and jokes, and he learns at an early age that bravado is a key element in gaining membership to the fratriarchy. But it may simply be that like the adolescent youths encountered by Corrigan (1975), prisoners are actively engaged in the social practice of doing nothing except marking their patch when hanging around in communal spaces. They have found a way of using the imposed system of association activity and creating a territorial, subcultural space reminiscent of those they would occupy on the outside.

INMATE RELATIONS

Inmate solidarity of the type and intensity described by early prison researchers such as Sykes is rare now; the drugs culture that exists in all prisons has created a "dog eat dog" environment in which individuals are unwise and unwilling to put their trust in fellow inmates. But pressure to fit in with the dominant culture is nonetheless strong, and conformity to types of behavior seems to result in a "move in a direction of solidarity" (Hood and Sparks 1970), which ameliorates some of the problems associated with life as an individual in a rigidly structured, closed social environment:

> I share a cell—that's my choice. . . . The main attraction of twoing-up is having someone to talk to. It's like therapy. I'd done a year on my own but to share with someone was quite attractive. I'd not really spoken to anyone for a year, only very shallow conversations. Same with Theo, the Dutch guy. Another Dutch man came in and it really opened up his world. He used to be in his cell all the time before. (David)

> You tend to get like hanging around with like. Drug dealers stick together—it's hip in here. I don't mix with the bag heads [heroin users] or house burglars—they're scum. . . . I'm choosy about whose company I keep. My closest friend here is my co-defendant but you can't really have friends in prison, just associates. (Tom)

> Some prisoners look up to others because of the crimes they've committed—mostly the would-be gangsters. You *can* have friends in prison. If you see another black person in prison you know you'll survive. They'll be bona fide friends because you're both convicted, you can talk, smoke draw, reason, share personal stuff. . . . We speak in jargon, lyrics. With my brothers, it's a safe environment. (Paul)

Absorption into one or other of the subcultures in prison and the resulting sense of belonging to a group with a strong identity (whether the primary identification is based on ethnicity, political or criminal ideologies, access to contraband economies, or some other variable) may provide partial explanation for high recidivism rates in most Western countries. In other words, the custodial experience provides a highly structured environment, which demands an adherence to an inmate code and provides ontological security based on mutual support and camaraderie for people who have otherwise found their life chances seriously diminished. This cohesive structure among similarly disadvantaged social misfits helps to compensate for the bleaker aspects of prison life (Hood and Sparks 1970):

> I've been here before so I'm used to it—I just see it as a break. . . . I had all the usual fears of violence and rape, and so on, but then I got here and found I knew half the people in here, so I was alright. (Michael)

Yet ironically, it is the very existence of male subcultures that weakens the hegemonic notion of masculinity to which disadvantaged men are culturally encouraged to aspire and that ensures the social reproduction of deprivation and marginalization. Inside the locally constructed lower working-class world, there is little room for deviation from the prescribed norms that characterize this group, and conformity is paramount. For example, it is arguable that young lower working-class men are increasingly less likely to form their identities on the basis of occupation and life chances and are more likely to get their sense of self through the kind of tribal, collective identity that is fostered by football, music, or some other "fanship." The difficulty that faces them is that all these identifications require conspicuous consumption of designer-label clothing and accessories, and it may be that young men in today's anomic society are fostering at an early age not the skills necessary to prepare them for a mundane working life in industry but rather the wells of ungratified desire which instill a sense of dissatisfaction with the gains to be made through legitimate means. Although it is not being suggested that all lower working-class males are unable to find ways of accomplishing masculinity in ways that do not involve crime, it might reasonably be assumed that those who do offend bring into prison with them a masculine ideology and commitment to a criminal subculture that prepares them for life inside. Once in prison, the intensity of the desirable male image is magnified further. As Gilmore notes, "the harsher the environment and the scarcer the resources, the more manhood is stressed as inspiration and goal" (Gilmore 1990, 224). Few environments offer a more intensely harsh, unproductive, and impoverished set of circumstances than the prison.

HEGEMONIC MASCULINITY IN PRISONS

The desire to prove one's manhood, which frequently leads to criminal behavior, conviction, and imprisonment, may itself, then, be a prerequisite to a successful adaptation to life inside. This may be particularly true of those who have committed very serious offenses, who might be said to import with them into prison the ideology of aggressive masculine values that precipitated their crimes in the first place. For example, while the many young, short-term, petty criminals that make up the prison population adhere to a particular style of masculinity, they are dismissed as "wannabes" by older, long-term, or life-sentence inmates who are equally keen to emphasize their own credentials as "proper" villains:

> It's a Mickey Mouse jail—full of young scallies and inadequates. It's mostly kids now, charging around and making a lot of noise. [This] could be the best prison in the country for long-termers to finish off their sentences, but it's spoilt by the short-termers on heroin. A lot of idiots and parasites really. Prisons have degenerated since the old days. They're just criminal factories now. (Ray)

> There are one or two bullies on the wing. They tend to pick on the weaker ones, those who look young or vulnerable. Every time you go to a new prison you let it be known that, while you're a good guy, you're not to be messed around. It's an aura: "don't pick on me." People pick up on that, they know you don't muck around with lifers. You put across that if you pick on me, shit will fly. You're picking on a piece of hard stuff. They can pick on me verbally, it's water off a

> duck's back. But no-one's going to go for me physically because they know what I'm capable of, what I'm in here for. For example, if someone goes into my cell I'll break their fingers. I think violence should never be used unless it is the pure last resort. But if someone asked for it, I'd resort to it. (Roy)

> [This prison] is like a children's home. You have a lot of wannabe gangsters in here—"plastic gangsters" we call them. I'm "Old Firm." We get respect. I'm well known inside and outside. I like the fact that I'm Mister Big both here and on the streets. (Dave)

Feminist writer Nicole Ward Jouve further illustrates the significance of the prevailing culture on the precipitation of serious offenses in her account of the circumstances surrounding the crimes of the serial killer Peter Sutcliffe (known as the "Yorkshire Ripper"), who killed thirteen women in the north of England between 1975 and 1980. She argues that "the whole aura of . . . aggressive maleness that surrounded Sutcliffe made his murders possible" (Ward Jouve 1988, 144). This aura was provided partially by a father who, Ward Jouve suspects, would rather have a mass murderer for a son than a closet homosexual and by friends of the offender who "regarded prostitute-bashing as a joke" (p. 144). Ward Jouve's exploration of Sutcliffe's relationships reinforces the point that hegemonic masculinity is not achieved solely through domination over women but is also constructed in relation to subordinated or less powerful men. In other words, achieving hegemony may depend on the relationship and interplay between the different definitions that a culture makes available at any given time. For example, in the context of the prison, the power achieved and held on to by those at the top of the prisoner hierarchy is to some degree legitimized, normalized, and sustained by its opposite number at the bottom. Put simply, the hegemonic masculinity at the apex of the hierarchy of power, represented most strongly by the professional criminal and armed robber, is culturally reinforced by its opposite number at the bottom—that is, the rapist and pedophile, who deviate from conventional heterosexual masculine norms. Furthermore, physical violence frequently endorses dominant cultural patterns. The fact that assaults on some inmates (by both fellow inmates and by officers) occur and are tolerated by those with the authority to intervene demonstrates that hegemonic values based on physical coercion are part of the complex horizontal and vertical relationships instituted between prisoners and prison officers and between these groups and what Sim calls the "technocrats who occupy powerful positions as governors, area managers and state bureaucrats in the Home Office" (Sim 1994, 102).[3]

Hegemonic masculinity in prisons, then, is clearly as bound up with aggression and violence as it is on the outside. That is not to say that the most violent men (in respect to their crimes or to their behavior in prison) are the most powerful inside; indeed, the volatile offender is more likely to be marginalized than respected. Nevertheless, a certain degree of "controlled aggression" is required to survive the psychological and physical rigors of imprisonment. Ascendancy achieved by means of threats, bullying, and predatory aggressiveness is not hegemony, but the necessity of establishing a no-nonsense, tough reputation on reception into a new institution is well documented in personal accounts of life inside. Of course, physical jostling for positions of power and status are common among lower working-class groups of males, but it is perhaps especially visible in prisons because they are such blatantly status-depriving environments and therefore create a particularly acute need for indices of relative status (Toch 1975, 64). But even after a tough facade has been established, it has to be maintained, and this in itself can be a great source of pressure. Toch notes that some inmates go to extraordinary lengths to accommodate an image of themselves that conforms to the hegemonic ideal but that when approached by nonjudgmental outsiders (such as university researchers), their manly self-portraits crumble and, indeed, are "relinquished with gratitude" (Toch 1975, 15); this is a finding supported by the participants in this study. Tony's comment was typical:

> I'm really glad I've talked to you. Sorry I was a bit uncooperative to start with, but you're naturally suspicious of people in here. I feel like I've got some really important things off my chest, though, talking to you. It's nice to be able to be myself for a change.

SELF AND IDENTITY

"Wearing a mask" is arguably the most common strategy for coping with the rigors of imprisonment, and all prison researchers will be familiar with the sentiment that inmates feel it necessary to adopt a facade while inside. But equally, they have probably been told that the presentation of a heavily managed "front" is impossible to sustain for prolonged periods inside prison. Indeed, it is arguable that the facility to discard the mask and "be oneself" is not only desirable but is absolutely necessary if a prisoner is to "get through" their sentence with their self-esteem reasonably in tact (Jewkes 2002). Self and identity—usually conceived as two sides of the same coin—can thus be distinguished. Self emphasizes difference and requires prisoners to draw on the specific interpersonal relations (family, work, style, cultural preferences, etc.) that mark them out as being distinct from the rest of the inmate population. Identity stresses similarity and requires inmates to hail the dispositions and resources that enable them to engage with and integrate into the prevailing inmate culture. Prisoners may be constantly engaged in these two interlocking forms of emotional endeavor (Craib 1998)—that is, the "internal" work of coping with conflict, fear, and disorientation and the "external" work of reconciling what goes on inside with the construction and maintenance of a culturally acceptable, masculine identity.

This distinction between the private sense of self and the public presentation of identity is usually conceptualized in terms of their "backstage" and "frontstage" settings, respectively (Goffman 1959; see also Giddens 1984). Backstage is where one's basic, personal ontological security system is restored and where the tensions associated with sustaining the particular bodily, gestural, and verbal codes that are demanded in this setting are diffused:

> I get angry and lonely, but not bitter. I know I can only blame myself. Thank God we're allowed CD players in here. I get rid of frustration by listening to Black Sabbath or Led Zeppelin very, very loud. You have to come over a bit harder in here; you have to stand tall and show you can't be intimidated. But at night you can get back in your pad and be yourself. It's the only thing that keeps me sane. (Dave)

> My private time is in the evening. I write letters between 9:30 and 10 every night. People know not to disturb me then. I write two sides of A4 every evening. I keep two diaries as well, one for my missus and one for me. That's good—an outlet. I'm terrified of losing Sharon. . . . She's my wife, my lover, my best friend, everything to me really. But I get this little . . . "belly feeling," I call it. Anxiety I suppose. That's why it's so important for me to keep writing to her, to let her know how much she means to me. (Craig)

> I become myself at lock up. I'm sometimes glad when 8 o'clock comes and you can lock yourself away. People handle it in different ways. I like to walk around the sports field and just reflect. Others smash a window or self harm or talk to their mates or the chaplain. (Ray)

Frontstage is where the public aspect of one's identity will be presented in social engagement with others. The public persona that individuals present when interacting with others inside prison may be a familiar guise, constructed and refined through a long process of socialization into male-dominated subcultures as a child, adolescent, and adult. For example, an inmate from the kind of lower working-class background from which prisoners are predominantly drawn might bring with him a type of knowledge, speech pattern, attitude, and so on, that will enable him to fit in to the inmate culture more easily than his middle-class counterpart. But a middle-class prisoner might feel more comfortable when dealing with figures of authority in the penal system because of shared values, life experiences, and educational background. However, imprisonment may involve disruption of the equilibrium between the two spheres, resulting in further damage to the individual's sense of well-being. If forced to share a cell with one or more other inmates, the prisoner may be continually in an enforced state of frontstage, with little opportunity to restore his interior sense of self. If locked up on his own for prolonged periods, on the other hand, he may suffer equally in his inability to engage in frontstage activity. This blurring of the boundaries between frontstage and backstage, together with the pressure for conformity and compliance, may undermine the inmate's personal and social identities, preventing both from functioning as they would in other circumstances:

> I hate prison because I have to pretend to be someone I'm not. In my cell I can be myself but as soon as I come out I have to stand differently, present myself differently. When I'm on the phone I have to remember to swap over to myself. . . . People can't spend enough time being their private selves in [prison]. . . . I feel like I've got a split personality. (Craig)

But whatever resources the new inmate is able to import into prison with him, many, regardless of their background and social class, will arrive at reception with a fairly consistent picture of what prison is like (often informed by media-generated images of violence and intimidation) and then proceed to adjust their perceptions as they observe and interact with other prisoners:

> Through watching others, through eavesdropping, through cautious conversation and selective interaction, a new inmate refines his understanding of what . . . prisoners look like, how they move, how they act. Despite his belief that he is different from these other prisoners, he knows that he cannot appear to be too different from them, if he is to hide his vulnerability. His initial image of other prisoners, his early observations, and his concern over how he appears to others thus provide a foundation for the identity he gradually creates through impression management. (Schmid and Jones 1991, 422)

> I remember for the first six months I was here, standing in the queue for meals, trying not to make eye contact with anyone in case they took it the wrong way. I'm a bit more relaxed now, but you still have to be on your guard the whole time. (Simon)

For some inmates the presentation of self will be a familiar, if not exaggerated, version of the social identity developed prior to entering prison. But as Schmid and Jones (1991) suggest, most new inmates feel vulnerable, and it might be argued that prisoners are not quite as adept at role playing and impression management as is sometimes assumed. In particular, not all inmates are able to conform to the superordinate version of masculinity that seems to ensure an easier passage through a prison career. For some, the projection of a false identity will, quite simply, be beyond their impression-management skills, and they will be forced to withdraw—literally and emotionally—into their private self (Goffman 1961a; Cohen and Taylor 1972):

> It's this macho thing that grinds you down. I think it's a shame really. I've been all over Europe and you just don't see it, it's something peculiar about British culture. In jail you're constantly on your guard. You have to be man enough to stand up for yourself or you get walked over. Prison is a brain drain—you have to be on your toes or just stay in your cell and try to be invisible. (George)

> Not everyone can cope with prison. Crime is itself often the result of poor socialization skills. There are people in here that you never, ever see. They're in

here because they have no social skills and they're antisocial while they're in here. What chance do they have? That's why there's so much self-harm and suicide in prison. (Garth)

Garth's comment reminds us that prison research can only take account of the survivors of the prison experience and that those inmates who have thought about taking their own lives while in prison (seventeen to eighteen percent of the total inmate population) report higher-than-average feelings of apathy, boredom, and lethargy (Liebling 1992). Worrall (2000) has criticized what she describes as the "outward bound mentality" of the prisoner-coping literature, arguing that the overriding expectation that prisoners should find ways of coping is incompatible with inmates' own expectations—some simply do not want to cope. And so it was for some of the men I interviewed who talked movingly of their suffering and losses and who had experienced periods of deep depression that were only exacerbated by the demands of the performative masculine culture. The desire to disengage from, or "tune out" of, prison routine was, in such circumstances, entirely understandable.

Even inmates who succeed in establishing a tough, no-nonsense reputation to survive the psychological and physical rigors of imprisonment may find their sense of the masculine changing as their sentence proceeds. For example, the importance of maintaining a "hard" front may diminish as the end of their sentence nears:

> I just want to keep my head down and stay out of trouble. I've been in bother before and had days added, . . . but now I can see my release day ahead of me, so I'm just seeing out the last few weeks, not getting into any bother. . . . I just stay in my pad, watch TV all day and sleep as much as possible. I've got nothing to prove anymore. (Matt)

Alternatively, prisoners may seek to reestablish and assert their masculinity throughout their sentences in more subtle ways than simply adopting an aggressive, "hard man" stance. For example, many inmates construct new identities as students or tradesmen:

> I tried to re-invent myself when I got sent down. I wasn't happy with my identity before I came in, I felt a failure. Now I need to prove I can do what I'm doing. I'm doing an Open University degree. . . . I read newspapers and watch TV, but select things that are a lot more intellectual than I would have before. It's all part of the re-invention of myself. I've matured more in the past five years than in the thirty-four years before. I'm studying Ancient Greek and I read proper newspapers. If I'd been put inside when I was sixteen I might have turned out a better person. I was a wimp when I came in; now I'm much more assertive. (Dave)
>
> I did an HND at Stafford [prison] in Business Studies. It gave me confidence and self-esteem. I achieved something. But generally in prison I have a sense of not having my responsibilities, not being a man. (Craig)

While not explicitly (hyper)masculine identities, the adoption of student, artisan, or tradesman identities nourishes the self and is typical of working-class cultures, particularly among the male, working-class unemployed (Sapsford 1983). "Scholar" and "work" identities also provide an alternative to the dominant masculine hegemony for middle-class prisoners, where skills ranging from the ability to read to the possession of legal knowledge may provide an opportunity to flaunt oneself symbolically in a kind of "psychological one-upmanship" (Cohen and Taylor 1972).

Also intrinsic to masculine rituals of display are symbols of conspicuous consumption, and although prisoners may earn as little as £7 a week it is nonetheless important to be visibly consuming if their adequacy as a man is to be upheld (Bostyn and Wight 1987). The influences of commodification can be seen in a variety of prisoners' possessions. For example, in the broader study from which this data is drawn (Jewkes 2002), it was noted that among a group of maximum-security inmates, one indicator of both lifestyle aspirations and the need to signal to the group something of one's preprison identity was footwear. Most inmates are young, street-wise urbanites, and they literally wear their masculine credentials on their feet. Their new and expensive designer-label trainers indicate a desire to fit in with the dominant norms and yet also suggest a degree of competitiveness; for some inmates, it is important not to get left behind in the rapidly moving worlds of fashion and footwear technology. By contrast, a middle-class Dutch prisoner serving time in a medium-security jail, while resigned to wearing his shabby and threadbare prison uniform, had on his feet a pair of elegant, highly polished, brown leather brogues. Not only aesthetic but also clearly expensive, his shoes, he admitted, were important for him to be allowed to wear, not only to maintain a sense of himself as a man of taste and culture but also to signal to the other inmates and, importantly, to the prison officers that he was "different, more refined, than they are."

Some commentators (e.g., Lefebvre 1971; Brittan 1977) have argued that conspicuous consumption is a new and vicious form of alienation whereby individuals are defined not by what they do (i.e., produce) but by what they own. For these critics, "lifestyle" is a symbol of the exploitation of mindless conformists at the hands of powerful manufacturers and marketers. However, such arguments neglect the very real effect of conspicuous consumption on many people's sense of self. For example, the adoption of particular designer clothing and footwear by large sections of the working classes (including prison inmates) is illustrative of the positive self-image that such symbolic gestures can generate in structural environments where self-esteem and aspiration are under constant assault. Bostyn and Wight (1987) understand this relationship well, arguing that "the goods people choose to buy are a physical expression (often not conscious) of their characters, or at least what they want to project as such" (p. 140). They emphasize the intrinsically masculine attributes of many commodities and suggest that one's identity as an adult, a father, and a man are inextricably bound up in commodities such as meat, machines, and alcohol. The deprivation of such items—particularly when associated with the inability to purchase them with a "man's wage"—emasculates the individual and attacks his sense of self-worth. Likewise, in prisons, the deprivation of material goods (Sykes 1958) arguably heightens the need for and value of consuming and spectacle, both as a restorer of the embattled and emasculated self and, more fundamentally, to bring color into an otherwise drab and uniform environment. Prison cells might be furnished with the aspirational symbols of media-saturated consumer capitalism—posters of glamour models and pop stars, pictures of expensive sports cars, hi-tech audio equipment and, increasingly, televisions—but to reduce these symbols to mere products of an exploitative ad-man's desire to take advantage of passive dopes who know no better negates the real sense of agency and empowerment that the choice, purchase, and use of these consumables can produce—albeit, that it is within a structure of domination and exploitation. Material aspirations and lifestyle choices might thus be interpreted as positive adaptations to confinement and are often considered sufficiently prized to guarantee status. But more importantly, such statements of style may nourish the self and counter the feelings of dependency and weakness that incarceration can foster.

References to feelings of emasculation among male prisoners are common (see, e.g., Sykes 1958; Goffman 1961a; Toch 1975), and, of course, the relative scarcity of women in men's prisons represents a problem for the presentation of the robust sexual appetite normally associated with manhood to the extent that some researchers have likened imprisonment to physical castration (Sykes 1958; Segal 1990). Because we partially define ourselves in relation to what we are not, the inmate's sense of identity is distorted by his predominantly male environment and undergoes a "disidentifying role," inducing a fear of losing his sense of masculinity (Goffman 1961b, 23). Isolated from the world of women who, by their very polarity, give the male world much of its meaning, the inmate is unable to seek reflection of his identity in the eyes of those who, by their "other-ness," traditionally give him a masculine sense of self. A common response to this problem among prison inmates is to take up bodybuilding, which may serve the purpose of attracting a mate or, conversely, of warding off potential advances. In prison, keeping physically fit is understandable, given the level of fear among inmates and prison officers. More than that, however, the serious pursuit of an excessively muscular physique is significant in terms of the presentation of self as a powerful and self-controlled individual. The body is constructed as a site of difference in relation to others who are physically less strong and is a key performative device. In institutions where standard prison clothing is issued, remodelling the body may be the primary means of asserting one's individual personality and gaining ground in an overtly competitive environment. It is a statement of presence and of power (which obviously makes it attractive to those who are marginalized or disempowered), and it represents the ultimate achievement of self-control and agency. Not only do individuals form an understanding of themselves by continually reworking their sense of self as they go through life, but their personal biography is also constructed partly through the systematic ordering of the body through fitness, shape, and diet (Giddens 1991). Put simply, the constructed, labored-over body is the locus of an undervalued presence in the world, albeit one that is open to reconstruction and the pleasures of narcissism:

> It holds the years back while you're in jail if you take care of yourself. You want to come out as fit if not fitter. You look better, feel better, and it shows *them* [the prison officers] that you can handle yourself. (Brian)
>
> In my last jail I had a role model—a boxer. He got me into training. He was the hardest man in the prison—everyone respected him, so they respected me because I hung around with him. Those of us who train together have camaraderie, we tell each other stories. The gym also helps me cope with stress. When I've had a bad day I go down there and work it off. After half an hour's circuit training or weights I feel better—and better about myself, I suppose. I'm quite vain to be honest with you! (David)

Like conspicuous consumption, then, bodybuilding has the slightly paradoxical benefit of both enhancing public image and nourishing a positive sense of self. It appeals to those inmates who wish to use the institution for whatever benefits might be available, including social interaction with others, or who wish to flaunt their strength in front of their guards and other inmates. But equally, it is a form of protection and preservation of self that appeals to those who prefer to withdraw from the inmate culture and who are attracted to a solitary, narcissistic pursuit that entails no relation to other inmates (Ward Jouve 1988).

It may be supposed, then, that even in the highly constrained environment of the prison society, there exist many permutations of the "proof" of masculinity to respond to the imperative for inmates to fashion a masculine "way of being" (Pronger 1990) as an adaptive stance to the patterns imposed on them by their environment. Indeed, an emerging theme in the literature on constructions of masculinity is that many social institutions organize masculine power through constructs of sexuality, socializing their inhabitants in the ways of "doing" heterosexuality as a means of validating their masculinity and gaining acceptance to the group:

> There's a lot of homophobia in prisons. [This unit] is full of vulnerable prisoners, grasses and nonces. There have been two punishment beatings over here in the last month—that's the nature of this prison. If you're gay, you keep it to yourself. You act tough and stay cool. You join in with the banter about the female screws and you keep your head down. The greatest tool a prisoner can have is to stay calm and in control and not show any vulnerability. (Paul)

However, as argued previously, such examples of impression management belie the real identity beneath and ignore the complex interaction between biological determinants, psychological processes, and social expectations. Not all prisoners will possess the "cultural capital" (Bourdieu 1977) necessary to sustain a superficial identity, and, even if they are able to present an acceptable public facade, it represents only half of the picture and misses entirely what goes on inside their bearer. As Craib comments, "*social* identities can come and go but *my* identity goes on as something which unites all the social identities I ever had, have or will have. . . . [It] overflows, adds to, transforms the social identities that are attached to me" (Craib 1998, 4; emphasis added). In short, identity is not just concerned with the outward presentation of self, but it is the ability to maintain inner sameness and continuity to maintain a sense of ontological security (Giddens 1984). Furthermore, while it may be the gift of some men to play at will with the conventions of gender, many others will be constrained from doing so by a variety of psychological and cultural impediments, especially in an environment as unpredictable, frightening, and alien as the prison.

CONCLUDING THOUGHTS

This article has argued that the overt masculinity evident in so many studies of imprisonment has parallels in the wider culture beyond the prison walls. Many studies have suggested that the criminal life of the offender begins with some degree of contact with delinquent or offending peers, through whom a criminal identity and perspective is acquired. Echoing Goffman's use of the term, Irwin (1970) states that any new phase of the offender's "career," including the frequently cyclical path through arrest, sentencing, imprisonment, and release, is structured by meanings and definitions brought to the phase from perspectives gathered earlier. Criminality as a learned response to the imperatives enforced by hegemonic masculinity is suggested in a number of inmates' autobiographical accounts and sociological studies of lower working-class culture show the excessive display of one's masculinity, including aggressive and violent behavior, to be a central feature of working-class life. It hardly needs to be stated that any previous contact or involvement with criminal perspectives and behavior systems prior to arrest will inevitably shape the new inmate's overriding prison identity and coping strategies.

But given the evidence for the brutalizing and psychologically damaging effects of imprisonment, it would be naive to suggest (as do Irwin and Cressey 1962; Irwin, 1970) that the prison is simply one functioning part of a wider criminal mechanism and that inmates only adapt to incarceration to the extent of it being another integrated episode within a long criminal career. Indeed, to suggest that the social life of a prison revolves entirely around essentialist male beliefs and criminal ideologies not only presupposes that the inmate culture is virtually identical across all male prisons regardless of category, physical location, and management policy, but is also tantamount to blaming the victims of the bullying, oppression, and fear that characterize many prisons (Stevens 1994). Whatever their circumstances, individuals are not mere bearers of structure; they are complex amalgams of several influences, responding to their life experiences with greater or lesser degrees of compliance and confrontation, defining their own individuality in terms of both cultural conformity and resistance. As Layder comments, "unique psychobiographical experiences will intersect with the dynamics of particular situations and the influence of wider social contexts to determine a person's behaviour" (Layder 1994, 210). In prisons, as in other spheres of life, the marking of "sameness" and "difference" is crucial to the construction of identity positions, and both may be reproduced and mediated through a range of symbolic systems and through forms of social inclusion and exclusion. For example, individuals may be marginalized (or accepted) on the basis of the crimes for which they are serving a prison sentence or for their stance on a particular aspect of the prison culture, such as drug use, or indeed, "otherness" might be conferred on much more mundane and spurious grounds. Although various types of masculinity are adopted to counter some aspects of marginalization (scholar, skilled tradesman, and expert in legal matters and prisoners' rights are common examples), an extreme construction of masculinity as an identity position is the most universal response to the imperative to conform to the lower working-class dominated prison culture. It is thus simultaneously a reflection of wider social norms and a response to the specific, unique properties of imprisonment. But not every inmate will conform to the hegemonic masculine ideal; as demonstrated, hegemonic masculinity carries no intrinsic meaning without the subordinated versions against which it is pitched.

It must be assumed, then, that behavioral patterns constructed around violence and manliness in prison are not simply a facsimile of the outside world, even among the underclass that provides the prison with the majority of its inmates. Criminal perspectives learned earlier in life combine with the pains of imprisonment to give rise to an enhanced or exaggerated form of masculinity. As a response to the label *prisoner*, with all its connotations of weakness, conformity, and the relinquishing of power, manliness (or a version of it) becomes the primary means of adaptation and resistance. The same forces that exist throughout the patriarchal world and that find their least sophisticated expression among underclass males exist in prison to sustain an equilibrium where power is held by those who maintain a hegemonic masculine front, amounting to an abhorrence of femininity (in men as well as women), aggressive homophobia, and a personal code of behavior based on confrontation and force rather than negotiation and respect; in short, a hypermasculinity in which "normal" values and behavioral patterns of powerful men take on an extreme form in the face of powerlessness against the institution.

NOTES

1. All quotes from prisoners are taken from interviews conducted by the author at two Category C prisons in the English Midlands in April 1999.

2. From the German *Männerbünde*, or men's league, coined by early German sociologists to denote the kind of fratriarchy described here.

3. Peter Sutcliffe has been assaulted several times by fellow inmates, which may be partially explained by the role of the tabloid press who give a high profile to some criminal cases and encourage other prisoners to place themselves in the role of vigilantes on behalf of society at large. The fact that the tabloids enjoy the highest circulation figures among the British press—reporting the lurid details of crimes against the most vulnerable members of society yet frequently failing to report subsequent assaults by some prisoners on their fellow inmates—is perhaps a further indication of the implicit sanction which society places on the exertion of hegemonic masculine values over weaker, subordinated ones.

REFERENCES

Bostyn, A. M., and D. Wight. 1987. Inside a community: Values associated with money and time. In *Unemployment: Personal and social consequences*, edited S. Fineman. London: Tavistock.

Bourdieu, P. 1977. *Outline of a theory of practice*. Cambridge, UK: Cambridge University Press.

Bowker, L. 1977. *Prisoner subcultures*. Toronto: Lexington.

Brittan, A. 1977. *The privatized world*. London: Routledge.

Brod, H. 1990. Pornography and the alienation of male sexuality. In *Men, masculinity and social theory*, edited by J. Hearn and D. Morgan. London: Allen & Unwin.

Charlesworth, S. 2000. *A phenomenology of working class experience*. Cambridge, UK: Cambridge University Press.

Cockburn, C. 1986. *Machinery of dominance*. London: Pluto.

Cohen, S., and L. Taylor. 1972. *Psychological survival: The experience of long-term imprisonment*. Harmondsworth, UK: Penguin.

Connell, R. W. 1987. *Gender and power*. Cambridge, UK: Polity.

Corrigan, P. 1975. Doing nothing. In *Resistance through rituals: Youth subcultures in post-war Britain*, edited by S. Hall and T. Jefferson. London: Hutchinson.

Craib, Ian. 1998. *Experiencing identity*. London: Sage.

De Certeau, M. 1984. *The practice of everyday life*. Berkeley: University of California Press.

Giddens, A. 1984. *The constitution of society*. Cambridge, UK: Polity.

———. 1991. *Modernity and self-identity*. Cambridge, UK: Polity.

Gilmore, T. 1990. *Manhood in the making*. New Haven, CT: Yale University Press.

Goffman, E. 1959. *The presentation of self in everyday life*. New York: Anchor.

———. 1961a. *Asylums: Essays on the social situation of mental patients and other inmates*. London: Penguin.

———. 1961b. On the characteristics of total institutions: The inmate world. In *The prison: Studies in institutional organisation and change*, edited by D. Cressey. New York: Holt, Rinehart & Winston.

Grapendaal, M. 1990. The inmate subculture in Dutch prisons. *British Journal of Criminology* 30:341-55.

Hood, R., and R. Sparks. 1970. *Key issues in criminology*. London: Weidenfeld & Nicolson.

Irwin, J. 1970. *The felon*. Englewood Cliffs, NJ: Prentice Hall.

Irwin, J., and D. Cressey. 1962. Thieves, convicts and the inmate culture. *Social Problems* 10 (1): 142-55.

Jewkes, Y. 2002. *Captive audience: Media, masculinity and power in prisons*. Cullompton, UK: Willan.

Layder, D. 1994. *Understanding social theory*. London: Sage.

Lefebvre, H. 1971. *Everyday life in the modern world*. London: Penguin.

Liebling, A. 1992. *Suicides in prison*. London: Routledge.

Newburn, T., and E. Stanko, eds. 1994. *Just boys doing business? Men, masculinities and crime*. London: Routledge.

Pronger, B. 1990. *The arena of masculinity: Sports, homosexuality and the meaning of sex*. New York: St Martin's Press.

Reisig, M. 2001. The champion, contender and challenger: Top-ranked books in prison studies. *Prison Journal* 81 (3): 389-407.

Remy, J. 1990. Patriarchy and fratriarchy as forms of androcracy. In *Men, masculinity and social theory*, edited by J. Hearn and D. Morgan. London: Allen & Unwin.

Sapsford, R. 1983. *Life sentence prisoners: Reaction, response and change*. Milton Keynes, UK: Open University Press.

Schmid, T., and R. Jones. 1991. Suspended identity: Identity transformation in a maximum security prison. *Symbolic Interaction* 14 (4): 415-32.

Scraton, P., Sim, J, & Skidmore, P. (1991) *Prisons under protest*, Milton Keynes: Open University Press.

Segal, L. 1990. *Slow motion: Changing masculinities, changing men*, London: Virago.

Sim, J. 1994. Tougher than the rest? Men in prison. In *Just boys doing business? Men, masculinities and crime*, edited by T. Newburn and E. Stanko. London: Routledge.

Stevens, D. J. 1994. The depth of imprisonment and prisonization: Levels of security and prisoners' anticipation of future violence. *Howard Journal of Criminal Justice* 33 (1): 137-57.

Sykes, G. M. 1958. *The society of captives: A study of a maximum security prison*. Norwood, NJ: Princeton University Press.

Toch, H. 1975. *Men in crisis*. Chicago: Aldine.

Tolson, A. 1977. *The limits of masculinity*. London: Routledge.

Ward Jouve, N. 1988. *The street-cleaner: The Yorkshire ripper case on trial*. London: Marion Boyars.

Willis, P. 1977. *Learning to labour*. Aldershot, UK: Gower.

Worrall, A. 2000. Life as a woman: The gendered pains of indeterminate imprisonment. Paper presented to British Society of Criminology conference, University of Leicester, UK, July 2000.

Yvonne Jewkes, Ph.D., is a senior lecturer in criminology at the University of Hull, U.K., and is the founding editor (with Chris Greer and Jeff Ferrell) of the new Sage journal Crime, Media, Culture: An International Journal.

[20]

SNAKES AND LADDERS: UPPER-MIDDLE CLASS MALE OFFENDERS TALK ABOUT ECONOMIC CRIME*

SARA WILLOTT
Staffordshire Universtiy

CHRISTINE GRIFFIN
University of Birmingham

MARK TORRANCE
Staffordshire Universtiy

This paper explores the ways in which male offenders in professional-status occupations prior to conviction construct and justify money-related crime. We report a detailed analysis, based in grounded theory and critical social-psychological discourse analysis, of a loosely-structured group interview with four offenders. The men constructed justifications for their offenses in terms of "breadwinning" for their immediate family and economic responsibility toward their extended "family" of employees and creditors. They represented their post-conviction decline in social status as being "dragged down" by envious "boys" in the state apparatus. They positioned themselves on moral high ground, despite having been inappropriately sent to the working class world of prison ("Dante's Inferno"). We contrast these accounts with those of less privileged male offenders.

Although the association between crime and social class is less clear-cut than, say, between crime and gender or crime and age (Messerschmidt, 1994), a closer look reveals an interesting, although complex, relationship. For example, Braithwaite (1979) found that more people from working class backgrounds are convicted of "conventional" crimes (i.e., those handled by the police rather than the bodies, such as Customs and Excise) than are those from the middle classes (see also Giddens, 1993). The dominant image of "nonconventional" economic crime is shaped by "newsworthy" scandals involving public personalities (Croall, 1992). However, these representations tend to depict exceptional individuals. Patterns of criminological research funding (Schlegel and Weisburd, 1992), selective

* The research reported in this paper was supported by the United Kingdom Economic & Social Research Council (Grant R000236020). We would like to thank Harriette Marshall, Jim Messerschmidt, Robert Bursik, and the anonymous *Criminology* reviewers for helpful comments on earlier drafts.

police surveillance (see Smith, 1983), political rhetoric, and media portrayal (Conklin, 1977) have served to focus public attention on conventional crimes (Coleman, 1985) and endorse the construction of dangerous lower class "criminal types." The economically privileged are, therefore, called to account for their crimes far less often (Levi, 1994). According to Poveda (1994), we are socialized to look through the legal lens of the state, whereby "the crimes of the powerful are concealed or obscured from view" (Poveda, 1994:4). However, as Beirne and Messerschmidt (1995) have pointed out, other types of crimes are committed largely by more powerful (invisible) people, which extract larger financial and physical burdens from their victims (see also Conklin, 1977). In other words, despite the overwhelming seriousness of "white-collar" crime, a number of factors have conspired to build and maintain a close association between criminality and working class status. Furthermore, once caught up in the legal system, "justice" tends to favor offenders from socially privileged positions (Conklin, 1977; Savelsberg, 1994). Given the association between criminality and "working class" status, we are arguing that there is a need to reexamine the accounts employed by offenders from a range of social class backgrounds and focus research on the less-visible crimes committed by economically privileged offenders.[1] Furthermore, we would argue that the relationship between crime and social class cannot be addressed in isolation from issues of gender and other systems of hierarchical difference (Braithwaite, 1991).

The phrase "white-collar crime" was introduced by Sutherland (1940), who argued for criminological theorizing that went beyond the narrow and unjust assumptions about what constituted criminality. Sutherland defined white-collar crime as "a crime committed by a person of respectability and high social status in the course of *his* occupation" [emphasis added] (Sutherland, 1949:9). In Sutherland's definition, the assumption is that the perpetrators would be men. Although Sutherland was the first to turn the spotlight on the previously hidden privileged law-breakers, he has been accused of ignoring important factors such as the ways in which crime is

1. It is useful at this point to briefly clarify our use of the idea of class in this paper. There has been considerable debate about the validity of class as a construct used by social scientists to define social groups (e.g., Giddens, 1993; Rose, 1998). In this paper, we describe research conducted with offenders that we refer to as "professional," broadly following Rose's revised socioeconomic classification (Rose, 1998). The key features of this group, for the present purposes, were that they were educated to a high level and had access to, and prior to conviction were active in, lucrative professions. More importantly, however, than our use of class in this paper to define our sample is that class is a construct used by people outside of the social scientific community to talk about themselves and the society in which they live. Given this, we might reasonably expect discourse around class to feature prominently in the ways in which these men described themselves and their offenses.

gendered (Messerschmidt, 1993). Recent exceptions apart, mainstream criminological research continues to sideline the intersections of class, race, and gender (Gelsthorpe and Morris, 1990). We therefore need to look elsewhere, in theoretical terms, to address the issue of why a disproportionate number of men are convicted of crime (Daly and Chesney-Lind, 1988).

Messerschmidt (1993) argues that "crime. . . can provide a resource for doing masculinity in specific social settings as well as contributing to a gendered line of action in which future accountability may be at risk (e.g., being an adequate breadwinner)" (Messerschmidt, 1993:85). Although some research has recently begun to explore the relationship between gender and crime (e.g., Dobash and Dobash, 1995; Newburn and Stanko, 1994), this research has tended to focus on crimes of violence rather than economic crime.[2] Research on the relationship between gender and economic crimes committed by more privileged men is even thinner on the ground (Levi, 1994). According to Levi, although the ratio of male-to-female offenders is not as high for white-collar crime as it is for other crimes, when the figures are broken down into, for example, minor and major fraud, it is the men in powerful occupational positions who are more likely to be convicted of the more serious crimes.

Previous research into class and crime has tended to ignore gender, and existing research into gender and crime has either focused on crimes of violence or sidelined intersections with class. Our interest in this paper is both in economic crime committed by socially privileged men and in how this is tied to gender and class. However, we are not seeking to uncover the causes of criminal behavior. Rather than using gender and class as constructs to explain offenders' actions, we are interested in the ways in which offenders explain their actions and, specifically, in the ways in which gender and class are implicated in the language they use when justifying offending. We elaborate on some of our reasons for adopting this approach in the following section.

THEORETICAL BACKGROUND

Based on the work of Austin (1961), Scott and Lyman (1968) argued that when people violate a social norm, they often make use of linguistic negotiating tools, which they term "accounts" to reestablish social equilibrium. These accounts can take the form of either excuses or justifications.

2. In this paper, we will use the term "economic crime" to indicate a range of financially motivated offenses, including offenses such as residential burglary, that are typically thought of as "blue collar" and offenses such as embezzlement and fraud, that are associated more with "white collar."

Excuses entail admitting wrongdoing but denying responsibility. Justifications entail admitting the action but denying that it was wrong, thus presenting the act morally acceptable. A justification can take a variety of forms, including appeals to higher loyalties, condemnation of those pointing the judicial finger, denial of injury, and sad tales of the recent past. Accounts need to be persuasive if they are to stand a chance of being accepted.

Starting from the reasonable assumption that white-collar offenders in particular will want to maintain a noncriminal self-concept (e.g., Conklin, 1977), Benson (1985) drew on Scott and Lyman's work to explore the ways in which this group accounted for their offenses. For most white-collar offenders, the conviction is their first experience of being labeled as morally deviant. As they are forced from their status as previously law-abiding and "professional" citizens, accounts can be employed to overcome this process of identity change in order to redefine themselves as socially and morally acceptable. Benson offered an individualized psychological explanation for offenders' (use of justificatory accounts in terms of a combination of impression management strategies (Goffman, 1959)) and a cognitive (re)interpretation of events inside the head. Benson concludes that in all probability, the offender engages in a combination of impression management and self-persuasion and that the two may well slide into each other.

The idea that people (and, specifically, economic offenders) use linguistic devices to maintain social equilibrium is paralleled by work in discursive social psychology (e.g., Billig et al., 1988; Potter and Wetherell, 1987). Central to this perspective is the understanding that identity is constructed and renegotiated through language operating in the context of social structures (anticipated by Mills, 1940). Identities are also constructed in relation to others, such that those in socially powerful positions are equipped to define what is "normal" and what is deviant. Language is responsible for maintaining, if not creating, power imbalance in the relationships among different social groups (e.g., Parker, 1990). The emphasis is less on creating a typology of accounts or testing these in experimental settings (e.g., Schlenker and Darby, 1981) than on an examination of accounts given in everyday conversation, against a backdrop of power relations. For example, Billig (1991) examined discrimination in the British Army. The highest ranking officer employed a sophisticated sociological account of how there was no "color bar" in recruitment, with all recruits judged on their merits rather than in terms of ethnic origin. He, thus, used a linguistic device both to justify the lack of black soldiers, and to deny personal prejudice. These discursive justifications, therefore, serve a purpose in talk and are set within a context of power relations. This is not to suggest, however, that people are helpless in the face of prevailing patterns of discourse. On a day-to-day basis, they have the opportunity to maintain, reinforce, or resist the ways in which language positions them (Butler, 1990).

Like Benson, therefore, this approach focuses on the way in which offenders use language to socially position, or reposition, themselves. Offenders are, however, not free to adopt any justificatory strategy they wish: They must draw on existing discursive resources (shared ways of speaking) to present a cohesive and plausible account of their actions. As far back as Sykes and Matza (1957), there was recognition that the ways in which language is used to smooth over deviation from social norms draws on constructions of both gender and class. Arguably, gender and class remain central to the ways in which people both define themselves and the society around them. It would seem reasonable, therefore, to assume that these constructs would feature in offenders' justification of their crime.

Therefore, the contribution of this paper is in exploring the ways in which the linguistic strategies that offenders adopt are both constrained and facilitated by existing discursive patterns. Specifically, we were interested in the ways in which the economically privileged convicted male offenders that we interviewed drew on pervasive discourses of masculinity and class to reposition themselves socially and to justify their criminal activity. In addressing this question, we are only tangentially interested in the causes of crime. It is also beyond the remit of this paper to fully examine the policy implications of these discursive patterns. Our focus is on the ways in which criminal activity is constructed and justified and how class and gender are implicated in the constructions employed by this group of male offenders.

The research we report is a detailed analysis of the talk of a small group of male professional economic offenders. However, before doing so, we will briefly outline some findings from interviews with working class men convicted of "blue collar" economic crime (typically, residential burglary). This will serve two purposes. First, the talk of these men provides an informative contrast with that of the professionals'. Second, it will allow us to illustrate what we see as some of the central features of discourses around class and gender.

MALE WORKING CLASS OFFENDER'S TALK ABOUT ECONOMIC CRIME

As part of a previous study exploring the experiences of men classified as long-term unemployed (Willott and Griffin, 1997), we looked at how unemployment impacted interviewees' understanding of their masculinity. Traditionally, what it means to be a man has been inseparable from going out to work and earning a living because of assumptions around men as family providers (e.g., Bernard, 1981) and because unemployment impacts where and how men spend their time and money (e.g., Wight, 1993). Paid employment, therefore, constitutes one of the main anchors for dominant versions of masculine identity. The removal of this anchor is likely to challenge men's construction of their masculinity (Connell, 1995; Morgan, 1992). Despite facing long-term unemployment, the men we interviewed did construct themselves as the family breadwinner and as belonging in the public rather than in the domestic sphere. Previous research has suggested that minor economic crime can fulfill a similar role to paid employment in maintaining gender identity, with unemployed men earning through so-called "fiddly jobs" (see also MacDonald, 1994). Moreover, when the cash-in-hand resource was unavailable, men in these studies talked about "more serious" crime as an option.

More recently, we interviewed groups of working-class men (defined as such according to Rose, 1998) convicted of economic crime.[3] These men did not have access to well-paid professional jobs and were mainly unemployed prior to conviction. They constructed themselves as breadwinners with loyalties to their immediate family, and these loyalties overrode their responsibility to be law-abiding citizens. The state was constructed as having reneged on the social contract made shortly after the Second World War, thus releasing them from some of their responsibilities to the state. Despite the payment of taxes, successive governments had increasingly failed to deliver full employment, adequate pensions and welfare payments, a well-resourced National Health Service, and so forth. They drew on the culturally familiar narrative of Robin Hood to justify who it was acceptable to steal from (i.e., the rich) and the intention behind the act (in terms of feeding the family—the poor). These men were, therefore, able to redirect the accusation of moral wrongdoing back to the state and position themselves as "decent" men forced into crime. Having been forced into crime by an unjust and corrupt state system, they also constructed themselves as the recipients of humiliation and robbery from those above them in prison. They, therefore, positioned themselves at the bottom of life's game board, playing an unfair game of snakes and ladders[4] against powerful others determined to keep them in their place.

The working class participants only talked about well-educated or socially privileged criminals when probed. These mainly working class men argued that there are times when it is excusable for a rich man to

3. For more detail of the accounts and illustrative narratives employed by this group, see Willott and Griffin (1999).

4. For the sake of readers unfamiliar with this children's boardgame, each player throws dice in order to move up the board. The arbitrary nature of the game is compounded by variously sized snakes and ladders, which catapult a player down or up the board, respectively.

steal; when "say you can get on a tread-mill. Or you [inaudible] or family needs and it can get out of control"(John, WC. 54). To steal from the poor or for a "high-flyer"(Manjit, WC.54) to thieve in order to maintain a high-cost lifestyle for themselves, however, was defined as "stinking greed"(Martin, WC.54). Perhaps these working class men did not initiate talking about criminals from a higher social class because the professional class offenders occupied a social stratum outside of their experience.

Manjit *But at the end of the day, they live in a massive, in such a. . .a high level of life-style, that's it's hard to relate to isn't it?*
Martin *Different world*

Extract 1: WC.55[5]

In contrast, the professional class offenders talked at great length about falling from their privileged world into the working class world of prison.

In summary, the working class offenders had access to three main discursive strategies to justify their crime. They could argue that they were fulfilling the traditional man-as-breadwinner position, they were redistributing wealth Robin Hood style, and they had been forced into crime, having been let down by a corrupt and unjust state who had reneged on their promises. It is reasonable to argue that offenders from a socially privileged and economically wealthy position would not have access to these strategies. How, then, would men such as this account for their involvement in economic crime?

MALE PROFESSIONAL OFFENDER'S TALK ABOUT ECONOMIC CRIME

The discourse we analyzed in this paper is taken from a group discussion with four participants, all serving custodial sentences at the same U.K. prison, and all convicted of economic fraud and fraud-related offenses. All participants had professional qualifications and were professionally employed at the time of conviction. Two were working in the legal profession, one was an accountant, and one in a medicine-related occupation. Although now barred from practicing in their particular professions and technically without employment at the time of interview, all of the men

5. *Transcription conventions* (taken in part from Potter and Wetherell, 1987): Full transcripts are available on request from the first author.
= Indicates the absence of a discernible gap between speakers.
. . . . . A pause of 1 second or more.
[ ] Square brackets indicate that some transcript has been deliberately omitted. Material in square brackets is clarifying information.
<u>*They*</u> A word or phase underlined indicates additional emphasis.
Extract identification: Group discussion; either working or professional class: text chunk within discussion.
All participant names are pseudonyms.

talked in terms of being able to find relatively well-paid jobs on release using previous social connections, even if the employment would be of lesser social status and salary than was their previous occupation.

One of the authors facilitated the discussion, which took place without a prison officer or any other third party present. Immediately prior to the group discussion, the researcher distributed signed letters on university letterhead assuring the participants that their identities would be concealed in reporting of the research. The discussion was unstructured, in the sense that participants were free to direct the conversation as they wished. The researcher opened the discussion by indicating that she was interested in the offenders' perspectives on their offenses, and she asked, as an opening question, whether they thought there was a connection between people needing or wanting money and committing offenses for financial gain. The researcher then kept her contributions to a minimum, talking only when directly asked a question, to ensure that participants were not talked over, or occasionally to allow space for emerging topics to be explored. Within the constraints of a recorded interview, therefore, we believe that the discourse sampled was as reasonably close to what might be expected in naturally occurring conversation. The interview lasted around 60 minutes and generated approximately 12,000 words of transcript.

ANALYSIS

In exploring the data, we adopted an analytic process used successfully in previous research that combines constructivist-grounded analysis (Henwood and Pidgeon, 1992) and critical discursive social psychology (e.g., Parker, 1990). The full details of this approach can be found in Willott and Griffin (1997). We will summarize it here.

The audiotaped discussions were first transcribed and imported into Atlas-ti,[6] a software package for the analysis of qualitative data. We started the process of analysis by both reading and rereading the transcripts and listening to the taped discussions. We then divided the discussion into 34 chunks and in so doing fixed the units of analysis for the whole analytic process. The size of each chunk varied from a few lines to a couple of pages, bounded by changes in topic introduced by either the facilitator

6. Atlas-ti for Windows 95 (Muhr, 1996) is a software package that facilitates the analysis of qualitative data. It supports the process of identifying and coding transcript segments (which may overlap) and the construction of nonhierarchical networks. Networks can be made of codes or, as analysis progresses, can be used to indicate relationships among lower level networks. The researcher, therefore, develops an understanding of the text through construction of a series of nested networks, each of which can be viewed diagrammatically within the program. Atlas-ti, therefore, supports the grounded theory principle of moving from data to theory but allows substantially more flexibility than, for example, NUDIST (Fielding and Lee, 1991).

or one of the discussants. We then coded all of the material using in vivo codes. "In vivo" is a grounded theory term meaning words or phrases used by the participants, such as "the man in the street" or "criminal." These codes were not theoretically laden but were simply a way of dividing large amounts of text into manageable units. Codes can be thought of as indicating the topic, or one of the topics, that participants addressed within the particular chunk of transcript. Each chunk of text was associated with between 1 and 6 codes, and we used 84 codes in total.

We then more or less arbitrarily selected one of the codes that we had associated with a reasonably large number of chunks of transcript. We identified different ways in which the discussants talked about this topic, moving toward a more theoretical understanding of the material. We looked specifically for inconsistencies, metaphors, anecdotes, contemporary proverbs, and what appeared to be deliberate omissions. Through these, we began to build a picture of the patterns within the men's discourse and how these ways of talking were used to construct persuasive arguments. Once we had a fairly clear understanding of the ways in which the men talked within the chunks of transcript associated with this first code, we then selected all units of text under a second in vivo code and repeated the process. We asked whether our model of the discursive patterns that we built when looking at the first topic was adequate to account for the ways in which the men talked about the second. Where this was not the case, we added to our model. We repeated this process for 12 different in vivo codes until we found that the model we had built was adequate as an account of most of the men's talk. Toward the end of this analysis, we also mapped out the ways in which each pattern of discourse related to other patterns.

The process that we have described draws heavily on grounded theory principles, such as moving between theory and data in an iterative fashion, the idea of reaching theoretical saturation and exploring the nature of links between theoretical categories. We also borrowed several specific strategies, such as the development of in vivo codes and regular and frequent memo writing. However, our approach differs from the traditional Glaser and Strauss (1967) position in which theory was assumed to develop from a theoretical vacuum and that detailed analysis of peoples' talk provides insight into what they really think (assumptions criticized by Henwood and Pidgeon, 1992). As we discussed above, we saw our interviewees' talk as strategic, focused on constructing a representation of themselves that was socially acceptable and drawing on discursive patterns already culturally present. The goal of our analysis, therefore, was not a unified theory, but a potentially complex network of interrelated and sometimes contradictory ways of talking. In this respect, our approach leans more on the epistemological assumption of critical discursive social psychology (e.g., Parker, 1990; Wetherell, 1995) than on traditional grounded theory.

RESULTS

In this section, we will examine the patterns of discourse recurrently drawn on by the professional class participants to construct their modus operandi. We have chosen to organize the results loosely around an analogy with the board game *Snakes & Ladders*, given that all of the men came up with several variations on the "life is like a game/gamble" metaphor (see also Benson, 1985). Another reason for choosing to organize the results in this way is that the working class men described more economically privileged offenders using phrases such as "high level" and "highflyer," whereas "trying to maintain a high social standing," "career ladder," "I was a good hit," "on a slippery slope," "taken down," "taken into the bowels of the earth," and "maintaining the moral high ground" were recurrently used by the professional class men to describe their serving a custodial sentence and their position in relation to other inmates.

PROFESSIONAL CLASS ACCOUNTS: RESPONSIBILITIES FOR THE FAMILY AND BEYOND

The professional class men used an extended version of the breadwinner discourse to account for their crimes by constructing themselves as the primary financial support for their wives and children, but they expanded this to include employees and their families.[7]

Francis *If it had just been me, I don't think. . . there would probably have been no need, to, to have to dig into these funds, because. . .*

Lawrence *I agree, if I was a single person, I would have just walked away, it wouldn't have concerned one.*

Rupert *Yeah, I think that is a strong factor, because although my family's grown up now, at the time this happened I had a young family. Then you look to your staff, who in turn have got responsibilities and young families themselves.*

7. All information that might reveal the identity of any participant has been obscured or omitted, such as participants' original name, their (prior) occupation, the specific offense, and the prison in which they were held.

Lawrence	*That was a big factor as well, from the staffing angle, that you felt that you were letting the staff down, and you were in the middle of a recession, which was vicious, and er. . . now of course, you realize that the staff don't give, er, two hoots, and so, again, you're naive I think, in feeling that those responsibilities are there, which no one's asking for.*
SW	*Right.*
Francis	*You see, none of us was taking this money to live a raucous life-style. . . A sort of selfish, you know, quixotic sort of life-style. Erm, it was as a genuine need to look after others, our families, our children, our borrowings, and erm, I think that's what took me a, it took me a long time to come to terms with the fact that, that I was a 'criminal'. And I think it was partly, largely because I was trying to help my own.*

Extract 2: PC.8

In the extract above, Lawrence and Francis are accounting for their crimes using an expanded version of the male breadwinner discourse. The position constructed by these professional class men was that of shouldering far greater responsibilities than merely those of a man with a wife and children to support. They are constructing themselves as patron to clients and protector of employees (and their families). Francis, Lawrence, and Rupert are arguing that they "dug into the funds" for the benefit of others rather than for themselves. To "dig into" conjures up very different connotations than does to "steal from." "Digging into funds" implies that the money did not belong to anyone in particular, but was a resource that could be justifiably drawn on when the "need" arose. These "others" in need were not just immediate family, but a wider circle of dependants. Francis is at pains to argue that the motivation was not "selfish" greed but arose from "a genuine need to look after others." Although there was never an explicit mention of "greed" in their discourse, an explanation solely around the "need" of others implies the negation of "selfish" greed. They are, therefore, contrasting their (unasked for) responsibilities for others with personal selfishness, as potential reasons for their involvement in economic crime. This group of men also talked about being "brought up to try, to shoulder responsibility. That's what you're taught through schools, through university or whatever" (Lawrence, PC.9). These four men returned to the theme of contrasting responsibilities repeatedly throughout the discussion:

Owen	*The real difference between what happens if a white-collar guy goes down or a professional guy goes down, as against a blue-collar worker, because for the blue-collar worker, it's devastating for him and his family. He's lost his job, his income might be department of social security benefits. So for his immediate family, yes, it is devastating. But for a guy to be run out of practice, like I was and like Francis was, it's not only devastating for that particular guy, but also for all his staff and their immediate families as well. . . . all your clients as well as your own family and the school fees and all the rest of it. So it seems to me that the knock-on effects =*
Rupert	*The net spreads wider doesn't it.*
Owen	*The effect's greater because there's more people dependent on you.*
Lawrence	*Responsibilities. . .*

Extract 3: PC.23

Not only do these professional class ("white-collar") men talk about shouldering greater responsibility than "blue-collar" (working class) workers, but as a consequence, they also construct themselves as the greater victims once convicted.

PROFESSIONAL RESPONSIBILITIES AND A HIGH SOCIAL STANDING

The professional class men talked not only about responsibilities to family, employees, small creditors, and their borrowings, but also an even wider responsibility to "The Profession" and a self-consciousness not simply about their individual standing within their particular profession, but also the standing of their profession relative to others and of all professions in relation to other occupations (see also Extract 5 below).

Lawrence	*Coming back to your question about economics and crime =*
Rupert	*White-collar crime is obviously much more related to economic factors. . .*
Lawrence	*So if you're trying to prove a criminality in terms of. . .*
SW	*That's not what I'm trying to do. . .*

Rupert	*I guess, perhaps the others [presumably the other three discussants] were subject to, a level of expectation in relation to social standing and the trappings that go with that. And felt obliged to achieve that, one way or another.*
SW	*Mm.*
Rupert	*Er, I think that is possibly a factor.*
SW	*Mm.*
Lawrence	*Yeas, which comes back down to arrogance, comes down to egoism, comes down to, you know, so are we out of sync there, in terms of. . . =*
Francis	*It may not just be that, Lawrence. There's also self-respect. I mean, is that arrogance, or egoism? . . .There is tremendous pressure on all of us to keep a standing and to keep a sort of presence, you know, among your peers. Erm, I was very conscious at one point that [name of profession] seemed to be doing, not as well as some of the other professions, and "what can I do about that." The only thing I could do was work harder, you know, it certainly wasn't to go [inaudible].*
Owen	*Yeah, I think the general standing of the professions has gone down over the last, what, fifteen years or so. Certainly since I've been involved in the [name of] profession. Looking at all the other professions, they all seem to have declined in terms of status, as much as the [name of] profession.*

Extract 4: PC.15

Rupert and Francis position themselves as "trapped" into certain expectations associated with their high social standing. Failure to meet these expectations of individual achievement would, they argue, reflect not only on their "presence" in the community, but also on the status of The Professions (to which they owe some further responsibility). Therefore, although these men constructed themselves as somewhere near the top of life's gameboard, life at the top necessarily entails some "trappings." Once again, there is a contrast between doing it for others (e.g., The Profession) and doing it for oneself (which equates with individual arrogance or ego). Then comes a moment of reflection in their discourse as Lawrence questions Rupert's causal analysis with the possibility of explaining their actions in terms of internal factors, such as egotism or arrogance. However, the other men do not take up this brief foray into talk about individual blame. Rather than pursuing this line, Francis swiftly returns to an explanation in terms of social pressure and responsibility toward others.

The men constructed themselves as both hapless pawns and proactive players in the game of life, occasionally alternating between these contradictory positions within a single sentence.

"THE POLITICS OF ENVY" FROM THOSE BENEATH

For the professional class men participating in the discussion, the decline of The Professions generally (which contributed to their personal downfall) was a recurring theme. A major factor in this decline, they argued, was the part played by "the decisions makers. . . the little people in state bureaucracy." Such that their fate was no longer decided by the "power of the law [but] controlled by those administrators"(Lawrence PC.20). All agreed with Lawrence as he developed the position that those working in The Professions are higher beings morally and should be judged on a different basis than "blue collar" workers.

Lawrence	*The Professions don't have any peak value now. They're just another business and they're judged along with the rest. And the people who are doing the judging don't see any particular enhanced value, whether you're a plumber or whether you're a lawyer."*
	Extract 5: PC.29
Lawrence	*The state machinery is a myth, OK! The state machinery consists of people. I didn't deal with a machine, I had individual people coming after me, who presumably—none of whom were married, none of them had any responsibilities—they were young, most of them were under 30 years old. They were the decision-makers in effect. . . . .* *You're up against people, who have their own ambitions and they will use you, as a foil to achieve it.*
SW	*Right, I mean=*
Rupert	*Do you think the politics of envy come into it?*
Lawrence	*Yes, very much so. I mean, I had a particularly vicious case officer, who was out-and-out chips on shoulders. . . You know, balance him up, how many. I mean, he came from a very underprivileged background, didn't understand a lot of the aspects [inaudible] of which my particular case was about. And one felt very clearly that he wanted me as a feather in his cap, as a, a. . . I was a good hit, as a [name of profession], as one of his successes.*
	Extract 6: PC.19

Lawrence is arguing in the extracts above that the new decision makers are men from the lower classes who are clawing their way up the ladder by shooting down men in the professions. Unlike themselves, these younger men have not shouldered the same responsibilities in terms of family and staff; they are not even providers, let alone superproviders. Such men failed to appreciate the delicate position of a man with professional and family responsibilities. They were talked about as ruthless in their pursuit of success and, therefore, presumably lacking in moral fiber. The professional class men are, therefore, constructing these "new boys" (Francis, PC.21) as young men without marital or employee responsibilities and from a lower social and moral class to themselves. This construction of moral, intelligent, and highly educated beings versus the amoral and ill-informed lower classes is echoed in Lawrence's description of Crown Court versus High Court judges below (Extract 9). They constructed themselves as deserving of respect and a high social standing in the public sphere. Furthermore, they argued that their efforts to stay at the top were being thwarted by the envy of the new boys on the block; the aspiring middle class men clambering up the hierarchy through their occupational positions in the state apparatus.

SLIPPING DOWN THE RECESSION SNAKE

So the professional class men were constructing themselves as shouldering a burden of responsibility for a wide circle of dependants and being chased by young, ambitious men in the state apparatus with "chips on shoulder" and presumably "something to prove." The financial context in which their personal demise was possible, they argued, was one of economic recession; a bombardment from wider external forces which left them vulnerable to attack.

SW *What happened in your case Owen?*

Owen *I was running a practice that was great during the good times, a [type of] practice, and then we hit the recession, which went on not for six months or a year, but year after year after year. And despite cutting back, couldn't erm, do sufficiently, and ended up taking clients' money to actually keep the firm going. That all culminated in stress and nervous breakdown an all the rest of it. So erm. . . for me, my crime was taking money, not for my personal benefit, but for the benefit of others, to keep the firm going. But ultimately I could see that the situation had to come to an end at some stage, and it was my responsibility.*

Extract 7: PC 10.5

Despite ending with an admission of personal responsibility, Owen uses impersonal passive terms such as "the recession" to position himself as a victim of circumstance. The recession is described as slowly sapping away at the firm's resources until he "ended up" taking clients' money; again implying little choice in the crime. This account positions Owen both as having little agency and simultaneously as actively "taking money." However, this contradiction is resolved by again drawing on a discourse of responsibility for and to others, taking the money "to keep the firm going. . .for the benefit of others." Time and again these men described the recession as an unstoppable and unforeseen external force, inducing stress and a consequent clouding of rational judgment in the victim, who was then drawn down into an economic and emotional vortex. The participants used phrases and metaphors such as "you just get sucked into it" (Francis, PC10.5), "bled me dry financially. . . a slippery slope" (Rupert, PC10.7), and "it became very vicious, like a rolling rock down a hill" (Lawrence, PC.12) . Metaphors such as these, in addition to the use of the passive voice again, paint an image of hapless pawns swept into criminal despair because they were in the wrong place at the wrong time.

"BECOMING A CRIMINAL": PROFESSIONAL CLASS MEN'S CONSTRUCTIONS OF THE (WORKING CLASS) CRIMINAL (UNDER) WORLD:

Francis	*You 'become' 'a criminal'—just as Rupert was saying—you're taken down and you're put in a cell. And you can't sit down in that cell—there's nowhere to sit—and someone will say "are'll bring youa cuppa tea ina-minute" [growling cockney accent] and you wait half an hour. And someone might put their head through the bar. . .*
Lawrence	*=and say "oh, you won't hang yourself then?"*
Francis	*Yes, yes. . . and you look up and there's an absence of light fittings in the place. . . .*
[laughter]	
	I mean, even the light bulbs are screwed into the ceiling, so. . . .
[more laughter]	
Lawrence	*So you read the graffiti. . .*
Francis	*And you're told to take your tie off in case you hang yourself!*
Rupert	*'Smasher woz 'ere, 1982' [growling cockney accent].*
Lawrence	*That's right, and the spelling is wonderful [sarcastic tone].*

Francis	*And you've got great butch female prison wardens. . . It's like going into the maelstrom, it's dreadful.*
Lawrence	*It's unreal. . . it is unreal.*
Francis	*Yes, it's like Dante's Inferno.*
Lawrence	*It's a hell of an experience.*

Extract 8: PC.32

These four men continued in the same vein for some time, describing their first experience of life as "a criminal" using phrases such as "the bowels of the earth," "jangling keys," and "from the calm of the court, down into the chaos" (Francis, 10.32). Being "taken down" is literally constructed as entering "hell." From the growling cockney accents to the comments about interior décor and the misspelled graffiti, this group of men were constructing the criminal world as not only as completely alien to their own, but also as vastly inferior, a working class, unsophisticated, hellish place where even traditional gender roles are turned on their head, with "great butch female wardens." They also argued that prison does not disrupt the life of a working class criminal, whereas "we have fallen out of the structure of our lives" (Lawrence, PC.24). In fact, Owen argued (PC.26), prison could well prove to be educational in the criminal career of the "blue-collar guy."

Rupert	*It's very humiliating, erm, I think we all found that. . . to be in the dock, branded as a common thief in the circumstances in which we committed our thefts. Maybe that's how it should be, I don't know. But it's very humiliating.*
Francis	*Well, Lawrence described how the judge probably saw a burglar one minute and then Lawrence the next, and that's exactly what it's like. That's one reason why, a couple of years ago we wanted to take motoring offenses out of the magistrates' courts, because you've got, you know, perfectly reasonable members of the public, who have driven too fast, er, in the company of common criminals. . . You know, burglars, rapists and muggers and all the rest of it.*
Lawrence	*I was talking with Owen just before we came, about the difference between Crown Court judges and High Court judges. I've had quite a dosage of both. The High Court judges are completely. . . . they're intelligent; they grasp the points very quickly. The Crown Court judges. . . different ball game. I mean those guys are used to dealing with=*
Francis	*=all they hear is a constant liturgy of depravity.*

Lawrence *Exactly, the real base aspects of crime, not white-collar crime, or, whatever you call it, fraud or whatever. . . .*

Extract 9: PC.30–31

Lawrence, Francis, Owen, and Rupert devoted much of their time to positioning themselves as "other" in relation to "real criminals." They positioned themselves as morally superior to the common thief, sometimes referred to as "lower class"(PC.24) or "the blue-collar worker"(PC.27). Having drawn a distinction between "perfectly reasonable members of the public" and "common criminals," a proximity to the latter was talked about as humiliating. They argued that they should have been judged on a different basis, or at least in a different court room from "burglars, rapists, muggers, and all the rest," given that their cases required intelligent understanding. The Crown Court judges, either through their stupidity or their constant exposure to "depravity," had apparently lost the ability to distinguish different sorts of crime and criminals; the moral difference, say, between a burglary and white-collar crime. The professional class men accounted for "common" or "blue-collar" crime using arguments that positioned working class criminals as other to and distant from themselves. They also argued that these men were motivated to commit crime as they blindly followed group norms: "speaking up for them in a funny sort of way, I think it is perceived among their peers, the sort of crimes they commit are not morally. . . I don't think they're in a moral dilemma"(Rupert, PC.27). The working class offenders were, therefore, constructed as amoral, or as not subject to the same dilemmas as professional class offenders.

BUNGLING AMATEURS IN CRIME

The professional class participants not only positioned themselves as "other" in comparison to "common" working class criminals, but also in contrast to "professional middle class criminals" or "fraudsters." These men argued that their incarceration was partly down to poor decision making: "the stress factor really. . .your efficiency is impaired. You need to operate at 120% efficiency to repair the damage. . . It may be that your conscience dilutes your efficiency" (Rupert, PC.7). "What you've got here [inside prison] are people that've screwed up, they've bungled in a crisis"(Lawrence, PC.9). Ordinarily, these men argued, they were "competent professionals in our Professions [but] we were bungling amateurs as far as getting caught was concerned"(Rupert, PC.6). This uncharacteristic bungling in a crisis could, Rupert suggests, be explained by a moral conscience, whereas a "professional" white-collar criminal,[8] they argued, is a

8. Professional, in this sense, refers to a recidivist from a higher social class,

breed apart; calculated, cynical, and "not concerned with the moral aspects" (Rupert, PC.7).

Rupert	*Well, some are more professional in being able to avoid getting caught. Although we may have been competent professionals in our Professions, we were bungling amateurs as far as avoiding getting caught is concerned.*
Lawrence	*Yeah, I think we were naive, I think the people out there that are most cynical and who approach it in a professional manner are less likely to get caught. Because they would stuff everybody else, and they would look after the criminal aspects because they were aware of that.*
Rupert	*=and they're one or two steps ahead of the game all the time, you know, they know what the consequences are and they know generally how to avoid them. . . I'm hardly in a position to take the moral high-ground, erm, but I personally don't find any credence in viewing at this distance, that some get away with it and some don't.*

Extract 10: PC.6

These four men positioned themselves in opposition to these white-collar professional criminals who, according to Lawrence, caught the media attention and thereby constructed all white-collar criminals as "out-and-out fraudsters. [Whereas] we just screwed up. . . . The implication is that [name of prison] is full of professional criminals, having their rest-cure and putting their heads together. . . There is this criminal type, white-collar guy. . . . he's a fraudster" (PC.34). Rupert defines himself as a competent member of "A Profession" (read: upstanding member of the noncriminal world who was good at his job but screwed up in a crisis) as opposed to a "professional fraudster" (read: a different and morally deviant being, belonging in the illegal underworld). "I'd make a useless white-collar criminal, because I had a morality" (Lawrence, PC.11). To describe themselves as "naive, bungling amateurs" in relation to criminal behavior is far from self-deprecating in this context. Lawrence is using "morality" as a discursive frame to distinguish himself not only from "blue-collar common criminals" but also from "professional white-collar criminals." Although these four men may have slipped down the longest snake on the board into the working class underworld of prison, unlike the professional fraudsters, they are able to position themselves as retaining the moral high

rather than a (former) member of one of "The Professions," such as doctors, lawyers, and accountants.

ground because they played a fair game. This positioning is illustrated by phrases such as "I'm hardly in a position to take the moral high-ground, erm, but. . .," the 'but' here speaks volumes.

Lawrence *What you've got here are people that've screwed up. They've bungled in an economic crisis and decided to run with it. And in many ways, they've tried too hard. . .*

Extract 11: PC.9

SUMMARY AND CONCLUSIONS

In summary, therefore, our interviewees were able to represent themselves as "not really criminal" in relation to their fellow inmates inside prison: "Real" criminals consisted of the working class inmates and a minority of socially privileged "Pro's." The working class or common criminals were constructed as stupid and as morally depraved, whereas the "professional" "white-collar criminals" or "out-and-out fraudsters" were represented as clever but again, immoral. Despite experiencing the degradation of "becoming a criminal" and being "taken down" into the working class underworld of prison, these men positioned themselves as retaining the moral high ground. To draw on the snakes and ladders analogy, our interviewees appear to represent themselves as having reached the final stretch in the game only to have the misfortune of sliding down a judicial-process snake. Our interviewees adopted four broad strategies to maintain this position. They represented themselves as breadwinners, as intellectually superior to the state, judicial, and legal system, which led to their prosecution, as morally superior, and as being the victims of circumstances outside of their control.

All of the men drew on the man-as-breadwinner discourse to account for or justify their involvement in economic crime. However, the professional class participants employed this discourse differently to the working class offenders. Both groups argued that as men, they were responsible for "bringing home the bacon" for their immediate families in their position as father and husband. "Man-as-family-breadwinner" is a well-documented and hegemonic pattern of discourse in the maintenance of traditional masculine identities (e.g., Bernard, 1981; Willott and Griffin, 1997). However, the participants from the socially privileged group used an embellished (or beneficent patron) version of the breadwinner discourse to talk about additional responsibilities toward a much wider circle of dependants, such as employees and small creditors.

In representing themselves as intellectually and morally superior to both their accusers and the "real" criminals, the (ex) professional men compared themselves favorably with the men in the state system who discovered their offense, the judges who convicted them, the "devious" white collar recidivists who did crime properly, and the majority of other (working class) inmates who belonged in prison. Geis (1982) quotes from Laite (a white-collar criminal and author) who described his fellow inmates as "foul-mouthed, sadistic riff-raff. . . different from me in a very basic and dangerous way" (p. 91). Their accusers were described as either Crown Court judges who were unable to distinguish depravity from white-collar crime or ambitious "new boys on the block," "the decisions makers. . . the little people in state bureaucracy"(PC.20) who were using them to claw their way up the ladder. These "upstarts" in the system came from an underprivileged background, and it was implied that they were without responsibilities or the technical knowledge and expertise or the credentials gained through postgraduate studies that they had under their belts. Connell (1993) argues that since the nineteenth century, we have witnessed a competition primarily between two dominant versions of masculine identities: expertise (see also Seidler, 1989, on masculine identity and rationality) and direct dominance. In speculating over the construction of a new variant of dominance-based hegemonic masculinity, Connell talks about "thrusting entrepreneurs" (Connell, 1993:614) or technocrats (operating through the indirect mechanism of financial administration) competing with the older vanguard of expertise-based masculinity (such as members of professional occupational bodies). Arguably, this historical analysis mirrors the competition reflected in the discourse of these socially privileged male offenders.

Finally, their being labeled as "a criminal" could be attributed to, they argued, an unlucky combination of forces beyond their control (such as the economic recession in the 1980s). Although the working class offenders justified their offenses as, in part, a result of being let down by the state system, their representation of the state was, in many ways, different. The working class men talked about the state as having reneged on a social contract and, therefore, giving them both little choice and almost moral freedom to violate certain laws in particular contexts. However, although there was no mention of a social contract, the professional class offenders did talk about Thatcher's government encouraging investment and leaving them high and dry when the recession hit.

As such, their accounts employed particular justifications. Many of these have been outlined as strategies by Benson (1985), Conklin (1977) and Scott and Lyman (1968), such as appeals to higher loyalties, condemnation of those who had pointed the finger at them, denying that their crimes had caused injury to others, offering sad tales of the recent past and claiming that they had simply "borrowed" or "dug into funds" rather than stolen the money. We realize, of course, that these accounts were employed by a small group of men in a specific social-historical context. This means, for example, that we cannot determine the extent to which they constructed their rationalizations after the offense and that the emphasis on morality during the court proceedings for these men would shape the context in which these accounts were elicited (Benson, 1985; Potter and Wetherell, 1987). For example, although the professional class men based their accounts solely around the "genuine needs" of others, the working class men debated the complex relationship between "need" and "greed" for men with more money than themselves. To some extent, this difference might perhaps reflect the greater emphasis on moral character during the process of degradation (Benson, 1985) for the professional men.

We are arguing that the men in our study actively constructed their identities from the resources available to them. The discursive patterns identified in this study are not limited to the talk of men who have committed offenses: the justificatory strategies that the men adopted are not constructed in a vacuum but draw on ways of talking that are already present within society. These resources are not class or gender neutral; they were "doing" specific, class-related forms of masculinity (see, for example, Donaldson, 1987; Pyke, 1996). More specifically, the men might be thought of as "doing professionalism," the particular kind of masculinity associated with rationality, knowledge, and technical expertise discussed by Connell (1993, 1995). Our approach builds on and to some extent moves away from that used by Benson (1985) and Scott and Lyman (1968). We are arguing that the findings reveal an interplay of identity work being accomplished around different versions of privileged and subordinated versions of masculinity (see Connell, 1995; Messerschmidt, 1997) in relation to class. Capitalism and patriarchy are intertwined (Messerschmidt, 1986), and there may be very little to distinguish discourse used to justify white-collar crime and law-abiding capitalist activity (Levi, 1994). Being an economic entrepreneur who takes financial "risks" in the workplace is socially legitimated, at least from the perspective of fellow professionals, because it is compatible with being the breadwinner both for immediate family and a wider "family" of employees. In the United Kingdom at least, management of financial risk and responsibility is associated with being a member of a particular professional class. Although there are notable exceptions, being professional is associated with being part of particular elite social networks based around family background and attendance at the "right schools," universities and (often exclusively male) clubs. This professional class is seen as encompassing not only the financial risk takers, but also the judicial system to which the risk takers are answerable should things go wrong. Levi, in his review of British white-collar crime (1993, 1994), concluded that when "people like us" came before the judgment of the court, although offenders were occasionally punished severely as an example to others or for letting their side down, the sentence was often tempered by empathy for their fall from grace and an understanding of the good motives that lay behind their moral lapse. Although such empathy is understandable, it is not acceptable that such empathy is "so seldom extended to those who have no grace from which to fall" (Levi, 1993:82). The discursive patterns outlined in this study, therefore, serve not only to provide professional class offenders with a strategy for justifying their actions, but also arguably reduce the perceived immorality of their offence in the eyes of society and, more seriously, in the eyes of the judicial system. This will serve to reinforce inequalities in the criminal justice system.

REFERENCES

Austin, John
1961 A plea for excuses. In J. Urmson and G. Warnock (eds.), Philosophical Papers. Oxford: Clarendon Press.

Beirne, Piers and James Messerschmidt
1995 Criminology (2d ed.). Orlando, Fl: Harcourt Brace.

Benson, Michael
1985 Denying the guilt mind: Accounting for involvement in a white-collar crime. Criminology 23(4):583–607.

Bernard, Jessie
1981 The good-provider role: Its rise and fall. American Psychologist 36:1–12.

Billig, Michael
1991 Ideology and Opinions. London: Sage.

Billig, Michael, Susan Condor, Derek Edwards, Mike Gane, David Middleton, and Alan Radley
1988 Ideological Dilemmas: A Social Psychology of Everyday Thinking. London: Sage.

Braithwaite, John
1979 Inequality, Crime and Public Policy. London: Routledge and Kegan Paul.
1991 Poverty, power, white-collar crime and the paradoxes of criminological theory. Australian & New Zealand Journal of Criminology 24:40–58.

Butler, Judith
1990 Gender Trouble: Feminism and the Subversion of Identity. New York: Routledge.

Coleman, James
1985 The Criminal Elite: The Sociology of White-Collar Crime. New York: St. Martin's Press.

Conklin, John
1977 Illegal but not Criminal: Business Crime in America. Englewood Cliffs, N.J.: Prentice-Hall.

Connell, Robert W.
1993 The big picture: Masculinities in recent world history. Theory and Society 22:507–623.
1995 Masculinities. Cambridge: Polity Press.

Croall, Hazel
1992 White Collar Crime: Criminal Justice and Criminology. Bucks: Open University Press.

Daly, Kathleen and Meda Chesney-Lind
1988 Feminism and criminology. Justice Quarterly 5(4):497–538.

Dobash, R. Emerson, Russell P. Dobash, and Lesley Noaks (eds.)
1995 Gender and Crime. Cardiff: University of Wales Press.

Donaldson, Mike
1987 Labouring men: Love, sex and strife. ANZJS 23(2):165–184.

Fielding, Nigel and Raymond Lee (eds.)
1991 Using Computers in Qualitative Research. London: Sage.

Geis, Gilbert
1982 On White-Collar Crime. Lexington, Mass.: Lexington Books, D.C. Heath

Gelsthorpe, Loraine and Allison Morris
1990 Introduction: Transforming and transgressing criminology. In Loraine Gelsthorpe and Allison Morris (eds.) Feminist Perspectives in Criminology. Milton Keynes: Open University Press.

Giddens, Anthony
1993 Sociology, 2d ed. Oxford: Polity Press.

Glaser, Barney and Anselm Strauss
1967 The Discovery of Grounded Theory. Chicago: Aldine.

Goffman, Erving
1959 The Presentation of Self in Everyday Life. Garden City, N.Y.: Anchor.

Henwood, Karen and Nick Pidgeon
1992 Qualitative research and psychological theorising. British Journal of Psychology 83:97–111.

Levi, Michael
1993 White-collar crime: The British scene. ANNALS, AAPSS 525:71–82.
1994 Masculinities and white-collar crime. In Tim Newburn and Elizabeth Stanko (eds.). Just Boys Doing Business?: Men, Masculinities and Crime. London: Routledge.

MacDonald, Robert
1994 Fiddley jobs, undeclared working and the something for nothing society. Work, Employment and Society 8(4):507–530.

Messerschmidt, James W.
1986 Capitalism, Patriarchy and Crime. Totowa: Rowan and Littlefield.
1993 Masculinities and Crime: Critique and Reconceptualization of Theory. Maryland: Rowan and Littlefield.
1994 Schooling, masculinities, and youth crime by white boys. In Tim Newburn, and Elizabeth Stanko (eds.). Just Boys Doing Business?: Men, Masculinities and Crime. London: Routledge.

1997 Crime as Structured Action: Gender, Race, Class, and Crime in the Making. Beverly Hills, Calif.: Sage.

Mills, C. Wright
1940 Situated actions and vocabularies of motive. American Sociological Review 5:904–13

Morgan, David H.J.
1992 Discovering Men. London: Routledge.

Muhr, Thomas
1996 Atlas-ti, for Windows 95: The Knowledge Workbench (release 4.0) [Computer software]. London: Scientific Software Development/SCOLARI, Sage

Newburn, Tim and Elizabeth Stanko (eds.)
1994 Just Boys Doing Business?: Men, Masculinities and Crime. London: Routledge.

Parker, Ian
1990 Discourse: Definitions and contradictions. Philosophical Psychology 3:189–203.

Potter, Jonathan and Margaret Wetherell
1987 Discourse and Social Psychology: Beyond Attitudes and Behaviour. London: Sage.

Poveda, Tony
1994 Rethinking White-Collar Crime. Westport, Conn.: Praeger.

Pyke, Karen
1996 Class-based masculinities: The interdependence of gender, class, and interpersonal power. Gender and Society 10(5):527–549.

Rose, David
1998 Commentary: Once more unto the breach: In defence of class analysis yet again. Work, Employment and Society 12(4):755–767.

Savelsberg, Joachim J.
1994 Constructing White-Collar Crime: Rationalities, Communication, Power. Philadelphia: University of Pennsylvania Press.

Schlegel, Kip and David Weisburd
1992 White-Collar Crime Reconsidered. Boston: Northeastern University Press.

Schlenker, Barry and Bruce Darby
1981 Use of apologies in social predicaments. Social Psychology Quarterly 44:271–278

Scott, Marvin and Stanford Lyman
1968 Accounts. American Sociological Review 33:46–62.

Seidler, Victor
1989 Rediscovering Masculinity: Reason, Language and Sexuality. London: Routledge.

Smith, David
1983 A Survey of Londoners. Police and People in London, Vol. 1. London: Policy Studies Institute.

Sutherland, Edwin H.
1940 White collar criminality. American Sociological Review 5:1–12.

1949 White Collar Crime. New York: Dryden Press.

Sykes, Gresham and David Matza
1957 Techniques of neutralization: A theory of delinquency. American Sociological Review 22:664–670.

Wetherell, Margaret
1995 Romantic discourse and feminist analysis: Interrogating investment, power and desire. In S. Wilkinson and C. Kitzinger (eds.). Feminism and Discourse: Psychological Perspectives. London: Sage.

Wight, Daniel
1993 Workers not Wasters: Masculine Respectability, Consumption and Unemployment in Central Scotland: A Community Study. Edinburgh, Scotland: Edinburgh University Press.

Willott, Sara A. and Christine Griffin
1997 Wham bam, am I a man? Unemployed men talk about masculinities. Feminism and Psychology 7:107–128.
1999 Building your own lifeboat: Male offenders talk about economic crime. The British Journal of Social Psychology 38(4):445–460.

Sara Willott is a Lecturer in Psychology at Staffordshire University. Her main interest is in the exploration of masculine identities. She has particularly focused on men whose gender identity was potentially threatened, the long-term unemployed, and men convicted of economic crime. This research has been published in *Feminism and Psychology* and *The British Journal of Social Psychology*.

Christine Griffin is a Senior Lecturer in Social Psychology at the University of Birmingham, United Kingdom. Her main research interests include young people's experiences and representations of youth and adolescence in the academic and popular domains; sexuality and gender relations, including constructions of masculinity; and the use of qualitative methods in critical social psychology. She has published widely in these and related areas and is the author of *Typical Girls?* (Routledge and Kegan Paul, 1985), and *Representations of Youth* (Polity Press, 1993). She is also a founding editor of the international journal, *Feminism and Psychology*.

Mark Torrance is a Senior Lecturer in Psychology at Staffordshire University. Originally trained in social psychology, he maintains an active interest in discourse analytic methodology. His main focus of research is the psychology of text production.

[21]

Managing Marginalised Masculinities: men and probation

SALLY HOLLAND & JONATHAN B. SCOURFIELD

ABSTRACT *This paper aims to offer some insights into the gendered nature of the work of probation officers. Much of the work of the British Probation Service is with marginalised men. In recent years there has been some discussion in academic and practitioner circles about the significance of the social construction of masculinity to probation practice. This paper reports a qualitative study of probation officers' constructions of masculinity. The study found conflicting discourses of masculinity, each with different implications for working with men.*

Most front-line criminal justice personnel spend much of their time managing marginalised men, and this is particularly true of probation officers. Their role is one of both promoting offenders' welfare and of social control. The contention of this paper is that there are conflicting discourses of masculinity current in the probation service with potentially very different implications for work with men who offend. We see discussions of gender in the probation service as important because the central task of the organisation can be characterised as one of managing marginalised masculinities.

The term 'marginalised masculinity' is taken from Connell's oft-cited framework for gender relations (Connell, 1987, 1995). It is men who indulge in what he calls a 'spectacular display' of 'masculine protest' that probation officers most commonly encounter. These are men who have restricted access to the power that a traditional working class man's job, such as manual labour, can give them. They usually cannot construct their masculinity through work, education, ownership of property or lasting consumer items. 'Jason', described below by his probation officer, represents very familiar gender practices:

> You've got here a lad who's bitten off another man's ear at one time and is even alleged to have eaten it. The way the media portrays your Arnold Schwarzenegger, the way to be a man, I don't think this lad's thinking has extended beyond that. He's tall, he's strong, he's powerful. The father built a gym out the back. Dad used to work out, his sons have worked out, that's being a man. This lad, if he has a new girlfriend, feels it's improper to walk down the road with that girlfriend. He has to walk in front of her because of the perception of friends ... He will now say that much of his behaviour is about

status and creating an image that his friends find acceptable, and he needs to feel important. (Interview twelve, female officer)

It can be argued that many men like Jason end up on probation because their communities are more policed and also because their behaviour is conspicuous, often deliberately so, and is amplified by reputation. They are stigmatised by the state and their communities, and they are genuinely a threat to the safety of people living in those communities. Their gender identity is central to their criminal behaviour. Messerschmidt (1993) writes that crime is a resource for doing gender. Our paper looks at crime, and at probation work, through the lens of gender. The causes of crime are, of course, complex and interconnected, and each event has its own interactional history. The discussion below will, however, pay particular attention to making connections between the work of probation officers and the social construction of masculinity.

As traced by May (1994), government policy in the last two decades has sought to move the probation service away from its tradition of improving the welfare of offenders, and towards the management of punishment in the community. The last government removed the requirement for probation officers to undergo social work training, and spoke of the need for ex-army and ex-police personnel to join the probation service. This was, in effect, a call for the masculinising of the organisation. There has also in recent years been renewed interest in the potential for probation to effect change in offenders' behaviour (Raynor & Vanstone, 1994). This renewed rehabilitative optimism has coincided with some attempts by the probation service to challenge criminal behaviours whose roots in the social construction of masculinity are particularly overt, such as sexual assaults, and violence against women (Warwick, 1991; Scourfield & Dobash, 1999).

Some criminologists are currently researching and theorising the link between constructions of masculinities and a wide range of crimes (e.g. Newburn & Stanko, 1994; Jefferson, 1996). Alongside this activity, there has been a call for probation officers to make masculinity explicit in their work (McCaughey, 1992; Buckley 1996). Such authors write of 'challenging', 'confronting' or 'deconstructing' masculinity. In the light of this new emphasis, the research reported below sets out to explore the constructions of masculinity within the Probation Service. The research studied how probation officers, who have an important role in the sentencing of some offenders and in their management in the community, understand men's crime and their work with men.

The Research Process

One of the authors, Jonathan Scourfield, conducted semi-structured interviews with 14 probation officers (six women and eight men) in South Wales. He also read 50 client files and 30 pre-sentence reports, chosen from districts other than those where the interviewed officers worked, so as not to hold up any individual officers to particular scrutiny. He was, at the time, a probation officer colleague of both those interviewed and those whose files and reports were studied.

The position of practitioner researcher is both privileged and problematic. Familiarity with the setting presents a challenge to the researcher who is seeking an open questioning perspective (McCracken, 1988). The researcher may be seen as belonging to a particular sub-group within the organisation, creating expectations in the participants of what the researcher may wish to hear. Conversely, the practitioner researcher may be able to gain in-depth information more quickly and participants may be more willing to be frank with a colleague than with an outside 'expert' (Hammersley & Atkinson, 1995).

The interviewer's sex and gender identity will also inevitably affect the research process (McKeganey & Bloor, 1991). It is possible that in this study the researcher might have been identified as a man with an interest in masculinity. If so, assumptions about his particular perspective might vary widely. In fact, he was little known to these particular respondents. Assumptions were probably made by interview respondents about required rhetoric on masculinity within the organisation. This is interesting in itself since it reveals something about an influential masculinity discourse.

The probation offices studied are all in the South Wales valleys. This is an area of major industrial decline. Employment opportunities for men in traditional men's jobs have declined considerably and levels of women's economic inactivity are some of the highest in the UK. A disproportionate number of probation clients live in particularly stigmatised hilltop council estates which are often remote from most services and from the next nearest community.

Although the prime focus of the study was constructions of masculinity, it was important to consider accounts of working with women as well, since masculinities are inherently relational, that is, they are constructed and produced in relation to femininities and other masculinities. The study was conducted on a relatively small scale, but did examine an element of probation culture in some detail. The themes discussed below, relating to how probation officers' understand men offenders and communicate with them, may reflect something of the wider occupational culture of the service outside of a few South Wales offices. Probation clients' constructions of masculinity were not studied. This would be an interesting angle to include in a study of probation culture, but was outside the scope of our research.

The interview and file recording data reveal some valuable insights into probation officers' accounts, for different audiences, of men and of work with men. Pre-sentence reports give background information about offence and offender to sentencers, and conclude with a sentencing proposal. Although their contents are confidential to the author, defendant, sentencer and lawyers, these reports can be seen as public accounts of masculinities. These data are discussed elsewhere with an emphasis on the difference between the constructions of masculinity in the interviews and in the documentary evidence (Scourfield, 1998). The discussion below focuses on spoken and written accounts together, to argue that three distinctly different and often conflicting discourses of masculinity can be found. These discourses are characterised as traditional (boys will be boys), new (explicitly challenging masculinity) and mainstream (implicitly challenging masculinity). We found that most probation officers in this study appeared to be negotiating more than one of these discourses in their professional lives. As Lupton and Barclay (1997, p. 9) write, 'within ... institutions there may be a number of competing discourses around a particular phenomenon'.

The concept of discourse is particularly useful for discussion of occupational culture. It conveys the idea of a body of concepts, values and beliefs within which people operate, which become accepted as knowledge. Middleton (1992, p. 142) writes that 'to speak legitimately of a discourse of masculinity it would be necessary to show that a particular set of usages was located structurally within a clearly defined institution with its own methods, objects and practices'. It can be argued that probation officers do have to negotiate discourses of masculinity according to Middleton's definition. Knowledge about men is located in institutional practices such as the writing of reports and records, court decisions, and reference to the medical and social sciences. We do not propose that our characterisation of different trends and approaches as separate discourses implies these are unassailable categories. To borrow the term Connell (1995) uses in relation to his hierarchy of masculinities, these are 'configurations of practice' (p. 81) rather than tightly bounded approaches.

Discourses of Masculinity

Traditional Discourse—Boys Will be Boys

Some of those interviewed found it difficult to talk about men as men. Qualitative interviews are often demanding for respondents, but this particular difficulty reflects the fact that the process of looking critically at masculinities is a new one. One probation officer said:

> I suppose the culture over the last few years has been ... gender awareness has been more female awareness as opposed to male awareness. (Interview nine, male officer)

Traditionally probation officers have not named men as men and have not had a critical perspective on masculinity. We describe four ways of working which we characterise as traditional masculinity discourse: ostensibly non-gendered causal explanations for crime; accepting explanations at face value; a men-centred approach; and an approach to sentencing that constitutes almost blanket mitigation, that is, a default strategy of attempting to avoid punitive sentencing. In relation to the concept of marginalised masculinity, it could be argued that this discourse emphasises the marginalisation of men who offend rather than their masculinity; their powerlessness rather than their use of power.

The study found evidence of the persistence of common-sense explanations for men's crimes in probation culture. A traditional probation discourse on men makes a simple causal link between men's behaviour and causal factors other than his gender identity, deflecting responsibility for his actions away from the man himself. So, for example, with a client on probation for constant harassment of a woman, including regular threats to kill her, the officer discussed alcohol, family relations and social skills, but not apparently anything about his views about this woman, or women in general (file 46). The pre-sentence reports studied were almost always framed within this traditional discourse. Alcohol and drugs were commonly used as single explanatory factors, in a rather deterministic way. So, for example, a report will describe a young man as stealing a car because he has taken some temazepam, and will conclude that if he takes the advice of a drug counsellor and reduces or stops his drug use he will not steal so many cars. A pre-sentence report author wrote that the client had changed from drinking cider to drinking beer 'because he recognised the adverse effect cider was having upon him and his relationship with his partner' (in file 14). Young men's behaviour is explained not with reference to the culture of the male peer groups in which context most offending takes place, and not in terms of the young men's claim to identity or power through their chosen behaviour, but rather in terms of simple causation by an external factor. Violence against women partners is, almost without exception, described with euphemisms such as 'volatile relationship', 'stress in the family' and 'domestic problems'. Again, intoxication is used as a simple causal connection to the damaging behaviour. Such causal accounts do not consider the man's agency in the violence.

Behind this simple connection may be an assumption that the disinhibiting effects of alcohol or drugs allow the natural aggressive social character of men to come out. Boys will be boys, when the mask slips. One interview respondent stated this belief overtly when he explained sexual violence by saying that 'men have a greater libidinal drive than women'. He concluded that when working with men who commit acts of violence (his own broad term), 'the best we can reasonably hope for [is to] make some effort to control it'. (*interview four, male officer*)

The traditional discourse of masculinity is offender-centred in the sense that offenders' explanatory accounts of their offences are usually accepted on face value. This is in keeping with the influential 'non-treatment paradigm' outlined in Bottoms and McWilliams' 1979 article, with its emphasis on a negotiated helping relationship rather than an agenda imposed by the officer. An exception to this acceptance of offenders' explanations on face value is the use of a psychodynamic model in a significant minority of cases. We see this too as rooted in a traditional masculinity discourse, insofar as it again suggests a link between men's behaviour and causal factors other than his gender identity, and deflects responsibility for a man's actions away from any sense of his own agency. Psychodynamic models held sway in social casework in the 1960s and 1970s (Mayer & Timms, 1970) and, though they have since been subject to some criticism, they are still, in our experience as practitioners, influential in the work of both the probation service and mainstream social work practice.

> Mr. Jones's childhood insecurities manifesting themselves in his obsessive relationship with his ex-wife that culminated in the conviction of Arson being reckless as to whether life is endangered. (Pre-sentence report in file 13)

> (the client has been influenced by) ... adverse influences of inconsistent relationships he experienced with his parents in former years, and he still clearly suffers from the alternating effects of rejections and reconciliations. (Report 9)

We also include within the traditional discourse a men-centred or masculinist approach. There are some officers, albeit a small minority of those interviewed, who are more comfortable working with men than women. They probably represent the historical tendency of the probation service to only cater in practice for men whilst not being aware that this is the case. One respondent explained how he saw the differences between men and women clients:

> The women are more, I would say, manipulative, perhaps more difficult to work with in specific areas ... to a great extent I would say that women tend to be less receptive to wanting to work closely, or even to have a working relationship at all ... they use the fact of their feminism, I think, they use that to some extent to try and get out of the situation ... [male] clients tell you they don't want to co-operate and there's no pretence about it ... that's the difference. (Interview one, male officer)

A reading of pre-sentence reports reveals that an area in which the traditional masculinity discourse is dominant is that of the approach to sentencing. It can be argued that, in the context of court culture, probation officers still tend to perceive their role as mainly one of mitigation. They are obliged to address the seriousness of the offence, but often have a different view of this from other court personnel. They are still perceived by other players in the sentencing process as mitigating, and this perception is understandable in view of the strong anti-carceral and minimum intervention traditions in the probation service, reflected in the practice of pre-sentence report writing. The experience of one of the authors of working as a probation officer was that exceptions to the mitigation role tended to be only in relation to either particularly morally repugnant physical violence offences or sexual offences where the prospect of repetition was seen to be a major risk.

There are debates here which are not being engaged with by the probation service in the area studied. For example, feminists have called for the further criminalisation of domestic violence, a crime that has traditionally not been processed by the criminal justice system. The almost blanket mitigation of men's behaviour by probation officers within the court setting runs contrary to this call and represents an area of probation practice which still appears to be largely governed by the traditional masculinity discourse. The attempt to mitigate is connected to a recognition of the marginal social status of most defendants that officers encounter in court, and perhaps also a willingness to accept that lasting harm has not been caused by the offending, but that the behaviour represents boys being boys, in a harmless kind of way. In some respects, the traditional discourse of masculinity could be characterised as recognising the marginalisation of men who offend, but not their masculinity. The data did not show explicit references to class and social deprivation in officers' talk nor in their documents, possibly because an awareness of the poverty of clients was assumed common ground between interviewer and respondent. The tradition of mitigating the harmful effects of the criminal justice system is, however, linked to a construction of clients as victims of an unjust society.

New Discourse—Explicitly Challenging Masculinity

Most of those interviewed showed some familiarity with the recent attention given in feminist-inspired academic and practitioner literature to the masculinity–crime connection and its implications for probation work. It was evident that discussion of these issues had a certain profile in the organisation. Most officers referred to the influences in men's upbringing, including family, peers, community and media, that encouraged a desire to dominate and to be seen to perform appropriately aggressive, independent masculinity. They commonly offered the examples of violence, both physical and sexual, and car crime, when talking about the distinctive features of men's crime. They talked about using these insights into the making of men in their work, sometimes explicitly, in the sense of announcing to clients that that was what they were doing.

> If a man's offences involve women—either against them or a knock on effect—I will make a point of raising it ... I will attempt to challenge, confront or just discuss those things. (Interview two, male officer)

> I adapted some exercises—'women/men are ...', 'women/men should be ...'. Their responses would then be discussed, trying to find out where their attitudes come from, what they're all about. (Interview seven, female officer)

> I'm linking with the bits of masculine behaviour that I personally find unacceptable ... that will bring him into conflict with the law. (Interview twelve, female officer)

Only a relatively small amount of case recording described this explicit addressing of masculinity. One officer showed a particular interest in working with violent men, whether or not they were on probation for violence, from the perspective of overtly discussing their views on being a man. Several other officers seemed occasionally to focus directly on their clients' masculinities, where the relevance of these was particularly stark. An innovative example of this was the spontaneous group discussion with a client and his friends, who had spoken of their intention of going out that day for a revenge attack on a group of young men from a neighbouring district. The discussion focused on their need to uphold the honour of their home area by using violence.

Distinctive general features of this new discourse on men include the influence of feminist critiques of male power, attention to the experiences of victims and a different approach to male cultures of crime. Several interview respondents talked about men's social power and the subordination of women. Examples include the following:

> Arran is a highly immature and volatile young man who is seeking to adopt the mantle of being 'hard'. (File 11)
>
> Used Duluth power and control wheels [a counselling tool] to try and get at Lee's use of his partner as a servant. (File 5)

This discourse has a rather different view of men's agency from the traditional discourse. Men are seen as responsible for their actions in the sense that part of socially constructed masculinity is a desire to control, to get their own way. However, some of the respondents' talk of damaging models of masculinity tends to see men as imprisoned by upbringing, and therefore not free to choose:

> He talked of feeling 'out of control' at times. Linked to family background—beaten by dad as was mother. (File 30)

The new discourse pays more attention to the experience of victims than does the traditional one. The importance of a victim perspective, for example in the writing of court reports, has been stressed in government guidance on probation work in recent years, and left realist criminology (e.g. Young & Matthews, 1992) has prioritised the experience of victimisation in the study of crime. Several interview respondents quickly moved on to the topic of victimisation of women and children when discussing the distinctiveness of men's crime. The new discourse requires a fresh look at the cultures of crime. It questions and challenges the explanations that men offenders themselves give for their behaviour, not accepting common-sense notions, but instead looking at the masculinities of individuals, peer groups and communities. There is an interest in how manhood is proven through conspicuous displays and in the controlling of women and children.

Many of the probation officers identified the local cultural context of their workplace as having an influence on local masculinities. Unemployment and traditional close-knit communities with specific local cultures were amongst the factors identified as influencing local men, whether clients, friends or themselves.

> I suppose it's an area where it's difficult for men to break out of the stereotypes and what's expected of them. Small valley communities with quite entrenched views of what men should do and what women should do, perhaps more so than other areas I've worked in. (Interview eleven, female officer)
>
> I see people now who I drink with, whose views about men and women frighten me and I see a lot of myself in the past in them. I think to myself 'fuck me, I used to be like that'. The language they use about women, about themselves, it's quite frightening. (Interview two, male officer)

Some of the comments about 'valleys men' suggested the connection between lack of economic status and assumptions of power and authority over others that is conveyed by the concept of marginalised masculinity:

> I don't what the strains are like on men trying to grow up in a situation where 25% of the valley are unemployed and yet there's still a culture of thinking that men go out to work and women don't. (Interview ten, female officer)

However, the new discourse can be seen to be more about masculinity than marginalisation; more about gender than class. It emphasises men's social power rather than their powerlessness.

Mainstream Discourse—Implicitly Challenging Masculinity

The renewed rehabilitative optimism of the 1990s, stimulated by effectiveness research such as that in McGuire's collection (1995) has arguably led to a change in emphasis in mainstream probation culture. The preoccupation has become 'what works'. It has been stated that the client–worker relationship has to be reformulated in the light of what is known about effectiveness (Raynor & Vanstone, 1994). Offence-focused cognitive-behavioural work has become an orthodoxy in many areas. The dominance of cognitive-behavioural approaches is reflected in many of the accounts of working with men in this study. A significant number of the accounts of practice in both files and interviews could be seen as implicitly challenging masculinities through practice that can broadly be labelled cognitive-behavioural. This label is very broad. As Saunders (1989) has written:

> There is no monolithic theory or integrated set of procedures that can be called 'cognitive-behavioural'. Rather the term covers a collection of principles and procedures that many practitioners have not attempted to link theoretically. (p. 77)

Most cognitive-behavioural therapy could be described as helping people see how their thoughts or beliefs trigger emotions, which in turn trigger actions, and helping them break these connections and therefore change their behaviour. Much of the practice described in probation officers' accounts draws on these ideas in some way, particularly in linking clients' beliefs with their actions, challenging the logic of those beliefs, and tracing the consequences of particular ways of thinking. File recording often refers to analysing clients' 'self-talk'. This refers to the cognitive-behavioural technique that focuses on the messages people give to themselves that predict particular behaviours are likely to result, as a response to the message.

This practice is ostensibly gender neutral in the sense that the therapeutic methods are intended for men and women alike. However, the data reveal that there are often-mentioned examples of methods, linked to cognitive-behavioural therapy, which perhaps do address masculinities, without necessarily naming them as such. Examples of these are:

- helping clients to see the consequences of their actions;
- discussion of the values on which their behaviour was based and alternatives to these values;
- helping them see the effects of what they had done on other people, particularly women and children;
- comparing their offending with pro-social aspects of their behaviour;
- encouraging them to talk about emotions instead of acting on them in a destructive manner;
- discussion of responsibilities.

Perhaps these techniques can be seen as addressing a masculinity which involves rigid thinking and internalised beliefs in the right to dominate others. These are some examples of how officers expressed this approach:

> Trying to get them often to locate what I consider to be their more female side, to look at their values, to look at why they are behaving in particular ways, why they think that's important and to consider whether those values are really

> being pushed on them by other people or whether they are what they really believe in ... I mean things like acknowledging feelings, thinking about ... how their families experience what they're doing. (Interview eight, female officer)
>
> Getting them to talk about their feelings, getting them to express what their beliefs are about themselves and about women. (Interview eleven, female officer)
>
> Working on him increasing self-control, understanding the effect he has on others, thinking about his reactions, taking slow steps. (Interview twelve, female officer)

There was some considerable overlap between the respondents who described using these approaches with men and those whose explanations of men's behaviour were also informed by feminism. We have characterised the mainstream approach as a separate discourse so as to emphasise the important difference between an explicit and an implicit challenging of masculinity. The discourse of 'what works' in probation does not specifically address men. The methods given prominence are intended to be gender neutral. Our data show, however, that they may have the unintended effect of challenging masculinity.

Obviously these characterisations of discourses of masculinity are not an attempt to create unassailable categories. They merely represent trends from the data which we hope have some theoretical coherence. Probation officers negotiate these conflicting discourses from day to day and many practise within all three. Accounts of practice in the interviews were most often within the new and mainstream discourses. File recording revealed both traditional and mainstream discourses and very little of the new discourse. The pre-sentence reports were written primarily within the traditional discourse of masculinity, with some evidence of the mainstream discourse but none of the new. Both file recording and report writing are an essential part of probation practice, whereas research interviews are not. This may suggest that there is relatively little explicit challenging of masculinities going on in practice, at least in the geographical area studied (Scourfield, 1998). However, many probation officers appear to be in the process of at least thinking about and discussing the possible implications of their understanding of masculinities for their practice, and some mainstream practice methods may have the unintended effect of challenging male clients' values and beliefs as men.

Gendered Identities and Occupational Culture

Respondents were asked questions which explored their personal gendered identities. Their responses revealed a rich variety of formative experiences that shaped them. The data suggest that in probation practice, occupational discourses of masculinity override the complexity of individual gendered identities.

The gendered experiences of the officers, and their retrospective construction of what influenced them, were very diverse, and defied simple categorisation. To provide just a few examples, one male officer talked of how important being brought up with women in 'the primary position' in the family was to forming his views on gender (interview six). One woman officer wanted to challenge people's gendered assumptions about her and about probation work by herself becoming an officer ('there must be something bolshy about me'). She said she used to be 'gleeful' if a client was surprised at having a woman officer. This same woman said she had been put off other types of social work partly because the men in these jobs were 'wimps' (interview ten). Another woman officer spoke of her awareness of crime as gendered stemming from her own experience of seeing her brother being given 'a lot more leeway' in the family home (interview fourteen). Another male officer said 'I think it's still better for the mother to be at home' (interview one). A few of the respondents overtly linked their gendered identities to local identity, sometimes also with implications of class background. One man said 'I'm a valleys boy, born and bred, and I believe in straight talking' (interview four). Because of this diversity within a small sample, to categorise the gender identities of the men and women respondents as, for example, Mac an Ghaill (1994) does for men teachers would be to oversimplify them.

Atherton's research (1990) showed a common culture of gendered assumptions about clients' lives, regardless of the sex of the officers. Although we did not set out to make rigorous comparisons between men and women officers, it is important in the context of discussing gendered identities to make some observations on this theme. We could tentatively claim that the new discourse of masculinity had a stronger hold on the women than the men, insofar as the women interviewed all engaged with this discourse, whereas two of the men seemed to be wholly free of it. Ambition, particularly when thwarted, was clearly a more important issue for the men than for the women. One man said:

> I regard myself as having made a bloody failure of my life, well and truly, and one of the clearest indications of that is the fact that I am a probation officer. It's proof positive of my mediocrity. (Interview four)

There were also common themes in the interview data, both about the respondents' gendered identities, and in relation to the gendered constructions of clients discussed in the previous sections. A common theme of respondents' gendered identities was that most said when they embarked on their probation careers they did not think of the job as one which was mainly about working with men. This testifies to the historical strength of the traditional discourse which did not recognise the masculinity of crime, seeing clients as people rather than (mostly) men.

It is interesting to note that, despite the diversity of gendered identities in the interview data and some possible differences emerging between women and men officers, we found individual men and women alike to be consistently constructing masculinity in their practice within limited discourses and fitting particular tasks. Pre-sentence reports by men and women were overwhelmingly written within the traditional discourse on men. Files reflected the traditional and mainstream discourses, and little of the new discourse. Rhetoric on masculinity in the interviews drew heavily on the mainstream discourse and, with the exception of two men, also drew heavily on the new discourse. We would suggest, in probation practice, that occupational discourses of masculinity tend to override the complexity of individual gendered identities.

The dominance of the traditional discourse in pre-sentence reports may reflect the discursive limits of the court setting. Emerson and Pacey (1992) write that:

> Decision-makers ... do not see and treat cases as self-contained, isolated entities, but rather as practical decision tasks embedded in known and foreseeable courses of institutional action. (p. 234)

For probation officers these 'known and foreseeable courses' will include the various sentencing options available to the court and the limited possibility of bringing about a positive outcome from a largely punitive criminal justice system. Probation officers will also be influenced by an established and largely traditional discourse on offending within the court setting. That rhetoric on masculinity in the interviews draws heavily on both new and mainstream discourses on men may suggest that these discourses currently have the status of dominant forms of knowledge in the organisation.

Discussion and Conclusions

This study did not set out to evaluate practice. We do not intend, therefore, to make prescriptive judgements on the basis of the data. There are, however, some interesting issues that might need discussion within the probation service. Perhaps probation officers need to consider the conflicting discourses of masculinity and how they impact on their own personal practice. Several respondents spoke of a general lack of honest debate about gender, in part because there are such divergent views around in the organisation. Honesty is certainly needed if the service is to grapple with the complexities of gender and crime.

Each of the discourses on men can be seen to have strengths and weaknesses. Of course, the traditional discourse is open to criticism from feminists for failing to deconstruct masculinities, thus reinforcing traditional justifications for abusive behaviour. Conversely, there is a risk that the new discourse of explicitly challenging masculinity may not recognise that probation officers are in the business of working specifically with marginalised men, not men in general. The marginalised status of the clientele should perhaps have implications for methods of intervention. The traditional discourse does take account of the very real welfare needs of men who offend. Whereas an extreme adoption of the traditional discourse would mean only helping men with these welfare needs, thus helping change marginalised masculinities into hegemonic ones, a caricature of the new discourse might involve treating all men clients as uniformly powerful, as if they make completely free choices, unaffected by other social factors, to abuse and dominate women, children and other men.

The care–control debate that has at various times raged in the probation service needs to be revisited in the light of feminist work on men's crimes. There are two new perspectives to enter the debate: a reclamation of men's agency in understanding masculinity and a pressure for criminalising abusive behaviour that has historically been excused by the criminal justice system. Both perhaps challenge a simplistic stance that 'punishment' is always wrong and that probation officers should always avoid a controlling role. It might be argued that the new discourse on men and probation presents a credible alternative both to what is perceived by much popular opinion to be the overly liberal approach of traditional probation, and also to the macho punitive approach that has become the rhetoric of the party political mainstream. There are risks, however, that the rhetoric of 'challenging' and 'confronting' masculinity could itself become a macho response (Sheath, 1990).

Perhaps tensions between discourses of masculinity are in fact strongly linked to care–control tensions inherent in the probation officer role; tensions which remain despite governmental action to emphasise the control function. In some respects, what we have labelled the traditional discourse on masculinity represents a traditional welfare approach, with an emphasis on mitigating the worst effects of a punitive system on socially marginalised clients. The new discourse, with its emphasis on male offenders' responsibility, and challenging or confronting them, has some common ground with the socially authoritarian consensus that the current government represents. The new discourse also brings back the idea of the probation officer defining the client's problem. This aspect of 1970s psychodynamic casework was criticised on the basis of the power imbalance involved (see Bottoms & McWilliams, 1979). An officer deciding that, despite a male offender's own explanations of his behaviour, s/he knows that it can *really* be explained by the social construction of masculinity, is returning to the tradition of 'probation officer knows best'. This basis for the probation relationship may well be entirely appropriate, indeed it is the theoretical basis on which we set out to write this paper, but feminist-inspired officers perhaps need to acknowledge that this is the basis on which they work.

The mainstream discourse, influenced by cognitive-behavioural work, is an interesting development in changing men. The very influential probation discourses of 'what works' and anti-oppressive practice are usually considered separately. Where they have converged, debates have focused on whether programmes that have been found to reduce reconviction rates are oppressive or liberating (Neary, 1992; Raynor & Vanstone, 1994). It is possible that, in fact, practice which is found to be effective in reducing reoffending is effective because it is helping to change masculinities, and is therefore anti-oppressive, without making this explicit (personal communication with Richard Thurston, April 1996). Probation officers need to consider whether the next stage should be to make it explicit, or whether the work is more effective because challenging masculinities is implicit and avoids making men defensive by addressing them as men.

There has been considerable discussion in probation services in recent years about the historical marginalisation of women from mainstream provision for offenders, although it is not clear whether services for women have improved because of this discussion. To echo Hearn's (1996) warning about the concept of masculinity/masculinities in academia, there is perhaps a danger that the new interest in masculinity and probation practice might have the effect of diverting attention away from women and making them invisible once more.

The different discourses outlined above can be seen to reflect different aspects of the concept of marginalised masculinity. The traditional discourse is more a discourse of class, marginalisation and powerlessness, whereas the new discourse is more a discourse of gender and power. The mainstream discourse is a discourse of pragmatism and effectiveness that is implicitly gendered. It could perhaps be argued that this is a reasonably healthy mix for an organisation which is subject to many different external pressures, and an organisation in which tensions between care and control are inherent. However, to return to our starting point, we recommend the concept of marginalised masculinity, in its fullest form, as a useful one to probation work, and one that could potentially help reconcile some of the strongest tensions over work with men that we found in the organisation.

Acknowledgements

We should like to thank Jonathan Scourfield's former employers for allowing time and access for the research referred to above and, in particular, those colleagues who agreed to be interviewed or to give access to their files and reports. We are also grateful for the support of a Cropwood Fellowship at the Cambridge Institute of Criminology and to Betsy Stanko, Richard Thurston and two anonymous referees for their valuable advice.

An earlier version of this paper was presented at two conferences during 1997, 'Constructing Social Work Practices' at the University of Tampere, Finland, and the British Criminology Conference at Queen's University, Belfast.

REFERENCES

ATHERTON, M. (1990) Sex stereotyping in probation practice, Unpublished MSc Econ thesis, Cardiff University.

BOTTOMS, A. & MCWILLIAMS, W. (1979) A non-treatment paradigm for probation practice, *British Journal of Social Work*, 9(2), pp. 159–202.

BUCKLEY, K. (1996) Masculinity, the Probation Service and the Causes of Offending Behaviour, in: T. MAY & A.A. VASS (Eds) *Working with Offenders* (London, Sage).

CONNELL, R.W. (1987) *Gender and Power* (Cambridge, Polity Press).

CONNELL, R.W. (1995) *Masculinities* (Cambridge, Polity).

EMERSON, R.M. & PACEY, B. (1992) Organizational Horizons and Complaint-filing, in: K. HAWKINS (Ed.) *The Uses of Discretion* (Oxford, Clarendon Press).

HAMMERSLEY, M. & ATKINSON, P. (1995) *Ethnography: principles in practice*, 2nd edn (London, Routledge).

HEARN, J. (1996) Is Masculinity Dead? A critique of the concept of masculinity/masculinities, in: M. MAC AN GHAILL (Ed.) *Understanding Masculinities* (Buckingham, Open University Press).

JEFFERSON, T. (Ed.) (1996) *Masculinities, social relations and crime*, Special edition of *British Journal of Criminology*, 26(3).

LUPTON, D. & BARCLAY, C. (1997) *Constructing Fatherhood. Discourses and experiences* (London, Sage).

MAC AN GHAILL, M. (1994) *The Making of Men: masculinities, sexualities and schooling* (Buckingham, Open University Press).

MAY, T. (1994) Probation and Community Sanctions, in: M. MAGUIRE, R. MORGAN & R. REINER (Eds) *The Oxford Handbook of Criminology* (Oxford, Oxford University Press).

MAYER, J. & TIMMS, N. (1970) *The Client Speaks* (London, Routledge and Kegan Paul).

MCCAUGHEY, C. (1992) Making Masculinity Explicit in Work with Male Offenders, in: P. SENIOR & D. WOODHEAD (Eds) *Gender, Crime and Probation Practice* (Sheffield, PAVIC).

MCCRACKEN, G. (1988) *The Long Interview* (Newbury Park, CA, Sage).

MCGUIRE, J. (1995) (Ed.) *What Works: reducing reoffending* (Chichester, Wiley).

MCKEGANEY, N. & BLOOR, M. (1991) Spotting the invisible man: the influence of male gender on fieldwork relations, *British Journal of Sociology*, 42(4), pp. 195–210.

MESSERSCHMIDT, J. (1993) *Masculinities and Crime: critique and reconceptualisation of theory* (Lanham, MD, Rowan and Littlefield).

MIDDLETON, P. (1992) *The Inward Gaze. Masculinity and subjectivity in modern culture* (London, Routledge).

NEARY, M. (1992) Some academic freedom, *Probation Journal*, 39(4), pp. 200–202.

NEWBURN, T. & STANKO, E.A. (1994) (Eds) *Just Boys Doing Business? Men, masculinities and crime* (London, Routledge).

RAYNOR, P. & VANSTONE, M. (1994) Probation practice, effectiveness and the non-treatment paradigm, *British Journal of Social Work*, 24, pp. 387–404.

SAUNDERS, D.G. (1989) Cognitive and Behavioural Interventions with Men who Batter: application and outcome, in: P.L. CAESAR & L.K. HAMBERGER (Eds) *Treating Men Who Batter: theory, practice and programmes* (New York, Springer).

SCOURFIELD, J.B. (1998) Probation officers working with men, *British Journal of Social Work*, 28(4), pp. 581–599.

SCOURFIELD, J.B. & DOBASH, R.P. (1999) Programmes for violent men: recent developments in the UK, *The Howard Journal of Criminal Justice*, 38(2), pp. 128–143.

SHEATH, M. (1990) 'Confrontative' work with sex offenders: legitimised nonce-bashing?, *Probation Journal*, 37(4), pp. 159–162.

WARWICK, L. (1991) *Probation Work with Sex Offenders* (Norwich, Social Work Monographs).

YOUNG, J. & MATTHEWS, R. (Eds) (1992) *Rethinking Criminology: the realist debate* (London, Sage).

[22]

TOWARDS SAFER SOCIETIES

Punishment, Masculinities and Violence Against Women

LAUREEN SNIDER

This paper seeks to look beyond criminalization models to examine what is known about building less violent societies, at the macro, middle and micro levels. It argues that criminalization is a flawed strategy for dealing with male violence against women caused by a failure to theorize social control adequately, a failure that has led feminists and other progressive social movements to mis-identify penality as synonymous with social control. The first part examines the realities of agendas of criminalization and increased punitiveness through incarceration rates. The second part seeks to explain the dependence on criminal law and institutions of criminal justice by feminists and new social movements. Focusing on wife assault and battery, it points out that strategies of criminalization have benefited privileged white women at the expense of women of colour, aboriginal and immigrant women, and points out problems with the failure to engender concepts of social control. The third part looks at what we know about policies, strategies and identities with the potential to transcend criminalization and facilitate social transformation, paying special attention to the construction, roots and maintenance of hegemonic masculinity. Overall it is argued that effective social control of aberrant behaviour must be sought outside criminal justice institutions, and that the feminist and progressive focus should shift towards examining how to create less violent people (particularly men), families, communities and societies.

The single minded pursuit of criminalization at the index of achievement for progressive social movements seems to me misconceived. (Cohen 1994: 105)

... the moral sentiments which are internalized by individuals do change over time, as new normative codes are legislated and new generations are socialized in accordance with them. (Garland 1990: 54)

Our [women's] status as a group relative to men has almost never, if ever, been changed from what it is. (MacKinnon 1992: 456)

* Department of Sociology, Queen's University, Kingston, Ontario Thanks to Elizabeth Comack, Carole LaPrairie, Gail Kellough and Stan Cohen for comments on earlier drafts, and to John Braithwaite and Peter Grabosky for providing a supportive climate at ANU, where this paper was born.

LAUREEN SNIDER

This paper is about praxis, domestic assault and the need to construct safer, more humane social orders. It is written, in part, to counteract the distressing tendency of progressive groups[1] such as feminism to embrace agendas of punishment, thereby reinforcing and legitimizing policies of coercive control which dominate the western world in the late twentieth century. This emphasis on punishment rather than amelioration has been noted by critics before, but few alternative models have been put forth,[2] in part, I suspect, because academics share the modernist predilection for cynicism over idealism, and for naming and blaming over strategizing on prevention. Criticism is so much easier—no one can prove negativism is misplaced, but it is easy to demonstrate that ameliorative social policies have not lived up to the expectations of those who originated them—contradictory and unrealistic as such expectations must be to survive the political process in modern democratic states. The rush to identify and punish bad guys is appealing as praxis because the politics of moral indignation, combined with the saleability of finger-pointing in sensation-seeking media, generates instant publicity, making this form of consciousness-raising comparatively simple. To effectively challenge beliefs that criminalization is *the* answer to problematic behaviour, and to develop and popularize strategies to change the policies, institutions and attitudes which reinforce violent responses in the first place, is an overwhelming task. The irony is that progressive academics, particularly feminists working in fields of criminology and law, have long acknowledged that deep-seated social problems such as domestic assault can only be ameliorated by ideological and structural change, the very time-consuming laborious process now being pushed into the background by policies of criminalization (Mandell 1994; Smart 1989; Mathiesen 1990). Decades of social science research, empirical and theoretical, critical and conservative, document the failure of criminal justice systems to improve the safety, life-conditions or life-chances of victims, or to transform offenders (Box 1983; Gottfredsen and Hirschi 1990; Rothman 1971, 1980; Ratner and McMullan 1987; Silberman 1980; Martinson 1974; McBarnet 1981; Garland 1990; Ericson and Baranek 1982).

In the area of domestic assault, such tendencies are particularly troublesome. With the supply of public monies getting smaller by the day, policies increasing criminalization virtually guarantee that money will be diverted from feminist shelters, consciousness-raising or empowerment programmes (Elias 1989; Matthews 1994) and channelled into criminal justice systems to finance compulsory arrest and/or charge policies. Counter-charging—the practice of laying charges against the complainant if there is *any* evidence of retaliatory violence or self defence—is endemic in many locales; it must now be counted a major deterrent to reporting offences. Worst of all, as we shall see, there is no persuasive evidence that reliance on criminal justice has made the female complainant safer or the male offender less violent, even in the short term (Sherman 1992; Marsh *et al.* 1982; Dobash and Dobash 1992; Dutton 1984;

[1] The term 'progressive' is inaccurate and pretentious. It seems to imply that only feminists and those on the left care about being humane, while people who identify with other parts of the political spectrum happily go about adding to the sum of human misery. This is obviously not true. However, it is difficult to find any collective term that is more accurate-as post-modernists correctly insist, all generalizing labels are inaccurate. As used in this paper, progressive refers to those people and groups whose work claims to be 'critical' (of patriarchy or capital) in theory, and transformative (counter-hegemonic) in praxis.

[2] Notable exceptions include the recent works of John Braithwaite and his co-authors (Braithwaite 1989, 1991, 1994, 1995, Braithwaite and Pettit 1990; Braithwaite and Daly 193); also Brickey and Comack 1987; and the harm-reduction and peace-making schools (Brants and Kok 1986; Dahl 1986; Pepinsky and Quinney 1991).

Caringella-MacDonald 1985, 1987, 1988). And, in the long term, the legacy of such policies is the creation of more misogynous men, more dependent women and more vulnerable family units, and the reinforcement of the impression, in media and public discourse, that the problem of domestic assault revolves around figuring out how to punish better, deeper and more. Surely, as feminists and academics, we have better suggestions to offer. Surely, even if the public demand for punitiveness is as overwhelming as right wing media and politicians insist (a dubious assertion, see Immarigeon 1991; Braithwaite and Mugford 1994), we should be challenging consensuses that reinforce law and order lobbies, laying the intellectual groundwork for counter-hegemonic battles and positing alternatives. Surely, as a minimum, we should be asking how to make the creation of safer societies a primary goal of social policy and progressive struggle.

That is the purpose of this paper. The first part examines the realities of agendas of criminalization through incarceration rates and increased punitiveness. The second part seeks to explain the dependence on criminal law and institutions of criminal justice by progressive groups and new social movements, particularly feminism. Focusing on wife assault and battery, it points out that strategies of criminalization have benefited privileged white women at the expense of women of colour, aboriginal and immigrant women, and examines our failure to theorize and engender concepts of social control. The third part offers preliminary thoughts on strategies with more potential to trenscend criminalization and nurture transformative, counter-hegemonic change. Two questions are addressed here: how do macro level factors reinforce violence in social orders, and how can communities be restructured and dominant maculinities and identities changed? In other words, what steps are required for people to *feel* safer, *become* less vulnerable, and *prevent* intergenerational cycles of recurring violence?

Before delving into the arguments, several points must be made about language and the use of categories, because this paper employs essentializing categories such as women, class, visible minorities and people of colour, and attempts generalizations beyond the particularities imposed by individual situations. In addition, data (empirical 'knowledge')[3] are used to develop arguments for and against certain theoretical perspectives. This is done despite the epistemological, ontological and practical limitations of statistics, on the one hand, and the risk, even the arrogance, of understating difference within the artificial, theoretically constructed collectivities employed on the other.[4] It is done because theory requires, at least initially, a

[3] Because it is awkward to put quotation marks around 'know' and 'knowledge' each time they are used, I have not done so. But they should be assumed, because 'knowledge' is never final and it is always fallible, a social construction bound by time and culture. Although this paper is aimed, in part, at constructing arguments that might be 'true', the more important goal is to offer alternative conceptions of reality that might be useful, in the struggle to create more humane and egalitarian social orders.

[4] Postmodern theories themselves need to he situated to be understood. The insistence that new social movements (nsms) have replaced class-based movements as vehicles of change came out of widespread disenchantment with the left, with the collapse of state socialism and electoral massacres (Hall 1988), and the recognition that global capitalism has robbed nation states of much of their economic and political power. Many on the left welcome the new focus on the politics of identity and on small-scale personal struggles. Foucoult's greatest contribution to modern theory was his insight that power is not centred exclusively in the state but dispersed throughout civil society: thus praxis operates through multitudinous theatres of resistance, to constituted authorities of every sort. For him, the key issue is personal identity (Foucault 1982: 211). Similarly, Laclau and Mouffe (1985, 1987), Magnusson (1992) and Offe (1987) celebrate the rejection of state theories, arguing that politics is 'inscribed upon the bodies' of human agents, and of the environment they inhabit (Carroll 1992: 16). It is not, in other words 'out there'. But it is not always clear whether such postmodernists have any vision of building new structures, economies or discourses, or if their only goal is resistance. Resistance to what, for whom, to what end: these are unanswered questions (Wood 1990: 78-9).

willingness to 'essentialise certain relationships as objects of knowledge which are not reducible to each other' (Carlen 1991: 14). This violates some postmodern canons (e.g. Winter 1992), but the value of this theoretical position—and others—must be judged by the validity and persuasiveness of the analyses produced (Garland 1995: 182), not by *a priori* and dogmatic prescriptions claiming, for example, that fragmentation and incoherence are all there is.[5] Such claims must be scrutinized just as severely as the positions they critique. Indeed, criminologists should be particularly wary of importing postmodern critiques in an uncritical fashion because they may have the unintended consequence of silencing progressive voices, thereby reinforcing hegemonic interests and agendas. Movement politics is hard work, it often requires a temporary suspension of disbelief, a sense of vision, of involvement in something bigger than oneself. 'Speaking for the other', with all its risks, embodies this claim and this need. Given the perilous state of western economies with record levels of inequality within and between nation states, ideologies celebrating greed in the guise of free market economic theory dominating the 'marketplace' of ideas, and spiralling rates of unemployment, progressive voices and alternative positions are desperately needed. When postmodernists deride such voices in the name of theoretical purity, they—we—risk weakening and destabilizing progressive movements. With mass media quick to publicize any evidence of dissent among leftist groups, the result is that hegemonic right-wing forces, unconcerned with the arrogance of appropriation of voice, monopolize public debate. Thus we see gun lobbies and law and order advocates skewing the definitions of right and left so violently that to be 'progressive' in the United States in the late twentieth century means favouring electronic monitoring and urinalysis instead of caning and chain gangs. Constantly interrogating strategies is essential, but progressives must balance the risks of sometimes speaking for others (an essentializing and arrogant thing to do) against the very real need to get counter-hegemonic positions *heard*.

This does not mean that the categories employed in this paper are to be understood as conveying Truth. Macro-level structures such as capitalism and patriarchy are not meant to be seen as having one universal 'meaning' or one inevitable behavioural, institutional or ideological consequence. But the events that result from the social relations of production or reproduction cannot be interpreted as purely random occurrences. To talk about capitalist economic systems or patriarchal relations means that certain gender identities, roles, languages, ideologies, ways of knowing and types of knowledge are reinforced, welcomed and otherwise *more likely to occur*. In any diverse collectivity, other ways of thinking, seeing and acting will be found, but they will usually be marginalized, derided, typically less common and certainly less influential, with fewer political, social or ideological 'coat-tails' (Smart 1992; Howe 1994; Butler 1990). Concepts and structures, be they criminal justice systems or patriarchal families, are neither monolithic entities that 'cause' behaviour (a determinist interpretation), nor constellations of actors whose interests and construction of reality have purely idiosyncratic implications (a pluralist/postmodern interpretation).

[5] Many postmodern pieces fail this test. They work well as critiques of dogmatism but fail when they lapse into Dogmatic generalizations such as those condemning all generalizations!

On the micro level, this understanding of structural forces is consistent with a long-accepted sociological truism commonly credited to Mead: 'everything is an interpreted thing and not a thing in itself' (Winter 1992: 793). Structures are real in the sense that they provide individuals with resources and meanings, and people construct identities from the structures that surround them (Giddens 1981). Ethnicity, class and gender direct—but none of them determine—the meanings individuals give to the structures. The selves people construct out of these meanings are mediated by social interaction and language. 'Genuine subjectivity is alienated from itself by the reified structures and collective myths of our society', as Boyle has said, but there remains 'a necessary dialectic between personal phenomenologies and structural theories of ideology' (Boyle 1985: 757). In the end, of an infinite variety of possible selves that could be constructed, those that are publicly validated in that social system are *most likely* to occur. Thus, if a given society differentiates among its members using categories based on age, skin colour, sex, class, language, religion and sexual orientation (or uses eye colour, mathematical skill or the ability to communicate with extrasensory beings), the identities most commonly adopted will reflect (but not mirror) these categories. The range of publicly validated selves, infinite in theory, varies in practice with the social and cultural resources available. People both act, and are acted upon, they are subject and object, oppressor and oppressed. The social context of the individual provides discursive, semiotic and linguistic reference points to allow identities to be formed, while cultural and structural resources provide the building blocks (Oyserman and Saltz 1993). This conceptualization of structure and agency accounts for—in fact it predicts—a wide range of differences among people occupying identical social categories (such as race, gender and class).

Criminalization as a Growth Industry

Rather than concentrating on building less violent social orders, the focus in western societies in recent years has been on discovering new ways to punish, and on delivering punishment more effectively. This section examines why punishment, through systems of criminal justice, has become the dominant guarantor of social order.[6]

Increasing penality through criminalizing behaviours that were formerly tolerated, abolishing parole and statutory remission, lengthening prison sentences, and replacing police and judicial discretion with mandatory charges and minimum sentences has become both symptom and symbol of the modern state. Penality, and the businesses and sciences that support it, is a growth industry (Christie 1993). The politics of law and order guarantees a steady supply of politicians promising to get

[6] As Foucault (1979) and Smart (1989) have pointed out, the disciplines of social science are indeed *disciplines*, and they are central to the promotion of penality. This is particularly true of criminology, which claims to produce useful, scientific laws. Walker (1993) asserts that criminological studies on discretion led to mandatory minimum sentencing and charging policies and to Model Sentencing Codes (thereby increasing sentence length). Similarly, Martinson (1974) receives credit (or blame) for tile shift in US prison philosophy from rehabilitation to detention. Such results were neither foreseen, nor necessarily desired by their authors. While empiricist, context-free research often lends itself most easily to such uses, there is no such thing as a study that cannot be used to promote punitive agendas, if only by 'proving' it is invalid!

'tough on crime'; arguing that these policies are futile, cruel or racist is electoral suicide. It is deeply ironic that the United States, one of the most violent and disordered countries in the developed world, and certainly among the least successful in controlling criminal behaviour, has become the world model for penal policy.[7] In the United Kingdom, the (then) shadow Home Secretary of the Labour Party copies the mandatory curfew policies adopted in Memphis, Tennessee to curb youth crime (*Sunday Times*, London, 2 June 1996: A6). In Australia, politicians in the 1995 elections in Queensland and New South Wales call for laws allowing householders to shoot intruders on sight and mandatory life sentences for repeat offenders, emulating California's 'Three Strikes' legislation. And yet, in New South Wales armed robbery fell by 19 per cent between 1983 and 1993, and those claiming victimization from assault fell from 3.4 per cent in 1983 to 2.5 per cent in 1993 (Australian Bureau of Statistics 1994; Wynhausen 1995).

Crime rates, whether measured by police statistics or victimization rates, are falling in Anglo-American democracies. Crimes of violence, for example, fell by 4 per cent in the United States in 1994 (Appleby 1995), with urban crime down most dramatically—1994 homicide numbers were at a 25-year low, and they dropped a further 33 per cent during the first six months of 1995. Murder rates dropped by 8 per cent in 1995: '21,597 murders were recorded in 1995, 13 per cent fewer than in 1991; and 'property crime fell by 1 per cent to 12 million offences, the lowest number since 1987' (Thomas, *Guardian Weekly*, 20 October 1996: 15). Even crack cocaine use is slowing: statistics from the National Assessment of Educational Progress report the percentage of US blacks from 18 to 25 admitting use declined from 3.1 per cent in 1991 to 0.7 per cent in 1993 (Appleby 1995). In Canada, homicide in 1994 dropped by 8 per cent, making the 1994 rate 2.04/100,000, the lowest in 25 years. Violent crime overall—premeditated murder, sexual assault, robbery and verbal threats—dropped by 3 per cent and even the number of incidents reported to police declined by 5 per cent (Hess 1995: A5).

Three caveats are in order. First, many violent crimes go unreported, particularly in poor or minority areas where inhabitants know that calling the police doubles the oppression, and households where women take regular abuse from violent partners in the privacy of the family are not uncommon (Rodgers 1994; Dutton 1984; Ontario 1982). Secondly, every country has enclaves where crime rates are simply irrelevant to people's daily experiences—aboriginal towns in Australia, for example, where 90 per cent of the women (females over 15) and 84 per cent of girls (under 15) have been sexually assaulted (Greer 1994: 65-6); similar conditions characterize some First Nations reserves in Canada (LaPrairie 1993: 240–1). And third, stranger homicides, in the United States, have increased. Because these are random and unpredictable, they

[7] Braithwaite's excellent article (1994) on model-mongers provides information on the dynamics of this process. Powerful actors—and countries—are modelled more than less powerful ones; the periphery copies the core. America's dominance allows it to shape everything from fashion trends to scholarship Intellectuals must publish in American journals and cite American examples. (For non-Americans, being an 'internationally recognized scholar' means being recognized in the United States as well as one's own country; Americans are generally spared this cumbersome necessity as recognition in the core alone is sufficient.) Should 'good' ideas have the temerity to appear in the periphery, they, and sometimes their originators, are appropriated by power-brokers in the centre, their ideas (inventions, etc.) then become seen as American, and are often reimported by the periphery.

generate more public fear than the possible violence of acquaintances.[8] But this is *not* the reality elsewhere. There is no evidence that stranger homicides are rising in Canada, for example, where 13 per cent of all homicides in 1994 involved strangers, a statistic that has remained constant for the past decade (Hess 1995a). Indeed, in virtually every country except the United States (where young men are most at risk), infants under the age of one—hardly a group targeted by strangers—have the highest victimization rates (Hess 1995*b*, citing Statistics Canada). But the fact that American trends and fear levels are at epidemic levels shapes perceptions of danger and influences social policy everywhere else.

And in the United States the punitive movement goes from strength to strength: in 1995 alone bills allowing caning for minor offences and laws to bring back whipping were announced in New York, California and Mississippi (Dettmer 1995).[9] The Omnibus Crime Bill passed by the US Congress in 1994 calls for 100,000 new police officers by the year 2000 and authorizes state spending of $7.9 billion for prison construction and boot camps. Corrections budgets are the fastest growing sector in state governments (Thomas 1994); prison spending totalled $25 billion in 1990, two and a half times more than in 1971. Rates of incarceration have risen from 230 per 100,000 in 1979 to 504 in 1991 (Christie 1993: 90). In Canada they rose from 100/100,000 to 111/100,000 in one decade, 1979 to 1989, and jumped to 130 per 100,000 by 1995, with average offender caseloads up 29 per cent (Brodeur 1996). European countries are catching up fast, with Northern Ireland at 109/100,000, the United Kingdom at 92, Germany at 82, and France holding the line at 78 per 100,000 (these are 1990 figures, and the Netherlands and Scandinavian countries remain comparatively low) (Christie 1993:91-93).

The United States continues to outpace the rest, however, with an incarceration rate for black males of 2,678/100,000, rising to 7,210/100,000 for those 25 to 29 years of age (all 1992 figures) (Walinsky 1995: 47). On any given day in the District of Columbia in 1991, 15 per cent of all black men aged 18 to 34 were in prison, 21 per cent were on probation or parole, and 6 per cent were awaiting trial or at large. Only 15 per cent of all black men living in Washington, it is estimated, would *not* be arrested at some point in their lives (Wallinsky 1995: 47). One of every 193 adults in the United States was incarcerated in the summer of 1994, with state prisons holding 919,143 men and women, and federal prisons holding 93,708 (Thomas 1994). Women still constitute a tiny percentage of prison populations in most countries (5.7 per cent in United States

[8] Because stranger homicides are less likely to result in arrests than intimate homicides, and because many official studies are based on arrested and/or convicted criminals (it being much harder to gather information on those who have not been apprehended), this increase has often been hidden in official rates. But homicide clearance rates, a good indicator, have dropped from 91 per cent in 1965 to 60.5 per cent in 1993 and 1994, dipping to 58.3 per cent in cities over one million. The FBI estimates that stranger homicides comprise 53 per cent of all urban homicides in the US (Walinsky 1995: 46), and that 'only' 12 per cent of urban homicides take place within the family. Some commentators suggest a feminist conspiracy covers this up because such a statistic downplays domestic assault. It seems unlikely. Women are still more likely to be victimized by men than the reverse. Separated or 'unfaithful' women still face much higher risks of being assaulted or killed than unfaithful or separated men (Rodgers 1994; Scutt 1983; Wearing 1990; Stubbs and Wallace 1994). And men who kill in the heat of passion' are still more likely to escape first degree homicide convictions than women who kill to avoid further abuse (Lees 1994). American figures reflect the high rates of homicide outside the family, not low rates *inside* it.

[9] The proposal was defeated in Mississippi when the 32-member black caucus, realizing which race was most likely to be whipped and mindful of its historic associations with slavery, took the unusual step of voting against the legislation as a block.

in 1989), but female rates of imprisonment are going up even faster than male rates. In US jails, rates rose by 95.3 per cent from 1984 to 1989 (male rates rose by 51 per cent); in federal and state prisons they increased 24.4 per cent (while men rose 'only' 12.5 per cent). The number of women incarcerated rose from 12,331 in 1980 to 40,566 in 1989, an increase of 229 per cent; men went from 303,643 to 669,489, up 120 per cent (Immarigeon and Chesney-Lind 1992: 2–4). This trend too is copied elsewhere—women's incarceration rates in the Australian state of Victoria more than tripled from 1979 to 1989 (Howe 1990*a*); similar increases took place in Canada (Johnson and Rodgers 1993).

Incarceration rates are but one component of a widespread weakening of civil liberties and an allied increase in state coercive powers. In the United Kingdom police powers have been enhanced and practices once seen as abuse have been normalized (Reiner 1992). In Canada maximum sentences have been lengthened, parole has become harder to get, and provinces are passing laws to allow the indefinite detention of repeat offenders. In Alberta and Ontario chain gangs have been proposed (Feschuk 1995). Over the last year the government of Alberta, citing public pressure to make inmates suffer,[10] has removed pool tables and colour televisions from provincial prisons, abolished pay for institutional chores, and cancelled conjugal visiting programmes (Feschuk 1995).[11] Several provinces as well as the federal government plan to ban (tobacco) smoking in prisons, a measure disguised as a health regulation which will have widespread punitive effects given the high percentage of inmates addicted to nicotine (Feschuk 1995: A7). In North America women guilty of 'substance abuse' are increasingly likely to be incarcerated, to safeguard the 'rights' of the foetus, a predicted collusion of medical and legal discourses that situates punitiveness even more deeply in the (female) body (Smart 1989; Edgley and Brissett 1990; Bagley and Merlo 1995). In the United States progressive lawyers, unable to argue for rights to shelter, welfare or health care for the destitute (all vitiated by Supreme Court decisions in the 1980s), are reduced to arguing for the constitutionally protected right to beg (Fudge and Glasbeek 1992: 59). (Surely the right to be homeless is next.) Protections against self-incrimination, laws disallowing evidence seized by pumping defendants' stomachs, laws banning the hiring of replacement workers or guaranteeing hard-won rights to organize collectively, to strike, or to minimum standards of education and health care, have been continuously eroded throughout Europe and North America (Bartholemew and Hunt 1990; Fudge and Glasbeek 1992).

[10] This is all the more ironic when one considers that provincial prisons in Canada are designed for offenders serving sentences under two years. The viscous criminals these crackdowns target, except for a small percentage awaiting trial on more serious offences, are doing time for non-payment of fines, traffic infractions such as driving under the influence (of alcohol) and shoplifting.

[11] Mercy is not dead, however. That same day a judge decided it was 'too harsh' to fire four Montreal police officers convicted of beating a Haitian taxi driver so severely he never regained consciousness. They were sentenced to 60 or 90-day jail terms, served on weekends, and 180 hours of community service (Picard 1995: A7). Rather than arguing for equity through increased punitiveness, the usual response of progressives, we might instead promote equity by advocating decreased incarceration for the poor and powerless, giving them the same treatment as offenders where mercy is shown to further agendas of hegemonic social control.

Understanding Feminist and Progressive Support

This section examines the process by which left-wing progressive groups have come to support agendas of punishment and the consequences and implications of this. In particular it asks why feminism, a transformative social movement with 'antimaterialist, antistatist, antibureaucratic' aims and 'humanistic, interpersonal and communitarian values' (Handler 1992: 697), has come to see penality as both a primary objective of struggle and a criterion of its success. The key to this question lies, it is argued, in a mis-identification of penality with social control. The result has been that all the instrumental and symbolic anti-violence messages which are more properly and effectively conveyed by processes of socialization, conscience-building, ostracism and shaming (components of social control), have been vested into penality, where they cannot be achieved and should not be sought.

Right-wing support for agendas of law and order is theoretically and historically consistent (Thompson 1963, 1975). On the left, protracted ideological struggles in seventeenth and eighteenth century Britain forged a 'respectable' working class whose identity depended, in part, on their sense of superiority to and difference from the despised 'rabble' in the criminal classes beneath them; Marx himself vilified criminals as the reactionary, bribable tools of the bourgeoisie (Garland 1985; Melossi 1980; Melossi and Pavarini 1981). However most social democratic parties in the 1960s and 70s advocated mildly progressive policies such as prison reform or even abolition, and campaigned to improve prison conditions and end capital punishment (Lea and Young 1984; Kinsey *et al.* 1985). Early second wave feminism opposed all forms of state punishment.[12] But not a decade later, criminalization and incarceration had become key goals of conservatives and progressives alike. For feminists this was, in part, a response to research revealing the full and horrendous extent of male attacks on women (Brownmiller 1975; Dobash and Dobash 1975); in part it reflected the extension of state funding as feminists in the 1970s and 80s reached the limits of volunteerism and turned to government for long-term funding of hot-lines, crisis centres and shelters. Control over hiring and policy passed to state agencies, resulting in mandatory record-keeping and reporting to police, individualistic and therapeutic approaches to women now constructed as 'clients', an end to political action and consciousness-raising, and the creation of constituencies of therapists, social workers and lawyers with vested interests in criminalization (Matthews 1994; Michaud 1992; Dobash and Dobash 1992; Ursel 1992; Dekeseredy and Hinch 1991). Though oppositional voices remained, calls for greater punitiveness were more easily heard than others, and coercive policies were eagerly adopted by governments seeking to legitimate agendas tightening control over underclass populations (Snider 1985).

Thus Anglo-American democracies over the 1970s and 80s revised laws and policies on sexual and domestic assault, increased sanctions and introduced mandatory response, arrest and charging policies (Roberts 1991; Caringella-MacDonald 1987; Marsh *et al.* 1982). Such policies led, as they always do, to greater surveillance and

[12] For example, feminists in Berkeley, California in the late 1960s were so opposed to the punitive arm of the state that the technique they adopted against rapists was to embarrass the offender by visiting his place of residence, en masse, with denunciatory placards (Matthews, 1994). An early version of shaming, perhaps.

criminalization of those who fit hegemonic definitions of 'the criminal', those whose lives are easiest to scrutinize and those least able to resist intrusions. One result has been intensified immiseration of lower class women, visible minorities, native and aboriginal women. These are the women most vulnerable to contempt of court charges and to counter-charging practices, and least able to resist state action or find the resources to leave violent partners (Macleod 1995). Compulsory criminalization of native men has accelerated cultural genocide, legitimizing the placement of native children into (white) foster families and spotlighting the 'inadequacies' of the native family (Monture-Okanee 1992). Arrest of the family breadwinner often deprives immigrant women and children of landed immigrant status and may lead to deportation, since dependence on the state (should welfare be sought) and criminal conviction (of the 'head' of the family) are both grounds for deportation (Martin and Mosher 1995; Pratt 1995). Immigrants with any irregularities in their papers are quickly declared unfit for citizenship and the entire family unit is shipped back to its country of origin. For women of colour in Britain, Canada and the United States, increased surveillance and criminalization means increased vulnerability to the actions of racist police and judicial authorities. They have reinforced already powerful stereotypes of black men as violent and black families as pathological, and threaten both family and community—the two bulwarks people of colour have had against an alien and hostile white world (Carby 1982; Williams 1987). And the ultimate irony is that poor and minority women are most deeply affected by the cuts in English language courses, welfare, day care, health care and education deemed necessary to pay for the higher criminal justice costs that policies of mandatory criminalization require (Elias 1989; Michaud 1992; LaRocque 1995). The $9.5 billion Canada spent on criminal justice in 1992 (up 23 per cent from 1989 to 1991), for example, would have built 1,900 state of the art elementary schools (Tripp 1996).

There is little evidence that increased criminalization has empowered women or made them safer in or outside the home. Indeed, the empirical debate over the success of mandatory arrest policies for batterers (Sherman 1992) revolves around whether arrested men are more or less likely to be reported for offences again.[13] Surely the better criterion of success is whether criminal justice intervention was the solution desired by the putative victim, and whether it made her life or that of her children better, subjectively or objectively. The high levels of contempt of court charges (laid against women who refuse to testify against the alleged batterer) and of counter-charges (laid against women deemed to have retaliated or defended themselves with physical force) can be read as evidence that this is not the case. Women in such situations who call police are usually seeking help to put an end to the violence and, despite a century of feminist activism, police are still the only 24-hour state-funded service with this mandate. This, not the failure of police and judges to respond punitively enough, or the undeniable misogyny that underlies much discretionary decision making, is the most tragic consequence of feminist reliance on criminalization. (See, in general,

[13] Being rearrested is deemed equivalent to reoffending. Of course it is not, since decisions to call in the authorities and report 'offenders' are contingent on social and political factors such as privacy levels afforded by place of residence, alternative resources available to the victim, the parties' past experiences with police, and others. Mandatory arrest policies never deprive police of *all* discretion—the power to respond initially, and to define the occurrence as the type of act covered by mandatory policies remains in their hands.

Braithwaite and Daly 1994; Tifft and Markham 1991; Caringella-Macdonald and Humphries 1991; Andrews *et al.* 1990; Ekland-Olson *et al.* 1984; Snider, 1990, 1994).

But it is not the only tragic consequence. Continued feminist support for criminalization is also fed by anger and fear. Whatever official crime statistics say about the chances of victimization, high female levels of fear and vulnerability are both real and rational, given the circumstances of many women's lives (Canada 1988; Rodgers 1994; Lea and Young 1984; Hanmer and Stanko 1985; Stanko 1990). But the conceptual leap from acknowledging fear to promoting incarceration is neither rational nor automatic. Feelings of vulnerability are not ameliorated by higher imprisonment rates—and anyway these rates are already much higher than commonsense perceptions (Roberts 1994; Sacco and Johnson 1990). Such feelings can be tackled, on the other hand, by social and structural changes which give people greater control over their surroundings. Graffiti, empty public spaces, the erosion of inner-city urban environments, the disappearance of professionals, local services and beat cops from neighbourhoods, the absence of recreational facilities, the erosion of public transit and the decline of employment opportunities (which produces fear-producing groups of young men hanging out in public places) all promote fear and, in some cases, increased criminal opportunities as well (Skogan 1990; Jackson 1989; Wilson and Kelling 1982). So does the richly deserved loss of faith in the integrity and accountability of economic, political and religious elites (Calavita and Pontell 1995; Calavita 1986, 1983; Levi 1993, 1987, 1984). Opportunities for counter- hegemonic struggle abound, but groups caught up in agendas of legalism and criminalization tend not to see them.

Indeed, criminal justice systems are probably the least effective institutions to look for transformative change. Even the staunchest advocates of incarceration do not argue that prisons are successful institutions, only that they punish well. The failure of correctional institutions to deter or rehabilitate has been repeatedly documented in studies ranging from the asylum in the sixteenth century to the penitentiary in the nineteenth to the modernist, management-oriented institutions of today (Rothman 1971, 1980; Garland 1990; Ignatieff 1978; Mathiesen 1990; Walker 1993; Feeley and Simon 1992, 1994). That prisons increase recidivism, nourish criminal subcultures, create 'schools for crime', impoverish prisoners' families and brutalize the keepers as thoroughly as the kept was recognized as early as 1820 (Foucault 1979).[14] Criminal justice systems appropriate personal problems, empowering states and court systems, not victims (Christie 1977; Braithwaite 1991). Prisons cannot provide jobs, someone to love you when you are depressed, to praise you when you do good things and administer the very real sanction of disapproval when you do not. Time inside makes those defined as offenders (disproportionately poor, native, minority men) more bitter,

[14] The history of Kingston Penitentiary, Canada's first, established in 1835, is typical. A decade after it opened, the first of a series of Royal Commissions into prison conditions decried the corruption of the warden, the sadistic and excessive use of whipping (the infamous 'cat o' nine tails'), the starvation of inmates, physical torture, and corruption of the guards, concluding that inmates were either driven insane or transformed from amateur into skilled criminals (Brown Commission Report 1849, in Cooper 1993: 48). Or consider the Kingston Prison for Women, Canada's only federal penitentiary for women, constructed in 1934 after a hundred years of reports recommending such a prison as a solution to all ills. The first Royal Commission Report to recommend its closure was issued in 1938, a scant four years later (Archambault Commission, in Cooper 1993· 43). And still we do not learn, for as I write plans to replace P4W with five regional facilities (and a healing lodge for Aboriginal women), are underway. The first of these opened three months ago, in Edmonton, Alberta. Meant to be an open facility allowing inmates to learn and grow, it is already under pressure to tighten control because of inmate 'escapes'.

unemployable, and typically more misogynist as well. Prisons are most successful at delivering pain–people suffer inside prisons, before and after them as well (as Feeley (1979) pointed out, the process is the punishment).

Recognizing the horrific human cost of violence against women, and seeking to focus public attention on this in the face of massive resistance, feminism sought the material and ideological resources (i.e. media attention and state monies) that criminalization provides, forgetting that symbolic denunciation is not the same as providing solutions. Naming problems (Spender 1980) and heaping moral opprobrium on offenders is no substitute for attacking causes,[15] and meaningful, transformative social change can only be achieved by transforming identities, groups and structures. Ultimately penality fails because 'the conditions which do most to induce conformity—or to promote crime and deviance—lie outside the jurisdiction of penal institutions' (Garland 1990: 289). Changing subcultures of belief and life-long patterns of behaviour is brutally difficult whether the target is crack users or City fraudsters. To do it humanely while respecting democratic norms of freedom of choice and action is almost impossible.[16]

For progressive groups with goals of amelioration and empowerment to embrace agendas of penality is significant. How we punish reveals much about dominant conceptions of social order, of gender, class, ethnic identity, and even of 'civilization' (Elias 1982, 1978). Focusing exclusively on monsters or folk devils, the 'otherness' of law-breakers and the futility of redemption speaks to manichean beliefs about the nature of people, about societies out of control where vengeance, the purposive infliction of pain, becomes the only response to nonconformity (Garland 1990: 276). Labelling every person who aggresses against another a 'criminal' is epistemologically absurd; locking them all up is fiscally impossible. Focusing massive amounts of time, resources and attention on creating instrumental knowledge and seeking technical fixes to problems without technical solutions has chilling socio-cultural ramifications. Such a quest marginalizes and silences those seeking emancipatory or critical knowledge or pursuing counter-hegemonic strategies (Habermas 1968/1971). Policies of criminalization, as fact and discourse, speak volumes about hierarchy and dominance, about 'proper' relations between the propertied and non-propertied, men and women, black and white and brown peoples. Entire subsets of laws—vagrancy, disorderly conduct, obstructing police and resisting arrest, prohibitions against disabling

[15] The following definitions are employed in this paper. Violence refers to the infliction of pain, harming others through the use or threat of force. It can be physical or non-physical, and prescribed (legal), for example when police use coercion to subdue suspects, or proscribed (illegal). It can be individual and one-on-one, as in robbery and assault; or collective/corporate, as in manufacturing cars that explode in rear-end collisions or carcinogenic medical implants. Criminal law typically focuses only on the individual, illegal act. Punishment is 'the legal process whereby violators ofthe criminal law are condemned and sanctioned in accordance with specified legal categories and procedures' (Garland 1990: 17). It includes the 'linked processes of law-making, conviction, sentencing, and the administration of penalties', the 'discursive frameworks of authority and condemnation', and the 'rhetoric of symbols' which represent the penal process to its audiences (Garland 1990: 17). Finally social control refers to: 'the complex of laws, processes, discourses and institutions involved in criminalizing and sanctioning behaviour' (Garland 1990. 10).

[16] The only other success of penality lies in its power to denounce, to convey social disapproval. Criminalization stigmatizes even the most powerful, on the rare occasions it is applied to their misdeeds (Pearce 1989, 1993; Braithwaite 1995) Thus, the evils of hazardous waste or employer negligence are more effectively conveyed through criminal rather than administrative law; the pronouncement of sentence is an august degradation ceremony in and of itself. A strategy of criminalization makes sense if seen as a consciousness-raising device to change public attitudes or highlight the misogyny permeating laws and practices such as the 'rule of thumb' on wife beating. However it can be argued that many of the ideological benefits are achieved from the publicity and struggle; it is 'success', defined as attaining state monies for criminalization, that is problematic.

electronic shackles or 'cheating' on urinalysis tests—celebrate the politics of authority (Schrecker 1990).[17]

One of the most serious consequences of the mis-identification of penality with social control, however, has been the paucity of theoretical attention paid to theorizing and engendering concepts of control. Social control, the discouraging of antisocial acts, is a prerequisite of social order. And while the acts deemed antisocial, the methods employed, the actors employing them and their effectiveness vary widely, all human collectivities attempt to control the practices and beliefs of those designated as members. Individual or self discipline is prescribed through the rewards and punishments of socialization; at the community level, social control is sought through processes ranging from verbal disapproval to ostracism and banishment. Punishment is an important component of social control, a shaming and socializing device with symbolic as well as instrumental functions (Garland 1990: 277-90; Polk 1994). But penality—institutions devoted to punishment through formal systems of criminal justice—is not the same thing, it has never been shown to be necessary to achieve social control and may well be counterproductive (Braithwaite 1989; Christie 1993).

The role and necessity of penality has seldom been explicitly debated, particularly by progressive groups (Pitch 1995). Professional literatures on penality abound; essentially non-reflexive, they calibrate with Foucauldian precision the exact amount of pain correlated with deterrence (rehabilitation having dropped out of fashion this decade) (Feeley and Simon 1992, 1994; Garland 1995). Public and political media, meanwhile, focus exclusively on denunciation and vengeance. To find arguments prescribing penality as an essential component of social control one must look to social theory, to the arguments of earlier scholars such as Durkheim and Freud. Durkheim saw penality as a prerequisite for social solidarity; he predicted that the need to punish would diminish as societies moved from mechanical to organic solidarity (Durkheim 1893, 1900). While this prediction has been shown to be incorrect (Grabosky 1984; Sorokin 1937), Durkheim's work is still being mined to great effect (Pearce 1989; Garland 1990), as it underlines the symbolic importance of penality as well as the individual and collective need to hold people/groups *accountable* for their deeds (not necessarily through criminalization).

Freudian arguments are less persuasive, as they rest on the assumption that the degree of repression required by modern industrialized societies is so great that creating a population of closet sadists must be considered a price of civilization. Because people in 'civilized' societies have to discipline themselves most of the time, they need assurance that those who do not do so suffer for their failure. Evidence that the price of non-repression is high is necessary to strengthen the psychic defences of the conforming majority against the ever-present temptation to misbehave (Garland 1990; Elias 1978, 1982). Such arguments, however, assume that criminality is

[17] Penality creates jobs, legitimizes professions, builds major indusuries. As Christie (1993) shows, the criminal justice system is one of the largest, most prosperous areas of the American economy, one of the few places where jobs can be had, careers built, towns made prosperous, and technological innovations perfected. Penal professionals have their own journals, jargon, conferences and all the detritus of established disciplines. Penal punishment has been refined and rendered scientific, the dispassionate field of experts removed from the emotional excesses of amateurs seeking vengeance and revenge (Garland 1990: 184-5).

undisciplined behaviour, that criminal acts are impulsive, pleasurable, aggressive and uninhibited. At a time when everything from complex corporate fraud to sleeping in the streets has been declared criminal, this is simply incorrect.[18] And, while it is possible that the levels of discipline demanded in industrialized societies do have a psychic cost, jumping on the bandwagon of psychological determinism to justify high levels of incarceration is unwarranted at this time. Dozens of competing explanations for modern infatuations with penality are available and many, such as the politics of law and order and its resonance with agendas of hegemonic control, are more parsimonious and persuasive.

But the most important problem with arguments that vengeful state action is psychologically or biologically necessary is their failure to theorize gender, their assumption that humans all have similar responses to the suppression of aggression, and identical propensities to act out aggressive urges. And yet, since the development of the modern state, women, particularly privileged white women, have consistently sought and benefited from higher levels of state control.[19] As the physically weaker sex, women have the most to lose when formal control breaks down, as rapes in Bosnia and assault levels in urban ghettos attest. First-wave feminist movements sought laws to criminalize alcohol and drug use, abolish prostitution, sterilize the 'feeble-minded', and create special reformatories for women and juveniles (Rafter 1983, 1985; Heidensohn 1992; Garland 1985; Ursel 1986; Chunn 1992). Nineteenth-century women were so enthusiastic about the potential of state control that they even took unwaged positions as social workers and police officers (Heidensohn 1992). Such roles were seen, and justified in rhetoric, as 'natural' extensions in the public sphere of women's main private role, that of socializing the young. Mothering is (among other things) a controlling role, whereby children learn to conform, restrain antisocial impulses, and accommodate the discipline demanded of contributing adults in that society. Historically, then, insofar as generalizations across race and class are possible, women in western societies over the last 100-odd years have resisted the idea that state or social control is necessarily a bad thing. Feminism in particular has sought to harness state power as a counterbalance to patriarchal power in the private sphere. Being assigned the primary responsibility for children in most cultures has made it essential for women to find ways to control the labour and actions of adult males, since patriarchal cultures make women dependent on men for sustenance and protection. The ability of women to be

[18] Arguments on the psychology of offenders are very much in fashion now (Gottfredson and Hirschi 1990). But it should be obvious that many criminal acts—producing, promoting and profiting from selling a drug known to cause cataracts or heart disease, for example, or hiring workers who cannot speak sufficient English to understand the warning labels on the cyanide they are using—require foresight, planning and discipline. Such crimes are more closely related to capitalism and cupidity than to drive fulfilment.

[19] I have purposively not defined social control because the definition is part of the problematic. It has been defined so narrowly that it includes only physical coercion, and so broadly every kind of influence, from socialization in family units to brainwashing in total institutions, is covered (Howe 1994: 65-6). Much feminist writing utilizes the broadest definition, implicitly or explicitly, and judges control negatively when exercised over women, positively when exercised by them. It is sometimes suggested that women are imprisoned in familial discourses, for example, because these are shaped by ideals of femininity originating in patriarchy (Howe 1994; Carrington 1990; Benhabib and Cornell 1987). However, if every kind of influence is seen as a patriarchal plot, what, then, is the absence of (social) control? What is the goal of resistance? Is it to create some kind of pre-social, Rousseauian 'natural' woman? Feminism needs to sort out which controls must be resisted and which embraced, rather than arguing (apparently) against all the processes of socialization.

financially—and therefore materially—independent of men is a new and still fragile phenomenon.[20]

The susceptibility of progressive groups to agendas of criminalization, then, and the allied failure to separate processes of control from institutions of penality, has had serious social consequences. Communities simply cannot be transformed into sane and civil places by installing cops on every corner or, for that matter, welfare workers in every home. Criminalization does not solve problems created by racism, de-industrialization or immiseration. It does provide satisfying outlets for much legitimate rage, but at the cost of leaving dominant groups unthreatened and dominant relations, of capital and patriarchy, unchallenged. The next section of the paper attempts to go beyond criminalization and examine the kinds of changes that might be sought, cultural and structural prospects with more potential to create truly safer societies.

Preliminary Thoughts on Ameliorative Strategies

Macro-level issues

If criminalization is not a solution to misogyny and violence, what is? This section of the paper examines what we know about building less violent societies, institutions and individuals. Ultimately such a goal requires change in the macro-level structures that maintain capitalism and patriarchy. But we have certainly learned by now that structural change does not guarantee that anything transformative will happen at micro levels. Conversely, the absence of macro-level change does not mean the absence of resistance or of significant counter-hegemonic victories at micro levels. Structures affect the chances and direction of change, they do not make it inevitable. However the present period of upheaval offers unique opportunities for transformative change due to the destabilization of institutions of governance, the ferment of opposing voices, the many groups vying to get 'their' solutions adopted. And much has been achieved over the last century, through mechanisms of struggle and resistance, the skilful deployment of mass media and electoral politics and the process Braithwaite calls 'model-mongering' (1994). Although much of this progress has been confined to the developed world, attitudes and behaviour, public opinion and law in a range of important areas have undergone radical change. There is less tolerance of corporate crime (Rossi *et al.* 1974; Cullen *et al.* 1982; Goff and Mason-Clark 1989), drunk driving, environmental pollution and interpersonal violence in general, particularly against women and children. Prejudice against visible minorities, homophobia and discrimination against women are now considered unacceptable by sizeable proportions of the population (which is not to say they have ceased to exist). The 1970s and 80s saw considerable

[20] Conversely it can be argued that men have suffered more than women in the civilizing process described by Elias and Durkheim since they represent the more aggressive sex Male definitions of 'normal' social control are often used—for example when the level of control applied to girls is described as oversocialization (Hagan 1991). The classic male dream of freedom involves escaping wives and children (deemed responsibilities), pursuing lives where sexual gratification and job-labour are casual, impulsive and commitment-free. Generations of popular culture and literature (male-dominated, aimed particularly at *young* men)—the 'Easy Rider', 'going down the road' Kerouac-style literatures, the frontier where 'a man can be a man'—all celebrate independence from the demands of civilization/women.

progress (as well as extensive backlash) in the centuries-old process of redefining the behaviour, attitudes, manners and sensibilities required of 'civilized' peoples (Spierenberg 1984; Elias 1978, 1982). Note, however, that many recent changes have been 'net-widening'—they created new behaviours to be abhorred and controlled, not new choices to be celebrated.[21]

Let us start at the macro level, examining what we know about building less violent social orders. Anthropological studies of non-western societies show that many, though certainly not all, nomadic small-scale hunting and gathering communities achieved high levels of gender equality and low levels of in-group interpersonal violence. Take the seventeenth century Huron, who lived on Georgian Bay in what is now the province of Ontario, for example. Each sex had a series of 'locations' in a complex kin structure with matrilineal nuclear families in a matrilocal longhouse tradition. There were distinct, but separate and equal tasks for men and women in agriculture, politics and marriage, with both sexes enjoying a relatively free choice of marital partner, provided clan and exogamy rules were respected. Divorce was common, but sexual and physical aggression were rare (Anderson 1991). Rape-prone societies, on the other hand, more frequently feature non-egalitarian relations in language, culture and in the distribution of resources. The absolute level of material affluence is not significant provided a certain minimum is maintained, but the distribution of goods is, particularly whether they are shared or monopolized by male elites. In rape-prone societies force becomes a means of achieving goods and status, and both competition and violence are keys to manhood. Gender differences between men and women are exaggerated, highly valued tasks are reserved for men and 'women's work' is denigrated. Socialization emphasizes roughness and cruelty, particularly towards boys who, it is believed, have to be toughened to survive. Women in rape-prone societies have few power bases of their own—few economic, political or spiritual arenas that confer status or power. Lacking personal or institutional power, trained to be compliant and submissive, females become easy and legitimate targets for male aggression (Harris 1991; Buchwald *et al.* 1993; Caringella-MacDonald and Humphries 1991; Knopp 1991; Archer and Gartner 1984).

Anthropological findings from tiny nomadic societies with minimal surplus or differentiation cannot be directly applied to industrialized capitalist states, highly stratified and specialized in every sense. And generalizing about patterns of crime and violence from such 'evidence' is even more difficult. However modernist obsessions with record-keeping mean that, while it is difficult to infer causality from the data, considerable information about individual and illegal violence in developed societies can be found in official statistics and victimization surveys. And, while statistics on official or state violence are harder to come by (because much of this violence is normative), incarceration rates provide a rough approximation for it as well. While most crime indicators are so dependent on levels of public education, public reporting and police priorities that they are virtually useless for international purposes, homicide statistics are the great exception, and relatively reliable comparisons can be made.

[21] Indeed, feminists do well to remember our own culpability—in privileging gender over race, for example, and ignoring the views of many minority women who would see racism as more significant than sexism in their lives (Greer 1994; Matthews 1994; Carby 1982; Williams 1987).

TOWARDS SAFER SOCIETIES

Thus we know, as discussed above, that English-speaking Anglo-American countries, particularly the United States, have the highest rates of both official and criminal violence. The least violent industrialized societies by the data are Japan, several countries in north-west Europe, and the Scandinavian countries. The latter all have comparatively homogeneous populations, and low levels of economic inequality. Comparing after-tax incomes for the top and bottom 10 per cent in 13 different nations, the United States has the most unequal distribution of income with a ratio of 5.94, Canada stands at 4.03, Australia at 4.01 and Britain at 3.8. The least unequal countries are Finland at 2.59, Sweden at 2.73, the Netherlands at 2.84, Austria at 2.88 and Norway at 2.93 (Kesterton 1995: A16). The ratio of the pay of a typical worker to that of a typical corporate Chief Executive Officer (CEO) is 1:16 in Japan, 1:21 in Germany, 1:33 in the United Kingdom, and a whopping 1: 120 in the United States (*Harper's* 1996: 46). While industrialized societies in general have wider gaps between rich and poor than hunting and gathering societies do, the clustering of less violent societies at the egalitarian ends of the scale is, to say the least, suggestive.

Less violent developed societies have superior social safety nets as well. The quality of life available to people on welfare or unemployment insurance in France or Norway, for example, is much higher than that allowed the subsidized poor in the United States, because France and Norway provide low cost medical care, education and housing in addition to income, while most American states do not. While unemployment due to corporate retrenchment and globalization of trade has occurred in all industrial countries, their effects have been offset, to some degree, by such subsidies. Moreover, the scale and speed of downsizing have been moderated—either because wholesale disposal of surplus employees was discouraged by stigma and shaming (as in Japan), or because union contracts forbid massive layoffs or made them prohibitively expensive (as in Germany, France and Scandinavia) (Abegglen 1975). While few studies have linked social policy directly to crime rates, a recent look at homicide in Norway argues that full employment policies and a relatively egalitarian income distribution can substantially offset the economic and personal strains of unemployment (Stack 1990). (Costs showed up, however, in higher rates of separation and divorce.) The fact that less violent societies have universal health care and parental leaves and more violent ones do not (or, if they do, the programmes are partial and poor), is also worthy of note. Unfortunately, this kind of evidence is suggestive at best. We do not know direction of causality, so we cannot say whether factors such as higher support for the unwaged 'cause' lower levels of violence or vice versa. Indeed, we cannot be certain any causal relationship exists—the apparent correlations could be serendipidous. But it does make *a priori* sense to hypothesize that desperate, distraught people are more likely to seek violent solutions to interpersonal problems, for both instrumental and expressive reasons.[22] With collective national or religious identities impaired throughout the west (despite the example of the former Yugoslav states), individual violent acts such as the lone gunman of Dunblane become the primary focus of law enforcement. And there is evidence (Grabosky 1984: 176–8) that violence and punitiveness go up in societies,

22 They are also more likely to take a job, any job, however menial and poorly paid. This explains, in part, why unemployment rates in the United States have typically been lower than in Europe and Japan, and why employers in general seek to keep support levels as low as possible

organizations and families as stress increases. An empirical scale of the 'degree of desperation' different societies create, linked to scales of various types of violence, would be a useful measure indeed.

Homogeneity of population is also associated with lower levels of individual and state violence. The people of Japan, Norway and Sweden are similar in religion, ethnicity, heritage and language. Denmark and the Netherlands exhibit more heterogeneity, with visible minorities and ethnic subcultures, yet they remain relatively non-violent societies. In contrast, violent societies such as the United States are extremely heterogeneous (but Canada, the most heterogeneous of all, has homicide rates one quarter those in the United States). Learning to live with difference (in skin colour, sexual orientation, language) without judging it or making it the basis of institutional and cultural ranking systems is clearly difficult for humans (as illustrated by evaluative distinctions made world-wide to differences of gender and age). Levels of population density vary independently, but lower internal levels of mobility are more common in less violent countries. Many people in European societies have roots in their parish, village or county that stretch back many generations. Once again we cannot say that homogeneity and geographic stability automatically produce less violent societies. Indeed, cohesive ethnic, national or religious groups may be more likely to generate *collective* violence against out-groups. But 'rootedness' and stability do appear to be associated with lower rates of individual and in-group violence (Christie 1993).[23] The retention of regional identities, the creation of localized cultural or religious bonds that encourage independence from mass culture, and the retention of alternate systems of allegiance alleviate psychic pressures on individuals in times of upheaval. They let some people find sources of meaning and satisfaction even when the forces of global capital (and other natural and unnatural disasters) have taken away economic resources. Alternate identities, then, offer people *psychological* cushions for psychic survival; social safety nets offer them *economic* cushions, both are significant. And both are connected to creating and nourishing less desperate populations.

It is painfully obvious, however, that western societies at present are racing in the opposite direction. Economic 'cushions' are under attack and income inequalities are increasing as nation states reduce deficits by eliminating social services, health care, minimum wages, worker protection laws and anything else that adds to the (corporate) cost of production. Removing social safety nets and public services is presented as necessary to allow developed countries (or the national and multinational corporations they shelter) to compete in cut-throat global markets. When capital, investment and jobs can easily be shifted from Birmingham to Bangladesh, they will go wherever the potential for short-term profits is highest, or so we are told. Currency speculators have become key players in this game of capital roulette. George Soros, for example, ex-Hungarian financier, acts as a 'global reality cop, pouncing on any government that overvalues or undervalues its currency' (Friedman 1995: A17). To appease investment-bankers and avert potentially disastrous runs on their currency, nation states have systematically begun campaigns to make their citizens less secure and more vulnerable, both psychologically and economically. Developed countries have entered a race to see who can create the most insecure, unhealthy and violence-prone population. The United

[23] This paper looks primarily at reactive, individual violence rather than aggressive collective violence, be it for territory, resources or empire expansion. Both kinds are important in the struggle against violence against women.

States is ahead at the moment—but it had a head start, with fewer universal social programmes to dismantle—and Canada, New Zealand and the United Kingdom are catching up fast.

Creating more desperate citizens is not always accomplished without resistance, as the 1995 strike of public sector workers in France and 1996 demonstrations in Germany illustrate. However the removal of public support systems is much farther advanced elsewhere. In Canada, for example, unemployment benefits and federal equalization grants, core programmes to alleviate regional inequality and allow survival outside metropolitan areas, have been dramatically pared. Since jobs are seasonal in much of the country, families would work in tourism or the fishery during the summers, and get by the rest of the year through unemployment insurance, odd jobs, self-sufficiency, lower levels of consumption and family and community networks. In the outports and fishing villages of Newfoundland, for example, the land was exploited for its meagre resources, the sea for the once bountiful cod. Housing costs were low because mortgages were uncommon; people built their own houses. Interpersonal violence, while not absent, was kept in check by a combination of culture and community traditions (Felt 1987). Thus Newfoundland, always the poorest province in Canada by measures of income, has long had the lowest homicide rates, at 0.69/100,000 in 1994, well below the Canadian average of 2.04, or the 3.08 found in the mobile, heterogeneous and affluent province of British Columbia (Hess 1995: A5). But NAFTA (the North American Trade Agreement) has made government payments to fishers challengeable as unfair trading subsidies. Cutting the deficit to avoid ruinous runs on the Canadian dollar has become the primary way of justifying cuts to federal transfer payments supporting medicare, education, child care and welfare. Public services are costly and inefficient; grants to poor people or provinces erode economic competitiveness and encourage dependence, according to right-wing think-tanks and politicians. But they also allow people to nourish their roots and remain in regions where they have traditions and histories, relatives and support networks. 'Subsidies' are important in creating less desperate people.

Psychological 'cushions', in the form of identification with values outside mass culture, are also under attack.[24] As many have pointed out, mass culture operates through consumerism, and consumerism works by creating and/or reinforcing personal and social insecurity. People with secure identities, independent of 'lifestyle', are harder for advertisers to manipulate, cannot be trusted to buy on cue, may fail to grasp that they are inadequate, inferior and socially irresponsible because they do not own the latest model cars, VCRs and Nikes. Consumerism has to create hierarchies and reinforce individual identities because if I have the fastest car or most fashionable clothes, you obviously do not. This is not a capitalist conspiracy, it is a natural correspondence of interests between privately owned media and capital. Like most ideologies, that of consumerism has a core of truth—many products do save labour, increase comfort levels and make life more pleasant. Add to this the socially created truths of consumerism,

[24] Earlier collective identities based in craft guilds have largely disappeared. Religion, a primary source of alternative value systems in many parts of the world, has been marginalized in much of Europe and Canada, and 'captured' by consumerism and capitalism in the United States (Bibby 1993). There has been talk about the potential of technology (the Net, for example) to recreate community and nourish alternate identities, but since it is still predominantly privileged classes, men, and increasingly commercial interests which are 'on line', it is unduly optimistic to see anything 'alternative' emerging here.

that not possessing certain 'things' leads other social actors to case aspersions on your trustworthiness, thrift or credentials as a human being, and you have a very persuasive set of beliefs. But societies made up of people whose identities are solely dependent on purchased commodities are very vulnerable to capital's periodic cycles of contraction and expansion. Combining greater dependence with fewer social and economic supports leads inevitably to greater desperation, and some of this will emerge as increased interpersonal violence.

The content of mass culture is another factor linking desperation to violence. Without exploring the byzantine and endless debates over whether violent videos or television programmes directly incite aggressive acts or produce desensitization, the omnipresence of these messages—the fact that a high percentage of people's leisure time, daily routines and interactions with others revolve around violent events (be they fictional, news events or sports)—indicates that the messages have, at minimum, the power to monopolize human attention. Of course the actual effects of violent media will vary by individual, class, gender, values and role in the community. The food we consume also has different effects depending on body type, mood, age, gender, weight and level of nourishment. But if 'you are what you eat', you are even more totally what you direct your attention to, what you think about, and value. And modern cultural diets promote insensitization, the quick 30-minute fix, lists of winners and losers, the unambiguous black and white solution. Compromise means selling out, complexity is denied and violence, when used by 'people like us', is a good thing, the only way to surmount omnipresent forces of evil and incompetence.

When all this is added up—polarized politics, an increased focus on individualism at the expense of community, greater heterogeneity, decreased equality and the loss of older identities to mass consumerism—it appears to be a recipe for ever greater violence, deprivation, desperation and pain. It is hard to figure out modes of resistance, let alone transformation. Political parties on the left are demoralized and riven with conflict, some of it between groups that should be allies—unions versus environmentalists, native people against feminists or gays. In the short term, pessimism about the potential of macro-level change in today's nation state or its components is unavoidable. As Glasbeek has characterized the present era: 'The employing classes have set out to roll back such gains as the working classes have made' (1995: 128). But none of these developments are new. Individualism, mass culture, consumerism and the decline of collective identities are part of the modernizing forces of industrialism and democracy, producing resistance as well as capitulation, gains as well as defeats. No structure is monolithic or impenetrable—or eternal. Because transformation is a dialectic process occurring from the bottom up as well as the top down,[25] the next section of the paper will look at the potential for change at micro and middle levels.

[25] Documentation of the relative futility of starting at the top, in this case with legal reform, is provided by Rosenberg's analysis of judicial activism in the United States (1991). In analyses of school desegregation, abortion, gender discrimination, criminal procedure, reapportionment and environmental protection laws, Rosenberg documents the failure of litigation to achieve substantive results *unless* other factors were present. Incentives for compliance, sanctions for non-compliance, and support from the institutions which would have to implement the reform were necessary prerequisites. In other words, legal victories only change lived realities if the ideological work has already been done, or is well underway.

Building less violent communities and families

The focus here is on ways of building less violent families. While the difficulty of promoting micro and middle-level patterns at odds with macro-level forces cannot be underestimated, it is essential to examine the context of subordination and understand the ways in which domination and violence are rooted inside the individual, in the patterns of daily life (Giddens 1981; Smart 1992; Foucault 1982). Thus, even while macro-level institutions are reinforcing one set of social relations, other social relations are undermining class and patriarchy, resisting and refusing hegemonic ways of thinking and acting. Macro-level transformation cannot be effective 'if the agents upon whom [transformative politics] depends continue to be governed and defined by the very social contexts they are trying to transform' (Winter 1992; 812). The objective, then, is to examine how practices can be changed to foster subjectivities and identities which reject violent, dominator/dominated roles.

On a purely mechanistic level, attention must be paid to techniques and patterns of socialization. Child-rearing patterns based on rewards or the withdrawal of approval are more effective (that is, long-lasting and efficient) than those based on physical punishment. Practitioners like Spock and Bowlby have demonstrated that guilt or shame-producing psychological sanctions lead to the development of conscience, while spanking and slapping, which operate primarily through fear of consequences, have erratic ėffects and sometimes produce retaliatory aggression. Effective socialization produces adults with strong internalized standards of behaviour who refrain from certain acts by 'choice', rejecting antisocial behaviours because they feel guilty or evil when they do certain things. Non-violent child-rearing techniques, then, produce better socialized individuals, but less violent people and families will result *only if* violent behaviours are targeted as guilt-producing behaviours, and prohibitions against violence are conveyed to miscreants by role models and significant others—teachers, employers, youth leaders and the like.

However, there is profound cultural resistance to wholesale and unqualified discouragement of individual aggression, particularly in the rearing of sons. Mothers as well as fathers, terrified of boys becoming 'wimps', send contradictory messages about the acceptability of bullying and aggression. Only when it becomes extreme, as in the recent murder of a three-year-old child in Britain by two ten-year olds, or when its targets are seen as undeserving, are violent acts unreservedly shamed. To understand why some boys grow up embracing violent acts and identities, others eschew them, and the majority flounder in the middle, one must examine the relationship between micro-level patterns of control and systems of patriarchy. Literature on domestic assault tells us that many of the violent men who have been studied are frustrated individuals who see women as easy, weak and available targets. They are often jealous and insecure, they believe in traditional sex roles and deny, to themselves and others, that their assaults have serious effects on the victimized. Frequently they witnessed or experienced physical or sexual abuse as children. Such men tend to see woman as objects whose duty is to make their men's lives easier, a duty women frequently fail to fulfil being 'by nature' unreliable, unfaithful, lazy, etc. Violence for them is instrumental as well as expressive, a method of resolving conflict, establishing dominance, and claiming male entitlement (Tifft and Markham 1991; Dobash and Dobash 1992, 1975; Dekeseredy and Hinch 1991; Ptacek 1988*a*, *b*; Stets 1988; Buchwald *et al.* 1993).

However such literatures are often class-biased, and they do not tell us a great deal about pivotal micro-macro links. Works of feminist psychology on the other hand, though typically ignoring structural factors, can be read for insight on the ways that patriarchy becomes embedded in personalities through conscious and unconscious processes of identity formation (Chodorow 1978, 1989). Men construct masculinities in the same way that all identities are built, by choosing among the options they see as available and satisfying for 'people like them', people who share their class, race, neighbourhood, family and society as well as gender. In heterogeneous western societies a wide range of masculinities is available, offering much choice—and much confusion. However, the patriarchal man—silent, equipped with the latest $225 Reeboks, emotionally constipated and physically strong—is still the ideal, especially in mass culture. Hegemonic masculinities on this model are heavily promoted in dominant media and sport, and constitute the identities most visible, accessible and appealing, particularly to boys lacking alternative male role models. Peer groups of adolescent males, alienated from mainstream authority, use sport, rap and mass culture extensively to develop ideas of what it means to be a man in this class, race, region, culture and time. Frequently this means borrowing the most violent and misogynous components of mainstream identities on offer. The price of questioning hegemonic masculinities can be high, producing feelings of uncertainty about one's own masculinity, rejection by peers, or even physical attacks. Given dominant value-systems that glorify power as an end in itself, and the undeniable fact that force is useful in getting one's way (for it offers immediate gratification without the need to grovel, negotiate or compromise and, in sexual matters, without vulnerability or risk of rejection), it can be hard for those who buy in to understand why anyone would reject the entitlement offered by hegemonic masculinities. When you can partake of an identity that allows you, by the simple fact of gender, to see yourself as stronger and smarter than half the world, entitled by birthright to deference and power if not wealth, why would you question such beliefs? Dissident males, who by their very existence show that these identities are cultural creations supporting privilege rather than biosocial necessities, threaten the entire structure.

Class and ethnic differences must be figured into this equation because they mediate the appeal of certain masculinities. Poor black or hispanic men in marginalized underclasses, for example, may find identities based on possession of turf or defence of honour appealing, or those that celebrate individualistic and collective force as badges of status, perhaps because a block of contested cityscape, a muscular body and a gun are among the few resources they can claim in such environments (Polk 1994). For men in urban ghettos to claim identities where self-esteem or peer status depends on the successful attainment of professional credentials or higher degrees (as many reformers insist they should) would be psychological and cultural suicide. The economic and educational resources necessary to play this game are simply not available to the vast majority, however intelligent and industrious. The success of the handful who might make it would come at the psycho-social expense of the many who would not.

White working-class American men (and a small percentage of black men) have seen their relatively privileged positions, good wages and strong unions, disappear in recent decades. Some of them have turned to militia-style movements celebrating turf and force (the equivalent of ghetto youth identities but more rural and collective), and/or to nationalistic identities based on citizenship, claiming entitlement as citizens of the richest, best, most powerful nation in the world. Working-class European men, typically less marginalized than urban underclasses in the United States, and better protected from the vagaries of the global marketplace due to the psychological and economic cushions instituted in such states in the post-war period, have often used sport, particularly football (soccer to North Americans), to underpin and reinforce concepts of manhood that contain notions of fair play in addition to celebrating toughness, physicality and the ability to take life's reverses stoically—'like a man' (Williams and Taylor 1994).

For middle-class North American white men, born into settings where masculinities can be centered in occupational success and higher education, dominant masculinities show wide generational splits. Adolescent middle-class masculinity is often premised on physical prowess, strength and sport (all linked to sexual success as a source of status), but with maturity job performance becomes paramount. In the merciless literally accurate language of the metaphor, occupational success 'separates the men from the boys'. Although phenomena such as the jobless recovery now threaten the economic prospects of the adult middle-class man, mainstream cultural goals of wealth, achievement and success through upward mobility were realistic goals for many decades. There was therefore less need, *as a class*, to cling to older masculinities stressing physical toughness, patriarchal notions based on the power of the male body. Men in this class were not so much learning to labour as learning to rule. This does not mean that middle or upper-class masculinities reject misogyny or violence on either the personal or professional level (Godenzi 1994); the difference is often one of packaging more than substance. Levi (1994) points out that the City (the financial centre of London) is personalized by corporate executives and traders as a bitch goddess, a fickle female promising much but delivering little. Phrases such as 'the City is a place for men, not for boys' (Levi 1994; 241) (and, therefore, not for women at all) suggest a subculture where exchange markets are exclusive boys' clubs, and trading and deals are dominance games, competitions for personal as well as occupational power. The self images of urban currency traders reek of machismo—the cowboy mystique, the swaggering recklessness of the quintessential '25-year olds in red suspenders', the 'bad boy' heroes such as Nick Leeson, the 28-year-old bond trader who single-handedly brought down Barings Bank, the power of a George Soros, who 'single-handedly broke the British pound' (Friedman 1995: A17). Such warrior power rivals that of earlier male heroes on the battlefields of Waterloo or the Plains of Abraham. Such identities celebrate dominance and patriarchy, but claims are based more on cerebral than physical power. This is hegemonic masculinity globalized.

In modern industrial societies diversity is omnipresent; the identities sketched here are no more than ideal types; the degree to which any particular man buys into them is always partial, fragmented and conditional. Identities and their appeal vary by occupational subculture and change over time. But key common themes can be traced. One is the need to keep certain spheres of thought and action separate and distinct, inviolate, strictly male. Another is the need to dominate one's physical and social environment. Yet another is the celebration of freedom and the related portrayal of women's and family demands—for commitment, labour, permanence—as constraint or fetters that the 'real man' must resist and control. A very libertarian rejection of state or female social control pervades western masculinities. Domination by bosses or wives must be resisted, but it is not clear why, to what end, freedom means freedom *from* rather than freedom *to*. Fears of control may also be related to male fears of emasculation which pervade myth, culture and language. However, as discussed earlier, obsessions with criminalization, in the meaning, implications and responses to formal and informal mechanisms of social control, have limited feminist attention to gender differences such as these.

On the level of praxis and policy, any prescription for changing dominant masculinities and identities must be highly speculative: we simply do not understand the roots of these identities, their relation to biology, psychology, the social relations of capitalism or social practice. But the fact that traditional masculine identities are everywhere under attack is a source of hope for those who seek ameliorative social change. It should, it *must* be possible to find ways of being manly that are not misogynous and do not require the repression of every human emotion except anger. It should not be necessary to denigrate male sexuality or insist that it be denied to address misogyny or assault, but it is essential to differentiate the sex drive from the need to dominate. To understand the limits as well as the potential for change it is useful to examine the decline and fall of traditional male spheres of action, male 'imperatives' to impregnate, provision and defend females and family groups (Gilmore 1990). These three have been central to male roles, male self-esteem and male identities, historically and cross-culturally, for thousands of years. There is no reason to believe they are epiphenomena, mere social constructions that can be wiped out by laws or political tinkering. Indeed it is more plausible to see the blockage and denial of 'maleness' symbolized by the denigration of these roles as fuelling the male rage that animates the late twentieth century. Right-wing, racist, militia-style social movements and the reactionary, punishment-oriented political regimes which are their psychological equivalents (both of which, surveys tell us, are supported by men more than by women), as symptomatic. Male movements such as Promise Keepers and the Million Man March, although different from each other, represent other attempts, by white and black men respectively, to struggle with these issues and reclaim male territory—in this case by redefining the responsibilities, distinctiveness and privileges that defined masculinity in the past.

In less than one generation male prerogatives to impregnate, provide and defend have been radically altered. Take the responsibility to provide for one's family: as we have seen, technologies making many working-class jobs obsolete combined with right-wing policies to accommodate capital's quest for higher profit margins have destroyed union solidarity, wages and benefits, and abolished thousands of jobs. Since few women occupied the well-paid unionized jobs in heavy industry or manufacturing that were the primary targets of this wave of downsizing, working-class men were the main losers. In the 1990s downsizing spread up the class ladder, this time men and women in middle management and public sectors took the hit. The ability to provide for oneself, let alone one's mates and children, was radically altered. Government programmes, the economic cushions, softened the blow to an extent in some European countries, but these are temporary measures at best. To make matters worse, women sometimes found it easier to secure new jobs—they are typically better educated, more willing to accept low wage positions and are sometimes viewed by employers as more reliable and less aggressive (positive traits in the job market of the 1990s for many Mcjobs). In the middle classes, the success of feminism in securing equal opportunity, independence and promotion for women in formerly male domains, while relieving economic stress for men lucky enough to have partners with good jobs, added new stress to the pain of redundance and new fuel to the fires of backlash (Falludi 1991).[26] In North America, women's wages rose relative to men's as various equity programmes made hiring women (and some minorities) beneficial, and their relative scarcity in many traditionally male professions such as science or engineering increased their market value. Thus in the 1990s, just when large numbers of middle-class white men began experiencing intense marginalization for the first time, middle-class women began making real, though often exaggerated, gains.

The imperative to impregnate has become less necessary as well. Advances in technology threaten to make males redundant, with frozen sperm, artificial insemination and test-tube babies replacing humans. Patriarchy's historical monopoly over reproduction and hence over women has been challenged, and contraceptive pills, IUDs and legalized abortion have allowed many women, in the developed world at least, to control when, how and with whom they will reproduce. Backlash and resistance, as in laws requiring the consent of a partner or parent to procure an abortion, or 'voluntary chastity' movements, have been largely unsuccessful. The arrival of AIDS has made heterosexual promiscuity, always the prerogative of men more than women, literally life-threatening. Meanwhile overpopulation has rendered patriarchal structures that value men for the number of (male) offspring they can sire increasingly unfashionable, particularly in first-world countries where each new person consumes 17 times his or her share of the world's resources.

The need to defend oneself or one's mate against natural enemies (fire, flood and wild animals) has largely disappeared as well, particularly in developed and urbanized countries. But the desire for enemies is obvious: invented villains permeate popular culture, and heroes are pressed into service to ward off everything from godless communists, aliens and marauding rapists to killer hurricanes and runaway submarines. Unfortunately fulfilling the male imperative to defend in non-fictive realities runs up against state monopolies over the control of arms and the exercise of interpersonal violence. Thus we see the almost religious significance attached by militia movements to the 'right' to bear arms, or the more recent but equally intense reaction to the banning of handguns larger than .22 calibre following the Dunblane massacre in Britain (*Guardian Weekly*, 'Guns Go Abroad', 8 December 1996: 24). Public restrictions on private arsenals are essential, but they also benefit women as a group more than men as a group, since women are the more fearful and vulnerable sex. State social control deprives men of the right and obligation to display their (generally) superior physical strength and greater aggressive capacity, and another component of male identity disappears.

So what kind of remedies should progressive movements seek? No one would deny that many of these developments are positive. For people in urban industrialized societies to use violence to settle disputes unleashes cycles of escalating aggression and

[26] Jobs for married women are not new—all but the most privileged have worked outside the home since the dawn of the Industrial Revolution (except during the most intense periods of child-rearing), but their wages were kept low by a combination of sexism and glass ceilings, and their jobs were more likely to be seen, by women as well as men, as secondary.

punishment, as life in many American cities today illustrates, where the wealthy barricade themselves inside armed enclosures and the poor kill each other off in the streets (or die in overheated tenements, too frightened to go outside or even open their windows, as in Chicago's 1995 heat wave). Only arms dealers and politicians who feed off fear benefit from this. And the answer is most certainly *not* to return to a time when female labour was even more underpaid and undervalued than it is now, or to sexual double standards that punished only women.

To my mind the evidence indicates that women, especially feminists, can play only minor roles in struggles to create and define less violent masculinities. The heavy misogyny found in male identity formation is too widespread, culturally and historically, to be wholly accidental. Blatant rejection of femininity and an exaggeration of male-female differences is a primary component of virtually every known male subculture (including those among gay men) (Jefferson 1994). Whether this is biologically or psychologically necessary is not known, nor is it particularly relevant from a utilitarian perspective. What matters is that, to have any appeal to rebellious adolescent males with much clearer ideas of what they reject than what they accept, alternate male identities must be *different* from female identities. It may turn out that the biosocial psychology of male humans, not to mention eons of evolution, make it important for boys to exaggerate gender differences in order to reject the mother-figure and distance themselves from the dependence of childhood. But there is no reason to suppose that the need to create identities that are distinctively different from women's implies a need to hate, devalue or dominate women. The latter are necessary components of patriarchy, not masculinity.

It also seems obvious that boys/men need roles, and therefore institutions and (sub) cultures, that allow them to be aggressive, risk-takers and adventurers (which does not mean that women should be denied such roles). There are few cultural or social spaces in developed societies where boys can be constructively adventurous or aggressive. Fantasy roles abound, from cyber-space to video games, but many of these exploit racism or homophobia rather than satisfying needs. With the disappearance of wild animals, frontiers and unexplored territory, the only adventurous legitimate *jobs* on offer are violent and destructive in nature (such as soldiers, police and/or criminals), or they are restricted to a privileged elite (space explorers today require doctorates in astrophysics). No wonder male police and prison guards cling so desperately to machismo images and subcultures, fighting academic and political directives which would replace warrior roles with service orientations (Heidensohn 1992; Reiner 1992). No wonder, too, that virtually all businesses and political organizations are gendered in ways that relegate women to secondary roles responsible for emotional scutwork, while men claim the adventurous, aggressive roles and the prestige, power and income such roles 'deserve' (Hochschild 1983). It is not functionality, capitalism, or the dictates of efficiency that require such subcultures or organizational divisions of labour.

Heterosexual women do have important parts to play in struggles to recast male identities. Too often women as mothers reward violence and toughness in their sons (and weakness in their daughters), or devalue emotionality and vulnerability in men with negative labels. Women as lovers and mates, particularly young women, cannot continue to respond erotically to machismo and reject men exploring alternate masculinities or those who have refused emotional castration. Feminism as a movement is well placed to problematize and consciousness raise around women's roles in reinforcing violent masculinities.

Because knowledge is a form of power, there are important tasks in this struggle for those in the academy as well. New male identities need to be wide-ranging, they will vary with class, ethnicity, orientation, religious identification, occupation and age (to name only a few factors), and they cannot be specified or prescribed in advance. They must be struggled for, forged by trial and error, and based in older masculinities and ways of being. But little is known about the structural and cultural forces forming masculinities and femininities, or about micro level processes which mediate the process of identity formation among individual men and women (Foucault 1982). Violence has historically been connected with dominance, and both with eroticism, but the roots and consequences of these links are unclear. We know little about the various agendas and interests animating struggles around masculinities today, and we have not adequately explored the social or political consequences of the different visions of male–female natures and relationships now vying for power. Some groups attempting to recast male and female identities, for example, take the partial, political and fragmented bits of biological knowledge we have about sex differences as facts, and argue for conservative policies on this basis (such as forcing women to stay home to bond with infants, or excluding them from higher education in mathematics because of alleged differences in left-right brain functions governing spatial abilities in men and women, for example). Naming the problems, specifying the implications and identifying the interest groups at play is a necessary first step to securing transformative changes and, even more crucial right now, to averting reactionary ones.[27] This is all part of the process of creating alternative models, of envisaging different ways of seeing to counter the dead weight of hegemony, for acceptance of the status quo rests heavily on notions that it constitutes the necessary and inevitable ordering of the world.

Directing greater attention to an 'ethics of care' might be a useful component of the process of constructing alternatives (Gilligan 1982; Smart 1989: 72–4; Kellough 1995). Kellough suggests that the intersecting values of capitalism and patriarchy have co-opted, through law, the common human urge to care for others and distorted it into a welfare/dependence frame. Women in particular are forced to choose between independence/autonomy and the obligation to care for others or nurture (Kellough 1995: 382–3). This is a false dichotomy because people must be nurtured (through socialization) in order to become autonomous, so caring and independence are intertwined not juxtaposed. Such a concept is useful insofar as it can be used as a counterbalance to voices advocating penality and revenge, and a challenge to tyrannies of the binary. 'Using the need of human beings for the caring attention of others' (Kellough 1994: 383) as a tool to evaluate macro-level processes (laws, structures, policies and institutions) focuses attention on new concepts of human rights, concepts

[27] The struggle for identity, the territory of internal or psychological change, is central to counter-hegemonic and ideological change. And it has not been claimed and politicized to the degree that structure-based change, now the apparently unchallengeable property of those who would make the world safe for profit maximization, has been. It may therefore be fertile soil politically, as well as essential knowledge.

based in collectivist and dualistic rather than individualistic zero-sum terms. We know so little about the activities central to caring, or the institutions and implications of such an orientation, compared to those central to punishing.[28]

An ethics of care also provides entry, on the level of praxis, for an overdue interrogation of the moral basis of capitalism, allowing renewed questioning of the conduct and obligations of capital. A long and difficult struggle a century ago secured minimum levels of health and safety in first-world workplaces and set in place a benificent cycle redefining the responsibilities of capital to both labour and 'society' (Snider 1993: 89–112; Carson 1970, 1980*a*, *b*; Paulus 1974). The rise of the global economy has reversed many of these gains. Such downsizing costs millions in direct and indirect costs, through welfare and unemployment benefits, forgone taxes, less productive workforces due to loss of morale, heightened insecurity, and other impacts (Pearce and Snider 1995*a*,*b*). It also has significant negative impact, through the removal of economic and psychological cushions on struggles, to create less violent populations. But the right of capital to create disposable people and communities has yet to be seriously scrutinized, much less targeted, by the demoralized political left or progressive social movements.

Conclusion

Creating alternative models and shifting attention away from criminal justice 'solutions' will not be easy. However, the present era represents a crossroads, a turning point where the potential for ameliorative change increases. It should be clear that criminalization, incarceration and increased punitiveness, while symbolically important, have reinforced right-wing agendas, with little to offer those seeking justice, transformation or remedial action. The failure to theorize social control has allowed a mis-identification of penality and control, and the obsession with punishment has diverted attention from examinations of the causes of violence and from explorations of ways to transcend criminalization to nurture counter-hegemonic change. The paper has explored these issues, asking in a preliminary way how macro-level factors reinforce violence in social orders, and how communities can be restructured and dominant masculinities and identities changed. As always, the bulk of the work remains.

[28] Much caring labour, in the private sphere and in mainstream organizations ranging from airlines to government, is done by and expected from women rather than men (Hochschild 1983). However the consequences and implications this has for social policy, child-rearing, economic reform, and violence are unknown. Do male subcultures and identities lose the potential to express and develop caring identities because of the dominance of women in these spheres? Are women denied the chance to develop more instrumental abilities? With what consequences? The empirical and theoretical territory of caring needs to he explored as carefully as the terrain of penality has been.

References

ABEGGLEN, J. (1975), *Management and Workers: The Japanese Solution*. Tokyo: Sophia University Press.

ADKIN, L. (1992), 'Counter-Hegemony and Environmental Politics in Canada', in W. Carroll, ed., *Organizing Dissent*, 135–56. Toronto: Garamond.

ADKIN, L. and ALPAUGH, C. (1988), 'Labour, Ecology and the Politics of Convergence', in F. Cunningham, S. Findlay, M. Kadar, A. Lennon and F. Silva, eds., *Social Movements/Social Change*, vol. 4, pp. 48–73. Toronto: Between the Lines and the Society for Socialist Studies.

ALDER, C. and WUNDERSITZ, J. eds., (1994), *Family Conferencing and Juvenile Justice*. Canberra: Australian Institute of Criminology.

ALLEN, J. (1982), 'The Invention of the Pathological Family: A Historical Study of Family Violence in New South Wales', in C. O'Donnell and J. Craney, eds., *Family Violence in Australia*, 1–27. Melbourne: Longman Cheshire.

ANDERSON, K. (1991), *Chain Her By One Foot: The Subjugation of Women 17th Century New France*. London: Routledge.

ANDREWS, D., ZINGER, I., HOGE, R., BONTA, J., GENDREAU, P. and CULLEN, F. (1990), 'Does Correctional Treatment Work? A Clinically Relevant and Psychologically Informed Mega-Analysis', *Criminology*, 28/3: 369–404.

APPLEBY, T. (1995), 'Crime plummeting across the U.S.', *The Globe and Mail*, Toronto, 13 July, A8.

ARCHER, D. and GARTNER, R. (1984), *Violence and Crime in Cross-National Perspective*. New Haven: Yale University Press.

ASTOR, H., (1994), 'Swimming Against the Tide: Keeping Violent Men Out of Mediation', in J. Stubbs, ed., *Women, Male Violence and the Law*. Monograph Series 6: 147–73. Sydney: Institute of Criminology.

AUSTRALIAN BUREAU OF STATISTICS (1994), *Crime and Safety in Australia*. Canberra: Supply and Services.

BAGLEY, K. and MERLO, A. (1995), 'Controlling Women's Bodies', in A. Merlo and J. Pollock, eds., *Women, Law, and Social Control*, 135–54. Boston: Allyn and Bacon.

BARTHOLOMEW, A. and HUNT, A. (1980), 'What's Wrong with Rights', *Journal of Inequality*, 9/1: 1–58.

BENHABIB, S. and CORNELL, D. eds. (1987), *Feminism as Critique: Essays on the Politics of Gender in Late Capitalist Societies*. Cambridge: Polity Press.

BIBBY, R. (1993), *Unknown Gods: The Ongoing Story of Religion in Canada*. Toronto: Stoddart.

BOX, S. (1983), *Power, Crime and Mystification*. London: Tavistock Publications.

BOYLE, J. (1985), 'The Politics of Reason: Critical Legal Theory and Local Social Thought', *University of Pennsylvania Law Review*, 133, April.

BRAITHWAITE, J. (1989), *Crime, Shame and Reintegration*. Melbourne: Cambridge University Press.

—— (1991), 'Inequality and Republican Criminology'. Paper presented at Annual Meeting of the American Society of Criminology, San Francisco, November.

—— (1994), 'A Sociology of Modelling and the Politics of Empowerment', *British Journal of Sociology*, 45/3: 445–79.

—— (1995), 'Corporate Crime and Republican Criminological Praxis', in F. Pearce and L. Snider, eds., *Corporate Crime: Contemporary Debates*, 48–71. Toronto: University of Toronto Press.

BRAITHWAITE, J. and DALY, K. (1994), 'Masculinities, Violence, and Communitarian Control', in T. Newburn and E. Stanko, eds., *Just Boys Doing Business: Men, Masculinity and Crime*, 189–213. London: Routledge.

BRAITHWAITE, J. and MAKKAI, T. (199 1), 'In and Out of the Revolving Door: Making Sense of Regulatory Capture'. Unpublished paper, Research School of the Social Sciences, Australia National University, December.

BRAITHWAITE, J. and MUGFORD, S. (1994), 'Conditions of Successful Reintegration Ceremonies', *British Journal of Criminology*, 34/2: 139–7 1.

BRAITHWAITE, J. and PETTIT, P. (1990), *Not Just Deserts: A Republican Theory of Criminal Justice*. Oxford: Oxford University Press.

BRANTS, D. and KOK, E. (1986), 'Penal Sanctions as a Feminist Strategy: A Contradiction in Terms?', *International Journal of Sociology of Law*, 14: 269–86.

BRICKLEY, S. and COMACK, E. (1987), 'The Role of Law in Social Transformation: Is a Jurisprudence of Insurgency Possible?', *Canadian Journal of Law and Society*, 2: 97–119.

BRODEUR, J-P. (1996), 'Penal Saturation', in T. O'Reilly-Fleming, *Post-Critical Criminology* 315–28. Scarborough, Ontario: Prentice Hall.

BROWNMILLER, S. (1975), *Against Our Will: Men, Women and Rape*. New York: Simon and Schuster.

BUCHWALD, E., FLETCHER, P. and ROTH, M., eds. (1993), *Transforming a Rape Culture*. Minneapolis, MN: Milkweed Editions.

BUTLER, J. (1990), *Gender Trouble*. London: Routledge.

CAIN, M. and HARRINGTON, C., eds. (1994), *Lawyers in a Postmodern World*. Milton Keynes, UK: Open University Press.

CALAVITA, K. (1983), 'The Demise of the Occupational Safety and Health Administration: A Case Study in Symbolic Action', *Social Problems*, 30/4: 437–48.

—— (1986), 'Worker Safety, Law and Social Change: The Italian Case', *Law and Society*, 20/20: 189–229.

CALAVITA, K. and PONTELL, H. (1995), 'Saving the Savings and Loans: U.S. Government Response to Financial Crime', in F. Pearce and L. Snider, eds., *Corporate Crime: Contemporary Debates*, 199–214. Toronto: University of Toronto Press.

CANADA, STANDING COMMITTEE ON JUSTICE AND THE SOLICITOR GENERAL (1993), *Crime Prevention in Canada: Toward a National Strategy*. Ottawa: Canada Communication Group, Publishing, Supply and Services.

CANADA, BUREAU OF COMPETITION POLICY (1989), *Competition Policy in Canada: The First Hundred Years*. Ottawa: Consumer and Corporate Affairs.

Canada (1988), *General Social Survey*. Ottawa: Statistics Canada.

CARBY, H. (1982), 'White Woman Listen! Black Feminism and the Boundaries of Sisterhood', *The Empire Strikes Back: Race and Racism in 70s Britain*. London: Hutchinson.

CARINGELLA-MACDONALD, S. (1985), 'The Comparability in Sexual and Non-sexual Assault Case Treatment: Did Statute Change Meet the Objective?', *Crime and Delinquency*, 31: 206–22.

—— (1987), 'Marxist and Feminist Interpretations on the Aftermath of Rape Reforms', *Contemporary Crisis*, 12/4.

—— (1988), 'Parallels and Pitfalls: The Aftermath of Legal Reforms for Sexual Assault, Marital Rape and Domestic Violence Victims', *Journal of Interpersonal Violence*, 3/2: 174–89.

CARINGELLA-MACDONALD, S. and HUMPHRIES, D. (1991), 'Sexual Assault, Women, and the Community: Organizing to Prevent Sexual Violence', in H. Pepinsky and R. Quinney, eds.' *Criminology as Peacemaking*, 98–113. Bloomington: Indiana University Press.

CARLEN, P. (1991), 'Crime, Class, Gender, Race and Racism: Some Reservations about Global and Gender-Centric Theories'. Paper presented at International Conference on Feminist Criminology, Mount Gabriel, Quebec, 18–21 July.

CARRINGTON, K. (1990), 'Feminist Readings of Female Delinquency', in J. Grbich, ed., *Feminism Law and Society,* 5–31. Bundoora: La Trobe University Press.

CARROLL, W. (1992), 'Introduction: Social Movements and Counter-Hegemony in a Canadian Context', in W. Carroll, ed., *Organizing Dissent,* 1–19. Toronto: Garamond.

CARSON, W. G. (1970), 'White Collar Crime and the Enforcement of Factory Legislation', *British Journal of Criminology, 10:* 382–98.

—— (1980*a*), 'The Institutionalization of Ambiguity: Early British Factory Acts', in G. Geis and E. Stotland, eds., *White Collar Theory and Research.* Beverly Hills: Sage.

—— (1980*b*), 'The Other Price of Britain's Oil: Regulating Safety on Off-shore Oil Installations in the British Sector of the North Sea', *Contemporary Crises,* 4: 239–66.

CHANTELOUP G. (1992), *The Canadian Environmental Protection Act: A Critical Analysis of the Role of Industry in the Legislative Process.* Unpublished MA thesis, Queen's University, Kingston, Ontario, August.

CHODOROW, N. (1978), *Reproduction of Mothering: Psychoanalysis and the Sociology of Gender.* Berkeley: University of California Press.

—— (1989), *Feminism and Psychoanalytic Theory.* Cambridge: Polity Press.

CHRISTIE, N. (1977), 'Conflict as Property', *British Journal of Criminology,* 17/1: 1–14.

—— (1993), *Crime Control as Industry.* London: Routledge.

CHUNN, D. (1992), *From Punishment to Doing Good: Family Courts and Socialized Justice in Ontario 1880–1940.* Toronto: University of Toronto Press.

CLARK, I. D. (1989), 'Legislative Reform and the Policy Process: The Case of the Competition Act'. Address given to the National Conference on Competition Law and Policy in Canada. Toronto: October.

COHEN, S. (1994), 'Postscript: If Nothing Works, What is our Work?', *Australia and New Zealand Journal of Criminology,* 27/1: 104–7.

COMACK, E. (1993), *Feminist Engagement with the Law: The Legal Recognition of the 'Battered Woman Syndrome',* CRIAW Paper No. 31. Ottawa: Canadian Research Institute for the Advancement of Women.

COOPER, S. (1993), 'The Evolution of the Federal Women's Prison', in E. Adelberg and C. Currie, eds., *In Conflict with the Law,* 33–49. Vancouver: Press Gang.

CUFF, J. (1995), 'TV violence pointless, silly issue', *Globe and Mail,* Thursday, 3 August: Cl.

CULLEN, F., LINK, B. and POLANZI, C. (1982), 'The Seriousness of Crime Revisited', *Criminology,* 20/1: 83–102.

DAHL, T. S. (1986), 'Taking Women as a Starting Point: Building Women's Law', *International Journal of Sociology of Law,* 14: 239–6 1.

DEKESEREDY, W. and HINCH, R. (1991), *Woman Abuse: Sociological Perspectives.* Toronto: Thompson Educational Publishing.

DETTMER, J. (1995), 'Vandals in America could take a Caning', *The Weekend Australian,* 18–19. March, B1.

DOBASH, R. E. and DOBASH, R. (1975), *Violence Against Wives: A Case Against the Patriarchy.* New York: Free Press.

—— (1992), *Women, Violence and Social Change.* London: Routledge.

DURKHEIM, E. (1893), *The Division of Labour in Society.* New York: Free Press (1964).

—— (1990), 'Two Laws of Penal Evolution', *University of Cincinnati Law Review,* 38 (1969): 32–60.

DUTTON, D. (1984), *The Criminal Justice System's Response to Wife Assault*, Report No. 26. Ottawa: Ministry of the Solicitor-General.

EDGLEY, C. and BRISSETT, D. (1990), 'Health Nazis and the Cult of the Perfect Body: Some Polemical Observations', *Symbolic Interaction*, 13/2: 257–79.

EDWARDS, A. (1994), 'The Tyranny of the Binary: Social Construction of Gender, Sexuality and Rape in Criminal Trials'. Paper presented at Australian Sociological Association Conference, Deakin University, Geelong, Victoria, 7–10 December.

EKLAND-OLSON, S., LIEB S., and ZURCHER L. (1984), 'The Paradoxical Impact of Criminal Sanctions: Some Microstructural Findings', *Law and Society Review*, 18/2: 159–78.

—— (1982), *State Formation and Civilization*. London: Oxford University Press.

ELIAS, N. (1978), *The Civilizing Process*. London: Oxford University Press.

ELIAS, R. (1989), 'Which Victim Movement: The Politics of Victim Policy', in W. Skogan *et al.*, eds., *Victims and Criminal Justice*. Berkeley: Sage.

ERICSON, R. and BARANEK, P. (1982), *The Ordering of Justice: A Study of Accused Persons as Dependants in the Criminal Justice Process*. Toronto: University of Toronto Press.

FALLUDI, S. (1991), *Backlash: The Undeclared War Against American Women*. New York: Doubleday.

FEELEY, M. (1979), *The Process is the Punishment*. New York: Russell Sage Foundation.

FEELEY, M. and SIMON J. (1992), 'The New Penology', *Criminology*, 39/4: 449–74.

—— (1994), 'The New Penology: Notes on the Emerging Strategy of Corrections and its Implications', *Criminology*, 30: 449–74.

FELT, L. (1987), 'Take the "Bloods of Bitches" to the Gallows: Cultural and Structural Constraint upon Interpersonal Violence in Rural Newfoundland', St. John's Institute of Social and Economic Research, Memorial University of Newfoundland.

FESCHUK, S. (1995), 'Alberta Jails no Place Like Home', *The Globe and Mail*, 15 July, A7.

FOUCAULT, M. (1979), *Discipline and Punish: The Birth of the Prison*. New York: Pantheon.

—— (1982), 'The Subject and Power', in H. Dreyfus and P. Rabinow, eds., *Michel Foucault: Beyond Structuralism and Hermeneutics*, 194–230. Chicago: University of Chicago Press.

FRENCH, M. (1985), *Beyond Power: On Women, Men and Morals*. New York: Summit Books.

FRIEDMAN, T. (1995), 'Sorry, but this Group of Seven doesn't make the grade', *The Glove and Mail*, Tuesday, 30 May, Al7 (reprinted from the *New York Times*).

FUDGE, J. (1990),'What Do We Mean by Law and Social Transformation?', *Canadian Journal of Law and Society*, 5: 47–69.

FUDGE, J. and GLASBEEK, H. (1992), 'A Politics of Rights: A Politics with Little Class', *Social and Legal Studies*, 1, 45–70. London: Sage.

GALTUNG, J. (1969), 'Violence, Peace and Peace Research', *Journal of Peace Research*, 6: 167–91.

GARLAND, D. (1985), *Punishment and Welfare: A History of Penal Strategies*. Aldershot, Hants: Gower.

—— (1990), *Punishment and Modern Society: A Study in Social Theory*. Oxford: Clarendon Press.

—— (1991), 'Punishment and Culture: The Symbolic Dimension of Criminal Justice', *Studies in Law, Politics and Society*, 11: 191–222.

—— (1995), 'Penal Modernism and Postmodernism', in A. Blomberg and S. Cohen, eds.' *Punishment and Social Control*, 181–209. New York: Aldine de Gruyter.

GIDDENS, A. (1981), *The Class Structure of Advanced Societies*, 2nd edn. London: Hutchinson.

GILLIGAN, C. (1982), *In a Different Voice: Psychological Theory and Women's Development*. Cambridge: Harvard University Press.

—— (1987), 'Moral Orientation and Moral Development', in E. Kittray and D. Meyers, eds., *Women and Moral Theory*. New Jersey: Rowan and Littlefield.

GILMORE, T. (1990), *Manhood in the Making*. New Haven: Yale University Press.

GLASBEEK, H. (1995), 'Preliminary Observations on Strains of, and Strains in, Corporate Law Scholarship', in F. Pearce and L. Snider, eds., *Corporate Crime: Contemporary Debates*, 111–31. Toronto: University of Toronto Press.

GODENZI, A. (1994), 'What's the Big Deal?', in T. Newburn and E. Stanko, eds., *Just Boys Doing Business?*, 135–52. London: Routledge.

GOFF, C. and MASON-CLARK, N. (1989), 'The Seriousness of Crime in Fredricton, New Brunswick: Perception towards White-Collar Crime', *Canadian Journal of Criminology*, 31: 19–34.

GOTTFREDSON M. and HIRSCHI, T. (1990), *A General Theory of Crime*. Stanford: Stanford University Press.

GRABOSKY, P. (1984), 'The Variability of Punishment', in D. Black, ed., *Toward a General Theory of Social Control*, 163–89. New York: Academic Press.

GREER, P. (1994), 'Aboriginal Women and Domestic Violence in New South Wales', in J. Stubbs, ed., *Women, Male Violence and the Law*, Monograph Series No. 6: 64–87. Sydney: Institute of Criminology.

HABERMAS, J. (1968/1971), *Knowledge and Human Interests*, trans. J. Shapiro. Boston: Beacon.

HAGAN, J. (1991), 'A Power-Control Theory of Gender and Delinquency', in R. Silverman, J. Teevan and V. Sacco, eds., *Crime in Canadian Society*, 4th ed, 130–36. Toronto: Butterworths.

HALL, S. (1988), *The Hard Road to Renewal: Thatcherism and the Crisis of the Left*. London: Verso.

HANDLER, J. (1992), Postmodernism, Protests and the New Social Movements', *Law and Society Review*, 26/4: 697–731.

HANMER, J. and STANKO, E. (1985), 'Stripping Away the Rhetoric of Protection: Violence to Women, Law and the State in Britain and USA', *International Journal of Sociology of Law*, 13: 357–74.

HANNAH-MOFFAT, K. (1995), 'To Charge or Not to Charge: Front Line Officers' Perceptions of Mandatory Charge Policies', in M. Valverde, L. MacLeod and K. Johnson, eds., *Wife Assault and the Canadian Criminal Justice System*. Toronto: Centre of Criminology: 35–47.

Harper's Magazine (1996), 'Does America Still Work? A *Forum* Discussion with R. Blackwell, A. Dunlap, G. Gilder, E. Luttwak, R. Reich and P. Tough', 292/1752: 35–47.

HARRIS, M. K. (199 1), 'Moving into a New Milennium: Toward a Feminist Vision of Justice', in H. Pepinsky and R. Quinney, eds., *Criminology as Peacemaking*, 83–97. Bloomington: Indiana University Press.

HEIDENSOHN, F. (1992), *Women in Control*. Oxford: Oxford University Press.

HESS, H. (1995*a*), 'Violent crime rate drops by 3%', *Globe and Mail*, 3 August, A1, and 5.

—— (1995*b*), 'Babies in first year risk murder most', *Globe and Mail*, 3 August, A5.

HOCHSCHILD, A. R. (1983), *The Managed Heart: Commercialization of Human Feeling*. Berkeley: University of California Press.

HOWE, A. (1990*a*), 'Sentencing Women to Prison in Victoria: A Research and Political Agenda', in J. Grbich, ed., *Feminism Law and Society*, 32–53. Bundoora, Victoria: LaTrobe University Press.

—— (1990*b*), 'The Problem of Privatized Injuries: Feminist Strategies for Litigation', in S. Silbey and A. Sarat, eds., *Studies in Law, Politics and Society*, 10: 111–42.

—— (1994), *Punish and Critique: Towards a Feminist Analysis of Penality*. London: Routledge.

HURTIG, M. (1991), *The Betrayal of Canada*. Toronto: McClelland and Stewart.

IGNATIEFF, M. (1978), *A Just Measure of Pain The Penitentiary in the Industrial Revolution*. London: Routledge.

IMMARIGEON, B. (1991), 'Beyond the Fear of Crime', in H. Pepinsky and R. Quinney, eds., *Criminology as Peacemaking*, 69–80. Bloomington, Indiana University Press.

IMMARIGEON, R. and CHESNEY-LIND, M. (1992), *Women's Prisons: Overcrowded and Overused*. San Francisco: National Council on Crime and Delinquency.

JACKSON, P. (1989), *Minority Group Threat, Crime and Policing: Social Context and Social Control*. New York: Praeger.

JEFFERSON, T. (1994), 'Theorising Masculine Subjectivity', in T. Newburn and E. Stanko, eds., *Just Boys Doing Business?*, 10–32. London: Routledge.

JOHNSON, H. and RODGERS, K. (1993), 'A Statistical Overview of Women and Crime in Canada', in E. Adelberg and C. Currie, eds., *In Conflict with the Law*, 95–116. Vancouver: Press Gang.

KELLOUGH, G. (1992), 'Pro-Choice Politics and Postmodernist Theory', in W. Carroll, ed., *Organizing Dissent*, 81–100. Toronto: Garamond Press.

—— (1995), *The Abortion Controversy: A Study of Law, Culture and Social Change*. Toronto: University of Toronto Press.

KESTERTON, M. (1995), 'Income Gaps', *The Globe and Mail*, Friday, 27 July, A16.

KINSEY, R., LEA, J. and YOUNG, J. (1986), *Losing the Fight Against Crime*. London: Basil Blackwell.

KNOPP, F. (1991), 'Community Solutions to Sexual Violence', in H. Pepinsky and R. Quinney, eds., *Criminology as Peacemaking*, 181–203. Bloomington, IN: Indiana University Press.

LACLAU, E. and MOUFFE C. (1985), *Hegemony and Socialist Strategy: Towards a Radical Democratic Politics*. London: Verso.

—— (1987), 'Post-Marxism Without Apologies', *New Left Review*, 166: 79–106.

LAPRAIRIE, C. (1993), 'Aboriginal Women and Crime in Canada: Identifying the Issues', in E. Adelberg and C. Currie, eds., *In Conflict With The Law*, 235–46. Vancouver: Press Gang.

—— (1995), 'Altering Course: New Directions in Criminal Justice. Sentencing Circles and Family Group Conferences', unpublished paper. Ottawa: Department of Justice

LAROCQUE, E. (1995), 'Violence in the Aboriginal Communities', in M. Valverde, L. MacLeod, K. Johnson, eds., *Wife Assault and the Canadian Criminal Justice System*, 104–124. Toronto: Centre of Criminology.

LEA, J. and YOUNG, J. (1984), *What is to be Done About Law and Order?* Harmondsworth, Middlesex: Penguin Books.

LEES, S. (1994), 'Lawyers' Work as Constitutive of Gender Relations', in M. Cain and C. Harrington, eds., *Lawyers in a Postmodern World*, 124–54. Milton Keynes, UK: Open University Press.

LEVI, M. (1984), 'Giving Creditors the Business: The Criminal Law in Inaction', *International Journal of the Sociology of Law*, 12: 321–33.

—— (1987), '"Crisis; What Crisis"? Reactions to Commercial Fraud in the United Kingdom', *Contemporary Crises*, 11/3: 207–21.

—— (1993), *The Investigation, Prosecution, and Trial of Serious Fraud*, Research Study No. 14. London: Royal Commission on Criminal Justice.

MACKINNON, C. (1992), 'Pornography, Civil Rights and Speech', in C. Itzin, ed., *Pornography: Women, Violence and Civil Liberties*. Oxford: Oxford University Press.

MACLEOD, L. (1995), 'Policy Decisions and Prosecutorial Dilemmas: The Unanticipated Consequences of Good Intentions', in M. Valverde, L. MacLeod and K. Johnson, eds., *Wife Assault and the Canadian Criminal Justice System*, 47–62. Toronto: Centre of Criminology.

MAGNUSSON, W. (1992), 'Decentring the State, or Looking for Politics', in W. Carroll, ed., *Organizing Dissent: Contemporary Social Movements in Theory and Practice,* 69–80. Toronto: Garamond.

MANDELL, M. (1994), *The Charter of Rights and the Legalization of Politics in Canada.* Toronto: Thompson Educational Publishing.

MARSH, J., GEIST, A. and CAPLAN, N. (1982), *Rape and the Limits of Law.* Boston: Auburn. House.

MARTIN, D. and MOSHER, J. (1995), 'Unkept Promises: Experiences of Immigrant Women with the Neo-Criminology of Wife Abuse', *Canadian Journal of Women and the Law,* 8/1 3–44.

MARTINSON, R. (1974), 'What Works? Questions and Answers about Prison Reform', *The Public Interest,* 35: 22–54.

MATTHEWS, N. (1994), *Confronting Rape.* London: Routledge.

MATHIESEN, T. (1990), *Prison on Trial.* London: Sage.

MAXWELL, G. and MORRIS, A. (1994), 'The New Zealand Model of Family Group Conferences', in C. Alder and J. Wundersitz, eds., *Family Conferencing and Juvenile Justice,* 15–43. Canberra: Australian Institute of Criminology.

MCBARNET, D. (1981), *Conviction and Law: The State and the Construction of Justice.* London: Macmillan

MELOSSI, D. (1980), 'Strategies of Social Control in Capitalism: A Comment on Recent Work', *Contemporary Crises,* 4: 381–402.

MELOSSI, D. and PAVARINI, M. (1981), *The Prison and the Factory: The Origins of the Penitentiary System.* London: Ink Links.

MESSERSCHMIDT, J. (1986), *Capitalism, Patriarchy and Crime: Toward a Socialist-Feminist Criminology.* Tolowa, NJ: Rowan and Littlefield.

MICHAUD, J. (1992), 'The Welfare State and the Problem of Counter-Hegemonic Responses Within the Women's Movement', in W. Carroll, ed., *Organizing Dissent,* 200–214. Toronto: Garamond.

MICHELMAN, F. (1979), 'Welfare Rights in a Constitutional Democracy', *Washington University Law Quarterly,* 3: 659–93.

MONTURE-OKANEE, P. (1992), 'The Violence We Women Do: A First Nations View', in C. Backhouse, ed., *Challenging Times: The Women's Movement in Canada and the United States.* Montreal: McGill-Queen's Press.

MOORE, D. and O'CONNELL, T. (1994), 'Family Conferencing in Wagga Wagga: A Communitarian Model of Justice', in C. Alder and J. Wundersitz, *Family Conferencing and Juvenile Justice,* 45–86. Canberra: Australian Institute of Criminology.

OFFE, C. (1987), 'Challenging the Boundaries of Institutional Politics: Social Movement Since the Sixties', in C. Maier, ed., *Changing Boundaries of the Political, Essays on the Evolving Balance between the State and Society, Public and Private in Europe.* Cambridge: Cambridge University Press.

ONTARIO LEGISLATIVE ASSEMBLY (1982), *First Report on Family Violence: Wife Battering.* Toronto: Standing Committee on Social Development, September.

OSBORNE, J. (1984), 'Rape Law Reform: The New Cosmetic for Canadian Women', in C. Schweber and C. Feinman, eds., *Criminal Justice Politics and Women: The Aftermath of Legally Mandated Change.* New York: Haworth Press.

OYSERMAN, D. and MARKUS, H. (1990), 'Possible Selves and Delinquency', *Journal of Personality and Social Psychology,* 59/1 112–25.

OYSERMAN, D. and SALTZ, E. (1993), 'Competence, Delinquency and Attempts to Attain Possible Selves', *Journal of Personality and Social Psychology,* 65/2: 360–74.

PAULUS, I. (1974), *The Search for Pure Food: A Sociology of Legislation in Britain.* London: Martin Robertson.

PEARCE, F. (1989), *The Radical Durkheim.* London: Unwin Hyman.

—— (1993), 'Corporate Rationality as Crime', *Studies in Political Economy,* 40: 135–62.

PEARCE, F. and SNIDER, L., eds. (1995*a*), *Corporate Crime: Contemporary Debates.* Toronto: University of Toronto Press.

—— (1995*b*), 'Regulation Capitalism', in *Corporate Crime: Contemporary Debates,* 19–47. University of Toronto Press.

PEPINSKY, H. and QUINNEY, R., eds. (1991), *Criminology as Peacemaking.* Bloomington: Indiana University Press.

PICARD, A. (1995), 'Officers shouldn't be fired, union says', *Globe and Mail,* Saturday, 15 July, A7.

PITCH, T. (1995), *Limited Responsibilities: Social Movements and Criminal Justice.* London: Routledge.

POLK, K. (1985*a*), 'Rape Reform and Criminal Justice Processing', *Crime and Delinquency,* 31/2: 191–205.

—— (1985*b*), 'A Comparative Analysis of Attrition of Rape Cases', *British Journal of Criminology,* 25/3: 280–94.

—— (1994), 'Family Conferencing: Theoretical and Evaluative Concerns', in C. Alder and J. Wundersitz, eds., *Family Conferencing and Juvenile Justice,* 123–40. Canberra: Australian Institute of Criminology.

PRATT, A. (1995), 'New Immigrant and Refugee Battered Women: The Intersection of Immigration and Criminal Justice Policy', in M. Valverde, L. MacLeod and K. Johnson, eds.' *Wife Assault and the Canadian Criminal Justice System,* 84–104. Toronto: Centre of Criminology.

PTACEK, J. (1988*a*), 'How Men Who Batter Rationalize their Behaviour', in A. Horton and J. Williamson, eds., *Abuse and Religion.* Lexington, MA: Lexington Books.

——(1988*b*), 'Why Do Men Batter Their Wives?', in K. Yllo and M. Bograd, eds., *Feminist Perspectives on Wife Abuse.* Newbury Park, CA: Sage.

RAFTER, N. (1983), 'Chastizing the Unchaste: Social Control Functions of a Women's Reformatory, 1894–1931', in S. Cohen and A. Scull, eds., *Social Control and the State.* Oxford: Martin Robertson.

—— (1985), *Partial Justice.* Boston: Northeastern University Press.

RATNER, R. and MCMULLEN, J., eds. (1987), *State Control: Criminal Justice Politics in Canada.* Vancouver: University of British Columbia Press.

REINER, R. (1992), 'Police Research in the UK: A Critical Review', in M. Tonry and N. Morris, eds., *Modern Policing.* Chicago: University of Chicago Press.

—— (1994), *Public Knowledge of Crime and Justice: An Inventory of Canadian Findings.* Canada: Department of justice.

ROBERTS, J. (1991), *Sexual Assault Legislation in Canada: An Evaluation Report,* vols. 1–9. Canada: Department of Justice, Minister of Supply and Services.

RODGERS, K. (1994), 'Wife Assault: The Findings of a National Survey', *Juristat,* 14/9, Canadian Centre for Justice Statistics, March.

ROSENBERG, G. (1991), *The Hollow Hope: Can Courts Bring About Social Change?* Chicago: University of Chicago Press.

ROSSI, P., BOSE, C. and BERK, R. (1974), 'The Seriousness of Crimes: Normative Structure and Individual Differences', *American Sociological Review,* 39: 224–37.

ROTHMAN, D. (1971), *The Discovery of the Asylum: Social Order and Disorder in the New Republic*. Boston: Little, Brown.

—— (1980), *Conscience and Convenience: The Asylum and its Alternatives in Progressive America*. Boston: Little Brown.

SACCO, V. and JOHNSON, H. (1990), 'Patterns of Criminal Victimization in Canada', in *General Social Survey Analysis Series*, No. 2. Ottawa: Statistics Canada.

SCHRECKER, T. (1990), 'The Political Enigma of Criminal Justice'. Paper presented at 1990 Annual Meeting, Canadian Political Science Association, Victoria, BC, May.

—— (1992), 'Facing the Risks of Decline: Can Canada Prosper in the Global Economy?', *Canadian Issues*, 14: 1–29.

SCIMECCA, J. (1991), 'Conflict Resolution and a Critique of Alternative Dispute Resolution', in H. Pepinsky and R. Quinney, eds., *Criminology as Peacemaking*, 263–279. Bloomington: Indiana University Press.

SCUTT, J. (1982), 'Domestic Violence: The Police Response', in C. O'Donnell and J. Craney, eds., *Family Violence in Australia*, 110–20. Melbourne: Longman Cheshire.

—— (1983), *Even in the Best of Homes*. Melbourne: Penguin.

SHERMAN, L. (1992), *Policing Domestic Violence: Experiments and Dilemmas*. New York: Free Press.

SILBERMAN, C. (1980), *Criminal Violence, Criminal Justice*. New York: Vintage.

SKOGAN W. (1990), *Disorder and Decline: Crime and the Spiral of Decay in American Neighbourhoods*. New York: Free Press.

SMART, C. (1989), *Feminism and the Power of Law*. London: Routledge.

—— (1992), 'The Woman of Legal Discourse', *Social and Legal Studies, 1*: 29–44.

SMITH, D. E. (1974), 'Women's Perspective as a Radical Critique of Sociology', *Sociological Inquiry*, 44/1: 7–13.

SNIDER, L. (1985), 'Legal Reform and Social Control: The Dangers of Abolishing Rape', *International Journal of the Sociology of Law*, 13: 337–56.

—— (1986), 'Legal Reform and the Welfare State', *Crime and Social Justice*, 24: 210–42.

—— (1990), 'The Potential of the Criminal Justice System to Promote Feminist Concerns', *Studies in Law, Politics and Society*, 10: 143–65.

—— (1993), *Bad Business: Corporate Crime in Canada*. Toronto: Nelson.

—— (1994*a*), 'Criminalization: Panacea for Men who Batter but Anathema for Corporate Criminals', in D. Currie and B. Maclean, eds., *Social Inequality, Social Justice*, 101–24. Vancouver: Collective Press.

—— (1994*b*), 'Feminism, Punishment and the Potential of Empowerment', *Canadian Journal of Sociology of Law*, 9/1: 75–104.

SOLOMON, S. (1995), *The Confidence Game: How Unelected Central Bankers are Governing the Changed Global Economy*. New York: Simon and Schuster.

SOROKIN, P. (1937), *Socio-Cultural Dynamics*. *New* York: American Book Company.

SPIERENBURG, P. (1984), *The Spectacle of Suffering*. Cambridge: Cambridge University Press.

SPITZER, S. (1979), 'The Rationalization of Crime Control in Capitalist Society', *Contemporary Crises*, 3/2: 187–206.

—— (1990), 'The Seductions of Punishment: Toward a Critical Criminology of Penality'. Paper presented to Annual Meetings of American Society of Criminology, Baltimore, November.

STACK, S. (1990), 'Homicide in Norway: A Time-Series Analysis'. Paper presented at the Annual Meeting of the American Society of Criminology, Baltimore, 7–10 November.

STANKO, E. (1990), *Everyday Violence*. London: Pandora.

—— (1994), 'Challenging the Problem of Men's Individual Violence', in T. Newburn and E. Stanko, eds., *Just Boys Doing Business?*, 32–45. London: Routledge.

STRAUSS, M. (1977*a*), 'Societal Morphogenesis and Intrafamily Violence in Cross-cultural Perspective', *Annals of the New York Academy of Sciences*, 285: 717–30.

—— (1977*b*), 'A Sociological Perspective on the Prevention and Treatment of Wifebeating', in M. Roy, ed., *Battered Women*, 194–238. New York: Van Nostrand Reinhold.

STRAUSS, M. and GELLES, R. J. (1990), *Physical Violence in American Families*. New Brunswick, NJ: Transaction Publishers.

STETS, J. E. (1988), *Domestic Violence and Control*. New York: Springer-Verlag.

STUBBS, J. (1995), '"Communitarian" Conferencing and Violence Against Women: A Cautionary Note', in M. Valverde, L. MacLeod, K. Johnson, eds., *Wife Assault and the Canadian Criminal Justice System*, 260–92. Toronto: Centre of Criminology.

STUBBS, J. and WALLACE, D. (1994), 'Domestic Violence: Impact of Legal Reform in New South Wales', in J. Stubbs, ed., *Women, Male Violence and the Law*, Monograph Series No. 6. Sydney: Institute of Criminology.

THOMAS, P. (1994), 'U.S. Prison Population, Continuing Rapid Growth Since '80s, Surpasses 1 Million', *The Washington Post*, 28 October, A3.

THOMPSON, E. P. (1963), *The Making of the English Working Class*. London: Gollancz.

—— (1975), *Whigs and Hunters: The Origin of the Black Act*. New York: Pantheon.

TIFFT, L. and MARKHAM, L. (1991), 'Battering Women and Battering Central Americans', in H. Pepinsky and R. Quinney, eds., *Criminology as Peacemaking*, 114–5 3. Bloomington, IN: Indiana University Press.

TOMBS, S. (1990), 'Industrial Injuries in the British Manufacturing Industry', *Sociological Review*, 38/2: 324–43.

—— (1995), 'Corporate Crime and New Organizational Forms', in F. Pearce and L. Snider, eds., *Corporate Crime: Contemporary Debates*, 132–46. Toronto: University of Toronto Press.

TRIPP, R. (1996), 'Dollars and Pain; The Economics of the Justice System', *Kingston Whig-Standard*, Monday, 25 November, A1.

URSEL, J. (1986), 'The State and the Maintenance of Patriarchy: A Case Study of Family, Labour and Welfare Legislation in Canada', in J. Dickinson and B. Russell, eds., *Family, Economy and State*, 150–91. Toronto: Garamond.

—— (1992), *Private Lives, Public Policy: 100 Years of State Intervention in the Family*. Toronto: Women's Press.

WALINSKY, A. (1995), 'The Crisis of Public Order', *Atlantic Monthly*, July: 39–54.

WALKER, S. (1993), *Taming the System. The Control of Discretion in Criminal Justice, 1950–1990*. Oxford: Oxford University Press.

WEARING, R. (1990), 'A Longitudinal Analysis of the 1987 Crimes (Family Violence) Act in Victoria'. Unpublished Report, Criminology Research Council, Canberra.

WHYNHAUSEN, E. (1995), 'Fuelling a Fear of Crime', *The Weekend Australian*, 18–19 March, 25.

WILLIAMS, J. and TAYLOR, R. (1994), 'Boys Keep Swinging: Masculinity and Football Culture in England', in T. Newburn and E. Stanko, eds., *Just Boys Doing Business? Men, Masculinities and Crime*, 214–34. London: Routledge.

WILLIAMS, P. (1987), 'Alchemical Notes: Reconstructing Ideals from Deconstructed Rights', *Harvard Civil Rights: Civil Liberties Law Review*, 22: 401–27.

WILSON, J. Q. and KELLING, G. (1982), 'Broken Windows', *Atlantic Monthly*, March, 29–38.

WINTER, S. (1992), 'Don't Trust Anyone Not Over the Sixties', *Law and Society Review*, 26/4: 789–818.

WOOD, E. (1990), 'The Uses and Abuses of "Civil Society",' *Socialist Register*, 62–81.

YEAGER, P. (1991), *The Limits of Law: The Public Regulation of Private Pollution*. Cambridge, MA: Cambridge University Press.

ZIPPER, J. and SEVENHUIJSEN, S. (1987), 'Surrogacy: Feminist Notion of Motherhood Reconsidered', in M. Stanworth, ed., *Reproductive Technologies*. Cambridge: Polity Press.

Name Index

Abegglen, J. 457
Acker, Joan 200–201, 360, 374–5
Acosta-Belén, E. 283
Adams, L. 156
Addelston, J. 364
Agnew, Robert 70, 168
Akerstrom, Malin 172–3
Altman, D. 60
Amin, A. 15, 20–21
Anderson, Elijah 172, 181, 290
Anderson, K. 456
Andrews, D. 451
Appleby, T. 446
Araki, N. 123
Arch, E.C. 201
Archer, D. 456
Archer, J. 298
Athens, Lonnie H. 138, 166, 169–70, 298, 308, 314–15, 324–5, 327
Atherton, M. 436
Atkinson, P. 316, 428
Auburn, T. 62
Auld, J. 274
Austin, John 403
Avary, D'Aunn Wester 170, 177–9

Badinter, E. 119
Bagley, K. 448
Bakunin, Mikhail 57
Balkin, J. 363
Baranek, P. 442
Barclay, C. 429
Barclay, G. 214
Barclay, L. 218
Baron, L. 125
Baron, R.A. 150
Baron, Stephen W. 168
Barrett, F.J. 360–61, 375
Barthes, Roland 41, 258
Bartholemew, A. 448
Baudrillard, J. 265
Bauman, Zygmunt 51, 263–5, 270
Bayley, D.H. 123
Beck, Ulrich 263, 265–7, 269, 273
Beier, A.L. 17, 19
Beirne, Piers 402
Bendelow, G. 314, 317, 323, 330–31
Benedict, J.R. 155–7
Benedict, Ruth 123
Benjamin, Jessica 32, 48–51
Benjamin, W. 265
Bennet, Trevor 168
Benson, Michael 404–5, 410, 421–2
Bernard, Jessie 406, 420
Bernard, Thomas J. 84
Berrill, K.T. 151
Berry, Chuck 342
Beynon, John 168–9
Billig, Michael 404
Bingham, D. 253, 255–7, 259
Bird, S. 361, 375
Birkbeck, Christopher A. 168
Birnbaum, H.J. 152–3, 155, 159
Bjorn, L. 374
Blanchard, W.H. 152, 158
Bloor, M. 429
Bogart, Humphrey 254
Boisjoly, Roger 196–9, 206
Bolton, J.L. 17
Bolton, R. 159
Bonilla, F. 283–4
Bornoff, Nicholas 125, 127
Bose, C.E. 284
Bostyn, A.M. 394
Boswell, A.A. 157–8, 160
Bottcher, Jean 169
Bottoms, A.E. 268, 274, 431, 437
Bourdieu, Pierre 6–7, 13–14, 18, 63, 315, 397
Bourgois, Philippe xvi, 281–96, 298
Bowker, L.H. 157, 385
Bowlby, Dr. 461
Bowles, S. 360, 363
Bowling, B. 214
Box, S. 442
Boyle, J. 445

Braithwaite, John 117, 123, 264, 268, 272, 401–2, 443, 451, 453, 455
Brake, M. 343
Brando, Marlon 341
Brandth, B. 361
Brannon, R. 157, 192
Breines, I. 65
Brewer, J.D. 361
Briggs, J. 17
Briscoe, S. 303
Brissett, D. 448
Brittan, Arthur 4, 173, 251, 394
Britton, D.M. 360
Britton, Paul 103
Brod, H. 383–4
Brodeur, J-P. 447
Brown, J. 215, 361–2
Browne, A. 14
Browning, Christopher 118
Brownmiller, S. 37, 449
Bryant, Martin 93–4
Buchbinder, D. 62
Buchwald, E. 456, 461
Buckley, K. 428
Buckley, R. 125
Bulbeck, C. 60
Bulger, James 96, 107, 109, 251
Bulman-Janoff, R. 134, 139
Burgess, A.W. 134, 152
Burnett, R. 214–15
Burr, A. 264, 266
Burris, B.H. 362
Burton, L. 282
Buruma, I. 126–7
Bush, George W. 40, 64
Butler, Judith 5, 294, 405, 444

Cain, M. 117
Calavita, K. 451
Callahan, Harry 255
Campbell, Anne 84, 291
Campbell, Bea 32–4, 50–51, 217, 270, 273, 276
Campos, R. 283–4
Canaan, Joyce 85
Capper, Suzanne 251
Carby, H. 450
Caringella-MacDonald, S. 443, 449, 451, 456
Carlen, P. 271–2, 444
Carmichael, G. 122
Carpenter, Cheryl 170
Carrigan, T. 58
Carson, W.G. 468
Casey, J.J. 267
Castoriadis, C. 35
Cavanagh, K. 313, 325
Chambliss, W.J. 13
Chandler, Raymond 254–5
Chappell, D. 120–22, 124
Charles, M.T. 371
Charlesworth, S. 382
Chase, A. 154
Cherry, K. 126
Chesney-Lind, Meda 403, 448
Chetkovich, C. 360
Chodorow, Nancy J. 32, 47–8, 64, 462
Christie, N. 445, 447, 451, 453, 458
Chubby Checker 342
Chunn, D. 454
Cialdini, R.B. 157
Clark, J. 298
Clarke, A. 254
Clarke, John 355
Clarkson, C. 135
Clatterbaugh, K. 205
Coates, D.L. 364
Cochran, Eddie 342
Cockburn, C. 204–5, 361, 374, 385
Coffey, S. 361
Cohan, S. 256
Cohen, Albert 172, 177
Cohen, Lawrence 134, 186–7
Cohen, Stan 235, 392, 394, 441
Cohn, C. 203
Coleman, James 402
Coleman, Will 185
Collier, Richard xii, xiii, 34, 38, 41–2, 93–114, 169, 217, 297
Collins, J. 298, 324
Collinson, D.L. 360
Collinson, M. 360
Collison, Mike xvi, 71, 169, 173, 263–79
Comstock, G.D. 151
Condon, J. 125
Conklin, John 402, 404, 421
Connell, R.W. xi, xiii, 4–9, 15, 19, 21, 23–5, 31, 33–42, 57–67, 71–2, 84, 117–19, 127, 134–5, 137–9, 144, 157, 192–4, 206, 218, 282, 297, 299, 308–9, 314, 316, 319, 330–31, 339, 352, 360, 362, 375, 383, 406, 421–2, 427, 429

Copes, Heith xv, 165–90
Corbett, C. 134, 139, 145
Cordess, C. 235
Cordilia, Ann T. 150, 168
Corrigan, P. 386
Cose, E. 375
Courtenay, W. 319
Coward, Rosalind 258
Craib, Ian 47, 390, 397
Crawford, A. 133, 135
Creed, B. 257
Cressey, D. 381, 397
Croall, Hazel 401
Cromwell, Paul 170, 177–9, 214–15
Crowther, C. 24
Cruz, S. 281
Cullen, F. 455
Cullen, Lord 105–7, 110
Curran, D. 117
Currie, E. 10–12
Curtis, R. 275
Cusson, M. 214, 259, 266, 272

D'Emilio, J. 150
Dagger, K. 121
Daly, Kathleen 403, 451
Damme, Jean-Claude van 251
Darby, Bruce 404
David, D.S. 192
Davies, B. 62
Davis, M. 266, 273–4
De Certeau, M. 386
De la Cancela, V. 290
Dean, James 341, 348
Decker, Scott 171–2, 175
Dekeseredy, W. 449, 461
Denborough, D. 65
Denzin, N. 215
DeParle, J. 282
Dettmer, J. 447
Devlin, A. 215, 217
Diamond, M. 237
Diamond, S. 118, 129
Diamond, T. 365
Dietz, J.L. 283
DiTomaso, N. 360
Dobash, R.Emerson 134, 230, 403, 442, 449, 461
Dobash, Russell P. 134, 230, 403, 428, 442, 449, 461
Dobrin, A. 11–12
Donaldson, Mike 34, 58, 63, 203, 422
Donnelly, N. 303
Dorn, N. 266
Douglas, Kirk 257
Douglas, Michael 257
Dower, John 118, 126
Doyle, David P. 84
Driscoll, A.K. 151
Dubinskas, F.A. 201, 204, 206
Dunning, E. 135
Durkheim, E. 453
Dutton, D. 442, 446
Dysart, D. 125

Easteal, P. 122–3
Eastwood, Clint 117, 255
Eckert, Paul 85
Eco, U. 252, 255, 265
Edgerton, R. 298
Edgley, C. 448
Edley, Nigel 31, 34, 39, 41–2, 44, 62, 218
Edwards, A. 118
Edwards, Ethan 253
Ehrhart, J.K. 152, 157
Ekland-Olson, S. 451
Elder, G.H. 215
Elias, Norbert 15, 17–19, 314, 317, 326, 331, 452–3, 456
Elias, R. 442, 450
Elliott, Anthony 34–5, 51
Ellis, Lori 172
Emerson, R.M. 436
Engelbrecht, G.K. 345–6
Enloe, C. 375
Ericson, R.V. 256, 442
Evans, J. 235
Evans, R. 122
Ezre, Edna 180

Fagan, J. 298
Faludi, Susan 32–4, 50–51, 59, 465
Farrall, Stephen xv, xvii, 213–46
Farrell, J.M. 160
Farrington, David P. 214–16, 218
Fast, I. 48
Featherstone, M. 265, 270
Feeley, M. 117, 451–3
Feeney, Floyd 168, 178
Feinman, C. 363
Feldman, A. 282

Felson, Marcus 134, 168, 186–7, 268, 272
Felson, R. 298
Felt, L. 459
Fenstermaker, Sarah 71, 169, 192–3
Ferguson, B. 282
Ferguson, M. 58
Ferraro, K. 133, 135
Feschuk, S. 448
Fletcher, J. 18–19
Florman, S.C. 205
Foley, Douglas E. 85
Foote, C.E. 230
Ford, John 253
Foucault, M. 451, 461, 467
Frank, A.W. 230
Franklin, Karen xiv, 149–64
Franz, B.T. 151
Freed, L.F. 343, 345–7, 353
Freud, Sigmund 32, 41, 45–8, 235, 453
Friedman, T. 458, 463
Frieze, I.H. 14, 134, 139
Frosh, S. 218, 233, 235
Fuchs, C. 257
Fudge, J. 448
Fusco, Cuso 338

Gadd, David xv, xvii, 39, 213–46
Gamson, J. 361
Garafolo, J. 186
Garland, D. 441–2, 444, 449, 451–4
Gartner, R. 456
Gates, Bill 39–40, 62
Geis, Gilbert 152–3, 421
Gelsthorpe, Loraine 403
Gerson, J. 361
Gibbon, E. 17
Gibbons, D. 117, 128
Gibbs, J.T. 11, 13
Gibbs, John J. 172
Gibson, Mel 256–7, 259
Giddens, Anthony 71, 88, 194, 256, 263–70, 272, 294, 391, 396–7, 401, 445, 461
Gidycz, C.A. 152–3
Giggs, J. 266
Gilligan, C. 467
Gilmore, D.D. 8, 14, 38, 40, 60, 118–19, 127
Gilmore, T. 384, 388, 464
Gintis, H. 360, 363–4
Girard, R. 16, 19
Giroux, H. 364
Gitlin, T. 254
Glasbeek, H. 448, 460
Glaser, Barney G. 316, 365, 409
Glaser, C. 337–8
Glassner, Barry 170
Glover, Edward 234
Godenzi, A. 463
Goff, C. 455
Goffman, Erving 270, 314, 319, 325–6, 330–31, 382, 385, 391–2, 395, 397, 404
Gordon, M. 133–4, 138
Gorz, A. 20
Gottfredson, M. 133, 135, 186, 214, 442
Grabosky, P. 453, 457
Graham, K. 298–9
Gramsci, Antonio 3, 5, 8, 15, 22, 31, 36, 57, 282
Grapendaal, M. 382
Greenfeld, L.A. 153
Greer, P. 446
Griffin, Christine xix, 401–26
Groth, A.N. 152–3, 155, 159
Groves, W. Byron 166
Gruber, J. 374
Guarnaccia, P.J. 287
Gurr, Ted R. 16

Haarr, M. 363
Habermas, J. 25, 452
Hacker, S. 205
Hagan, J. 270–71, 274–5
Hagedorn, John 71
Hagell, A. 251
Hale, C. 250
Haley, Bill 342
Hall, G.C.N. 153
Hall, Steve xii, xiii, 3–29, 34, 57, 59, 61–5, 218, 235, 258
Hamilton, J.W. 152
Hamilton, Thomas 93–7, 99–110
Hamilton, V. 123
Hammersley, M. 428
Hanawalt, B.A. 16
Handler, J. 449
Hanmer, J. 451
Hannerz, U. 13
Hardy, George 199
Hark, I.R. 256
Harpur, R.S. 347
Harris, Eric 156
Harris, M.K. 456

Harris, R. 364
Hawkins, G. 12–13
Hawks, Howard 253
Hazlehurst, K. 124
Hearn, Jeff xi, 34, 38, 61–3, 360, 438
Hebdidge, D. 265–6
Heidensohn, F. 363, 454, 466
Heise, L. 153
Henican, E. 154, 156
Henwood, Karen 408–9
Herek, G.M. 150–51, 160
Herodotus 17
Hess, H. 446–7, 459
Hill, C. 17
Hinch, R. 449, 461
Hindelang, Michael 134, 186
Hirschi, T. 214, 264, 442
Hobbs, Dick xvii, 8, 15, 21, 24, 135, 169, 216, 219, 232, 266, 274, 298, 309, 313, 315–17, 321, 330, 332
Hobdell, Kathy xiv, 133–48
Hochschild, A.R. 58, 466
Hochstetler, Andy xv, 165–90
Hodge, R. 251–2, 254, 258–9
Hoff, L.A. 143
Holden, C. 214
Holland, Janet 87
Holland, Sally xix, xx, 427–39
Hollway, Wendy 65, 219–22, 233
Holmlund, C. 256–7
Holmstrom, L.L. 134, 152
Holt, R. 17
Homel, R. 298
Honaker, David 166
Hood, R. 387
Hood, Robin 406–7
Hood-Williams, J. 46–7, 219, 236
Hope, T. 275
Horne, R. 8, 10, 13–15, 20–21, 24
Horowitz, R. 328
Horsley, W. 125
Hoshino, K. 123
Hough, M. 133–4
Howe, A. 444, 448
Hudson, R. 24
Huff, C.R. 291
Hughes, M. 214–15
Hughes, R. 122
Huithwaite, Z.M. 351–2
Hummer, R.A. 157
Humphries, D. 451, 456
Hunt, A. 448
Hunt, J. 324, 331, 362–3
Hutchinson, I.L. 11
Hyatt-Williams, A. 235

Ignatieff, M. 451
Immarigeon, B. 443
Immarigeon, R. 448
Ingham, M. 4
Irwin, John 173, 180, 381, 397
Itzin, C. 259

Jackman, M. 360
Jackson, Bo 80–81
Jackson, David 107, 169–70
Jackson, P. 451
Jacobs, Bruce 166, 171–3
Jaggar, A. 283, 294
James, Oliver 4, 10, 21
Jameson, Frederic 50, 256–7
Jarrett, Robin L. 282
Jefferson, Tony xii, xiii, xv, 31–57, 59–62, 64–5, 135, 167, 172, 213, 217, 219–22, 231–3, 235, 237–8, 263, 269, 294, 297, 308, 317, 428, 466
Jennings, J.L. 230
Jewkes, Yvonne xviii, 381–400
Johnson, B.D. 275
Johnson, H. 448, 451
Johnson, Lynton 342, 344, 350
Jones, R. 392
Jones, T. 135
Juni, S. 157
Jupers, T.A. 157–8
Jurik, N.C. 362–4

Kael, Pauline 255
Kanin, E.J. 153, 158
Kanter, R.M. 201, 203, 368
Kappeler, S. 250, 259
Katz, Jack 14, 150, 166, 169, 174, 232, 259–60, 264, 266–8, 271
Katz, M. 282
Kaufman, M. 65, 157
Kelling, G. 451
Kellough, G. 467
Kelly, L. 133–4, 230
Kennedy, Leslie W. 168
Kerfoot, D. 200, 203, 362

Kersten, Joachim xiv, 117–31, 169, 173
Kessler, S. 192
Kesterton, M. 457
Kibby, K. 298
Kilpatrick, D. 139
Kimmel, M.S. xi, 4, 58, 60, 157, 361
King, A. 324, 326
King, M.B. 12
Kinsey, R. 449
Klebold, Dylan 156
Klein, Melanie 32, 46–7, 220, 236
Knight, B.J. 214
Knight, R. 152
Knights, D. 200, 203, 362
Knopp, F. 456
Kondos, Angelo Peter 351
Koss, M.P. 152–3
Kraemer, S. 235, 237
Kramer, R.C. 191
Kühne, H. 120–21
Kupers, T. xix

Lacan, Jacques 41, 47
Lafree, Gary 168
LaGrange, R. 133, 135
Lang, E. 298
LaPrairie, C. 446
Larkin, Philip 44
LaRocque, E. 450
Lasch, C. 20–21, 264
Lash, Scott 263–6, 272–4
Laub, John H. 70, 150, 214–16, 231, 238
Laumann, E.O. 59
Lauritsen, J. 136
Layder, D. 398
Layton, Lynne 32, 48
Lea, J. 10–11, 449, 451
Lea, S. 62
Lebra, T.S. 126
Lee, Bruce 251
Leeson, Nick 463
Lefebvre, H. 265, 394
Lefkowitz, B. 156, 160
Leibrich, J. 214–15
Leidner, R. 360
Leitner, M. 267
Leonard, K.E. 218
Levi, Michael 4, 402–3, 422–3, 451, 463
Levine, Felice J. 70
Lewes, K. 45, 65
Lewis, Oscar 282
Lewis-Fernandez, R. 287
Liebling, A. 393
Lippitt, R. 150
Lister, S. 12, 314, 321, 325, 332
Little Richard 342
Little, D. 117
London, W. xix, 157–8
Luckenbill, David F. 84
Lund, Bob 199–200, 207
Lundgren, Dolf 257
Lupton, D. 218, 309, 429
Lyman, Stanford 317, 325, 403–4, 421–2
Lynch, Michael 166
Lyng, Stephen 259, 264, 270, 321

Maanen, J. van 365
Mabin, A. 343
McAndrew, C. 298
Mac an Ghaill, Mairtin 32–4, 40, 50–51, 59, 87, 218, 436
McBarnet, D. 442
McCall, Nathan 159
McCarthy, B. 157
McCaughey, C. 428
MacCleod, Jay 172
McConnell, M. 197, 202
McCoy, Sherman 40
McCracken, G. 428
MacDonald, M. 16
MacDonald, Robert 406
McGuire, J. 434
MacInnes, J. 13, 15, 31, 41–4, 47
McKeganey, N. 429
McKenna, W. 192
MacKinnon, C. 441
MacLeod, L. 450
McMullan, J. 442
McRobbie, A. 233
McWilliams, W. 431, 437
Maddern, P. 17
Maguire, M. 10, 133–4, 139, 143, 145–6
Maher, L. 275
Maier, M. 192
Malamuth, N.M. 153
Malony, Mike 340, 342, 348–9
Mandel, E. 255
Mandell, M. 442
Mann, Anthony 253
Mannheim, H. 274

March, J.G. 201
Marchand, M.H. 60
Markham, L. 451, 461
Marlowe, Philip 254
Marsh, J. 442, 449
Marsh, P. 298
Marshall, J. 150
Martin, D. 450
Martin, K. 360, 364
Martin, Katherine A. 87
Martin, P.Y. 157, 360–62
Martin, S.E. 361–5
Martinson, R. 442
Maruna, Shadd 150, 170, 173, 213–14, 216–17, 221, 230–31, 238
Marx, Karl 22, 449
Mason, Jerry 199–200, 207
Mason-Clark, N. 455
Mathiesen, T. 442, 451
Matthews, N. 442, 449
Matthews, R. 433
Matza, David 150, 272, 405
Mauer, M. 281
Mauss, M. 314, 316, 321
Mawson, A.R. 150, 153
Maxfield, M. 133, 135
May, T. 428
Mayer, J. 431
Mayhew, P. 133, 135
Mayor, Gwen 103
Meisenhelder, T. 214
Meléndez, Edgardo 283
Meléndez, Edwin 283
Mellor, P.A. 18–19, 325
Melossi, D. 449
Menkel-Meadow, C. 118, 129
Mennell, S. 18
Merighi, J.R. 11, 13
Merlo, A. 448
Merrill, L. 153
Merton, R. 266
Merwe, General van der 351
Mesrine, J. 269
Messerschmidt, James W. xii, xiii, xv, 4, 6, 15, 37–8, 60, 63, 69–92, 117–18, 127–8, 167, 169, 172, 179, 191–212, 217–19, 275–6, 282, 298, 308, 313, 324, 331, 362, 375, 401–3, 422, 428
Metz, Christian 252
Michaud, J. 449–50
Middleton, P. 429
Millar, W.B. 271
Miller, Jody xvi, 167, 172, 219
Miller, Walter 172
Millham, J. 151
Milliken, F.J. 205
Mills, C. Wright 238, 404
Minsky, R. 44–6, 234–5
Mirrlees-Black, C. 267
Mitchell, J. 50
Miyazawa, K. 120–21, 126
Miyazawa, S. 123
Moffitt, T. 214
Mohanty, C.T. 283
Monaghan, Lee F. xvii, 298, 309, 313–34
Monture-Okanee, P. 450
Mooney, Katie xviii, 331, 335–56
Moore, D. 309
Moran, A. 122
Morash, M. 363
Morgan, David H.J. 4, 60, 72, 134, 169, 195, 208, 361, 406
Morgan, J. Pierpont 64
Morrell, R. 65
Morris, Allison 403
Mosher, J. 450
Mott, J. 267
Moynihan, Daniel 282
Muehlenhard, C.L. 153
Mugford, S. 268, 443
Mukherjee, S. 121
Mulloy, Lawrence 199
Mulvey, Laura 252–3
Murtaugh, Roger 257

Naffine, N. 297
Naples, N. 57
Nardi, P.M. 159
Neale, S. 253
Neary, M. 438
Nelson, T.S. 152, 157
Nettlton, S. 331
Newburn, Tim xi, 4, 12, 37, 118, 139, 251, 386, 403, 428
Newson, E. 251
Nielsen, H.B. 64
Noble, G. 252
Norman, S.G. 346

O'Malley, P. 263, 266, 268–9

O'Sullivan, C.S. 39, 152, 158–9
O'Toole, L.L. 156–7
Ogasawara, Y. 360
Olson, James 170, 177–9
Ormrod, S. 204
Osborn, S.G. 214
Oyserman, D. 445

Pacey, B. 436
Padavic, Irene xviii, 359–79
Paredes, A. 283, 293
Parker, H. 218, 264, 266–7, 270
Parker, Ian 404, 408, 410
Pattman, R. 35, 41
Patton, C. 151–2
Patton, Michael Q. 70
Paulus, I. 468
Pavarini, M. 449
Pearce, F. 453, 468
Pearson, G. 266–7
Peiss, K. 361
Pérez, S. 281
Petersen, Ann C. 85, 309
Peterson, David 168
Pezzin, L.E. 214
Pidgeon, Nick 408–9
Pierce, J. 360
Pike, D.L. 364
Pingel, F. 149, 154
Pinsonneault, P. 214
Pitch, T. 453
Plant, Martin 269, 271
Plant, Moira 269, 271
Pleck, J.H. 157
Pointing, J. 143
Polansky, N. 150
Polk, G.C. 152–3
Polk, K. 14, 118, 298, 453, 462
Pontalis, J.B. 44
Pontell, H. 451
Potter, Jonathan 404, 422
Poveda, Tony 402
Pratt, A. 450
Preble, E. 267
Presley, Elvis 341–2
Prokos, Anastasia xviii, 359–79
Pronger, B. 396
Propp, Vladimir 252
Ptacek, J. 14, 62, 461
Punch, M. 365
Purpel, D. 364
Pyke, Karen 422

Quigley, B.M. 218

Rafter, N. 454
Rainwater, L. 282
Ramírez, R. 283
Ratner, R. 442
Rawlings, P. 144
Ray, Johnny 342
Ray, R.B. 255
Raynor, P. 428, 434, 438
Redhead, S. 270
Redl, F. 150
Reiner, R. 448, 466
Reisig, M. 382
Remy, J. 383–4
Rengert, George 170
Renzetti, C. 117
Resick, P. 134
Reskin, B. 361
Rice, T.W. 364
Richardson, D.R. 150
Richardson, L. 367
Rideau, W. 158
Rifkin, Jeremy 20
Riger, S. 133–4, 138
Riggs, Martin 257
Rivera-Batiz, F.L. 283
Roberts, J. 449, 451
Robins, D. 135, 137
Rodgers, K. 446, 448, 451
Rodríguez, C.E. 283–4
Roper, M. 58
Rose, David 406
Rose, N. 266
Rosich, Katherine J. 70
Roskey, M.L. 158
Rossi, Peter H. 168, 455
Rothman, D. 442, 451
Rotundo, E.A. 157
Rowland, W. 250
Rozee-Koker, P. 152–3
Rudberg, M. 64
Ruggerio, V. 24
Rumgay, J. 229
Runcie, Robert 93
Runyan, A.S. 60
Russakoff, D. 156

Russell, Brian 207
Russell, Kurt 256–7
Russell, S.T. 151
Russo, N.F. 153
Ryan, Michael 94, 98

Sabo, D. xix, 157–8
Sacco, Vincent 168, 451
Saco, D. 117–18
Saltz, E. 445
Sampson, Robert J. 70, 136, 150, 214–16, 231, 238
Sanday, P. 152–3, 155, 158
Sanders, J. 123
Sandler, B.R. 152, 157
Santiago, C. 283
Sapsford, R. 394
Sassen, S. 284
Saunders, D.G. 434
Saunders, K. 122
Savage, S. 361
Savelsberg, Joachim J. 402
Sayers, Charles Thomas 351
Schlegel, Kip 401
Schlenker, Barry 404
Schlesinger, P. 259
Schmid, T. 392
Schrag, J.L. 153
Schrecker, T. 453
Schutz, A. 325, 330
Schwartz, G. 328
Schwarzennegger, Arnold 249, 251, 256–8, 427
Schwendinger, H. 13
Schwendinger, J. 13
Scott, J. 294
Scott, J.C. 360
Scott, J.W. 360
Scott, Marvin 317, 325, 403–4, 421–2
Scott, Sue 72
Scourfield, Jonathan B. xix, xx, 427–39
Scraton, P. 383
Scully, D. 153
Sedgwick, E.K. xiv
Segal, L. xii, 251, 353, 395
Seidler, Victor 137, 421
Shapira, Z. 201
Shapland, J. 133, 136, 139, 144
Shaw, Clifford 70
Sheath, M. 437
Shelley, Peggy L. 172
Shepherd, J. 133, 135
Sherman, L. 442, 450
Shilling, Chris 18–19, 86, 313–14, 318–19, 322, 324–5, 331
Shimada, S. 125
Shover, Neal 84, 166, 168–73, 177, 179, 181, 214–15
Silberman, C. 442
Sim, J. 383, 389
Simon, J. 451, 453
Simpson, Sally S. 172
Sinatra, Frank 342
Skidmore, P. 383
Skogan, W. 451
Sluka, J.A. 282
Smart, B. 265
Smart, C. 442, 444, 448, 461, 467
Smit, D. 343
Smith, David 214, 402
Smith, P. 117
Snider, Laureen xx, 441–79
Sommers, I. 214
Soothill, K. 120
Sorokin, P. 453
Soros, George 458, 463
South, N. 266
Spade, J.Z. 157–8, 160
Sparks, Richard xv, xvi, 249–61, 387
Spierenberg, P. 456
Spock, Dr. 461
Stack, C. 282
Stack, S. 457
Stallone, Sylvester 249, 251, 256–7
Stanko, Elizabeth A. xi, xiv, 4, 12, 37, 118, 133–48, 386, 403, 428, 451
Starbuck, W.H. 205
Steadman, H. 298
Stella, Simonetta P. 348
Stets, J.E. 461
Stevens, D.J. 398
Stirratt, M. 364
Stossel, John 370
Strange, C. 219
Straus, M. 125
Strauss, Anselm L. 316, 365, 409
Sue, S. 153
Summers, A. 122
Sutcliffe, Peter 389
Sutherland, Edwin H. 70, 170, 173, 402
Swerdlow, M. 374

Swindler, Ann 178
Sykes, Gresham M. 382–3, 386, 395, 405
Szalacha, L.A. 160

Tamura, M. 123
Tasker, Y. 257
Taylor, Ian 12, 15, 20–21, 23, 25, 274–5
Taylor, J. 125
Taylor, L. 392, 394
Taylor, R. 463
Taylor, S. 24
Teten, A.L. 153
Thatcher, Margaret 421
Theweleit, K. 256
Thomas, P. 446–7
Thomas, William I. 70
Thommeny, J. 298
Thompson, Arnie 199
Thompson, C. 214–15
Thompson, E.H. 157
Thompson, E.P. 449
Thompson, Robert 96, 107
Thornberry, T. 216
Thorne, Barrie 59, 85, 87, 192, 194
Thurston, Richard 438
Tifft, L. 451, 461
Timms, N. 431
Toch, H. 328, 390, 395
Tolson, Andrew 201, 348, 385–6
Tompkins, Jane 253, 259
Tomsen, Stephen xii, xvi, xvii, 63, 297–311, 313, 316–17, 322, 325–6, 328, 332
Tonry, M. 282
Torrance, Mark xix, 401–26
Tripp, D. 251–2, 254, 258–9
Tripp, R. 450
Trompf, G.W. 16
Tunnell, Kenneth 179
Turney, B. 215, 217
Tyler, M. 24
Tyson, Mike xiii, 219–20

Urry, J. 268
Ursel, J. 449, 454

Vanstone, M. 428, 434, 438
Vaughan, D. 191, 204
Ven, P. van de 151
Venables, Jon 96, 107
Venter, H.J. 354
Vidich, A. 315
Vitello, P. 156
Volz, R. 59

Wacquant, L. 282, 314, 316, 322, 332
Waddington, P. 321, 327
Wajcman, J. 204–5
Walby, S. 62
Waldorf, D. 275
Walinsky, Adam 447
Walker, J. 122, 124
Walker, S. 451
Walkerdine, V. 233
Walklate, S. 37, 217, 219
Walters, G.D. 268
Ward Jouve, Nicole 389, 396
Warde, A. 265, 269
Warr, M. 133, 214
Warren, C.A.B. 365
Warwick, L. 428
Wasilchick, John 170
Watson, J. 331
Wayne, John 137, 253, 257
Weaver, A. 316
Webb, Ferdinand 355
Webster, C. 22
Weinberger, L.E. 151
Weisburd, David 401
Weissman, E. 155
Wellman, D. 338
Wells, S. 298–9
West, Candace 71, 169, 192–3
West, D.J. 214
West, G.W. 214
West, P. 298–9
Westbury, V. 122
Westwood, Sallie 169, 181
Wetherell, Margaret 31, 34, 39, 41–2, 44, 62, 218, 404, 410, 422
Whitehead, S. 34, 320
Wight, Daniel 394, 406
Wikberg, R. 158
Williams, C. 360–61
Williams, J. 463
Williams, P. 450
Williams, S. 314, 317, 323, 330–31
Willis, Bruce 251, 256
Willis, Paul 13, 40, 205, 266, 272–3, 360, 385
Willott, Sara xix, 401–26
Wilson, J.Q. 275, 451

Wilson, W.J. 10, 12
Winlow, Simon xvii, 13–15, 22, 24, 169, 298, 309, 313–16, 318, 323, 325–6, 330–31
Winter, S. 444–5, 461
Wolfe, Tom 40
Wolferen, K. van 123, 125
Wolfgang, M.E. 14
Wood, Julian 87
Worrall, A. 393
Wortman, C. 143
Wright, James D. 168
Wright, Richard 166, 168, 171–2, 175
Wynhausen, E. 446

Yancey, W. 282
Young, J. 11, 433, 449, 451

Zimmerman, Don H. 71, 169, 192
Zimring, F.E. 12–13
Znaniecki, Florian 70
Zulehner, P.M. 59